THE HUMAN BODY

Its Anatomy and Physiology

C. H. BEST

C. B. E., M.A., M.D., D.Sc. (Lond.),
F.R.S., F.R.C.P. (Canada)
Professor and Head of Department of Physiology,
Director of the Banting-Best Department of
Medical Research, University of Toronto

N. B. TAYLOR

V.D., M.D., F.R.S. (Canada), F.R.C.S. (Edin.),
F.R.C.P. (Canada), M.R.C.S. (Eng.), L.R.C.P. (Lond.)
Formerly: Professor of the History of Medicine
and Medical Literature, University of Western
Ontario, London, Canada; Professor of
Physiology, University of Toronto

THE HUMAN BODY

Its Anatomy and Physiology · Fourth Edition

HOLT, RINEHART AND WINSTON
New York · Chicago · San Francisco · Toronto · London

Copyright 1932, 1948, © 1956, 1963, by Holt, Rinehart and Winston, Inc.

All rights reserved

Library of Congress Catalog Card Number: 63-7312

ISBN: 0-03-011655-4

Printed in the United States of America

1234   081   9876

Cover: Anatomical drawing by Andreas Vesalius (1514-1564)

Preface to the Fourth Edition

When the first edition of this text appeared, in 1932, it was the authors' belief that physiology should not be valued solely as a technical study, but should be considered rather as a desirable addition to any student's general knowledge, whatever the career for which he is being prepared. The passage of thirty years has not changed this belief; in fact, more than ever, the layman cannot consider himself well informed and still remain ignorant of basic physiology and some of the more recent advances in physiological science. Therefore, this book has been planned to meet the needs both of those students who must acquire a firm grounding in physiology in order to continue their studies in this and related fields, and of those students who intend to go no farther in the area.

Readers will find that this edition is a careful revision of the previous one, which, in turn, was a greatly altered and expanded version of the first two editions. With the aim of bringing material up to date, within the framework of the original scope and aim of the text, a simplified account has been given of the nucleic acids, DNA and RNA, together with a discussion of the very live question of their significance in the processes of heredity. Again, reflecting scientific progress of the last seven years, information on problems pertaining to space flight has been added. The section on the structure and physiology of the cell has been expanded; atherosclerosis has been more fully dealt with and the moot question of diet in relation to its development discussed; and a short outline of the collagen diseases has been included. In a number of instances practical applications of scientific facts have been added. Many new illustrations were prepared for this edition, and a number of the old figures have been redrawn or modified. The Glossary has been expanded and revised.

It is with pleasure and gratitude that we acknowledge the careful reading of the manuscript by Professor Richard C. Wolf of the University of Wisconsin. The text has benefited from his criticisms and suggestions.

N. B. T.

Toronto, Canada
February, 1963

Contents

ix

GENERAL PRINCIPLES

PART I

1
Atoms and Molecules

THE ATOM

All matter, living or nonliving, is made up of inconceivably small particles called **atoms.** Atoms may therefore be looked upon as the building material from which everything we see, feel, touch, and taste is made. Atoms make up the air we breathe and our food and water.

Atoms are of different types; an atom of iron, for instance, is different in size and in weight from an atom of gold, and a gold atom is different again from one of silver, of copper, or of carbon. Materials that are each composed entirely of one type of atom, such as iron, gold, calcium, phosphorus, sodium, carbon, oxygen, etc., are called **elements.**

The atom itself is made up of minute particles or units of electricity —**protons, electrons,** and **neutrons.** Protons are units of positive electricity, whereas electrons are units of negative electricity. Neutrons are electrically neutral. Electrons are believed to revolve at high speed in concentric orbits around a central core or **nucleus** composed of protons and neutrons (Fig. 1.1). The protons and neutrons are held together in two pairs to form **alpha particles,** which are shot out at high velocity from radioactive atoms. The nucleus of the atom is made up of alpha particles.

The atom may be compared to a miniature solar system, the electrons representing the planets and the nucleus the sun. If the atom could be enlarged until its nucleus was the size of a baseball, the electrons would be the size of golf balls whirling around the nucleus at high speed and separated from it by a distance of several miles.

The atom, then, is mostly empty space; the electrons are held in their orbits at these relatively immense distances from the nucleus by powerful forces. It has been estimated that if these forces could in some way be annulled so that the electrons and nuclei of all the atoms in our bodies came together into a compact mass, we would shrink to a speck

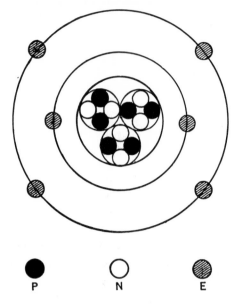

Fig. 1.1. The structure of an atom of carbon. *P*, protons; *N*, neutrons; *E*, electrons. A pair each of protons and neutrons make up an alpha particle.

P   N   E

scarcely visible to the naked eye. Truly, "we are such stuff as dreams are made on."

The properties of any particular type of atom depend upon the number of protons in its nucleus. An atom of iron, for example, possesses more protons than an atom of oxygen or carbon or calcium but fewer than an atom of copper or zinc. One proton more or less in an atom is sufficient to alter completely its character and the properties of the mass of substance of which the atom is a part. The protons are all alike; it is their *number* that makes the differences among atoms. The number of electrons in an atom equals the number of protons; the atom as a whole is, therefore, electrically neutral.

This concept of the atom leads up to the conclusion that the infinite variety in the world around us is simply a matter of the numbers of protons and electrons in the atomic structure. The greatest number of protons or electrons in any atom is only 101, and the smallest is 1 (hydrogen). The other atoms have numbers in an almost unbroken series in between.

The movements of our muscles, the beating of our hearts, the digestion of our food, the heat of our bodies, and even our thoughts are the result of the motions of atoms of different kinds—carbon, hydrogen, oxygen, etc.—coming together at one moment in different sets and combinations and separating again at another. Chemical change is occurring ceaselessly in our bodies; as Lavoisier, the great French chemist, said more than a century and a half ago, *"La vie est une fonction chimique."* [1]

[1] "Life is a chemical function."

Carbon, of all the atoms, is the most characteristic of life.[2] It is the very essence of animal and vegetable matter and has made possible the development of living things. Had the earth been created without carbon, which seems such a commonplace substance, there would have been a desolation of rock and water for all eternity. Never would a tree or even a blade of grass, much less the human race, have come into being.

Isotopes. The atoms of any single element, say, of oxygen or chlorine, have not all exactly the same weight, as has been taught for many years. The atomic weights of the elements as given in standard tables are average or mean values for immense numbers of atoms. For example, the atomic weight so given for chlorine is 35.45. But no individual atom has this weight; some have a weight of 35, others a weight of 37. These atoms of different weights are called **isotopes**; many are radioactive like radium; that is, they have unstable nuclei that shoot out particles or "rays" at very high velocities (20,000 to 100,000 miles per second). The different weights of isotopes are due to their possessing different numbers of **neutrons** in their nuclei; the number of protons and electrons in the atoms of any given element is the same.

Radioactive isotopes are produced artificially and are now widely used in medicine, as, for example, the destruction of the tissue of malignant growths, and in biochemical experiments; isotopes of iodine are employed in the treatment of toxic goiter.

MOLECULES

When two or more atoms become joined together, the particle that results is, of course, larger and heavier than one composed of a single atom. It is then called a **molecule**. For example, sodium (Na) and chlorine (Cl) atoms combine to form sodium chloride (NaCl—table salt); two atoms of hydrogen (H) combine with one of oxygen (O) to form a molecule of water (H_2O); or an atom of carbon (C) unites with two of oxygen to form a molecule of carbon dioxide (CO_2). The molecules so formed, and of course the substances they constitute, are entirely different in character from the separate atoms. The element sodium is a caustic solid and chlorine a highly irritating and poisonous gas, whereas sodium chloride is a relatively mild and harmless substance essential for most living processes. Again, hydrogen and oxygen are gases, but they unite to form water.

When the molecules of a compound break down into the atoms of which it is composed, the process, or **chemical reaction**, involved is called **decomposition**. When, for example, a compound of mercury and oxygen (a red powder known as mercuric oxide) is heated to a high temperature,

[2] Charcoal, coal, the diamond, and the "lead" in a pencil are examples of pure carbon.

the original metal appears. The oxygen with which the mercury was combined is split off from it and escapes. Frequently decomposition and combination proceed simultaneously—for example, when two compounds are brought together in solution and two compounds quite different from the original ones are formed. Thus, sodium chloride and silver nitrate react to form silver chloride and sodium nitrate. The four types of atoms have undergone a rearrangement. Such a reaction is called **double decomposition.** Chemical changes or reactions are, therefore, of three main types—combination, decomposition, and double decomposition.

Molecules may contain two atoms only or a very great number. Very many different kinds of atom may be present in the larger molecules. It is large and heavy molecules such as these that comprise the protein materials of the living body. The molecules of the fats and of some carbohydrates are also hundreds of times larger and heavier than a molecule of, say, sodium chloride. Could a molecule of certain proteins be enlarged to the size of a pea, the molecule of sodium chloride, if magnified proportionately, would be no larger than a pinhead.

Molecules are in constant motion. They are ceaselessly changing their positions, moving to and fro, or bouncing about like a number of rubber balls thrown upon a hard floor. In solid materials these movements are less lively than in liquids and gases, and are probably of an oscillatory nature only. In gases the movements have no limits. Air, for instance, is a mixture mainly of the molecules of the three gases oxygen, nitrogen, and carbon dioxide. And no matter how still the air may appear to be, the molecules are in ceaseless motion, colliding with one another or with solid objects and flying off again in another direction. If confined within a bottle or other vessel, they beat against the vessel's wall and, when allowed to escape, start on an erratic journey that may take them anywhere—even to regions miles above the earth.

In liquids the motions of the molecules are less rapid, though just as ceaseless. Heat speeds up the movements; cold slows them down. In liquids and in solids the molecules are closely packed; in gases their distances from one another are much greater. By compression the molecules of gas may be brought closer together, and the gas pressure rises; if the molecules are packed densely enough, liquefaction or even solidification of the gas occurs.

Colloids. When enormous numbers of atoms become grouped together, the molecule becomes so large that it can be faintly seen and its movements detected by an extremely powerful microscope (ultramicroscope). Such huge molecules are spoken of as **colloid particles** (Gk. *kolla,* glue), and the substance they compose is called a **colloid.** Often such a molecule is too large to pass through the pores of an animal membrane, such as parchment, frog's skin, or the intestinal wall. The molecules of proteins, starches, and fats are of such a size. These large molecules have a tendency to cling together, as grains of clay cohere to form lumps. In this way relatively colossal particles are formed.

Colloidal solutions. Molecules massed together in this way, or even very large single molecules, form solutions that differ in several respects from those of the smaller molecules, which make up such substances as common salt, cane sugar, copper sulfate, etc. We therefore speak of these solutions as **colloidal solutions** and of the solutions of salt, cane sugar, etc., as **crystalloid**, or **true solutions.**

Liquid glue or gelatin, boiled starch or liquid rubber, India ink, white of egg in water, and blood serum are examples of colloidal solutions. Many colloidal solutions readily change to a more or less solid state when treated in certain ways. When glue or gelatin, for instance, is dissolved in hot water, solidification or jellying occurs when the solution cools. This change in state is due to the fact that the relationship of the colloid particles to the water in which they were dissolved becomes reversed. In the fluid condition the particles are separated from one another and surrounded by the water. In the solid state the particles cannot move, for they have become joined together to form a meshwork that encloses the droplets of water (Fig. 1.2). The fluid state is termed **hydrosol**; the gelatinous state, **hydrogel**.

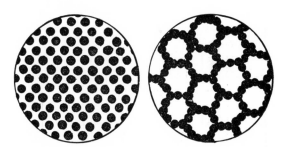

Fig. 1.2. Diagram to show the rearrangement of the particles when a sol changes to a gel.

Brownian movements. The English botanist Robert Brown in 1828 observed under a powerful microscope random and erratic movements in a colloidal solution. These so-called *Brownian movements* are due to the molecules of water, or the small molecules of crystalloids in the solution, colliding at high speed with the large colloidal particles and knocking them about.

Ions. When two atoms combine they do so by sharing between them one or more of the electrons in the outer ring of each atom. As long as the chemical substance is in the **solid** state the atoms are held together by electrostatic forces, but the molecules of certain substances, such as sodium chloride (NaCl), hydrochloric acid (HCl), and sodium hydroxide (NaOH), when dissolved in water undergo **dissociation** or **ionization**. That is, the atoms, or certain groups of atoms, separate from one another and become electrically charged. When sodium chloride, for example, is dissolved in water, the sodium atom loses an electron—that is, a negative charge—to chlorine and, consequently, becomes electrically positive. The chlorine atom, since it gains an electron, becomes electrically negative. Such charged atoms move swiftly through the solution and are called **ions** (Gk. *ion,* going) .

Other substances behave in a similar manner. Hydrochloric acid dissociates into the positively charged hydrogen ions (H^+) and the negatively charged chlorine ions (Cl^-), and sodium hydroxide into positive sodium ions (Na^+) and negative hydroxyl ions (OH^-). Water itself is very slightly dissociated into H^+ and OH^- ions.

Substances whose molecules behave in this way when dissolved in water are called **electrolytes.** When an electric current is passed through a solution of an electrolyte, the negative ions ($^-$) travel to the point where the current enters the solution (**anode**) and the positive ions ($^+$) move to the point where the current leaves the solution (**cathode**) . The negative ions are therefore called **anions** and the positive ions, **cations.** Thus, when a current passes through a solution of sodium chloride (NaCl), the sodium cations (Na^+) collect at the cathode and the negative ions (Cl^-) at the anode (Fig. 1.3) . This effect is called **electrolysis.**

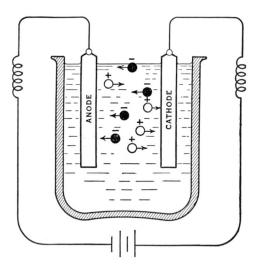

Fig. 1.3. Electrolysis. As an electric current passes through a solution of sodium chloride (NaCl), the positively charged ions (Na^+), or cations, move to the cathode and the negatively charged ions (Cl^-), or anions, to the anode.

Diffusion. When two solids are placed in close contact no interchange of molecules take place between them. But when two samples of a gas of different concentrations are brought together, molecules of the sample with the higher concentration move to the one with the lower concentration until the molecules are evenly mixed and the two samples are of uniform concentration. Thus, when a pungent gas, such as bromine, is released into a closed room, it can be smelled after a time in all parts of the room even though there are no air currents to mix it with the air. This process, which also occurs, though much more slowly, between certain liquids and substances in solution, is due to the spontaneous movements of the individual molecules or ions and is called **diffusion.** Crystalloids diffuse rapidly as compared with colloids, which do so very slowly or not at all. Diffusion occurs also across certain membranes.

Dialysis. It has just been stated that, whereas crystalloids are readily diffusible and will pass through a membrane such as parchment, the colloids, which are nondiffusible, are held back. It is possible, therefore, to separate crystalloids from colloids in a solution containing both. The process of separating these two substances by means of a membrane is called **dialysis.**

Let us suppose that a bag or tube of parchment is filled with a solution of sodium chloride containing a colloid, such as gelatin, and immersed in water or a weaker solution of salt. Molecules of salt pass rapidly through the membrane from the stronger solution to the water, or weaker solution, surrounding the bag. Water molecules pass in the opposite direction to take the place of the salt molecules. This interchange of molecules continues until the solutions on the two sides are of uniform salt concentration. If the solution surrounding the bag is repeatedly removed and replaced by pure (that is, distilled) water, the salt is finally completely removed from the solution within the bag, leaving only the colloid material.

Osmosis, osmotic pressure. Membranes differ considerably with respect to their permeability to molecules of various sizes. Some allow the passage of small molecules of water and crystalloids but are impermeable or nearly so to the larger colloid molecules. Other membranes again, although permeable to water molecules, are impermeable to the larger ones, such as those of salt or sugar. A membrane that will permit the transfer of water but not of a substance dissolved in the water is called semipermeable to that specific solution. Such a membrane behaves as though it were a sieve with a mesh or openings of a certain definite size. Any molecule smaller than the openings will pass through; larger molecules will be barred.

Now if water should be separated from a solution of sugar by a semipermeable membrane that allows water but not the sugar molecules to pass through it, water will pass into the sugar solution but the sugar molecules cannot pass out. The sugar solution becomes diluted and increases in volume, and if it were in a tall narrow container its level would rise; that is, its pressure would be increased. The sugar molecules act as though they "attracted" or "drew" the water molecules across the membrane. This process in which water is transferred across a semipermeable membrane is called **osmosis,** and the pressure thus created is called the **osmotic pressure.** By means of an *osmometer,* a specially constructed chamber made of rigid walls and a membrane supported by resistant but porous material, enormous pressures can be developed through osmosis (Fig. 1.4). The greatest pressures are developed by solutions of crystalloids; the pressure developed by colloids is very small.

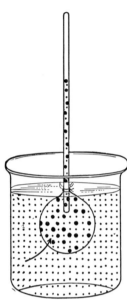

Fig. 1.4. Osmotic pressure. A sac formed of a semipermeable membrane is fastened to one end of a glass tube. The large dots represent sugar molecules; the small ones, water molecules. Water passes through the "pores" of the membrane as indicated by the arrow. The pressure within the sac rises as shown by the height of the fluid column in the glass tube.

Water molecules always pass through a semipermeable membrane from the weaker to the stronger solution. The stronger solution has the greater osmotic pressure and is called **hypertonic;** the weaker solution is called **hypotonic.** Two solutions are said to be **isotonic** if they exert equal osmotic pressures. When isotonic solutions are placed on either side of the membrane, no water accumulates on either side and no osmotic pressure is developed.

Osmosis in vital processes. The principles of dialysis, osmosis, and osmotic pressure are of the utmost importance in living processes. The various structures of the body are made up of 60 to 90 percent water, in which are dissolved many crystalloid and colloid substances. Food elements, minerals, enzymes, vitamins, and hormones pass by diffusion from the blood through the walls of the capillaries into the fluids surrounding these vessels and bathing the cells of the tissues. The envelopes of the tissue cells and the walls of the capillaries themselves are semipermeable membranes of different types; thus they act in a selective manner toward the various substances dissolved in the blood and body fluids. Osmosis, therefore, enters largely into the processes involved in the interchange of fluid between the blood and the fluid of the tissues, as well as between the tissue fluid and the interior of the cells. It plays an essential part as well in the production of urine. The absorption of water from the soil by the roots of plants and trees and the rise of sap in the stems and trunks also depend to an important degree on osmotic forces.

Acids and bases. Hydrogen ion concentration. pH. Everyone knows in a general way the characteristics of an **acid.** Acids have a taste usually described as sour—like vinegar or lemon juice; they turn blue litmus paper red. Lye (sodium hydroxide) and slaked lime (calcium hydroxide, used in making mortar) are common examples of **bases.** They usually have a bitter taste and they turn red litmus blue. Lye and certain other bases are also called **alkalies.** The terms **basic** and **alkaline,** are, therefore, often used interchangeably. Strong solutions of both acids and bases are highly destructive to animal and vegetable tissues.

Acids and bases combine to form compounds called **salts,** which are neither acid nor basic. Thus,

$$\underset{\substack{\text{hydrochloric}\\\text{acid}}}{\text{HCl}} \quad + \quad \underset{\substack{\text{sodium}\\\text{hydroxide}}}{\text{NaOH}} \quad \rightarrow \quad \underset{\text{salt}}{\text{NaCl}} \quad + \quad \underset{\text{water}}{\text{H}_2\text{O}}$$

Acids and bases therefore neutralize one another.

The term **reaction** is used in referring to the acid or alkaline character of a chemical or its solution; the term is applied as well to the body fluids. Hydrochloric acid, vinegar, urine, and sweat have an acid reaction, whereas lye, lime, blood, milk, and the tissue fluids are alkaline in reaction. A **neutral** reaction is one that is neither acid nor alkaline.

The true acidity or alkalinity of a solution depends upon its concentration in free hydrogen or free hydroxyl atoms (that is, in hydrogen or hydroxyl ions). (See p. 8.) A 10-percent solution of hydrochloric acid is more acid than a 10-percent solution of acetic acid. The hydrochloric acid tastes more sour and is more destructive to living tissues. This is because it has a higher concentration of hydrogen ions. Nearly all (80 to 97 percent) of the molecules of hydrochloric acid are dissociated into hydrogen ions (H^+) and chlorine ions (Cl^-), whereas the molecules of acetic acid are dissociated to a relatively small degree (1.4 percent).

An alkaline solution also contains hydrogen ions but in relatively low concentration; the hydroxyl ions are in excess. An acid solution contains hydroxyl ions but only in relatively low concentration. In a neutral solution the concentrations of the two kinds of ions are equal. It follows, then, that the acidity, alkalinity, or neutrality of a solution can be expressed by stating its concentration in hydrogen ions alone, the hydroxyl ion concentration being disregarded. The sum of the concentration of H and OH ions is always the same; when the concentration of one ion is high, that of the other is correspondingly low.

It has become customary to express the hydrogen ion concentration by the symbol pH and a figure from 0.00 to 14.00. Water or a neutral solution is pH 7.00. The acidities range downward from this to pH 0.00; the alkaline range is upward to pH 14.00. The numbers, it will be seen, run in reverse order to the H ion concentrations. The *lower* the pH the *greater* is the hydrogen ion concentration and the greater the acidity. Thus, a solution of pH 1.00 has a greater H ion concentration than one of pH 6.00 and is, therefore, more acid. Moreover, the pH 1.00 solution has not simply six times the H ion concentration of pH 6.00 but several thousand times more.

In the same way, pH 14.00 indicates a much lower H ion concentration, and consequently a much more alkaline solution, than pH 8.00 (Fig. 1.5). The blood and body fluids are slightly alkaline—about pH 7.40.

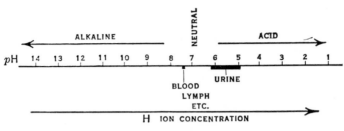

Fig. 1.5.

2
Protoplasm

Protoplasm is the stuff of which all living things are made. Anything composed of protoplasm is or has been alive. It is necessary, then, that we should know all we can about a substance that constitutes the very essence of living matter—a substance that goes to the making of a green leaf, of a worm, or of a man. The "stuff and substance" of brain, muscle, bone, and sinew is protoplasm.

Protoplasm is a gelatinous substance composed largely of water (around 75 percent) and protein (around 25 percent). It is structureless and actually fluid or semi-fluid, for under a powerful microscope particles can be seen to move through it more or less freely. The streams or currents that can sometimes be seen within its substance also indicate its fluid nature. Besides protein it contains various essential minerals—calcium, sodium, potassium, magnesium, etc.—and small amounts of sugar (glucose), starch (glycogen), and fatty materials.

Proteins are colloids—that is, large molecules grouped together or very large single molecules. Protoplasm is, then, a colloidal solution, and like such solutions, it changes to the solid state under certain conditions. After death it loses its fluid nature. Protein molecules are made up of the atoms of carbon, nitrogen, oxygen, and hydrogen, some sulfur, and usually a little phosphorus. To the carbon, protoplasm owes its wonderful versatility. Without carbon, life in the numberless forms in which we know it could never have evolved. Carbon atoms, unlike the atoms of any other element, have the extraordinary ability to link themselves into chains and rings and to add to these the atoms of other elements. When it is recalled that the addition of a single atom to a molecule may completely change its character, one can realize what tremendous possibilities for variation in form, minute structure, and function are bound up within protoplasmic material.

The modern chemist makes use of this characteristic of the carbon atom, and in his laboratory imitates in a measure the wonders that

13

through the ages nature has wrought from protoplasm. Using a raw material derived from prehistoric life—coal tar—he links the carbon atoms into rings and chains to create substances differing widely in their propperties—antiseptics, anaesthetics, headache powders, perfumes and flavors, various brilliant dyes, plastics, photographic materials, and many other things in general use today. Or, starting with cotton or wood pulp (cellulose) and attaching nitrogen, sulfur, or other atoms here or there to the carbon, he can make explosives, celluloid, paints, or artificial silk.

Below are shown some of the ways in which carbon atoms link themselves and other atoms together.

$$
\begin{array}{cc}
\text{H} & \text{H--H--H--H--H--H} \\
| & \quad\;|\;\;\;|\;\;\;|\;\;\;|\;\;\;|\;\;\;| \\
\text{H--C--H} & \text{H--C--C--C--C--C--C--H} \\
| & \quad\;|\;\;\;|\;\;\;|\;\;\;|\;\;\;|\;\;\;| \\
\text{H} & \text{H--H--H--H--H--H}
\end{array}
$$

$$
\begin{array}{c}
\text{H} \\
| \\
\text{C} \\
\diagup \quad \diagdown\!\!\diagdown \\
\text{H--C} \quad\quad \text{C--H} \\
\| \quad\quad\quad | \\
\text{H--C} \quad\quad \text{C--H} \\
\diagdown \quad\quad \diagup \\
\text{C} \\
| \\
\text{H}
\end{array}
$$

The structure of the molecule of a coal-tar (aniline) dye is given in Figure 2.1, which is reproduced merely to illustrate the complexity of the arrangement of the atoms in a carbon compound.

The loss or addition of an atom from or to a molecule will alter its entire nature. The mere change in position of one of the atoms will do the same. The number of ways in which the atoms making up protoplasm —carbon, hydrogen, oxygen, nitrogen, and sulfur—can be combined is unlimited. Indeed, the chemical compounds that nature might create from these atoms exceed in number the stars in the Milky Way. So it may be realized how nature's laboratories have, from this raw material, produced types of life infinitely varied in structure and function.

DIVISIONS OF PROTOPLASM

Microscopic life. Until some 300 years ago muscle, skin, bone, and other tissues of our bodies were thought to be little more than lumps of material, without any fine texture or structure. They were supposed to be simply masses of pulp, without any division into small pieces. It is not surprising that this should be the belief of the scientists before the seventeenth century, since no one then could look into a piece of muscle or skin or liver and see just how it was made up. A Dutch biologist, Anton Leeuwenhoek, was one of the first to use the microscope to examine all kinds of living things (Fig. 2.2). His single-lensed instrument was a very poor affair compared with the powerful compound microscopes of today, which magnify the object thousands of times.

But to Leeuwenhoek it was a miracle worker, a weaver of fantastic tales—but tales that, strange and weird and almost unbelievable as they were, nevertheless were true. This lens brought him worlds that had been closed to all eyes since the beginning of time. So absorbing and fascinating were the dramas which unfolded before his eyes that he gave up his life to the study of this world of the "infinitely little." His great work describing what he had seen was published in 1669.

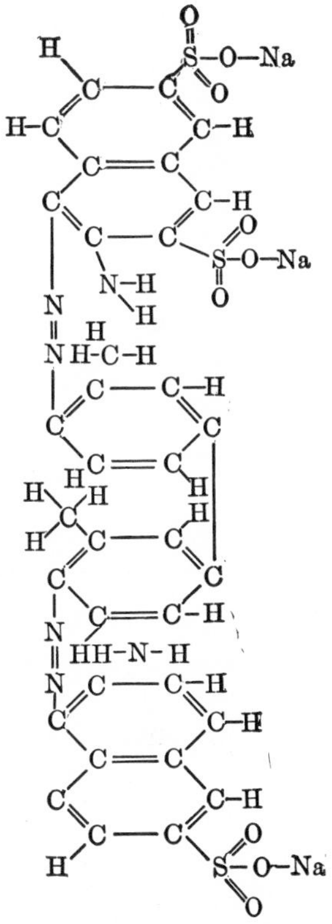

Fig. 2.1. Formula of an aniline dye, showing the complicated arrangement of the great number of carbon, hydrogen, nitrogen, and other atoms.

Nothing was too commonplace for him to examine; little escaped his scrutiny, and nothing was examined that did not furnish its surprises. Dust, earth, sea water, ditch water, all showed millions of tiny forms of life—little animals—*animalculae* he called them. Everywhere was teeming life; almost nothing was quite motionless. Blood was no longer what it appeared to be to the naked eye—simply a richly red fluid—but was seen to be a colorless liquid in which were suspended pale pink coin-shaped bodies — the **corpuscles** — that were whirled along like tiny rafts through finely delicate channels. We now call these channels **capillaries.**

Cell structure. It was later discovered that the tissues of our bodies that make up the muscles, skin, kidney, heart, liver, or other organs were not textureless but were made of a delicate fabric of millions upon millions of globular, columnar, cuboid, spindle-shaped, or irregularly shaped bodies. These bodies we call **cells.** We now know that these cells are composed of protoplasm, and we know that they are used together in sheets, tubes, or rounded masses, as in a tiled floor or in a piece of masonry, to form the many different parts of our bodies. It was not until 1838, more than a century after Leeuwenhoek's day, that a cell of the body was clearly described. One of the earliest published illustration of tissue cells is shown in Figure 2.3.

Fig. 2.2. Microscope used by
scientists of the 17th century.

Cells, though of many different types, sizes, and shapes, resemble one another in their appearance. The general plan of structure is the same in all. In order that the reader may form an idea of the cell's structure, we cannot do better than describe the amoeba—a microscopic animal found in ponds and ditches. Its entire body consists of but a single cell (Fig. 2.4).

The amoeba. The amoeba is a tiny piece of protoplasm; yet when pinched, pricked, or touched with something hot or with a crystal of salt, it shows by a movement that it is alive. It is therefore said to be **irritable.** This is a word which physiologists use in a very special sense to denote the reaction of a living thing in response to a change in its environment. Such a change is called a **stimulus.** Technically, then, the word *irritable* means the ability to respond to a stimulus.

The amoeba breathes and digests food, rids its body of waste materials, and moves from place to place. Yet no particular part of its body has been set apart as lungs, stomach, kidneys, or limbs. The protoplasm of which its body is molded is a Jack-of-all-trades. It can do all these things, which in higher animals are performed by special organs. The amoeba's entire body or any part of it may be given over to the task at hand, whether this be seizing and digesting its food, moving from one place to another, breathing, or ridding itself of waste materials (see also p. 148).

Though the tissues of the human body, whether nervous, muscular, glandular, or what not, are built mainly of protoplasm, this material has undergone in each type of tissue certain changes that endow it with the ability to carry out some specific duty. Such **differentiation,** as it is called, has enabled the cells of which the different organs are

Fig. 2.3. A reproduction of one of the published drawings of tissue cells.

composed to perform a particular function, whether this be secretion (gland), contraction (muscle), conduction (nerve), or the manufacture of hormones (endocrine), with the highest degree of efficiency.

Under the microscope the amoeba appears as an irregularly shaped scrap of living jelly. The irregular outline of the cell can be seen to

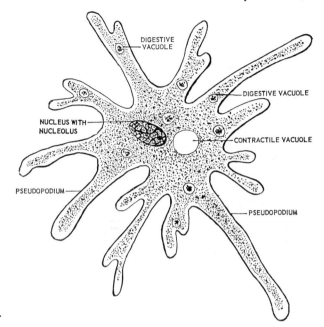

Fig. 2.4. An amoeba.

change from time to time, and, as we watch, we soon see that there is a purpose in these changes. One or two little peninsulas of protoplasm will be seen to jut out from the amoeba's body into the water surrounding it. These protrusions of protoplasm are called **pseudopodia** (Gk. *pseudopodium,* false foot). At another moment the pseudopodium is drawn back, only to be thrust out again at another part of the amoeba's circumference. The movements enable the animal to reach its food or to move away from a spot which is not suitable for it to live in. Figure 2.5 shows an amoeba chasing a small globular organism and trying to engulf it. The white cells in human blood and the cells in some other tissues of the body are able to move about in the same way, but most of the cells of the body are firmly fixed.

In or near the center of the amoeba can be seen a round or oval

Fig. 2.5. An amoeba endeavoring to engulf a small organism, which, on account of its shape, at first slips from the amoeba's grasp. *(After Jennings.)*

object which remains distinct from the main body of the cell. This is called the **nucleus.** The body of the cell surrounding the nucleus is called **the cytoplasm.** There is to be seen within the cytoplasm, usually not far from the nucleus, a small cavity called a **vacuole,** which constitutes the digestive system of the amoeba. Enzymes poured into it from the cytoplasm digest food particles that the organism has captured. The vacuole can be observed to alter in size and shape from time to time. A small body within the nucleus is called the **nucleolus.**

When the amoeba is killed and its body stained with a blue dye, it is found that the nucleus stains much more deeply than the cytoplasm. The reason for this difference is that the nucleus contains a material called **chromatin** (Gk. *chroma,* color), which absorbs the dye more readily. The chromatin material appears as dark-colored threads or strands that interlace in a complicated way with one another to form a fine network within the nucleus; it belongs to a class of compound proteins containing nucleic acid, the *nucleoproteins* (Ch. 30). Though the outline of the amoeba changes from time to time, none of its substance becomes lost; that is, the cytoplasm does not become dissolved by the water to disappear gradually, as a small piece of ordinary jelly would be, but holds together. This is because the amoeba, like the cells of which our bodies are made, possesses some firmer material at its boundary—a kind of **membrane**—that prevents the cytoplasm from breaking up and disappearing. This outer layer is also frequently referred to as the cell envelope or cell wall.

With the exception of the vacuole, the different parts described above for the amoeba—namely, the nucleus with its chromatin, the cytoplasm, and the cell membrane—are to be found in nearly all animal cells.[1] Most cells also possess a small body, called the **centrosome,** situated in the cytoplasm close to the nucleus. When the cell is stained with a suitable dye, a minute structure—the **centriole**—is seen near the center of the centrosome. Figure 2.6 shows a typical cell of the body of a higher animal. Close to one side of the nucleus is a circumscribed network of interlacing strands known as the **Golgi apparatus.** Little is known of its function. The black dots, **inclusion bodies,** are specks of food material.

TISSUES AND CELLS

Different parts or organs of the body behave differently. The duties one type of tissue has to perform are quite different from the duties performed by another type. The reason that one tissue or organ, such as the stomach, can digest food, and another organ, such as a muscle, can move a limb, is that the cells making up each organ are different. There

[1] The only exception to this is the fully developed red blood cell of man and higher animals, which has no nucleus.

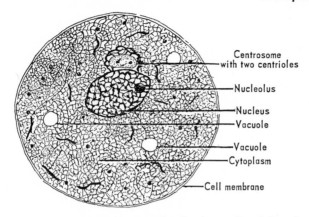

Fig. 2.6. Diagram of a typical cell. The small rod-shaped bodies in the cytoplasm are known as mitochondria and the black dots as inclusion bodies. The mesh surrounding the centrosome represents the Golgi network. For a description of the nature of these structures and their possible functions see a text on histology; also p. 418.

are four main types of cell—*epithelial, muscular, nervous,* and *connective*. The term **tissue** is a very general one, applied to any material derived from animal or vegetable life and consisting of cells that are grouped together in masses. When it is desired to be more explicit and to indicate the general type of cell of which a certain tissue is composed, one of the particular names just mentioned, or some other qualifying term is added. Thus we speak of *epithelial* tissue, *muscular* tissue, *nervous, fatty,* and *bony* (or *osseous*) tissues, etc. More specific terms, such as liver (*hepatic*) tissue, kidney (*renal*) tissue, etc., are also used.

Muscular tissues and nervous tissues will be described in Chapters 4, 24, and 33.

Epithelial tissue. The epithelial tissues serve the purpose of protection. They cover the surface of the body (skin) and line the nose, throat, windpipe, stomach, and intestines. The various glands of the body are also composed of epithelial cells that have acquired special powers to manufacture juices (secretions). Typical epithelial cells are oblong in shape and appear under the microscope as short and thick, or tall and narrow, blocks set side by side upon a thin membrane (**basement membrane**) and a thin layer of connective tissue. The term **columnar** is given to epithelial cells that are higher than they are broad. They are often, as in the case of those lining the respiratory passages, surmounted by delicate hairlike structures called **cilia** (Fig. 2.7, *left*). The cilia, which are about $\frac{1}{3500}$ inch long, sway continuously to and fro so that their surface looks like a wheat field undulating in a breeze. The waves, however, travel only

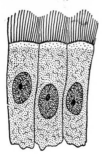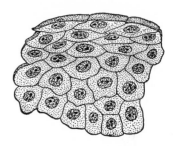

Fig. 2.7. *Left,* three columnar epithelial cells; *right,* several layers of epithelial cells (stratified squamous epithelium) from the mucosa of the mouth. Semidiagrammatic. The superficial layer is of the squamous type; deeper cells are cuboid in shape.

toward the exterior—upward in the lower air passages and downward in the nose. Thus the cilia serve to sweep dust and other small particles and mucus from the surfaces of the air passages.

Epithelial cells that are shaped like cubes are called **cuboidal**. Again, in some regions, such as the skin, the covering of the eyeball, and the walls of the air sacs in the lungs, they are flat and scalelike. This type is called **squamous** (L. *squama,* a scale) ; they usually form the outermost layer of a type of tissue called *stratified epithelium,* composed of several layers of cells of graded thicknesses. (See Fig. 2.7, *right.*)

The linings of the nose, throat, windpipe, stomach, and intestines are called **mucous membranes,** and consist of a layer or layers of cells lying upon a foundation of connective tissue and a few muscle cells. Many of the epithelial cells in these situations form drops or globules of mucus—an almost clear, watery, or somewhat slimy fluid—within their bodies. The globules burst from time to time, pouring their contents upon the surface of the mucous membrane. Epithelial cells of this nature are in reality like little **mucus glands.** From their appearance when filled they have received the name **goblet cells** (Fig. 2.8) . When the cells are inflamed, their secretion is increased many times. We are all familiar with the "running" nose of the common cold and with the expectoration of

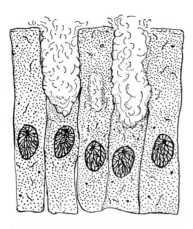

Fig. 2.8. Goblet cells discharging mucus. Mucus is shown forming in the middle cell.

mucus which accompanies a "cold in the chest." The thick fluid comes largely from the goblet cells.

One type of epithelial cell is extremely thin, thinner even than the squamous cells mentioned above, being no more than 0.0001 inch thick. Such cells are found laid edge to edge to form delicate linings for the arteries, veins, and heart. The smallest blood vessels, the capillaries, are tubes composed entirely of a single layer of these cells. These cells also cover the membranes of the thorax (**pleurae**), of the abdomen (**peritoneum**), and of other cavities. The name **endothelial** is given to this type of epithelial cell (Fig. 2.9).

Connective tissue. Connective tissue serves a supporting function, and above all is a repair tissue. Highly specialized cells, such as those of the nervous system, and of muscle, lose the power to multiply shortly after birth. Therefore, when such cells are destroyed by accident or disease they are not replaced. The defect is repaired by connective tissue consisting largely of fibers. A *scar*, or *cicatrix*, is a compact mass of fibrous

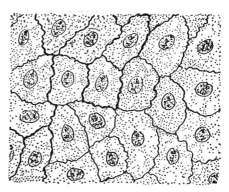

Fig. 2.9. Endothelial cells.

connective tissue that restores a defect caused by the destruction of other more highly specialized cells. When, for example, the skin is accidentally cut, its natural elasticity draws the edges of the wound apart and the space between is filled with a clot of blood consisting of blood cells and a network of fibrin threads (Ch. 7). Soon the clot is penetrated by fine blood vessels that convert it into a red, highly vascular granular tissue called *granulation tissue.* The granulation tissue is soon invaded by primitive connective tissue cells called **fibroblasts** (Gk. *blastos,* a germ, sprout, embryo) that develop into mature, elongated fibrous cells. These, with the passage of time, become firm and tough, and stitch the wound, at it were, and draw its edges closer together. This process is called healing by granulation or **second intention,** but when an operation wound is sutured and the edges of the skin are brought accurately together it is said to heal by **primary union** or **first intention.**

The primitive cells in the connective tissue—the *fibroblasts*—respond vigorously to various forms of chronic irritation, either of a chemical or a mechanical nature. An example of this propensity is cirrhosis of the liver, in which the highly specialized hepatic cells are strangled by an overgrowth of fibrous tissue. The connective tissue reaction may be induced by various chemical agents, such as alcohol, chloroform, or the

fumes of carbon tetrachloride (a cleaning fluid and fire extinguisher).
Increase in the connective tissue—*fibrosis*—of the lung also occurs in
miners and others whose occupations entail the inhalation of irritating
dusts. The fibrosis interferes with pulmonary function and encourages
the development of tuberculosis. In these and other examples of fibrosis
that could be cited, the so-called chronic irritation is really a persistently
repeated mild injury, and it is this that induces the connective tissue
proliferation.

Connective tissue cells differ greatly in shape and size, and form
tissues correspondingly diverse in structure, consistency, and function.
Some of these cells, as already indicated, are long and fibrous; others,
round or oval and filled with fat; still others undergo mineralization
(chiefly by calcium and phosphorus) and form bone. The chief divisions
of the connective tissue class are

Fibrous	Cartilaginous
Areolar	Elastic
Adipose	Hemopoietic (bone marrow and lymphoid tissue)
Osseous, or bony	[2] Neuroglial (of central nervous system)

Fibrous tissue is strong and tough, consisting mainly of long fibers
that form protective and supporting structures, such as ligaments, muscle
tendons, the capsules about joints, membranes or aponeuroses in various
situations, and the fasciae between muscle bundles or separating groups
of muscles.

Areolar tissue is a relatively soft, loose form of connective tissue
consisting of a network of interlacing fibers with numerous fat cells in

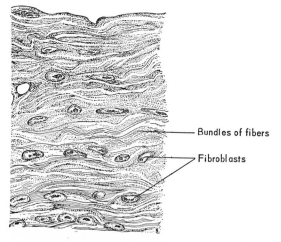

Fig. 2.10. Fibrous connective
tissue.

Bundles of fibers

Fibroblasts

---

[2] There is some difference of opinion as to whether neuroglia should be classed as
connective tissue or as nervous tissue. Functionally it is the connective tissue of the
central nervous system; but it is derived from ectoderm as is other nervous tissue,
whereas connective tissue proper is mesodermal in origin.

its mesh. Many of its fibers are highly elastic; others are tough, inelastic, and strong, resembling those in fibrous tissue. Areolar tissue also contains large mobile cells that, like some of the white blood cells, have a "scavenging" function. Areolar tissue is what one might call a "packing" tissue; it fills up spaces between organs, separates parts of organs from one another, and acts as a buffer or cushion; it is found beneath the skin, forms the outer coats of arteries and veins, and makes a bed for the internal organs. It is found in almost all parts of the body.

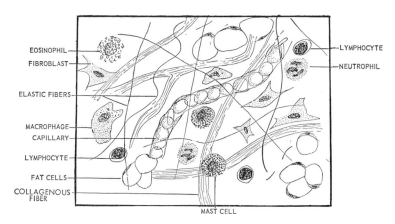

EOSINOPHIL
FIBROBLAST
ELASTIC FIBERS
MACROPHAGE
CAPILLARY
LYMPHOCYTE
FAT CELLS
COLLAGENOUS FIBER
LYMPHOCYTE
NEUTROPHIL
MAST CELL

Fig. 2.11. Areolar connective tissue.

Fatty, or adipose, tissue contains relatively few fibers, being made up mainly of areolar tissue whose cells have been greatly enlarged by the accumulation of fat in their cytoplasm; this distends the cell and flattens the nucleus against the cell boundary (Fig. 2.12). Adipose tissue serves many purposes. In the subcutaneous tissues it insulates the deeper structures against cold, cushions bony parts, rounds out the contours of the body; it serves as padding around and between the internal organs, especially of the abdomen. It also provides a store of potential energy. Food in excess of the body's requirement is stored as fat, which is often a burden to the individual or a detriment to his health (see *obesity,* Ch. 30).

Cartilage, or gristle, is a firm bluish or yellowish substance consisting of scattered groups of large cells with prominent nuclei and a ground substance that may be homogeneous or interlaced with fibers. In the former instance it is known as **hyaline** (glasslike) **cartilage,** in the latter as **fibrocartilage.** If it contains a large proportion of elastic fibers it is called **fibroelastic** cartilage. In the embryo most of the skeleton is first laid down in hyaline cartilage which, later, is replaced by bone.

Hyaline cartilage covers the ends of bones within joints, serving to buffer shocks and provide smooth surfaces upon which the bones can

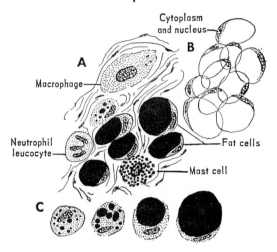

Fig. 2.12. Adipose tissue. Fat cells have been stained black using osmic acid. A, general connective tissue being converted to adipose tissue by the accumulation of fat; B, fat cells of adipose tissue from which the fat has been removed by ether; C, stages in the development of a fat cell.

slide. The thyroid, cricoid and nasal cartilages, and the lower part of the nasal septum are of the hyaline type. *Fibrocartilage* composes part of the intervertebral discs (p. 40), the semilunar cartilages of the knee joint, and the cartilage of the symphysis pubis. Certain small cartilages (cuneiform and parts of arytenoid, Ch. 22) of the larynx, the epiglottis, the pinna or auricle, and the outer part of the external auditory meatus are composed of *fibroelastic* cartilage.

Elastic connective tissue contains fibers that stretch readily but return to their original length when released from the stretching force. This type of tissue composes ligaments around freely movable joints, such as the ankle and the articulations of the vertebral column. The arteries, especially those of large and medium size, are plentifully supplied with elastic fibers.

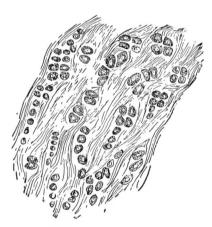

Fig. 2.13. A section of cartilage.

Mast cells, which bear a resemblance to the basophil granular leukocytes, are found in areolar tissue distributed along the course of the small blood vessels. Their cytoplasm is packed with large dark granules that almost or completely hide the nucleus. They produce heparin (Ch. 7).

The principle protein of the fibers and ground substance of fibrous connective tissue and cartilage is **collagen.** It is also contained in bone and most other types of connective tissue. Extracted by boiling water from hides, bones, cartilage, hoofs, etc., of animals, it is marketed as glue, size, or jelly powders, hence its name (Gk. *c(k)olla,* glue) .

There is a group of disorders characterized by an overgrowth of fibrous connective tissue, or by some abnormality in its development, distribution, or composition. These disorders, now generally known as the **collagen diseases,** include *rheumatoid arthritis, acute rheumatism,* and certain affections of the arteries *(periarteritis nodosa)* , skin *(sclero-derma)* , or muscles *(fibromyositis)* . The discovery a few years ago that the hormone of the adrenal cortex or the adrenocorticotropic hormone of the pituitary gland relieved the arthritic conditions, suggested that the adrenal cortex, in some way, influenced the growth and development of the collagenous tissues. But the action of the hormone upon arthritis is more probably of a pharmacological nature; that is, it acts rather as a remedial drug than by correcting a hormone deficiency, for the beneficial effect is induced only by doses much larger than those required in adrenal insufficiency (Ch. 40) , nor is arthritis a characteristic of this disease.

Bony, or osseous, tissue will be described in the next section, *hemopoietic tissue* in Chapter 8, and *neuroglial tissue* with the nervous system.

PHYSIOLOGICAL PROPERTIES OF PROTOPLASM

Protoplasm in its simplest form, as in the body of the amoeba, is endowed with four abilities. It is just these abilities that we recognize as the outward and visible signs of life. They are **irritability** (which, as has been explained, is the power to react to a stimulus) , **growth, metabolism,** and **reproduction.**

In the higher forms of life, protoplasm as a whole has lost the self-sufficiency it retains in the lower forms. Persons in a modern civilization no longer grow their wheat, grind their flour, and bake their bread. They no longer clothe themselves in homespun garments, or fell the trees and hew the timber for their dwellings. Each of these different tasks is performed by specially trained persons who are generally of little use in fields other than their own. So it is with protoplasm when it becomes "civilized" and comes to live in rows upon rows of cells. No longer can any one type of cell perform all the vital duties, as the amoeba does. Labor is divided, and certain groups of cells become highly trained for special purposes.

Nerve and muscle cells, for instance, have, so to speak, educated themselves to respond very quickly to stimulation. They are consequently called the **irritable tissues.** They cannot, however, reproduce themselves, and it is only in early life that they grow. In higher animals and man a special group of cells has been set aside, segregated from the rest of the cells of the body for the special purpose of reproduction, a very complicated process described in Chapter 48. The amoeba and other one-celled organisms, in order to perpetuate their kind, simply divide into two equal parts. They are immortal, for the parent, as well as the new cells, continues its existence.

Living cells of all kinds, whatever their duties, are tiny chemical laboratories. Within their protoplasm are carried out the most complicated chemical reactions—oxidations, decompositions, and combinations of various types. When food is oxidized by the tissues heat is generated. Each cell might be thought of as a stove of microscopic size, but whose fuel is the carbon of food instead of wood or coal. When a handful of sugar is thrown into the fire it flares up, and we say that it has burned or has undergone combustion. Oxygen was consumed in the burning, so, chemically speaking, the sugar was *oxidized,* its carbon to carbon dioxide (CO_2), and its hydrogen to water (H_2O). Fat burns with a much hotter flame. Meat burns with great difficulty, but it too will be consumed in a hot fire. Both meat and fat also require oxygen for their combustion. The heat produced keeps the body warm, maintaining a constant temperature at about 98.6° F. Thus, when we say that a certain food is **metabolized,** we mean that it is oxidized by the cells of the tissues, with the production of heat. The process itself is called **metabolism.** The quantity of heat produced is expressed in Calories.

Metabolism, however, embraces chemical processes other than the oxidation of food. The term may be applied to any chemical process occurring in living tissues. So we may speak of the oxidation or other chemical change undergone by carbohydrate in the cells (but not in the intestinal tract) as *carbohydrate metabolism,* by protein as *protein metabolism,* and so on. The cells derive from the blood the substances they require and manufacture entirely new materials. The breakdown of molecules into small chemical groups is called **catabolism** (Gk. *cata,* down); **anabolism** (Gk. *ana,* up) is the term for synthetic processes. The digestive glands, for example, form secretions of various sorts containing enzymes and acids or bases; other complex and very powerful substances known as *hormones* are formed by the cells of the endocrine organs (Ch. 38). The synthesis of new tissue during growth and for the repair of worn-out tissue parts is also included under the term metabolism.

Chemical functions are not confined to animal cells, for they are performed also by plant life. The yeast cell, for example, converts sugar into alcohol and carbon dioxide; and the microorganisms of disease manufacture various poisonous substances called **toxins.**

A phenomenon that requires a word here but will be treated more fully later, is the generation of electricity during activity. An electrical current is set up in all types of tissue—nervous, muscular, or glandular—when they become active.

In the earlier divisions of the fertilized egg (Ch. 49) all cells are similar in appearance, but they possess immensely different potentialities. As development proceeds, groups of cells go their different ways, becoming greatly dissimilar in shape, structure, and function. They aggregate in masses to form the several organs of the body, each ingeniously constructed for the special functions it has to perform. This process whereby tissues and organs are developed along special lines is called **differentiation.** Its guiding principle is chemical, and resides in certain groups of cells called *organizers, activators,* or *evocators.*

In the process of differentiation not all types of cell are endowed in equal degree with the four faculties given above. Nerve and muscle cells have developed the property of irritability to the highest state of proficiency; bone cells excel in the ability to draw minerals from the blood; bone and red blood cells have little power to generate heat, whereas the cells of the liver which carry out numerous chemical processes have a very high metabolism and produce large quantities of heat.

After cells, except those of the sex glands, have undergone differentiation, that is, have reached maturity in form and function, they are no longer capable of reproduction. *Mature* cells, whether they be of nervous or of muscular tissue, red blood cells or epithelial cells, or even connective tissue cells, are incapable of reproducing their kind; but the various connective tissues and the epithelial tissues have a store of primitive cells upon which to draw. Therefore, bone, blood, and skin, but not nervous or muscular tissue, are able to regenerate and replace cells that have been destroyed.

HOW DIFFERENT PARTS OF THE BODY ARE NOURISHED

We have seen how the amoeba obtains its food. But the cells of the body cannot roam about looking for food; the food must be carried to them. This task is performed by the blood. The blood acts as the waiter who brings the food from the cooks in the kitchen to the guests in the dining room. The cells of the stomach and intestines are the cooks of the body. They prepare the food and give it to the blood, which then gives a little to every cell in the body. Each cell oxidizes what it receives and gets from it energy to do useful work.

THE SKELETON AND
THE MUSCULAR SYSTEM
PART II

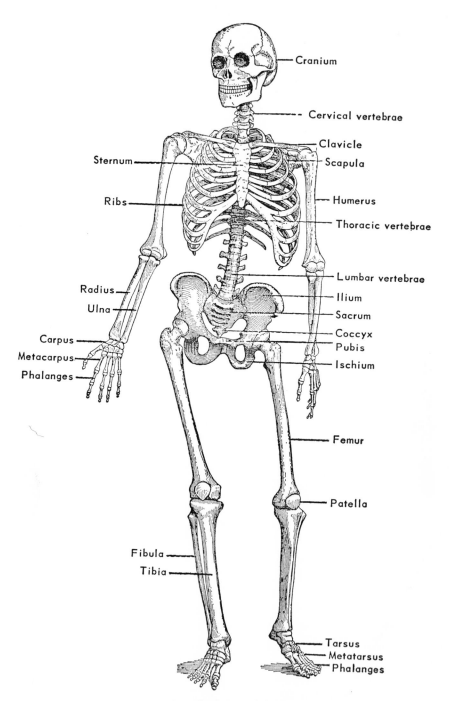

Fig. 3.1. The human skeleton.

3
The Skeleton

GENERAL DESCRIPTION OF BONES

The bony structure of the body is called the **skeleton** and consists of 200 bones of various shapes and sizes (Fig. 3.1). The bones are bound together by strong fibrous tissue, but the junctions between many of the former permit a limited degree of movement of one bone upon another and are called **joints.** In vertebrates—that great group of animals possessing a backbone or vertebral column—the skeleton is covered by soft tissues, muscles, fat, vessels, nerves, etc., and is therefore called an **endoskeleton.** In many invertebrate forms, such as lobsters, crabs, oysters, clams, snails, etc., the skeleton, which is formed on an entirely different plan, is on the outside of the soft tissues; and though the material of which it is composed is hard and calcareous in nature, it differs from bone. Such protective coverings are called **exoskeletons.** In animals still lower in the scale of life, such as worms, there is no skeleton of any kind, and some vertebrates, such as fish (scales) and turtles (carapace), have an endo- as well as an exoskeleton.

The *functions* of the endoskeleton of vertebrates, including man, which from now on will be called simply the skeleton, are (a) *protective,* (b) to afford a framework for the support of the various soft structures of the body, (c) to serve for the attachment of muscles, and (d) to provide a readily available storehouse of essential minerals, for example, calcium and phosphorus.

The protective purpose of the skeleton is seen especially in the skull, vertebrae (spinal column), thorax (ribs and breast bone), and in the bones of the pelvis (hip bones). The central nervous system, heart and lungs, kidneys, liver, and pelvic organs are thus well guarded from external violence. The anterior part of the abdomen is about the only region containing vital structures that does not appear to be adequately protected.

31

The form and rigidity the bony framework gives to the soft structures are obvious. Through its giving attachment to muscles, the bones such as the long bones of the arms and legs are converted to strong levers, tools, or weapons that can be used for work, locomotion, or defense. The bony framework of the body is not static in its composition in the sense that the minerals of which it is so largely composed remain fixed without interchange with the other constituents of the body; *the skeleton is composed of living tissue,* its materials being constantly dissolved and passed into the blood stream, and being replenished from other tissues and from food.

The minute structure of bone, or osseous tissue. Bone contains a large proportion of mineral matter, chiefly calcium and phosphorus (as tricalcium phosphate and calcium carbonate) but also smaller amounts of magnesium and traces of fluorine, chlorine, and iron. Some bones, like those of the limbs, are developed by the deposition of minerals in cartilage. Others, such as some bones of the cranium (Ch. 3), are formed by the mineralization of membranous tissue.

Two types of osseous tissue enter into the construction of the long bones of the limbs. The **shaft,** or **diaphysis,** of a limb bone consists of a tube of hard *compact* bone, while the ends, or **epiphyses,** are composed of *cancellous (spongy)* bone, covered by a shell of compact bone.

A section of compact bone from the shaft of the femur (thigh bone) is shown in Figure 3.2. The heavily mineralized substance is laid down in groups of from six to eight concentric tubular plates called **lamellae** that enclose numerous narrow channels known as **Haversian canals.**

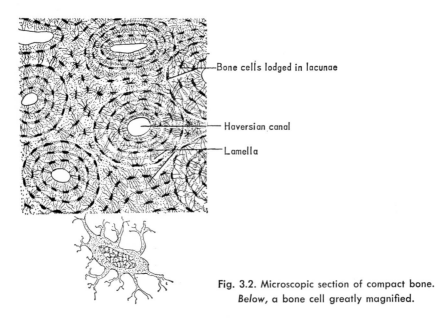

—Bone cells lodged in lacunae

— Haversian canal

—Lamella

Fig. 3.2. Microscopic section of compact bone. *Below,* a bone cell greatly magnified.

These run parallel to the long axis of the bone and carry branches of the nutrient artery, nerves, and some loose areolar tissue. Spaced at short intervals between the lamellae are small cavities, the *lacunae* (not to be confused with Howship's lacunae mentioned below) from which fine canaliculi radiate and connect with the Haversian canals and with other lacunae. Thus a rich system of anastomosing channels penetrates the bone matrix, which transmits nutrient fluid transuded from the blood vessels into the substance of the bone. The Haversian canals also communicate with the inner and outer surfaces of the bone through channels known as the *canals of Volkmann*. The longitudinal tubular space (medullary cavity) running *down the center* of a long bone (Fig. 3.3) such as the humerus or femur, is filled with a soft, fatty substance known as **yellow marrow.**

The bone cells belong to the connective tissue class, and are of three types—**osteoblasts, osteoclasts,** and **osteocytes.** The first two of these are present in the developing bone; the last, in formed bone. The *osteoblasts* are large, plump cells usually found in a single row beneath the periosteum, from which they arise. They are mainly responsible for the formation of bony tissue.

The *osteoclasts* are multinucleated giant cells found where bone is being resorbed. They lie in shallow depressions—*Howship's lacunae*—that they appear to have excavated on the bone surface. The administration of parathyroid hormone (Ch. 40) causes resorption of bone and increases the number and activity of the osteoclasts.

As new bone is laid down beneath the periosteum during normal growth, or in the repair of a fracture, the osteoblasts become included in the new-formed material and differentiate into *osteocytes,* the permanent cells of mature osseous tissue. These cells are lodged in the lacunae

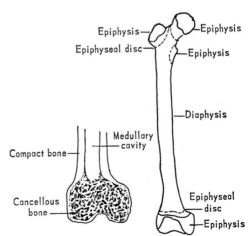

Fig. 3.3. The main parts of a typical long bone.

mentioned above; their slender processes penetrate into the canaliculi radiating from the lacunae.

Cancellous bone is made up of slender bars of osseous tissue called trabeculae that interlace with one another (Fig.3.4), and give a sponge-like pattern to the bony structure. The spaces between the trabeculae are filled with a soft, dark red tissue called the **red marrow** that is responsible for the manufacture of red blood cells, granular leucocytes, and probably also of the blood platelets (Fig. 3.5). This substance consists of a mass of immature red blood cells and granular leucocytes mostly in the later stages of their development, as well as the forerunners of the platelets—the **megacaryocytes**

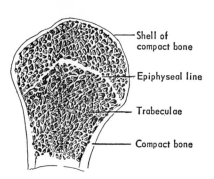

Fig. 3.4. Cancellous bone; section through head of humerus to show trabeculae and epiphyseal line.

(labels in figure: Shell of compact bone; Epiphyseal line; Trabeculae; Compact bone)

(Ch. 8) and a few mature erythrocytes and leucocytes. The ribs and bodies of the vertebrae as well as the ends of the long bones are composed of cancellous bone covered by a thin layer of compact bone. In the cranial bones, spongy bone is also found sandwiched between two layers of dense bone.

The membrane covering the exterior of the bone is called the **periosteum;** that lining the medullary cavity, the **endosteum.**

The development and growth of bone. In the embryo the greater part of the skeleton is primarily patterned in hyaline cartilage developed from the embryonic connective tissues (the mesenchyme). Some bones of the skull (frontal, parietal, squamous and tympanic parts of the temporal, some parts of the sphenoid, the vomer, nasal, zygomatic, and most of the maxilla) and part of the collar bone are developed from membrane. *Ossification,* or *osteogenesis,* that is, the replacement of the cartilage model by one of bone, occurs through the activities of the osteoblasts (see above) both beneath the periosteum and in foci within the cartilage called **ossification centers.** Each bone is developed from one or more ossification centers; only the smallest bones, such as the lacrimal and nasal bones and the carpal and metatarsals, are formed from one center.

The cartilage in which the future bone is modeled is not converted directly into bone. In the first stage toward the formation of bone, the cartilage degenerates and is replaced by a calcified material known as *osteoid (bonelike) tissue.* This calcification process is the work of the osteoblasts, which abstract the mineral from the blood and lay it down with organic material. An enzyme known as *phosphatase,* also produced

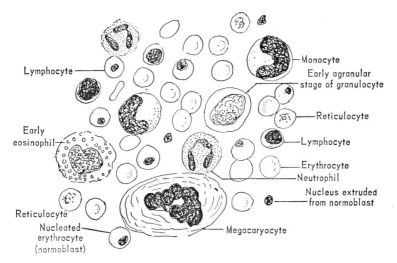

Lymphocyte

Early
eosinophil

Reticulocyte

Nucleated
erythrocyte
(normoblast)

Monocyte
Early agranular
stage of granulocyte

Reticulocyte

Lymphocyte

Erythrocyte
Neutrophil

Nucleus extruded
from normoblast

Megacaryocyte

Fig. 3.5. Smear of red bone marrow drawn from sternum by needle puncture.

by the osteoblasts, is essential to the process. Later the osteoid tissue is replaced by true bone as a result again of osteoblastic activity.

The ossification centers appear at widely different ages. In any given bone the first center to appear is called the *primary center;* those appearing later are called *secondary centers.* That part of a bone developed from the primary center, which in the case of a long bone corresponds to the shaft of the bone, and mentioned above, is called the *diaphysis.* The part formed from a secondary center is called the *epiphysis;* in the long bones these are situated at the ends of the bone; but in other bones the secondary centers appear in various situations, and the part of the bone that is ossified from each of these centers is also called an epiphysis (Fig. 3.3) .

With very few exceptions, for example, the distal end of the femur, all the epiphyseal or secondary centers do not appear until after birth. Many make their appearance in infancy or childhood, but some not until puberty, and the medial end of the collar bone not until between the 18th and 20th year.

The primary centers of the great majority of the bones appear before birth. The bones of the carpus are notable exceptions, the times of appearance of the centers of the different carpal bones varying from 6 months after birth to 14 years.

A long bone, such as the humerus or femur, grows in thickness through the activity of the osteoblasts derived from the periosteum, the new-formed bone being laid down in layers on the bone's outer surface. At the same time that new bone is being added on the outside, bone resorption is taking place on the inner surface, that is, on the wall of the medullary cavity. Hence the shaft of the bone does not increase excessively in thickness and encroach upon the central cavity; the cavity, rather, widens step by step with the deposition of osseous tissue subperiosteally.

The bone grows in length by multiplication of cells within the cartilage model, mainly toward the ends of the shaft. As already stated, the cartilage is first calcified and the osteoid tissue is later replaced by true bone through the activity of the osteoblasts of the ossification center. At the same time bone is being formed by the ossification centers of the epiphyses. As the new bone of the shaft and epiphyses gradually increases, only a thin zone of cartilage is left between the two. This is called the **epiphyseal plate** or **disc.** For some time the disc remains unossified, and during this time it is the only means whereby the bone can grow lengthwise. Though the cartilage cells within the epiphyseal plate multiply, it does not increase in thickness because the older cells at its boundaries become ossified. Thus cartilage growth within the disc, which would expand it, is balanced by bone formation at the boundary. The inevitable result is lengthening of the bone. Finally, the cartilage of the epiphyseal plate is replaced by bone, and firm union of epiphyses and diaphysis is thus ensured. This marks the time when the bone has reached its adult length; it is incapable of further longitudinal growth.

There is a very definite time set for the fusion of the epiphyses and diaphysis of each particular bone. Thus, the upper epiphysis (head) of the humerus fuses with the diaphysis (shaft) at 21 years of age for males and at 18 years for females, whereas the main parts of the os coxae (hipbone) fuse in both sexes at about the 17th year. The epiphyseal cartilage is a weak link in a bone, and until complete osseous union between epiphyses and diaphysis has occurred violence may cause a separation at this point instead of fracture of the bone. *Separation of an epiphysis* is therefore not uncommon in children.

The details of the growth of flat or irregularly shaped bones, such as the scapula, hipbone, and sacrum, which are ossified from a number of centers (eight or nine for the scapula, and eight for the hipbone) are very complicated, but the general principles are the same as those described for the long bones.

The "molding" or "sculpturing" of a bone into its characteristic adult shape is the result of two opposing processes—bone formation and bone resorption—that is, the solution and removal of bone substance at one point and bone formation at another. The factors involved in bone resorption are imperfectly understood. For a long time it was thought that the osteoclasts were primarily the active agents, that they, as it were, "gnawed" the bone and removed it piecemeal. The gathering of these cells at sites where the bone was undergoing active resorption, their lodgment in small excavations (Howship's lacunae, see above) on the surface of the bone, as well as the bone resorptive action of the parathyroid hormone (Ch. 40), accompanied by the appearance of large numbers of osteoclasts, all taken together, seemed to strengthen this theory. But bone resorption may occur in the complete absence of osteoclasts and, when present, they do not appear to exercise any phagocytic action. Nevertheless, though a belief in the primary importance of the osteoclasts in the process is not now entertained, these cells do apparently exert an influence in some way upon the resportion of bone.

Though normally the bones cease to grow in length, breadth, and thickness after the epiphyses and diaphyses have fused, the osseous tissue, given the appropriate stimulus, is capable of localized growth. This is seen in the union of fractures; the newly formed tissue that cements together the fragments of the broken bone is called *callous;* it is produced by the periosteum. Also, the bosses and ridges on a bone where the muscles are attached become more prominent in muscular subjects as a result of the stimulus provided by the pull of the contracting muscles. Overgrowth of bone may occur as abnormalities; bony spurs (exostoses) and the thickening and enlargement of bone in osteitis deformans and acromegally are examples of such.

The figure of 200 given previously for the bones of the skeleton does not include the three minute bones, or ossicles, of the ear, nor the small bony nodules known as **sesamoid** bones developed in some tendons (Gk. *sēsamoeidēs,* shaped like sesame seeds), nor are the *sutural* or *Wormian*[1] bones included.

The bones of the skull and vertebral column are sometimes referred to as the **axial** skeleton, and the bones of the limbs the **appendicular** skeleton.

Before describing the separate bones it will be necessary to define certain terms that will be used and have not already been explained.

Terms referring to direction and position. The so-called **anatomical position** of the body is standing with the palms of the hands turned to face forwards (Fig. 3.6). The aspect of the body showing the face, chest, palms of the hands, abdomen, etc., is called **anterior.** The back of the body is called the **posterior** aspect. Four principal **planes** of the body are recognized and known as the **median, sagittal, coronal,** and **transverse** planes. The *median plane* passes longitudinally through the center of the body, and might be represented by a board in this position with its edges directed anteriorly and posteriorly, and its two broad surfaces directed to the right and left. A *sagittal plane* is either the median plane or any other vertical plane to either side of and parallel to it. The *coronal,* or *frontal, plane* is any plane passing through the body at right

---

[1] These are small irregular bones sometimes found in joints (sutures) of the skull.

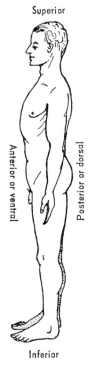

Superior

Anterior or ventral

Posterior or dorsal

Inferior

Fig. 3.6. The anatomical positions to which the various terms anterior, posterior, ventral, dorsal, etc., refer.

angles to the median or to a sagittal plane. A *transverse,* or *horizontal, plane* is one that passes horizontally at right angles to the median plane. The anterior surface of the arms (the body being in the anatomical position) is called the **volar** surface. The term **plantar** means in the direction of or related to the sole of the foot. The term **ventral** is applied to a direction toward the anterior surface of the human body or to the under surface of an animal, while **dorsal** means toward the back of the body. A direction toward the midline of the body is called **medial,** one toward either side is termed **lateral.** Thus, in describing the positions of two structures or of two parts of a structure, the one is said to be medial or lateral to the other according to whether the one is nearer or farther than the other from the midline. In speaking of a structure or part, such as a limb, artery, or nerve, any point nearer its origin is referred to as being **proximal** to a more distant point which is said to be **distal** to the former point. Thus, the shoulder is proximal to the elbow, but the elbow is distal to the shoulder, and the ankle is distal to the knee or hip. The body resting on its back is said to be in the **supine** position; lying with the face down is called the **prone** position.

Terms used in connection with bones, joints, and various soft tissues. **Aponeurosis** (pl. *aponeuroses*) is a tough, smooth, broad fibrous sheet, of a white, opalescent, or glistening appearance. It is most frequently attached to large, broad muscles, such as those of the abdominal wall. **Articulation** is the apposition of two bones to form a joint; it also means, of course, the formation of words, speech (L. *articulus,* a joint; but also a knob, the knot of a tree, a moment in time, or a division or part of a speech) . **Crista** is a sharp ridge resembling a cock's comb (L. *crista,* crest of a bird) . Duct is a narrow tube, usually applied to one that carries off the secretions of a gland. **Facet** is a small, smooth, flat or slightly depressed area on a bone that is usually a point of contact with another bone or other hard structure. **Fascia** (pl. *fasciae*) is a sheet of tissue composed of connective tissue fibers and areolar tissue that serves to cover or envelop various organs, to separate muscles or parts of muscles, or to intervene between the skin and deeper tissues. **Fissure** is a furrow, deep groove, or cleft. **Foramen** (pl. *foramina*) is a perforation, hole, or opening in a bone, membrane, or any other structure. **Fossa** (L., a trench or ditch; pl. *fossae*) is a shallow depression. **Ganglion** (Gk., a tumor) is a collection of nerve cells in the brain, but especially on a nerve trunk. In the latter situation (such as on a posterior root ganglion) it usually forms a distinct swelling. The term is also a surgical one applied to a small swelling on the back of the wrist derived from a tendon sheath. **Lamella** (L., pl. *lamellae*, diminutive of *lamina*) is a thin flat plate. **Lamina** (L., pl. *laminae*) is a layer, plate, or stratum. **Ligament** (L. *ligamentum*, a bandage or bond) is a cord, sheet, or band of strong connective tissue, situated most commonly about or within a joint that it serves to support and aids in holding the bones together. **Membrane** is a flat, thin sheet of pliable material that covers other structures, envelops an organ or part, or lines one of the body cavities. The term is a very comprehensive one. A membrane may be highly cellular like the mucous or synovial membranes, or be composed mainly of connective tissue fibers. Again, it may consist of a single layer of thin, flat epithelial (endothelial) cells. **Raphe** (Gk., a seam) is a line of union, usually fibrous between two similar structures. **Septum** (L., an enclosure or barrier) is a partition, generally of connective tissue, dividing a cavity or separating the parts of any organ or tissue. **Sinus** (L., a basin) a cavity or hollow (such as a nasal sinus), an expanded part, a small vessel (such as in the liver), or one of the large intracranial veins. **Tendons** are tough cords or ribbons of fibrous connective tissue to which muscle fibers are fused and through which a muscle exerts traction upon the bone into which it is inserted. **Theca** (Gk., a box) is a sheath such as encloses a tendon or a Graafian follicle of the ovary. **Tubercle** (L. *tuberculum*, diminutive of *tuber*, a swelling) is a small rounded elevation on a bone, in pathology also applied to similar swellings in skin, lung, and other soft tissues. **Tuberosity** is a rounded prominence on a bone, usually somewhat larger than a tubercle.

DESCRIPTIONS OF INDIVIDUAL BONES

Bones of the vertebral column (spinal column or backbone)

The vertebral column is composed of a long series of separate bones called **vertebrae** (sing. *vertebra*), linked together by ligaments and bound by muscles to form a strong support for the head and trunk, and indirectly to provide rigidity for the suspension of the limbs (Fig. 3.1, 3.7). It is capable of assuming, through the contraction or relaxation of muscles, either a high degree of rigidity or great flexibility. Besides its supporting function, the vertebral column is given the equally important duty of protecting the spinal cord to which each vertebra furnishes a complete and stout ring of bone; the whole series of vertebrae provide,

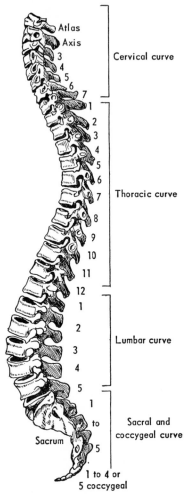

Atlas
Axis
3
4
5
6
7

Cervical curve

1
2
3
4
5
6
7
8
9
10
11
12

Thoracic curve

1
2
3
4
5

Lumbar curve

1
to
5

Sacral and
coccygeal curve

Sacrum

1 to 4 or
5 coccygeal

Fig. 3.7. The human vertebral column.

as it were, a hollow bony cylinder in which the spinal cord is enclosed. There are 34 vertebrae—7 **cervical** (neck), 12 **thoracic**, or **dorsal** (back of thorax), 5 **lumbar** (small of back), 5 **sacral** (fused to form the sacrum), and 5 **coccygeal** (fused to form the coccyx) (see below).

The greater number of the vertebrae are constructed upon a common plan, though variations of this basic design, more or less pronounced, are found between the vertebrae of different regions of the spinal column. A typical vertebra consists of two principal parts called the **body** and the **vertebral arch**. The *body*, situated anteriorly, is a thick disclike mass of cancellous (spongy) bone with a thin covering of compact bone; it is convex horizontally in front and concave behind where it helps to form the **spinal canal** containing the spinal cord. The vertebral bodies are laid flat upon one another, like a stack of coins, to form a more or less vertical column, a disc of fibrous cartilage intervening between each two adjacent ones. The *vertebral arch* completes posteriorly a ring of bone that, with the bodies and arches of the other vertebrae, forms the spinal canal (see Fig. 3.10). The space enclosed by this bony ring is called the vertebral foramen. The arch consists of two **pedicles**, two **laminae**, a spinous process, two **transverse processes** and four **articular processes**. The pedicles are two bars of bone that spring from the body and incline backwards. The laminae are a pair of broad plates arising from the pedicles; they meet and fuse in the midline behind, and from their point of fusion the spinous process, which points backward and downward, is developed (Figs. 3.7, 3.10 to 3.12). The transverse processes project laterally and posteriorly on each side from the junctions of the pedicles with the laminae. The articular processes are also arranged in this fashion; there are a superior and an inferior pair. The superior project upward with their articular facets facing backward; the inferior project downward, their articular surfaces facing forward. The articular processes articulate with the processes of the vertebrae above and below, the superior with the inferior of the vertebra above, the inferior with the superior of the vertebra below.

The **cervical vertebrae** (numbered 1 to 7 from top to bottom) are smaller than the vertebrae of other regions. The spinous processes of most of the cervical vertebrae are short and split at their tips; the first, second, and seventh are exceptions: the vertebral bodies are small and oval (Figs. 3.8, 3.9). The first and second cervical vertebrae have very special and

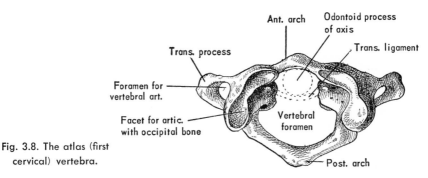

Fig. 3.8. The atlas (first cervical) vertebra.

distinctive features and are given specific names. The first is called the **atlas** (for, like the Greek god who bore the heavens upon his shoulders, it supports the head). It is an irregular ringlike bone possessing neither a body nor a spinous process. The anterior and posterior halves are called, respectively, the **anterior** and **posterior arches.** Joining the arches

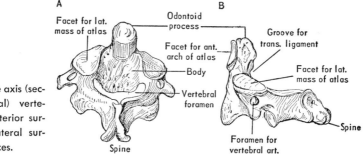

Fig. 3.9. The axis (second cervical) vertebra. A, posterior surfaces; B, lateral surfaces.

on either side is a **lateral mass** consisting of a transverse process, and a large, oval, smooth surface that articulates with the occipital bone of the skull. The posterior aspect of the anterior arch shows an articular surface (facet) that makes contact with a corresponding facet on the anterior surface of the odontoid (toothlike) process of the second cervical vertebra, called the **axis** (Figs. 3.8, 3.9). The odontoid process serves as a pivot upon which the atlas and the head can be rotated. It is a stout, conical, upright column arising from the body of the vertebra. The odontoid process of the axis, as mentioned above, is provided with a facet for articulation with a similar facet on the atlas; it is held in position by a ligament that passes behind it and is attached on either side to the lateral mass of the atlas. The body of the axis is small and largely hidden by the odontoid process. The pedicles and laminae are stout; the latter give origin to the strong ligaments of the neck—**ligamenta flava**. The spine is relatively large but the transverse processes are small.

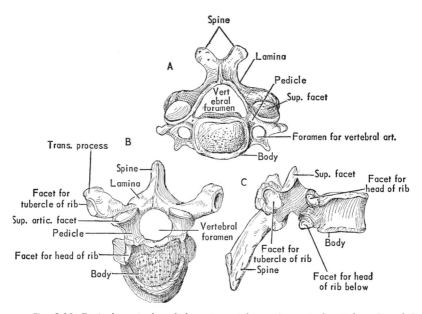

Fig. 3.10. Typical cervical and thoracic vertebrae. A, cervical vertebra; B and C, thoracic vertebra, superior and lateral aspects, respectively.

The **thoracic vertebrae**, 12 in number, are intermediate in size between the cervical and lumbar vertebrae. The bodies are shaped somewhat like a conventionally depicted heart. An upper and a lower facet is seen on each side of the body for articulation with the heads of the ribs—the upper facet with the rib of the same number, the lower facet with the rib below. A third facet is present on the transverse process of each side that articulates with the tubercle of the rib of the same number. The vertebral foramen is small and circular (Figs. 3.10, 3.11).

The **lumbar vertebrae**, 5 in number, are much larger than the thoracic; they have thick, heavy, oval bodies, long, thin transverse processes (except the fifth), and short spines that project almost horizontally backward (Fig. 3.12).

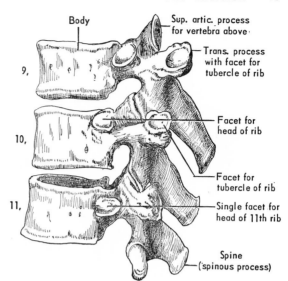

Body

Sup. artic. process
for vertebra above

9,

Trans. process
with facet for
tubercle of rib

10,

Facet for
head of rib

Facet for
tubercle of rib

11,

Single facet for
head of 11th rib

Spine
('spinous process)

Fig. 3.11. The ninth, tenth, and eleventh thoracic vertebrae.

The sacrum completes the bony pelvis. It represents 5 vertebrae fused into a single bone. It is a large, massive, very irregular structure, but as a whole is triangular or wedge shaped, with its base directed upwards; its long axis is curved with the concavity facing forwards, that is, toward the pelvic cavity (Figs. 3.7 and 3.13).

The coccyx, or tail bone, which is composed of several (usually 5) rudimentary vertebrae fused together, is a small triangular bone that articulates by its base with the lower end of the sacrum (Fig. 3.13; muscle origins are colored pink, insertions blue).

The ribs are 24 bowed bones (12 on each side) that, with the thoracic vertebrae behind and the sternum in front, form the thorax or framework of the chest. Starting above they are numbered 1 to 12 in numerical correspondence with the thoracic vertebrae. The first 7 ribs are called true ribs because they are connected in front through the costal cartilages with the sternum. The lower 5 are termed false, since the eighth, ninth, and tenth have a common connection with the sternum, each being joined to the costal cartilage of the rib above, while the

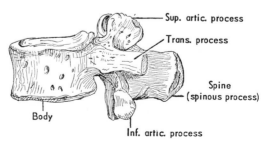

Sup. artic. process

Trans. process

Spine
(spinous process)

Fig. 3.12. A typical lumbar vertebra.

Body

Inf. artic. process

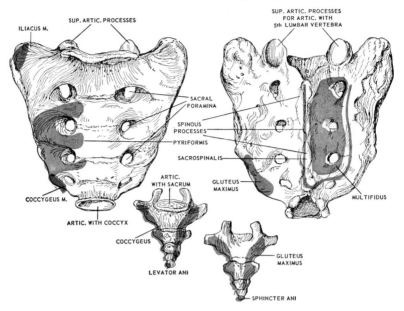

Fig. 3.13. The sacrum (upper figures) and coccyx (lower figures). *Left,* anterior, or pelvic, surfaces; *right,* posterior surfaces.

eleventh and twelfth, also called **floating ribs,** have no connection at all with the sternum.

A typical rib, such as the sixth, has an **anterior end** that shows a cuplike depression into which fits the outer end of the costal cartilage, and a **posterior** or **vertebral** end that presents, for description, a **head, neck,** and **tubercle.** The main part of the rib is called the **shaft.** The head, or posterior extremity, shows two small, smooth areas (facets) for articulation with the thoracic vertebrae above and below; through a short ligament the head is attached between these areas to the intervertebral disc. The neck is the short, constricted portion in front of the head, and is marked off from the shaft by the **tubercle,** a small elevation with a facet for articulation with the transverse process of the corresponding vertebra. The shaft is thin and flat with sharp upper and lower borders; it is bowed outwards and somewhat twisted as well. The arch shows a somewhat sharp bend, called the **angle,** about 2 inches in front of the tubercle (Fig. 3.14) .

The first, second, tenth, eleventh, and twelfth ribs show special features. The first and second are relatively short, especially the first, and show sharp curvatures. The surfaces of their flat and broad shafts look upwards and downwards and are not twisted.

The sternum (L., chest) , **or breast bone,** is an elongated, flat bone resembling a Roman sword, occupying the center of the front of the chest. The upper, somewhat triangular part, is called the **manubrium** (L., handle) and the lower, pointed part, the **xiphoid** (Gk., sword) **process**, or **ensiform** (L., sword) **cartilage.** The upper border of the manubrium shows a shallow concavity—the **suprasternal notch.** The main part of the sternum between the manubrium and the xiphoid process is known as the **body,** or **gladiolus** (L., sword). The upper 10 ribs are connected to the sternum through 7 bars of cartilage, called the **costal cartilages** (Fig. 3.15).

The vertebral column and the thorax as a whole. The vertebral column presents four curves: **cervical** convex forwards; **thoracic** convex backwards; **lumbar** convex forwards; and **pelvic,** or **sacral,** with its convexity backwards. The convexities are thus directed alternately forward and backward. The thoracic and pelvic curves are termed primary since they appear in early fetal life, the cervical and lumbar curves are secondary, or compensatory. The cervical curve appears when the baby is able to sit up; the lumbar when he commences to walk (Fig. 3.7).

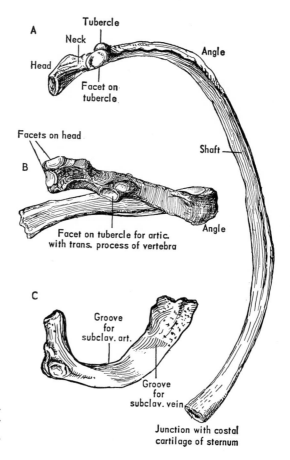

Fig. 3.14. Typical ribs. A and B, fifth rib, inferior and posterior aspects, respectively; C, first rib.

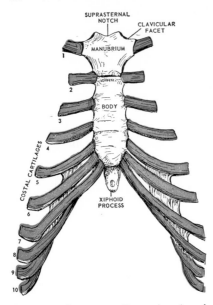

Fig. 3.15. The sternum (breast bone) and costal cartilages (in blue).

There are three fairly common deformities of the spine: *lateral curvature (scoliosis), kyphosis,* and *lordosis.* The normal spinal column observed from behind, is almost perfectly straight; there is no deviation to either side. But as a result of faulty habits of posture, from weakness of muscles (for example, as may result from anterior poliomyelitis) or certain other causes, a lateral curvature may develop that is most commonly situated with the middle of the curve in the lower dorsal (thoracic) and upper lumbar regions. The convexity of the curve may be directed either to the left or to the right. Compensatory curves with their convexities having directions opposite to that of the main, or primary, curve develop in the spinal column above and below the latter. Kyphosis is usually an exaggeration of the normal backward convexity in the dorsal region; it is sometimes called "humpback." Lordosis, or "hollow back," is an exaggeration of the forward convexity in the lumbar region (Fig. 3.16).

Spinal ligaments. Short but stout ligaments pass between the vertebral spines. The most important are in two sets, the **interspinous** and **supra-**

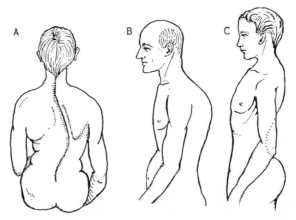

Fig. 3.16. Three common abnormalities of the spine. A, lateral curvature, or scoliosis; B, bowed back, or kyphosis; C, hollow back, or exaggerated lordosis.

spinous ligaments, respectively. The supraspinous ligaments of the cervical vertebrae are especially stout and strong and together form a thick cord called the **ligamentum nuchae,** or the **nuchal ligament.** In quadrupeds the nuchal ligament is an important aid; in the horse, for example, it lies beneath the mane and aids in holding up the head against gravity. Other ligaments bind the fronts and back of the vertebral bodies together; still others, called **ligamenta flava** because of their yellow color, stretch between the laminae of the vertebrae.

Bones of the head

The bony framework of the head is called the **skull.** The skull, exclusive of the bone of the lower jaw, is usually known as the **cranium.** Sometimes the word skull is also restricted to this part of the head, and is thus used synonymously with cranium. The upper, domed part of the skull is called the **skullcap,** or **calvaria.** There are 22 bones entering into the formation of the skull. All, with the exception of the lower jaw, or **mandible,** are immovably fixed in position. Of these, 15 bones form the skeleton of the face and the hollow, globular portion that encloses the brain; 7 other bones, though entering into the structure of the facial part of the head, are deeply situated, and do not contribute to the contours of the face. A list of the bones of the head is given below. The skull as a whole is shown in Figures 3.36 to 3.38.

BONES OF THE HEAD

1 frontal bone 2 parietal bones (right and left) 2 temporal bones (right and left) 1 occipital bone 1 sphenoid bone 1 ethmoid bone	Dome (calvaria), sides and base of skull
2 maxillae (sing. maxilla) 1 mandible (lower jaw) 2 zygomatic bones (cheek bones) 2 nasal bones	Bones of the face proper
2 palatine bones 1 vomer 2 lacrimal bones 2 inferior conchae	Bones that enter into structure of face but do not appear on surface.

The frontal bone is a large bone that is shaped somewhat like a cockleshell, which forms the forehead and upper part of the **orbit** (eyesocket) (Fig. 3.17). Its convex surface is covered by skin and the forepart

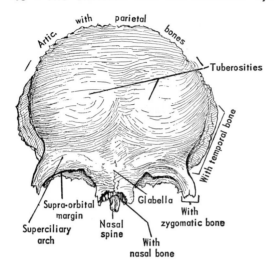

Fig. 3.17. The frontal bone, external surface.

of the scalp. A little above each orbit is an arched elevation called the **superciliary arch.** Above each of the latter a bosslike elevation, the **frontal tuberosity,** is to be seen. A short distance below the superciliary arches, curved rims of the bone form the **supraorbital margins.** On each side a horizontal plate (*orbital plate*) extends backward from the latter and constitutes the roof of the orbit. Between the supraorbital margins, a short, broad, notched tongue of bone projects downward and articulates on each side with a nasal bone and the nasal process of a maxilla. This part of the bone, which is referred to as its **nasal part,** ends below in a sharp spike called the **frontal spine.** The latter forms part of the septum of the nose; it articulates behind with the perpendicular plate of the ethmoid bone. Above the base of the nasal part and between the superciliary arches is a slight elevation called the **glabella.** The frontal bone between the superciliary arches and including their inner portions consists of two thin plates that enclose between them relatively large spaces known as the **frontal air sinuses.** Behind, the frontal bone is joined to the two parietal bones by a serrated (saw-toothed) articulation called the **coronal suture.** In the young infant the frontal bone is in two separate lateral halves separated by the frontal suture; the two halves commence to unite in the second year. In the infant skull, where the coronal and sagittal sutures meet (this latter suture is described below), is a rather large lozenge-shaped gap in the skull bone that is covered only by membrane and the tissues of the scalp. It is called the **anterior fontanelle.** It closes about the middle of the second year (Fig. 3.18).

The **parietal bones,** one on either side of the dome of the skull, are somewhat bowl shaped, with their concave surfaces facing toward the brain. They are joined in the midline by a saw-toothed joint that runs

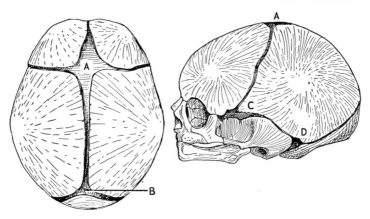

Fig. 3.18. The skull at birth. *Left,* superior aspect. A, anterior fontanelle; B, posterior fontanelle. *Right,* lateral aspect. A, anterior fontanelle; C, anterolateral fontanelle; D, posterolateral fontanelle.

anteroposteriorly and is called the **sagittal suture.** They are joined to the frontal bone by the coronal suture, and to the occipital bone by the lambdoid suture (Fig. 3.19). In the infant skull, a triangular space closed by membrane only is situated at the junction of the lambdoid and sagittal sutures. It is called the **posterior fontanelle,** and is much smaller than the anterior fontanelle. Also, its time of closure is much earlier than that of the latter, namely, between the second and third months after birth. Two other fontanelles—**anterolateral** and **posterolateral**—are situated at the inferior angles of the parietal bone on each side of the infant skull. They are shown in Figure 3.18.

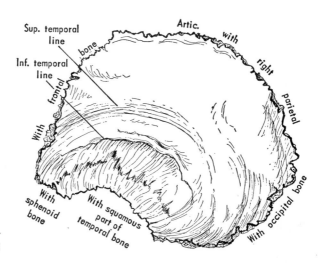

Fig. 3.19. The left parietal bone, external surface.

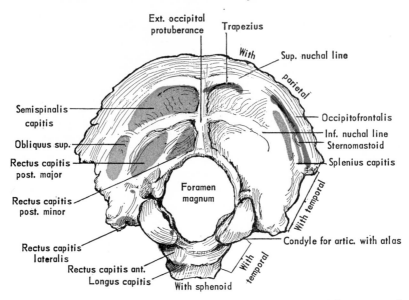

Fig. 3.20. Outer surface of occipital bone. It should be understood that groups of muscles—trapezius, occipitofrontalis, semispinalis, recti, etc.—though represented on one side only for the sake of simplicity are actually bilateral. In this and other figures muscle origins are colored pink, insertions blue.

The occipital bone forms the back of the skull and the posterior part of the base. The basal part supports the lowermost part of the brain (the medulla oblongata, Ch. 37) and is perforated by a large opening called the **foramen magnum** through which the brain becomes continuous with the spinal cord (Fig. 3.20). On either side of the anterior part of the foramen is a smooth, obliquely set, almond-shaped area, called the **occipital condyle.** The condyles rest upon corresponding areas of the atlas vertebra. About midway between the margin of the foramen magnum and the upper, or lambdoid, border of the bone is a prominent elevation called the **external occipital protuberance.** It can be felt as a distinct bump in the living subject. A corresponding rough elevation is present on the interior of the bone; it is known as the **internal** *occipital protuberance*. Arching outwards from each side of the external occipital protuberance is a ridge called the *inferior nuchal line*. Similar ridges— the *superior nuchal lines*—are situated a little above and posteriorly. The *trapezius* muscle takes origin from the superior nuchal line of the same side, while into the inferior nuchal line the *superior oblique* and *rectus capitis, major* and *minor,* are inserted.

The temporal bones are situated on the sides and base of the skull. Each consists of a thin, flat portion called the **squamous part,** a stout, wedge-shaped mass called the **petrous part,** a lower posterior portion

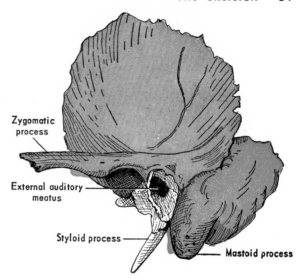

Zygomatic
process

External auditory
meatus

Styloid process

Mastoid process

Fig. 3.21. The outer surface
of the left temporal bone.
Pink, squamous part; blue,
mastoid part; uncolored,
tympanic part.

called the **mastoid portion,** and a curved plate lying below the squamous part and in front of the mastoid process called the **tympanic part** (Fig. 3.21). The *squamous part* is placed almost vertically at the side of the skull. A horizontal bridgelike bar of bone known as the **zygomatic process** springs from its lower part and, running forward, articulates with the temporal process of the zygomatic bone. The *petrous part* is nearly horizontal and directed obliquely inward and forward. It is wedged between the sphenoid and occipital bones, forming part of the base of the skull. It contains the organs of hearing and equilibrium. The *mastoid part* is thick and forms that part of the skull behind the ear. The part immediately behind the outer opening (meatus) of the ear is continued downward as a heavy, conical projection called the **mastoid process,** which contains numerous air cells; these communicate with the middle ear, and inflammation of the latter not infrequently extends into them causing the condition known as *mastoiditis.* The *tympanic part* is situated below the squamous part and in front of the mastoid process; it forms the lower half of the bony part of the external auditory meatus; that is, the external bony canal of the ear that is closed at its inner end by the eardrum or tympanic membrane (see Fig. 3.22).

A slender process about 1 inch long projects downward and a little forward from the under aspect of the bone in the region of the tympanic part and in front of the mastoid part. It is called the **styloid process,** and gives origin to three elongated slender muscles that descend to the tongue, neck, and pharynx.

The sphenoid bone is an unpaired bone forming part of the base of the skull; it is situated in front of the basilar part of the occipital bone.

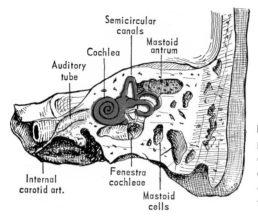

Fig. 3.22. Section through the temporal bone to show inner half or so of the middle ear and the internal ear (pink), beyond which is imagined as seen through the inner wall of the middle ear. (See also Ch. 46.)

Its shape has been compared to that of a bat with outspread wings. It has a body from which spring two larger and two much smaller **wings,** and two **pterygoid processes** that project downward from the body where this is joined to the large wings. On the upper, or intracranial, aspect of the body is a deep depression called the **sella turcica** (Turkish saddle) which lodges the hypophysis cerebri, or pituitary body. The sella turcica is bounded in front by an oval elevation (**tuberculum sellae**) and behind

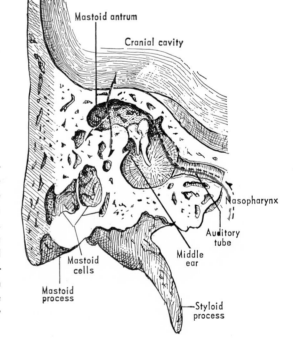

Fig. 3.23. Showing how infection may spread from the nasopharynx to the middle ear, mastoid cells, and even to the meninges of the brain. The narrow passage leading from the middle ear is called the aditus of the mastoid antrum. Fine canals lead from the latter to the mastoid cells; the whole system is lined by mucous membrane.

by a square bony plate called the **dorsum sellae.** The optic nerve and ophthalmic artery are transmitted through a round opening—the **optic foramen**—situated at the base of the lesser wing (Fig. 3.24).

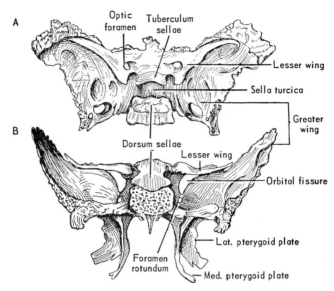

Fig. 3.24. The sphenoid bone (intercranial). *A,* posterior aspect; *B,* superior aspect.

The zygomatic (old term *malar*), **or cheek bone,** is a quadrilateral bone that forms part of the outer wall and floor of the orbit and the prominence of the cheek. It articulates with the frontal, the maxilla, and the temporal bones (Figs. 3.25 and 19.6).

The nasal bones are two small bones placed side by side between

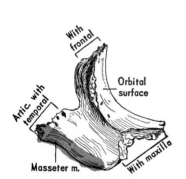

Fig. 3.25. The left zygomatic bone, medial surface; lateral surface shown in Figure 3.37, green.

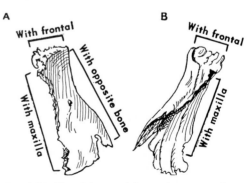

Fig. 3.26. The right nasal bone. A, outer surface; B, medial surface.

the frontal processes of the maxillae. They articulate above with the frontal bone and together form the bridge of the nose (Fig. 3.26).

The **ethmoid bone** is very light and porous, and cuboidal in shape (Fig. 3.27). It is located in the front part of the base of the skull and contributes to the formation of (a) the medial walls of the orbital cavities (eye sockets), (b) the septum of the nose, and (c) the roof and outer walls of the nasal cavities. It is composed of (1) a horizontal perforated plate called the **cribriform plate**, (2) a **perpendicular plate**, and (3) a lateral mass, called the **labyrinth**, on either side. The cribriform plate fits into the central notch (**ethmoid notch**) in the anterior part of the frontal bone; its numerous perforations, or foramina, transmit the olfactory nerves from the nasal cavity to the brain. From the upper surface of this plate a triangular spur of bone projects upwards into the cranial cavity; it is called the **crista galli** (cock's comb). The perpendicular plate is directed downward from the cribriform plate and forms the upper part of the nasal septum. Each labyrinth consists of a number of air sinuses, the **ethmoid sinuses,** situated between two vertical bony plates, the lateral of which forms a part of the medial wall of the orbital cavity; the medial plate of the labyrinth contributes to the formation of the outer wall of the corresponding nasal cavity. It is a thin lamina continuous above with the under surface of the ethmoid bone; its lower part is convoluted or rolled, and is called the **middle nasal concha** (L., a shell). Above the middle concha is a deep groove or furrow called the **superior meatus** (passage) of the nose; above it again is a curved plate of bone known as the **superior nasal concha** (*turbinate bones* are older names for the conchae).

The **inferior nasal conchae** are separate bones; they are two curved laminae lying horizontally, one on each lateral wall of the nasal cavity. The lateral aspect of the bone presents a longitudinal furrow or concavity that forms part of the inferior meatus of the nose (Fig. 3.28).

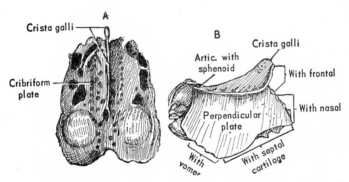

Fig. 3.27. The ethmoid bone. *Left,* superior aspect; *right,* right lateral aspect (right labyrinth removed).

The vomer is a thin quadrilateral plate that forms the back and lower part of the nasal septum (Fig. 3.29).

The palatine bones are two bones shaped, respectively, somewhat like the letter L and a reversed L (⌐), and situated in the posterior part of the nasal cavity between the pterygoid processes of the sphenoid bone and the two maxillae. Each pos-

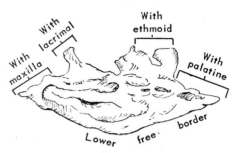

Fig. 3.28. The right inferior nasal concha, medial surface.

sesses a horizontal and a vertical plate. The palatine bones aid in the formation of the floor and outer wall of the nasal cavity, the roof of the mouth, and the floor of the orbital cavity. Each bone has *two processes*—

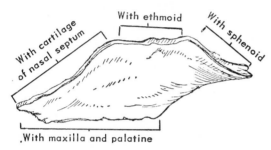

Fig. 3.29. The vomer, left lateral aspect.

orbital and sphenoidal—and a **tubercle** (also called the pyramidal process). The orbital process is directed upwards and outwards from the perpendicular plate, its lateral surface contributing to the formation of the floor of the orbital cavity. The sphenoidal process points upward and inward and articulates with the sphenoid. The tubercle projects backward, downward, and laterally from the point of union of the horizontal and perpendicular plates (Fig. 3.30).

The lacrimal bones are two very small, delicate bones; each assists in the formation of the front part of the medial wall of the orbital cavity and, together with the frontal process of the maxilla forms a groove (lacrimal groove) that

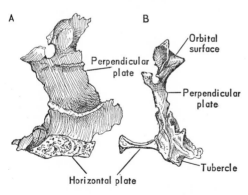

Fig. 3.30. The palatine bones. *A,* medial aspect of bone of left side; *B,* posterior aspect of bone of right side.

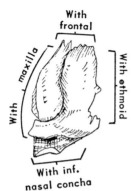

With frontal

With maxilla

With ethmoid

With

With inf. nasal concha

Fig. 3.31. The left lacrimal bone, lateral surface.

lodges the lacrimal sac and nasolacrimal (tear) duct (Fig. 3.31).

The maxillae (upper jaw bones) form a large part of the face; they carry the upper teeth. Each bone contributes to the formation of the roof of the mouth, the floor of the orbital cavity, and the floor and outer wall of the nasal cavity (Figs. 3.32 and 3.36). The *body* of the bone constitutes its greatest part and contains a large, pyramidal air space called the maxillary sinus (old term *antrum of Highmore*). The maxilla has four processes—zygomatic, frontal, alveolar, and palatine—that spring from the body. The zygomatic process arises from the upper and lateral parts of the body. It articulates with the zygomatic bone. The frontal process projects upward to occupy a position between the nasal and lacrimal bones and forms a part of the outer wall of the nasal cavity. The alveolar process is a thick, curved horseshoe-shaped process projecting downward from the lower limit of the body. It contains sockets for the lodgment of the upper teeth, 8 in number, on each side. The palatine process lies horizontally and projects toward the midline where it articulates with the corresponding process of the maxilla of the opposite side. It forms, with its fellow, the anterior three quarters or so of the bony palate, and part of the floor of the nose. It articulates behind with the horizontal plate of the palatine bone. The process, near its medial free edge, is raised into a ridge—the nasal crest—that, with the corresponding ridge of the opposite maxilla,

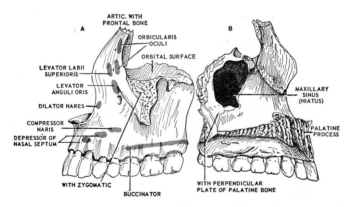

Fig. 3.32. The left maxilla. *A*, external surface; *B*, medial surface. The large opening into the maxillary sinus shown here is much reduced in the intact skull by the encroachment of other bones—ethmoid, lacrimal, palatine, and inferior concha.

forms a groove into which is fitted the lower edge of the vomer. In front, the ridges of the two bones form an upward-projecting spine called the **nasal spine.** The two palatine processes sometimes fail to meet in the mid-line and leave a gap—a developmental anom-aly known as cleft palate, which is frequently accompanied by a harelip (Fig. 3.33).

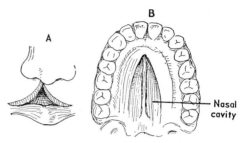

Fig. 3.33. A, single right-sided harelip; B, cleft palate.

The **mandible (or lower jaw)** is a large, strong bone forming the chin and sides of the face. It consists of a hori-zontally curved *body* and two flat, broad processes called **rami** (sing. *ramus*) that project upwards, with a slight inclination backward. The body forms the chin and is strongly arched. It has 16 sockets for the lodgment of the lower teeth. A perforation on its anterior surface—the **mental foramen**—on each side a little distance from the midline gives exit to the mental nerve and vessels. The ramus on each side has two processes at its upper extremity, separated by the concave upper margin of the bone. The anterior process, known as the **coronoid,** is flat and triangular; it projects upward and slightly forward. The pos-terior process, called the **condyloid,** is more prominent and somewhat hook shaped and has a rounded upper end that articulates with the base of the skull, where it fits into a depression—the **articular fossa**—of the temporal bone. Movement of the head of this process within the fossa permits the opening or closing of the jaw (Fig. 3.34) .

The **hyoid bone,** though strictly speaking not a bone of the face, is usually described along with the facial bones for convenience. It can be plainly felt by the fingers placed on the neck below the chin. It is a small, fragile, U-shaped bone, and is suspended from the styloid processes

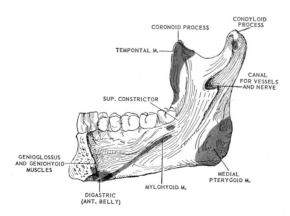

Fig. 3.34. The inner surface of the right mandible. (See also Figure 3.36.)

of the temporal bones by the **stylohyoid ligaments**. It consists of a quadrilateral *body* and two elongated processes, or horns, on each side called the **greater** and the **lesser cornua**. The hyoid gives attachment to muscles of the tongue and pharynx and other small muscles of the neck, such as the mylohyoid, omohyoid, and thyrohyoid. The hyoid bone is of medicolegal interest since in murder by strangulation it is frequently fractured (Fig. 3.35).

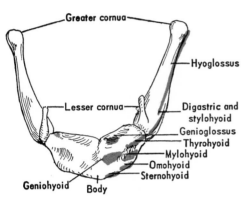

Fig. 3.35. The hyoid bone.

The **paranasal sinuses** are a system of air spaces within the maxillae and the frontal, sphenoid, and ethmoid bones that communicate with the nasal cavities. They have been touched upon in the descriptions of the respective bones, but will be described more fully in Chapter 19.

The skull as a whole. The skull is poised upon the summit of the vertebral column where it rests upon the atlas vertebra, the occipital condyles making contact with the articular surfaces on the lateral masses of the axis.

The bones of the adult skull, with the exception of the mandible, are joined so intimately to one another that no movement between them is possible. The unions between the bones are very irregular and with their numerous indentations and projections resemble the shore lines on a map. The serrated joints (see p. 74) are called **sutures** (L. *sutura,* a seam). The sutures are quite evident in young persons but in the aged they tend to become indistinct or obliterated, the bones becoming fused with one another.

The brain case, that is, the part of the skull containing the brain, is composed of the frontal, parietal, temporal, and occipital bones together with those bones forming the base of the skull.

In infancy and childhood the skull, as compared with the adult skull, represents a much larger proportion of the skeleton. In other words, the child's skull is nearer its adult size than is any other part of his skeleton. The brain and skull grow rapidly up to the seventh year, and most rapidly during the first 18 months after birth. Growth slows after the seventh year up to the time of puberty when another period of rapid enlargement of the brain and consequently of the skull occurs.

The shape of the skull varies considerably between individuals and it has long been recognized that the anteroposterior and transverse proportions are racial characteristics. Negroes and some East Indian tribes have long heads, whereas the Dutch, Albanians, some Chinese, the Eskimos, and some tribes of American Indians have heads with short anteroposterior diameters. Between these two extremes are Europeans of the Nordic races and some East Indians. The term *doliocephalic* is given to the long heads and *brachiocephalic* to the short or round heads (the Cromwellian "round heads" were so called only because they cut their hair short). There is no racial difference in the capacity of the brain case.

The four views of the skull—the front, the side, the base, and from above—are called, respectively, the **norma frontalis, norma lateralis, norma basilaris,** and **norma verticalis.** The first three of these are shown in Figures 3.36 to 3.38.

When the upper part of the skull bone and the brain are removed and the interior of the base of the skull exposed, the contours of the bones composing the latter mark it off into three areas called the **anterior, middle,** and **posterior cranial fossae.** The anterior fossa is formed by the orbital plate of the frontal bone, the cribriform plate and crista galli of the ethmoid, and the lesser wings and anterior part of the body of the sphenoids. The middle fossa is formed by the greater wings and a part of the body of the sphenoid bone, and by the temporal bone (petrous part). The posterior fossa is formed mainly by the occipital bone, but also, to a minor extent, by the petrous part of the temporal and the posterior part of the sphenoid where it joins the occipital.

The **orbital cavity** is formed by the mosaiclike fitting together of parts of 7 bones: frontal, lacrimal, sphenoid, ethmoid, zygomatic, and the maxilla (Figs. 3.36, 3.37).

Bones of the upper limb and shoulder

The **scapula, or shoulder blade,** is a large, flat, triangular bone that occupies, one on each side, the upper and lateral two thirds or so of the posterior chest wall, extending from the second to the seventh ribs. From its posterior surface projects a prominent, elongated, oblique shelflike ridge called the **spine of the scapula,** which marks off this aspect of the bone into an upper and a lower, much larger part, called respectively, the **supraspinous** and **infraspinous fossa.** The lateral end of the spine is expanded and overhangs the shoulder joint; it is called the **acromion.** The lateral angle of the shoulder blade is thick and broad, and is called the **head of the scapula.** It is concave, for the reception of the head of the humerus, the hollow being named the **glenoid cavity.** A somewhat hooked, beaklike process projects forward from the upper border of the head; it is called the **coracoid process** (Fig. 3.39).

The **clavicle, or collar bone,** is a slender, elongated bone lying horizontally at the root of the neck; it can be felt just beneath the skin. It serves to brace back the shoulder and to transmit a part of the weight

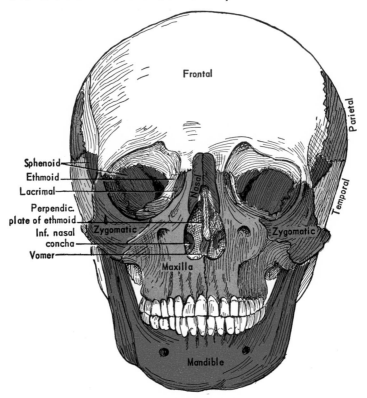

Fig. 3.36. The skull, norma frontalis. Pink: maxilla, parietal; blue: spenoid, nasal mandible; yellow: temporal; green: zygomatic, inferior nasal concha; orange: lacrimal, vomer; uncolored: frontal, ethmoid.

of the arm to the axial skeleton. It presents a double curve, its outer part being concave forwards and its inner portion convex forwards. It articulates at its inner end with the manubrium of the sternum and at its outer end with the acromion of the scapula (Fig. 3.40).

The humerus is the bone of the arm (shoulder to elbow). Its upper end is composed of a **head** and two prominences called the **greater** and **lesser tuberosities.** The head is smooth and hemispherical and in life is covered by hyaline cartilage. It is directed inward, backward, and upward to fit into the glenoid cavity of the scapula. The tuberosities are placed anteriorly, the *greater* to the outer side of the *lesser*. They are separated by a longitudinal groove—the **bicipital groove**—that lodges the tendon of the long head of the biceps muscle. The lower expanded, somewhat triangular extremity articulates with the bones of the forearm; its outer part, called the **capitulum,** with the head of the radius; its inner (medial), pulley-shaped part, called the **trochlea,** with the concavity on the upper end of the ulna. The prominences, one on either side of the lower end,

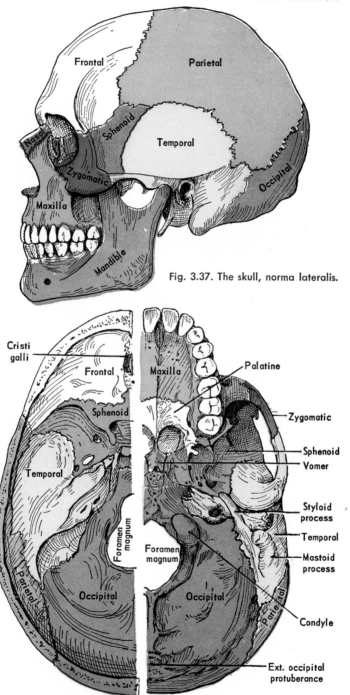

Fig. 3.37. The skull, norma lateralis.

Fig. 3.38. The skull, norma basalis. *Left,* internal surface; *right,* external surface.

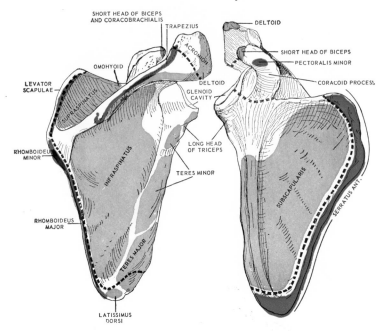

Fig. 3.39. The right scapula (shoulder blade). *Left,* posterior surface; *right,* anterior (costal) surface. Broken lines show epiphyseal lines.

are called, respectively, the **medial** and **lateral epicondyles.** The medial epicondyle is the more prominent of the two and can be felt in the living subject immediately beneath the skin (Fig. 3.41).

The **radius** is the lateral bone of the forearm. Its shaft is slender above, but widens below, and is slightly bowed with the convexity outwards; its lower end shows a pronounced expansion, with a small, downward, pyramidal projection on its outer side, called the **styloid process** (Figs. 3.42, 3.43). The upper end, or *head,* of the bone is disc shaped; the small, concave, upper aspect articulates with the capitulum of the humerus. Medially, the head articulates with a shallow depression, the **radial notch,** on the ulna. A little below the inner part of the head

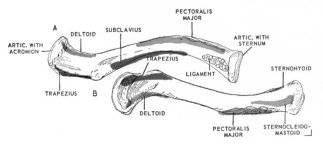

Fig. 3.40. The right clavicle. *A,* inferior aspect; *B,* superior aspect.

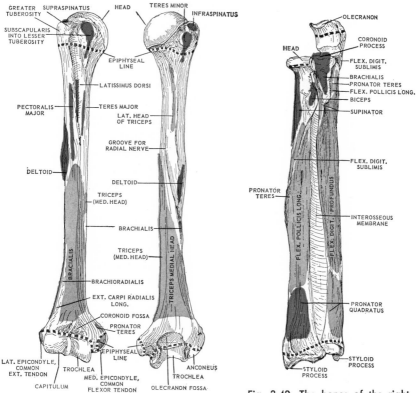

Fig. 3.41. The right humerus. *Left,* anterior aspect; *right,* posterior aspect.

Fig. 3.42. The bones of the right forearm, anterior aspect; radius at the left, ulna at the right.

is a rough oval elevation called the **tuberosity,** into which the tendon of the biceps is inserted. The portion of the bone between the head and the tuberosity is called the neck (Fig. 3.42).

Fracture through the lower end of the radius is known as *Colles's fracture.* Of all fractures it is one of the most common, and is caused by a fall upon the palm of the hand, the weight of the body being thus suddenly transmitted through the radius to the ground. The styloid process of the ulna, as a result of the pull upon it by attached ligaments, is usually broken off as well. The wrist shows a characteristic deformity that has been compared to a turned-down fork, this appearance being given by the prominent hump on the back of the wrist and the concavity formed by the volar aspect of the wrist and hand. The hand is also displaced outwards.

The ulna lies on the medial side of the forearm. It has a stout, hook shaped, upper extremity, the concavity of which looks forward and articulates with the trochlea of the humerus. The back and upper part of

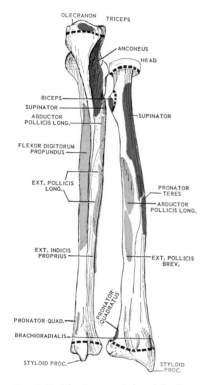

Fig. 3.43. The bones of the right forearm, posterior aspect; ulna at the left, radius at the right. The bones are separated, interosseous membrane not shown.

the hooklike upper end forms the prominence of the elbow and is called the **olecranon;** its uppermost part is bent forward like a beak that fits into a depression on the back of the lower end of the humerus above the trochlea. The lower part of the concave articular surface forms a prominent forward projection called the **coronoid process.** The articular surface itself, formed by the anterior surface of the olecranon and the upper surface of the coronoid process, is called the **trochlear notch.** Adjoining this on its lateral side is a smaller articular surface known as the **radial notch,** which lodges the side of the head of the radius. The lower end of the ulna is small, little broader than the shaft of the bone, and has a small, rounded, downward projection on its inner side; this is called the **styloid process** (Figs. 3.42, 3.43).

Bones of the wrist (carpus) and hand

The carpus. The **carpal,** or **wrist, bones** form two rows of four bones each. They are small and of different irregular shapes. The proximal row consists of the **scaphoid** (boat shaped), **lunate** ([half]moon shaped), **triquetral** (triangular), and **pisiform** (like a pea), respectively, starting from the outer side. The distal row is made up of the **trapezium** (table), **trapezoid** (like a table, quadrilateral), **capitate** (round, like a head), and **hamate** (hooked), respectively, from the outer side. The outer three bones of the proximal row together form a smooth, arched, upper surface that articulates with the lower end of the radius and a disc of cartilage below the ulna (Fig. 3.44).

The metacarpus. The metacarpal bones are five elongated bones that form the framework of the body of the hand (palm and back). They are referred to by numbers, starting from the lateral (thumb) side. Their expanded proximal ends, or **bases,** articulate with the distal row of carpal bones as well as with one another on one or both sides. The first metacarpal (metacarpal of the thumb) is an exception, in that it does **not** articulate with the second metacarpal (metacarpal of the index). The

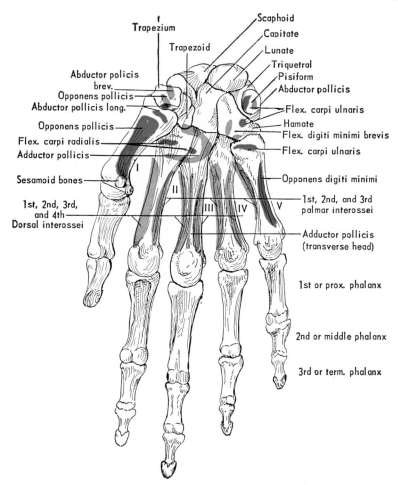

Fig. 3.44. The bones of the right hand, anterior (volar, or palmar) aspect. Roman numerals refer to the metacarpal bones.

distal ends, or **heads,** of the metacarpals are smooth and rounded and articulate each with the proximal end of the first phalanx of the thumb or a finger. The heads of the metacarpals form the knuckles (Fig. 3.44).

The phalanges (sing. *phalanx*), the thumb and finger bones. There are three bones for each of the four fingers, and two for the thumb. They are numbered one to three from the proximal to the distal end of the fingers, or one and two for the thumb. The **base,** or proximal end, of each bone is broader than the adjoining **shaft.** The distal end, or **head,** of each phalanx is smooth and resembles a pulley (except the terminal ones that form the tips of the fingers and thumb). The base of the first phalanx articulates with the head of the corresponding metacarpal, that of the second phalanx with the head of the first, and the base of the third (in the case of fingers) with the head of the second. The third, or terminal, phalanx is considerably shorter, more slender than the others, and somewhat tapered.

Bones of the hip and lower limb

The bones composing the hip and lower limb are the **os coxae, femur, patella, tibia, fibula,** the **tarsals, metatarsals,** and **phalanges** of the foot.

The os coxae, or hipbone (old term *os innominatum*), is a large, massive, irregularly shaped bone with a pronounced constriction in the middle where is situated a cup-shaped depression called the **acetabulum** (Fig. 3.45); this hollow lodges the head of the femur. The hipbones contribute largely to the formation of the pelvic cavity. Each bone develops in three separate parts, called the **ilium,** the **ischium,** and the **pubis,** that are joined by cartilage in early life along a Y-shaped line within the acetabulum. Bony union commences at about 12 years, but is not complete until between 20 and 25 years. The names of these parts of the bone are retained to describe it in the adult. The *ilium* (pl. *ilia*) is the upper expanded, or flared part of the bone. The bone is narrowed below, where it forms part of the acetabulum. The upper border of the ilium

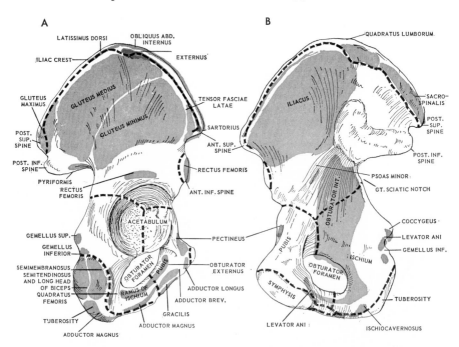

Fig. 3.45. The right os coxae (hipbone). A, external surface; B, medial surface.

forms a thick, curved rim called the **iliac crest,** which is easily felt at the level of the waist in the living subject. This rim ends anteriorly and below in a projection that can be felt in the upper part of the groin, and that is called the **anterior superior iliac spine.** There is a less conspicuous elevation on the anterior border below the latter and just above the acetabulum known as the **anterior inferior iliac spine.**

The posterior border of the ilium also shows two prominences—the **posterior superior** and **posterior inferior iliac spines.** At the inferior spine the posterior border turns sharply forward and forms with the posterior border of the ischium a broad bay, called the **greater sciatic notch.**

The upper and anterior part of the inner surface of the ilium is moderately concave, and is called the **iliac fossa.**

The *pubis* (pl. *pubes*) forms the anterior lower part of the os coxae. It consists of a flat *body* and two bars of bone that spring from it, known as the **superior** and **inferior rami.** The upper border of the body is called the **pubic crest.** The superior ramus is joined in the acetabulum to the ilium and the ischium. The inferior ramus is directed downward, outward, and backward, and becomes continuous with the ramus of the ischium. The pubis is joined in front to its opposite fellow through a cartilaginous joint known as the **symphysis pubis,** which can be felt beneath the skin at the lowermost point of the trunk.

The *ischium* (pl. *ischii*) is sharply curved and forms the lower and posterior part of the hipbone. Its upper termination is joined to the ilium and to the superior ramus of the pubis in the acetabulum. The anterior lower and less massive part, called the **ramus,** is, as just mentioned, continuous with the inferior ramus of the pubis. The lower, heavy curved part, situated between the upper part of the bone and the ramus is called the **body;** its lowest part is rough and prominent, and is called the **tuberosity;** it supports the trunk in the sitting position. The pubis and ischium together form a ring of bone that encloses a space called the **obturator foramen.**

The girdle of the lower limb differs from that of the upper; whereas the shoulder girdle consists of two pairs of bones, clavicles and scapulae, the lower girdle consists of the two hipbones, which articulate with the spinal column through the joint between the ilium and the sacrum—the **sacroiliac joint.**

The pelvis (a basin) is a stout, bony ring composed of the two hipbones, which form the front and sides, and the sacrum and coccyx, which complete it behind; it encloses the pelvic cavity and supports the vertebral column. It is, in turn, supported, in the standing position, by the lower limbs. It consists of a **false** and a **true pelvis,** separated by an imaginary oblique plane passing from the prominence of the sacrum downwards and forwards to the upper end of the symphysis pubis (Fig.

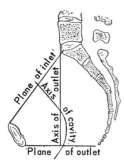

Fig. 3.46. Diagram of the female pelvis from the side to show the planes and axes.

3.46). The false pelvis is formed by the upper expanded portion of the ilium of each side. The true pelvis is the smaller part, lying below and behind the **pelvic inlet,** which is the space bounded by the prominence of the sacrum, the anterior and lower parts of the two ilia, and the superior rami of the pubes. The true pelvis encloses the pelvic cavity which contains the pelvic colon, rectum, urinary bladder, and, in the female, the uterus, ovaries and vagina. The **pelvic outlet** is the space bounded by the tip of the coccyx, the tuberosities, and the inferior rami of the pubes. The latter form the **pubic arch,** which lies below the symphysis pubis.

The planes of the pelvic inlet and outlet make different angles with the horizontal so that the axis of the true pelvis is curved, with its concavity forward (Fig. 3.46). A knowledge of the anatomy of the pelvis of the female, which differs in particulars from that of the male (Fig. 3.47), is of essential importance in understanding the birth mechanisms. Sex differences are more pronounced in the pelvis than in any other part of the skeleton. The bones of the female pelvis are lighter and more finely

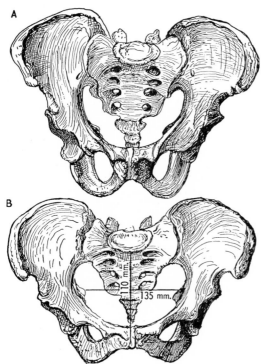

Fig. 3.47. The male (A) and female (B) pelves compared, with the diameters of the inlet of the true pelvis in the female.

formed than those of the male, and the areas of muscular attachments less strongly marked. The iliac fossae of the female are less concave, the ilia more vertically placed and the curves of the iliac crests less conspicuous; the pelvic cavity is shallower and broader due to the relative shortness of the sacrum, and to its greater width. The female pubic arch is broader and rounder, the two pillars of the arch forming an angle of at least 90°, whereas the male pelvic arch is usually less than a right angle.

Deformities of the pelvis may be a cause of difficult labor. There are several types of such deformities, the most commonly being rickets in early life, or an associated deformity of the spine, such as scoliosis or lordosis. The normal diameters of the female pelvis are as follows: **anteroposterior** (from the tip of the coccyx to the lower part of the symphysis pubis), 109 to 110 mm; **transverse** (across the widest part of the outlet), about 135 mm. Marked reduction in either or both of these diameters is called a **contracted pelvis**.

The femur, or thigh bone, is the longest and strongest of all the bones. It has a cylindrical **shaft,** a **head** (upper end), and two large

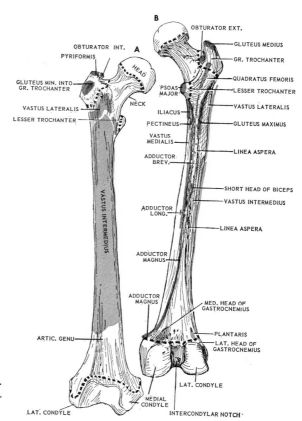

Fig. 3.48. The right femur. A, anterior surface; B, posterior surface.

masses of bone at its lower end called the **medial** and **lateral condyles.** The shaft is narrowest in its middle part but is expanded in its upper and lower parts. The head, which is smooth and rounded, fits into the acetabulum of the hipbone. It is joined to the shaft at an angle of 125° by a short length of bone called the **neck** (Fig. 3.48). This part is a not uncommon site of fracture, especially in old persons in whom it tends to become less dense, more or less porous, and consequently, weak. A large boss of bone is situated on the outer side of the junction of the shaft with the neck; it is called the **greater trochanter.** A much smaller, conical elevation, called the **lesser trochanter,** projects medially and backwards from the posterior aspect of the junction of neck and shaft. Running down the posterior surface of the shaft from the lesser trochanter is a rough ridge called the **linea aspera;** in the lower third of the shaft the latter divides into two, one passing toward each condyle.

The lower end of the femur articulates with the tibia (leg bone) by the two condyles mentioned above, which are smooth and rounded, like two rockers, and move upon the upper surface of the tibia. The *patella* articulates with the lower end of the femur just above the middle of the tibial articulation. The two condyles are separated behind by a deep depression called the **intercondylar notch.**

The patella, or kneecap, a large sesamoid bone (p. 37), is developed in the tendon of the principal muscle (quadriceps femoris) on the front of the thigh, where it crosses the knee joint to be inserted into the tibia. The patella is a relatively flat, roughly round bone with a pointed lower part, or apex. Its posterior surface is smooth for articulation with the femur, being molded to the condyles. The patella is fastened to the tibia by the ligamentum patellae, which is really the terminal part of the tendon of the quadriceps femoris muscle (Fig. 3.49).

The tibia is the medial of the two bones of the leg (knee to ankle)

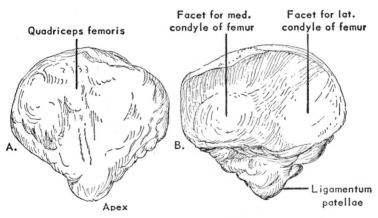

Fig. 3.49. The right patella. A, anterior surface; B, posterior surface.

(Figs. 3.50, 3.51). It is much thicker and stronger than the fibula, which lies to its outer side; it transmits the weight of the body to the ground. The *upper end* of the tibia broadens out to form a massive structure formed like an inverted prism. The two masses of bone on either side are called the **lateral** and **medial condyles**, the upper, smooth surfaces of which articulate with the corresponding condyles of the femur. The lateral condyle, the more prominent of the two projects like a shelf, on the under surface of which is a facet for articulation with the head of the fibula. A boss on the front of the bone at the upper end of the shaft is called the **tubercle**; the ligamentum patellae is inserted into its upper half. The **shaft** of the tibia shows anteriorly a sharp, slightly curved crest lying just beneath the skin and popularly called the **shin**. The *lower end* of the tibia is moderately expanded and, medially, is continued downwards into a tapered projection called the **medial malleolus**. This is easily identified as it, too, lies just beneath the skin. The smooth, concave

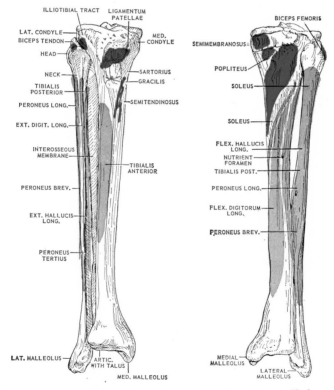

Fig. 3.50 *(left)*. The bones of the right leg, anterior aspect; fibula at the left, tibia at the right.

Fig. 3.51 *(right)*. The posterior aspect of the bones of the right leg. Small blue areas, semimembranosus; large blue area, popliteus.

under surface of this part of the tibia articulates with the talus or first bone of the tarsus. The lateral surface of the lower end of the tibia is held in close relation with the fibula by a strong ligament.

The fibula is the long, slender bone lying to the outer side of the tibia. Unlike the tibia, it does not transmit the body's weight; for the greater part of its length it is buried beneath the muscles of the leg. Its upper end is expanded into a somewhat flat, triangular head that articulates with the tibia just beneath the lateral condyle. A stout fibrous sheet —the *interosseous membrane*—stretches between the bones of the leg; it is fastened to the opposed borders of the shafts of the bones. The lower end of the fibula is prolonged downwards well beyond the level of the medial malleolus (of the tibia); this projection is called the **lateral malleolus.** The inner side of the lateral malleolus has a smooth surface for articulation with the side of the talus. The medial and lateral malleoli form the two well-known prominences, one on either side, at the ankle.

Fracture of the lower part of the fibula and separation of the medial malleolus, often with tearing of neighboring ligaments, is known as *Pott's fracture.*[2] It is usually caused by a slip on uneven ground causing a sharp turn of the ankle. The loss of the bracing action of the fibula causes the foot to be displaced outwards (Figs. 3.50, 3.51).

The tarsus corresponds to the carpus and the **metatarsals** to the metacarpals, the bony framework of the foot being built upon a plan similar to that of the hand. The number of phalanges is the same for the toes as for the fingers and thumb but, of course, they are much shorter and thinner. There are 7 tarsal bones—the **talus, calcaneum,** placed proximally, and a distal row of 4 bones named, from the outer to the inner side of the instep, the **cuboid** and the **lateral, intermediate, and medial cuneiforms.** The **scaphoid bone** is wedged between the front part of the talus behind and the 3 cuneiforms in front (Fig. 3.52).

The talus is a large, stout bone, and enters largely into the formation of the ankle joint, possessing a smooth, pulleylike upper surface that articulates with the under surface of the lower end of the tibia. The talus surmounts the calcaneum, articulating with it principally by a large concave surface (Fig. 3.53).

The calcaneum, or *heel bone,* as just mentioned, articulates and supports the talus. It articulates in front with the cuboid bone. Behind, it is stout and rounded and projects beyond the bones of the leg to form the heel. The **tendo calcaneus** (*Achillis*) is inserted into its posterior surface (Fig. 3.54).

The metatarsal bones form the anterior half or so of the instep and the corresponding part of the sole of the foot. Their distal ends, or

---

[2] Percival Pott, a famous surgeon of the eighteenth century, suffered this fracture himself. His name has also been attached to several other conditions, for example, Pott's disease, Pott's tumor, Pott's gangrene, and Pott's aneurysm.

heads, are smooth and rounded, and articulate with the bases of the phalanges. Their proximal ends, or *bases,* articulate with the distal row of tarsal bones, and, excepting the first (metatarsal of the thumb), with their immediate neighbors. Between its head and base a metatarsal bone is roughly cylindrical and slightly curved; this area is called the *shaft* (Fig. 3.52).

The arches of the foot are the result of the tarsal and metatarsal bones forming a strong **longitudinal arch,** the piers of which are the calcaneum behind the heads of the metatarsals in front. The summit is the superior articular surface of the talus, to which the weight of the body is transmitted through the tibia. The arch of the foot receives support in its lateral portion from the strong tendon of the peroneus longus muscle of the leg (Ch. 5) and several stout ligaments.

The longitudinal arch of the foot really consists of two arches, a **medial** and a **lateral,**

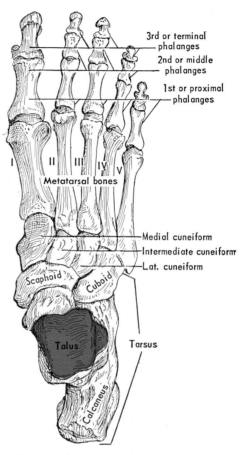

Fig. 3.52. The bones of the right foot. Articular surface of talus in blue, it articulates with the lower end of the tibia.

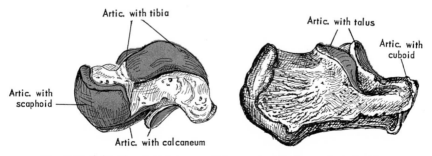

Fig. 3.53 *(left)*. The right talus, medial aspect; articular surfaces in blue.
Fig. 3.54 *(right)*. The right calcaneum, medial aspect; articular surfaces in blue.

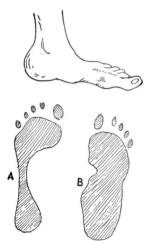

Fig. 3.55. Flat foot. *Above,* medial aspect. *Below,* A, impression made by normal left foot; B, by flat right foot.

the former being formed by the calcaneum, the inner bones of the tarsus, and the first, second, and third metatarsals; the latter by the calcaneum, the outer bones of the tarsus, and the fourth and fifth metatarsal bones. The foot is also arched transversely but to a less pronounced degree.

Obliteration or pronounced lowering of the arches of the foot is known as *flat foot,* or *pes planus;* nearly all the plantar surface of the foot then comes into contact with the ground (Fig. 3.55). The foot is often turned outward (everted) as well. The arches of the foot are not developed until after early childhood.

The foot serves two purposes: (1) the obvious one of supporting the weight of the body, and (2) providing a strong, arched lever for walking, jumping, etc.

JOINTS AND BURSAE

Joints, or articulations

A joint is a junction between two bones. In some joints, such as those of the shoulder and hip, considerable freedom of movement between the bones is permitted; in others, movement is restricted to two dimensions and varies in range with different joints. In still others, such as those of the skull, no movement at all is possible. A typical joint has the following construction: the articulating surfaces of the opposed bones are smooth, reciprocally shaped to carry out most easily a particular movement, and covered with a thin layer of cartilage (**articular cartilage**). A strong envelope of fibrous tissue, the **capsular ligament,** surrounds the joint, helping to hold the bones in position. This and the parts of the bones within the joint not covered by cartilage are lined by a delicate membrane, the **synovial membrane;** the joint cavity enclosed by these structures contains a lubricating fluid, the **synovia,** or **synovial fluid** (Fig. 3.56). In some joints, such as the hip and knee joints, the bones are held together by a ligament or ligaments within the joint itself (Fig. 3.57).

Many joints do not conform entirely to the foregoing description but differ in certain particulars. The flat curved bones forming the skull, for example, are joined by the locking together of saw-toothed (serrated) edges, fibrous tissue, but no cartilage being interposed between them. These joints are called **sutures.** The principal sutures are the **coronal,** between the frontal and the two parietal bones; the **sagittal,** running anteroposteriorly between the two parietal bones, and the **lambdoid,**

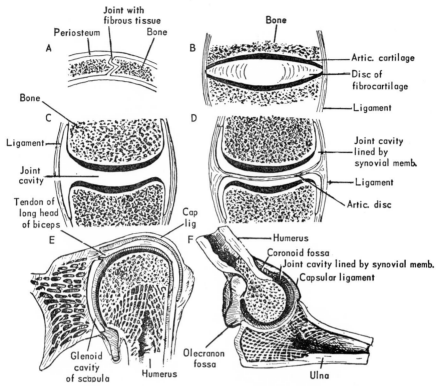

Fig. 3.56. Six types of joint. *A*, section through the sagittal suture of the skull; *B*, cartilage joint; *C-F*, synovial joints; *C*, simple synovial joint; *D*, synovial joint with articular disc of fibrocartilage, as in joints between the vertebral bodies; *E*, shoulder (ball and socket) joint; *F*, ginglymus, or hinge, joint between the humerus and ulna.

between the two parietal bones and the occipital bone. In some joints, called the **cartilaginous joints,** the bones are covered by a layer of hyaline cartilage, and, in addition, a disc of fibrocartilage is interposed that, being fastened to the layer of hyaline cartilage, aids in holding the bones together. This type of joint is found between the vertebral bodies. **Synovial joints** are those such as the shoulder, elbow, hip, knee, ankle, etc., that are lined by a synovial membrane, except over the articular cartilage, and contain synovia; they have the general construction of the typical joint described above; this class includes most of the joints of the body. Most synovial joints are either the **ball and socket type,** such as the shoulder and hip joints; or **hinge joints** (also called **ginglymus joints**) , such as the elbow, knee, and ankle. In the shoulder joint, the head of the humerus articulates with the glenoid cavity of the scapula, and in the hip joint, the head of the femur is received by the acetabulum of the os coxae; both these joints permit a wide range of movement.

The bones forming the hip and knee joints are held together by ligaments within the joint cavity itself. In the hip joint, a short round

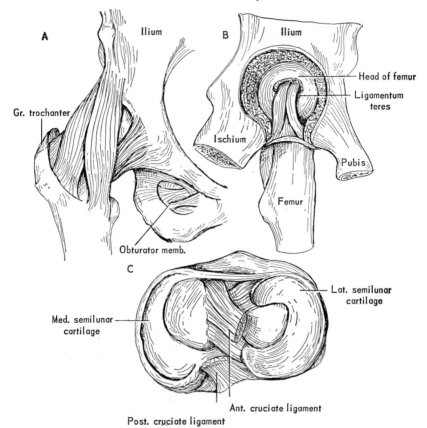

Fig. 3.57. The exterior, A, and interior B, of the hip joint, inner wall (pelvic) of socket removed; C, the interior of the knee joint, showing upper surface of tibia.

ligament called the **ligamentum teres** passes from about the center of the head of the femur to the bottom of the acetabulum. The femur and tibia are held together within the knee joint by two ligaments called the **anterior** and **posterior cruciate ligaments** (Fig. 3.57). These two strong ligaments run from bone to bone in an oblique anteroposterior direction and cross one another, hence their names. To be mentioned for their practical importance are the articular cartilages of the tibia. They are semilunar in shape; detachment of one or both of these structures is not infrequent an injury of the knee joint, especially in football players and other athletes.

The joints between the bodies and processes of the vertebrae, individually, permit of only slight movement, but, acting together, they allow considerable bending and twisting of the spinal column. The joint surfaces of the vertebrae are covered by a thin layer of hyaline cartilage. The vertebrae are bound together by strong ligaments and by discs composed of a broad annual band of fibrocartilage enclosing a softer, highly elastic substance called the **nucleus pulposus** (Fig. 3.58). This central portion is especially well developed in the lumbar region. A displaced nucleus pulposus pressing on sensory nerve roots as they issue from the spinal cord is a common cause of severe back pain.

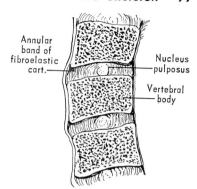

Fig. 3.58. Intervertebral disc with nucleus pulposus.

Several general terms relating to joint injuries or disease should be defined. *Dislocation* or *luxation* is a complete separation and displacement of the bones of a joint; *subluxation* is an incomplete dislocation. *Arthritis* means the inflammation of a joint, including the capsule, ligaments, and synovial membrane. *Synovitis* is an inflammation more or less confined to the synovial membrane.

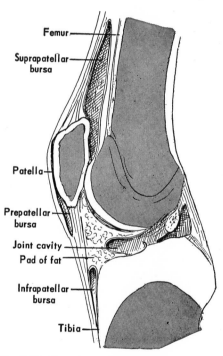

Fig. 3.59. Three bursae about the knee joint. Subcutaneous infrapatella bursa not shown.

Bursae

In various situations in the body, but most commonly where pressure is naturally exerted or where a tendon rides over a bony surface, small sacs are developed containing a little fluid. Such bursae (L. sing. *bursa*, a purse) are to be found over the acromion process of the scapula, about the knee joint, over the olecranon process of the ulna, and at the back of the heel between the calcaneum and the tendo calcaneus. There are four bursae near the front of the knee joint: the **suprapatellar**, between the quadriceps extensor tendon and the femur; **prepatellar**, between the patella and the skin; and two **infrapatellar**, *deep* and *subcutaneous*, situated, respectively, between the tibia and the ligamentum patellae, and between the tibia and the skin.

Inflammation of a bursa is called *bursitis*. The bursa between the patella and the skin not infrequently becomes inflamed as a result of injury; the condition is popularly known as "housemaid's knee" (since often caused by work in the kneeling position) (Fig. 3.59).

4

The Muscular System, Functional Anatomy and Physiology

GENERAL DESCRIPTION OF MUSCULAR STRUCTURE; TYPES OF MUSCLE

There are three types of muscular tissue; namely, (1) *smooth, non-striated,* or *involuntary,* (2) *striated, skeletal,* or *voluntary,* and (3) *cardiac [heart] muscle,* or *myocardium.* Cardiac muscle, though of course involuntary, is striated, and will be described with the heart.

Smooth muscle largely composes the walls of the various digestive organs (esophagus, stomach, intestine, etc.) and of other hollow structures, urinary bladder, ureters, uterus, etc. It is found also in a great number of other situations, such as in the skin, blood vessels, in the capsules and partitions of solid organs, and in glands. It is also called involuntary because we have no conscious control over the activity of this type of muscle. The terms **striated** and **nonstriated** or **smooth,** refer to the microscopic crossbands seen in skeletal muscle but that are absent from involuntary muscle. Smooth muscle, however, shows very fine longitudinal lines, or striations, that, even with a powerful microscope, are ill-defined (Fig. 4.1). Smooth muscle possesses certain special physiological properties that will be considered with the digestive organs (Ch. 24).

Striated, skeletal, or voluntary muscle

Striated muscular tissue is that substance with which we are all familiar as flesh, or lean meat. Its solid constituent is nearly all protein which is about 20 percent of the whole. The remaining 80 percent or so

78

is water in which various minerals, sodium (chloride and bicarbonate), potassium, calcium, magnesium, etc., are dissolved. Its coloring matter is a pigment closely resembling hemoglobin and called **myoglobin.**

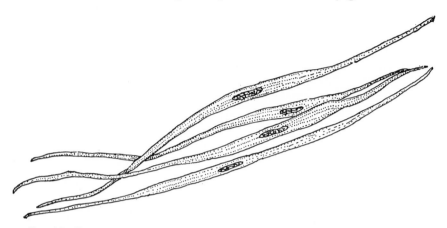

Fig. 4.1. Microscopic appearance of smooth (nonstriated or involuntary) muscle cells from the wall of the intestine, separated by teasing.

The minute (microscopic) structure of striated muscle. Striated muscle cells are long and slender. They vary greatly in length from a millimeter or so, as in the case of those of the stapedius muscle in the middle ear, to 50 mm or even more. On account of their relatively great length in comparison with their diameter (10 to 100 microns) the cells of muscle are usually called muscle fibers. Nevertheless, it is evident that muscle cells do not run through the entire length of most muscles. They are joined together in series by having their ends, which are tapered, applied to one another side by side. In large muscles great numbers of such fibers are bound together by connective tissue sheaths into bundles called **fasciculi** (sing. *fasciculus*).

Upon close examination under the microscope a striated muscle fiber shows a series of alternating light and dark transverse bands. Each fiber is ensheathed by a delicate membrane called the **sarcolemma** (*sarx,* flesh [muscle]; *lemma,* husk), and running through its entire length are a great number of fine parallel filaments—the **myofibrils.** The latter are embedded in the cytoplasm, usually referred to as the **sarcoplasm.** Each myofibril is constituted of a number of alternating light and dark sections. They are called the *I* and the *A* (or the *J* and the *Q*) discs, respectively (Fig. 4.2). A narrow dark line known as the *Z* line, or Krause's membrane, divides each light, or *I*, disc transversely into halves. The discs in all the myofibrils lie in line across the fiber, light to light and dark to dark; they are the cause of the characteristic striation of skeletal muscle. The myofibrils are the most minute parts of the muscle that can be seen with the ordinary microscope, but even these, delicate as they are, can be shown by means of the electron microscope to consist of a large number of fine threads of protein material called **actomyosin** (p. 94). These infinitely fine threads are called **micellae**. They are the essential contractile elements of muscle.

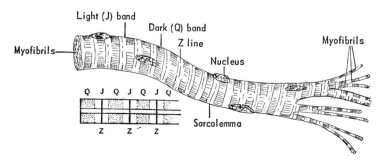

Fig. 4.2. Microscopic appearance of a striated (voluntary or striped) muscle fiber; lower sketch shows striations diagrammatically and drawn to larger scale.

The striated muscle fiber contains one or more nuclei just beneath the sarcolemma; in a long fiber several nuclei may be seen. In having its nuclei placed near its outer boundary, the striated muscle fiber differs from most other cells, in which the nuclei are centrally situated. Each muscle fiber is separated from its neighbors and is completely enveloped by a thin investment of connective tissue. This sheath which lies outside the sarcolemma is called the **endomysium**. A connective tissue layer, the **perimysium,** also encloses groups of muscle fibers, holding them in bundles. The envelope of connective tissue surrounding the entire muscle is called the **epimysium** (Fig. 4.3).

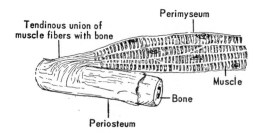

Fig. 4.3. A bundle of muscle fibers blending through tendon with the periosteum. Semidiagrammatic; muscle fibers and bone not drawn to same scale.

General anatomical features of skeletal muscle. *Origins and insertions.* Most skeletal muscles, as the name implies, are attached to bony structures, though a few, such as those of the face, are attached to skin; others are attached to cartilage and some to ligaments or to other muscles. One of the bones to which a muscle is attached is usually held more or less stationary by the action of other muscles; the **prime mover** (see below) thus is provided with a fixed point for its contraction. This attachment of the muscle is usually called its **origin.** The other extremity of the muscle, especially of a limb muscle, is most usually attached to a bone that moves upon some type of joint when the muscle contracts; this attachment is called the **insertion** of the muscle. In the case of the muscles of the limbs and of certain other parts, the muscles are situated with their insertions distal to their origins (that is, more toward the fingers or toes), and when the muscle contracts its insertion moves toward its origin, which remains stationary (Fig. 4.4). Most voluntary muscles are inserted not directly into the bone, but through the medium of a strong, tough, inelastic fibrous cord called a **tendon** (or sinew, in popular language, Fig. 4.3). Tendons vary greatly in length, in man, from a fraction of an inch to more than a foot. Sometimes a muscle has a tendon at each of its extremities.

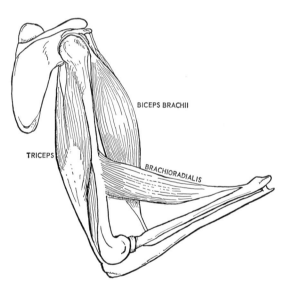

Fig. 4.4. Drawing to show the action of muscles crossing a joint. When the biceps brachili and brachioradialis contract they pull upon the radius and flex the arm at the elbow; when the triceps contracts the elbow is straightened (extended).

Shapes and fiber patterns. Muscles are of many shapes and sizes. Their shapes are variously described as **fusiform** (spindle shaped), **quadrilateral** or **rhomboid, triangular, straplike** (such as the long muscle on the front and inner side of the thigh and knee), and **pennate** (like a feather) in which the fibers pass from either side to a central tendon that they join obliquely (Fig. 4.5). This arrangement of the fibers is called **bipennate.** In other muscles only one half of a feather is represented, the fibers passing obliquely to only one side of the tendon; they are called **unipennate.** In most muscles the fibers pass in a direct line— the line of pull—from origin to insertion.

When a muscle, for example, the biceps of the arm, contracts, it

Fig. 4.5. Four different types of arrangement of the fibers in voluntary muscles. Diagrammatic; description in the text.

appears to increase in volume, and the ancient and medieval physicians thought that such actually occurred. But it has been shown conclusively that no increase in the volume of a muscle occurs when it contracts.

Muscular movements. Muscles that bend a limb at a joint, such as those that raise the thigh at the hip joint or bend the elbow or knee, are called *flexor muscles* (or **flexors**). Those that straighten the limb, lower the thigh at the hip joint or straighten the arm at the elbow or the leg at the knee are called *extensor muscles* (or **extensors**). Muscles that move the limb or other part in a direction away from the mid-line of the body or of a limb are called **abductors,** and those executing the opposite movement—that is, bringing the limb or other part toward the mid-line of the body or of a limb are known as **adductors.** There are also muscles that **rotate** a limb. In the case of the movements at the ankle joint, confusion is avoided by adding the qualifying **plantar** and **dorsi-** to the word **flexor.** Thus, moving the foot upward upon the ankle joint is called **dorsiflexion;** depressing the foot toward the ground is called **plantar flexion.** *Dorsiflexors* and *plantar flexors* are corresponding terms given to the muscles that carry out these movements (Fig. 4.6). Turning the forearm so that the palm of the hand faces forward is called **supination;** turning it to bring the palm to face backward is called **pronation.**

A *sphincter* is a muscle whose fibers run circularly around the orifice of a muscular tube or other hollow organ. When it contracts, the entrance or outlet from the organ is closed, much as the mouth of a bag is tightened by a drawstring. The lower end of the esophagus, the outlet from the stomach, the anal orifice, the distal end of the ureter, the neck of the urinary bladder, and the urethra are all guarded by sphincters.

In performing a given movement, such as bending the leg at the knee or the arm at the elbow, the several muscles carrying out the movement act as a "team." In bending the arm at the elbow, for example, the muscles that execute the actual movement, biceps, etc., are called **prime movers,** but we shall see (Ch. 34) that the oppositely acting muscles, in this instance the triceps, must relax; they are called **antagonists.** The functions of these muscles are of course reversed when the elbow is extended, the triceps now being the prime mover and the biceps antagonist. **Fixation muscles** are those that hold stationary the bone or

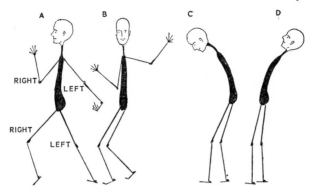

Fig. 4.6. Diagrammatic representation of various movements. *A,* extension of fingers of right hand, flexion at right shoulder and elbow and at right hip and knee; flexion of fingers and wrist of left hand, extension at left shoulder and elbow and at left hip and knee; plantar flexion of right foot at ankle, dorsiflexion of left foot. *B,* adduction of right arm at shoulder, abduction of left arm; abduction of right thigh at hip, adduction of left thigh; dorsiflexion of toes. *C,* flexion of neck and trunk. *D,* extension of neck and trunk.

bones giving origin to the muscle, thus enabling it to apply its force most effectively to the bone into which it is inserted. For example, in flexing the elbow, the muscles about the shoulder hold the humerus, clavicle, and scapula steady as the flexors contract. Muscles that hold a joint that is crossed by the tendon of the prime mover in the best position for its action are called **synergists.** Thus, when the muscles (flexors of the fingers and wrist) that clench the fist contract, there is a tendency for the wrist to be sharply flexed. Normally this does not occur, because the muscles on the back of the forearm (extensors of the wrist), whose tendons cross the back of the wrist, contract, thus give rigidity to this joint.

The manner in which the nerves end in the muscles will be described in Chapter 34.

PHYSIOLOGY OF MUSCLE

The muscle fiber is a highly differentiated cell whose prime function is to contract, that is, to shorten, and thus to move the limbs or other part of the body. The power of a muscle and the amount of work it can perform is dependent upon the innumerable primary functional units of which it is composed, namely, the infinitely minute micellae constituting the muscle fibers.

Method of recording contractions of an isolated muscle. Our knowledge of the physiology of muscular contraction has been gained largely from

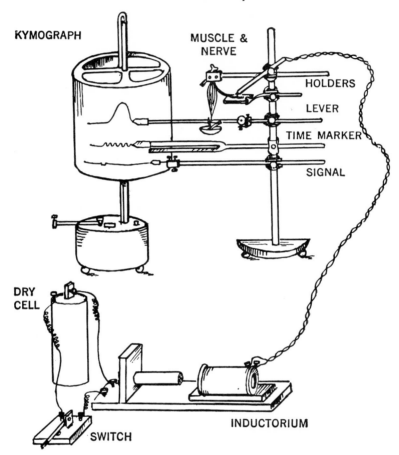

KYMOGRAPH

MUSCLE & NERVE

HOLDERS

LEVER

TIME MARKER

SIGNAL

DRY CELL

INDUCTORIUM

SWITCH

Fig. 4.7. Showing apparatus for stimulating an isolated frog's muscle and the method of recording the contraction. The electrical connections of the signal magnet have been omitted.

studies of the isolated muscle of the frog. The muscle of the calf—the **gastrocnemius**—is the one most generally employed. This muscle is attached above to the lower end of the thigh bone (femur) and below, through a strong tendon called the tendo calcaneus or tendon of Achilles, to the bone of the heel. In preparing the muscle for an experiment, it is removed from the animal together with its nerve supply (the sciatic nerve) and the lower end of the femur. The preparation is then suspended by fixing the section of bone in a clamp and fastening the lower tendinous end of the muscle to a light lever, as shown in Figure 4.7. The lever is adjusted so as to make light contact with the surface of a revolving drum, motivated by clockwork and covered with smoked paper. This instrument is called a *kymograph*. As the drum revolves, the soot is removed by the point of the lever, thus tracing a white horizontal line so long as the lever remains stationary. Any shortening (contraction) of the muscle causes an upward movement of the lever which then inscribes a curve on the rotating drum.

A tuning fork of the required frequency of vibration (for example, $\frac{1}{100}$, $\frac{1}{50}$ second) is arranged with a writing point to mark the time intervals at the bottom of the tracing, or some device run by clockwork may be used. A signal magnet is also set up in the primary circuit of the inductorium (see below) to indicate the instant that the stimulating current, which also activates the signal, is made or broken.

The inductorium. An induced electric current is usually employed in classroom experiments for stimulating muscle and nerve; it can be finely graded in strength, and a series of rapidly repeated shocks can be applied to the excitable tissue. The instrument employed for this purpose is called an *inductorium,* which consists of two cylindrical spools or coils of wire called *primary* and *secondary* (Fig. 4.8). The primary coil consists of an iron core wound around by a few turns of thick wire. It receives current from a dry cell, a switch or key being interposed in the circuit. The secondary coil is composed of many turns of fine wire. Its core being hollow, it is capable of being slid like a sleeve over the primary coil. It runs on parallel metal bars and can be pivoted as well around its transverse axis. When the current from the dry cell enters the primary coil, a current is induced in the secondary coil. The low electromotive force of the primary circuit is transformed to the high electromotive force of the induced current which is led off to stimulating electrodes fastened to binding posts, one on either end of the horizontal bars along which the secondary coil slides. The primary circuit may be

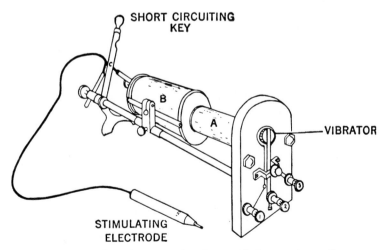

Fig. 4.8. The inductorium. A, primary coil; B, secondary coil.

made and broken by means of the key, or by the rapid movements of an automatic *interrupter,* or *vibrator,* on the instrument itself. Nerve or muscle can then be stimulated by a series of rapidly alternating make and break induced currents. The break shock of the induced current is more effective as a stimulus than is the make shock. The current induced in the secondary coil is increased or diminished by sliding this coil toward or away from the primary coil. The induced current can also be graded by rotating the secondary coil upon its pivot, and altering the angle it makes with the primary coil. When the secondary and primary coils have their long axes at right angles to one another, there is no induced current. A current is induced as the secondary coil is moved from the right angle toward the horizontal position, and increases steadily the farther it is turned in this direction, reaching a maximum for any given distance from the primary coil when the long axes of the two coils are in line.

The muscle "twitch," the simplest muscular contraction. Muscle responds to any one of four types of stimulus—*electrical, mechanical, thermal,* or *chemical.* It may be stimulated directly by placing electrodes on its surface, or indirectly through its nerve, as occurs naturally in the body. When stimulated experimentally in either of these ways and with a single stimulus, for example, a make or break shock, the muscle contracts, and, having raised the writing lever to a certain height, relaxes again and allows the lever to return to its original position. Thus a curve similar to that shown in Figure 4.9 is inscribed. This simple brief contraction is called a muscle **twitch**; it is due, of course, to the shortening (contraction) in unison of the numerous fibers of which the muscle is composed. A simple contraction or twitch does not occur in the living animal under ordinary physiological conditions, but the reflex contraction of the extensor muscles of the thigh caused by a tap on the patella tendon (knee jerk)

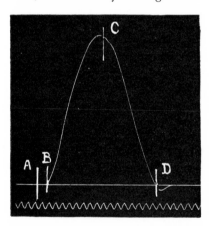

Fig. 4.9. Record of a muscle twitch. A-B, latent period; B-C, contraction phase; C-D, relaxation phase. Time indicated by lower tracing ($1/100$ sec) caused by a vibrating tuning fork. (After Stirling.)

is of this nature. The curve shown in Figure 4.9 is marked off into three parts to represent corresponding phases of the muscular response. The stimulus was applied at *A;* shortening of the muscle commences at *B* and relaxation at *C.* The distance from *A* to *B* indicates the period elapsing from the application of the stimulus to the commencement of the contraction. This is called the **latent period**; its duration is about 0.01 second. The next period (B to C), during which the lever rises from the horizontal line (base line) to the summit of the curve, is the **contraction phase**; it lasts for approximately 0.04 second. The part of the curve from C to D represents the **relaxation phase**; this has a duration of about 0.05 second.

As determined by the method described above, the total duration of the contractile process of the frog's gastrocnemius muscle, including the latent period, is found to be about 0.1 second. The muscles of warm-blooded animals have considerably shorter contraction times.

The latent period of the muscle, as measured from the instant of stimulation of its nerve, is made up of (a) the very brief interval during which the initial chemical changes are occurring in the muscle fiber and tension is being developed, (b) the time taken for the impulse to travel along the nerve from the point of stimulation to the muscle, and (c) the time required to overcome the inertia of the lever. The last mentioned, (c), can be almost entirely eliminated by refined methods of recording, for example, some form of recording in which the contraction of the muscle moves a mirrored surface; this reflects a beam of light that is photographed. The light beam, which is substituted for the material lever, is free from inertia. Furthermore, its length can be such that great magnification of the movements of the reflecting surface can be obtained. The true latent period of muscle—that is, the interval between the stimulation of the muscle fiber and the commencement of the shortening process—varies between 0.0025 and 0.004 second.

Relationship of force of contraction to intensity of stimulus. If a series of stimuli of gradually increasing strength is applied directly to the muscle, contraction curves of graded heights will be obtained (Fig. 4.10). The weakest stimulus that will excite the muscle is called the **minimal, or threshold, stimulus.** As the strength of each successive stimulus is increased, a greater and greater response is obtained from the muscle. Ultimately, a point is reached where the muscle contracts maximally—that is, no further increase in the height of the contraction curve results from increasing the strength of the stimulus. This is called the **maximal stimulus.**

The "all or none" law. This law, which is described more fully in

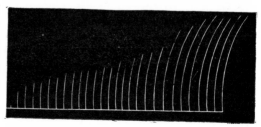

Fig. 4.10. Record of a series of contractions caused by a succession of stimuli of graded strength. The muscle lever traced each of these lines while the drum of the kymograph was at rest, and was then moved by hand to a fresh position after each contraction.

Chapter 33, states that any stimulus that excites a tissue causes a maximal response. The grading of the muscular response to stimuli of graded strength, as just described, appears to contradict this statement. The explanation is that a muscle is composed of a number of units—the muscle fibers. Since the force of the contraction of the whole muscle is dependent upon the number of fibers excited by the stimulus, a strong stimulus excites a larger number of fibers than does a weak one, and with a maximal stimulus the current spread to involve all the fibers. Studies made upon a *single* muscle fiber have shown that it does not respond by graded responses as the strength of the stimulus is increased. It responds maximally or not at all; that is, it obeys the "all or none" law.

Summation and tetanus. If a second stimulus is sent into an isolated frog's muscle within the latent period of the first, no obvious effect is produced. If, however, the second stimulus is applied while the muscle is contracting in response to the first stimulus, it contracts again; the second contraction is added to the first, the shortening of the muscle being then greater than that caused by a single stimulus. The greatest effect of the second stimulus is observed when it is applied to the muscle near the height of the contraction caused by the first. This phenomenon, whereby one contraction is added to a previous one to produce a greater total shortening of the muscle, is called **summation** (Fig. 4.11). A third contraction may be added to a second, a fourth to a third, and so on. When the stimuli sent into a frog's gastrocnemius muscle are at a slower rate than from 15 to 30 per second, the individual contractions can be distinguished—that is, they are not completely fused. The contraction curve shows smaller or larger waves synchronous with the rate of stimulation. At rates of stimulation higher than this the responses are completely fused, the contraction curve being perfectly smooth. The curve rises to a maximum height considerably greater than that caused by a single stimulus, and remains at this height as long as the stimulation lasts or until the muscle becomes fatigued. A sustained contraction of this nature is called **complete tetanus.** The contraction caused by slower rates of stimulation, and in which the individual responses are distinguishable, is referred to as **incomplete tetanus.**

The rate of stimulation at which complete fusion of the contractions occurs varies with the speed at which a given type of muscle normally contracts. Thus, rapidly acting muscles require a higher rate of stimulation to produce tetanus than do more slowly acting muscles, and the rate required by smooth muscle is slowest of all (5 stimuli per second). In the rapidly acting muscles of the wings of insects, contractions are not fused until the rate of stimulation reaches about 300 per second and upward, and even a human eye muscle (internal rectus) requires a stimulation rate of 350 per second.

Treppe, or the "staircase" phenomenon. When a muscle is stimulated

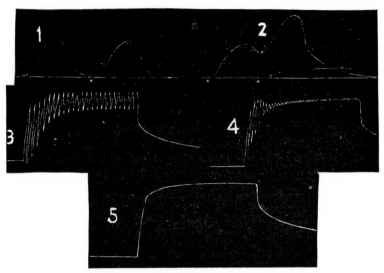

Fig. 4.11. Illustrating summation and tetanus. 1, two separate contractions of equal amplitude, the second stimulus being applied after relaxation of the muscle; 2, summation, the second stimulus being applied at a shorter interval after the first than in 1; 3 and 4, incomplete tetanus caused by a series of stimuli applied at short intervals apart; 5, complete tetanus resulting from a still more rapid rate of stimulation, the individual muscular responses being completely fused. *(After Stirling and Howell.)*

repeatedly at regular intervals, the first few contractions of the series increase successively in amplitude. This phenomenon, first described (see heart muscle) by an American physiologist in 1870, is due, apparently, to the beneficial effects exerted upon the irritability of the muscle by the chemical products of the first few contractions, and by the rise in temperature (Fig. 4.12).

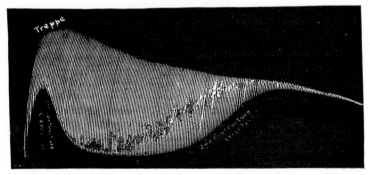

Fig. 4.12. Illustrating treppe, contracture, and fatigue. The muscle was stimulated at intervals of one second. The contractions are very close together because the kymograph drum was moving slowly. *(After Howell.)*

Effect of loading on muscle contraction. A muscle contracts more forcibly if suitably loaded. The increase in the height of the contraction increases up to a point with each weight added to the scale pan suspended from the muscle as shown in Figure 4.7. The force of the contractions then decreases again as the load is gradually increased (Fig. 4.16). For an isolated frog's muscle the maximum height is attained at a loading weight of between 30 and 50 grams. When a loaded muscle is stimulated to contract, the first effect is a sudden lengthening of the muscle fibers. This sudden stretch causes tension in the muscle that is immediately followed by shortening. The stretching of the fibers in some way enables the muscle to mobilize more energy than is possible for the unweighted muscle. The same phenomenon occurs in cardiac muscle (Ch. 14). Throughout the shortening of the muscle the tension remains constant. This type of contraction is therefore called **isotonic** (Gk. *isos,* equal + *tonus,* tension). But if the muscle is loaded with a weight that it is unable to lift or is attached to a stiff spring that it cannot bend, only a very slight shortening of the muscle fibers can occur. Such a contraction is called **isometric** (Gk. *isos,* equal + *metron,* measure).

In the body the muscles execute both types of contraction. The isometric type is seen in those muscles that maintain the body's posture, such as the extensors on the front of the thigh. These exert a constant pull upon the leg, and thus hold the limb in the extended position to afford a firm support for the body. The movements of the limbs, as in walking, lifting objects with the hands, or throwing a ball, are brought about by isotonic contractions.

Fatigue. If *direct* stimulation of an excised muscle—that is, with the electrodes placed upon the muscle—be continued after the contractions have reached their maximum amplitude, the irritability of the muscle gradually becomes depressed due to the accumulation of lactic acid (Fig.

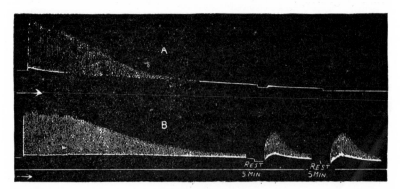

Fig. 4.13. Showing the effect of oxygen lack upon the onset of fatigue. Records from a pair of sartorius muscles of frog, stimulated at 1-second intervals. A, in nitrogen; B, in oxygen. (After Fletcher.)

4.13). The concentration of lactic acid at which loss of irritability of the muscle occurs, and at which it fails to respond to stimulation, is around 0.5 percent.

The onset and development of this state of **fatigue** are more rapid the higher the rate of stimulation. Isolated muscle, or one in the intact animal the blood supply of which has been occluded, also fatigues more rapidly than one receiving an adequate oxygen supply. Oxygen is required for the removal of the lactic acid produced during contraction. In the muscle deprived of its blood supply this does not readily occur. Lactic acid accumulates, and it is to such accumulation that the loss of irritability of the muscle is attributed (see p. 95).

When a muscle is stimulated not directly but *through its nerve,* fatigue supervenes much sooner—long before the lactic acid concentration has reached the value at which it depresses muscular irritability. We know that nerve is highly resistant to fatigue. There must, then, be a third structure or tissue in the nerve-muscle preparation that is peculiarly susceptible to fatigue; this is the junction between nerve and muscle—the **myoneural junction**—which exhibits the properties of a synapse (Ch. 34). The early fatigability of the myoneural junction can be demonstrated by a simple experiment. If the nerve to the muscle is stimulated repeatedly until the muscle fails to respond, a stimulus of the same strength as before applied directly to the muscle causes a vigorous contraction (Fig. 4.14).

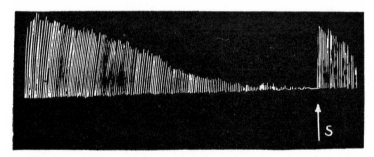

Fig. 4.14. Illustrating the ready fatigability of the myoneural junction, i.e., before the muscle itself. The muscle was stimulated *through its nerve* to the arrow, S, and then *directly.*

Electrical changes in muscle. Like nerve and other excitable tissues, an action potential is developed in muscle when it contracts, the active region of the muscle being negative to the inactive region. A current of injury can also be demonstrated when one electrode is placed on a crushed or cut end of the muscle, the other on the uninjured surface, and the two electrodes connected through a galvanometer (see Fig. 33.4). The action current or the current of injury in muscle can be used to

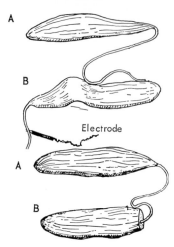

A

B

Electrode

A

B

Fig. 4.15. The rheoscopic preparation. See text.

excite the nerve of another isolated muscle. This so-called **rheoscopic preparation** is shown in Figure 4.15. When muscle *B* (upper sketch) is stimulated to contract, a twitch of *A* occurs as the wave of contraction passes beneath its nerve which touches the contracting muscle at two points. Similarly, if a part of the nerve of muscle *A* (lower sketch) is laid on the cut surface of muscle *B*, and another part is made to touch the uninjured surface of *B*, a slight twitch of *A* occurs each time the latter contact is made.

Muscular work and efficiency. Work, as defined by the physicist, is the product of the load (expressed in grams, kilograms, or pounds) and the vertical distance (in millimeters, centimeters, meters, or feet) through which it is raised. According to the units of distance and weight employed, the work is expressed in gram-millimeters, gram-centimeters, kilogram-meters, or foot-pounds.

The isolated muscle can be made to perform work by stimulating it to contract and lift a weight. A load consisting of a known weight is attached to the lever at the point of attachment of the muscle, which is then stimulated. The height above the baseline of the tracing inscribed by the lever is measured. This measurement, however, is not the actual distance through which the weight has been raised, for the shortening of the muscle has been magnified by the lever. The distance as measured must, therefore, be divided by the magnification of the lever, which is usually five.

The work performed by the gastrocnemius muscle of the frog is most suitably expressed in gram-millimeters. For example, a muscle that lifts a weight of 1 gram to a height of 2 mm does 2 gram-millimeters of work. The muscle when loaded with a heavier weight may not raise it so high, yet may do more work. Thus, if it lifts a weight of 4 grams only 1 mm it does 4 gram-millimeters of work. Starting with a light load and gradually adding to it for a number of successive contractions, it is found that the work performed increases up to a maximum and then falls off. There exists, therefore, an optimum load, that is, a load with which the muscle performs the maximum amount of work (Fig. 4.16). Since the work, as just defined, is the product of the load and the lift, no work is done by an unloaded muscle when it contracts; nor by one that contracts against a weight that it is unable to lift. In both these instances, however, there is an expenditure of energy that is derived from chemical processes taking place in the muscle; all of this energy appears ultimately as heat.

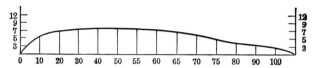

Fig. 4.16. Diagram to show the method of measuring muscle work. Heights of contractions along vertical lines, weights in grams along the horizontal line. (After McKendrick.)

Of the total energy expended by any machine, part appears as mechanical work and the remainder is dissipated as heat. The efficiency of the machine is defined as the percentage of the total energy that appears as work. Thus:

$$\text{Efficiency} = \frac{\text{work}}{\text{total energy (work + heat)}}$$

As mentioned above, a muscle contracting isometrically or without a load performs no work, all the energy being dissipated as heat. Contracting with an optimum load, on the other hand, muscle has an efficiency of from 25 to 30 percent, which compares favorably with that of the best type of gasoline engine. By measuring the heat produced by a muscle during its contraction and the work done, its efficiency can be readily calculated from the equation given above. In making the calculation, the energy appearing as work and as heat must, of course, be expressed in the same units. We may express the work in heat units (for example, microcalories). Now, the heat equivalent of a gram-millimeter is 0.00235 microcalorie. Therefore, if the heat produced is 8.4 microcalories, and the work performed is 1200 gram-millimeters, then the total energy expenditure expressed as heat can be calculated as follows:

Heat produced = 8.4 microcalories
Work = 1200 gram-millimeters
Heat equivalent of the work = 1200 × 0.00235 = 2.8 microcalories
Total energy expenditure therefore = 8.4 + 2.8 = 11.2 microcalories.
   The efficiency is 2.8/11.2 = 25 percent

Muscle tone. In the healthy body the skeletal muscles are constantly maintained in a state of slight partial contraction known as **tone, or tonus.** Those muscles that support the body in the standing position, such as the extensor muscles of the thigh, leg, neck, and back, show the greatest degree of tone. Tone is a reflex phenomenon, the adequate stimulus for its elicitation being a stretching force. The particular spinal reflex involved is called the **stretch reflex.** This extremely sensitive reflex evokes a contraction in response to the least increase in muscle length. Muscle tone is also under the control of higher centers in the brain and severe disturbances—either an increase, decrease, or complete loss—in tone faculty occur in a number of nervous diseases.

The chemical constitution of muscle. Fresh muscular tissue, which composes the lean part of beef, pork, etc., contains about 20 percent of protein and around 75 percent of water. The remaining 5 percent is made up of minerals and various organic compounds (glycogen, glucose, lipids, steroids, and nonprotein nitrogenous compounds). The principal mineral in the muscle cell (fiber) is potassium, which has a concentration of around 400 mg per 100 grams; magnesium, phosphorus, sodium, and calcium are present in much lower concentrations. The chief nonprotein nitrogenous substances are **creatine, phosphocreatine, adenosinetriphosphate,** and **urea.** The main proteins composing the contractile elements of muscle (the micellae) are **myosin** and **actin.** These two proteins are in very close functional association in the micellae; the combination, known as **actomyosin,** is of essential importance in the contractile process.

The pigment of muscle, called **myoglobin,** or **muscle hemoglobin,** is closely allied chemically, as well as functionally, to hemoglobin.

The chemistry of muscular contraction. Muscle derives the energy for its contraction, ultimately, from the combustion of carbohydrate; in the final step of this process oxygen is consumed and carbon dioxide (CO_2) and water (H_2O) produced. The actual contraction of the muscle, however, is brought about by the explosive separation of a molecule of phosphoric acid from **adenosinetriphosphate** (abbr. ATP). **Adenosinediphosphate** (ADP) is thus formed. This reaction is the very first to occur when the muscle fiber contracts. The molecule of phosphoric acid split off from ATP combines with glycogen, of which a considerable store is present in the muscle fiber. Instantaneously with the acquisition of phosphoric acid, the glycogen splits off a molecule of phosphorylated glucose called **glucose phosphate** that is converted through a series of intermediate reactions to **fructose diphosphate** (that is, fructose combined with two molecules of phosphoric acid). The fructose diphosphate passes through a series of complicated reactions to form lactic acid. After the transfer of phosphorus from ATP to glycogen, and the formation of ADP, **phosphocreatine** splits into **creatine** and **phosphoric acid.** The liberated phosphorus is taken up by ADP, and ATP is reformed. Thus:

$$\text{phosphocreatine} \rightarrow \text{creatine} + \text{phosphoric acid}$$
$$\text{phosphoric acid} + \text{ADP} \rightarrow \text{ATP}$$

The conversion of ATP to ADP as just stated is the immediate source of the energy for the contraction of the muscle fiber. From the breakdown of phosphocreatine is derived the energy for the reformation of ATP from phosphoric acid and ADP. Phosphocreatine is also resynthesized, the energy for the resynthesis being derived from the breakdown of glucose phosphate to lactic acid.

Of the lactic acid produced, one fifth is oxidized to carbon dioxide and water. The remainder (four fifths) is resynthesized to glycogen in the liver, muscles, and other tissues of the body. Each of the chemical changes described above is dependent upon a specific enzyme.

The first three of the reactions occurring in muscle and tabulated below, namely, the removal of phosphate from ATP, the breakdown of phosphocreatine, and the breakdown of glycogen to lactic acid, can be carried out in the absence of oxygen. The removal of lactic acid (by oxidation) and the resynthesis of glycogen can occur only in the presence of oxygen. There are therefore two phases in the contractile process, a **nonoxidative, anaerobic,** or **contraction phase** and an **oxidative, aerobic,** or **recovery phase.** This latter is necessary to restore energy-producing substances and permit continued contraction of the muscle.[1]

A SUMMARY OF THE CHEMICAL CHANGES OCCURRING IN MUSCLE DURING ITS CONTRACTION AND RECOVERY

(a) Adenosinetriphosphate (ATP) yields
- phosphoric acid
- +
- adenosinediphosphate (ADP)

immediate energy for contraction

(b) Phosphocreatine yields
- creatine
- +
- phosphoric acid

energy for resynthesis of ATP (ADP + phosphoric acid)

(c) Glycogen to lactic acid through glucose phosphate, fructose diphosphate and a number of enzymatic reactions

energy for resynthesis of phosphocreatine

(d) Oxidation of $\frac{1}{5}$ lactic acid produced

energy for resynthesis of remainder ($\frac{4}{5}$) of lactic acid to glycogen

In so far as its energy relationships are concerned, the muscle fiber has been compared to a submarine that, while submerged, is driven by energy stored in electric batteries, oxygen not being required; this period corresponds to the anaerobic phase of the process in the muscle. The

[1] A muscle deprived of oxygen (that is, in an atmosphere of nitrogen) is, therefore, capable of responding to stimulation for a considerable time. Lactic acid, however, is not removed by oxidation and resynthesis to glycogen, but, accumulating, reduces the irritability of the muscle. The concentration of lactic acid at which the muscle fails to respond is around 0.5 percent. This is called the *lactic acid maximum*. When oxygen is supplied to a muscle fatigued by repeated stimulation in nitrogen, the lactic acid is removed and the irritability of the muscle restored.

batteries are recharged when the submersible reaches the surface, oxygen then being necessary. This corresponds to the aerobic or recovery phase of the muscle.

Heat production in muscle. When a muscle contracts heat is produced. The muscular tissues constitute one of the main sources of the heat of the body (Ch. 29). In an isometric contraction in which no work is performed all the energy of the chemical reactions occurring in the muscle appears as heat. Of this heat, part is produced during the activity of the muscle (**contraction heat**), and part after contraction and relaxation are over and the muscle is being restored to its original state; this is called **recovery heat.** The contraction heat is generated in the absence of oxygen, that is, anaerobically, whereas the recovery heat is produced only aerobically, and is due mainly to the oxidation of lactic acid formed during contraction.

Oxygen debt. In strenuous muscular exercise of brief duration, only a fraction of the oxygen required for the recovery phase of the contracting muscles is breathed during the course of the exercise. For example, the oxygen requirement for a race of 100 yards, which takes only a few seconds to run, is 6 liters or more. Yet the quantity of oxygen that can be absorbed in this time is less than 1 liter. Indeed, a short race can be run with the breath held. In other words, the sprinter goes into debt for oxygen during the race, and pays up later. Thus the oxygen consumption after the exercise period is much higher than during an ordinary period of rest. The extra oxygen is utilized in the removal of the lactic acid produced during the exercise. The size of the oxygen debt for any piece of work is determined by measuring the oxygen consumption of the after-period of exercise, and subtracting from the result the figure for the oxygen consumption of a corresponding period of rest. During very strenuous muscular effort the oxygen debt may amount to 15 liters or more.

The ability of the muscles to contract without receiving the full oxygen requirement until the work has been completed has an obvious advantage. Short periods of strenuous exercise can be undertaken that would otherwise be impossible, for the respiratory and circulatory systems are quite unequal to the task of furnishing, during the exercise, the great volume of oxygen that is ultimately used in the recovery process. The maximum quantity of oxygen that can be delivered to and consumed by the tissues of a large healthy man is not more than about 2 liters per minute and, for most persons, considerably less than this.

In light exercise no oxygen debt is incurred. The lactic acid is removed as it is produced; in other words the body, in so far as oxygen consumption is concerned, "pays as it goes." Lactic acid production and removal are nicely balanced; a "steady state" becomes established shortly after the start of the effort. At this time a person engaged in an athletic performance of some duration, such as running, rowing, etc., breathes with less effort. As the expression goes he has got his "second wind."

The source of energy for muscular work. We have seen that the energy for the contraction of the isolated muscle is ultimately derived from carbohydrate. Glycogen is broken down through glucose phosphate and fructose diphosphate to lactic acid. In the numerous studies of the respiratory exchange of the isolated gastrocnemius muscle of the frog during contraction, respiratory quotients of 1.0 (Ch. 28, footnote 2) are obtained. In the intact animal, carbohydrate is also the fuel for short bouts of muscular exercise. After a sprint, for example, a fall in blood sugar may occur, and the ingestion of glucose prior to a race is now recognized as a valuable means of postponing fatigue and enhancing muscular performance. In prolonged and exhausting work the carbohydrate stores become depleted; fat is then burned to furnish the required energy. Protein apparently is not utilized in muscular exercise, or, if so, to a very small extent.

5

The Muscular System (continued), Descriptions of Individual Muscles

There are a very great number of different muscles, and in a book of this scope those of lesser importance can be described but briefly. Most of the muscles will be considered in groups in accordance with their locations. Those concerned with respiration, digestion, and the genital functions are dealt with more appropriately in the chapters devoted to the physiology of these subjects. The muscles of the middle ear are described in Chapter 46.

As an aid in the study of the origins and insertions of muscles, the figures of the bones in Chapter 3 should be consulted.

MUSCLES OF THE HEAD; MUSCLES OF FACIAL EXPRESSION AND MASTICATION

Muscle of the scalp

The **occipitofrontalis** is a broad musculofibrous sheet that covers the upper part of the cranium from the eyebrows to the back of the head. It has two anterior and two posterior bellies connected by a strong fibrous sheet called the **epicranial aponeurosis**, which covers the upper part of the skull. The two anterior bellies of the muscle arise, one on either side, from the frontal bone. The posterior bellies take origin from the occipital bone and the mastoid processes of the temporal bones (Fig. 5.1). *Actions:* the scalp is drawn backwards by contraction of the occipital bellies; the frontal bellies acting from above raise the eyebrows, and in a stronger movement the skin of the forehead is transversely wrinkled. Thus, surprise, horror, or fear is expressed. Acting from below the frontal bellies cause frowning.

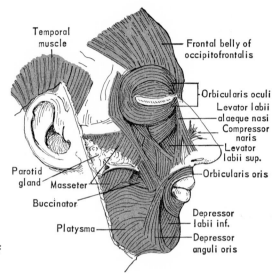

Fig. 5.1. Principal muscles of the head.

Muscles of the eyelids

The orbicularis oculi is composed of muscle fibers that sweep around the opening of the eyelid. It is located in the upper and lower eyelids and extends over the temporal region and downwards over the cheek. Its *action* is to close the eye, as in sleep or in winking. Such movements involve only the part covering the lids, but firm closure of the eyes and wrinkling of the skin are caused when the whole muscle contracts.

The corrugator is a small, triangular muscle lying beneath the inner part of the orbicularis oculi. Its *action* is to cause vertical wrinkles in the skin of the forehead, as in frowning.

Muscles of the nose and mouth

The dilator naris arises from the maxilla and is inserted into the ala nasi—the soft tissue of the nostril. Its *action* is to dilate the nostril.

The compressor naris arises from the maxilla above the incisor teeth and runs upwards and inwards to the bridge of the nose. Its *action* is to narrow the nostril.

The orbicularis oris has no bony attachment. Its fibers, which surround the opening of the mouth, are derived in part from the other oral muscles (Fig. 5.1) and from the skin.

The risorius arises from the fascia over the posterior part of the cheek and is inserted into the skin at the angle of the mouth.

The **buccinator** is the principal muscle of the cheek, bridging the gap between the upper and lower jaws. It arises from the maxilla and mandible opposite the molar teeth.

The other muscles about the mouth arise from neighboring bone, maxilla, zygomatic, or mandible, and are inserted into the skin of the upper or lower lip, or at the angle of the mouth.

The *actions* of **levator labii superioris** (elevator of the upper lip), **levator anguli oris** (elevator of the angle of the mouth), **depressor labii inferioris** (depressor of the lower lip), and **depressor anguli oris** (depressor of the angle of the mouth) are well described by their names. The orbicularis oris closes the lips and compresses them against the teeth. The buccinator presses the cheek against the teeth and pushes food between them, thus aiding in mastication. Another action, from which it derives its name (L. *buccina,* a trumpet), is to force air from the mouth, as in blowing a wind instrument. The *risorius* retracts the angle of the mouth laterally to produce a grinning expression (L. *risor,* laughter).

All the muscles of the nose and mouth just described are supplied by branches of the *facial nerve.*

Muscles of mastication

The **masseter** is a stout quadrilateral muscle arising from the zygomatic process of the maxilla and the zygomatic arch, and is inserted into the lower half of the ramus of the mandible. A deeper portion of the muscle is inserted into the coronoid process and the upper half of the ramus of the mandible. The masseter is a powerful muscle. *Actions:* it elevates the mandible and brings the lower teeth against the upper. It is supplied by branches of the *mandibular nerve.*

The **temporalis** is a strong, fan-shaped muscle that arises from the temporal fossa on the side of the head and is inserted into the inner surface, apex, and anterior border of the coronoid process of the ramus of the mandible. Its *action* is to elevate the mandible and close the mouth. It is supplied by branches of the *mandibular nerve.* The contractions of both the temporalis and the masseter can be felt by firmly closing the jaws and placing the fingers on the side of the jaw or on the temporal region (Fig. 5.2).

The **pterygoideus lateralis** takes origin from the greater wing of the sphenoid bone (upper head of muscle) and the lateral surface of the lateral pterygoid plate (lower head). The fibers converging pass backwards and laterally to be inserted into the neck of the mandible and the capsule of the mandibular joint (Fig. 5.2). The **pterygoideus medialis** arises from the medial surface of the lateral pterygoid plate, from the tubercle of the palatine bone, and from the maxilla. Its fibers pass

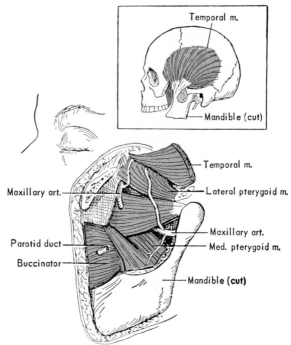

Fig. 5.2. *Lower drawing, muscles of mastication on the left side; the masseter muscle and most of the ramus of the mandible have been excised. Inset shows the temporal muscle (redrawn from Gray: Text-book of Anatomy & Physiology).*

laterally and backwards to be inserted into the medial surface of the ramus and angle of the mandible. The *action* of the pterygoid muscles is to protrude the mandible. The medial muscle also elevates the mandible while the lateral muscle depresses it, thus assisting in opening the mouth. When the two muscles on one side act together and alternately with those of the opposite side, a side to side motion is given to the mandible, as in grinding the food between the teeth. The pterygoids are supplied by branches of the *mandibular nerve.*

Muscles of the tongue and pharynx are described in Chapter 25.

MUSCLES OF THE NECK

Superficial lateral muscles

The platysma is a broad, thin, superficial muscular sheet that arises on each side from the fascia overlying the upper parts of the pectoralis major and deltoid muscles (pp. 113, 115). Its fibers run obliquely upward and forward to the lower part of the face where they are inserted into the border of the mandible and the subcutaneous tissue and skin. It is a very weak muscle and serves to lessen the hollow between the lower jaw and the neck. Its *actions* are to cause oblique wrinkling of the skin of the neck and to draw the lower lips downwards; it may assist in depressing the jaw. It is supplied by the *facial nerve* (Figs. 5.1, 5.10).

The **trapezius** is a large, flat, triangular muscle that covers the posterior part and a little of the side of the neck and the upper part of the back. It arises from the external occipital protuberance and the part of the bone lateral to the latter, from the ligamentum nuchae, and from the spines of the seventh cervical and of all the thoracic vertebrae. The fibers converge laterally and are inserted into the outer part of the clavicle, and into the acromion and spine of the scapula. The muscles of the two sides form a trapesium or quadrangular figure, hence the name. Its *actions* are to steady the scapula during movement of the upper arm. Acting with other muscles in the neighborhood, it assists in rotating the scapula, elevating it or retracting it, so as to brace the shoulder. It is supplied through the *accessory nerve* and the *third and fourth cervical nerves* (Figs. 5.1, 5.7).

The **sternocleidomastoideus** is commonly referred to simply as the **sternomastoid.** It is the most prominent muscle of the neck in the living subject and especially in lean persons, for it is seen as a diagonal column beneath the skin running from behind the angle of the jaw to the manubrium of the sternum, where the muscles of the two sides come close together. The muscle arises by two heads—from the upper part of the manubrium and from the inner third of the clavicle (Gk. *kleis* [*kleid-*], clavicle) and is inserted into the mastoid process of the temporal bone. By its *action* the head is drawn downward toward the corresponding shoulder, or it may rotate the head to turn the face to the opposite side. When both muscles act together the head is bowed forward, or raised from the ground if the body is lying on its back. In difficult breathing, these muscles may also aid the ordinary muscles of respiration in raising the thorax, while the head is fixed by other muscles (Fig. 5.3).

Suprahyoid muscles

The suprahyoid muscles lie on the anterior aspect of the neck between the lower jaw and the hyoid bone.

The **digastric,** as its name indicates, has two bellies—anterior and posterior—connected by a tendon that is held in close relationship to the hyoid bone by a loop of fibrous tissue. The anterior belly is attached to the mandible on one side of the chin; the posterior belly to the mastoid process. The two bellies thus bound a triangle just below the mandible (Fig. 5.3).

The **stylohyoid** arises from the styloid process of the temporal bone and is inserted into the body of the hyoid bone. The **mylohyoid** is in part covered by the anterior belly of the digastric. With its opposite fellow, which it meets in the mid-line, it forms the floor of the mouth. It

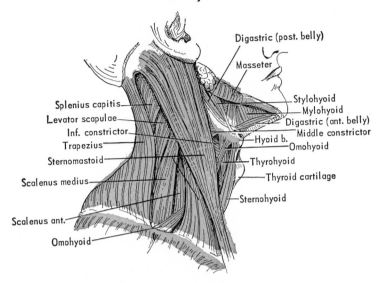

Digastric (post. belly)

Masseter

Splenius capitis

Levator scapulae

Inf. constrictor

Trapezius

Sternomastoid

Scalenus medius

Scalenus ant.

Omohyoid

Stylohyoid

Mylohyoid

Digastric (ant. belly)

Middle constrictor

Hyoid b.

Omohyoid

Thyrohyoid

Thyroid cartilage

Sternohyoid

Fig. 5.3. Superficial lateral muscles of the neck.

originates from the inner surface of the mandible and is inserted into the body of the hyoid bone (Figs. 5.3, 5.27). The **geniohyoid** is a slender muscle that arises from the inner surface of the mandible on one side of the chin. It is inserted into the hyoid bone. *Actions:* the suprahyoid muscles exert a steadying action upon the hyoid bone during movements of the tongue, during mastication, talking, and swallowing. During the latter act the mylohyoid raises the floor of the mouth and, with the other muscles, elevates the hyoid bone. The nerve supply of the anterior belly of the digastric is by a branch of the *inferior dental nerve* (branch of mandibular), the posterior belly by a branch of the *facial nerve*. The stylohyoid is also supplied by the facial nerve; the mylohyoid by a branch of the inferior dental nerve, and the geniohyoid through the *hypoglossal nerve.*

Infrahyoid muscles

The **sternohyoid** arises from the inner end of the clavicle and the manubrium of the sternum, and is inserted into the body of the hyoid bone. The **sternothyroid** lies under cover of the former muscle, arising from the manubrium and the cartilage of the first rib. It is inserted into the thyroid cartilage. The small **thyrohyoid,** running from the thyroid cartilage to the hyoid bone, may be considered the continuation upward of the sternothyroid. The **omohyoid** consists of two bellies, an upper attached to the hyoid bone, and a lower arising from the upper border of the scapula. The two bellies are connected at nearly a right angle by a short tendon that is fixed in position by a fibrous attachment to the clavicle and the first rib (Fig. 5.3). *Actions:* the sternohyoid depresses the hyoid bone after it has been elevated by the suprahyoid muscles; the sternothyroid depresses the larynx; the thyrohyoid depresses the hyoid bone or elevates the larynx; the omohyoid is a depressor of the hyoid bone, and may also serve as an accessory muscle of respiration when inspiration is difficult. The infrahyoid muscles are supplied by branches of the *hypoglossal nerve.*

Anterior vertebral muscles

The **longus cervicis, longus capitis, rectus capitis anterior,** and **rectus capitis lateralis** are situated on the anterior aspect of the cervical and upper thoracic vertebrae. They are attached above to the atlas vertebra or the occipital bone, and below, to the transverse processes of the cervical vertebrae. *Actions:* the first three of these muscles bend (flex) the head forward; the last bends it to the same side. The nerve supply for the anterior vertebral muscles is from the *cervical nerves.*

Lateral vertebral muscles

The **scalene muscles,** scalenus anterior, medius, and posterior comprise this group (Fig. 5.3). They arise from the transverse processes of the cervical vertebrae, excepting the atlas and axis, and descend to the root of the neck where they are inserted, the anterior and the medius into the first rib, and the posterior, which is really the posterior part of the scalenus medius, into the second rib. *Actions:* the scaleni bend the cervical part of the vertebral column to the same side; the anterior muscle also bends the neck forward and rotates it to the opposite side. If the upper attachments of these muscles are fixed, they, acting from above, raise the first and second ribs, and thus aid the elevation of the thorax in difficult breathing. They derive their nerve supply through the *cervical nerves.*

MUSCLES OF THE TRUNK

Deep muscles of the back and posterior aspect of the neck

The deep muscles of the back and back of the neck constitute a most complex system (Fig. 5.4). Taken as a whole they extend from the back of the sacrum to the back of the skull.

The **splenius capitis** takes origin from the lower half of the ligamentum nuchae and, ascending, is inserted under cover of the sternomastoid into the mastoid process and the occipital bone.

The **splenius cervicis** arises from the spines of the third to sixth

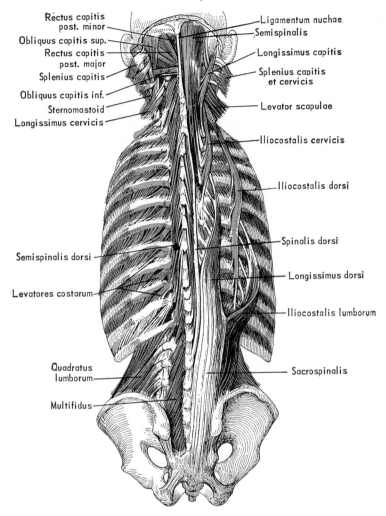

Rectus capitis
post. minor

Obliquus capitis sup.

Rectus capitis
post. major

Splenius capitis

Obliquus capitis inf.

Sternomastoid

Longissimus cervicis

Ligamentum nuchae.

Semispinalis

Longissimus capitis

Splenius capitis
et cervicis

Levator scapulae

Iliocostalis cervicis

Iliocostalis dorsi

Spinalis dorsi

Longissimus dorsi

Iliocostalis lumborum

Sacrospinalis

Semispinalis dorsi

Levatores costarum

Quadratus
lumborum

Multifidus

Fig. 5.4. Deep muscles of the back and back of the neck.

cervical vertebrae and is inserted into the transverse processes of the upper two or three cervical vertebrae.

The sacrospinalis is a large, powerful muscle that lies in the groove at the side of the spinal column. It arises from the surface of a broad, strong tendon through which it becomes attached to the spinous tubercles of the sacrum, the spines of the lumbar and the eleventh and twelfth thoracic vertebrae, and the posterior part of the crest of the ilium. It forms a fleshy mass in the lower lumbar region, but separates in the upper lumbar region into three muscular columns, a *lateral,* an *intermediate* and a *medial,* called, respectively, **iliocostocervicalis, longissimus,** and **spinalis.** The fibers of each of these columns have different attachments at three levels and are therefore described as consisting of three parts in sequence from below upwards. The attachments of the upper and middle parts and the middle and lower parts overlap. *Actions:* the action of the sacrospinalis, in general, is to straighten the back or to bend it backwards. When the thoracic part of the muscle of one side contracts, the back is bent, or rotated, to that side only. The cervical part of the muscle draws the head backward or turns it with chin directed to the same side. The nerve supply is from the *cervical, thoracic,* or *lumbar nerves* in accordance with the levels of the various parts of the muscle.

Muscles of the anterior and lateral walls of the abdomen; the inguinal canal and rings

The principal anterolateral muscles of the abdomen are the *external oblique, internal oblique, transversus,* and *rectus*[1] (Fig. 5.5). The first three of these form three strata, the muscle fibers composing each running in a different direction and thus reinforcing one another.

The external oblique is the most superficial; its fibers arise from the lower eight ribs and run downwards and forwards to cover the lateral and anterior aspects of the abdomen, and end in a strong, broad aponeurosis through which the muscle gains attachment to the pubis and the anterosuperior iliac spine. The lower fibers of the muscle are attached directly to the crest of the ilium. The aponeurosis meets that of the opposite muscle in the mid-line of the abdomen, where a stout, longitudinal, tendinous structure, called the **linea alba,** is formed. The border of the aponeurosis in the groin, where it stretches from the anterior superior iliac spine to the pubis, is folded backward so as to form a thick band with a grooved upper surface; this band is called the **inguinal** (or *Poupart's*) **ligament.**

The internal oblique is thinner and weaker than the external oblique under which it lies. It arises from the lateral two thirds of the grooved surface of the inguinal ligament, from the anterior part of the iliac crest, and from the lumbar fascia. The majority of the fibers pass upwards and medially, but the most posterior ones ascend almost vertically to be inserted into the lower three ribs; those arising from the inguinal ligament arch downwards across the spermatic cord (in the male) or round ligament of the uterus (in the female), and are inserted through a tendon into the pubis. The remaining fibers, which constitute the bulk of the muscle, fan out and end anteriorly in an aponeurosis that splits into two layers to enclose the rectus abdominis; the layers join again at the linea alba.

---

[1] These English names are in most common us; the full Latin terms are, respectively, *obliquus abdominis externus, obliquus abdominis internus, transversus abdominis,* and *rectus abdominis.*

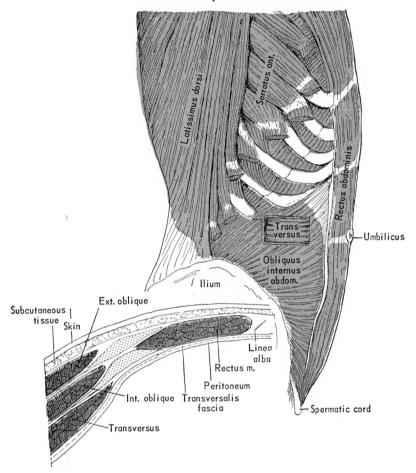

Fig. 5.5. Muscles of the abdominal wall, obliquus externus removed and an opening cut in obliquus internus to show transversus muscle. *Lower drawing* shows a cross section of the abdominal wall on one side of the mid-line.

    The transversus abdominis is the deepest muscle of the abdominal wall. Its fibers runs transversely. It arises from the outer half of the inguinal ligament, from the anterior part of the iliac crest, and from the twelfth rib and the costal cartilages of the lower six ribs. The muscle ends anteriorly in an aponeurosis that, except for its lower part, is inserted into the linea alba. The lower part of the aponeurosis joins the tendon of the internal oblique muscle; this *conjoint tendon* is inserted into the pubis. Lying deep to the transversus muscle is the transversalis fascia; it is separated from the peritoneum only by a layer of areolar tissue (Fig. 5.5).

    The rectus abdominis is a long, straplike muscle running the entire length of the abdomen just to one side of the mid-line. It takes origin from the pubis and from the ligaments covering the front of the symphysis pubis, and is inserted into the cartilages of the fifth, sixth, and seventh ribs. Only the linea alba intervenes between it and its fellow of the opposite side. A strong sheath encloses the muscle. Behind, the sheath is formed by the posterior layer of the aponeurosis of the internal oblique and the aponeurosis of the transversus; the anterior wall of the sheath is formed by the anterior layer of the aponeurosis of the internal oblique and the aponeurosis of the external oblique fused together (Fig. 5.5).

Actions of the anterolateral abdominal muscles. The anterolateral abdominal muscles, when they contract, raise the pressure in the abdominal cavity and thus aid in such acts as emptying the stomach (in vomiting), the bladder, or rectum, or in the expulsion of the child during parturition. They may also aid in the expiratory phase of respiration by pressing upon the viscera and raising the diaphragm. At ordinary times their elasticity and tonic contraction support and maintain the viscera in their normal positions. If the pelvis is fixed, the rectus and oblique muscles raise the trunk from the lying-down position and flex the lumbar vertebrae; contraction of the muscles of one side alone bends the trunk to that side.

The posterior abdominal muscles, the psoas major and minor, and the iliacus, are more suitably described with the muscles of the lower limb.

The inguinal canal. The inguinal canal is a passage about 4 cm long that runs from the deep to the superficial inguinal ring obliquely downwards and medially parallel to and just above the inguinal ligament. In the male it transmits the spermatic cord, and in the female, the round ligament of the uterus (Fig. 5.5). In front it is covered by the skin, superficial fascia, and the external oblique muscle, and in part by the fibers of the internal oblique. Behind is the conjoint tendon of the internal oblique and transversus muscles; its floor is formed by the inguinal ligament and its roof by arched fibers of the internal oblique and transversus muscles.

The inguinal rings. At the upper and outer end of the inguinal canal, midway between the anterior superior iliac spine and the symphysis pubis, is an oval opening in the transversalis fascia known as the **deep inguinal ring;** it is the inlet of the inguinal canal and transmits the spermatic cord in the male and the round ligament in the female. The abdominal surface of the ring is slightly depressed and covered by the peritoneum. The **superficial inguinal ring** is the outlet of the inguinal canal. It is somewhat triangular in shape with its base on the pubic crest. The spermatic cord or the round ligament pass through it to the scrotum or the labium majus.

The deep inguinal ring is a weak part of the abdominal wall and is a common site of *rupture,* or *hernia.*[2] A sudden increase in abdominal pressure, as occasioned, for example, in lifting a heavy weight, may force a knuckle of bowel or other abdominal structure through it and down the canal, from which it may emerge through the superficial inguinal ring and enter the scrotum in the male or the labium majus in the female. This is called *indirect inguinal hernia.* In *direct inguinal hernia,* the structure pushes before it the wall of the canal between the two rings, traverses the lower part of the inguinal canal, and emerges from the superficial inguinal ring (Fig. 5.5). In either type of inguinal hernia, the peritoneum is pushed ahead of the hernia and stretched, so as to almost completely enclose it; this is called the *hernial sac.* (See also *femoral hernia,* Ch. 13).

In the fetus, up to a month or two before birth, the testes are situated in the abdomen. The inguinal canals are the natural passage through which they descend to the scrotum. They complete their journey shortly before birth. Sometimes one testis, or both, fails to reach its permanent position, remaining in the abdomen or traversing only a part of the inguinal canal. This developmental anomaly is called *undescended testis,* or *cryptorchidism.*

Muscles of the pelvis

The pelvic muscles are the **obturator internus, pyriformis, levator ani,** and **coccygeus.** The first two muscles mentioned will be described with the muscles of the lower limb, as will the **psoas major, psoas minor,** and **iliacus,** which, though partly in the abdomen and pelvis, are inserted into the femur (Fig. 5.6).

The **levator ani** arises in front from the pelvic surface of the body of the pubis to one side of the symphysis, and behind, from the spine of the ischium, and the fascia covering the obturator internus muscle. The fibers pass backwards and downwards across the anal canal and the side of the prostate gland (in the male) and of the vagina (in the female) to be inserted into the perineal body and the coccyx. Many of the fibers join in the mid-line with those of the opposite muscle to form a large part of the floor of the pelvis. *Actions:* the levator ani, with its fellow of the opposite side, supports the pelvic viscera and constricts the lower end of the rectum, thus aiding in the retention of the feces; in the female, the two levatores ani act as a sphincter to the vagina. The nerve supply is from the *fourth sacral nerve* and the *pudendal nerve.*

---

[2] *Rupture* is not a good term, for very rarely is there any tearing of tissue. The canal normally is a potential passage from the abdominal cavity.

The term *hernia* is applied to the protrusion of any organ, part of an organ, or other structure through a defect in a natural wall of the body. Thus, the protrusion of brain substance through a defect in the skull is called a cerebral hernia, and of an abdominal structure through the muscular wall of the abdomen at the umbilicus (navel), an umbilical hernia.

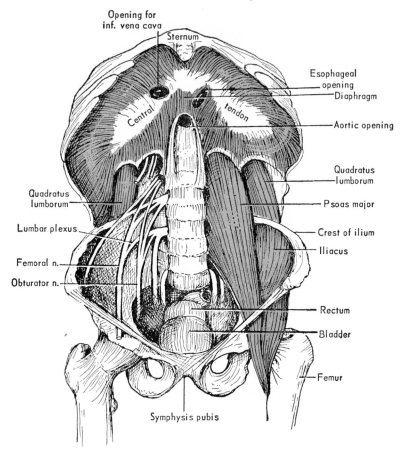

Fig. 5.6. Muscles of the posterior abdominal wall and pelvis.

The coccygeus muscle lies posterior to the levator ani and arises from the spine of the ischium; it is inserted into the side of the coccyx and lowest part of the sacrum. Its *action* is to give support to the coccyx and pull it forward after it has been pressed backward during defecation or parturition. It is supplied by branches of the *fourth and fifth sacral nerves.*

Muscles of the perineum; the perineal body

The perineum is the region lying between the tip of the coccyx behind and the pubis in front; on either side, near its middle, is the tuberosity of the ischium. The posterior part of this region contains the outlet of the anal canal (anus) ; the anterior part contains the urinary orifices and the external genital organs. The former is called the *anal region;* the latter the *urogenital region.*

The only muscle in the **anal region** to be described here is the **external anal sphincter;** it is the same in both sexes and consists of muscle fibers arranged in an ellipse surrounding the anus just beneath the skin. It arises from the tip of the coccyx by a narrow tendon and is inserted into the perineal body in front of the anus, where its fibers blend with other muscles in the region. It serves to keep the anus closed, except during defecation or the passage of flatus.

The muscles of the **urogenital region** differ in the two sexes. In the male they are the **transversus perinei superficialis** and **profundus,** the **bulbospongiosus, ischiocavernosus,** and **sphincter urethra.** The corresponding muscles of the female are given the same names but show certain differences in disposition and arrangement appropriate to the genital structures of the female. These muscles will be more fully described in Chapter 49 (they are shown in Figs. 5.30, 5.31).

The perineal body is a fibromuscular node (L. *nodus,* a knot) in the midline of the perineum about $1/2$ inch in front of the anus. It is the point of meeting and attachment of eight perineal muscles—the **sphincter ani externus, bulbocavernosus,** and, on each side, the **transversus** (superficial and deep) and the **levator ani muscles.** The perineal body is therefore a most important structure in maintaining the integrity of the pelvic floor, especially in women, in whom it may be torn through during parturition.

MUSCLES CONNECTING THE UPPER LIMB WITH THE TRUNK

Muscular connections of the upper limb with the vertebral column

The **trapezius,** one of this group of muscles, has already been described with the lateral muscles of the neck; it is also a superficial muscle of the back.

The **latissimus dorsi** is a broad triangular sheet of muscle that arises from the spines of the lower six thoracic vertebrae, from the lumbar fascia, through which it gains attachment to the spines of the lumbar and sacral vertebrae, from the crest of the ilium, and from the three lower ribs (Figs. 5.5, 5.7, 5.8). The fibers cover a large part of the back and converge toward the side of the chest, where they become twisted upon themselves and, with the teres major, form the posterior fold of the armpit (axilla); they end in a stout tendon that is inserted into the bottom of the bicipital groove of the humerus. *Actions:* the latissimus dorsi adducts the arm, rotates it inwards, and draws it backwards, and aids in lowering it against resistance. It is an important muscle in rowing and swimming. It also, by compressing the chest, takes part in sharp expiratory acts, such as coughing, sneezing, or blowing. It is supplied by the *nerve to the latissimus dorsi,* derived from the brachial plexus.

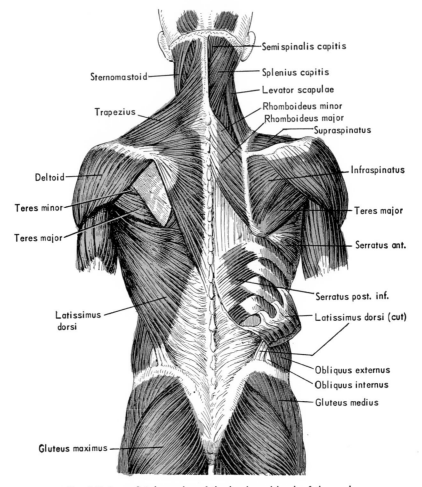

Fig. 5.7. Superficial muscles of the back and back of the neck.

The rhomboideus major and rhomboideus minor are two relatively short, quadrilateral parallel muscles running obliquely between the vertebral column and the scapula. The rhomboideus major arises from the spines of the thoracic vertebrae, second to fifth, and is inserted into the medial border of the scapula. The rhomboideus minor takes origin from the lower part of the ligamentum nuchae and the spines of the seventh cervical and first thoracic vertebrae (Fig. 5.7). It is inserted into the triangular area at the medial end of the spine of the scapula.

The levator scapulae arises from the transverse processes of the atlas and axis, and of the third and fourth cervical vertebrae; it is inserted into the upper part of the medial border of the scapula. *Actions:* the rhomboids and the levator scapulae act to steady the scapula in the

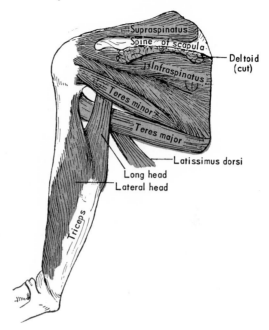

Fig. 5.8. Muscles of the back of
the scapula and arm.

various movements of the upper limb. Acting with other muscles, they
aid in retracting, bracing, or depressing the shoulder. These three muscles are supplied by branches of the *cervical nerves.*

Muscular connections of the upper limb with the anterior and lateral thoracic walls

The pectoralis major is a powerful triangular muscle covering the
upper half or so of the anterior wall of the chest (Fig. 5.9). It arises from
the inner half of the anterior surface of the clavicle, from the anterior
surface of the lateral half of the sternum as far down as the sixth or
seventh costal cartilage, from the costal cartilages of the upper seven ribs,
and from the aponeurosis of the obliquus externus abdominis. The
fibers pass outwards, converging to end in a tendon that is inserted into
the outer lip of the bicipital groove of the humerus. *Actions:* the pectoralis major, acting as a whole, adducts and medially rotates the arm,
or draws the arm forwards or medially if it has been extended (that is,
held forward or backward). The clavicular fibers alone come into play
when the arm is flexed at the shoulder; they draw the arm down. The
muscle is supplied by the *fifth to eighth cervical nerves* and the *first
thoracic nerve.*

The pectoralis minor is a much smaller muscle than the pectoralis
major and lies beneath the latter (Fig. 5.10). It arises from the third,

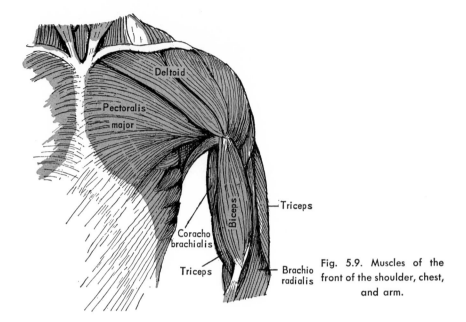

Fig. 5.9. Muscles of the front of the shoulder, chest, and arm.

fourth, and fifth ribs, and the fascia covering the external intercostal muscles; it is inserted into the coracoid process of the scapula. *Actions:* the pectoralis minor acts with the serratus anterior to draw the scapula forward and laterally. In conjunction with the rhomboids and levator scapulae, it rotates the scapula so as to depress the point of the shoulder. It is supplied by the *seventh and eighth cervical,* and the *first thoracic nerves.*

The subclavius is quite a small muscle that passes from the first rib at its junction with the costal cartilage to a groove on the under surface of the middle third of the clavicle. Its *action* is to draw the point of the shoulder forward and downward, and to hold the clavicle firm during movements of the shoulder joint. It is supplied by the *fifth and sixth cervical nerves.*

The serratus anterior lies over the upper and lateral part of the chest between the scapula and the ribs. It arises by fingerlike bundles of fibers (called *digitations*) from the outer surfaces of the upper eight or nine ribs, and the fascia covering the internal intercostal muscles. The lower four digitations alternate (or interdigitate) with muscular slips of the external oblique muscle (obliquus externus abdominis). The fibers passing backwards are inserted into the anterior (costal) surfaces of the medial border, and the superior and inferior angles of the scapula. *Actions:* the serratus anterior draws the scapula forward and operates in such movements as pushing or punching. Those fibers inserted into the

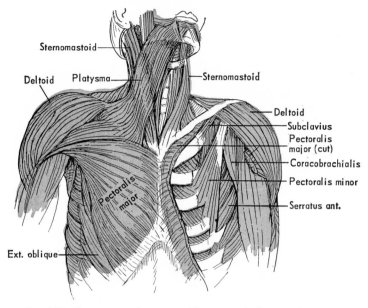

Fig. 5.10. Showing muscles exposed by removal of pectoralis major.

inferior angle act with the trapezius to rotate the scapula and thus to assist in raising the arm above the head. It is supplied by the *fifth, sixth, and seventh cervical nerves.*

MUSCLES OF THE UPPER LIMB

Muscular connections of the shoulder girdle (clavicle and scapula) with the arm

The **deltoid** is a thick muscle that covers and rounds out the shoulder (Figs. 5.7, 5.9, 5.10). It arises from the outer third of the clavicle, from the acromion, and from the spine of the scapula. The fibers converge to form a thick triangular mass, and end in a thick tendon that is inserted into an elevation on the outer side of the shaft of the humerus near its middle. *Actions:* the principal action of the deltoid, as a whole, is to raise the arm from the side; it is assisted in this movement by the supraspinatus. The anterior fibers of the deltoid, acting with the pectoralis major, draw the arm forward and rotate it medially. The posterior fibers, in conjunction with the latissimus dorsi and teres major, draw the arm backward and rotate it laterally. The deltoid is supplied by the *circumflex nerve.*

The **subscapularis** takes origin from the anterior (costal) surface of the body of the scapula. Its fibers converge laterally to be inserted into the lesser tuberosity of the humerus and the capsular ligament of the shoulder joint. It is supplied by the *fifth and sixth cervical nerves* (Fig. 5.11).

The supraspinatus takes origin from the supraspinous fossa of the scapula and is inserted into the uppermost facet on the greater tuberosity of the humerus (Figs. 5.7, 5.8).

The infraspinatus occupies the infraspinous fossa of the scapula, arising from its medial two thirds; its fibers converge to a tendon that crosses the superior aspect of the shoulder joint and is inserted into the middle facet on the greater tuberosity of the humerus and into the capsule of the shoulder joint. It is supplied by the *suprascapular nerve* (fifth and sixth cervical nerves) (Figs. 5.7, 5.8).

The teres minor is a slender muscle that arises from the flat area on the dorsal surface of the scapula along its lateral border (see Fig. 3.36).

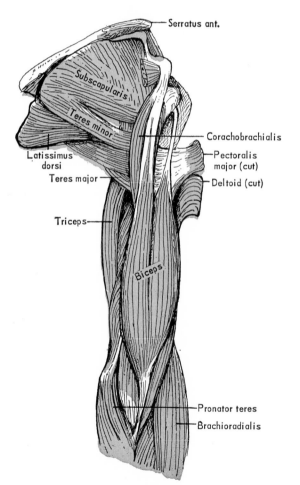

Fig. 5.11. Muscles of the posterior wall of the axilla (from the front) and the front of the arm.

It is inserted into the lowest facet on the greater tuberosity of the humerus and into the capsule of the shoulder joint. It is supplied by the *circumflex nerve.*

Actions of the subscapularis, supraspinatus, infraspinatus, and teres minor. The main action of these four muscles is to hold the head of the humerus firmly in the glenoid cavity during the movements of the arm brought about by other muscles, for example, the deltoid.

The **teres major** is a short, stout muscle that takes origin from the dorsal aspect of the inferior angle of the scapula and is inserted through a flat tendon into the medial lip of the bicipital groove of the humerus. *Action:* the teres major draws the arm backward and medially, and rotates it medially. It is supplied by the *subscapular nerve* (fifth and sixth cervical nerves).

Muscles of the arm[3]

The **coracobrachialis** arises from the tip of the coracoid process by a tendon common to it and the short head of the biceps, and is inserted into an impression on the medial aspect of the humeral shaft near its middle (Fig. 5.9). *Action:* the coracobrachialis draws the arm forward and medially. It is supplied by the *musculocutaneous nerve* (seventh cervical nerve).

The **biceps** (brachii [of the arm]) is the large, fleshy mass on the front of the arm. As indicated by its name (L. *bi,* double + *caput,* head), it arises by two heads, a short and a long. The *short head* arises from the tip of the coracoid process by a tendon common to it and the coracobrachialis. The *long head* arises within the shoulder joint from an elevation above the glenoid cavity; it arches over the head of the humerus in a special synovial sheath, and descends in the bicipital groove of the humerus. The tendons are continued downwards into two muscular bellies that, though closely applied to one another, are separable throughout their length; they end about 3 inches above the elbow in a flat tendon that is inserted into the posterior part of the tuberosity of the radius. *Action:* the biceps flexes the elbow joint and is a strong supinator of the forearm as well. The long head presses downward upon the head of the humerus and thus antagonizes the tendency of the deltoid to cause the humeral head to slip upward. The biceps is supplied by the *musculocutaneous nerve.*

The **brachialis** arises from the lower half of the anterior surface of the humerus. Its fibers, converging as they descend, are inserted through a thick tendon into the tuberosity and coronoid process of the ulna.

---

[3] In anatomy, the words *arm* or *upper arm* (brachium) mean the upper limb between the shoulder and the elbow; the *forearm* (antebrachium) is the member from the elbow to the wrist.

Action: the brachialis flexes the elbow joint. It is supplied by the *musculocutaneous nerve.*

   The triceps is the large muscle on the back of the arm. It arises by three heads—long, lateral, and medial (Figs. 5.8, 5.11). The *long head* takes origin through a flat tendon from a tubercle below the glenoid cavity of the humerus; the *lateral head* from a ridge on the posterior surface of the upper part of the humeral shaft as far down as the upper part of the spiral groove; and the *medial head* from the posterior surface of the humeral shaft below the spiral groove. The muscle fibers end about the middle of the arm in a broad tendon composed of two aponeurotic sheets, the more superficial of which covers the lower part of the muscle while the deeper one penetrates the muscle substance. The two layers of the aponeurosis fuse above the elbow and are then inserted into the upper part of the posterior surface of the olecranon. *Action:* the triceps is the extensor muscle of the forearm (that is, it straightens the elbow). The long head assists in drawing the humerus backwards and adducting it when the arm is extended.

Muscles of the forearm (antebrachium)

   The muscles of the forearm are very numerous. They will be described in two main groups: (a) those on the anterior aspect of the forearm (*anterior antebrachial muscles*); and (b) those on the posterior aspect (*posterior antebrachial muscles*). Each main group is divided further into a *superficial* and a *deep* lot. A classification follows below.

   The first five muscles listed (all the superficial anterior antebrachial muscles) arise by a common tendon from the medial epicondyle of the humerus.

MUSCLES OF THE FOREARM

Anterior aspect

Superficial group	Pronator teres Flexor carpi radialis Palmaris longus	Flexor carpi ulnaris Flexor digitorum sublimis
Deep group	Flexor digitorum profundus Flexor pollicis longus	Pronator quadratus

Posterior aspect

Superficial group	Brachioradialis Extensor carpi radialis longus Extensor carpi radialis brevis Extensor digitorum	Extensor digiti minimi Extensor carpi ulnaris Anconeus
Deep group	Supinator Abductor pollicis longus Extensor pollicis brevis	Extensor pollicis longus Extensor indicis

1. Anterior antebrachial muscles

The **pronator teres** arises by two heads—humeral and ulnar—the *humeral head* arising by the common tendon just mentioned; the much smaller *ulnar head* takes origin from the medial border of the coronoid process of the ulna. The two heads, after joining, pass obliquely to be inserted through a flat tendon into the lateral aspect of the shaft of the radius near its middle. *Action:* the pronator teres pronates the forearm and hand; that is, it rotates the radius upon the ulna, thus turning the hand medially so that the palm, at the end of the movement, faces backward. The pronator teres is supplied by the *median nerve* (sixth and seventh cervical nerves) (Fig. 5.12).

The **flexor carpi radialis** arises through the common tendon and gives rise near its middle to a long tendon of insertion that passes into the palm, to the base of the second metacarpal bone, and by a separate slip to the base of the third metacarpal bone. The tendon occupies a groove (lined by a synovial sheath) on the trapezium. *Action:* the flexor carpi radialis flexes the wrist and aids in abducting the hand. It is supplied by the *median nerve.*

The **palmaris longus** is a weak, slender muscle that is often absent. Its long, slender tendon is inserted into the flexor retinaculum (p. 127) and the central part of the palmar aponeurosis. *Action:* the palmaris longus aids in flexing the wrist.

The **flexor carpi ulnaris,** like the flexor carpi radialis, has an ulnar head as well as a humeral origin through the common tendon. The *ulnar head* arises from the medial border of the olecranon and the upper two thirds of the posterior border of the ulna. Its tendon is inserted into the pisiform and hamate bones, and the base of the fifth metacarpal bone. *Action:* the flexor carpi ulnaris flexes the wrist and adducts the hand. It is supplied by the *ulnar nerve* (Fig. 5.12).

The **flexor digitorum sublimis** arises by two heads—humeroulnar and radial. The *humeroulnar head* takes origin by means of the common tendon from the humerus, from the ligament of the elbow joint, and from the medial side of the coronoid process of the ulna. The *radial head* arises from the anterior border of the radius, between the tuberosity and the insertion of the pronator teres. The muscle divides into four parts, each of which ends in a tendon, for insertion into the proximal and middle phalanges of the fingers. Opposite the bases of the proximal phalanges each tendon splits into two ribbonlike strips. The two parts of each slip become turned on their long axes so that their surfaces are reversed; then reuniting, they partially cross with one another and redivide (Fig. 5.14). Each division is inserted into the sides of the middle phalanx. The buttonholelike slit caused by the first splitting of the tendon transmits the tendon of the flexor digitorum profundus. The

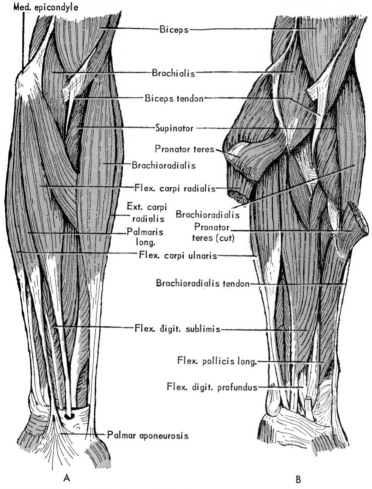

Med. epicondyle

Biceps

Brachialis

Biceps tendon

Supinator

Pronator teres

Brachioradialis

Flex. carpi radialis

Ext. carpi radialis

Brachioradialis

Palmaris long.

Pronator teres (cut)

Flex. carpi ulnaris

Brachioradialis tendon

Flex. digit. sublimis

Flex. pollicis long.

Flex. digit. profundus

Palmar aponeurosis

A

B

Fig. 5.12. Muscles of the front of the forearm. A, superficial muscles; B, deep muscles.

turning of the slips and their reunion form a groove in which the latter tendon slides. *Action:* the flexor digitorum sublimis flexes the fingers, first the middle phalanges and then, with continuing action, the proximal phalanges. It may also assist in flexing the wrist. It is supplied by the *median nerve.*

The flexor digitorum profundus contributes largely to the fleshy mass on the ulnar side of the forearm, but underlies the superficial flexors. It arises from the upper three quarters of the medial and anterior aspects of the shaft of the ulna, from a depression on the medial side of the coronoid process, and through an aponeurosis from the posterior border of the ulna. The muscle fibers end in four tendons that pass through the slits in the tendons of the flexor digitorum sublimis, and occupy the grooves formed by these tendons, to be inserted into the palmar aspect of the bases of the distal phalanges of the four fingers. *Actions:* the flexor digitorum profundus flexes the distal (terminal) phalanges after the middle phalanges have been flexed by the tendons of the flexor digitorum sublimis; it also aids in flexing the wrist. Its medial part is supplied by the *ulnar nerve,* and its lateral part by the *median nerve.*

The **flexor pollicis longus** arises from the anterior surface of the radius, the interosseous membrane, and usually from the medial border of the coronoid process of the ulna. Its tendon is inserted into the palmar surface of the base of the distal phalanx of the thumb. *Actions:* the flexor pollicis longus flexes both phalanges of the thumb. It is supplied by the *median nerve.*

The **pronator quadratus** arises from the anterior surface of the lower part of the shaft of the ulna and is inserted into the lower quarter of the anterior surface and border of the radius. *Actions:* it serves to hold the lower ends of the radius and ulna together and to prevent their separation by an upward force applied through the carpus; it has but little action as a pronator, despite its name. It is supplied by a branch of the *median nerve.*

2. Posterior antebrachial muscles

The **brachioradialis** arises from a ridge above the lateral epicondyle of the humerus. It forms the lateral boundary of the cubital fossa, the triangular space in front of the elbow joint. The muscle ends a little above the middle of the forearm in a tendon that is inserted into the outer aspect of the radius just above the styloid process. *Actions:* the brachioradialis flexes the elbow joint. It stands out prominently when an attempt is made to flex the forearm against a resistance. It is supplied by the *radial nerve* (Fig. 5.13).

The **extensor carpi radialis longus** (**or longior**) arises from the ridge above the lateral epicondyle of the humerus and to a much less extent from the common extensor tendon (see below). Its long tendon is inserted into the dorsal surface of the base of the second metacarpal bone; the tendon occupies a groove on the back of the radius behind the styloid process. It is supplied by the *radial nerve.*

The **extensor carpi radialis brevis** (**or brevior**) lies beneath the preceding muscle. It arises from the lateral epicondyle of the humerus by a tendon shared with the next three extensor muscles—the *common extensor tendon.* Its tendon is inserted into the dorsal aspect of the bases of the second and third metacarpal bones. This muscle and the preceding one act synergically with the flexors of the fingers, with the extensor carpi

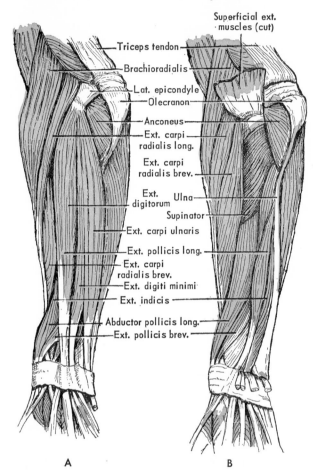

Fig. 5.13. Muscles on the back of the forearm. *A*, superficial muscles; *B*, deep muscles.

ulnaris (extension of the wrist), and with the flexor carpi radialis (abduction of the hand). It is supplied by the *radial nerve*.

The extensor digitorum arises by the common extensor tendon from the lateral epicondyle of the humerus. It gives rise to four tendons, each of which is inserted in a complicated manner into the bases of the middle and distal phalanges of a finger. A triangular fibrous membrane, called the *dorsal digital expansion,* covers the dorsal aspect of the metacarpophalangeal joint and the base of the proximal phalanx (Fig. 5.14). Each tendon of the extensor digitorum passes down the middle of this membrane; near the base of the second (middle) phalanx the tendon splits into three parts. The middle part is inserted into the base of the second phalanx, while the lateral and medial parts join the dorsal digital expan-

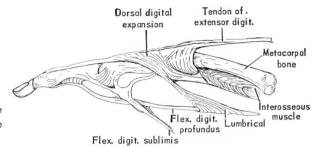

Fig. 5.14. Showing the arrangement of the tendons of a finger.

sion. The two side parts join again more distally, and the single tendon is then inserted into the base of the terminal phalanx. *Actions:* the extensor digitorum extends the fingers at the metacarpophalangeal and interphalangeal joints, and thus opens the hand; it may also assist in extending the wrist. The muscle is supplied by a branch (posterior interosseous) of the *radial nerve.*

The **extensor digiti minimi** is usually connected to the medial side of the preceding muscle and also arises by the common extensor tendon. Its tendon splits into two as it crosses the back of the hand and joins the dorsal digital expansion of the proximal phalanx of the little finger. *Action:* the extensor digiti minimi extends the little finger and helps to extend the wrist. It receives a branch (posterior interosseous) of the *radial nerve.*

The **extensor carpi ulnaris** arises by the common extensor tendon from the posterior border of the ulna through an aponeurosis common to it and to the flexor carpi ulnaris and flexor digitorum profundus. It is inserted into the ulnar side of the base of the fifth metacarpal bone. *Actions:* the extensor carpi ulnaris steadies the wrist during flexion of the fingers and, in conjunction with the flexor carpi ulnaris, adducts the hand; contracting with the flexor carpi radialis (longus and brevis) it extends the wrist. It is supplied by the *posterior interosseous nerve.*

The **anconeus** is a small triangular muscle lying on the back of the elbow. It takes origin by an individual tendon from the lateral epicondyle of the humerus. Its fibers fan out from their origin and are inserted into the side of the olecranon and upper quarter of the shaft of the ulna. *Action:* the anconeus assists the triceps in extending the elbow. It is supplied by the *radial nerve.*

The **supinator** arises in two parts—one tendinous and one muscular —from the lateral epicondyle of the humerus, from ligamentous structures in the neighborhood, and from a linear elevation (*supinator crest*) on the upper part of the lateral surface of the shaft of the ulna and the triangular depression in front of it. It is inserted into the upper third of the lateral surface of the radius. The muscle is thus partially wrapped around the radius. *Actions:* the supinator supinates the forearm, rotating the radius so as to turn the hand forward. It is supplied by the *posterior interosseous nerve* (Fig. 5.13).

The abductor pollicis longus arises from the lateral portion of the posterior aspect of the middle quarter of the shaft of the ulna, from the adjacent part of the interosseous membrane, and from the middle third of the posterior surface of the radius. Its tendon is inserted into the lateral side of the base of the metacarpal bone of the thumb. *Actions:* acting with the abductor pollicis brevis, the abductor pollicis longus abducts the thumb; or, acting with the extensor pollicis (longus and brevis), it extends the thumb at the carpometacarpal joint. It and the next two muscles are supplied by the *posterior interosseous nerve.*

The extensor pollicis brevis arises from the posterior surface of the radius immediately below the radial origin of the abductor pollicis longus, and from the adjacent part of the posterior surface of the interosseous membrane. It is inserted into the base of the metacarpal bone of the thumb. *Action:* the extensor pollicis brevis extends the proximal phalanx of the thumb, and when the latter is fully extended extends the metacarpophalangeal joint.

The extensor pollicis longus arises from the middle third of the lateral portion of the posterior surface of the ulna and from the interosseous membrane, and is inserted into the base of the distal phalanx of the thumb. The tendon of this muscle, as it crosses the outer border of the wrist, lies about ¾ inch dorsal to the extensor pollicis brevis; when the thumb is fully extended, the former tendon becomes prominent and a depression between the two tendons appears. This is called the "anatomical snuff box." It was the practice of snuff users to place a little of the tobacco in this depression and draw it up the nose. The space contains the radial artery. *Action:* the extensor pollicis longus extends the distal phalanx of the thumb; it also abducts the thumb and rotates it laterally, and acting in conjunction with the extensor pollicis brevis and the abductor pollicis longus, it aids in extending the metacarpal bone and the proximal phalanx of the thumb.

The extensor indicis arises from the upper part of the lower third of the posterior surface of the ulna and the interosseous membrane. It joins the tendon of the extensor digitorum that goes to the first (index) finger. *Action:* the extensor indicis aids in extending the first finger and in extending the wrist. It is supplied by the *posterior interosseous nerve.*

Muscles of the hand

The muscles of the hand are usually described in three groups.

Short muscles of the thumb ⌠Abductor pollicis brevis   Flexor pollicis brevis
(lateral part of the palm) ⌡Opponens pollicis   Adductor pollicis

| Short muscles of the little finger (medial part of the palm) | Palmaris brevis
Abductor digiti minimi | Flexor digiti minimi
Opponens digti minimi |
| Muscles of the middle of the palm | Interossei | Lumbricales |

The first and second groups form two fleshy masses called, respectively, the **thenar**, which is the larger, and the **hypothenar eminences**.

The **abductor pollicis brevis** lies on the outer side of the thenar eminence. It arises from the ligament in front of the wrist joint (flexor retinaculum), and from the trapezium and scaphoid bones of the carpus. It is inserted into the outer (radial) side of the base of the proximal phalanx of the thumb (Fig. 5.15). *Action:* the abductor pollicis brevis moves the thumb forward at right angles to the palm and rotates it inward. It is supplied by a branch of the *median nerve*.

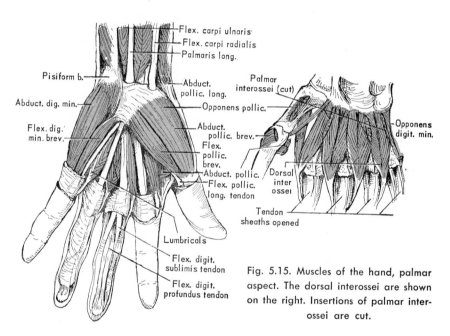

Fig. 5.15. Muscles of the hand, palmar aspect. The dorsal interossei are shown on the right. Insertions of palmar interossei are cut.

The **opponens pollicis** lies beneath the preceding muscle; it arises from the ligament in front of the wrist and from the trapezium. It is inserted into the metacarpal bone of the thumb along the entire length of its outer border. *Action:* the opponens pollicis flexes the metacarpal bone of the thumb and rotates it toward the palm, so that the thumb can touch the tip of any of the fingers. It is supplied by a branch of the *median nerve*.

The **flexor pollicis brevis** forms the inner part of the thenar eminence. It arises from the ligament in front of the wrist, and from the trapezium. It is inserted into the outer side of the base of the proximal phalanx of the thumb. *Action:* the flexor pollicis brevis flexes the proximal phalanx of the thumb and, with continuing action, flexes and inwardly rotates the metacarpal bone. It is supplied by both the *median* and *ulnar nerves.*

The **adductor pollicis** arises by an oblique and a transverse head. The *oblique head* takes origin from the capitate and trapezium bones, the bases of the second and third metacarpal bones, and the ligaments of the carpus; its tendons joins the tendons of the first palmar interosseous, and the transverse head, and is inserted into the inner side of the base of the proximal phalanx of the thumb. The *transverse head* arises from the palmar surface of the third metacarpal bone and is inserted with the oblique head. *Action:* the adductor pollicis draws the thumb into the palm of the hand. It is supplied by a branch of the *ulnar nerve.*

The **palmaris brevis** lies just beneath the skin of the hypothenar eminence. It arises from the ligament in front of the wrist and from the palmar aponeurosis, and is inserted into the skin of the inner border of the hand. *Action:* the palmaris brevis wrinkles the skin of the inner part of the palm and deepens the hollow of the palm.

The **abductor digiti minimi** forms the ulnar border of the hypothenar eminence. It arises from the pisiform bone, and is inserted into the base of the proximal phalanx of the little finger and into the dorsal digital expansion of the extensor digiti minimi. *Action:* the abductor digiti minimi abducts the little finger by pulling on the proximal phalanx.

The **flexor digiti minimi** arises from the hook of the hamate bone and from the ligament on the front of the wrist joint; it is inserted into the base of the proximal phalanx of the little finger. *Action:* the flexor digiti minimi flexes the proximal phalanx of the little finger.

All the muscles of the little finger receive their nerve supply from the *ulnar nerve.*

The **interossei** (sing. *interosseus*) are in two sets, *palmar* and *dorsal,* of four muscles each, occupying or partly covering the space between the metacarpal bones (Fig. 5.15). The **dorsal interossei** are bipennate in the arrangement of their fibers, and arise from the sides of the metacarpals between which they lie; they are inserted into the bases of the proximal phalanges and into the dorsal digital expansions. The second and third muscles are inserted into the proximal phalanx of the second (middle) finger, one on each side of its base. The first dorsal interosseus is inserted on the outer (radial) side of the base of the proximal phalanx of the index finger, and the fourth into the inner (ulnar) side of the base of the proximal phalanx of the ring finger. **The palmar interossei** arise from the palmar surfaces along one or another side of the metacarpal bones. The first arises from the ulnar side of the base of the metacarpal bone of the thumb, and is inserted into the base of the corresponding proximal phalanx. The second arises from the entire length of the ulnar side of the palmar surface of the second metacarpal bone, and is inserted into the base of the corresponding proximal phalanx. The third and fourth take origin from the radial sides of the fourth and fifth metacarpal bones, and are inserted into the bones of the corresponding proximal phalanges (that is, of the little and ring fingers). The middle finger, while it receives the insertion of two dorsal interossei, does not receive a palmar muscle. *Actions:* the dorsal interossei are abductors of the fingers, drawing them to either side from an imaginary line running longitudinally through the middle finger, while the palmar muscles adduct the fingers towards that line. Acting with the lumbricales, both sets of interossei flex the proximal phalanges. The first palmar interosseus flexes and adducts the thumb at the metacarpophalangeal joint. Both sets of interossei are supplied by branches of the *ulnar nerve.*

The lumbricales (Fig. 5.15) are four small muscular bellies that arise from the tendons of the *flexor digitorum profundus* muscle. Each is inserted into the lateral margin of the dorsal digital expansion of the corresponding extensor digitorum tendon, and into the base of the proximal phalanx. *Action:* the lumbricales assist the interossei in flexing the fingers at the metacarpophalangeal joints, and exert traction upon the tendons of the flexor digitorum profundus. Those of the first and second fingers are supplied by branches of the *median nerve,* of the third and fourth by the *ulnar nerve.*

DEEP FASCIAE OF THE UPPER LIMB

The brachial fascia forms an investment for the muscles of the arm, and the antebrachial fascia for the muscles of the forearm. These fasciae send partitions (septa) between the various muscles, and are attached to bony prominences. At the wrist the antebrachial fascia is thickened in front and behind to form two broad bands that hold the tendons in position (Fig. 5.14). The anterior band is called the flexor retinaculum; the posterior one, the extensor retinaculum. A strong fascia called the palmar aponeurosis covers the flexor tendons and invests the muscles of the palm of the hand. Only its central portion is tough and thick; this part is triangular in shape. Its apex blends with the flexor retinaculum and gives insertion to the tendon of the palmaris longus muscle. Its base divides into four slips, one for each finger. The lateral and medial parts of the aponeurosis cover the muscles of the thenar and hypothenar eminences, and are relatively thin.

MUSCLES OF THE LOWER LIMB

Muscles of the iliac region

The psoas major arises from the transverse processes of all the lumbar vertebrae, from the bodies of the twelfth thoracic and the third, fourth, and fifth lumbar vertebrae, from the intervertebral discs, and from the tendinous arches bridging the constricted portions of the bodies of the lumbar vertebrae. The muscle descends across the brim of the true pelvis to end in a tendon that, after receiving the fibers of the iliacus on the lateral side, is inserted into the lesser trochanter of the femur (Fig. 5.6). *Action:* the psoas major acts in conjunction with the iliacus; the two muscles are frequently referred to as the *iliopsoas.* The psoas major is supplied by branches of the *second, third, and fourth lumbar nerves.*

This muscle is of clinical interest because, in acute abdominal conditions it may undergo reflex contraction with consequent flexion of the thigh on the abdomen. Also, in tuberculous disease of the lumbar or lower thoracic vertebrae, purulent material may track down within the sheath of the muscle and appear as a subcutaneous swelling (cold abscess) in the upper and inner part of the thigh.

The psoas minor, which lies in front of the preceding muscle, arises from the bodies of the twelfth thoracic and first lumbar vertebrae and the intervening intervertebral disc, as well as from the inner surface of the ilium. It is inserted into the pubis. *Action:* the psoas minor assists, though weakly, in flexing the trunk. It is supplied by a branch of the *first lumbar nerve.*

The iliacus arises from the upper two thirds of the iliac fossa and the iliac crest, from the lateral mass of the sacrum, and from the anterior sacroiliac and iliolumbar ligaments (Fig. 5.6). Its fibers are inserted into the lateral side of the tendon of the psoas major. *Action:* with the psoas major, the iliacus flexes the thigh upon the pelvis; contracting together, they bend the trunk forward, or raise it from the recumbent to the sitting position. The iliacus is supplied by branches of the *femoral nerve.*

Muscles of the thigh

As a convenience in description, the thigh muscles are divided into three groups.

Anterior femoral muscles	Tensor fasciae latae Sartorius	Quadriceps femoris Articularis genu
Medial femoral muscles	Gracilis Pectineus Adductor longus	Adductor brevis Adductor magnus

Posterior femoral muscles	Biceps femoris	Semimembranosus
	Semitendinosus	

1. Anterior femoral muscles

The **tensor fasciae latae** arises from the anterior 2 inches or so of the iliac crest, and from the anterior superior spine of the ilium and the concave margin of bone immediately below. It is inserted between the two layers of the iliotibial tract (p. 140) about one third of the distance down the outer side of the thigh. *Action:* the tensor fasciae latae draws upon the iliotibial tracts and aids in extending the knee, steadies the pelvis on the head of the femur, and the femoral condyles upon the tibia. It is supplied by the *superior gluteal nerve* (fourth and fifth lumbar, first sacral) (Fig. 5.16).

The **sartorius** is a long, straplike muscle (the longest in the body) that arises from the anterior superior iliac spine and part of the notch immediately below; it crosses to the medial side of the thigh and then descends to the medial side of the knee, whence a flat tendon curves forward and, broadening out into an aponeurosis, is inserted into the upper and medial part of the shaft of the tibia. *Action:* the sartorius aids in flexing the thigh on the pelvis, and the leg on the thigh. It also acts as an abductor and lateral rotator of the thigh. It is supplied by the *femoral nerve*.

The **quadriceps (four-headed) femoris** is the main muscle on the anterior aspect of the thigh and consists of four parts called the *rectus femoris, vastus lateralis, vastus medialis,* and *vastus intermedius* (Fig. 5.16).

The **rectus femoris** arises by two tendinous heads from the anterior inferior iliac spine and from the ilium above the acetabulum. The tendons join and expand into an aponeurosis from which the muscle fibers, arranged in a bipennate manner,

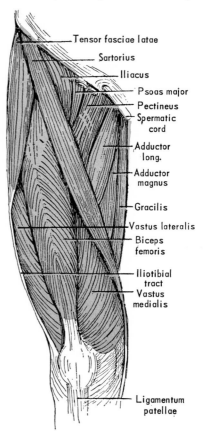

Fig. 5.16. Superficial muscles on the front of the right thigh.

arise. The fibers end in a stout tendon that is inserted into the upper part of the patella. The **vastus lateralis** takes origin from the greater trochanter of the femur and from the linea aspera by a broad aponeurosis that covers the upper three quarters of the anterior surface of the muscle. It is inserted by a flat tendon into the lateral border of the patella. The **vastus medialis** arises from the femur along the lower part of the trochanteric line, the spiral line, and from the linea aspera, and is inserted into the medial side of the patella. The **vastus intermedius** arises from the anterior and lateral surfaces of the upper two thirds of the femoral shaft and is inserted through an aponeurosis into the lateral border of the patella and the lateral condyle of the tibia. It lies under the cover of the rectus.

The tendons of the four parts of the quadriceps femoris join in the lower part of the thigh to produce a stout tendon that is inserted into the upper part of the patella (which is developed as a sesamoid bone). From the lower end, or apex, of the patella the tendon is continued as the *ligamentum patellae,* which is inserted into the tubercule of the tibia.

Articularis genu (**subcrureus**) is a small muscle that arises from the lower part of the anterior aspect of the femoral shaft, and is inserted into the synovial membrane of the upper part of the knee joint.

2. Medial femoral muscles

The **gracilis** is a thin, flat muscle, broad above but narrow below. It arises from the body and inferior ramus of the pubis and part of the ramus of the ischium. It is inserted into the medial surface of the shaft of the tibia below the condyle. *Actions:* the gracilis flexes the leg and rotates it inwards; it may also adduct the thigh. It is supplied by the *obturator nerve* (Figs. 5.17, 5.18).

The **pectineus** is a four-sided muscle. It arises from the superior ramus of the pubis and is inserted into the posterior surface of the shaft of the femur a short distance below the lesser trochanter. Its *action* is to adduct the thigh and flex it on the pelvis. It is supplied by the *femoral nerve*.

The **adductor longus** arises by a slender tendon from the front of the body of the pubis near the symphysis, and is inserted into the middle third of the linea aspera of the femur.

The **adductor brevis** arises from the front of the body of the pubis and from its inferior ramus, and is inserted into the femur near the insertion of the pectineus.

The **adductor magnus** takes origin from the inferior ramus of the pubis, and from the ramus and tuberosity of the ischium. It is a large, fan-shaped muscle; its fibers, for the most part, are directed downward and outward, and are inserted into the linea aspera and the medial supracondylar line and condyle of the femur.

Actions of the adductor longus, brevis, and magnus. The three muscles last described are strong adductors of the thigh; they also rotate the thigh outwards, and flex it upon the pelvis. They are well developed in horseback riders as they are essential for maintaining a firm grip on the saddle. These muscles not infrequently become sore or suffer injury from such exercise. All three muscles are supplied by branches of the *obturator nerve.*

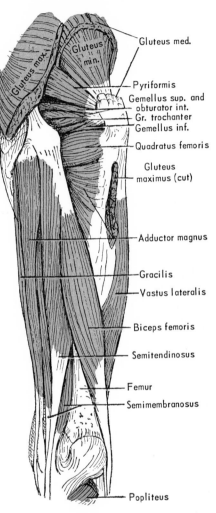

3. Posterior femoral muscles

The **biceps femoris** arises by two heads, a long and a short. The *long head* takes origin with the semitendinosus by a common tendon from the tuberosity of the ischium, and from a ligament passing from the latter to the sacrum (sacrotuberous ligament). The *short head* arises from the linea aspera and lateral supracondylar line of the femur. The two heads merge into a tendon that is inserted into the outer side of the head of the fibula and, to a smaller extent, into the lateral condyle of the tibia. The biceps femoris and the next two muscles are called the *hamstrings.*

The **semitendinosus**, so called from its very long tendon of insertion, arises with the biceps femoris by a common tendon from the tuberosity of the ischium. The muscle fibers end near the middle

Fig. 5.17. Muscles on the back of the thigh.

of the thigh in a tendon that curves forward around the inner side of the knee to be inserted into the upper part of the medial surface of the tibia, near the insertions of the sartorius and gracilis.

The **semimembranosus** takes origin by a thick tendon from the tuberosity of the ischium above and on the outer side of the common tendon of origin of the other two hamstrings; the tendon expands into a broad aponeurosis from which the muscle fibers arise and end in a second aponeurosis. The latter narrows to a tendon that is inserted into the back

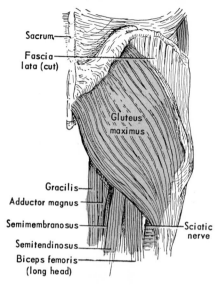

Sacrum

Fascia
lata (cut)

Gluteus
maximus

Gracilis

Adductor magnus

Semimembranosus

Semitendinosus

Biceps femoris
(long head)

Sciatic
nerve

Fig. 5.18. Superficial muscles of the gluteal
region (buttock).

of the medial condyle of the tibia (Figs. 5.17, 5.18).

Actions of the hamstring. Pulling from above, the hamstrings flex the knee; acting from below, they aid in drawing the trunk backwards or in raising it from a stooping position. They serve also to steady the pelvis upon the head of the femur and thus to maintain erect posture. The hamstrings are supplied by branches of the *sciatic nerve.*

Muscles of the gluteal region or buttock

The **gluteus maximus** is the large superficial muscle that forms the rounded mass of the buttock (Fig. 5.18). It arises from the posterior surface of the ilium, from the aponeurosis of the sacrospinalis muscle, from the posterior surface of the sacrum and the side of the coccyx. Its superficial fibers pass over the greater trochanter of the femur and are inserted into the iliotibial tract; its deeper fibers are inserted into the gluteal tuberosity of the femur. *Actions:* the gluteus maximus, acting from above, extends the thigh on the pelvis; acting from below, it raises the trunk upon the thigh, as in lifting a weight from the ground. It is an important muscle in maintaining erect posture, supporting the pelvis upon the head of the femur. It is supplied by the *inferior gluteal nerve.*

The **gluteus medius** is largely overlapped by the preceding muscle. It arises from the outer aspect of the ilium and is inserted into the greater trochanter of the femur.

The **gluteus minimus** arises from the outer surface of the ilium below the origin of the gluteus medius, by which it is completely covered; it is inserted into the greater trochanter. *Actions:* the glutei (medius and minimus) abduct the thigh and rotate it inwards. Both muscles are supplied by the *superior gluteal nerve.*

The **pyriformis** arises within the pelvis from the anterior surface of the sacrum (Fig. 5.17). Passing out of the pelvis through the greater sciatic foramen, the muscle is inserted by a round tendon into the greater trochanter. *Action:* the pyriformis rotates the thigh laterally. It is supplied by branches from the *first and second sacral nerves.*

The **obturator internus** arises within the pelvis from the bone surrounding the obturator foramen and from the obturator membrane (the membrane that covers over the obturator foramen). Leaving the pelvis through the lesser sciatic foramen, it is inserted by a flat tendon into the front part of the medial surface of the greater trochanter (Fig. 5.17).

The superior gemellus arises from the spine of the ischium, the **inferior gemellus** from the tuberosity of the ischium; the tendons of both these muscles blend with the tendon of the obturator internus and are inserted with it.

The quadratus femoris is a small quadrilateral muscle lying below the gemellus inferior; it arises from the tuberosity of the ischium and is inserted into the crest on the posterior surface of the femur below and medial to the greater trochanter.

The obturator externus arises from the hip bone, where it forms the inner margin of the obturator foramen, from the rami of the pubis and the ramus of the ischium, and from the obturator membrane. The fibers pass backwards and converge to a tendon that is inserted into the depression on the medial side of the greater trochanter (trochanteric fossa). *Actions:* the preceding five muscles rotate the thigh outwards. They are supplied by branches of the *lumbar and sacral nerves* (third lumbar to second sacral).

Muscles of the leg. Crural muscles

The muscles of the leg are grouped for purposes of description into three groups, *anterior, lateral,* and *posterior.*

Anterior muscles of the leg (Anterior crural)	Tibialis anterior Extensor hallucis longus	Extensor digitorum longus Peroneus tertius
Lateral muscles of the leg (Lateral crural)	Peroneus longus	Peroneus brevis
Posterior muscles of the leg (Posterior crural)	Gastrocnemius Soleus Popliteus Flexor hallucis longus	Plantaris Flexor digitorum longus Tibialis posterior

1. Anterior crural muscles

The tibialis anterior (Fig. 5.19) form the fleshy mass on the lateral side of the shin. It takes origin from the outer condyle and the upper two thirds of the outer side of the shaft of the tibia, as well as from the neighboring part of the interosseous membrane. Its fibers end in a tendon that passes to the inner side of the foot, and is inserted into the medial and inferior surfaces of the medial cuneiform bone, and the base of the first metatarsal bone. If the foot is lifted from the ground and the ankle strongly dorsiflexed, the tendon stands out and can be traced as it crosses the medial side of the ankle joint. The muscle can also be felt on the front of the leg when it contracts. *Action:* when the foot is not weighted by the body, that is, if it is off the ground, the tibialis anterior dorsiflexes the foot. When the body is standing, this muscle acting from above raises the bones into which it is inserted—the first metatarsal and middle cuneiform—and rotates them laterally. It thus accentuates the longitudinal plantar arch and inverts[4] the foot. Pulling from below, the tibialis anterior draws the leg forward at the ankle joint and this prevents overbalancing backward.

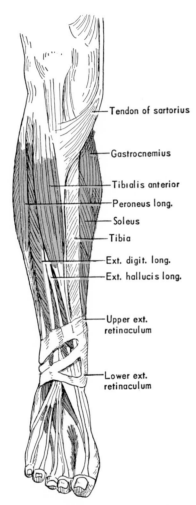

Tendon of sartorius

Gastrocnemius

Tibialis anterior

Peroneus long.

Soleus

Tibia

Ext. digit. long.

Ext. hallucis long.

Upper ext. retinaculum

Lower ext. retinaculum

Fig. 5.19. Anterior crural muscles.

The **extensor hallucis longus** (Fig. 5.19) takes origin from the anterior surface of the middle two quarters of the fibula and the adjoining part of the interosseous membrane. It is inserted into the dorsal (upper) surface of the base of the distal phalanx of the great toe. *Action:* the extensor hallucis longus dorsiflexes the phalanges of the great toe and with continued action assists in dorsiflexing of the foot. Its tendon stands out prominently in the living subject when the great toe is dorsiflexed.

The **extensor digitorum longus** is a slender muscle lying on the lateral side of the anterior aspect of the leg. It arises from the lateral condyle of the tibia, the upper three quarters of the anterior surface of the fibula, and the upper part of the interosseous membrane. At the ankle joint its tendon divides into four, each of which goes to one of the four outer toes, where it is inserted in a manner similar to that already described for the tendons of the extensor digitorum going to the fingers. *Actions:* the extensor digitorum longus dorsiflexes the outer four toes and with continued action dorsiflexes the foot.

The **peroneus tertius** arises from the lower third or so of the ante-

---

[4] Turning the foot so as to raise its inner border is called inversion; the opposite movement of raising the outer border of the foot is called eversion. The latter is a much more restricted movement than inversion.

rior surface the fibula and the adjoining part of the interosseous membrane; it is inserted into the dorsal aspect of the base of the fifth metatarsal bone. This muscle is really a part of the extensor digitorum longus. *Action:* the peroneus tertius dorsiflexes and everts the foot.

All the anterior crural muscles are supplied by the *anterior tibial nerve.*

2. Lateral crural muscles

The **peroneus longus** (Fig. 5.19) arises from the head and the upper two thirds of the lateral surface of the shaft of the fibula. Its tendon commences about the middle of the leg and passes behind the outer malleolus, crosses the outer side of the calcaneum obliquely to the side of the cuboid bone, then traverses the under surface of the latter and crosses the sole diagonally to be inserted into the base of the first metatarsal bone and the medial cuneiform bone. *Action:* the peroneus longus aids in steadying the tibia upon the talus (first bone of the tarsus, Ch. 3), and through the position of its tendon is an important factor in maintaining the arches of the foot. It can also evert the foot when it is not bearing weight (Fig. 5.24). The peroneus longus is supplied by the *musculocutaneous nerve.*

The **peroneus brevis** takes origin from the lateral surface of the fibula in its lower two thirds. It lies under cover of the preceding muscle. Its tendon runs behind the lateral malleolus, in front of the peroneus longus tendon; it runs along the side of the calcaneum and is inserted into the base of the fifth metatarsal bone. *Actions:* the peroneus brevis aids in everting the foot and prevents overinversion, thus protecting the ligament on the outer side of the ankle. It is supplied by the *musculocutaneous nerve.*

3. Posterior crural muscles

The **gastrocnemius** (Fig. 5.20) is the most superficial and the most prominent muscle of the calf. It takes origin by two heads. The *lateral head* arises from the back of the femur along the supracondylar line and from the outer side of the lateral condyle. The *medial head* takes origin from the posterior part of the medial condyle of the femur and from the bone immediately above it. Both heads are also attached to the capsular ligament of the knee joint. About the middle of the leg the two heads end in a broad aponeurosis that narrows and is joined by the soleus tendon to form the *tendo calcaneus* (tendo Achillis). The latter is inserted into the posterior aspect of the calcaneum (heel bone). The gastrocnemius is supplied by the *medial popliteal nerve.*

The **soleus** (Fig. 5.20) lies beneath the gastrocnemius. It arises from

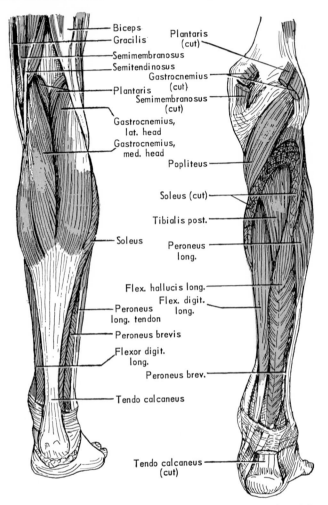

Fig. 5.20. Posterior crural muscles. *Left,* superficial muscles; *right,* deep muscles.

the posterior aspects of the head and upper quarter of the shaft of the fibula, from the middle third of the medial border of the tibia, and from a fibrous band between the upper parts of the tibia and fibula. Its tendon joins that of the gastrocnemius to form the tendo calcaneus. It is supplied by the *medial popliteal* and *posterior tibial nerves. Actions:* the calf muscles are powerful plantar flexors of the foot. The gastrocnemius supplies the main propulsive force in walking, running, or jumping, while the soleus serves chiefly in maintaining the posture of the leg upon the foot.

The plantaris is a weak, unimportant muscle in man. It consists of a small, spindle-shaped belly that takes origin from the posterior aspect of the femur above the external condyle, and ends in a long, slender tendon that is inserted into the posterior part of the calcaneum. *Action:* the plantaris acts in conjunction with the gastrocnemius. It is supplied by the *medial popliteal nerve.*

The **popliteus** lies at the back of the knee joint. It arises from the lateral condyle of the femur and from the posterior ligament of the knee joint. Its fibers run obliquely to their insertions into the upper fourth of the posterior surface of the tibia, above the origin of the soleus. *Action:* the popliteus assists in flexing the knee joint. It is supplied by the *medial popliteal nerve.*

The **flexor hallucis longus** arises from the middle part of the posterior surface of the fibula and from the interosseous membrane. Its tendon occupies a groove that crosses the posterior surfaces of the tibia and talus, and the undersurface of a projection (sustentaculum tali) on the medial aspect of the calcaneum. It is inserted into the plantar surface of the base of the distal phalanx of the great toe.

The **flexor digitorum longus** arises from the middle three quarters of the posterior surface of the shaft of the tibia. Its tendon runs behind the medial malleolus and forward along the side of the calcaneum. In the sole the tendon, after receiving a slip from the flexor longus hallucis, broadens out and is joined by the flexor longus accessorius. It immediately divides into four tendons that are inserted into the bases of the distal phalanges of the four outer toes. *Actions:* with the foot off the ground, the flexor hallucis longus and the flexor digitorum longus flex the toes. With the foot bearing the weight of the body, these muscles steady the heads of the metatarsal bones, which serve as the fulcrum of the lever through which the body is raised and propelled in walking, running, or jumping. Both of the preceding muscles are supplied by the *posterior tibial nerve.*

The **tibialis posterior** (Fig. 5.20) arises from the posterior surfaces of the shafts of the tibia and fibula and the interosseous membrane. Its tendon curves forward behind the medial malleolus to the foot and is inserted mainly into the medial aspect of the navicular bone. It also sends slips of insertion to several other bones of the carpus—talus, cuboid, and the three cuneiform bones—and to the bases of the second, third, and fourth metatarsal bones. *Actions:* the tibialis posterior is a strong inverter of the foot, and also is an important muscle in maintaining the longitudinal arch of the foot. It contributes a steadying effect upon the balance of the leg on the foot, counteracting any inclination to overbalance laterally. It is supplied by the *posterior tibial nerve.*

Muscles of the foot

The muscles of the foot consist of a *dorsal* muscle, the *extensor digitorum brevis,* and four layers of *plantar* muscles, from the most super-

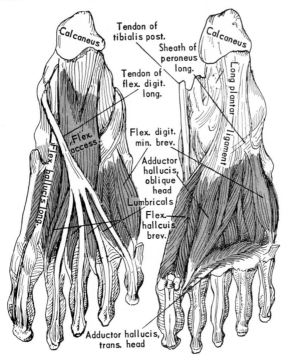

Fig. 5.21. Muscles of the sole of the foot. *Left*, intermediate or second layer; *right*, deep or third layer.

ficial to the deepest, as follows: (a) *abductor hallucis, flexor digitorum brevis*, and *abductor digiti minimi;* (b) *flexor digitorum accessorius* and *lumbricales;* (c) *flexoris hallucis brevis, adductor hallucis*, and *flexor digiti minimi brevis;* (d) *interossei* (Fig. 5.21).

The **extensor digitorum brevis** arises mainly from the outer and upper surfaces of the calcaneum and ligaments in the neighborhood. Its fibers end in four tendons, the most medial of which is inserted into the dorsal surface of the base of the proximal phalanx of the great toe. The remaining three tendons are inserted into the tendons of the extensor digitorum longus, going to the second, third, and fourth toes. It is supplied by a terminal branch of the *anterior tibial nerve. Action:* the extensor digitorum brevis is an extensor of the toes.

The **abductor hallucis** arises from a tubercle on the medial surface of the calcaneum, from the flexor retinaculum (p. 127), and from the plantar aponeurosis. It is inserted into the base of the proximal phalanx of the great toe. It is supplied by the *medial plantar nerve.*

The **flexor digitorum brevis** arises from the tubercle on the medial aspect of the calcaneum and from the plantar aponeurosis. Its fibers end in four tendons that divide, unite, and redivide and are inserted in the same way as are the tendons of the *flexor digitorum sublimis* of the forearm. It is supplied by the *medial plantar nerve.*

The **abductor digiti minimi** arises from the sides and under surface of the calcaneum, and from the plantar aponeurosis. Its tendon is inserted into the outer side of the base of the proximal phalanx of the little toe. It is supplied by the *lateral plantar nerve.*

The **flexor digitorum accessorius** arises by a *medial fleshy* and a *lateral tendinous head.* The former arises from the medial surface of the calcaneum, the latter from a tubercle on the outer surface of the bone and from the long plantar ligament. It is supplied by the *lateral plantar nerve.*

The **lumbricales** arise from the tendons of the *flexor digitorum longus.* They are inserted as in the case of those of the hand into the dorsal digital expansions of the outer four toes. The first (most medial) lumbrical is supplied by the *medial plantar nerve,* the others by a branch of the *lateral plantar nerve.*

The **flexor hallucis brevis** takes origin from the under surface of the cuboid bone, the adjacent part of the lateral cuneiform bone, and the tibialis posterior tendon. It gives rise to two tendons that are inserted into the sides of the base of the proximal phalanx of the great toe. It is supplied by the *medial plantar nerve.*

The **adductor hallucis** takes origin by an oblique and a transverse head. The *oblique head* arises from the second, third, and fourth metatarsal bones, and is inserted into the lateral side of the base of the proximal phalanx of the great toe. The *transverse head* takes origin from the ligaments of the third, fourth, and fifth toes, and blends with the tendon of the oblique head. It is supplied by a branch of the *lateral plantar nerve.*

The **flexor digiti minimi brevis** arises from the plantar surface of the base of the fifth metatarsal bone and is inserted into the lateral side of the base of the proximal phalanx of the little toe.

The **interossei** of the foot are arranged very similarly to those of the hand and, as in the latter, are in two groups—four *dorsal,* but only three *plantar.* The **dorsal interossei** are bipennate muscles that arise from the adjacent borders of the metatarsal bones between which they lie. Their slender tendons are inserted into the dorsal expansions and bases of the proximal phalanges. The base of the phalanx of the second toe receives the tendon of the first interosseus on its medial side, and that of the second interosseus on its lateral side. The lateral sides of the proximal phalanges of the third and fourth toes receive the tendons of the third and fourth interossei, respectively. The **plantar interossei** lie beneath the third, fourth, and fifth metatarsal bones and arise from the bases and medial sides of these bones; their tendons are inserted into the medial sides of the bases of the corresponding phalanges and into the dorsal digital expansions.

Actions of the muscles of the foot. In most instances the muscles of the foot have actions described by their names. Thus, the abductor hallucis abducts the great toe, and the adductor hallucis adducts it. The flexor digitorum brevis assists in flexing the toes; the abductor digiti minimi abducts the little toe, and so on, for the other muscles. But the most important functions of the foot muscles are to steady the toes and bind them into a strong base of support, and to maintain the arches of the foot.

DEEP FASCIAE OF THE LOWER LIMB

A stout fascia called the **fascia iliaca** covers the psoas and iliacus muscles. The deep fascia investing the thigh is known as the **fascia lata**. Above and laterally, it is thick and strong, and forms a stout band down the outer side of the thigh known as the *iliotibial tract,* which splits in its upper part into two layers; between these the tensor fasciae latae muscle is inserted (Fig. 5.16). The fascia lata is strong about the knee joint, but thin and weak over the posterior and medial aspects of the thigh. Behind and laterally, it is attached to the iliac crest and the back of the sacrum; in front it is fixed to the inguinal ligament and the superior ramus of the pubis. In the upper and medial part of the thigh there is an oval gap in the fascia lata called the *saphenous opening.* The long saphenous vein passes through this to join the femoral vein.

The **deep fascia of the leg** is thickened at the ankle where it forms bands that hold the tendons in place as they cross the joint. The bands, five in number, are named, respectively, *superior extensor retinaculum, inferior extensor retinaculum, flexor retinaculum, superior peroneal retinaculum,* and *inferior peroneal retinaculum* (Figs. 5.19, 5.20). The superior extensor retinaculum holds in place the tendons of the tibialis anterior, the extensor hallucis longus, extensor digitorum longus, and the peroneus tertius as they cross the front of the ankle. The inferior extensor retinaculum is a Y-shaped band lying distal to the forementioned. The flexor retinaculum extends from the inner malleolus to the calcaneus, and binds down the tendons of the tibialis posterior, flexor digitorum longus, and flexor hallucis longus, as well as the posterior tibial vessels and nerve. The superior and inferior peroneal retinacula lie on the outer side of the ankle; the peroneus longus and peroneus brevis pass beneath it.

The **plantar aponeurosis** is an exceedingly strong fascial covering for the muscles of the sole. Its thickest and strongest part is centrally placed. This is composed of white connective tissue fibers running mainly in the long axis of the foot, but reinforced by many transverse fibers. This central portion is narrower behind where it is attached to the calcaneum than in front where it divides into five parts that diverge and pass one to each toe. The medial and lateral parts of the aponeurosis are thin, and cover the muscles on the corresponding sides of the sole.

THE BONES AND MUSCLES AS LEVER SYSTEMS

A lever is a strong bar or other rigid structure that can be moved about a fixed axis called the **fulcrum**, and through which a force can be transmitted. Levers are of three classes. In a lever of the *first class,* the fulcrum is situated between the applied force and the object to which the force is transmitted (such as a weight to be raised, Fig. 5.22*A*). Examples are, a seesaw, scissors, or a pump handle. In levers of the *second class* (Fig. 5.22*B*), the weight to be moved is situated between the force and the fulcrum, as in a nutcracker, a wheelbarrow, or in raising a weight upon a plank having one end resting upon the ground (fulcrum). In levers of the *third class,* the force is applied between the fulcrum and the weight, as when a ladder is raised by grasping it near the middle while one end rests upon the ground (Fig. 5.22*C*).

Many bones, especially the long bones of the limbs, act as levers, the attached muscle or muscles furnishing the power. Levers of the first class are employed in the body for stability. The best example is the head poised upon the atlas (fulcrum), the weight being the front or the back of the head, and the force being supplied by the muscles of the neck. There are few levers of the second class in the body; an example is depressing the lower jaw against a resistance (as when the teeth are stuck together by taffy), the fulcrum being the joint between the mandible and the temporal bone of the skull, and the force being supplied by the muscles that lower

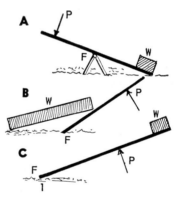

Fig. 5.22. Showing the three classes of lever: first *(A),* second *(B),* and third *(C); W,* weight; *F,* fulcrum; *P,* power.

the jaw. The foot, in walking, also serves as an arched lever of the second class, the fulcrum being the heads of the metatarsal bones; the power is furnished by the calf muscles attached to the calcaneum. The weight that is raised is that of the body through the tibia.

Most of the levers in the body are of the *third class.* An example of the operation of such a lever is the flexion of the forearm. The elbow joint is the fulcrum, the force is provided by the biceps muscle attached to the upper part of the radius, and the weight to be lifted is the more distal part of the forearm or an object grasped by the hand. (See also p. 611.)

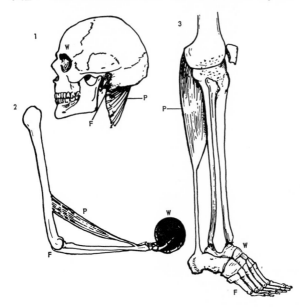

Fig. 5.23. Showing the three classes of lever in the human body: first (A), second (B), and third (C); W, weight; F, fulcrum; P, power. Semidiagrammatic.

The structures shown in Figures 5.24 to 5.31 are described in other sections of the book.

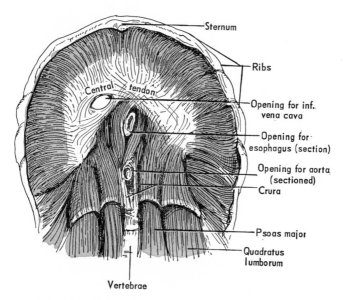

Sternum

Ribs

Central tendon

Opening for inf. vena cava

Opening for esophagus (section)

Opening for aorta (sectioned)

Crura

Psoas major

Quadratus lumborum

Vertebrae

Fig. 5.24 *(Above)*. The diaphragm viewed from below.

Fig. 5.25 *(Below)*. The intercostal muscles.

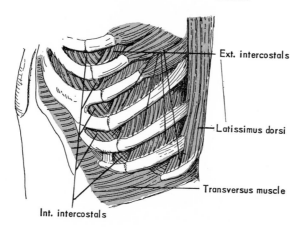

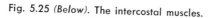

Ext. intercostals

Latissimus dorsi

Transversus muscle

Int. intercostals

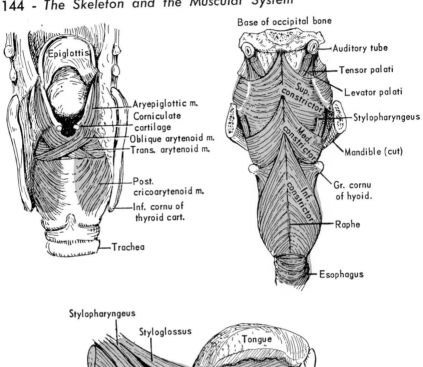

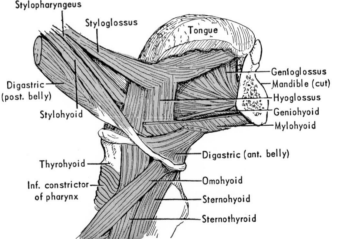

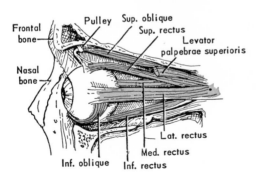

Fig. 5.26 *(Upper left)*. Muscles on the posterior aspect of the larynx.

Fig. 5.27 *(Upper right)*. Muscles of the pharynx from behind.

Fig. 5.28. *(Center)*. Muscles of the tongue and throat, mucosa of tongue partly removed.

Fig. 5.29 *(Left)*. The ocular muscles.

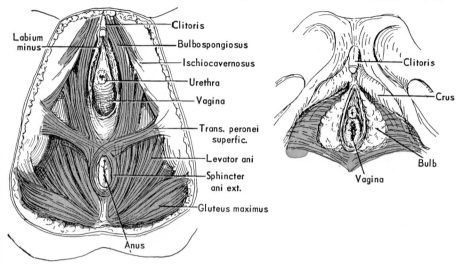

Fig. 5.30 *(Above).* Muscles of the female perineum and labia majora, skin and subcutaneous tissue removed. *(Right)* sketch of deeper structures.

Fig. 5.31 *(Below).* Muscles of the male perineum.

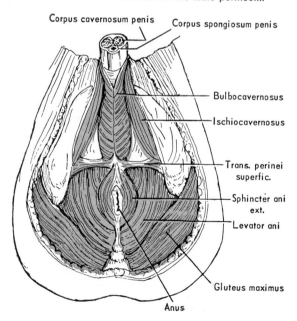

THE FLUIDS OF
THE BODY
PART III

6

The Functions and Composition of the Blood

The fluids of the body fall into two main categories; namely (a) the red fluid within the blood vessels—the **blood** and (b) the colorless fluid outside the circulatory system—the **extravascular fluid.** Of the extravascular fluid, a part lies within and is a constitutent of the cells of the tissues generally; it is called *intracellular fluid.* The remaining part of the extravascular fluid is called *extracellular fluid.* The latter comprises the fluid in the small spaces between the cells, the fluid in the serous cavities (pleural [Ch. 19], peritoneal [Ch. 27], pericardial sac [Ch. 12], etc.), the cerebrospinal fluid, and the fluid (lymph) within the lymph vessels.

This chapter and the three that follow will be devoted to a description of the blood. The extravascular fluids will be dealt with in Chapter 9.

FUNCTIONS OF THE BLOOD

In order to understand the functions of the blood, let us study for a moment a creature composed of only a single cell, such as the amoeba (Ch. 1). It lives in water, and the water that bathes its surface serves for this organism those purposes that for higher forms of life, having bodies composed of millions of cells, are carried out by the blood and other extra cellular fluids. For example, the single-celled amoeba requires oxygen, and this gas simply passes by diffusion from the water in which the creature lives into the interior of its body. The amoeba forms carbon

148

dioxide, and this gas, as it is produced, passes directly out into the surrounding water. Nourishment is obtained also in this direct and simple fashion, and in the same way waste materials formed within the cell are cast away. Similarly, the amoeba's temperature and its water supply are governed by water in which it lives.

The human body is composed of millions and millions of cells, each of which is not fundamentally different from an amoeba. The elemental needs of each cell of this community of cells are no greater and no less than those of the one-celled animal. No cell of the body can exist for long without oxygen. Every cell forms carbon dioxide, which must be eliminated from its protoplasm and from the body. Nourishment must be provided upon which each cell may feed, and waste materials must be removed if the cells are not to become poisoned and die. But we know that in the bodies of higher animals the cells are packed together in masses and lie at a distance from the surface. They cannot possibly satisfy their essential needs in the simple fashion of the amoeba. Some primitive forms of life, such as the sponges, though made up of many cells, get over this difficulty by the development of canal systems that course through their bodies and open upon the surface. Through these canals the ocean waters in which the sponge lives flow freely in and out to bring oxygen and nourishment to the interior cells and to carry carbon dioxide and waste products away. Such a device may be looked upon as the first attempt at a circulation. It is an open system and, of course, very imperfect. In higher forms of animal life the circulation is closed, and the channels are filled, not with water, but with a fluid highly specialized for the performance of those duties that every body cell demands.

Approximately 70 percent of the substance of the animal body is made up of fluids. Fluids fill the spaces between groups of tissue cells and bathe every cell (Ch. 9). The colorless fluid in these places moves sluggishly, much as water seeps through marshy ground. It is not kept within definite channels or canals and is therefore spoken of simply as the **tissue fluid,** or the **interstitial fluid.** On the other hand, that bright red fluid that we know as blood courses swiftly through a system of tubes —**arteries, capillaries,** and **veins** (Ch. 12). In the largest of these tubes— the arteries—the blood flows at the rate of a mile or more per hour. The blood, however, as we shall presently see, is only semifluid; it contains a large number of solid particles—the blood cells—that are evenly mixed with the fluid. The smallest blood vessels—the capillaries—are made of the very thinnest and most delicate of membranes. The wing of a mosquito is a coarse, heavy material compared with the membrane that forms the wall of a capillary. The capillary walls are porous and allow fluid, but not the red cells, to pass from the blood and mix with the fluid in the tissues. They also permit tissue fluid to enter the blood stream and mix with the blood. Thus, it can be easily understood how oxygen and nourishing substances are conveyed from the blood to the cells of the tissues, and how, on the other hand, carbon dioxide and waste materials[1] can be carried from the tissue cells to the blood.

The blood flowing through the capillaries, and the interchange of materials between the fluids of the tissue and of the blood, call to mind a brook trickling through a marshy meadow. The water of the marsh, though apparently still, is kept fresh and sweet, and vegetation flourishes as a result of the revivifying stream flowing through its midst.

The functions of the blood and tissue fluids are summarized below.

1. *Respiration:* the transportation of oxygen from the air in the lungs to the capillaries, and of carbon dioxide from the capillaries to the lungs. The capillary blood delivers the oxygen to the fluid of the tissues which, in turn, carries carbon dioxide from the cells to the blood in the capillaries.

2. *Nutrition:* the conveyance of food materials—glucose, amino acids, and fats (Ch. 30) —from the intestine to the tissues.

3. *Excretion:* the carriage of waste products from the tissues to the kidney and intestine.

4. *Regulation of the body temperature* (Ch. 29) .

5. *Maintenance of the water content of the body.* This duty is shared, of course, by the tissue fluids.

6. *Protection against disease.* The blood and tissue fluids contain certain chemical substances, antitoxins, etc., that are the basis of the body's defense against germs and other injurious agents (Ch. 11) . The blood also serves as a medium through which hormones (Ch. 38) manufactured by the several ductless glands are carried to all parts of the body.

The quantity of blood. The blood in the body of a man of average size has a volume of about 6 liters. It makes up about 9 percent of the total weight of the body. This quantity varies very little in health.

THE COMPOSITION OF THE BLOOD

The blood is a bright red fluid consisting of a suspension of cells— the corpuscles—in an almost colorless fluid. The corpuscles are of two main types—red and white. The red corpuscles are many times more numerous than the white. Both types will be described in the following chapters.

If blood is shed and collected in a small glass tube, it soon sets into a jelly or **clot.** Certain measures can be taken, however, that will prevent the blood from clotting, and when this is done it will be found that the blood cells, after a time, have settled toward the bottom of the tube,

---

[1] These are unoxidized elements of food, mostly remnants of protein, such as urea, uric acid, etc.; they are carried in the blood to the kidneys and excreted in the urine.

much as finely divided clay settles from water. The setting of the corpuscles can be hastened very greatly by placing the tube of blood in a machine called a *centrifuge*. This machine spins the tube of blood in a circle in the same way that milk is spun in a separator. When the tube is removed, the blood will be found to have separated into a lower red and nearly solid portion, and an upper straw-colored fluid (Plate I*a*). The lower mass is composed entirely of the blood cells, which, being heavier, have been forced to the bottom of the tube. The upper portion is the fluid part of the blood. It is called **plasma.** The plasma amounts to about 55 percent of human blood; the cells make up the remaining 45 percent or so.

The following are the chief constituents of the blood:

I. Plasma
Water, 92 percent

Proteins
- Fibrinogen
- Serum globulin
- Serum albumin

Inorganic substances
- Chlorides, carbonates, and phosphates
- Sodium
- Potassium
- Calcium
- Magnesium

Nutritive materials
- Glucose, fats (Ch. 30)
- Amino acids (Ch. 30)

Various antibodies, hormones, and enzymes
Waste materials   Urea, uric acid, etc. (Ch. 30)

II. Solid elements
Red cells, or erythrocytes
White cells, or leucocytes
Platelets, or thrombocytes

The plasma. In composition and general appearance the plasma resembles very closely the fluid filling the tissue spaces and bathing the individual cells. The proteins are dissolved in the plasma in much the same way as gelatin or white of egg, which are types of protein, may be dissolved in a weak solution of salt. The proteins give to the plasma a certain "stickiness," or *viscosity,* which water or saline alone does not possess. As we shall see later, this viscosity of the plasma aids in maintaining the blood pressure (Ch. 15).

Since the proteins are colloids, those principles governing the behavior of colloidal solutions (Ch. 1) apply to the blood plasma.[2] Fibrino-

[2] The capillary wall is a semipermeable membrane in so far as the proteins of the plasma are concerned (Ch. 1). The latter, especially the albumin, therefore, exert a definite though small osmotic pressure.

gen has a special function to perform in the coagulation of the blood (Ch. 7). The osmotic pressure of the plasma depends mainly upon the serum albumin. Thus, since water is drawn from the tissues and held within the blood vessels, the volume of the blood is maintained at the normal level (Ch. 15). From the serum globulin immune substances are manufactured that are essential for the defense of the body against the microorganisms of disease (Ch. 11).

The various inorganic constitutents of the plasma—sodium, calcium, potassium, phosphates, and sodium bicarbonate—are absolutely essential for the proper functioning of the body cells. The proportions of these several salts do not vary appreciably in health, but serious disturbances arise if their percentages rise above or fall below the normal level.

When a specimen of living tissue is removed from the body of an animal for study, it must be kept moist or it will die almost immediately. Pure water, since it does not contain the essential salts, is not suitable for this purpose, and the cells are killed. A watery solution may be made up containing sodium chloride, calcium chloride, and potassium chloride in the same proportions as they exist in the plasma. This fluid, known as Ringer's solution after the physiologist who first used it, when employed to bathe the tissue, keeps it alive and capable of performing its normal functions for a comparatively long time. Sodium bicarbonate is added to the solution to serve a purpose similar to that which it serves in the body; namely, the neutralization of acids formed in metabolic processes, and the maintenance of the normal alkalinity.

The glucose, fats and fatty acids, and amino acids in the plasma are the food materials being carried to the tissues of the body. Some of these materials supply the energy for the performance of work, others go to build up the body of the growing animal, and still others are used to repair the wear and tear of the tissues. These substances are derived from the starches, sugars, fats, and proteins of the food, which has been digested in the stomach and intestines. Urea, uric acid, and other waste materials derived from the protein of food and body tissues (Ch. 32) are excreted in the urine.

7

The Red Blood Cells.
Hemoglobin. Anemia.
Blood Clotting. Hemorrhage.
Transfusion. Carbon Monoxide
Poisoning

RED BLOOD CELLS, OR ERYTHROCYTES

The red cells of the blood are called **red blood corpuscles, or erythrocytes** (Gk. *erythros,* red + *kytos,* cell) . Under the microscope erythrocytes appear as faintly pink discs. They owe their color to a pigment called **hemoglobin,** which will be considered in more detail later. The deep red color of blood as seen by the naked eye is due to the great numbers of these pigmented cells massed together. The mature human erythrocyte is different from any other cell of the body in that it possesses no nucleus.[1] If the cell is examined carefully under the microscope, a shallow, saucerlike depression can easily be made out in its center (Plate I*b*) . The depression or hollow occupies the greater part of the body of the cell and is present upon both surfaces, making the cell much thinner toward the center than around its circumference, which forms a circular lip. As a consequence the cell, when seen edgewise, has an outline something like a dumbell or a doubly clubbed rod.

The size and number of red cells. The red cell is about 0.0003 inch in

---

[1] The red corpuscles in the blood of some lower forms—for example, the frog—contain a nucleus.

diameter and no more than 0.0001 inch thick.[2] Looked at under the microscope, a film of blood appears as a mass of these small rounded objects, crowded together so that each one touches, or almost touches, its neighbor. Sometimes the cells cling together with their broad surfaces applied to one another, and the edges only are seen, so that they resemble a pile of coins. Such an arrangement of the cells is spoken of as a **rouleau** (pl. *rouleaux*) (Plate I*b*).

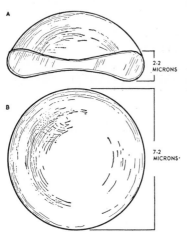

Fig. 7.1. Showing the form and structure of a red blood cell. A, sectioned; B, from above.

A cubic millimeter of a man's blood contains from 5 to 5½ million red cells. A cubic millimeter is about ¹⁄₂₅ drop. The blood of a woman contains about half a million fewer cells per cubic millimeter than the blood of a man. The number of cells in all the blood of a man of average size is no less than 25 trillion (25,000,000,000,000). If laid flat, edge to edge and one layer deep, all the cells in the human body would cover an area of about 3,500 square yards.

The life history of the red cells. The red cells are manufactured by the **red marrow** of such bones as the ribs, vertebrae, and the diploe of the skull. In children red marrow in the ends of the long bones of the limbs share this function. The red cell develops through several stages before it is finally turned out as a finished product and discharged into the general circulation. In its earliest stage it is a very large cell with a large nucleus but no pigment. Later it becomes smaller, gains hemoglobin, and finally loses its nucleus. In a healthy man it does not escape from the bone into the general circulation until it has reached this last stage. The cells of this stage—that is, the youngest cells in the circulation—show, when stained with a special dye, a fine blue network or reticulum. They are therefore called **reticulocytes.** They soon lose this reticulated appearance, becoming mature erythrocytes within a few hours after their discharge from the bone marrow.

The erythrocyte has a short life. It is driven completely around the body at high speed once or twice a minute and is subjected to many stresses and strains. It becomes old and worn out in service and finally breaks up in the blood stream. Its life span has been estimated at 90 to

---

[2] These measurements are more usually expressed in microns (μ). A micron is ¹⁄₁₀₀₀ millimeter. The diameter of the red cell is around 7.2 μ and its thickness 2.2 μ. These are mean figures; normally the diameters of the red cells in a specimen of blood vary from 6 to 9 μ, but there are few to be found as small or as large as these. The greatest number will have a diameter of 7.2 μ (Fig. 7.1).

125 days. The fragments of the worn-out cells are removed from circulation by certain large scavenger cells in the spleen. Fresh erythrocytes are turned out by the bone marrow to replace the millions of cells that disappear each day.

HEMOGLOBIN

The pigment of the red cell is a complex protein called **hemoglobin.** It is the all-important constituent of the cell. Without hemoglobin the erythrocyte would be worthless. Of the many substances composing the human body, hemoglobin is one of the most interesting. If it were not for this pigment, our skins would be almost as white as paper—or a sickly putty color. Chemists have studied this material very carefully and have found out some strange things about it. They have discovered, in the first place, that it is a close relative of the coloring material of plants. The green color of plant life is due to a pigment that resembles hemoglobin. The plant pigment is called **chlorophyl.** This pigment is just as important to the plant as hemoglobin is to animals. By means of chlorophyl and the sunlight, plants are able to build up starches and sugars from the water of the earth and the carbon dioxide of the air. It was also found that the brilliant colors of the feathers of some birds, the colors of their eggs, and many other hues in nature were due to pigments that resemble closely the pigment of our blood. Hemoglobin, however, is different from these pigments in one very important particular. It contains **iron.** The blood of a man contains enough iron to make a 2-inch nail. As Ruskin says, "Is it not strange to find this stern and strong metal mingled so delicately in our human life that we cannot even blush without its help?"

Iron. The iron of hemoglobin gives this pigment the power, which other similar pigments have not, to carry oxygen. We know than an iron nail soon becomes red with rust. The nail rusts because the oxygen in the air forms a chemical union with the iron of the nail. So, too, the oxygen of the air in our lungs joins with the iron in the hemoglobin and turns it a brighter red. But there is an essential difference between the combination of oxygen with the iron of the nail and its union with the iron in hemoglobin. The iron rust (iron oxide) will not give up the oxygen again except under very drastic treatment.

The oxygen that combines with hemoglobin in the lungs, on the other hand, is released again with ease when the red cell reaches the capillaries. We do not say, therefore, that the hemoglobin (or the iron in it) has been *oxidized,* for that implies a firm and stable union. Instead we speak of it as being **oxygenated.** When hemoglobin loses its oxygen and becomes a darker red, it is called **reduced hemoglobin.** When the red cell is returned to the lungs and the hemoglobin takes up another load of oxygen and flashes red again, it is called **oxyhemoglobin** (see also Ch. 20).

Other constituents of hemoglobin. Iron makes up only a small part of the hemoglobin molecule. Two other substances form its greater part—a pure pigment part called **porphyrin** and a protein called **globin**. When porphyrin and iron are combined together without globin, the substance is called **hematin**. Hematin is found in onions, spinach, cabbage, and several other vegetables, in wheat, oatmeal, yeast, meats, etc. It is apparent, then, that our bodies derive an abundance of this substance from food.

But, unfortunately, the hematin present in food cannot be used to any important extent by the body for the manufacture of hemoglobin. Yet, provided that the diet contains adequate amounts of iron and of globin, which is present in protein foods, especially meats, the cells of the tissues have no difficulty in synthesizing the necessary amount of hemoglobin for newly formed red cells. Liver, kidney, beef muscle, and chicken gizzard are especially rich in hemoglobin-building material. Iron is usually present in adequate amounts in a liberal and well-balanced diet, but it is sometimes necessary to take additional amounts in the form of tablets or solutions. Children and women are especially likely to require extra iron.

The following scheme shows the main features in the structure of hemoglobin:

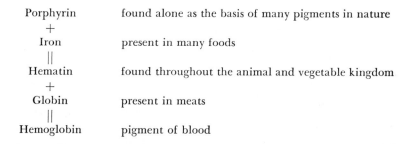

Porphyrin	found alone as the basis of many pigments in nature
+	
Iron	present in many foods
‖	
Hematin	found throughout the animal and vegetable kingdom
+	
Globin	present in meats
‖	
Hemoglobin	pigment of blood

The importance of hemoglobin. Hemoglobin has the property of combining loosely with oxygen to a greater extent than any other substance known. One hundred parts of water can absorb about 0.38 parts of oxygen. The blood plasma, which is mostly water, absorbs about the same amount. One hundred parts of blood (plasma + red cells), on the other hand, absorb about 20 parts of oxygen. The blood of a man's body will absorb a liter of oxygen—an amount that would fill a space, say, the size of a grapefruit. An equal amount of plasma will absorb no more than could be held within a robin's egg. It is apparent, therefore, that, if the circulating fluid of the body were all plasma, its bulk would have to be some 50 times greater than it is, in order that the tissues might be supplied with the necessary amount of oxygen. The blood makes up only about one eleventh of the body's weight. If it were not for hemoglobin, the blood would have to be 2 or 3 times the weight of the solid tissues.

In the jellyfish, which possesses no hemoglobin but nevertheless requires oxygen, the fluid portion of its body exceeds many times the solid material. Similarly, a man, instead of needing, as he does, only about 5 quarts of blood, would need, if he had no red blood cells, some 75 gallons of circulating fluid to carry the oxygen to his tissues. In order to pump this great quantity of fluid around the body, a huge heart, having a capacity of some 2 gallons or more, would be necessary. Weighted down by his great heart and blood vessels, and swamped by a sea of body fluid, he would be left incapable of an active life. Next to oxygen itself, iron—since it is the essential part of hemoglobin—is probably the most important element in the lives of higher animals.[3]

Variations in the number of red cells. Anemia. When the red cells are reduced in number, the condition is spoken of as *anemia.* Since the function of the red cell is to carry oxygen from the lungs to the capillaries, from which it is distributed to the cells of the tissues, persons suffering from anemia may not be able to get enough oxygen fully to satisfy their needs. They become breathless when any exertion, sometimes even the mildest, is attempted.

There are several causes of anemia—namely, *poor nutrition,* especially a lack of first-class protein food or of vitamins, or a low content of iron in the diet; *repeated hemorrhages; defective function of the red bone marrow;* or *the destruction of blood cells by some toxic substance in the circulation,* either formed in the body or ingested. In health, red cells are produced continuously, for they have a comparatively short life (3 to 4 months) and the old or dead cells must be replaced by young, healthy ones from the bone marrow. A perfect balance must be struck between loss from natural causes and replacement by new cells, in order that the red cell population shall remain numerically unchanged. Anemia, therefore, may arise in three principal ways: by (1) loss of erythrocytes from the vessels, or their excessive destruction in the circulation, (2) defective function of the bone marrow, or (3) lack of the proper materials for erythrocyte manufacture, the normal wastage being uncompensated.

Pernicious anemia is a very severe type of blood disease caused by depressed function of the bone marrow. Until recent years it was invariably fatal. In this disease the bone marrow fails to receive a substance essential for its normal function, and supplied by the liver. It is called the **hematinic principle,** or more usually now, **vitamin B_{12}.** The average size of the erythrocytes in pernicious anemia is greater than normal; they

---

[3] One hundred cubic centimeters (cc) of human blood contain about 15 grams of hemoglobin, and 1 gram of hemoglobin combines with 1.34 cc of oxygen. This ratio is spoken of as its **oxygen capacity.**

are abnormal in other ways and have a short life. Thus, the number of red cells in the circulation falls to a low level,[4] and unless the disease is arrested, the patient cannot obtain a sufficient quantity of oxygen to sustain life. The usual way in which this type of anemia is now cured is by supplying the patient with vitamin B_{12}.

The discovery of this cure is an interesting story of research. A few years ago Dr. G. H. Whipple and his associates in Rochester, N Y., found that dogs made anemic by repeated bleeding manufactured more red cells on a diet of liver than when sustained on any other food. As an outcome of these experiments, Drs. Minot and Murphy of Boston gave liberal amounts of cooked liver to patients suffering from pernicious anemia. This diet was found to increase the number of erythrocytes in a spectacular manner, to restore their normal form, and to put the patient on the road to recovery. Pernicious anemia has now been removed from the list of fatal diseases. An extract of liver or vitamin B_{12} given by injection is a specific cure for the disease.

Vitamin B_{12} is widely distributed in nature; it is present in liver, yeast, and many of the ordinary foodstuffs. It is found in the large intestine of normal persons, as well as of those suffering from pernicious anemia. Since, then, there is no lack of this vitamin in the diet, Why, it may well be asked, does pernicious anemia ever develop? The answer can be given in simple terms. The victim of the disease cannot make use of the vitamin that he receives. But the cause of his failure is a more complicated matter. The red bone marrow is deprived of vitamin B_{12}, indispensable for the production of mature erythrocytes, because its absorption from the intestine is inadequate. Normal gastric juice contains an enzyme required for vitamin B_{12} absorption. The gastric glands of the pernicious anemia patient show atrophy, and both this enzyme and pepsin-hydrochloric acid are absent from his gastric juice. The deficit of the gastric glands is the key and primary lesion in the disease. Though large oral doses of vitamin B_{12} will cure pernicious anemia, a certain quantity being absorbed apparently without the aid of the specific gastric enzyme, a minute amount—a mere fraction of a milligram—is effective when given parenterally (intramuscularly).

Before the mechanism underlying the disease was finally clarified, the essential substance in normal gastric juice was called the **intrinsic factor,** and that in the food (that is, vitamin B_{12}) the **extrinsic factor.** It was then known that liver tissue was rich in the extrinsic factor; here it is stored by the healthy body and drawn upon as required by the bone marrow.

Pernicious anemia can also be brought under control by the oral administration of a preparation of defatted and powdered hog's gastric

[4] The quantity of hemoglobin in the blood of a victim of this disease may be only a quarter or less of the normal.

mucosa, which contains in utilizable form the enzyme that the patient lacks.

More recently it has been discovered that another factor of the vitamin B complex—*folic acid,* also known as *pteroylglutamic acid*[5]—is also effective in restoring the blood of the pernicious anemia patient to normal. But folic acid is much less valuable than vitamin B_{12} because it does not prevent or arrest the neurological changes (degeneration of the fibers of the posterior columns of the spinal cord) often such a prominent and serious feature of the disease.

Hypochromic, or *microcytic, anemia,* a much less severe type, results from a shortage of iron or of first-class protein in the diet. A deficiency of certain vitamins, especially of some factors of the B complex or of vitamin C, may also occasionally be responsible for an anemia of this type. Anemias arising in these ways are usually readily cured by correcting the nutritional fault. The erythrocytes in this form of anemia are smaller than the normal and contain less hemoglobin than in health but are not very greatly reduced in number, whereas, as mentioned above, in pernicious anemia the cells are actually larger than normal and each cell contains more hemoglobin than do normal cells. Now, the essential defect in anemia is the reduction in the oxygen-carrying pigment hemoglobin. In pernicious anemia the reduction in hemoglobin is due to the reduced number of red cells (even though each cell holds more than the normal amount of hemoglobin). In the anemia resulting from a lack of iron or other dietary essential, the reduction of hemoglobin is due both to the reduction in the number of cells and, in greater degree, to the smaller amount of hemoglobin in the individual cells. This latter type is, therefore, called **hypochromic** (Gk. *hypo,* under + *chroma,* color) or **microcytic** (Gk. *micros,* small + *kytos,* cell), whereas anemias such as pernicious anemia are called **hyperchromic** (Gk. *hyper,* above) or **macrocytic** (Gk. *macros,* large).

The number of red cells is sometimes permanently increased above the normal as a result of disease. There may be as many as 12 million or more in each cubic millimeter of blood.[6]

An increase in the number of red cells may occur in health. For instance, when one performs a piece of hard physical exercise, the red cells may increase by 10 or 15 percent within a few minutes; a rise in the temperature of the environment also results in an increase in the number of red cells. These increases in the red corpuscles are a result of the escape of large reserves of red cells from the spleen (Ch. 8) or other regions where red cells are stored. After the exercise is over, or when the air temperature falls again, the cells return to the storehouses.

A visitor to a mountainous region also increases the number of his

---

[5] Both vitamin B_{12} and folic acid are present in normal liver tissue.

[6] This disease is called *polycythemia.* Its cause is unknown.

red cells very rapidly when a height of 8000 feet or more above the sea is reached. This increase, too, is due to the discharge of red cells from the spleen into the circulation. The reduction in the oxygen of the blood not only causes contraction of the spleen but also stimulates the manufacture of red cells by the bone marrow. Thus, persons who live in the rarefied air of mountainous regions have permanently a greater number of red cells (up to 8 million per cu mm) than those who live at lower altitudes. Their bone marrow is increased in amount.

The body's aim in increasing the number of red cells in the circumstances mentioned above seems clear. It has already been mentioned that the red cells give the blood its ability to carry oxygen. During muscular exercise more oxygen is required; at high altitudes the air holds less oxygen, and consequently there is less of it available for the body. In either of these instances an increase in the number of red cells will enable the blood to take up more oxygen from the air, and so to carry more to the cells of the tissues than would otherwise be possible.

COAGULATION, OR CLOTTING, OF BLOOD

If a blood vessel is opened and a small amount of blood collected in a test tube, it will remain perfectly fluid for 5 or 6 minutes. After this time the tube may be turned upside down, yet the blood will not be spilled. It will have been converted into a firm red jelly. The blood is then said to have coagulated, or clotted. If this blood jelly is allowed to stand for half an hour or so longer, a further change will take place. The blood will become separated into a small, firm red mass—the *clot*—and a clear yellowish fluid—the serum—which surrounds it. When, after this so-called *retraction* of the clot, the latter is examined under a powerful microscope, fine threads may be seen, forming a meshwork in which the red and white cells are held. The fine threads are composed of a protein called fibrin (Plates I*c* and I*e*). They were formed when the blood clotted and, by their contraction afterwards, have entrapped the cells as in a net. This has caused the separation of the clot from the serum. The whole process resembles somewhat the clotting of milk. The milk first loses its fluidity; later there follows a separation into curds and whey.

We all at one time or another have had a finger pricked or cut, or a tooth pulled. Such small injuries involve the opening of tiny blood vessels and the escape of blood. But little blood is lost, for soon after the blood escapes clotting occurs in and around the opening in the vessel, and the small hemorrhage ceases. If closure of the wound did not occur, death would certainly follow. The blood would have ebbed away drop by drop, and nothing could have stopped the steady drip. If we make even a tiny puncture in a full hot-water bottle, we know that within a short time most of the water will leak out. In the same way a large part of the blood would escape from the body from the smallest wound. Clotting of the blood is therefore an important factor in the arrest of hemorrhage, though by no means the only one (p. 164).

Very complicated physical and chemical changes underlie the clotting of blood, and many years have been spent by several investigators in unraveling the intricacies of the process. The actual jellying of the blood, so obvious to the naked eye, is due to the conversion of the soluble fibrinogen of the plasma (Ch. 6) into the insoluble threads of fibrin. The several processes leading to this final change will be described as simply as possible.

Four substances—**prothrombin, calcium, thromboplastin,** and **fibrinogen**—are essential for the clotting of the blood. Should any of these be absent, the blood remains fluid after it has been shed. The actual change in the blood when it clots is the conversion of the soluble fibrinogen to the insoluble fibrin. We have just seen that fibrin appears in the form of fine threads that entangle the cells of the blood. But cells are neither necessary for nor an integral part of the clotting process. Plasma quite free from cells clots as firmly as whole blood, the only difference being that the clot is white instead of red.

The first three substances mentioned above are required to bring about the change of fibrinogen to fibrin. In the presence of calcium, prothrombin is acted upon by thromboplastin and converted to the active enzyme called **thrombin**. Prothrombin is produced by the liver; it is present in the circulating blood but is inactive. The blood also contains calcium, but free thromboplastin is absent. Thromboplastin is contained in all the solid tissues. When blood escapes from a vessel it is inevitable that tissue cells are injured and thromboplastin freed. The thromboplastin acts with the calcium upon the prothrombin, changing it to thrombin. The thrombin then acts upon the fibrinogen and converts it to fibrin.

The sequence of events is summarized below:

prothrombin + thromboplastin + calcium = thrombin
(inactive)

thrombin + fibrinogen = fibrin
(active)

The blood as it flows in the blood vessels does not clot, because there is no free thromboplastin available to convert the prothrombin to thrombin. The blood glides along the smooth lining of the arteries and veins without injury, which would cause thromboplastin to be liberated. Any small amount of thrombin that might be produced in the circulating blood is neutralized by an antagonistic substance known as **antithrombin,** which is present in low concentration in the circulating blood. Thus, clotting within the vessels (**intravascular clotting, or thrombosis**), which would cause instant death, is guarded against.

Intravascular clotting is easily induced in animals by injecting thromboplastin into the circulation. An extract of any tissue may be used as a source of thromboplastin, but one prepared from lung or thymus is especially rich in this material.

The platelets when injured also liberate a substance that hastens the clotting process.

Anticoagulants. Substances that prolong or prevent the coagulation of the blood are called **anticoagulants.** Among such substances are **citrates** and **oxalates,** which combine with the calcium of the blood and prevent it from acting in the clotting mechanism; **hirudin,** an extract from the mouth glands of leeches; certain **dyes; dicumarin,** a material formed in decaying clover silage; and **heparin,** produced in the liver, lungs, and other tissues of mammals.

Dicumarin and heparin are of especial interest. The first of these has been shown to be the cause of bleeding in farm animals fed upon spoiled clover. It acts as an anticoagulant by reducing the prothrombin concentration of the blood. Heparin is a very powerful anticoagulant normally present in the body. Its function in the body is not known with certainty, but apparently it is not produced for the purpose of preventing coagulation within the vessels, for only insignificant amounts are present in the blood. Heparin antagonizes the action of thrombin, but it is different from the antithrombin already mentioned as being present in the circulating blood.

Vitamin K. In order to manufacture prothrombin the liver must be supplied with vitamin K. When the body lacks this vitamin the concentration of prothrombin in the blood falls to a low level and the blood clots very slowly. In such circumstances, dangerous bleeding may result from a trivial wound (see above). Some newborn babies bleed to death as a result of the mother's suffering from a deficiency of vitamin K. The hemorrhagic state is treated by the administration of this vitamin. A few hours after birth the newborn manufactures its own vitamin K, an effect for which bacteria in the intestine are responsible. Prevention of the disease consists of giving adequate amounts of the vitamin to the mother for some time before delivery.

Hemophilia. Hemophilia is a hereditary disease in which the blood does not clot, or does so very slowly. A victim of this disease may die of a very trivial wound, for it may be impossible to staunch the bleeding. A person with this disease is known popularly as a **bleeder.** The sufferers are always boys or men. But, though the disease appears only in the male members of a family, it is transmitted to the next generation only by the females. For instance, if a father is a bleeder, neither his sons nor his daughters will have the disease. His daughters, nevertheless, but not his sons, may transmit it to their sons, but not to their daughters; the latter, in turn, may again transmit it. In brief, the disease skips a generation; the grandsons of a bleeder may be affected but not his sons, daughters, or granddaughters. Color blindness and some other afflictions are inherited in an identical way.

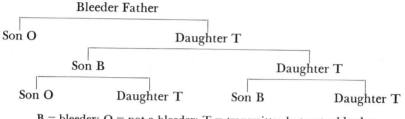

B = bleeder; O = not a bleeder; T = transmitter but not a bleeder.

HEMORRHAGE

The escape of blood from the blood vessels, from whatever cause, is spoken of as **hemorrhage.** The blood may escape from the body, as after the infliction of an open wound that severs the blood vessels, or it may pass into the tissues and so not be visible. A **cerebral hemorrhage,** for example, is the result of the rupture of a small vessel in the brain and the spilling of blood into the brain substance. Or, the bleeding may occur into one of the hollow organs, such as the stomach, in which case the blood is usually vomited, or into the intestine. Lastly, hemorrhage may occur into the lungs, and the blood may then be coughed up. When the blood appears upon the surface of any part of the body, the hemorrhage is called *external.* When the blood enters the tissues or one of the body cavities, we speak of *internal,* or *concealed, hemorrhage.*

The bleeding may be from an **artery,** from **capillaries,** or from a **vein.** When the bleeding is external, the type of vessel from which the blood escapes can usually be determined easily, since the bleeding from each kind of vessel, as a rule, shows distinctive characteristics—but a description of these must be postponed until the physiology of the circulation has been described (Part 4).

Whatever may be the cause of the hemorrhage, the effects upon the victim of the accident are the same, provided the loss of blood from the vessels is sufficiently great and occurs rapidly; the general effects are not very different whether the hemorrhage is internal or external.

General effects of hemorrhage. 1. *A great drop in the blood pressure occurs* if a large quantity of blood is lost within a short time. On the other hand, should the bleeding be slower, a large quantity may be lost with but little drop in pressure. It is easy to understand the reason for this; we know that if a water main should burst suddenly, the water pressure would fall very quickly, whereas a small leak in a water pipe would cause little change. However, anemia may result from slow bleeding.

2. *The breathing and pulse rate become rapid;* the increase in the pulse rate is often a valuable sign of internal bleeding.

Unless the loss of blood is very great, the body is able to overcome to a large extent these ill effects of hemorrhage. An animal may lose a quarter of the total amount of blood in its body and yet recover. A man would probably survive after the loss of a similar proportion of his blood. When a vessel is opened, protective measures immediately and automatically come into play. Further hemorrhage is checked, and an endeavor is made to use to best advantage the blood that still remains. Finally, the body strives to replace the blood that has been lost.

Means employed by the body to check hemorrhage and replace the blood.
1. *Closure of the wound* in the vessel and the stoppage of further bleeding is aided by the formation of a clot of blood. The fall in blood pressure that occurs at this time enables the clot to form more easily. In addition, the vessel's channel becomes narrower, since the artery wall contains elastic fibers that shorten when cut, while the wall of the vessel about the rupture or cut contracts and the opposed surfaces of the inner lining become stuck together.

2. *The reduced quantity of blood* following a sharp hemorrhage is used to the greatest possible advantage. The small arteries in regions of the body such as the skin, muscles, etc., which are not vital importance, are contracted. In this way the smaller quantity of blood that remains is directed to regions such as the heart muscle and vital parts of the brain. These parts must, of course, be supplied with oxygen at all costs.

3. *Contraction of the spleen* may add a pint or more of blood to the general circulation to make up for that which has been lost.

4. *The blood vessels* draw upon the tissues to supply them with fluid in sufficient volume to replace the lost blood. Though the tissue fluid contains no red cells, it enables the vessels to be better filled, and so the blood pressure may rise again to near the normal level. Due to altered relationships between osmotic pressure and blood pressure (Ch. 1), the passage of fluid into the vessels from the tissues occurs within a remarkably short time after the blood has been shed. When a pint or more of blood is removed from a person for transfusion purposes, the lost fluid is replaced within an hour or two. The removal of water from the tissues accounts for the intense thirst from which the subjects of hemorrhage suffer. The tissues, including those of the mouth and salivary glands, become drier than usual. This arouses the sensation of thirst. The drinking of fluids is for this reason a valuable measure in aiding nature's efforts to restore the volume of the blood to normal.

5. *The number of red cells* is restored to normal as rapidly as possible. Since at first the blood volume is replenished to a large extent by

tissue fluids, the blood is at this time poorer than normal in red cells, and thus is paler. It may be several days or weeks, according to the recuperative powers of the individual, the amount of blood lost, diet, etc., before the number of red cells returns to normal.[7] The bone marrow increases its production and, in its haste to increase the red cell population of the blood, may in many cases turn out cells that are not quite mature. Reticulocytes and even a few nucleated cells may for this reason be found in the blood stream.

Artificial means employed for the restoration of the blood volume after hemorrhage. If the amount of blood that has been shed is so great that the body is unable to meet the emergency unaided, some fluid must be injected into the patient's veins to act as a substitute for the lost blood. The fluids that have been used for this purpose are the following:

1. Saline solution
2. A solution of a suitable colloid material
3. Human serum or plasma
4. Human blood

1. *Saline solution* is a 0.9-percent solution of sodium chloride (ordinary salt) in sterile water. It has been used extensively in the past but has not proved very successful. Its shortcomings have been recognized since World War I. The chief fault of saline is that it seeps through the thin membranous walls of the capillaries and floods the tissues. A short time after it has been injected, the blood volume is no greater than before. The molecule of sodium chloride is too small to be held back by the capillary wall. It exerts little or no osmotic pressure and, consequently, cannot retain water within the circulation.

2. *Colloidal solutions of nonhuman origin*—gum acacia, isinglass and gelatin, etc.—have been tried as substitutes for blood. Of course such substitutes do not carry oxygen in any important amount, since they do not contain red cells. But in many instances of hemorrhage it is not necessary to replace the red cells, for the body possesses many more than are absolutely required to sustain life. A large quantity of blood can be removed from an animal by bleeding without causing death, provided that the blood volume can be quickly restored and the blood pressure raised to near the normal level. This can be done with a cell-free fluid having as osmotic pressure of nearly the same value as that of plasma. The same holds true for man. The important thing is to restore the blood volume and thus raise the blood pressure (Fig. 7.2)

A solution, in order to be a suitable blood substitute, must not escape too freely from the circulation, as saline does. Its molecules should

---

[7] It has been found that after 400 cc of blood have been drawn for transfusion purposes 50 to 60 days elapse before the number of red cells returns to normal. Good food, iron, and an adequate supply of vitamins will reduce the time required for the restoration of the normal erythrocyte concentration.

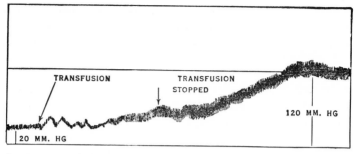

Fig. 7.2. Record of the blood pressure of a dog that was bled to the extent of 50 percent of its total blood volume and then given a transfusion with a 6-percent solution of isinglass. The blood pressure, as a result of the loss of blood, fell to the very low level of 20 mm Hg and the animal was on the point of death when the transfusion was started. The time from the commencement of the transfusion to the point where the blood pressure was restored to normal was about 10 minutes. *(Taylor and Moorehouse.)*

be as nearly as possible the size of the molecules of the plasma proteins and consequently should exert nearly the same osmotic pressure. The solution should, of course, have no toxic effect and cause no rise in temperature. Isinglass, prepared from the air bladders of fish, gelatin, or dextran (a carbohydrate), answers these requirements most satisfactorily in so far as artificial—that is, nonhuman—blood substitutes are concerned. These materials are used as 5- or 6-percent solutions in saline.

3. *Human serum or plasma* from voluntary donors came into extensive use during World War II. After the blood has been drawn and allowed to clot (unless plasma is to be used), it is centrifuged to separate the serum, which is then dried in bottles under a high vacuum. The dry mass that remains consists of the proteins and salts, and requires only the addition of distilled water to make a fluid ready for use as a blood substitute. Human serum in the dry form has the great advantage that it can be shipped conveniently and does not deteriorate even after several months. The process of preparation must, of course, be carried out under the most exacting conditions in order to ensure sterility. When plasma is used, an anticoagulant is added to the blood before it is centrifuged.

4. *Human blood* is obviously the ideal fluid for the replacement of the blood that has been lost, for it furnishes erythrocytes in addition to restoring the volume of the blood. In severe hemorrhage or shock (Ch. 11) it is superior to any other transfusion fluid. Nevertheless, its use is accompanied by very grave danger to the patient unless special precautions are taken. This danger lies in the fact that the mixing of the bloods of different individuals sometimes caused the red cells to mass together (Plate I*d*). This is spoken of as **agglutination.** Some of the small vessels —the capillaries—have a very fine caliber indeed. They may be so narrow that they will permit the red cells to pass along only in single file. It is

easily seen, then, that if a number of cells become "glued" together into masses, they will, upon reaching these fine vessels, block them and prevent a flow of blood through the regions these vessels normally supply. Occlusion of the vessels of the brain, heart, or lungs in this way may cause almost instant death.

The agglutinated cells disintegrate and the hemoglobin, which escapes into the plasma, is excreted by the kidney. Being insoluble in the acid urine, it blocks and damages the fine tubules of the kidney and thus brings urine formation to a standstill. In many, if not in most instances, this is the cause of death following the transfusion of unsuitable blood.

Before the blood of one person (the donor) can be injected into the veins of another (the recipient), the bloods of the two individuals must be tested to see whether they react in the manner described above. Samples of the two bloods are diluted with saline; they are mixed together, and the mixture is examined under a microscope.[8] If the corpuscles become agglutinated, the donor's blood is unsuitable; it is termed **incompatible.** Another individual whose blood is **compatible** must then be found who will offer his blood for transfusion.

The incompatibility of two bloods may even be detected with the naked eye; for, when the bloods are mixed, if agglutination has occurred, the cells form groups large enough to be seen and appear like grains of cayenne pepper floating upon the surface of a clear fluid. If the bloods are compatible, this does not occur, for the cells remain separate from one another and so cannot be seen by the unaided eye. The mixture remains a uniformly clear, pinkish fluid, just like any sample of diluted blood.

The bloods of all races of the world fall into four groups, according to their agglutinating reactions. The reaction relationships between the groups are rather complicated and can be touched upon only lightly. The four groups are designated, respectively, by the letters O, A, B, and AB. Nearly 90 percent of persons of European stock belong to either group O (45 percent) or group A (42 percent); only 10 percent belong to group B, and 3 percent to group AB. The compatibility or incompatibility of the blood of one group with the blood of any one of the other three has been studied exhaustively and is known in a general way. Thus, the blood of group A in the great majority of instances is compatible with the blood of group AB, but is incompatible with the blood of group B. Also, group O blood is compatible with the blood of any one of the other three groups. That is to say, the blood of a person belonging to group O would not, in most cases, be agglutinated when transfused into a patient belonging to any of the other groups. For this reason, members of group O have been called **universal donors.** It is never safe,

---

[8] The most exact and safest method of testing, known as *cross matching*, is usually carried out. It consists in mixing the diluted blood of the donor with the serum of the recipient, and then the diluted blood of the recipient with the serum of the donor.

however, to act upon this assumption, for exceptions occur and a dangerous if not a fatal reaction may result. Before transfusion the two bloods (donor's and recipient's) must be tested directly as mentioned above.

The incompatibility of the bloods of two persons belonging to certain of the groups given above is a type of **antigen-antibody reaction.** The corpuscles contain the antigen, the antibody is contained in the serum (Ch. 11). The latter being an agglutinating antibody is called an **agglutinin;** the antigen is called an **agglutinogen.** We may also speak of the agglutinin that agglutinates the corpuscles of group A as **anti-A,** and those that react with the cells of group B as **anti-B.**

The reactions between the corpuscles and sera of the four blood groups is shown in tabular form below.

Corpuscles	Serum			
	O	A	B	AB
O	—	—	—	—
A	+	—	+	—
B	+	+	—	—
AB	+	+	+	—

+ means agglutination; — means no agglutination.

The Rh factor. Besides the antigens just described, which are generally referred to as the ABO groups, several others have been discovered within the last few years. The most important of these is called the Rh factor, from its having been discovered in the blood of a species of monkey known as *Rhesus* which is used in laboratory experiments. This antigen is found in the blood of 85 percent of persons of European stock. Blood that contains it is called **Rh positive;** blood that does not possess this factor is called **Rh negative.** The Rh factor has been the cause of many transfusion accidents in the past. When the history of these accidents was studied, it became clear that they had occurred either in persons who had received a transfusion some time before the one that had caused the reaction, or in women who had been recently delivered; not infrequently the baby was stillborn. It was also revealed that all the patients had Rh-negative blood and that those of the first group had received transfusions of Rh-positive blood. The first transfusion had caused the production in the patient's serum of an Rh antibody that destroyed the cells received in the second transfusion. The reaction caused when a woman recently confined is transfused is due to the baby being Rh positive (inherited from the father) and the mother Rh negative; the fetus in the uterus has therefore immunized the mother against the Rh antigen. In

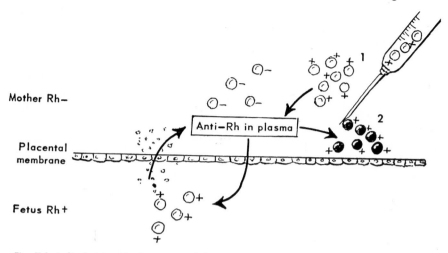

Fig. 7.3. *Left,* showing the formation of the anti-Rh factor in the mother's blood (Rh−) by antigen from fetus (Rh+), a reaction occurring when the mother is transfused with Rh+ blood; the anti-Rh factor is transmitted across the placenta to fetal blood and causes hemolysis. *Right,* showing the effect on injected cells of transfusions of Rh+ blood into an Rh− patient; (1) indicates a first blood transfusion of Rh+ blood into an Rh− patient, the anti-Rh factor formed as a result causes a reaction (2) with cells of a second transfusion.

other words, the latter has crossed the placenta into the maternal circulation and caused the production of an antibody (anti-Rh factor) that, if the mother should receive a transfusion of Rh-positive blood, causes the destruction of the injected cells.[9] Another damaging result of Rh incompatibility is the hitherto usually fatal disease of the blood of the unborn and newborn child known as *Erythroblastosis fetalis,* or *hemolytic disease of the newborn.* It is due to the anti-Rh factor produced in the mother's blood having crossed the placenta to cause destruction of the fetal red cells. This disease rarely occurs in a first pregnancy. Apparently, two or more pregnancies in which this type of incompatibility exists are required in order for a sufficient amount of antibody to be produced (Fig. 7.3).

CARBON MONOXIDE POISONING

Hemoglobin combines with other gases besides oxygen. One of these is coal gas, or carbon monoxide (CO), which is present as an impurity in the ordinary gas used for cooking and heating. It is also given off from

[9] It will be recalled that though the fetal and maternal bloods do not mix, an interchange of certain materials occurs across the placental membrane. These substances include, apparently, fragments of the fetal corpuscles (antigen) and maternal antibodies.

the exhaust of an automobile engine. In a remarkably short time a sufficient quantity of the gas may be produced by an engine to render the air in a closed garage deadly poisonous.

Carbon monoxide is worthless for living cells. If part of the hemoglobin has already combined with this gas, the pigment then cannot combine with as much oxygen. In other words, if the cargo space of the red cell is already partly occupied by the valueless gas, the cell is unable to take on a full load of oxygen. Death will result when the oxygen load is reduced below what is necessary to keep the cells alive. A victim of carbon monoxide poisoning, therefore, dies because a large proportion of his blood has been rendered useless—just as surely as if it had escaped from the body through hemorrhage.[10]

Thus, carbon monoxide is a deadly poisonous gas because it prevents the carriage of oxygen to the tissues.

There are three other facts that make carbon monoxide dangerous.

1. Hemoglobin combines much more easily with carbon monoxide than with oxygen. Should the blood be offered carbon monoxide and oxygen in equal amounts, it will combine with 250 parts of the former gas for every 1 of the latter. Consequently, though the air contains plenty of oxygen and only a small proportion of carbon monoxide, the blood loads up with the latter gas. Carbon monoxide has no smell, taste, or color. It is therefore impossible for anyone to detect it by ordinary means.

It was the practice in coal mines and during tunneling operations in World War I to use a canary or a mouse to reveal the presence of a dangerous concentration of carbon monoxide. If the air was contaminated by this gas, the small animal, owing to its higher metabolism, would succumb long before a man would be seriously affected, and in this way warning was given of the danger.

2. Carbon monoxide gas, when it combines with hemoglobin, forms a compound that, unlike oxyhemoglobin, is broken down again with the greatest difficulty. That is, hemoglobin not only combines very readily with carbon monoxide but releases it again only very slowly. Resuscitation of a victim of carbon monoxide poisoning is for this reason very difficult, even though artificial respiration is carried out in fresh air.

3. When the brain does not receive enough oxygen, the mind develops strange ideas and notions that may lead a person to perform foolish acts or become very stubborn and unreasonable. For this reason he may remain in an atmosphere containing carbon monoxide, though he knows the danger and might easily escape. Later, paralysis of the lower part of the body may occur, and the victim is then unable to remove himself before unconsciousness supervenes.

---

[10] Carbon monoxide also poisons protoplasm directly, bringing living processes to a standstill. The concentration of the gas for this action is much higher than that required to cause death by combining with the hemoglobin.

8

The Spleen. The White Blood Cells, or Leucocytes. The Platelets

THE SPLEEN

The spleen is an organ about the size of a man's fist, lying behind and below the stomach (Fig. 8.1). The blood is contained within a spongelike tissue called the **splenic pulp** into which the blood vessels, arterioles, and venules open. The fine interlacing partitions in the pulp of the spleen are called **trabeculae.** This spongelike structure enables the organ to hold a relatively large quantity of blood—about one eighth of the total amount in the body. The spleen is furnished with bands of smooth muscle that both encircle it and pass through its substance. It also contains islands of tissue of the same structure and function as that composing the lymph nodes (Ch. 10).

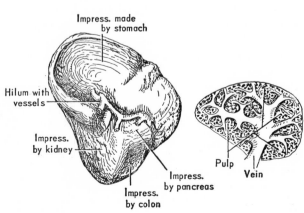

Fig. 8.1. The visceral surface of the spleen, with vessels leaving and entering the hilum. Section of spleen on right, showing pulp of spleen and tributaries of splenic vein.

Impress. made by stomach

Hilum with vessels

Impress. by kidney

Impress. by colon

Impress. by pancreas

Pulp

Vein

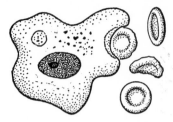

Fig. 8.2. Giant cell (macrophage) of the spleen engulfing a red cell.

The functions of the spleen have been touched upon incidentally in preceding pages, but some additional details may be given here. The spleen contains certain very large cells known as **macrophages** (Gk. *macros*, large + *phago*, I eat). These cells are among the most interesting in the body. Unlike most other cells, they are capable of moving from place to place and apparently live an independent existence. They resemble the amoeba (Ch. 2); they lurk in the pools of blood found throughout the spongelike substance of the spleen and are able to devour wornout erythrocytes, microorganisms, or fine particles of almost any foreign material. They are about eight times the size of a red cell, so that any red cell that has become old or has lost its vitality falls prey to them readily (Fig. 8.2). It is these cells that are responsible for the removal of the fragments of broken-down red cells from the circulation. For this reason the spleen is sometimes spoken of as the graveyard of the red cells. There is no evidence that the macrophages of the normally functioning spleen destroy young and healthy cells.

The spleen also serves as a receptacle for a large quantity of blood, which has a high concentration of red cells. In times of stress or emergency, when the body requires a greater quantity of circulating fluid and a greater number of erythrocytes—at high temperatures, during muscular exercise, at high altitudes, or in cases of poisoning by such gases as carbon monoxide—the muscle fibers, with which the spleen is liberally supplied, contract and force the extra blood into the general circulation, very much as fluid is squeezed from a sponge (Fig. 8.3). In this way, when the body is in urgent need of oxygen, millions of red cells, each with a full load of oxygen, come to its assistance.

In the embryo, erythrocytes and all types of leucocytes are produced in the spleen, but after birth the spleen, in health, manufactures only lymphocytes.

Fig. 8.3. Changes in the volume of the spleen as a result of emotional excitement. (After Barcroft.) Left: R, rest; C, dog sees cat. The numbers represent the relative sizes of the dog's spleen. Right; —·—·—, rest; ——————, smells cat; . . . ., hears cat; ——————, sees cat; — — —, chases cat.

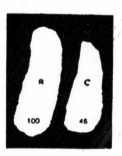

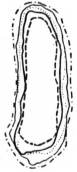

WHITE BLOOD CELLS, OR LEUCOCYTES

The white blood cells are larger on the average than the red cells and differ from the latter in other ways. They possess a nucleus; they contain no hemoglobin; and most of them can propel themselves from place to place. The leucocytes are much less numerous than the red cells. Only about 8000 are contained in a cubic millimeter of blood, so they are outnumbered 600 to 1 by the red cells. When a smear of blood is examined under the microscope, the white cells are seen sparsely scattered among the red cells. The different varieties of white cells are shown in Plate IIa and Figure 8.4.

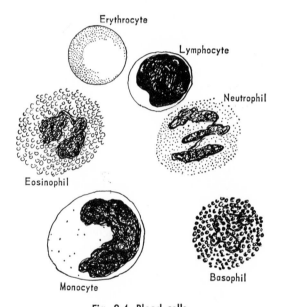

Fig. 8.4. Blood cells.

There are three main types of these cells: (1) *polymorphonuclears, or granulocytes;* (2) *lymphocytes, nongranular leucocytes,* or *agranulocytes;* and (3) *monocytes.* All varieties of granulocytes are produced in the red bone marrow only. The lymphocytes are formed in lymphoid tissue—the lymph nodes, spleen, etc.

Polymorphonuclears have a nucleus with from two to five parts (Fig. 8.5). The nucleus resembles a skein of yarn that has been twisted and bent so as to form knobs called **lobes,** connected by strands or threads. The number of lobes increases as the cell becomes older. In the youngest cells the division of the nucleus into two lobes is just commencing. A little later two lobes are clearly evident. In the next oldest cells three lobes have developed, and so on, until in the oldest cells the nucleus is comprised of five lobes. The ages of the cells as indicated by the number of nuclear lobes are termed the stages of Arneth (Fig. 8.4). The polymorphonuclears also differ from the lymphocytes in that their protoplasm is speckled with fine particles, or granules. They are therefore known also as **granulocytes.** According to the manner in which these granules take up certain dyes, three types may be recognized:

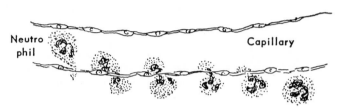

Fig. 8.5. Diapedesis.

1. Those containing granules that stain a violet color with neutral dyes are called **neutrophils.**

2. Those with granules that stain red with acid dyes, such as eosin, are called **eosinophils** (Plate IIa).

3. Those with granules that stain blue with basic dyes are known as **basophils.**

The neutrophils are by far the most numerous, constituting from 65 to 70 percent of all the white cells. The eosinophils and basophils are very few in number, the former constituting no more than 3 or 4 percent of the white cells, and the latter 0.5 percent.

Lymphocytes have a single large nucleus surrounded by a narrow rim of cytoplasm. They are about the size of an erythrocyte or a little larger, and constitute around 25 percent of all the white cells. A large mononuclear, nongranular white cell, called at one time the *large lymphocyte,* is really a lymphoblast; that is, a young or primitive lymphocyte. It is found in the lymphoid tissues but rarely in normal blood.

An increase in the number of lymphocytes (**lymphocytosis**) often accompanies chronic infections. They are also increased in the disease known as *infectious mononucleosis.* A decrease in the number of these cells in the circulation is called **lymphopenia.** It occurs in pneumonia and certain other acute infections.

Monocytes are large cells very much resembling the lymphoblasts. Their nucleus is usually deeply indented or horseshoe shaped, and their cytoplasm contains very fine granules. They are found only in small numbers in blood—about 8 percent of all white cells. They, like the neutrophil leucocytes, are phagocytic, though they are more active in chronic than in acute inflammatory processes.

An increase of the leucocytes above the normal number is called **leucocytosis,** which may be caused by any acute inflammatory condition, especially if septic in nature. In appendictis, for example, a count of the leucocytes is an important diagnostic aid.

Whereas leucocytosis is a normal defense reaction, **leukemia** is a malignant increase, often enormous (up to over 500,000 per cu mm), in the number of leucocytes. It is really a sarcoma of the leucocyte-forming tissues (bone marrow or lymphoid structures). The disease may involve the granulocytes (*myelogenous leukemia*), the lymphocytes (*lymphatic leukemia*), or the monocytes (*monocytic leukemia*). Not only is there a great increase in the number of white cells but they are abnormal, being of a primitive type, that is, in an early stage of their development.

Not only bacteria but also many materials that the body is better without—any useless refuse—are devoured and removed by the neutrophils. When, for instance, the tail and gills of the tadpole disappear as it develops into a frog, the neutrophyl leucocytes are responsible for the removal of these structures, which are of no further use. It is in this way also that dead tissue— even diseased bone—is separated from the living, or a dead tooth loosened. These cells, therefore, are often called the body's scavengers. Actually they serve as the tissues' first line of defense against invading bacteria. **Phagocyte** (Gk. *phago,* I eat + *k(c)ytos,* cell) is a more technical term by which these cells are known. The scavenging function itself is called **phagocytosis** (Fig. 8.6).

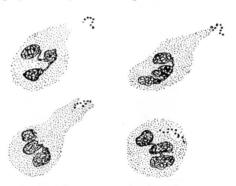

Fig. 8.6. Phagocytosis. Sketches of a neutrophil at 1-minute intervals engulfing a group of bacteria.

Certain synthetic drugs used in medicine sometimes cause a disease known as **agranulocytosis** (meaning the absence, or great reduction in number, of granulocytes). The disease is usually fatal because the body is unable to defend itself effectively against virulent microorganisms. Some of the drugs that cause agranulocytosis are of the greatest value in the treatment of disease, but this unfortunate action that they sometimes exert must always be borne in mind.

The functions of the leucocytes. The neutrophils very much resemble the amoeba, described in Chapter 2. Like the microscopic animal found in ponds or ditch water, these white cells of the blood can move from place to place. They wander about. They are not confined within the blood vessels, but leave the circulation through the joints between the endothelial cells of the capillary walls—an action called *diapedesis*—and move freely through the body fluids to any point to which by some un-known influence they may be attracted. They protrude, like the amoeba, a small part of their substance, and with this, as though it were a tongue, hand, or foot, they seize food or draw themselves along. These prehensile or locomotory parts, improvised at the moment, are called **pseudopodia** (Gk., false foot).

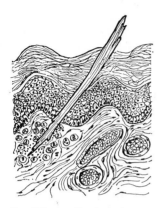

Fig. 8.7. A collection of neu-trophils around a germ-carry-ing rose thorn embedded in the skin.

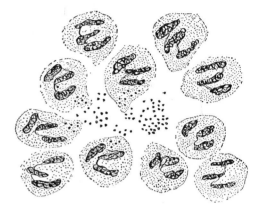

Fig. 8.8. Neutrophils surrounding and ingesting bacteria.

This propensity of the neutrophil leucocytes can be readily demon-strated by injecting a solution of fine particles into the subcutaneous tissues of a laboratory animal. If a watery suspension of finely ground charcoal is injected and the tissue examined a short time later, a swarm of neutrophils will be found collected at the point of injection. Moving about, here and there, they ingest the carbon grains until their cytoplasm is filled with them. This activity of the neutrophils makes them of the greatest value to the body. They defend it from the attacks of germs and materials injurious to the other cells, which are not nearly so well able to protect themselves.

The Russian scientist Metchnikoff discovered the action of the neu-trophils about 70 years ago and wrote vivid descriptions of what he saw under the microscope when they were carrying out their work. He drove a small rose thorn beneath the skin of a young starfish. Next day he observed that the sharp point of the rose thorn was surrounded by large numbers of leucocytes.

Exactly the same thing happens when a splinter runs into one's finger. The white cells are attracted to the spot and devour any bacteria that have been carried into the tissue; the splinter is dislodged by the removal of injured tissue surrounding it (Fig. 8.7). When microorganisms pass through the barrier of the skin and enter the deeper tissues, an alarm in some mysterious way is sounded instantly throughout the body. Millions of white cells, which have been hidden away like troops in reserve, are rushed to the threatened spot. They vigorously attack the bacteria (Fig. 8.8), and though large numbers of the invaders are destroyed, many leucocytes too fall victims to the deadly bacterial toxins.

The mixture of dead leucocytes, fluids, and bacteria together form a yellowish matter that is generally known as **pus.** The area hollowed out of the tissue and filled with this material is called an *abscess.* The number of white cells in the blood at this time may be 20,000 or 30,000, instead of the normal of 7000 or 8000. If it were not for the large numbers of leucocytes that surround an infected area, living germs would soon enter the blood; blood poisoning (*septicemia*) would result. Life or death is very often decided by the way in which these leucocytes do their work.

The lymphocytes are the source of the *gamma globulin* of the blood plasma that is closely associated with the production of various antibodies and is therefore of great importance in the development of immunity against bacterial and viral infections. The plasma globulin is produced directly from the substance of the lymphocytes. Their cytoplasm dissolves into the tissue fluids and eventually is taken up by the blood plasma. This process of serum globulin production through lymphocyte dissolution is under the influence of the hormone of the adrenal cortex. An injection of the hormone causes an increase in gamma globulin and antibody production, and a decrease in the number of circulating lymphocytes. It also causes a pronounced reduction in the number of circulating eosinophils (**eosinopenia**). Little is known of the function of the eosinophils, but they are increased in number in certain diseases, notably allergic states, such as asthma, and in infestation with intestinal worms and some other parasitic affections.

BLOOD PLATELETS

The blood platelets are small, flat, colorless cells or cell-like structures[1] about half the size of a red corpuscle. They number about 250,000 per cu mm of bood (Plates I*e* and II*a*). They are important elements in the blood-clotting process (Ch. 7). It is generally believed that the platelets are formed in the red bone marrow.

[1] Not all authorities are agreed concerning the precise origin of the platelets.

9

The Extravascular Fluids,
The Lymphatic System

EXTRACELLULAR AND INTRACELLULAR FLUID

The fluid lying outside the blood vessels is colorless, since it does not contain hemoglobin and, for the most part, contains no cells. It lies in the spaces between the tissue cells—the so-called **tissue spaces**— and in the serous cavities (pleural and peritoneal cavities, pericardial sac). It includes, as well, the cerebrospinal fluid within the skull and spinal canal, and the fluid known as lymph, contained within the lymphatic system. The extravascular fluid in these situations is called **extracellular,** for a still larger amount of water is contained within the tissue cells. This is called the **intracellular** fluid. The blood plasma, of course, is also extracellular.

All these fluids consist mainly of water, and it is usual to speak of them as extracellular or intracellular water. They vary somewhat in composition in different situations. The fluid of the tissue spaces (the **tissue,** or **interstitial, fluid**) is fluid that has filtered from the blood plasma through the capillary wall. It, therefore, closely resembles the plasma in its composition; but it has a much lower concentration in protein. The lymph drained from the tissue spaces is identical in composition with the tissue fluid, whereas the lymph in the lymphatics of the abdomen (thoracic duct) usually contains a considerable quantity of fatty material.

The animal body is composed largely of water; the total water of the body amounts to about 70 percent of its total weight. This total body water, which is the water of the blood plus the extravascular water (extracellular and intracellular), can be measured in the human subject by injecting intravenously a substance that mixes with or is dissolved in the

178

water throughout the body, and that can be detected in a sample of blood drawn shortly after the injection and analyzed. From the degree of dilution of the injected substance in the sample, the total body water can be readily calculated. If one wishes to know separately the amounts of intracellular and of extracellular water, a substance is injected that is dissolved in and uniformly distributed throughout the extracellular water of the body, but *does not enter the cells.* The figure for the amount of extracellular water subtracted from that of the total water gives the volume of the intracellular water.

Normal values. The partitions of the body water and their values as percentages of the body weight are shown in Figure 9.1.

Water balance. The values for the body water and its several divisions remain remarkably constant in the healthy adult. This depends upon a nice balance of the water intake and output. During growth, however, or during a period of convalescence from an illness, when new tissue is being formed or tissue is being repaired and the body weight is increasing, water is retained; that is, the output of water is less than the intake. This is because a large volume of water is laid down with the protein of the newly formed tissue, and for purposes incident to the increase in the size of the body.

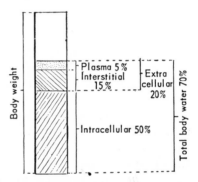

Fig. 9.1. Diagram showing the divisions of the body water.

The water intake. Water is taken into the body in food and drink. The former, either solid or semisolid, supplies the body with a considerable quantity of water. Lean beef yields a relatively large amount of water, as does also carbohydrate though apparently dry. Of the three foodstuffs, only pure fat, such as butter, is almost or quite devoid of water. But, paradoxically, pure fat supplies much more water to the body than *pure* protein (raw meat is 25 percent protein and 75 percent water) or pure, perfectly dry starch. The water of pure protein or starch, though not present in these substances themselves, *is formed when they are metabolized in the body.* This is called the **water of metabolism.** It is explained in Chapter 28 that the oxidation of the carbon of the food produces carbon dioxide (CO_2), while oxidation of the hydrogen yields water (H_2O). Thus, 100 grams of fat, when oxidized in the body, produce 107 grams of water, and in the metabolism of the same amount of pure starch or protein, 41 and 55 grams of water, respectively, are formed. From an ordinary mixed meal, the body derives daily about 350 grams of water from the oxidation of the foodstuffs.

The total daily water intake from all sources averages about 2500 cc.

Only about 1000 cc of this is taken as pure water or as beverages, such as coffee, tea, milk, beer, etc.

The water output. In order that the water balance be maintained, the output of water must, of course, exactly equal the intake. This extremely nice adjustment is dependent largely upon the sense of thirst, which regulates the intake. The water output by the several routes is given in the following table. The output is also regulated through the posterior lobe of the pituitary gland.

	cc
Skin (loss by sweating or evaporation of water)	500
Expired air (that is saturated with water)	350
Urine	1500
Feces	150
Total	2500

These values are for a normal body temperature and average air temperature and humidity. In hot climates, the water loss from the skin and lungs may be several times greater than the average figure given, reaching, in extremely high temperatures, several liters daily.

Dehydration. Reduction of the total body water below the normal level is called **dehydration.** It may be due to the following:

1. *The simple deprivation of water,* as in persons shipwrecked or lost in an arid country; or to the refusal to drink, as in the insane.

2. *The excessive loss of water* from the body, as in severe diarrhea or vomiting; or to high fever in which the loss through skin and lungs is excessive and the patient too weak to drink sufficient water, his need being not recognized by his attendants.

3. *The depletion of salt* and the subsequent loss of water. Fluid can be retained in the body only as an isotonic solution (Ch. 1); that is, its osmotic pressure, due to dissolved salts, must be the same as that of the plasma, neither higher nor lower. Consequently, if substances (electrolytes) are lost from the body, water must be excreted as well, in order that the body fluids shall remain isotonic. Dehydration from this cause, sometimes called secondary dehydration because water is lost secondarily as a result of the loss of electrolytes, may result from the removal of normal secretions in excessive amounts, or following repeated injections of glucose solution, electrolytes then being leached, as it were, from the body.

THE LYMPHATIC SYSTEM

The lymph vessels, or lymphatics, commence at the periphery as a close network of very fine vessels (Figs. 9.2, 9.3). They drain away the fluid that has passed through the walls of the capillaries into the spaces of the tissues. The nature of this fluid—the *lymph*—contained in the lymphatic system has been described.

Traced centrally (that is, toward the root of the neck), the lymph vessels increase progressively in size through the confluence of the smaller lymph channels. They are not smooth like the arteries and veins but have a nodular appearance due to the presence of constrictions at regular intervals along their course. The constrictions are due to the attachment of valves on the interior of the walls of the vessels that direct the flow of lymph. The lymph vessels are disposed in a superficial and a deep set; in the neck and limbs the former run with the superficial veins, the latter with the main vessels and nerves. In the abdomen and pelvis they are in close relation to the aorta and its branches.

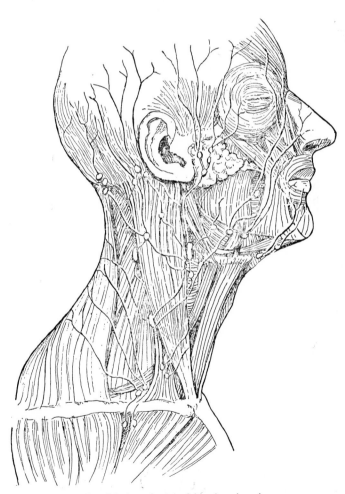

Fig. 9.2. Lymphatics of head and neck.

Only a few of the largest of the lymphatics have been given specific names; the two main vessels are called the *thoracic duct* and the *right lymphatic duct*.

The thoracic duct commences in the lower part of the abdomen in a saclike enlargement called the *cisterna chyli,* situated at the level of the upper two lumbar vertebrae, and on the right side of the abdominal aorta. The lymphatic trunk then ascends through the abdomen and thorax to the junction of the left internal jugular and subclavian veins (Fig. 9.3). Its contents are thus returned to the blood. The thoracic duct receives tributaries from both lower limbs, abdomen, left half of the thorax, left upper limb, and left half of the head and neck. In the abdomen this vessel receives lymph from the intestines and liver, as well as from other abdominal viscera; a certain proportion of digested fat, which is not absorbed directly into the blood (portal system), passes into the lymph of the thoracic duct; the lymph in this situation is more usually, however, referred to as **chyle.** It is turbid or milky in appearance after a meal containing much fat. The fine lymph vessels of the intestinal villi (Ch. 27) are called **lacteals** (L. *lac,* milk) from the milky appearance of their contents.

The right lymphatic duct drains lymph from that part of the body not tributary to the thoracic duct, namely, the right side of the head and neck, the right upper limb, and the right side of the thoracic wall. This vessel runs downwards in the lower part of the neck and empties into the blood stream at the point where the right internal jugular vein joins the right subclavian vein.

The lymph nodes, which are sometimes, though less suitably, called lymph glands, are almond- or bean-shaped structures situated at strategic points in the course of the lymph vessels. In two situations especially, the lymph nodes can be readily felt in the healthy subject—above the inner condyle of the humerus, and in the groin. But nodes are to be found in groups or chains in all parts of the body in the course of the lymphatics draining the various organs and areas, for example, running down the neck, below the lower jaw, at the nape of the neck, above the clavicle, in the axilla, in the thorax, in the abdomen and pelvis, and behind the knee. They are too numerous to describe in detail but are shown in Figures 9.2 and 9.3.

Structure of the lymph vessels and lymph nodes. The walls of the large lymph vessels consist of three coats, an *external* of connective tissue, a *middle* of smooth muscle, and an *inner* of a single layer of endothelial cells. The medium-sized vessels have no middle coat, and the finest vessels —the lymph capillaries—are composed of endothelium alone, the continuation of the inner coat of the larger vessels.

The lymph nodes have a slight depression on one side, called the *hilum,* where the lymph vessels leave, and blood vessels and nerves enter

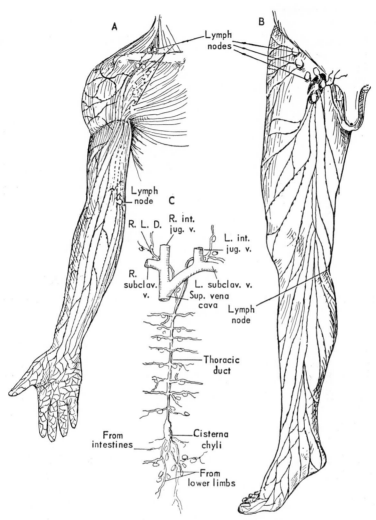

Fig. 9.3. Lymphatics, A, of upper limb; B, of lower limb. C shows entrance of thoracic duct and right lymphatic duct into subclavian vein. R. L. D., right lymphatic duct.

or leave. Within the node is a meshwork of connective tissue trabeculae, the spaces of which are filled with masses of densely packed lymphocytes (Fig. 9.4). Such *lymphoid tissue,* as it is called, is not peculiar to the lymph nodes but is found also in other situations, such as the thymus, spleen, tonsils, and adenoids (in the nasopharynx), and in the intestine. The collections of lymphoid tissue in the intestinal wall are known as *lymphatic nodules.*

After passing through the mesh of a lymph node, the lymph is col-

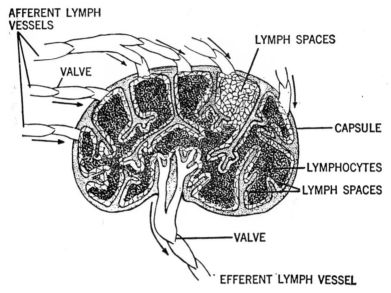

AFFERENT LYMPH VESSELS

VALVE

LYMPH SPACES

CAPSULE

LYMPHOCYTES

LYMPH SPACES

VALVE

EFFERENT LYMPH VESSEL

Fig. 9.4. Diagram of lymph node, sectioned to show internal structure; one area free of lymphocytes to show lymph spaces.

lected again by a number of lymph channels that spring from the convexity of the node and there join to reform the lymphatic trunk.

Functions of the lymph nodes. The lymph nodes perform three highly important functions: 1. They act as *filters* of the lymph in its course from the various organs and tissues to the point where it is returned to the blood. Any particulate matter, which includes microorganisms, is caught and held in the nodes and thus prevented from entering the blood stream. If it were not for these filters, general infection of the blood by pathogenic bacteria would be of common occurrence. When the foot, or any part of the lower limb or genitalia becomes infected, the nodes in the groin become swollen and tender, due to the localization there of the infecting organism. If the hand or arm is the seat of an infection, or the scalp or neck, the nodes at the elbow and axilla in the former instance, and those down the neck in the latter, may be involved similarly.

Within the nodes the bacteria are attacked and destroyed by large phagocytic cells (Ch. 8). The lymph nodes, therefore, must be looked upon as important elements of defense against the invasion of the blood by bacteria traveling the lymphatic paths. This function constitutes a second defense line, the leucocytes at the actual site of infection usually bearing the first shock of the attack.

2. *The production of lymphocytes.* Whereas the red marrow of the bones produces the red cells of the blood and the granular leucocytes, the lymphocytes are formed in the lymph nodes.

3. *The production of plasma protein.* Through the disintegration and dissolution of the lymphocytes which they contain in large numbers, the lymph nodes produce plasma globulin. This protein of the plasma is closely associated with the immune bodies (antibodies) through which bacteria and their toxic products are destroyed and antidoted. The disintegration of the lymphocytes within the lymph nodes and the production of antibodies appear to be controlled by the adrenocorticotrophic hormone of the pituitary body (Ch. 39). This immunizing function of the lymph nodes constitutes a third line of defense against infective agents.

The last two functions are not confined to the lymph nodes; the nodes possess these two functions because they are composed of lymphoid tissue. The manufacture of plasma globulin and of lymphocytes are functions of lymphoid tissue in general.

10

The Control of the
Reaction of the Blood
and Other Body Fluids

Reaction is a term that is used by the chemist in referring to the acid or alkaline nature of any solution (Ch. 1). A solution of sodium bicarbonate (baking soda), for example, has an alkaline reaction; acetic acid (vinegar) has an acid reaction. The reaction of the blood and tissue fluids is weakly alkaline. They have a pH around 7.43.

We hear much these days of "an acid condition of the system," "acidosis," "acid blood," and so on. The patent-medicine advertisers speak glibly of such conditions without having any clear idea of what they are saying. It cannot be stated too definitely that the blood never becomes acid except, rarely, in certain diseases when death is only a few hours away. Even then the pH falls only a little below 7.00, the neutral point.

With two exceptions, no fluid or tissue of the body is ever acid in reaction. The exceptions are the lining of the healthy stomach during the secretion of gastric juice, at which time the cells of the gastric glands have an acid reaction, and the fluid within the tubules of the kidney. But gastric digestion and the formation of urine are very specialized processes, and in so far as reaction is concerned the stomach and kidney are in a different class from other organs. In health, the reaction of the blood remains remarkably constant at about pH 7.43 and only in very serious disease does it become less alkaline.

Yet acids are continuously being formed in our bodies. Carbon dioxide, which is produced in the tissues by the burning of foodstuffs, acts, when dissolved in the blood, as a weak acid (**carbonic acid**). Lactic acid—an acid almost the same as that found in sour milk—is produced

186

in the muscles when they contract and in other active tissues. Large amounts of both carbonic and lactic acids are formed during muscular exercise, but unless the exercise is very severe the acid is quickly neutralized or removed—almost as soon as it is produced. Small amounts of hydrochloric, sulfuric, and other strong acids are being formed at all times in other active tissues. Consequently, the blood and tissues are always being threatened with having their reaction changed to acid, but as a result of other chemical changes that neutralize these acids immediately, no alteration of the blood reaction actually occurs.

In the first place, carbon dioxide, since it is a gas, is quickly eliminated from the body in the breath. We all know how one puffs and pants after muscular exercise. Lactic acid and other acids that cannot be got rid of as gas are neutralized in the blood and tissue fluids, both of which contain a fairly large amount of sodium bicarbonate. Any acid such as hydrochloric, tartaric, or lactic, when it comes into contact with sodium bicarbonate, is neutralized, and at the same time that neutralization occurs carbon dioxide is formed. The carbon dioxide evolved in the body by the action of acids upon sodium bicarbonate, just like the carbon dioxide produced when the foodstuffs are oxidized (Ch. 28), stimulates the respirations (Ch. 21) and is thus readily eliminated from the body.

The reaction between lactic acid and sodium bicarbonate is shown below. The neutral sodium lactate that results is removed by the kidneys. Thus:

sodium bicarbonate + lactic acid =   carbon dioxide   +   sodium lactate
                                    (removed by lungs)   (removed by kidneys)

The kidneys remove other acids from the body as well. The blood coming to the kidneys is alkaline, but the urine, which is derived from the plasma by filtration (Ch. 32), is acid. The kidney retains base and excretes acid and so aids in preserving the alkaline reaction of the body fluids. This is a most important function of the kidney, and one that is gravely impaired in severe kidney disease.

The alkali reserve. The alkaline substances in the blood and other body fluids, chiefly sodium bicarbonate, that serve to "buffer" acids and maintain the normal pH of these fluids is called the **alkali reserve.** In conditions in which there is an excessive production of acids, such as diabetes and nephritis, the alkali reserve is reduced. In other states, such as persistent vomiting (loss of hydrochloric acid), the alkali reserve is increased. A fall in the alkali reserve is called **acidosis;** a rise, **alkalosis.** There is no similar change in the reaction of the body fluids, owing to the buffering action of the alkali reserve. But should this reserve be reduced to the vanishing point, the pH falls; the condition then is called **acidemia.** If a great increase in bicarbonate occurs the pH of the body fluids rises; the term **alkalemia** is then applied.

11

Defensive Mechanisms Against Disease. Chemotherapy. Antibiotics. Surgical Shock. Anaphylaxis and Allergy

INFECTING AGENTS

Man, animals, and plants are constantly liable to attack by many lower forms of life—namely, **bacteria; fungi,** or **molds** (which cause ringworm and other affections of the skin) ; and **protozoa.** These latter are the infecting organisms in some of the most virulent of human diseases, such as *malaria, amoebic dysentery, African sleeping sickness,* etc. Bacteria and fungi belong to lower orders of the vegetable kingdom. Protozoa are unicellular animal forms (Fig. 11.1) .

The viruses, another large group of infecting agents, are the cause of a number of well-known diseases, such as *measles, mumps, chickenpox, shingles (herpes zoster), influenza,* one type of *pneumonia, anterior poliomyelitis (infantile paralysis), rabies, psittacosis* (a disease of parrots and allied species transmissible to man) , and the *common cold.* They are also responsible for several diseases of plants and even attack bacteria.

It is the general opinion that viruses are not living bodies but immense molecules, or groups of molecules, of nucleoprotein on the border line between the animate and the inanimate worlds. Though viruses vary considerably in size they are all smaller than the smallest of the bacteria that they sometimes infect and destroy, being then known as *bacteriophage.* Most viruses are invisible under the ordinary microscope, but show up as oval or round bodies under the electron microscope. They

188

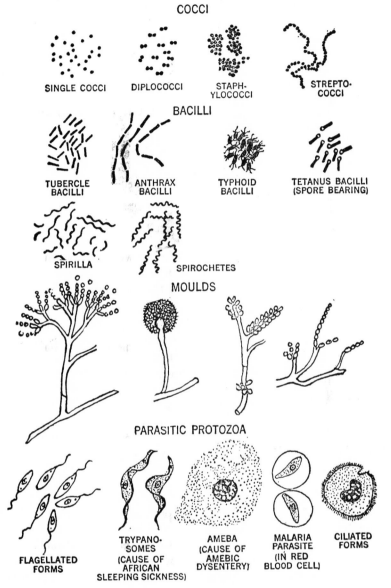

COCCI

SINGLE COCCI   DIPLOCOCCI   STAPH-YLOCOCCI   STREPTO-COCCI

BACILLI

TUBERCLE BACILLI   ANTHRAX BACILLI   TYPHOID BACILLI   TETANUS BACILLI (SPORE BEARING)

SPIRILLA   SPIROCHETES

MOULDS

PARASITIC PROTOZOA

FLAGELLATED FORMS   TRYPANO-SOMES (CAUSE OF AFRICAN SLEEPING SICKNESS)   AMEBA (CAUSE OF AMEBIC DYSENTERY)   MALARIA PARASITE (IN RED BLOOD CELL)   CILIATED FORMS

Fig. 11.1. Some pathogenic microorganisms.

pass through a fine filter and are therefore usually referred to as the **filterable viruses.** Viruses have one property in common with living organisms; they are capable of growth. But unlike bacteria they cannot be cultured apart from living cells; the hen's egg is the usual medium employed for this purpose. The intensely virulent nature of these bodies is evident from the fact that, in the case of one at least, the particular disease of which it is the cause can be transmitted by as small an amount as 1 cc of a solution containing it in a dilution of only 1 part in 10 billion.

The types of bacteria are innumerable, but fortunately only a small proportion cause disease. Also, only a relatively few kinds of fungi and protozoa threaten man or animals. Several bacterial forms are actually beneficial to man and some are even essential for human welfare. Those, for example, that inhabit the intestinal tract effect the final breakdown of food material with the formation of gas that, together with the bulk the bacteria themselves add to the feces, stimulates the bowel movements. Other bacterial forms present in the intestine are capable of synthesizing several factors of the vitamin B complex, as well as vitamin K.[1] From others again, and from molds, anti-infective substances of various kinds have been isolated (p. 197).

Bacterial forms. The commoner types of disease-producing (pathogenic) bacteria can be classified, on the basis of their microscopical appearances, into four main groups: **cocci** (sing. *coccus*), **bacilli** (sing. *bacillus*), **spirilla** (sing. *spirillum*), and **spirochetes** (Fig. 11.1).

The cocci are dotlike bodies that appear singly; in pairs (*Diplococcus,* a species of which causes lobar pneumonia); in clumps, like grapes (*Straphylococcus*); or in chains (*Streptococcus*). These last two types are the cause of acute pyogenic inflammatory conditions. One strain of *Streptococcus* is the cause of scarlet fever.

The bacilli are rod-shaped organisms; some examples are the *typhoid, tetanus,* and *diphtheria* bacilli, and the *tubercle bacillus.*

Spirilla are slender organisms possessing a shape like the shaft of a corkscrew.

The *spirochetes,* one genus of which is the cause of syphilis, have a slender spiral structure.

Reactions of the tissues to infecting agents

A pathogenic organism or virus shows, as a rule, a highly selective action with respect to the tissue that it or its toxin injures, and the symptoms characteristic of the disease it causes are the manifestations or the results of such injury, or represent the reaction of the tissue cells to invasion by the particular type of microorganism or virus. The toxin of the tetanus bacillus, for example, singles out nervous structures, lowering the "resistance" at synaptic junctions, so that a relatively mild stimulus —a mere touch, a faint sound, or a light—may cause widespread muscular responses. The viruses of rabies and anterior poliomyelitis also

---

[1] It sometimes happens that a patient receiving an antibacterial agent ("sulfa" drug or antibiotic, see below), especially when given by mouth, develops a deficiency in a certain vitamin or vitamins as a result of the destruction of intestinal bacteria.

direct their attack to the central nervous system, the former injuring nerve centers in the brain, the latter destroying chiefly the motor cells of the spinal cord. The typhoid bacillus directs its main attack to the mucous membrane of the small intestine; the tubercle bacillus had a predilection chiefly for pulmonary, bone, and joint tissues (though almost any tissue may be attacked). The bacteria of general septic infections, the staphylococci and streptococci, show much less selectivity of action, for they may cause an inflammatory condition in any tissue (see also p. 173). The spirochete of syphilis is also devoid of selective action; skin, bone, nervous, or any other tissue may be attacked. The reactions of the tissues it attacks are, however, as are also those of the tubercle bacillus, quite characteristic. The infected tissues react to both of these types by attracting small round cells, mostly lymphocytes, which form masses around the invading organism. Thus, a tubercle is formed in the case of tuberculosis, or a tumorlike structure called a **gumma** if spirochetes are the invading organisms.

The processes of immunity. The body is capable of putting up a defense that is in part or entirely successful against the inroads of most of the bacteria and viruses. The protection when it develops fully is called **immunity.** One who has suffered from an attack of smallpox, for example, cannot (except, perhaps, in the rarest instance) contract the disease again. With respect to that particular disease he is immune. Vaccination also confers immunity against smallpox.

The defenses of the body against the various disease-producing (pathogenic) organisms depend upon the activity of living cells. Cells, such as the neutrophil polymorphonuclear leucocytes and certain wandering cells of the reticulo-endothelial system, exert their protective action in an obvious, overt, or, one might say, mechanical way; they ingest the bacteria. The phagocytic property of the neutrophil leucocytes has already been described in Chapter 8. The immunity that the leucocytes confer is nonspecific, for they attack various types of bacteria indiscriminately, though they are particularly active against the pus-producing (**pyogenic**) forms. Other cells of the body, especially the lymphocytes in the lymphoid tissue, generally, throughout the body, produce and liberate chemical substances, closely associated with the globulin of the plasma, that have a *specific* neutralizing or destructive action upon the agent causing the disease. These substances, which go under the generic term **antibodies,** are, as it were, made to order, each for protection against only one pathogenic agent. Thus the antibody that is responsible for immunity against smallpox is inactive against measles or any other infectious disease. There are several types of antibody, namely **antitoxins,** that combine with and neutralize the bacterial poison, a substance generally called a **toxin.** Others, called **cytolysins** or **bacteriolysins,** destroy the foreign cell itself; to this group belong the **specific hemolysins** (Ch. 7) which cause the destruction of the red cells of one species when injected into the blood of another. **Agglutinins**, with which we are familiar, they having been also referred to in connection with the blood groups (Ch. 7), render bacteria innocuous by clumping them together in a mass. Agglutinins are produced in the blood of a patient suffering from typhoid fever. Some **precipitins** form an insoluble compound with the bacterial toxin and with foreign proteins.[2]

The foreign agent—whether a red cell in incompatible blood, a tissue cell of another species, a bacterial cell, or a virus—that stimulates the tissue cells of the **host** (that is, of the infected person or animal) to produce the antibody is called an **antigen** (Gk. *anti*, against + Gk. root *gen*, to form or produce). The response of the tissues of the host to the antigen and the production of the antibody, together with the reaction between the two, is called the **antibody-antigen reaction.** Paul Ehrlich of Berlin (1854-1815) many years ago sought to explain this reaction and the immunity it conferred by what has come to be known as Ehrlich's *side-chain theory* of immunity (Figs. 11.2, 11.3). Thus, in the case of

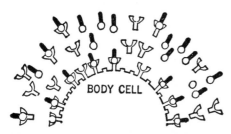

Fig. 11.2. Diagram illustrating the production of antitoxin according to Ehrlich's side-chain theory. ♦ = toxin; black, toxophore group; blank circle, haptophore group. ⅄ = receptors or haptins of body cell that join with the haptophore group of the toxin and through which the latter exerts its harmful effect upon the cell. Under the stimulus of the toxin (antigen), receptors are produced in excess, and escaping into the general blood stream, constitute the antitoxin.

immunity due to an antitoxin, he conceived that the protoplasm of the tissue cells, stimulated by the antigen, formed and put forth active chemical groups, or side chains, called **receptors**, or **haptins**; these combined with the bacterial toxin, and being thus linked to the tissue cells, brought about the injury characteristic of the disease. But the tissue cells produced an excess of such receptors which, becoming detached, passed into the general circulation, where they combined with toxin before it could reach and damage the cells. These free receptors constituted the antitoxin. The same conception could be made to embrace other types of antibody. Ehrlich suggested that the toxin molecule possessed two active chemical groups: one, known as the **toxophore** group, was responsible

---

[2] A delicate and specific test for human blood in medicolegal (murder) cases is based on the precipitin reaction. A rabbit is given a series of injections of a solution of human blood or serum. When the serum of the rabbit which, as a result of the injections, has developed a precipitin active against human serum, is added to a specimen of the suspected blood (for example, from stains on clothing, a presumed weapon, etc.) dissolved in a test tube, a slight cloudy precipitate appears if the material in question is human blood. If it is the blood of an animal the solution remains clear.

for its injurious action; the other, called the **haptophore** group, united with the cell receptor, or haptin, and thus enabled the toxin to bring its action to bear upon the tissue cell.

Three types of immunity are recognized—*natural, active,* and *passive.* **Natural immunity,** also called inborn, or innate, is that which has not been acquired by a previous attack of the disease, or in any other way. Thus, we are naturally immune to some diseases that afflict animals, and they possess a natural immunity to a great many human diseases— for example, measles and typhoid fever, to mention only two. Many persons appear to be naturally immune to anterior poliomyelitis and to some other human diseases.

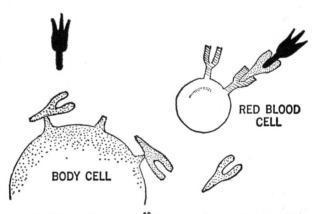

Fig. 11.3. Diagram illustrating the production and action of specific cytolysins, hemolysins, bacteriolysins, etc. According to Ehrlich's theory a substance destroyed by heat and called the *complement* ( ) is present in nearly all normal sera. It becomes joined to the receptor ( ) of the foreign cell by means of another substance called the *amboceptor* ( ), *intermediary,* or *immune body.* When this union takes place the foreign cell is destroyed. The amboceptor, which is not destroyed by heat, is produced by the body cells of the animal receiving the injection of antigen, e.g., foreign cells, bacteria, blood cells, or tissue cells of another species; it is specific, having a destructive action only upon the kind of cells that were injected. The complement is nonspecific; its nonspecificity can be demonstrated in the following way. When the immune serum is heated, the complement but not the amboceptor is destroyed and the serum loses its cytolytic action; this is immediately restored, however, by adding any normal serum.

RED BLOOD CELL

BODY CELL

Active immunity is that which has been developed as a result of the activity of the body's own cells, as when a person has recovered from an attack of an infectious disease, or has had the antigen administered by injection as explained below.

Immunity produced by the injection of an antibody, for example, diphtheria antitoxin, formed in the body of an animal or of another person is called **passive.** Diphtheria antitoxin is produced by the horse into which the toxin (antigen) of diphtheria has been injected. Serum from such animals is employed in treating diphtheria in patients suffering from this disease. In a similar way, serum from patients who have recently recovered from a disease, such as measles, scarlet fever, or anterior poliomyelitis, is used to immunize passively another person suffering from the same disease.

It is not always easy to say whether a person who has been exposed to some infection or other but does not "catch" it, is *naturally* immune to the disease or has been actively immunized against it by having at some time previous contracted it in such a mild form that it was not recognized. An apparently natural immunity probably occurs in this way to the virus of anterior poliomyelitis and to the typhoid bacillus.

Active immunity may be conferred artificially in order to prevent persons from contracting a disease should they be exposed to it. They are injected (**inoculated**) with an emulsion of bacteria that have been killed by heat or chemical means. The toxin is not destroyed, and it is the essential antigenic substance. Such preparations of dead bacteria are called **vaccines.** This method of immunization is employed against typhoid fever and infections with pyogenic organisms. Other methods of vaccination are practiced for protection against smallpox and rabies. Immunization against smallpox is carried out by infecting the subject with a mild form of the disease known as cowpox.[3] The lymph of calves that have been inoculated with the disease is pricked or lightly scratched into the subject's skin. In the case of rabies (hydrophobia) the victim of the disease is inoculated with a solution of the virus that has been weakened by drying and aging. Finally, the toxin of the causative organism, for example, that of diphtheria or of tetanus (lockjaw), may be rendered nontoxic by chemical treatment without destroying its antigenic properties—that is, its ability to stimulate antibody production. In other words, the toxophore groups, but not the haptophore groups of the toxin are destroyed. Immunizing agents prepared in this way are called **toxoids.** By the administration of diphtheria toxoid to young children, deaths from diphtheria, which used to run into high figures annually, have been reduced almost to the vanishing point.

---

[3] Vaccination against smallpox has a long history; it was practiced in Eastern countries, especially China and India, many hundreds of years ago. The method employed before Jenner was a rather dangerous procedure. But considering the terrible ravages of smallpox, it was justified. In this old method, the person whom it was desired to protect against smallpox was inoculated with a little material (sometimes first dried) from a pustule of a patient recovering from the disease. The virus, being in a weakened state, caused, except rarely, a mild form of the disease in the inoculated person. This method was introduced into England in the eighteenth century. Edward Jenner, an English physician, originated the modern method of vaccination against smallpox in 1796. The idea came to him from the remark of a milkmaid, "I cannot take the smallpox for I have already had the cowpox." The truth of this statement was known generally among the country people of the district. Jenner accordingly inoculated a boy of eight years, named James Phipps, with pus from the hand of a dairymaid infected with cowpox. Two months later Jenner inoculated the boy with smallpox virus. This, the crucial test, proved the efficacy of vaccination; Phipps did not contract smallpox. An outstanding example of the value of vaccination against smallpox is afforded by the statistics of the Franco-Prussian War (1870). In the Prussian Army, but not in the French, vaccination was practiced. Only a few Prussian soldiers died of smallpox, but several thousand French soldiers succumbed to the disease.

Pain and rest

The pain and temporary loss of function of an inflamed or injured part are definitely protective provisions. Though we may think that pain has been imposed upon us by a malicious Nature and could be dispensed with, we would soon be destroyed were it not for the warning that it gives of injury or of a threat of injury. In a certain nervous disease affecting the afferent fibers in the spinal cord that carry impulses giving rise to the sensations of pain and temperature from the hands, the patient is continually damaging his fingers; sores develop from such injuries, which are neglected because they cause no discomfort. It is also true that the most potent stimulus for evoking a protective reflex, such as jerking the hand away from a hot object, is a painful one. In the case of the eye, our most valuable sense organ, the winking reflex that shields the eye is extremely sensitive. Even the sight of an approaching object that might injure the eye will elicit the reflex; a stimulus that would result in nothing more than a mild sensation of touch if directed to any other part of the body surface, when applied to the cornea, the anterior surface of the eye, instantly causes reflex closure of the eyelid. The cornea is richly supplied with pain fibers that have a very low threshold; almost any stimulus, except the very blandest, such as a gentle jet of warm water, if it gives rise to any sensation at all, causes pain.

Of an importance as a protective device, nearly as great as that of pain, is the suspension of function in an injured structure. Rest, whether of a broken bone or a lung, enables the *healing power of Nature* (*vis medicatrix naturae*) to exert most effectively its beneficent action. In some instances, such as in pulmonary tuberculosis, where one lung is solely or predominantly affected, man, by artifice, does what Nature cannot, or fails to do. The severely damaged lung is immobilized—that is, put at rest by collapsing it (as by the injection of air into the pleural cavity of that side) or by cutting one phrenic nerve and thus paralyzing the corresponding half of the diaphragm. So, also, a broken bone is immobilized by putting it in splints, and inflamed eyes are protected by a bandage or dark glasses (though some natural protection is afforded by contraction of the pupil and closure of the eye lids) .

A recapitulation of other protective mechanisms

There are a number of other defensive measures that the body can take against the variety of adverse conditions and dangers occurring in an ever-changing environment. Among such provisions of Nature, most of which have been or will be dealt with elsewhere in this book, are the coagulation of the blood and the other reactions that tend to ensure against fatal hemorrhage (Ch. 7) ; the protection against a general blood infection afforded by the lymph nodes; the cilia and mucus of the upper respiratory passages as well as the cough reflex, which serve to prevent the entrance of foreign material into the finer airways of the lungs (Ch. 21); and the reactions of the sympatho-adrenal system (Chs. 37, 40).

Finally, it should be mentioned that in order that the various safeguards shall serve their purposes most effectively, since they are manifestations of living cells, all physiological processes must be maintained in states of prime efficiency. Unless this is so, the normal biochemical balance of the internal environment (homeostasis, p. 562) is not secured. When the general health is undermined, a way is opened for invasion by pathogenic microorganisms. Diabetic patients, for example, are especially susceptible to infection, and victims of this malady, and of nephritis and other general diseases are often carried off, not directly by the disease itself, but by some "intercurrent infection" such as pneumonia, or a septic condition.

CHEMOTHERAPY

Chemotherapy is the treatment of disease by the administration of a chemical compound, in many instances synthetic, by means of which the causative microorganisms are destroyed within the body of the patient, or their multiplication arrested. The science of chemotherapy has made enormous strides within the last 15 or 20 years. The aim of the investigator in this field is to prepare a chemical compound that is selectively active against one or more types of pathogenic organism, but, in the dosage used, exerts little or no toxic action upon the patient.

Paul Ehrlich, the founder of the science of chemotherapy, introduced some 40 years ago an arsenical compound having a destructive action upon the spirochetes of syphilis. It was named *Salvarsan,* or arsphenamine. It was also commonly known as "606" (six-o-six) because it was the last of a long series of compounds (presumably 606) that had been experimented with in the search of a cure for syphilis. Several compounds of arsenic and antimony have since been synthesized that are active against the protozoan organisms of malaria, African sleeping sickness, and other tropical diseases.

The "sulfa" drugs. In 1928, it was discovered by the German scientist Dr. Domagk that **prontosil,** a red dye, when administered to mice enabled them to withstand an injection of pathogenic bacteria that was ordinarily lethal. It was found later that a chemical group containing sulfur was the active antibacterial agent. This compound was prepared separately; it is colorless and known as sulfanilamide. The use of this drug and its derivatives—the so-called *"sulfa,"* or **sulfonamide drugs**—has opened up a fresh vista in chemotherapy. Several bacterial diseases from which the death rate was extremely high have been treated with these compounds with spectacular success. A large number of derivatives of sulfanilamide have been synthesized, such as **sulfapyridine, sulfathia-**

zole, and **sulfadiazine,** to mention those in most common use. The sulfonamides are not equally active against different bacterial forms. One drug may be active against one group of bacteria but fails against another group.

Antibacterial agents such as the "sulfa" drugs do not kill the bacteria like antiseptics or other chemicals, such as the arsenical compounds. *They prevent the bacteria from multiplying.* They are **bacteriostatic**[4] (L. *statos,* standing) rather than **bacteriocidal** (L. *caedo,* I kill) .

ANTIBIOTICS

An entirely new class of highly effective antibacterial agents has come into prominence within recent years. These substances, known as **antibiotics,** are obtained from other living organisms, especially fungi, molds, and bacteria. It was through a happy accident and alert observation that the first of these principles was discovered. In 1929, Dr. (later Sir) Alexander Fleming, an English bacteriologist, noticed that the growth of a culture of staphylococci that had been exposed to the air of the room was arrested in the neighborhood of a growth of a mold that had fallen upon the same culture plate. He suggested that the mold had produced a substance inimical to the bacteria. Dr. (later Sir) H. Florey and his associates at Oxford instituted a series of experiments during World War II that resulted in the isolation of the antibacterial principle from the mold. The mold had previously been identified as *Penicillium notatum;* the active principle was, therefore, called **penicillin.** Both Fleming and Florey received the Nobel Prize in 1945.

A number of antibiotic principles have since then been isolated from various molds and bacteria. The most valuable of these agents are **streptomycin, aureomycin (chlortetracycline), tyrothricin, terramycin (oxytetracycline),** and **erythromycin.** Streptomycin is obtained from the funguslike bacteria *Streptomyces;* it is active against the tubercle bacillus and a number of other pathogenic bacteria. Aureomycin is furnished by another species of *Streptomyces;* it is active against some virus infections and several types of bacteria. Tyrothricin is derived from a bacterial form found in milk and soil; it is especially valuable for local application in staphylococcic and streptococcic infections of the skin. Terramycin is obtained from another species of *Streptomyces.* Most of the antibiotics are bacteriostatic in their action, but some are also bacteriocidal. Others are active against pathogenic fungi.

---

[4] The mode of action of sulfanilamide is believed to be as follows: a factor of the vitamin B complex, para-aminobenzoic acid, is an essential requirement for some enzyme system in the bacterial cell. Owing to the similarity of their chemical structures, the "sulfa" drug and the vitamin compete for inclusion in the enzyme system. When the drug is taken up by the latter, the entrance of the vitamin into the system is "blocked." The enzyme is thus rendered inactive, and the bacteria are unable to multiply.

Pathogenic organisms show a remarkable adaptability to the action of various agents employed against them. They tend to become gradually resistant and can then tolerate larger doses of the antibacterial substance. When this occurs, the physician's strategy, when feasible, is to attack with some other antibacterial substance. Another person may become infected with the resistant bacteria. When, for example, infection is derived from a patient with tuberculosis treated with streptomycin, the effectiveness of this very valuable drug, in so far as the second infected person is concerned, is very greatly reduced.

SURGICAL SHOCK

A patient who has suffered a severe injury or has undergone an extensive operation may a few hours later (between 3 and 5) pass into a grave state variously known as **surgical, traumatic, secondary,** or **delayed shock.** The condition is commonly associated with the loss of a considerable quantity of blood. It is characterized by a very low blood pressure, a pale, cold, and clammy skin, and extreme weakness. The volume of circulating blood is greatly reduced, and this, whether due to the loss of plasma or blood into the tissues at the site of the injury or to external hemorrhage, as indicated above, is believed to be the cause of the symptoms. Treatment, therefore, is directed toward restoring the blood volume to normal by the transfusion of blood or an effective blood substitute. This aim can be attained if the shock is not too profound and treatment begun early. Shock is then said to be *reversible* and the patient recovers. But if the patient's condition is very grave from the start or treatment has been too long delayed, all restorative measures are unavailing; shock is then *irreversible.* Hemorrhage alone without excessive tissue damage causes identical symptoms—in this case the term *hemorrhagic shock* is applied.

ANAPHYLAXIS AND ALLERGY

When an animal is injected parenterally with a foreign protein, it becomes hypersensitive to that particular protein; if given a second minute dose of the protein 10 days or more later, it is overwhelmed by an intense reaction from which it quickly dies. The hypersensitive state is called *anaphylaxis,* and the characters of the reaction vary with the species; the guinea pig, for example, dies of asphyxia (bronchiolar spasm), whereas the dog succumbs to congestion of the liver and intestines. The effects are due, it is believed, to the release of histamine from the tissue cells—an antigen-antibody reaction—the first dose of protein (antigen) having caused the production of a specific antibody having this effect. *Allergy* and *serum sickness,* though much milder in their manifestations, are essentially similar in nature.

CIRCULATION OF THE BLOOD

PART IV

12

General Plan of the Circulatory System

The circulatory system of the body resembles in several ways a municipal water system. The water system consists of a pump and a complete set of closed metal tubes or pipes. In the living circulatory system the heart is the pump, and the closed tubes are of four kinds— **arteries, arterioles, capillaries,** and **veins** (Figs. 12.1, 12.2; see also Figs. 12.6 to 12.8). The arteries, being strong, thick-walled tubes, may be compared to the large water mains of the city. The small arteries and the arterioles, into which the larger arteries divide, carry the blood from the heart to all parts of the body, and may be compared to the narrow pipes carrying water from the street mains to the faucets. The veins carry the blood laden with waste materials, and are therefore comparable to the drains of an artificial system. The heart and vessels form a complete circle through which the blood flows (Plate II*b*).

It has not always been known that the blood travels in a circle. It seems so obvious to us today and is taken much as a matter of course, but for many hundred years it was universally believed that the blood simply ebbed and flowed like a tide away from and back to the heart. The scientific world waited until, more than 300 years ago, William Harvey, an English physician, discovered that the blood made a complete circuit from the heart to the tissues through the arteries, then through the tissues, and back again to the heart through the veins (p. 210). But, though Harvey's experiments furnished the proof for this, it took half a century more for many people to accept this apparently simple fact, so firmly entrenched were the old beliefs.

The parts of the circulatory system will now be described in more detail.

200

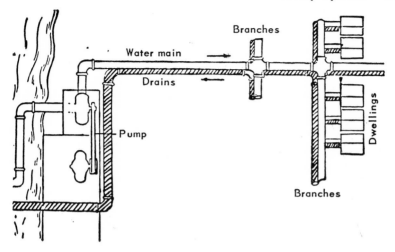

Fig. 12.1. Plan of a water system.

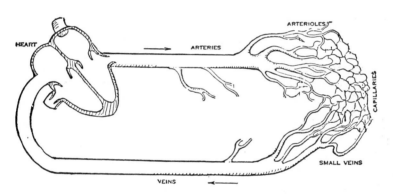

Fig. 12.2. Diagram of the circulatory system. Compare with Fig. 12.1.

THE HEART

The heart is a hollow muscular organ lying with its center a little to the left of the mid-line of the chest (Fig. 12.3). The muscle of the greater part of the heart is very thick and forms thick bands, which are interlaced with one another and twisted into rings, loops, and whorls to form very strong walls (Fig. 12.4).

The human heart and the hearts of higher animals are divided by a complete wall, or **septum,** composed mostly of muscle, into a right and a left half. Each half is again divided into an upper and a lower part by a horizontal partition. The upper chambers are called **atria** (sing.

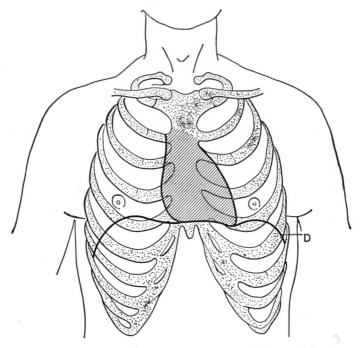

Fig. 12.3. The position of the heart in relation to the front of the chest wall. *D*, diaphragm.

atrium) or **auricles**[1]—right and left. The lower ones are called **ventricles** —right and left.

The two sides of the heart are completely separated—that is, the chambers of the right side have no direct communication with their companions on the left, because of the septum mentioned above; but the auricle and the ventricle of the same side open into each other. This opening is guarded by valves (Plate II*b*).

The right atrium, or auricle, receives blood from the great veins (superior and inferior **venae cavae**), which drain the blood from the head, neck, and arms above, and from the trunk and legs below. The right ventricle pumps blood *into* the lungs; the left atrium, or auricle, receives blood *from* the lungs; the left ventricle pumps its contents *into* the great artery or aorta. This artery gives off branches, which in turn rebranch, like the limbs and twigs of a tree, to convey the blood to all parts of the body (Ch. 13). Thus, in reality, there are two circulations, a *greater,* or **systemic,** through the body as a whole, and a *lesser,* or **pulmonary,** through the lungs. The heart serves as a two-cylinder pump situated between and connecting the two systems.

[1] Auricle is an older term but still in use, especially by physiologists.

The systemic circulation serves to carry oxygen and food materials for distribution to all parts of the body, and to remove carbon dioxide and the waste products of metabolism from the tissues. The pulmonary circulation is for the purpose of "ventilating" the blood—that is, for the elimination of carbon dioxide into the air of the lungs, and the absorption of oxygen.

The ventricles make up the greater part of the heart. They have thick walls, the muscle of the left ventricle being thicker than that of the right chamber, since it has more work to do. The walls of the auricles are comparatively thin. The ventricular muscle consists of numerous stout bundles that are arranged more or less concentrically so that when they contract the ventricular cavity is almost obliterated and the blood expelled (Fig. 12.4 and 14.2).

The valves and other structures in the cardiac interior will be described in Chapter 14.

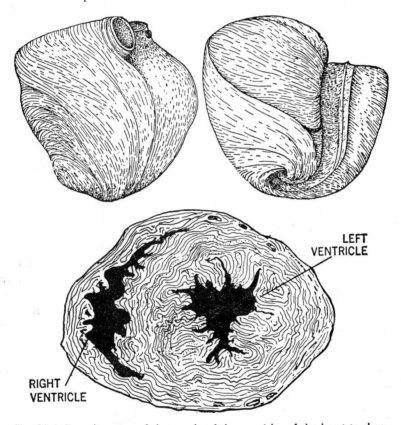

Fig. 12.4. Top, dissection of the muscle of the ventricles of the heart to show the arrangement of the muscle fibers. (Redrawn from Mall.) Bottom, cross section of heart through the ventricles.

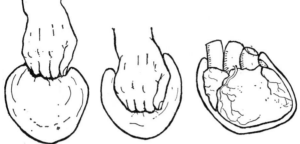

Fig. 12.5. Showing the manner in which the serous pericardium is formed.

The pericardium encloses the heart. It consists of two concentric membranous sacs, an inner *serous* and an outer *fibrous*. The **serous pericardium** is thin and delicate, and composed of a single layer of flat endothelial cells supported by a small amount of loose areolar tissue. It has been pushed in (invaginated) on one side by the developing heart so as to bring its walls into contact, endothelial surface to endothelial surface, thus forming a double layer. The inner (*visceral*) layer is adherent to the heart; the outer (*parietal*) layer is bound to the inner surface of the **fibrous pericardium** by areolar tissue, thus forming a smooth lining for the latter. The fibrous pericardium blends above with the sheaths of the great vessels entering and leaving the heart, and is anchored below by a broad base to the upper surface of the diaphragm. It is also attached in front by fibrous bands to the posterior aspect of the sternum. The heart moves freely within the pericardium, the smooth surfaces of the serous pericardium, lubricated by a film of fluid, gliding easily over one another.

The construction of the serous pericardium may be made clearer by a homely illustration. If we should take one of those transparent plastic bags now used as containers for fruit and vegetables, and press a fist into its side (not into its cavity) and mold it around the hand, we would have a rough imitation of the serous pericardium. The fist would represent the heart, the layer of the plastic envelope next the skin would suggest the inner layer of the serous pericaridum (epicardium) adherent to the heart, while the outer layer of the plastic envelope would correspond to the serous layer that lines the fibrous pericardium. The latter might be represented by a rough bag outside the plastic sac (serous pericardium).

The main functions of the pericardium are to anchor the heart in position with the chest, and to prevent overdistention of its cavities. Inflammation of the serous pericardium is called *pericarditis.* When the fluid between the two layers of the serous pericardium is greatly increased, the condition is called *pericarditis with effusion;* the accumulation of fluid may be so great as to interfere with the action of the heart.

THE BLOOD VESSELS

The arteries

The arteries are comparatively large tubes that carry the blood from the heart to the most distant parts of the body. Their thick, tough, strong walls are composed of elastic material that allows them to stretch and recoil. The largest arteries in the body are the **pulmonary,** which carries blood from the right ventricle to the lungs, and the **aorta,** which leaves the left ventricle. The course and branches of the aorta are described in Chapter 13. All but one of the arteries of the body carry bright red blood —that is, blood that has passed through the lungs and has received a load of oxygen from the inspired air. This one exception is the pulmonary artery. It carries to the lungs dark blood that has been brought by the veins from the tissues to the heart. The tissues have removed some of the oxygen from the blood as it passed through them, depriving it of its brilliant color—that is, the oxyhemoglobin has been converted to reduced hemoglobin (pp. 155, 300, 310).

The structure of the arteries. The walls of the arteries consist of three **coats,** or **tunics,** an inner, middle, and outer. The inner coat is called the **tunica intima,** the middle one the **tunica media,** and the outer one the **tunica adventitia** (Fig. 12.6). The tunica intima is a delicate lining—a single layer of endothelium. The tunica media is composed of smooth muscle and elastic connective tissue fibers, and is many times thicker than the lining endothelium. The tunica adventitia consists of connective tissue that carries small vessels and nerves to nourish and motivate the vascular wall. In the largest arteries, the proportion of elastic tissue is much greater and the proportion of muscular tissue much less than in the small and medium-sized arteries.

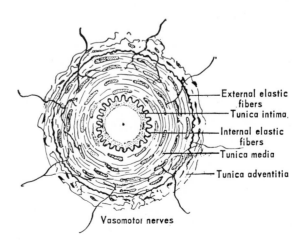

External elastic fibers
Tunica intima
Internal elastic fibers
Tunica media
Tunica adventitia

Vasomotor nerves

Fig. 12.6. Section through a small artery.

Degenerative diseases of the arteries. The arteries in later life may become stiff, hard, and brittle due to atrophy of the muscle of the tunica media and the deposition of lime salts. This type of arterial degeneration is most commonly seen in old age. The affected arteries are compared to pipe stems from their feel under the skin. In a more serious form of arterial degenerative disease the tunica intima is attacked; thickened areas appear that later break down into a soft material composed of cholesterol and other lipids (p. 412). This *atheromatous change* (Gk. *athērē,* porridge) leads to weakening of the arterial wall, especially in the larger and medium-sized arteries that are exposed to high pressure. Rupture may result if high blood pressure exists as well, or the blood within the vessel may clot (thrombosis). Such atheromatous changes are very common after middle age, and are the usual cause of the chief vascular emergencies, namely, *cerebral hemorrhage* and *coronary thrombosis.*

In the latter instance, clotting of the blood is encouraged by the roughening of the normally smooth endothelial lining of the artery by the atheromatous areas. This disease—*atherosclerosis*—causes more deaths each year in the Western world than do all other diseases combined, and there has been much controversy as to its cause. In the victims of coronary disease the concentration of cholesterol in the blood is consistently higher than in other persons. Elevation of blood cholesterol—*hypercholesterolemia*—is readily induced by a diet rich in animal fats, for example, butter, cream, eggs (yolk), and liver, which contain saturated fatty acids and relatively large amounts of cholesterol. Most vegetable fats and oils, on the contrary, whose fatty acids are unsaturated and contain no cholesterol, do not have such an effect. They and carbohydrates actually lower the blood cholesterol. Reasoning from these facts, the theory has been put forward that in those persons with hypercholesterolemia, the cholesterol was taken up in excessive amounts into the cells of the arterial lining and, accumulating there, produced the atheromatous patches. A diet high in animal fats was therefore thought to be conducive to the development of atherosclerosis, and was to be avoided.

It is doubtful, however, that a high cholesterol diet is of essential importance in causing atherosclerosis. Cholesterol is synthesized in the body, and it seems more likely that the disease is due to some hereditary fault—either of synthesis or breakdown—in cholesterol metabolism. It is suggestive in this connection that, though the disease is readily produced in rabbits and chickens by high cholesterol feeding, it cannot be produced in monkeys by this means. There are other factors concerned in the production of the disease, the most important being high blood pressure (arterial hypertension). The constant strain put upon the vessels encourages and accelerates the atheromatous process. Small hemorrhages into the intima followed by thrombosis in the minute vessels in the arterial wall may well be the initial change.

The arterioles

Arterioles is the name given to the very smallest tubes of the arterial system (Fig. 12.7). These vessels are little thicker than a hair (about 0.2 mm in outside diameter). Their walls are relatively rich in smooth muscle disposed circularly around the vessels. These muscle fibers can contract and close off the tube, or they can relax and so make the channel of the arteriole wider. In accordance with the comparison made above between the circulation of the blood and a municipal water system, the arterioles represent the faucets in our houses, which can be opened or closed.

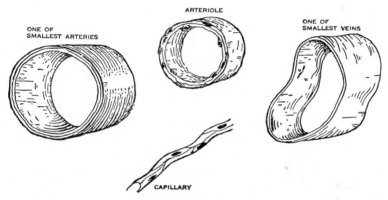

ONE OF SMALLEST ARTERIES

ARTERIOLE

ONE OF SMALLEST VEINS

CAPILLARY

Fig. 12.7. Sections of the four types of blood vessels—arteries, arterioles, capillaries, and veins. Though the different drawings are not made accurately to scale, some idea of the actual sizes of the vessels may be gained if the reader thinks of the small artery on the left as being about the diameter of a fine needle. The largest arteries in the body—the aorta and the pulmonary—are each, in an adult, a little over 1 inch in diameter where they leave the heart.

The capillaries

The capillaries lie between the arterioles and the veins. They are the finest blood vessels in the body, being less than one tenth the width of an arteriole. Their walls have no muscle but are made of the thinnest and most delicate material—a single layer of endothelial cells (Ch. 2). The blood, after leaving the arterioles, must pass through the thousands upon thousands of these fine tubes in order to reach the veins. The living color of our skins is due to the blood in the capillaries. When the skin becomes flushed and hot, the capillaries are filled with blood; when the skin is pale and cool, these vessels are narrower and hold less blood. When the skin is scratched, the blood that oozes from the trivial wound comes from these minutely narrow vessels (see also Ch. 18).

The veins

The veins are the drainpipes of the circulatory system. They collect the blood from the capillaries in the tissues and carry it to the heart. The veins near the capillaries are quite small, but by the joining together of small veins to form larger ones—like tributaries of a river—the blood, as it flows toward the heart, passes into progressively larger vessels. The largest veins in the body are the **superior vena cava** and the **inferior vena cava.** Both of these pour the blood into the right atrium. The superior vena cava drains the blood from those parts of the body above the level of the heart—head, neck, and arms. The inferior vena cava drains the blood from those parts of the body below the level of the heart. The blood of the lungs is brought into the left auricle by the four **pulmonary veins.** The blood in the pulmonary veins is bright red because it has just taken on a load of oxygen from the air in the lungs. These are the only veins in the body, therefore, that contain fully oxygenated blood (see p. 272). The blood in all the other veins has given up part of its oxygen to the tissues and so is a darker red owing to the reduced hemoglobin. Anyone can see the dark color of the blood in the veins on the back of the hand or on the forearm. The color, as it shows through the skin, has a bluish tint. Many of the larger veins have valves that aid the flow of blood toward the heart (Fig. 12.8).

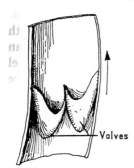

Fig. 12.8. A pair of valves in a large vein. The arrow points in the direction of the blood flow, that is, toward the heart.

THE COMPLETE SYSTEM

In order that he may understand the two circuits of the blood—the systemic and the pulmonary—the reader should refer to Plate II*b* and read carefully the following description of a red cell's voyage.

Imagine that the cell, having been ejected by the left ventricle into the aorta, has just started upon its journey around the body. Speeding down the great artery (aorta) at the rate of a foot or two per second together with millions of its fellows, it soon reaches a branch in the vessel and may turn along it, or may pass to some one or other branch beyond.

When the arteries branch into smaller twigs, many channels lie open to the cell. Whichever path it takes, sooner or later the red cell comes to a region where the channel is very narrow—so narrow, indeed, that it may brush the walls on either side or may have to be squeezed along. The corpuscle has now reached the smallest of all the blood vessels—the capillaries.

The stream here is flowing much more slowly than in the large arteries, and the red cell idles along at the rate of about 1 inch per minute. Compared with the rushing arterial river that the red cell has just left, the capillary stream is sluggish. Here, also, the walls of the vessels are so thin as to be transparent, and the cells of the tissues shine clearly through on either side (Plate IIIb).

The capillary vessels are so minute, indeed, that ten or more could be laid side by side upon a hair. Yet, if we were to take the cross sections of all these delicate tubes in all the tissues of the body and add them together, we should find that the sum was 500 to 1000 times greater than the cross section of the one large artery—the aorta—by which the blood left the heart. In other words, the bed of the stream over which the blood flows has become tremendously expanded in the region of the capillaries. It is as though a swiftly moving river had flood a tract of marshy ground furrowed by innumerable channels. This explains the slowness of the stream in the capillary region, for it is a principle of the flow of fluid through a closed system of tubes that the stream is slowed in passing through a broader passage, and is quickened when it traverses a narrower one.

The red cell, having journeyed through the capillary, enters somewhat larger vessels again—the **small veins,** or venules. As it reaches larger and larger venous tributaries its speed increases, for the reason given above; soon it is carried into one or another of the great veins (superior or inferior vena cava) and enters the right auricle of the heart. The speed of the red cell in the large vein where it opens into the right auricle is not greatly less than the speed of the blood in the aorta, because the diameters of the two large veins added together is not so much greater than the diameter of the latter vessel. Having reached the right atrium, it has now made a complete round of the systemic, or greater, circulation. In its slow passage through the capillaries it has given up to the tissues a part of the oxygen load with which it entered the aorta. So, by the time it has returned to the heart, the red cell has lost its scarlet color and is a darker red (Fig. 12.10). No interchange of fluid, respiratory gases, or of nutritive or waste materials occurs except as the blood traverses the capillaries.

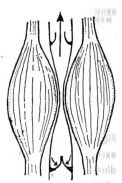

Fig. 12.9. Showing how the contracting muscles of the lower limbs in conjunction with the venous valves act as force pumps to drive blood toward the heart.

After entering the right ventricle, it is ejected into the large pulmonary artery and so enters the pulmonary, or lesser, circulation. In the lungs the red cell passes through capillaries again. There it becomes exposed to the air that has been inspired, and takes on a load of oxygen.

Leaving the capillaries as before, it enters a small vein and then successively larger veins to reach the left auricle through one of the four large **pulmonary veins.** Finally the left ventricle receives it, and the red cell has returned to the point from which it started half a minute or so ago—for that is about the time the red cell takes to make a tour of both circulatory systems. During exercise, however, the velocity of the blood is greatly increased.

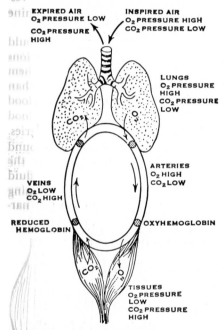

EXPIRED AIR
O₂ PRESSURE LOW
CO₂ PRESSURE HIGH

INSPIRED AIR
O₂ PRESSURE HIGH
CO₂ PRESSURE LOW

LUNGS
O₂ PRESSURE HIGH
CO₂ PRESSURE LOW

ARTERIES
O₂ HIGH
CO₂ LOW

VEINS
O₂ LOW
CO₂ HIGH

REDUCED HEMOGLOBIN

OXYHEMOGLOBIN

TISSUES
O₂ PRESSURE LOW
CO₂ PRESSURE HIGH

Fig. 12.10. Schematic diagram to show the exchange of the respiratory gases—carbon dioxide and oxygen. For the sake of simplicity the pulmonary and systemic circuits are combined into one circle and the heart omitted.

Emphasis should be laid upon certain points in the foregoing account. The right side of the heart contains only venous blood—that is, blood that has passed through the capillaries of the systemic circulation and so has given up part of its load of oxygen to the tissues. A quarter or so of its hemoglobin is in the reduced state (Ch. 7).

The left side of the heart contains only arterial blood, or blood that has passed through the capillaries of the lungs and has taken up nearly a full load of oxygen. Fully 98 percent of its hemoglobin is oxygenated (oxyhemoglobin). It has already been said that arteries carry blood away from, and veins carry blood to, the heart. The pulmonary artery, which conveys blood from the right ventricle to the lungs, and the pulmonary veins, which carry blood from the lungs to the left auricle, are therefore correctly named. Nevertheless, in one particular the pulmonary artery resembles a vein—it contains reduced, or so-called venous, blood. The pulmonary veins, on the other hand, contain oxygenated or arterial blood, and in this they resemble arteries. These are the only exceptions to the rule that an artery contains oxygenated, and a vein reduced, blood.

William Harvey and the discovery of the circulation of the blood. By a series of simple experiments William Harvey (1578-1657) showed that the blood must take the course just described. He pointed out that the valves of the heart were so fashioned that the blood could go in only one direction; that there could be no to-and-fro movement as was supposed by the medical men of his time. He saw that when the pulmonary veins in the living animal were tied, no blood entered the left ventricle; when the pulmonary artery was similarly obstructed, no blood passed through the lungs. Thus, he proved that the blood was driven from the right to the left ventricle, that is, through the pulmonary circuit.

The course of the blood through the systemic circulation was deduced from the following experiments. Compression of the aorta was followed by damming of blood in the left ventricle, which became dilated and labored in its beat. When, on the other hand, the great veins entering the right auricle (superior and inferior venae cavae) were tied, the right chambers of the heart collapsed, since they received no blood. When a large superficial vein was compressed (Fig. 12.11) it became swollen with blood on the side of the obstruction farther from the heart and empty on the near side; compression of an artery caused the pulse to disappear in that part of the artery beyond the point of pressure. Undoubtedly then, Harvey argued, the blood must be carried from the heart in the arteries and toward the heart in the veins.

The fetal circulation is described in Chapter 49.

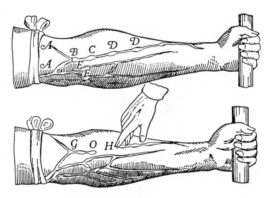

Fig. 12.11. Illustration of an experiment of William Harvey from his great work published in 1628, *De motu cordis et sanguinis* (the movement of the heart and blood). When a vein was compressed by the finger it collapsed on the side toward the heart and became distended with blood on the other side.

13
Descriptions of Individual Arteries and Veins

As we have seen, the blood has two outlets from the heart—from the left ventricle into the aorta, and from the right ventricle into the pulmonary artery. The pulmonary artery will be described in Chapter 18.

THE AORTA

This large vessel, through its branches and the innumerable divisions of the vascular tree, the trunk of which it represents, distributes oxygen-laden blood to the capillaries of all parts of the body, with the exception of the greater part of the lungs. From its origin at the left ventricle, the aorta ascends for 5 cm or so and then forming an arch descends close to the vertebral column through the thorax and abdominal cavity. This vessel, in man, has a diameter at its origin of over an inch (3 cm). The aorta is described in four parts: (a) the *ascending aorta,* (b) the *arch of the aorta,* (c) the *thoracic aorta,* and (d) the *abdominal aorta.*

The ascending aorta is about 5 cm (2 inches) long, and gives rise to only two branches, which supply the heart muscle itself. These are the *right* and *left coronary arteries;* they are described in Chapter 18 (Fig. 13.1).

The arch of the aorta is formed by the turning of the vessel from an upward to a downward course. In other words, it is interposed between the ascending and the descending portions. It gives off three large *branches* that supply the head, neck, and upper limb; these are the

212

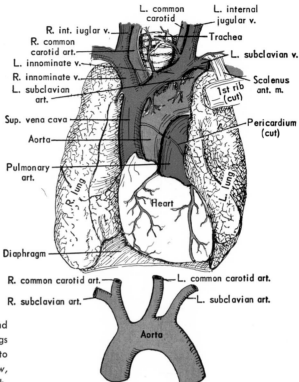

L. common carotid

L. internal jugular v.

R. int. iuglar v.

R. common carotid art.

L. innominate v.

R. innominate v.

L. subclavian art.

Sup. vena cava

Aorta

Pulmonary art.

Diaphragm

Trachea

L. subclavian v.

Scalenus ant. m.

1st rib (cut)

Pericardium (cut)

R. lung

L. lung

Heart

R. common carotid art.

R. subclavian art.

L. common carotid art.

L. subclavian art.

Aorta

Fig. 13.1. The heart and great vessels; the lungs have been retracted to expose the heart. *Below,* branches of aortic arch.

innominate artery, the *left common carotid artery,* and the *left subclavian artery.*

The innominate artery is the first and largest branch of the arch of the aorta. After coursing for about 2 inches (4 to 5 cm) upward, backwards, and to the right, it divides into the right common carotid and the right subclavian arteries.

ARTERIES OF THE HEAD AND NECK

The common carotid arteries

As just outlined, the *right* carotid arises from the innominate artery whereas the *left* springs directly from the aortic arch (Figs. 13.1, 13.2). The distribution of the two vessels is the same on both sides of the body. As a rule, the common carotids give off no branches in their course but divide into the *external* and *internal carotid arteries* in the neck at the upper border of the thyroid cartilage. Branches of these vessels supply the head and neck.

The external carotid artery

The external carotid artery ascends, one on either side, to a point in front of the ear midway between the mastoid process and the angle of the jaw, where, embedded in the parotid gland, it ends by dividing into the *superficial temporal* and *maxillary arteries.* The external carotid artery supplies blood to the muscles of the neck, to the pharynx, thyroid gland, tongue, face, and scalp, through the following branches: the *ascending pharyngeal, superior thyroid, lingual, facial,* and *posterior auricular,* in this order from below upwards.

The superficial temporal artery, the smaller of the terminal branches of the external carotid, sends twigs to the parotid gland, the masseter and temporalis muscles, and the upper part of the side of the face.

The maxillary artery supplies the upper and lower jaws, the muscles of mastication, the palate, nose, orbit, and the external and middle ears (Figs. 13.2, 5.2, Ch. 5). Through its branch the **middle meningeal artery** it supplies the dura mater, and through its **inferior dental branch** blood is distributed to the teeth of the lower jaw; its **superior dental branch** supplies the teeth of the upper jaw. The middle meningeal branch is important surgically, for it may be torn by a blow upon the head, even though no fracture of the bone occurs; pressure of the escap-

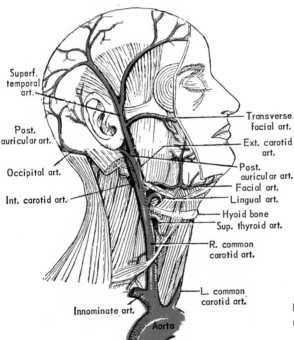

Superf. temporal art.

Post. auricular art.

Occipital art.

Int. carotid art.

Transverse facial art.

Ext. carotid art.

Post. auricular art.

Facial art.

Lingual art.

Hyoid bone

Sup. thyroid art.

R. common carotid art.

L. common carotid art.

Innominate art.

Aorta

Fig. 13.2. Arteries of the right side of the head and **neck.**

ing blood then causes loss of consciousness and paralysis, which must be relieved by trephining the skull.

The internal carotid artery

At its origin from the common carotid, the internal carotid artery shows a slight dilatation called the *carotid sinus* (Figs. 13.2, 13.3) which is of great physiological importance (Ch. 5). The internal carotid ascends to the base of the skull and enters the cranial cavity through a canal in the petrous portion of the temporal bone, called the *carotid canal.* In its cervical course (from its origin to the base of the skull) it gives off no branches. Its *branches* supply the middle ear through the **caroticotympanic branch,** which arises from the vessel in the carotid canal; the pituitary body; the orbit through the *ophthalmic artery;* and the brain through the *anterior* and *middle cerebral arteries.*

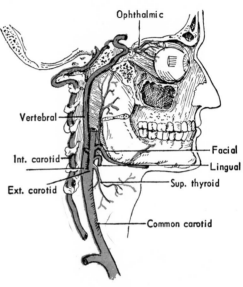

Fig. 13.3. The vertebral artery and deeper branches of the carotid arteries.

The ophthalmic artery (Fig. 13.4) is given off from the internal carotid within the cranial cavity and enters the orbit through a foramen (optic foramen) that also transmits the optic nerve. It sends a branch to the eyeball that supplies the retina and other coats of the eye; it also sends branches to the muscles of the eye, the lacrimal gland, and other structures of the orbit. The branch supplying the retina is called the **central artery of the retina** which, running forward in the center of the optic nerve, appears in the middle of the optic disc (Ch. 41). It is readily seen in the living subject by means of an instrument known as the ophthalmoscope.

The anterior cerebral artery springs from the internal carotid artery at the inner end of the fissure of Sylvius (lateral cerebral sulcus) which is described in Chapter 37. Through its **anterior communicating branch** the anterior cerebral artery is joined to its fellow of the opposite side. It gives off **central** and **cortical branches.** The former supply the brain substance in the depth of the cerebrum, and the latter are distributed to the anterior two thirds or so of the medial surface of the hemisphere and to the upper part of the lateral surface (Fig. 13.5).

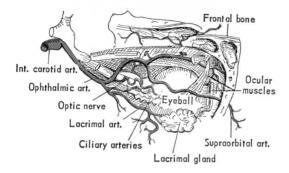

Fig. 13.4. The right ophthalmic artery and its branches, orbital cavity viewed from above.

The middle cerebral artery is the largest branch of the internal carotid artery. It runs laterally for a short distance in the fissure of Sylvius, and then turning backward and upward breaks up into branches that supply a large part of the cerebrum. **Central branches** are distributed to the interior of the brain; one of these, which supplies the internal capsule (Ch. 37), is called the "artery of cerebral hemorrhage," because its rupture is the most common cause of apoplexy, or what is popularly known as a "stroke." The **cortical branches** of the middle cerebral artery are distributed over the greater part of the lateral surface of the hemisphere.

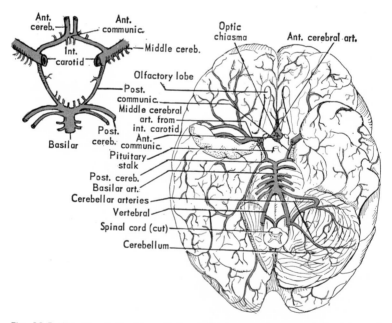

Fig. 13.5. Arteries at the base of the skull; the anterior part of the temporal lobe and most of the cerebellum on the left have been excised. Enlarged drawing of arterial circle (circle of Willis) on the left.

The circulus arteriosus, or circle of Willis, is a ring of anastomosing vessels at the base of the brain formed by the anterior and middle cerebral arteries in front, joined by an anterior communicating artery; and the posterior cerebral arteries behind, joined by a posterior communicating artery (Fig. 13.5). These anastomoses prevent the brain from being deprived of blood even though two of its main vessels should be occluded.

ARTERIES OF THE UPPER LIMB

The subclavian artery

All the blood that reaches the upper limb is delivered by this large artery. It arises on the *right* side as a division of the innominate (the common carotid being the other division) and arches outward; the highest point of the arch lies about 2 cm above the right clavicle. The *left* subclavian springs directly from the arch of the aorta and arches to the left (Fig. 13.1). Each artery crosses the front of the first rib and enters the axilla or armpit. From the outer border of the first rib to the lower border of the teres major muscle (which is the lower limit of the posterior wall of the axilla) the name of the vessel is changed to the *axillary artery*. From the lower border of the teres major the artery is continued down the arm and the name again changed to the *brachial artery*. The four major branches of the subclavian artery are the (1) *vertebral,* (2) *internal mammary,* (3) *thyrocervical,* and (4) *costocervical.*

The vertebral artery runs upwards through the foramina in the transverse processes of the first (upper) six cervical vertebrae and enters the cranial cavity through the foramen magnum of the occipital bone (Fig. 13.3). It gives off branches that supply the spinal cord and cerebellum. Before it enters the skull it sends several branches to neighboring muscles. Within the cranial cavity the vertebral arteries of the two sides converge toward the lower border of the pons, where they join to form a single trunk called the *basilar artery.*

The basilar artery, after a short course upward in a median groove on the anterior surface of the pons, divides into the right and left **posterior cerebral arteries** (Fig. 13.5) which, with the *posterior communicating arteries,* complete the circle of Willis. The basilar trunk sends branches to the pons and, through the posterior cerebrals, supplies the occipital lobe and part of the temporal lobe of the cerebral hemisphere.

The internal mammary artery descends into the thorax behind the upper six costal cartilages close to the border of the sternum. It sends branches to the pericardium, pleura, upper intercostal spaces, diaphragms, thymus, mammary gland, and to muscles of the neck and scapular region.

The thyrocervical artery supplies branches to the thyroid gland, to various muscles of the neck and scapular region, and to the larynx, trachea, and esophagus.

The **costocervical artery** sends branches to the upper intercostal spaces and to the posterior muscles of the neck.

The **axillary artery**, the continuation of the subclavian artery into the axilla, gives off branches to the muscles on the upper part of the chest, about the shoulder and posterior wall of the axilla, and to the humerus and shoulder joint (Fig. 13.6).

The **brachial artery**, the continuation of the axillary artery into the arm, lies at first on the medial side of the arm, but inclining forward as it descends comes to occupy the **cubital fossa** on the front of the elbows (Figs. 13.6, 13.7). The cubital fossa is the triangular space at the bend of the elbow bounded laterally by the brachioradialis muscle and medially by the pronator teres. The brachial artery supplies the muscles of the arm and gives off a branch called the **nutrient artery** which penetrates the humerus. Its largest branch, which is given off near its commencement, is called the **profunda brachii;** this turns backwards, then runs behind the humerus in the spiral groove with the radial nerve to the outer side of the bone; it here divides into an *ascending* and a *descending branch* and supplies the deltoid and triceps muscles.

The **ulnar artery** is the larger and the inner of the two terminal divisions of the brachial artery. It is placed deeply in its upper part, being covered by the deep head of the pronator teres. It becomes more superficial about the middle of the forearm. Crossing the medial side of the wrist just beneath the subcutaneous tissue and skin, it passes under

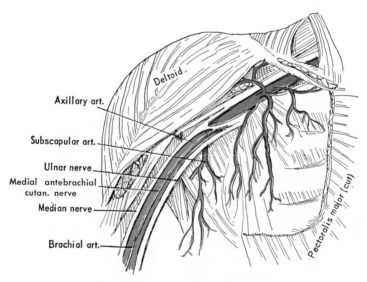

Fig. 13.6. The axillary artery and commencement of the brachial artery.

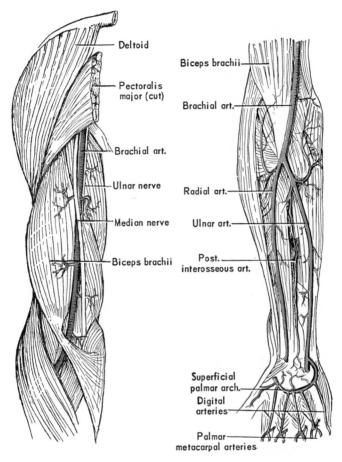

Fig. 13.7. *Left,* arteries of the arm and, *right,* forearm.

the palmaris brevis muscle and then, after giving off a **deep branch,** crosses the palm as the **superficial palmar arch.** A short distance from its origin, the ulnar artery gives off the two **ulnar recurrent arteries, anterior** and **posterior,** which turn upwards and supply structures about the elbow joint. At a little lower level, the **common interosseous artery** arises which, at the upper border of the interosseous membrane, divides into an **anterior interosseous** and a **posterior interosseous artery.** They descend on the respective surfaces of the membrane to the level of the wrist.

The **radial artery** is the lateral and smaller terminal branch of the brachial artery. Near its commencement it gives rise to a **radial recurrent artery** that supplies the elbow joint and neighboring structures. Just above the wrist the radial artery becomes quite superficial. It lies upon

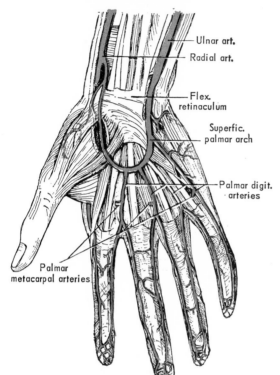

Fig. 13.8. Arteries of the right
hand, palmar aspect.

the lower end of the radius to the lateral side of the flexor carpi radialis.
It is this part of the artery that is generally used for feeling the pulse. In
the palm, branches of the radial artery supply the carpus, the adjacent
sides of the thumb and index finger, and the corresponding interosseus
muscles. The terminal part of the radial artery joins the deep branch of
the ulnar artery to form the *deep palmar arch.*

The **superficial and deep palmar arches** (Fig. 13.8) are arterial
arches of the palm with their convexities directed toward the fingers.
The **superficial arch,** as already mentioned, is formed by the superficial
terminal branch of the ulnar artery and is usually completed by a twig
from a branch of the radial artery. Four branches spring from the arch
and run forward: the other three branches go to the clefts between the
fingers and, after being joined by branches from the deep palmar arch,
divide into branches for the adjacent sides of the digits; the fourth
branch goes to the medial side of the little finger. The **deep palmar arch**
is formed by the deep branch of the ulnar artery and the terminal part
of the radial artery; it lies upon the proximal ends of the shafts of the
metacarpal bones. It supplies branches that, as mentioned above, join the
digital branches of the superficial palmar arch. Other branches pass back-

wards through the interosseous spaces to the dorsum of the hand, where they anastomose with other small branches of the radial artery.

ARTERIES OF THE THORAX DERIVED FROM THE THORACIC AORTA

The thoracic aorta, the continuation downwards of the aortic arch, commences at the lower border of the fourth thoracic vertebra and extends to the aortic opening in the diaphragm, through which it passes, and is continued as the *abdominal aorta.* The thoracic aorta supplies the pericardium, esophagus, bronchi, the lower nine intercostal spaces, and the mammary gland. These branches are named, respectively, *pericardial, esophageal, bronchial,* and *posterior intercostal.*

ARTERIES OF THE ABDOMEN AND PELVIS DERIVED FROM THE ABDOMINAL AORTA AND ILIAC ARTERIES

The abdominal aorta

The abdominal aorta commences at the opening of the diaphragm and descends in front of the vertebral column to the fourth lumbar ver-

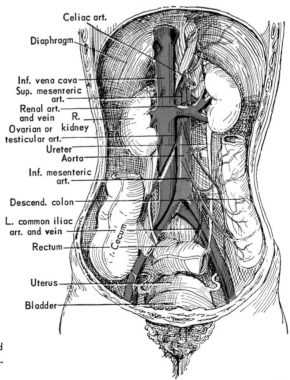

Celiac art.

Diaphragm

Inf. vena cava
Sup. mesenteric art.
Renal art. and vein   R.
Ovarian or kidney
testicular art.
Ureter
Aorta
Inf. mesenteric art.

Descend. colon

L. common iliac art. and vein

Rectum

Cecum

Uterus

Bladder

Fig. 13.9. Arteries and principal veins of the abdomen.

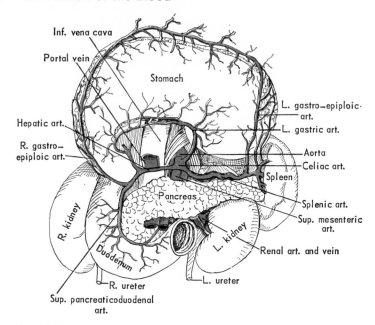

Inf. vena cava
Portal vein
Stomach
L. gastro-epiploic art.
Hepatic art.
L. gastric art.
R. gastro-epiploic art.
Aorta
Celiac art.
Spleen
Pancreas
Splenic art.
R. kidney
Sup. mesenteric art.
L. kidney
Renal art. and vein
Duodenum
R. ureter
L. ureter
Sup. pancreaticoduodenal art.

Fig. 13.10. The celiac artery and its branches; the stomach is turned upwards to show its posterior surface.

tebra, where it ends by dividing into the *right* and *left common iliac arteries* (Fig. 13.9).

The main branches of the abdominal aorta are the *celiac, superior mesenteric, renal, testicular* (male) or *ovarian* (female), and the *inferior mesenteric arteries,* in this order from above downwards.

The **celiac artery** is a short, wide branch that springs from the aorta ½ inch or so below the opening of the diaphragm, and divides into the *left gastric, hepatic,* and *splenic arteries* which supply the organs indicated by their names (Figs. 13.9, 13.10).

The **left gastric artery** also supplies the lower part of the esophagus and anastomoses with the *right gastric,* a branch of the hepatic artery.

The **hepatic artery** supplies the liver; the greater curvature, body, and pyloric region of the stomach through its **right gastric branch;** and the duodenum and pancreas through its **gastroduodenal** and **superior pancreaticoduodenal** branches. The liver is dependent for its oxygen supply upon the hepatic artery. Though a large volume of blood is carried to the liver by the portal vein, the blood in the latter vessel has a low content of oxygen that is quite inadequate to maintain the hepatic tissue in a normal, healthy state.

The **splenic artery,** which runs a tortuous course to the left along the upper border of the pancreas, divides into three or four short arteries that enter the spleen and supply its substances. It gives branches to the stomach and pancreas before entering the spleen.

The **superior mesenteric artery** springs from the aorta a little below the origin of the celiac artery (Fig. 13.11). It supplies the entire small intestine with the exception of the first part of the duodenum. It also supplies the cecum, the ascending colon, the greater part of the transverse colon, and sends branches to the pancreas through its **pancreatico-duodenal branch.** The branches of this artery are carried to the intestine between the layers of the mesentery, forming a succession of arches the parts of which anastomose freely with one another. The **inferior mesenteric artery** is smaller than the superior and is the last large branch to arise from the abdominal aorta before its division (Fig. 13.12). It supplies the terminal part of the transverse colon, the descending and pelvic colons, and the greater part of the rectum. Its continuation, which is now called the **superior rectal artery,** supplies the remainder (lower part) of the rectum.

The **renal arteries** are two short, wide vessels that supply the kidneys. They arise a little below the origin of the superior mesenteric artery.

The **testicular or ovarian arteries** pass, one on either side, to the corresponding testis or ovary.

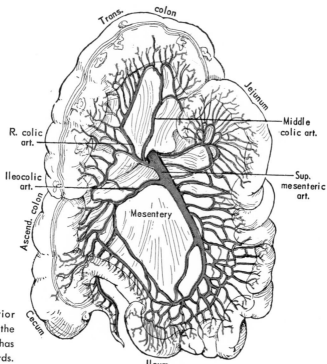

Fig. 13.11. Superior mesenteric artery; the transverse colon has been turned upwards.

The **common iliac arteries, right** and **left,** are the terminal divisions of the aorta and are about 2 inches long. Each divides at the level of the intervertebral disc between the last lumbar vertebra and the sacrum, into an *internal* and an *external iliac artery.*

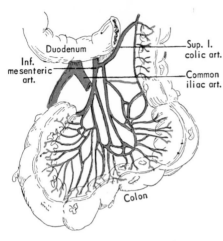

Fig. 13.12. The inferior mesenteric artery, intestine sectioned at duodenojejunal junction.

The **internal iliac artery** divides into an *anterior* and a *posterior trunk* (Fig. 13.9). The **anterior trunk** gives off branches that supply the urinary bladder, the lower part of the rectum, and in the female, the uterus (**uterine artery**) and the vagina (**vaginal artery**). Through a branch called the **obturator artery** it supplies the iliacus, obturator externus, and other muscles about the hip, as well as the hip joint itself. Through one of its terminal branches known as the **internal pudendal artery,** blood is delivered to the external generative organs (vulva and clitoris, or penis). The other terminal branch—the **inferior gluteal artery**—supplies the muscles and skin of the buttock and back of the thigh. The **posterior trunk** of the internal iliac supplies branches to several muscles of the pelvis and about the hip, to the sacrum, and to the gluteal muscles.

The **external iliac artery,** the larger of the two divisions of the common iliac, is continued into the thigh as the **femoral artery.** It gives off only a few, relatively small branches to the lower abdominal wall (**inferior epigastric artery**), and to the pubic region and groin (**pubic and cremasteric arteries**).

ARTERIES OF THE LOWER LIMB

The femoral artery

As mentioned above, this artery is the continuation of the external iliac artery, commencing behind the middle of the inguinal ligament. It descends on the front and inner side of the limb to the junction of the middle and lower thirds of the thigh, where it passes to the posterior aspect through an opening in the adductor magnus muscle and descends behind the knee joint as the *popliteal artery* (Figs. 13.13, 13.14). The upper 3.5 cm or so of the femoral artery are enclosed in a prolongation

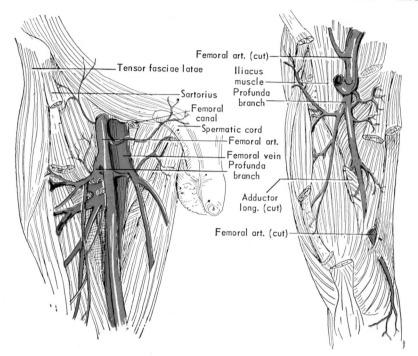

Fig. 13.13. The femoral artery and its branches on the anterior aspect of the thigh.

downwards of the fasciae of the abdominal cavity. It is called the *femoral sheath* and consists of three compartments. The femoral artery occupies the lateral compartment and the femoral vein the middle one. The medial compartment, also known as the *femoral canal,* contains areolar tissue, lymph vessels, and a lymph node. The upper end of the canal, which is situated behind the inguinal ligament, is called the *femoral ring,* and like the inguinal canal and inguinal rings is a weak part of the abdominal wall (Ch. 5). A knuckle of bowel or other abdominal structure may be forced down the canal, appearing as a swelling on the upper and inner part of the thigh. This is known as *femoral hernia.*

The branches of the femoral artery, with one exception, are relatively small and supply the lower part of the abdominal wall, the external generative organs and perineum, and muscles in the upper part of the thigh. The exception is a large artery called the **profunda femoris,** which springs from the femoral trunk 3.5 cm below its commencement. It plunges deeply among the muscles of the thigh, passing behind the femoral trunk and the femoral vein to the inner side of the femur. It terminates in *perforating branches,* which passing backward close to the bone supply the posterior muscles of the thigh.

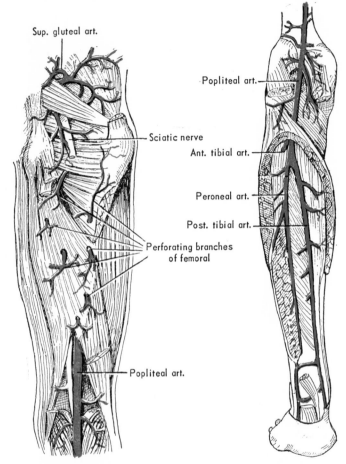

Sup. gluteal art.

Popliteal art.

Sciatic nerve

Ant. tibial art.

Peroneal art.

Post. tibial art.

Perforating branches of femoral

Popliteal art.

Fig. 13.14. Left, arteries on the back of the thigh and, *right*, leg.

The popliteal artery, the continuation of the femoral artery from the opening in the adductor magnus muscle to the back of the knee joint and through the popliteal space, gives branches to the knee joint and to the muscles and skin in the vicinity (Fig. 13.14). The *popliteal space,* or fossa, is the diamond-shaped space behind the knee bounded above laterally by the biceps femoris muscle and medially by the semitendinosus and the semimembranosus, and below by the two heads of the gastrocnemius. At the lower border of the popliteus muscles the popliteal artery ends by dividing into the *anterior* and *posterior tibial arteries.*

The anterior tibial artery, the smaller of the two divisions of the popliteal, commences at the lower border of the popliteus muscle and pierces the upper part of the interosseous membrane to reach the front of the leg (Figs. 13.14, 13.15). It lies on the anterior surface of the interosseous membrane for most of its course, but in the lower third of the leg is in contact with the tibia. It crosses the ankle to the dorsum of the foot and is here called the *dorsalis pedis artery.*

The dorsalis pedis artery passes to the first interosseous space, where it turns downward and enters the sole to complete the **plantar arch;** but a little before the change in its course it gives off a branch called the **arcuate artery** which arches outward across the bases of the metatarsal bones (Fig. 13.15). This vessel gives off from its convexity three **dorsal metatarsal arteries** which pass forward on the dorsal interosseous muscles to the clefts between the outer four toes. After being joined by branches of the plantar metatarsals, each divides into two, to supply the adjacent sides of the toes. A fourth dorsal metatarsal branch goes to the outer side of the little toe. The adjacent sides of the first and second toes are supplied by a branch that springs directly from the dorsalis pedis just after its arcuate branch has been given off.

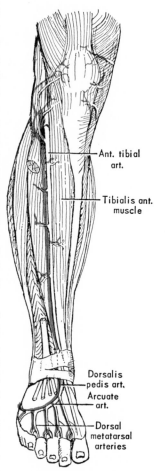

Fig. 13.15. The anterior tibial artery and arteries on the dorsum of the foot.

The **posterior tibial artery,** which is the larger division of the popliteal artery, descends on the medial side of the back of the leg (Fig. 13.14). It passes behind the medial malleolus into the sole and divides into the *medial* and *lateral plantar arteries.* About 1 inch (2.5) cm below its origin the posterior tibial artery gives off a large branch called the **peroneal artery,** which supplies the muscles of the calf and both bones of the leg. The peroneal artery ends in the region of the ankle and heel by breaking up into branches for the supply of neighboring structures.

The **medial plantar artery** runs forward with the medial plantar nerve on the medial side of the sole and of the great toe; it sends branches to join the first, second, and third plantar metatarsal arteries.

The **lateral plantar artery,** a considerably larger vessel than the preceding, crosses the sole obliquely with the lateral plantar nerve to the base of the fifth metatarsal bone. It then turns inwards again to the space between the bases of the first and second metatarsal bones where it anastomoses with the dorsalis pedis artery. Thus an arch, known as the **plantar arch,** is formed with its convexity directed forward and laterally. Branches from it, called the **plantar metatarsal arteries,** supply the sides of the toes and send twigs through the interosseous spaces to join the dorsal metatarsal arteries as already mentioned.

VEINS OF THE SYSTEMIC CIRCULATION

(The pulmonary veins are described in Chapter 18.)

Veins of the heart muscle

Most of the blood delivered to the heart muscle by the coronary arteries is drained into the right auricle by the **coronary sinus** which receives, in turn, blood through veins ascending on the surface of the heart. The remainder of the blood of the cardiac muscle is drained by small vessels that open directly into the auricles and ventricles.

Veins of the head and neck

The veins of the skull bone. Between the two tables of skull bone (that is, the diploe) is a system of veins called the **diploic veins.** They drain into the meningeal veins and the sinuses of the dura mater.

The intracranial veins. The **meningeal veins** accompany the corresponding meningeal arteries and run in the dura mater. They communicate with the superior sagittal sinus and other intracranial sinuses. The **cerebral veins** drain the substance of the cerebral hemispheres, and the more superficial ones run, for the most part, in the fissures and sulci of the cortex and empty into the sagittal sinus. The deeper cerebral veins drain the interior of the cerebrum. Two large veins **(internal cerebral)** join to form a short trunk in the mid-line called the **great cerebral vein;** it empties into the straight sinus.

The intracranial sinuses. The large veins contained between the layers of the dura mater are called *sinuses* (Fig. 13.16). There are a large number of sinuses, the most important being the *superior sagittal, inferior sagittal, straight, transverse* (paired), *sigmoid* (paired), *occipital,* and *cavernous* (paired.)

The **superior sagittal sinus** runs from the crista galli (of ethmoid bone) backwards in the mid-line just beneath the skull bone, which it grooves, to the internal occipital protuberance of the occipital bone; here it curves to one or the other side and continues as a *transverse sinus.* The posterior end of the sagittal sinus is dilated and is known as the *confluence of the sinuses,* but is commonly known by its older and more fanciful name, *torcular Herophili* (L., wine press of Herophilus, an Alexandrian physician of the third century B.C.).

The **inferior sagittal sinus** runs in the falx cerebri and is continued behind into the *straight sinus.* The latter sinus is continued into that *transverse sinus* which is *not* the continuation of the superior sagittal sinus (see above).

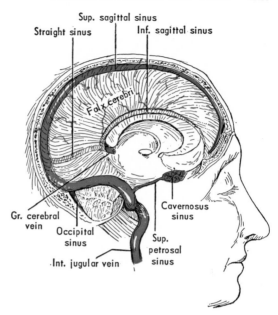

Sup. sagittal sinus
Straight sinus   Inf. sagittal sinus

Gr. cerebral vein
Occipital sinus
Cavernosus sinus
Sup. petrosal sinus
Int. jugular vein

Fig. 13.16. The intracranial sinuses.

The transverse sinuses, right and left, commence at the internal occipital protuberance. One (usually the right) is the continuation of the superior sagittal sinus, the other is the continuation of the straight sinus. Each transverse sinus runs laterally and forwards to the petrous part of the temporal bone, whence it is continued as the **sigmoid sinus.** The latter bends downwards and inwards, grooving the mastoid part of the temporal bone and the adjacent portion of the occipital bone, and then curves forward to end in the internal juglar vein, through which the venous blood is carried down the neck from the cranial cavity.

The cavernous sinuses are situated one on either side of the body of the sphenoid bone. Each is interlaced by numerous filaments that give it a spongy character; it receives blood from the orbit (through the superior ophthalmic vein) and from some of the cerebral veins, and communicates with veins of the face. This sinus is of considerable clinical importance for it may become infected and the blood within thrombosed (clotted) as a result of infection spreading from the orbit, nose, or face.

The internal jugular vein is the great vein of the neck. It descends from the base of the skull, where it commences as the continuation of the sigmoid sinus, to the sternal end of the clavicle (Fig. 13.17). Here it joins the subclavian vein to form the innominate vein. It lies in close relationship to the carotid artery. It receives tributaries from the face, mouth, pharynx, and thyroid gland (through common, facial, lingual, pharyngeal, and thyroid veins). The right lymphatic duct empties into it on the right side where it joins the subclavian; at this point on the left side the thoracic duct opens into it.

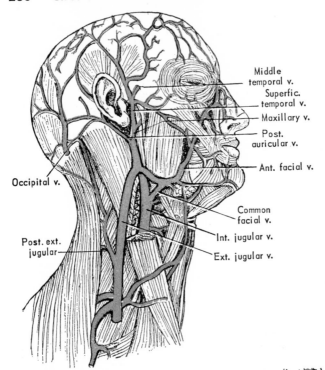

Middle
temporal v.

Superfic.
temporal v.

Maxillary v.

Post.
auricular v.

Ant. facial v.

Occipital v.

Common
facial v.

Int. jugular v.

Post. ext.
jugular

Ext. jugular v.

Fig. 13.17 (above). Principal
veins of the head and neck.

Fig. 13.18 (right). Superficial veins
on the dorsum of the hand.

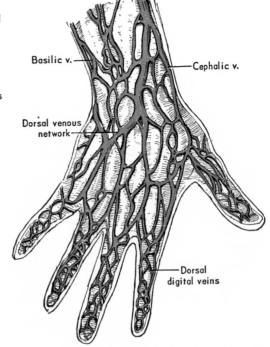

Basilic v.

Cephalic v.

Dorsal venous
network

Dorsal
digital veins

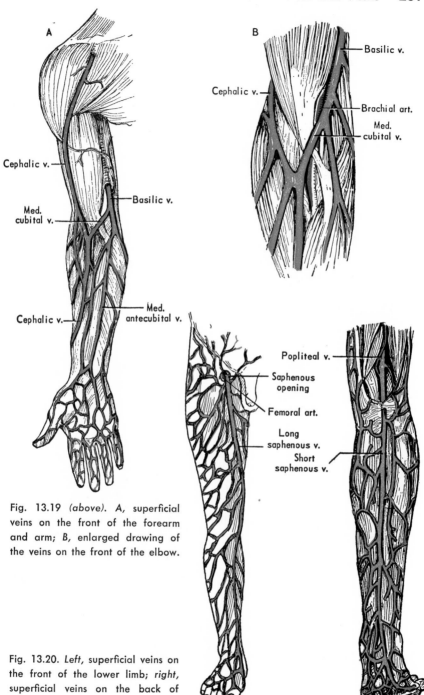

A

Cephalic v.

Med.
cubital v.

Basilic v.

Cephalic v.

Med.
antecubital v.

B

Cephalic v.

Basilic v.

Brachial art.

Med.
cubital v.

Popliteal v.

Saphenous
opening

Femoral art.

Long
saphenous v.

Short
saphenous v.

Fig. 13.19 *(above).* A, superficial veins on the front of the forearm and arm; B, enlarged drawing of the veins on the front of the elbow.

Fig. 13.20. *Left,* superficial veins on the front of the lower limb; *right,* superficial veins on the back of the leg.

The external, posterior external, and anterior jugular veins lie more superficially than the preceding. The external jugular vein commences at the angle of the lower jaw, being formed by a vein (*posterior auricular*) descending from behind the ear and the posterior division of the facial vein (Fig. 13.17). It empties into the subclavian vein. It drains a large part of the face and scalp. The posterior external jugular and the anterior jugular are small, superficial veins on the side and front of the neck, respectively, which empty into the external jugular vein.

The anterior facial vein drains a large part of the side of the face, nose, lips, and chin; it joins the anterior division of the posterior facial vein near the angle of the jaw to form the common facial vein, which empties into the internal jugular vein.

The posterior auricular and superficial temporal veins descend, respectively, behind and in front of the ear. They drain a large part of the scalp and join below the pinna to form the posterior division of the posterior facial vein. The blood drained by the superficial temporal vein flows into a short vein called the maxillary vein before reaching the posterior facial vein. The other tributary of the maxillary vein drains a deep plexus lying in relation to the pterygoid muscles.

Veins of the thorax

The innominate veins are formed, one on each side, by the confluence of the internal jugular and subclavian veins. They receive blood from the vertebral, internal mammary, and inferior thyroid veins. The veins of the two sides join to form the superior vena cava (Fig. 13.1). This latter large vein opens into the right auricle and carries all the blood from the head, neck, both upper limbs, and thorax.

Other small veins of the thorax that should be mentioned are the two internal mammary veins accompanying the corresponding artery, and the azygos vein which ascends in front of the right side of the vertebral column to the level of the fourth thoracic vertebra, where it arches forward and empties into the superior vena cava. It receives blood from the intercostal spaces of the right side, and the superior and inferior hemiazygos veins. The latter drain the left intercostal spaces.

Veins of the upper limb

The veins of the upper limb are in two sets—a *deep* and a *superficial*. The *deep veins* accompany the corresponding arteries and are called venae comitantes (sing. *vena comitans*). They usually run in pairs, one on each side of the artery. Starting in the hand, the venae comitantes of the smaller arteries join to form veins of progressively greater diameter, and in the arm the two trunks, lying one on each side of the brachial artery, are called the brachial veins; they are the upward continuations of the radial and ulnar veins, which accompany the arteries of the same name. The brachial veins empty into the **axillary vein,** the large vein of the axilla lying alongside and medial to the axillary artery.

The subclavian vein is the continuation of the axillary vein; it joins the internal jugular vein to form the **innominate vein.**

The superficial veins of the upper limb commence as a network of small veins just under the skin of the fingers, and become confluent at the bases of the fingers, especially on the dorsum (Figs. 13.18, 13.19). The larger veins so produced form a network in the palm and on the back of the hand. The latter, known as the **dorsal venous plexus,** is quite evident in the living subject. It is drained by two venous trunks, the **cephalic** vein on the radial side, and the **basilic** vein on the ulnar side. These two veins drain the anterior surface of the forearm, the cephalic vein from the wrist, the basilic vein from the upper part of the forearm. The venous plexus of the palm is drained by the **median antebrachial vein** which ascends near the middle of the anterior aspect of the forearm. Just below the elbow it joins the basilic vein.

In front of the elbow the cephalic vein gives off a short oblique branch that joins the basilic vein, then continues up the outer side of the front of the arm to a point below the clavicle, where it passes deeply between the pectoralis major and deltoid muscles to empty into the axillary vein.

The basilic vein ascends on the inner side of the front of the arm, at about the middle of which it passes deeply and, ascending to the axilla, is continued as the axillary vein.

Veins of the lower limb

As in the case of the upper limb, the superficial veins of the lower limb commence as small veins of the digits that form networks on the dorsum and the sole of the foot. The blood from the foot is drained by the two veins called the *long* and the *short saphenous.*

The long saphenous vein is the longest vein of the body, extending from the inner border of the foot to the upper part of the thigh (Fig. 13.20). It drains the sole and dorsum of the foot, and ascends in front of the medial malleolus, then on the side of the leg, knee, and thigh; in the upper part of the latter it inclines to the front and ends by joining the femoral vein in the femoral sheath about 3 cm below the inguinal ligament.

The short saphenous vein commences behind the outer malleolus and ascends in the middle of the calf to the back of the knee joint, a little above which it empties into the popliteal vein.

The saphenous veins are of considerable surgical interest because they are susceptible to dilatation and sacculation, the condition being known as **varicose veins.** The tendency of these veins to become varicose is due to the weight of the long column of blood that they are called upon to support in the standing position. Any circumstance that causes a resistance to the upward flow of venous blood, as by pressure upon the pelvic veins by the pregnant uterus or a tumor, increases this tendency. Normally the valves in the veins break the long blood colums into smaller sections and in this way considerably relieve the vein wall from the weight of blood, but once any marked dilatation of the vein occurs, the leaves of the valves fail to meet and perform this function and the dilatation of the veins then progresses more rapidly and becomes more pronounced.

The **deep veins,** like those of the upper limb, accompany the corresponding arteries and are named similar to their companion arteries. Thus, there are the **anterior** and **posterior tibial veins**[1] in the leg which unite to form the **popliteal vein** at the back of the knee; the latter, after passing through the opening in the adductor magnus opening, becomes the **femoral vein.** The femoral vein at the inguinal ligament becomes the **external iliac vein.**

Veins of the pelvis and abdomen

Here, again, the veins accompany the corresponding arteries and drain the organs or areas that the latter supply. There are the **external** and **internal iliac veins** which unite to form the **common iliac vein.** The common iliac veins of the two sides unite to form the *inferior vena cava* (Fig. 13.9).

The **inferior vena cava** is the great vein of the abdomen and corresponds in the venous system to the abdominal aorta in the arterial system. It ascends on the right side of the abdominal aorta, and passing through an opening in the diaphragm, empties into the right atrium of the heart. It drains blood from the lower half of the body, with the exception of the stomach, intestines, and spleen. The blood from these organs drains into the *portal vein* as described in the next paragraph.

The **portal vein** is formed by the union of the **superior mesenteric and splenic veins.** Besides these, the chief tributaries of the portal vein are the **right** and **left gastric veins.** The blood from the large intestine also reaches the portal vein, for the **inferior mesenteric vein** which collects blood from the large bowel is a tributary of the splenic vein. The portal vein is peculiar in that, though like other veins it drains a capillary area, it breaks up again in the liver into a capillary network. Thus all the products of the digestive processes are carried to the liver where the blood comes into direct contact with the hepatic tissue and undergoes changes preparatory to their utilization by the general tissues of the body. The blood, after passing through the liver, is carried by a number of short vessels—the **hepatic veins**—to the upper part of the inferior vena cava.

---

[1] The anterior and posterior tibial veins run in pairs, as *venae comitantes;* the anterior tibial veins are the continuation of the venae comitantes of the dorsalis pedis artery.

14
The Action of the Heart

The heart is a highly efficient pump. For its size it is capable of performing an almost incredible amount of work. It is also able automatically to adjust its performance to the amount of work it is required to do. A powerful man doing heavy work or running a race may pump 6 gallons of blood from his heart in a minute. It would take about three ordinary water buckets to hold that amount of blood, and it would take more than a minute to fill them from a hand pump many times larger than the heart. Moreover, this great quantity of blood is thrown from the heart against a high pressure. If we could tap the great artery—the aorta—and allow the blood to escape in a straight vertical pipe between 5 and 6 feet high, the blood would be forced to the top. The heart has two "cylinders"—the left and right ventricles—both of which discharge their contents at each beat. The heart derives its power from the contraction of muscular tissue that, as we have seen, composes its walls.

The heart valves. A pump, in order to drive fluid through a system of tubes, must be able to raise a pressure within its cylinder, and must possess valves so that no energy is wasted by forcing the fluid in a wrong direction (Fig. 14.2 and Plate II*b*). The valves of the heart are thin membranous leaves, placed at the openings from atria to ventricles and at the openings of the aorta and the pulmonary artery (Fig. 14.1). They are opened and closed by the pressure of blood on one or the other of their surfaces. Each set of valves will open in one diretion only; those between each atrium and ventricle open downward into the ventricle; they are called the **atrio-** (or **auriculo-**) **ventricular valves.** Those guarding the openings into the aorta and the pulmonary artery open into these vessels, and are called the **semilunar valves,** or, more particularly, the

235

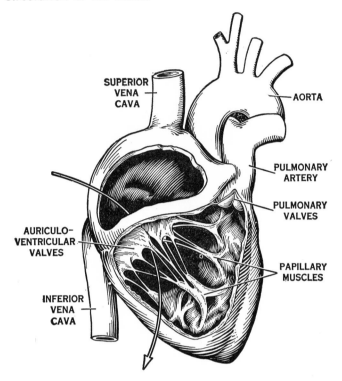

Fig. 14.1. The right side of the heart with the wall of the atrium and ventricle cut away to show the pulmonary and right atrioventricular valves, the papillary muscles, and cords running from these to the valve leaves. The arrow passes through the opening between atrium and ventricle.

aortic or **pulmonary valves. Mitral** and **tricuspid** are also names given, respectively, to the left and right atrioventricular valves.

Cords (**chordae tendineae**), like ropes of a parachute, run from the valve leaflets to fleshy pillars (**papillary muscles**) that arise from the walls of the ventricles. These cords prevent the valves from being forced upward into the auricle when the ventricle contracts (Fig. 14.1). But neither they nor the papillary muscles have any action in closing the valves. When the contraction occurs, the pressure within the cavity of the ventricle rises, and the valves between the auricle and ventricle are closed. As the pressure mounts still higher, the valves at the openings of the arteries (pulmonary and aorta) are forced open, and the blood rushes into these great arterial mains. When the ventricles relax again, and the pressure within these chambers falls below that existing in the great arteries, the valves close. The pressure in the ventricles continues to fall for a while, and when it falls below the pressure in the auricles, the valves in the floor of these chambers open and allow blood again to fill the ventricles.

The filling of the ventricles, the closure of one pair of valves followed by the opening of the other pair, the outrush of blood from the ventricles, and finally the relaxation and refilling of the ventricle are repeated again and again with perfect regularity 70 times or so each minute.

THE WORK OF THE HEART

Cardiac output

As in the case of other machines, the work of the heart is computed from the height (blood pressure) to which a weight (quantity of blood) is raised. The heart is the most industrious and indefatigable worker of the body. At every beat the left ventricle of a man at rest exerts a force sufficient to lift a weight of over 2 ounces to a height of over 5 feet. Each hour it does an amount of work equivalent to raising a weight of 500 pounds to the same height. The work performed in 24 hours by the left ventricle alone of a man lying quietly in bed equals that required to raise the weight of his body to the top of a 40-story building.

During strenuous muscular exercise, the heart's work is increased many times, for it not only pumps out more blood per minute but does so under a higher pressure. The quantity of blood that the heart pumps into the arteries each minute is called the **cardiac output,** or the *minute volume of the heart.* A healthy man can increase his cardiac output from around 5 liters per minute during rest to over 20 liters during very strenuous exercise. In order for the heart to perform this amount of work the flow of blood through its own arteries (**coronary arteries**) must be increased enormously to furnish its muscle with the necessary quantity of oxygen (Ch. 18).

The cardiac cycle, or beat

The series of different actions that the heart performs in succession is spoken of as its **cycle,** or **beat.** Starting with any one of the separate actions or movements of the heart, the sequence of cardiac events that takes place until that particular action commences to repeat itself constitutes a **cardiac cycle.** The contraction of the heart is called **systole;** its relaxation is called **diastole** (Fig. 14.2). A comparison between the heart muscle and a skeletal muscle may be drawn to show these two phases of the cardiac cycle. If the reader will grasp the biceps of one arm with the opposite hand and alternately bend (flex) and unbend (extend) his elbow, he will feel the muscle become firm and round when it contracts, and flat and soft when it relaxes. Though the biceps is solid, not hollow like the heart, its contraction corresponds to the systole of the ventricle, and its relaxation to the diastole.

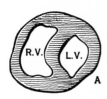

Fig. 14.2. Sections of ventricles. A, during diastole; B, during systole. R.V., right ventricle; L.V., left ventricle. (After Ludwig.)

In order to follow the successive acts performed by the heart, let us start at that moment when the ventricle is relaxed (diastole) (Fig. 14.3A) ; that is, at the end of the ventricular contraction (systole), at the moment when the semilunar valves at the openings of the arteries have just closed and the atrioventricular valves have not yet opened. The blood at this time pours into the auricles; a fraction of a second later the valves between auricles and ventricles open, and the blood streams into the ventricles (Fig. 14.3B). Soon the ventricles are filled or nearly filled. The atria at this moment contract to give an extra spurt to the blood and practically empty themselves into the ventricles (Fig. 14.3C). As though at a signal, the ventricles contract. At once the valves of the atria close, but the semilunar valves have not yet opened. The muscles of the ventricles continue to contract, and press upon the mass of blood in the ventricles. The pressure within the ventricles rises to a great height— a pressure sufficient to support a column of mercury 5 inches (120 mm) high, or to throw a stream of blood or water to a height of 5 feet or more. The valves guarding the arteries are forced open, and a flood of blood pours along the aorta and all the arterial channels (Figs. 14.3D and E). After their brief contraction the ventricles relax again; then the pressure within their cavities falls, the higher pressure in the arteries closes the semilunar valves, and this cycle comes to an end. Another cycle begins immediately.

Cardiac muscle. Functionally, the heart muscle, or *myocardium,* resembles smooth muscle since it contracts rhythmically and involuntarily, and is controlled by autonomic nerves. Yet it bears a likeness to skeletal muscle in that its fibers are cross striated. It differs, however, from both the smooth and skeletal varieties, for its fibers are not entirely separate; they are connected by slips to form a continuous sheet, or *syncytium,* throughout which a contraction spreads without interruption. Cardiac muscle, in common with skeletal muscle, shows treppe and the "all or none law" (Ch. 4). But it has a long refractory period, being inexcitable during systole; it cannot, therefore, be tetanized. Though the auricles and ventricles are separated superficially by fibrous tissue, they are continuous within the heart through the atrioventricular bundle (Ch. 16).

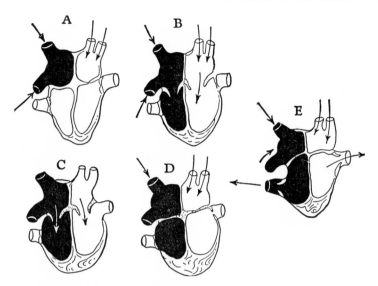

Fig. 14.3. Diagram to show different phases of the cardiac cycle. *A,* atria filling, valves between atria and ventricles closed, ventricle relaxed, valves at arterial openings closed; *B,* valves between the atria and the ventricles have opened and blood is pouring into the ventricles which are still relaxed; *C,* atria contract and empty into the ventricles which are filled to capacity; *D,* ventricles contract and close the opening into the atria, the pressure then rises rapidly and when sufficiently high to overcome the pressure in the pulmonary artery (or the aorta in the case of the left ventricle) the valves guarding the orifice of the artery open (in this sketch the valves are still closed; the ventricle is therefore a completely closed cavity); *E,* the semilunar valves have been forced open and the blood is now being forced into the pulmonary system (or aorta). The left side of the heart is drawn as though empty in order to show more clearly the positions of the valves, but it must be remembered that whatever is occurring on the right side of the heart is occurring at the same instant on the left side.

The pulse

Each beat of the heart causes a pulse in the arteries that can be felt as a light tap or impact if one presses a finger lightly over any large artery. The most usual place to feel for the pulse is over the radial artery at the wrist. But it must not be thought that the radial is different from any other artery in so far as the pulse is concerned. It is usually chosen simply because it is conveniently situated. The heart rate, and therefore the pulse rate, of a man at rest mentally and physically is about 70 per minute. When hard work is done the pulse quickens, and in very strenuous exercise it may rise to 180 per minute. Emotion and excitement also cause an increase in the pulse rate. In ill health, fever is the most common cause of rapid pulse.

It is a general rule that the smaller the animal the more rapid is its heart rate—that is, the shorter is the heart's cycle. An elephant's heart beats only about 25 times per minute; a mouse or a canary has a heart rate of 1000 or more per minute. The action of a baby's heart is about twice as fast as that of a full-grown man. It is impossible to count the heart rate of very small animals by the ordinary means; special electrical methods are employed to record it.

Students often misunderstand the nature of the pulse because they think that the beat is caused by the *flow* of the blood in the radial artery. The pulse is actually a wave set up in the *walls* of the vessels and in the blood contained within them, by the systole of the ventricle. The nature of the pulse may be made clear by means of an illustration. If an elastic band is stretched between two rigid supports and struck lightly or plucked at one end, a coarse vibration or wave travels to the opposite end. The impact upon the wall of the aorta by the blood discharged from the ventricle travels through the walls of the arterial system in a similar manner. The highly elastic wall of the aorta is expanded by the contents of the ventricle but immediately recoils again. Thus, a wave of expansion and recoil —a wave with a high- and a low-pressure phase—is set up and transmitted at high velocity even to the smallest arteries (Fig. 14.4).

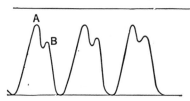

Fig. 14.4. A record of the pulse wave; A, crest due to the sharp expansion of the artery by blood discharged from heart; B, secondary wavelet known as the *dicrotic wave*.

The more elastic the walls of the vessels, the more slowly does the pulse wave travel. The speed of the wave is, therefore, considerably greater in an old person than in a child, because the arterial walls become stiffer and harder and consequently less elastic with advancing years.

The speed of the pulse wave is quite independent of the speed of the blood itself. We can demonstrate this fact by tying off a large artery. The blood in the vessel is brought to a standstill, yet the pulse is not abolished and its speed is not at all reduced (Fig. 14.5). The mass of blood ejected by a beat of the heart does not reach a peripheral artery (for example, the radial) until a fraction of a second *after* the arrival of the pulse wave that the ejected blood had started.

The apex beat and the heart sounds

The heart muscle becomes harder and more· rounded in form when it contracts. During systole it bulges forward, rotates a little to the right, and presses against the chest wall between the fifth and sixth ribs, at a

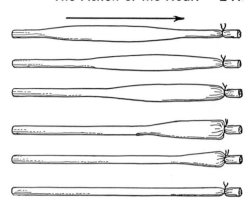

Fig. 14.5. Successive stages in the transmission of the pulse in a ligated artery.

point a little to the right and below the left nipple. A slight, soundless tap caused by the heart as it touches the chest wall can be felt in this spot with the fingers placed flat against the skin. It is called the **apex beat.**

The sounds that are heard when the ear is pressed against a person's chest, or when a special instrument known as a stethoscope is employed, are made within the heart itself. There are two sounds heard in quick succession; a slight pause follows, and then they are repeated. The sounds resemble the syllables "lub" and "dup," for the first sound lasts longer, is softer, and has a deeper pitch than the second, which is short, sharp, and of higher pitch. The first sound ("lub") is composed mainly of two sounds blended together. These are (1) the vibrations set up by the contraction of the heart's muscle, and (2) the vibrations caused by the valves between the atria and ventricles closing and their leaflets being put under tension by the pressure created in the ventricles at the commencement of systole. The second sound ("dup") is purely valvular in origin; that is, it is due to the vibrations set up by the closure of the valves at the openings of the pulmonary artery and aorta.

So long as the valves come together tightly and accurately, no blood can leak through in the wrong direction, and the heart performs its work with the efficiency of a good pump. Disease, however, not uncommonly attacks one or more sets of valves, causing them to become deformed, stiff, or partly destroyed. The affected valve may then be unable to close as tightly as it should in order to prevent the leakage of blood. Or it may not open freely, and so offer an impediment to the flow of blood through the opening it is supposed to guard. In either instance, the heart does its work less efficiently.

A heart with a defective valve is at a mechanical disadvantage; it must do more work than the healthy heart in order to maintain the circulation in any circumstances, but especially during muscular exercise. Its muscle becomes thicker, or **hypertrophied,** and its cavity **dilated.** These changes enable the heart in most instances to compensate for its handicap, and provided that the heart muscle itself does not fail, good health may be enjoyed for years by one whose heart has a valvular defect. Exercise even of a severe nature will not injure a healthy heart, but it may be dangerous for a person with a diseased heart valve and a hypertrophied or weakened heart muscle to undertake strenuous muscular work.

When a set of valves is diseased, the clear sound caused by the closure of healthy valves is no longer heard. There is heard, instead, a rushing or swishing sound, resulting from the leakage backwards of the blood, or from the obstruction to the flow of blood through the opening. The physician, by listening to the beats of the heart, can detect these unusual sounds, called heart **murmurs,** and thus locate the diseased valve. Rheumatic fever and certain contagious diseases, especially scarlet fever, are most commonly responsible for the deformities of the heart valves.

When the edges of a valve fail to meet accurately and form a tight seal, a part of the blood is allowed to leak back into the chamber from which it has just been driven; the blood is said to *regurgitate* and the valve—auriculoventricular, aortic, or pulmonary—is termed **incompetent.** When stiffening or deformity of a set of valves causes an impediment to the flow of blood from an auricle to a ventricle, or from a ventricle into the aorta or pulmonary artery, the narrowing due to such defect is called **stenosis.** Hence, *mitral* (left auriculoventricular valves), *tricuspid* (right auriculoventricular valves), *aortic,* and *pulmonary stenosis* are terms for narrowing at the various orifices of the heart.

15
The Arterial Blood Pressure

William Harvey proved that the blood made a circuit through the body—that it was ejected from the left ventricle into the arteries and returned to the right side of the heart by the veins. Yet he did not know that the blood circulated at a high pressure—or, if he held any opinion upon the matter, he made no comment. He probably thought, with the men of his day, that the blood currents were somewhat sluggish streams—that the flow through the arteries resembled the flow of water through canals or drains rather than the swift rush of fluid through closed pipes.

An English clergyman, the Rev. Stephen Hales, in 1733, was the first to demonstrate the high pressure of the blood in the arteries. He inserted a small brass tube into a large artery of a horse and connected the small tube to an 8-foot glass tube placed in a vertical position. When the clamp was removed from the artery, the blood rushed into the tube and rose nearly to the top. The top of the column of blood was observed to fluctuate up and down at each beat of the heart.

Since Hales' day much more convenient methods of taking the blood pressure have been devised. Instead of a long empty tube, a small tube bent into the form of a U with the bend filled with mercury is now employed (Fig. 15.1). This instrument is called a **manometer**. The blood presses upon and raises the mercury, which, being some 13½ times heavier than blood, rises only a few inches instead of several feet. For this reason it is customary to express the amount of the blood pressure in terms of the height in millimeters of the column of mercury (abbreviated as mm Hg[1]) that it will support. Thus we speak of the blood as having

[1] Hg is the symbol for *hydrargyrum*, mercury.

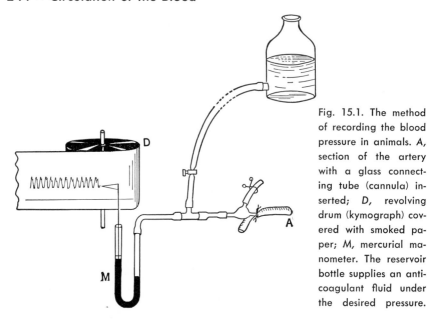

Fig. 15.1. The method of recording the blood pressure in animals. A, section of the artery with a glass connecting tube (cannula) inserted; D, revolving drum (kymograph) covered with smoked paper; M, mercurial manometer. The reservoir bottle supplies an anticoagulant fluid under the desired pressure.

a pressure of 120 to 150 mm Hg, as the case may be. There were no anesthetics in Hales' day, and so the animal must have suffered pain. Today whenever it is necessary to demonstrate directly the blood pressure in an animal, an anesthetic is always used, and no pain is ever occasioned.

Systolic and diastolic pressures. When the aortic valves are open and the ventricle contracts and forces blood into the arteries, it is apparent that the pressure in the arteries must reach its highest point. When, on the other hand, the heart relaxes and the aortic valves close, the pressure must decline again. Just before the next contraction of the heart occurs, the arterial pressure must reach its lowest level. Since the heart's contraction is called systole and its relaxation diastole (Ch. 14), the highest point of pressure in the arteries is termed the **systolic pressure** and the lowest point is called the **diastolic pressure**. The **mean pressure** is usually taken as the average of these two values (Fig. 15.2).

Fig. 15.2. The phases of the arterial blood pressure.

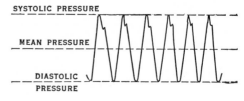

SYSTOLIC PRESSURE

MEAN PRESSURE

DIASTOLIC PRESSURE

HOW THE BLOOD PRESSURE IS CREATED AND MAINTAINED

Practically every part of the body must receive a regular supply of oxygen, or the cells that compose it will very soon deteriorate and finally die. To deliver this supply of oxygen, blood must be moved swiftly and under sufficient pressure so that it may be forced into the most distant regions of the body. If the blood pressure falls below a certain level, the tissues will be supplied with blood very poorly, or not at all. The brain will no longer carry out its functions; unconsciousness, ending in death, will result. It is important, then, to inquire into the means by which the stream of blood is kept at the necessary pressure.

In order to understand the factors upon which the arterial pressure depends, let us return to the comparison that was made on page 200 between the circulation and a municipal water system. The complete water system that serves the houses of a city consists in reality of two divisions. These are the pump and the large water mains on the one hand, and the drains on the other (Figs. 12.1, 12.2). Between these two divisions are a large number of separate faucets. When a faucet is opened, water flows out and is collected and carried away by drain pipes, which in many cities empty their contents into the same large body of water from which the pump is fed. In the water mains the pressure is many times greater than in the drains.

The circulation of the body is also divisible into a high-pressure system—the arteries—and a low-pressure system—the capillaries and veins. The pressure in the latter vessels is only a fraction of that in the arteries. Between the two systems a number of small vessels are situated, which at one time may open widely, and at another time may be tightly closed. These vessels, called **arterioles**, were discussed in Chapter 12. The walls of these fine tubes are composed of muscle fibers, which run circularly around them. When these muscular rings contract, the caliber of the vessel is reduced, less blood can flow through it, and we say the vessel has **constricted** (p. 263). When the muscle relaxes, the caliber of the tube becomes larger, more blood escapes into the capillaries, and we say the vessel has **dilated**. The arterioles therefore correspond to the faucets in the water system, a greater or a smaller quantity of fluid being permitted, in each instance, to pass from the high- to the low-pressure system. Figure 15.3 shows the fall in pressure that occurs in the circulatory system from the left to the right side of the heart.

The following factors are responsible for maintaining the arterial blood pressure:
1. Pumping action of the heart
2. Peripheral resistance
3. Viscosity of the blood

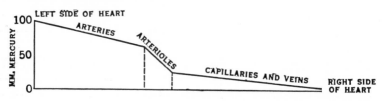

Fig. 15.3. Graph of the arterial blood pressure throughout the circulation. Note the very low pressure of blood entering the right auricle and the sharp drop in pressure in the region of the arterioles.

4. Quantity of blood in the arterial system

5. Elasticity of the arterial walls

We shall say a few words about the role played by each.

Pumping action of the heart. The arterial pressure will be raised if the quantity of blood that the heart discharges into the arteries each minute (cardiac output) is increased. This is obvious; since the arteries will contain more blood, the blood will distend their walls more fully. Should the pump expel less blood in a given time, the pressure will fall. These statements, however, hold true only provided the four other factors mentioned above remain unchanged. Like any other pump, the heart may increase the quantity of fluid discharged during any period by increasing the quantity that it expels at each beat while the number of beats per minute remains the same; or it may increase the discharge by beating more frequently while the quantity of blood discharged at each beat remains the same. Again, it may increase both the rate of its beat and the quantity discharged at each beat.

Peripheral resistance. This time-honored term is applied to the resistance that the great number of small arterioles offer to the flow of blood out of the arterial system into the capillaries and veins. We all know that it is more difficult to drive fluid along a narrow tube than along a wide one because there is more friction. It has already been mentioned that the arterioles can, since they have muscles in their walls, be constricted or dilated. The resistance to the flow of blood will be greater and less blood will therefore pass in any given time from the arterial system when the arterioles are constricted than when they are dilated. Just as the pressure in a town's water system would fall sharply if the faucets in all the houses were suddenly opened at once and more water allowed to flow into the sinks and drains, so, when the arterioles are dilated and more blood streams into the capillaries and veins, the arterial pressure falls; when the arterioles are narrowed, the pressure rises. Of course, in the arterial system the pressure does not for long continue to rise or to fall, but does so only until the volume of blood entering the arteries from the heart and leaving by the arterioles is again equal. The arterioles may therefore be compared to a dam in a river; when the dam is raised or lowered, after a time, the same volume of water flows over it as before.

Under ordinary circumstances the arterioles are never either fully dilated or completely closed, but in a state somewhere in between. This partial contraction of the vessel walls is called *vascular tone* and is dependent mainly upon nerves (Ch. 17) but also on the inherent contractile power of the smooth muscle of the arteriolar walls, for their tone is not completely and permanently abolished by cutting all nerves supplying the vascular muscle. The caliber of the small vessels is also acted upon by hormones and other chemicals in the blood.

Viscosity of the blood. Perhaps the simplest way to define the term **viscosity** is to say that it refers to the thickness or stickiness of a fluid. Fluids such as syrup and molasses are many times more viscous than water; blood is five times more so. A viscous fluid flows more slowly along a tube than other fluids, and more force is required to drive it through, since more friction is developed between its molecules. If two syringes are filled, one with water and the other with a heavy oil, it will be found that a very much greater force must be exerted upon the plunger, and a greater pressure must be created in the barrel of the syringe to force out the oil than to drive the water from the syringe nozzle. The oil has a higher viscosity than the water. In the same way, the viscosity of blood, being higher than that of water, aids in keeping the blood pressure at the usual level; the blood flows less freely through the fine arterioles than would water or saline.

Quantity of blood in the arterial system. It is quite apparent that any pressure system must contain a sufficient amount of fluid to fill its channels before any degree of pressure can be developed. The walls of the arteries can be stretched, so in reality the system can be overfilled. The more blood, therefore, that is contained in the arteries and the more their walls are stretched, the greater will the pressure be. If blood is lost by hemorrhage, the pressure will fall; fluid injected into the circulation causes the pressure to rise (Ch. 7).

Elasticity of the arterial walls. The arteries are plentifully supplied with elastic tissue fibers. In the normal healthy body the arterial system is overfilled, the walls of the vessels being at all times slightly stretched. At each beat (systole) of the heart an extra amount of blood is discharged from the ventricle and the walls are stretched still further. When the heart pauses again—that is, during its diastole—the stretched walls of the arteries recoil to their previous state almost as readily as a rubber band that has been released from a stretching force. When the walls recoil in this way, they press upon the blood and force it onward through the arterioles during the pause of the heart. That is to say, the blood pressure does not fall to zero between beats—the diastolic pressure is maintained, and the flow of blood into the capillaries and veins is continuous, and not in squirts. The capillaries and veins, therefore, unlike the arteries, do not pulsate. In a water system the pipes are made of non-elastic, rigid material, but we know that, though the water is forced into the system by a pump that works intermittently like the heart, the water flows from the faucets in a continuous stream, not in jets. This effect is obtained either by pumping the water up to a reservoir situated at a considerable height, from which it flows steadily by gravity to the faucets, or by employing a standpipe. The standpipe is a large vertical cylinder closed at its upper end and originally filled with air. When the water was allowed to fill the system the air was driven to the closed end of the cylinder and there compressed by the rising water. Thus entrapped, the air acts as an elastic cushion against which the water is forced by each beat of the pump. The pneumatic cushion as it expands after each beat forces the water along the supply pipes in a continuous stream to the faucets.

In the circulation another factor is required to convert the fluctuating pressure in the arteries to an even flow in the capillaries and veins. The arterioles must be in at least a moderate state of constriction. They should offer a certain resistance to the flow of blood, thus causing the arterial walls to stretch, which is saying again that the arterial system is overfilled. When the arterioles become widely dilated, the capillaries in certain regions, such as at the base of fingernail, pulsate, as indicated by intermittent flushing of the fingernail synchronous with the heart beats. Hence, both factors, elastic walls and the resistance offered by partially closed arterioles, are required to maintain the diastolic pressure and thereby drive the blood in a continuous stream into the capillaries and veins. If the arterial walls were rigid or the small vessels dilated to the maximum, there would be no diastolic pressure and only an intermittent systolic pounding on the vascular walls.

The normal blood pressure levels

The blood pressure varies considerably in different species but there is no consistent relationship between its height and the size of the animal. It is higher in the dog than in man, and if we should determine the arterial pressure of an elephant and of a mouse we should find little difference between the two measurements. The blood pressure in cold-blooded animals is, however, much lower than in mammals.

Though the arterial blood pressure of a young man of about 20 years of age is usually given as 120 mm Hg systolic and 80 mm diastolic, it shows a considerable range—from 110 to 122 mm Hg—among healthy persons. It is somewhat lower in women than in men, and much lower before puberty than after, reaching the adult level around 17 years of age.

VARIATIONS IN THE BLOOD PRESSURE

Physiological. It is usual for the arterial blood pressure to rise steadily with advancing years, though many authorities deny that it is a purely physiological process. Nevertheless it occurs in a large proportion of perfectly healthy persons. While a blood pressure of 140 mm Hg, for example, in a young man or woman would be considered abnormally high, it would arouse no serious concern in a person of 60 years of age. A permanently low blood pressure—between 90 and 115 mm Hg—occurs in a certain percentage of the general population and causes no ill effects. It is considered indeed to be conducive to or at any rate associated with long life, and is therefore heartily approved by insurance companies.

Normally a slight rise in the diastolic pressure occurs when a person rises from the recumbent to a sitting or a standing position; it is due to the reflex constriction of the arterioles. This response counteracts the effect of gravity upon the circulation and prevents the brain from being deprived of an adequate blood supply. But even a healthy person may experience a feeling of faintness if he rises too quickly after a lengthy period of recumbency, as when, awakened by the ring of the alarm clock, he jumps suddenly out of bed. The vascular reflex mechanism taken unawares does not respond with its usual briskness.

Muscular exercise is the commonest cause of a physiological rise in blood pressure. In very strenuous muscular effort the systolic pressure may reach a level of 180 mm Hg. In addition to reflex vasoconstriction and an increase in the output of blood by the heart, there occurs a discharge of adrenaline into the blood stream which augments the nervous factors. Very strong *emotion,* such as *anger, fear,* or *excitement,* has a similar though usually less pronounced hypertensive effect.

Pathological. In the disease known as high blood pressure, or **hypertension,** the blood pressure is considerably above the normal level for the person's age. It is permanently as high or higher than that of a healthy man performing strenuous muscular exercise. The systolic pressure may be 300 mm Hg or more, and the diastolic over 150 mm Hg when the patient is at rest. If it were possible to place a long glass tube in the artery of such a person, as Stephen Hales did in the artery of a horse, the blood would rise to a height of more than 12 feet instead of between 5 and 6 feet as it would in a healthy man.

The elevated arterial blood pressure is the result of increased peripheral resistance, that is, of undue narrowing or constriction of the arterioles throughout the body—the capillaries and veins are not involved in the general vasoconstriction. These are undisputed facts but the cause of the increase in peripheral resistance is not known with certainty; however, the experiments of Dr. Harry Goldblatt of Cleveland have made it very probable that in one type of the disease at least, some interference with the blood supply to the kidneys is responsible. It has been recognized for many years that high blood pressure is common in severe disease of the kidneys. Doctor Goldblatt produced permanent hypertension in dogs, comparable in all respects to hypertension in man, by narrowing the main artery to the kidney, using a silver clamp especially devised for the purpose. When the artery is narrowed in this way the kidney secretes a substance known as **renin** into the blood stream which results in constriction of the arterioles throughout the body. Thus, the peripheral resistance is increased. Such an effect, it will be understood from what has been said in regard to maintaining the normal blood pressure, must inevitably result in hypertension.

The strain and extra work thrown on the heart by the increased peripheral resistance results in dilatation of the heart (left ventricle) and hypertrophy of its muscle.

Low blood pressure is known as **hypotension.** The blood pressure may drop to a dangerously low level during *general anesthesia, surgical shock,* or *severe hemorrhage.* A profound fall may also result from some sudden emotional disturbance, and cause *fainting.* A permanently low blood pressure is also not unusual in debilitating diseases. In one rare form of hypotension, called *postural hypotension,* the blood pressure falls when the standing or sometimes even the sitting position is assumed. As mentioned above, the normal response to such a change in position is a *rise* in pressure.

Measurement of the blood pressure in man

If we wish to measure the blood pressure of a human being, we must do it indirectly, that is, without opening an artery, as may be done in animals. The measurement is made in the following way. An airtight, flat rubber bag, covered with cotton cloth, is wrapped around the arm above the elbow (Fig. 15.4). The cuff, or armlet, as it is called, is provided with two rubber tubes, which open into its interior. One of the tubes is connected with a *manometer,* which consists of an upright glass tube of mercury, fixed to a millimeter scale. The other tube of the armlet is attached to a small rubber bulb provided with a valve. By means of the bulb and tube, the armlet can be inflated and a pressure created in its interior. The air pressure is recorded by the manometer. It is evident that if we can counterbalance the pressure in the large artery of the arm with air pressure and read from the manometer the value of the air pressure used, we will know the value of the blood pressure in the artery. It is simply a matter of applying an amount of air pressure from without that will just balance the pressure within the large (brachial) artery of the arm. The pressure in the armlet is therefore raised by means of the bulb until no blood can pass to the section of artery below the cuff. This is indicated by the disappearance of the pulse at the wrist. The examiner then listens with a stethoscope over the artery just below the armlet as he gradually reduces the air pressure; he lowers the air pressure by cautiously releasing the valve on the tubing near the bulb. The instant that the artery opens a little and allows blood to escape below the cuff, a faint tapping sound is heard. The height of the mercury column of the manometer is read at this moment; the reading represents the **systolic** pressure. The examiner continues to lower the air pressure slowly until a soft murmur is heard; all sound then disappears. The manometer reading at the instant that the change in the sound occurs gives the **diastolic pressure.**

The blood pressure varies in different parts of the circulation. It is highest in the great arteries, such as the aorta and its branches, and lowest in the great veins opening into the right ventricle. That is to say, there is a gradual fall in pressure throughout the systemic circulation from the left to the right ventricle. The pressure in the aorta is over 120 mm Hg, whereas it is less than 1 mm Hg in the venae cavae (Fig. 15.3).

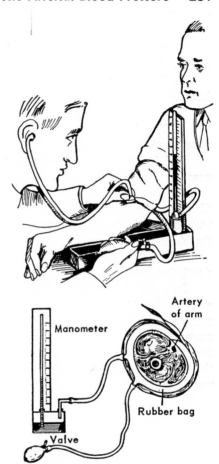

Fig. 15.4. *Top,* the manner in which the blood pressure is measured in man; this is called the *auscultatory* method. *Bottom,* a cross section of the arm with the armlet wrapped around it and connected with the manometer.

THE DIFFERENCE BETWEEN ARTERIAL AND VENOUS BLEEDING

When an accident has occurred and blood is lost, it is often important to know whether the hemorrhage is due to the opening of an artery or of a vein, since the means used to arrest the bleeding may be somewhat different in the two instances. The distinguishing features between arterial and venous hemorrhage are summarized below.

When an *artery* is opened:

1. The blood is a brighter red.

2. The blood escapes under high pressure—usually in spurts or pulses.

3. Compression of the tissues between the bleeding point and the heart stops the bleeding. Pressure beyond (distal to) this will not stop it.

When a *vein* is opened:

1. The blood is darker in color, for it contains a large proportion of reduced hemoglobin.

2. The blood flows more slowly; it does not escape in jets but appears to "well up."

3. The hemorrhage is arrested upon the application of pressure distal to the bleeding point. Moderate pressure applied between the wound and the heart increases rather than diminishes the bleeding, since the blood is flowing toward the heart.

When the bleeding is from *capillaries,* the blood is bright and oozes slowly from the wound. The blood soon clots.

In severe hemorrhage of any kind, either external or internal, the patient should be kept perfectly quiet and free from excitement or anxiety of any sort, so that the blood pressure may be kept low. For this reason no stimulant of any sort should be given. It is a common error to give alcohol in some form or other at this time; this will only increase the force of the heart, tend to elevate the blood pressure, dilate the vessels, and increase the bleeding. (See also Ch. 7.)

16
The Origin of the Heartbeat

If we watch the heart of a living frog, we may observe waves of contraction originating near the great veins where they enter the heart, and passing over the auricles and the ventricles in regular order. In the heart of man and of higher animals this wave of contraction is so rapid that its progress cannot be observed by ordinary means. The actual contraction of the muscle fibers of the heart is preceded, by a small fraction of a second, by an electrical change. The electrical changes can be recorded by means of an instrument known as an *electrocardiograph* (see below) and the action of the heart thus studied with precision. The underlying cause of the contraction or beat of the heart has been a question that has absorbed the interest of philosophers and scientists from the earliest times. The ancients thought that the heart's movements were presided over by a vital spirit, which entered the ventricle, and like steam or vapor, inflated the heart, and then, condensing again, caused the heart to collapse. That the heart was a muscle, which contracted when it apparently collapsed, and relaxed when it appeared to become inflated, never seems to have occurred to them. It was William Harvey who showed his generation that the heart, by virtue of its muscular walls, contracted and relaxed with an alternating rhythm and discharged the blood like any pump.

THE SEARCH FOR THE CAUSE OF THE HEART'S ACTION

The difficult problem still remained to be solved. What caused the heart to beat—what force started the rhythmical contractions? What was the nature of the hidden power that drove the pump? When it was dis-

253

covered later that the heart was supplied with nerves, it was thought that these were responsible for the heart's contractions in much the same way as nerves cause any other muscle of the body to contract. It was soon discovered, however, that the heart continued to beat after its nerves were divided. Ordinary muscle, of course, becomes paralyzed when its nerves are cut. So the heart's contractions could not be explained in this simple way. Also, the heart of the embryo chick commences to beat several days before any nerves or nervous tissue have grown into it. Again, it was thought that the blood itself, flowing through the heart, furnished the stimulus and in some mysterious way impelled it to beat. But again it was soon discovered that the heart would beat for a long time after it had been removed from the body, even though it contained no blood. If a rabbit is killed, and its heart immediately removed and a warm solution (Ringer's) containing calcium, sodium, and potassium chlorides and charged with oxygen is run through it, regular beating may continue for several hours (Figs. 16.1, 16.2). The isolated human heart, in the same way, has been made to beat for many hours after death. Far from being the very vulnerable organ it is thought to be, the heart in reality can be made to perform its work for a longer time after the death of the body than most other organs. The heart of a chicken has been known to beat after the other tissues of the body are dead and quite cold, even though no measures have been taken to keep the heart alive. The frog's heart removed from the body also continues to beat for some time. The power to contract rhythmically must lie within the heart muscle itself, for even strips cut from the ventricle will continue to contract for several minutes.

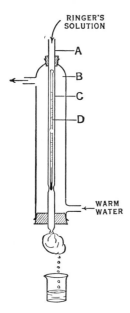

Fig. 16.1. The method of perfusing the isolated mammalian heart. Ringer's solution flows down the narrow tube under a pressure of about 120 mm Hg; the lower end of this tube is tied into the aorta so that the fluid will flow into the coronary arteries; surrounding the narrow tube is a glass water jacket through which warm water circulates.

Why the heart beats is a problem scientists have not yet solved. It is a mystery as darkly hidden as life itself. When the egg is developing into the chicken, the tiny scrap of growing tissue that is not yet a heart but that will become the heart can already be seen to be beating with a regular, even flicker.

We do know, however, that the beat in the full-grown heart starts in a little island of special tissue in the upper part of the right atrium called the **sinuatrial (sinuauricular) node,** and then passes as a wave over the rest of the heart. We know, also, that, each time the heart beats, a current

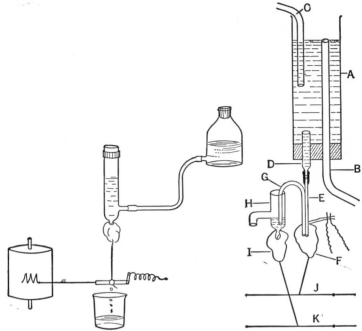

Fig. 16.2. Showing other methods of perfusing the heart. *Left,* a simplified method of perfusing the frog's heart, which has no coronary circulation; the fluid may therefore be delivered directly into the ventricle. The beats of the heart are recorded by means of a light lever that writes on the revolving drum (upstroke, systole; downstroke, diastole). *Right,* method for demonstrating the liberation of acetylcholine from the endings of the vagus. When the vagus of heart F is stimulated, the chemical as it is liberated passes in the perfusion fluid by tube G to vessel H and thence to heart I, which slows (see Ch. 17). A, reservoir; B, overflow tube; C, inlet tube; D, outlet tube; E, delivery tube to heart F; J and K, recording levers.

of electricity passes through it. The origin of the beat in the sinuatrial node and the passage of the contraction wave to other parts of the heart will now be described.

The sinuatrial (or sinuauricular) node. The sinuatrial node is a small island of specialized tissue. Its construction differs from that of the surrounding heart muscle, being composed of a primitive type of muscle cell and numerous nerve fibers. It lies in the upper part of the right auricle near the superior vena cava (Fig. 16.3). Here the heartbeat originates. This little knot of tissue might be called the "heart of the heart," for in it occur rhythmical chemical changes that supply the "spark" or **impulse** for each systole. The rest of the heart follows its bidding. The sinuatrial node sets the pace, and on this account is called the *pacemaker* of the heart. If it sends out a rapid stream of impulses, the heart beats quickly. If the rate at which it generates the impulses is

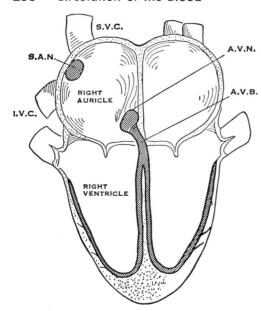

Fig. 16.3. Diagram of the conducting system of the heart. I.V.C., inferior vena cava; S.A.N., sinuatrial node; S.V.C., superior vena cava; A.V.N., atrioventricular node; A.V.B., atrioventricular bundle.

slower, the heart, too, beats more slowly. If the sinuatrial node is removed, the heart for a time ceases to beat.

THE HEART IMPULSE

The nature of the impulse. Though the exact nature of the impulse arising within the node is unknown, some very interesting and important features have been discovered about it. We know very little of the changes within the node that give rise to the impulse; nevertheless, once it has arisen, we may learn many things about its effects. We may know no more concerning the origin of a spark of fire or a flame, but we may watch it spread and see the results of its action. So it is with the impulse of the heart—though much of its inner nature is hidden from us, we have some knowledge of how it behaves and what it does.

Generated within the cells of the special tissue of the node, the impulse travels swiftly (1 to 5 meters per second) throughout the heart, stimulating the muscle in its course. The impulse is always accompanied by an electrical current. In animals the current may be demonstrated and its strength measured by connecting two parts of the heart, while it is beating, to a *galvanometer*—an instrument for recording electrical currents. The actual contraction of the heart muscle follows immediately upon the passage of the current over it. It cannot be said that the impulse and the electrical change are one and the same thing. Yet the two go hand in hand, and so invariably does the electrical change accompany the impulse that the former is taken as a certain sign of the latter.

The passage of the impulse from the sinuatrial node to the different regions of the heart. The swift message sent out from the node radiates in all directions through the muscular tissue of the auricle, making each muscle fiber that it traverses contract. Toward the lower part of the inner wall of the right auricle and above the valves opening into the right ventricle, a second node of special tissue is situated (Fig. 16.3). This is called the **atrioventricular** (or **auriculoventricular**) **node.** It gives rise to a bundle of tissue known as the **atrioventricular bundle,** which, descending to the upper part of the partition (**septum**) between the two ventricles, divides into a right and a left branch. Each of these branches divides into numerous fine twigs, which interlace with one another to form an intricate network known as the **Purkinje system,** which is spread over the interior of the ventricles. The atrioventricular node, like a receiving station, picks up the impulses radiating through the atrial muscle from the sinuatrial node. The bundle relays the impulses again along its branches and the numerous fine endings of these, to the individual muscle fibers of the ventricle. If the bundle should be severed or diseased so that no impulse can pass along it, the ventricle is completely cut off from the control of the pacemaker of the heart—that is, from the sinuatrial node. Division of the bundle completely interrupts communication between the auricles and the ventricles. Disease of the bundle, which gradually renders it incapable of transmitting impulses, is not uncommon. The condition is spoken of as *heart block.* The ventricles in such circumstances, however, do not, as might be expected, cease to beat. Since the block occurs gradually, they are given warning before being thrown entirely upon their own resources. They generate impulses of their own and beat independently but at a rate slower than that of the auricles.

THE ELECTROCARDIOGRAPH

The electrocardiograph[1] is an instrument used to record the electric current generated in the human heart. Solutions of various salts (electrolytes), such as sodium, potassium, and calcium chlorides, enter largely into the composition of the blood and tissue fluids. Such solutions are excellent conductors of electric currents (Ch. 1). The electrical changes generated in the heart muscle during its contraction are, therefore, readily conducted to remote parts of the body. In order to record the heart currents it is only necessary to connect two parts of the body with the instrument. The parts of the body employed for this purpose are the right arm and left arm, the right arm and left leg, or the left arm and left leg. These paired members are connected in turn, and in each

---

[1] The electrocardiograph is a type of galvanometer. Its moving part (the shadow of which is photographed and constitutes the record) is a fine filament of spun glass that has been silvered to make it electrically conductive.

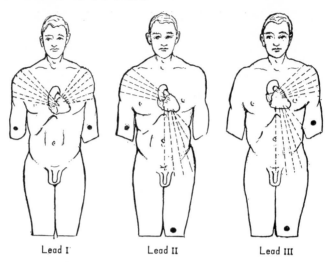

Lead I   Lead II   Lead III

Fig. 16.4. Showing the electrical currents generated by the contracting heart. Black circles represent the electrodes leading to the electrocardiograph.

instance a photographic record is made of the electrical effects of the cardiac contraction. Each pair of connections is referred to as a *lead* and denoted by the Roman numerals I, II, and III, in the order given above. A fourth connection—between the chest overlying the heart and the left leg—is usually recorded as well. The actual connections are made by means of wires running from the electrocardiograph to small metal cups held by suction on the skin, which has been previously moistened with saline or some other conductive substance (Fig. 16.4).

Figure 16.5 shows an enlarged drawing of an electrocardiographic record, or *electrocardiogram,* as it is usually called. This record has been taken from lead I, but electrocardiograms taken in other leads look very much the same to an untrained observer. At each beat of the heart the currents pass through one limb (arm or leg) of the subject, through the electrocardiograph, and back to the body through the subject's other limb; thus, the circuit is completed. Ever since the instrument was invented the waves of its record have been designated simply by the letters *P, Q, R, S,* and *T.* The wave *P* is caused by contraction of the auricles, and the waves *Q, R,* and *S* by the contraction of the ventricles.[2] The *T* wave is produced during the relaxation of the ventricles. When the heart is diseased the waves may be abnormal in shape or position. Thus, the physician is often able to gain valuable information concerning the condition of the heart.

---

[2] The electrical changes precede the actual contraction by a small fraction of a second, so that it is not strictly accurate to say that the waves are caused by the contraction.

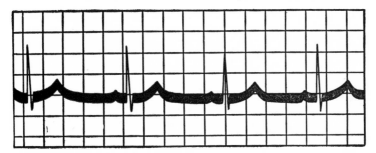

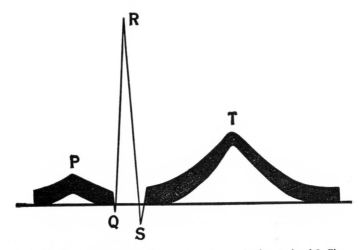

Fig. 16.5. An electrocardiogram. *Top,* a normal record taken in lead 1. The horizontal lines represent tenths of millivolts, the upright lines fifths of seconds. *Bottom,* a series of curves (a complete cardiac cycle) enlarged. The different waves are known simply by the letters P, Q, R, S, and T. The wave P is caused by the contraction of the auricles; Q, R, and S by the contraction of the ventricles; and T by the relaxation of the ventricles.

17
The Regulation of the Circulation

CONTROL OF THE HEART

It has been shown in the foregoing chapter what a self-reliant organ the heart is—how it has the power to perform its work though removed from the body, and to what a large extent it holds within its boundaries the organization for its government. Nevertheless, it is a small state within the larger kingdom of the body, and as such is under the control of the brain. We all know that the heart may beat faster as the result of mental excitement or emotions of various kinds. Messages of which we are unaware constantly pass from brain to heart (through **efferent nerves**) and from heart to brain (through **afferent nerves**) to direct and control cardiac action.

The nerves that carry efferent messages are of two types: (1) those that slow the heart, the **vagus nerves,** and (2) those that make the heart beat more quickly, the **accelerator,** or **augmentor, nerves.** Both these types of nerve, like those controlling the blood vessels (Ch. 17), belong to what is known as the **autonomic,** or **involuntary, nervous** system (Ch. 37). The vagus nerves belong to the **parasympathetic** division and the accelerators to the **sympathetic** division of this system.

The vagus nerves. These nerves, two in number, arise in the *hindbrain,* or **medulla oblongata** (Ch. 37), and descend on either side of the neck. The vagus, as its name implies, is a wandering or vagrant nerve, in the sense that it travels far afield, and its branches go to many parts of the body. It passes through the thorax into the abdomen and in its course gives branches to the lungs, heart, stomach, intestines, etc. At present we are concerned only with its branches to the heart (Plate IIIc).

The function of the vagus nerves is to slow the heart and reduce the force of its beats. They serve as "brakes" to prevent the heart from racing at an unnecessarily rapid speed. Unlike the brakes on an automobile, which are brought into play only occasionally, the vagus nerves are always in action to a greater or less extent. In this action they are like brakes that are adjusted too tightly and are always dragging just a little. Or they may be compared to the reins by which a driver keeps a constant curb upon a spirited horse, for they are always exerting a restraining influence upon the action of the heart. In physiology, a continuous action of this nature is called **tone.**

When the vagus nerve of an animal is stimulated strongly, especially by an electric current, the heart is stopped—but it may start to beat again though the stimulus is continued. This phenomenon is called "the escape of the heart" from vagal control.

The accelerator, or augmentor, nerves. The fibers of the accelerator nerves also arise in the medulla oblongata, but they reach the heart by passing down the spinal cord and emerging in the upper part of the thoracic region. From here they pass to ganglia of the sympathetic cord (Ch. 37) and thence to the heart. They have an action opposite to that of the vagus. They increase the rate and force of the heartbeat. As the vagus nerves act to rein in the heart, so the accelerators serve to whip it up. The accelerators are also in continuous action. That is, they too possess tone. Only a very bad driver indeed would rein in a horse at the same time that he was applying the whip, or would drive a motor car with the brakes gripping. Yet that is the way the brain, through the vagus and accelerator nerves, governs the rate of the heart. The vagus is always slowing the heart; the accelerators are always speeding it up. This arrangement, however, possesses certain advantages. The constant effects of the two nerves upon the heart are delicately balanced one against the other. When, for example, the action of the vagus is reduced and the effect of the accelerator is increased, a more pronounced—and prompter—acceleration of the heart is brought about than would otherwise be possible.

Chemical effects of vagus and accelerator nerves. The effects of the two sets of nerves governing the action of the heart are brought about by the action of chemical substances produced by the arrival of nerve impulses at the nerve endings. This surprising discovery is a relatively recent one. The substance produced when the vagus becomes active is called **acetylcholine.** This chemical resembles in its action the drug known as *muscarine,* found in poisonous mushrooms. Both these substances act to slow or stop the action of the heart. The action of acetylcholine is not confined to the heart; it affects many other structures, such as blood vessels, stomach, intestines, iris, etc., and it is liberated from the endings of the nerves supplying these parts (Fig. 16.2) .

It has just been stated that the action of the vagus is continuous, which means that acetylcholine is continuously being produced in small amounts. Why then, it may be asked, does it not enter the general circulation and produce its effects upon other organs? Again, one may ask, How can the heart suddenly increase its rate of beating if this chemical is present and active? The explanation is that the minute amount of acetylcholine produced at the vagal endings by each impulse is destroyed again in a small fraction of a second by an enzyme called **cholinesterase.**

The accelerator nerves and other nerves of the sympathetic nervous system also bring about their effects through the production of a chemical. This substance, if not identical with adrenaline (Ch. 40), resembles it very closely. It is destroyed much more slowly than acetylcholine and, entering the general circulation, produces slight side effects upon other structures of the body. But these minor effects do not cause any physiological disturbance. The chemical substance liberated at the ends of sympathetic nerves was originally called **sympathin.**

CONTROL OF THE BLOOD VESSELS

Those very small blood vessels through which the blood streams from the arteries into the capillaries and veins—the **arterioles**—are also under the control of the autonomic nervous system, whose fibers innervate the smooth muscle in the arteriolar walls (Fig. 17.1).

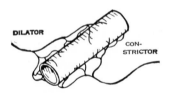

Fig. 17.1. Nerves going to the wall of an arteriole.

That the nervous system governs the caliber of the small blood vessels is a fact that everyone must have observed. We have all seen the skin flushed with blood as the result of excitement, embarrassment, or shame. We may also have seen the face become pale with fear, anger, or pain. We know, often much to our chagrin, that we can no more prevent these changes than we can alter the beating of our hearts. The blood in the countless capillary vessels gives the skin its color and warmth. When the muscular walls of the arterioles relax, such vessels dilate, the capillaries in consequence become distended with blood, and the skin becomes red and hot.

But nerve impulses cause changes in the caliber of the vessels quite apart from emotional states. Cold, heat, injury, etc., will induce constriction or dilatation of the cutaneous vessels; and variations in the diameters of the arterioles and capillaries of interior parts are occurring from time to time in accordance with the degree of activity of the different tissues and organs, and the quantity of blood that they require. Dilatation of the vessels is an inevitable accompaniment of acute inflammation, and is responsible for its most characteristic signs; namely, redness, heat, and swelling. The muscle fibers of the arterioles may be compared to the muscle of the heart, in that the nerves by which they are supplied have opposite actions. One of these sets relaxes the muscle and so causes the vessel to dilate; they are called **vasodilator nerves.** The other set stimulates the muscular rings, causing them to contract and thus narrow or constrict the arterioles; they are called **vasoconstrictor nerves.** The vasoconstrictors belong to the sympathetic division of the autonomic nervous system; the vasodilators are derived from both the sympathetic and the parasympathetic divisions. Under usual conditions the two sets of nerves are active at the same time, their opposed effects being nicely balanced one against the other. The vessels are thus maintained in a state of partial constriction or tone (p. 261).

The nervous control of the blood vessels is of very great importance to the various functions of the body. All parts of the body do not require an equal supply of blood at the same time. One organ or tissue may be at rest while another is active. In the latter instance more fuel is burned, and more oxygen is required; therefore, resting tissues receive less and active tissues more blood. The nerves of the arterioles enable this unequal distribution of blood to be brought about. For instance, in muscular exercise the active muscles may require 10 times the quantity of blood that will satisfy them during rest. The arterioles in other regions of the body are therefore narrowed, while those that carry blood to the muscles are dilated. A great volume of blood flows through these sluice gates into the active tissue. In the same way, after a meal the blood is turned into the digestive organs from other regions such as the muscles and brain, which in consequence are less abundantly supplied. The withdrawal of blood from the brain may account for the lazy feeling and drowsiness that follow a heavy meal. The role that the blood vessels of the skin play in regulating the body temperature will be dealt with in a later section (Ch. 29).

REFLEX EFFECTS ON HEART AND BLOOD VESSELS

Many afferent nerves when stimulated cause changes in the caliber of the small blood vessels (arterioles and capillaries). For example, if the large (sciatic) nerve of the lower limb is cut across and its upper end stimulated strongly, constriction of the vessels will result. A weaker stimulus applied in the same way may cause the vessels to dilate. If the effect upon the vessels is widespread and pronounced, a rise or a fall in the blood pressure may follow. These effects upon the vessels are brought about by reflexes. The impulses set up in the afferent fibers of the stimulated nerve travel to the brain, where they connect with efferent neurons (see Ch. 34 for the description of a reflex). Impulses discharged from the latter are conveyed by vasoconstrictor or vasodilator nerves to the small vessels.

Cold, heat, pain, ultraviolet light, massage, and other types of stimulus are capable of bringing about such reflex effects. They can be easily demonstrated in man. If one hand is put into cold water, for example, the vessels not only of the chilled hand but of the opposite hand as well are constricted. Or if a breeze from a fan is allowed to blow upon the skin of the back, the mucous membranes of the nose, throat, and bronchi become pale as a result of reflex vasoconstriction.

The aortic nerve. Reflex changes in the rate of the heart can also be induced. Stimulation of one type of afferent nerve may slow the heart, whereas stimulation of another type may cause acceleration. The vagus gives off a branch high in the neck that contains afferent fibers only. It is called the **cardiac depressor,** or **aortic nerve.** Stimulation of this nerve causes reflex slowing of the heart, dilation of blood vessels throughout the body, and as a consequence of these effects, a fall in blood pressure. This nerve ends in the walls of the aorta, its fine branches extending from the arch of the vessel as far as the heart (Fig. 17.2).

The sinus nerve. The sinus nerve has a function very similar to that of the aortic nerve. It is a branch of the glossopharyngeal nerve, and ends by fine filaments in the wall of the carotid sinus, which is a slight dilation of the common carotid artery at the point where it divides into the internal and external carotids. When stimulated, the sinus nerve also causes slowing of the heart, general dilation of the minute vessels, and a fall in blood pressure (Fig. 17.3).

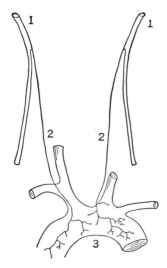

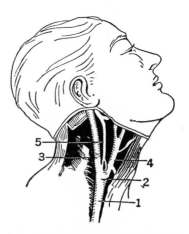

Fig. 17.2. The distribution of the aortic nerve. 1, section of vagus nerve going to the heart; 2, aortic nerve; 3, arch of the aorta.

Fig. 17.3. The sinus nerve (branch of the glossopharyngeal nerve) ending in the carotid sinus. 1, common carotid artery; 2, carotid sinus; 3, internal carotid artery; 4, external carotid artery; 5, sinus nerve.

Pressure is the physiological stimulus for the aortic and sinus nerves. Their endings in the aorta and carotid artery are extremely sensitive to changes in the pressure of blood within these vessels. In the living animal it is through this sensitivity that they fulfill their function of governing the rate of the heart and moderating the blood pressure—that is, preventing its rising too high or falling too low.

Because of the constant stimulus of the blood pressure upon the nerve endings, nerve impulses at low frequency—say 15 per second—are continually traveling up these nerves to the brain, from which impulses are discharged along the vasoconstrictor and vasodilator nerves to the blood vessels. Thus, in health, the blood pressure is maintained reflexly at a comparatively constant level. Should there be a tendency for the blood pressure to rise unduly, the frequency of the impulses increases— that is, the nerve endings are stimulated more strongly. Thus the heart is slowed, the vessels are dilated, and the blood pressure is prevented from rising to an extreme height. This reflex is not, however, all-powerful, for though active in hypertension (Ch. 15) it cannot keep the blood pressure within normal limits.[1]

Any tendency toward a fall in blood pressure causes a reduction in the frequency of the impulses, indicating a weaker stimulation of the nerves. As a consequence, the heart rate is increased, the vessels are constricted, and the blood pressure is prevented from falling or is raised again toward normal. Owing to their governing action upon the circulation, the aortic and sinus nerves are often called the **moderator nerves.**

---

[1] Similarly, in severe hemorrhage or surgical shock it is incapable alone of restoring the blood pressure to normal. Also in muscular exercise during which the blood pressure rises sharply, these reflexes apparently are in abeyance, or other, more powerful regulating mechanisms overrule them.

18

The Circulation in Certain Special Regions of the Body. The Effect of Gravity Upon the Circulation

CAPILLARY CIRCULATION

The capillaries are the smallest vessels of the circulatory system. They lie between the arterioles on the one side of the system and the veins on the other (Fig. 12.2). The caliber of one of these tubes may be less than the diameter of a red blood corpuscle (7 microns). Ten or more of these microscopic tubes could be laid side by side upon a hair. If all the capillaries of the human body could be joined in line, they would form a strand invisible to the naked eye but some thousands of miles in length. The length of each capillary, however, is less than half a millimeter. These vessels form a maze of connecting channels in the tissues (Plate III*b*). If the tongue or the toe web of a living frog is examined under the microscope, the red cells can be seen as they are carried through these tiny channels. For the most part, the cells pass along in single file, the vessels being too narrow to accommodate two abreast (Fig. 18.1). Some of the vessels at times may be so narrow that the corpuscle is squeezed along and pressed into a sausage shape.

Independent movement of capillaries. Until recent years it was believed that the capillaries were unable of themselves to change their diameters. It was thought that their calibers did not alter except in a passive way— that is, simply as a result of the blood entering from the arterioles and distending them. Since their walls are made of a single layer of thin,

266

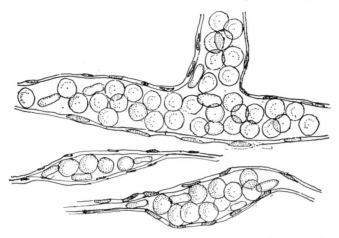

Fig. 18.1. Capillary calibers. In the uppermost figure the corpuscles are moving freely through the dilated vessel. In the middle figure a group of cells are pocketed by contraction of the capillary wall on either side, and not even plasma can pass. In the lowermost sketch cells are trapped but plasma flows through the vessel; this is called *plasma skimming*.

flattened endothelial cells (Ch. 2), and muscle fibers are entirely absent, it seemed impossible that they could constrict or dilate. It is now known, however, that the more proximally placed capillaries (that is, those nearest the arteriole that feeds them), at any rate, are provided with smooth muscle by means of which they can control from time to time the quantity of blood that enters the capillary network. These vessels are called *precapillaries*. Their diameters, like those of the arterioles, are controlled by vasoconstrictor and vasodilator nerve fibers.

The effects of mechanical and chemical stimuli upon the capillaries. The caliber of the arterioles and capillaries can be altered in other ways than through the nervous system. Should any capillary, even one beyond (distal to) the precapillaries, be stimulated mechanically—that is, by pressure or contact applied directly to the skin—it may contract so firmly that the blood within it is expelled. This effect may be shown upon the human skin. If a pencil is drawn very lightly over the skin of the back of the hand, a faint white line will appear in 3 or 4 seconds along the path taken by the pencil point. The narrow blanched area is due to the closure of the capillaries within it.

The capillaries are especially susceptible to the action of chemical substances. **Acids,** such as lactic and carbonic, formed in metabolic processes cause dilatation. Acetylcholine is also a dilator of capillaries. Alkalies, the hormone of the pituitary (**pituitrin**), and adrenaline cause constriction. In muscular exercise lactic and carbonic acids are formed

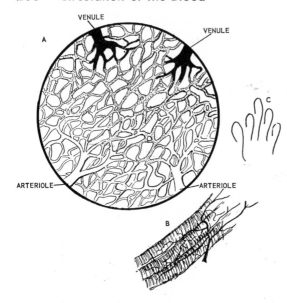

VENULE

VENULE

A

ARTERIOLE

ARTERIOLE

C

B

Fig. 18.2. Capillary patterns. A, capillary network in skin; B, capillaries to muscle fibers; C, capillary loops as seen at base of human fingernail under low power of microscope.

which, by dilating the small vessels in the muscles, increase greatly the flow of blood through them and thus provide for an adequate supply of oxygen. These acid products of metabolism serve a similar purpose in other active tissues—for example, glands, brain, etc.

Histamine, a chemical substance found in almost every tissue of the body, is a powerful dilator of capillaries and arterioles. A small dose injected into an animal's circulation may cause death as a result of widespread vasodilatation and a profound fall in blood pressure. Histamine is present in considerable amounts in the cells of the human skin but is "locked up" and under ordinary conditions does not escape into the general circulation. It is believed, however, that the redness and swelling that follow stimulation of the skin, as by a pin scratch and other mechanical stimulants, the application of heat—for example, scalding or scorching—and the sun's rays (sunburn), are caused by histamine or a histaminelike substance that the injury has caused to be liberated from the cells of the skin. The histamine then acts upon the small vessels. Sometimes in extensive mechanical stimulation of the skin the quantity of histamine or a closely similar substance escaping into the general circulation may be sufficient to cause a slight fall in blood pressure. Liberation of such a chemical is responsible in part, at least, for the heat, redness, and swelling associated with infective inflammatory conditions of the skin.

CIRCULATION THROUGH THE HEART MUSCLE

The heart muscle receives its blood supply through the **coronary arteries.** These are two vessels, right and left, that arise from the beginning of the aorta and, passing outward on either side, encircle the base of the heart. They are the first branches given off by the aorta. The trunk of the left coronary artery descends upon the anterior surface of the heart. The trunk of the right coronary descends upon the posterior surface (Plate IV*c*). Both vessels divide into branches that plunge into the substance of the heart. The blood, having passed through the arterioles and capillaries of the heart muscle, is collected again into veins, which join together to form larger vessels. The greater proportion of the blood, after it has passed through the arterioles, capillaries, and veins of the heart muscle, is emptied into the right auricle mainly by a single large vein—the **coronary sinus.** The coronary circuit is one of the shortest in the whole body. The blood takes only 2 or 3 seconds to pass from the arterial to the venous side; for instead of having to pass through distant parts of the body, such as the hand or foot or head, to reach the right auricle, it is short-circuited through the coronary system from the aorta to the right side of the heart. The heart, as we have seen (Ch. 14), performs, for its size, an enormous amount of work. In order to do this it must be richly supplied with blood. It would very soon fail should the streams of blood that irrigate its muscle and furnish it with oxygen and nourishment dry up. Indeed, the heart muscle ceases to contract within a second or two after its blood supply has been arrested. When this occurs, death follows almost instantly. The abrupt arrest of the circulation to a *part* of the heart muscle is a common cause of death in persons, especially men, over 50 years of age. It is caused by the clotting of blood in a branch of a coronary artery, which is usually the seat of atheromatous changes (Ch. 12). The condition is known as *coronary thrombosis,* or *coronary occlusion.*

Angina pectoris (breast pain) is another grave disease of the coronary arteries due to insufficiency of the blood supply to the heart muscle as a result of narrowing of the vessels, usually by atheromatous disease. It is marked by severe, often agonizing, pain beneath the lower part of the sternum, radiating down the left arm, to the lower jaw, and sometimes to the right arm as well. It is brought on, as a rule, by some muscular effort that increases the work of the heart and therefore the requirement of the heart muscle for oxygen; owing to the state of the vessels this cannot be fully supplied. A chemical substance formed and accumulated in the heart muscle as a result of the oxygen deficiency is believed to be the direct cause of the pain. Strong emotion, anger, fear, or sexual excitement may also precipitate an attack.

When the healthy heart is called upon to perform a greater amount of work, as in strenuous muscular exertion, an enormously greater volume of blood flows through its substance. During bodily rest the quantity of blood that traverses the coronary vessels of the human heart is only a small fraction of the blood flow through the rest of the body. During muscular exercise the blood supplying the heart muscle may be increased several fold, constituting then a larger proportion of the total blood flow. When very heavy work is performed, 2 liters of blood may flow through the coronaries each minute; this is nearly half as much as flows through the entire body during rest.

CIRCULATION THROUGH THE BRAIN

The cerebral circulation is peculiar. It differs from the circulation through other regions of the body (except the bone marrow) because the brain is enclosed in a rigid, unyielding encasement of bone—the skull. The blood enters the skull by the **carotid** and **vertebral arteries** and leaves by the **jugular veins.** The kidneys, the muscles, the liver, or any other part of the body may hold more blood at one time than at another, because these organs can swell upon occasion and accommodate the extra supply; their vessels can dilate. Or their vessels can constrict, in which case the organ shrinks. The quantity of blood within the skull, on the other hand, can be altered very little from time to time.

This may be made clear by means of a model. Suppose that a hole is bored in the bottom of a glass flask or bottle and a length of rubber tubing fitted into the opening so made. The flask is then packed with a fine-meshed sponge and filled with water. The neck of the vessel may then be closed with a cork, into which another length of rubber tubing is fixed, and arrangements may be made for water to be pumped into the sponge-filled flask by one tube and out by the other. Such a model would imitate fairly well the cerebral circulation (Fig. 18.3). The flask and its contents represent the skull filled by the brain with its blood vessels and fluid. One tube represents the carotid artery, the other the jugular vein. It is, of course, a foregone conclusion that, once the flask is filled, it will be utterly impossible to increase the quantity of fluid within it at any time. The speed at which the fluid travels through the flask and the meshes of the sponge can be increased or reduced by altering the force of the pump. But, since fluid cannot be compressed and the walls of the flask are unyielding, very little change in the volume of the contents can occur.[1]

Now let us suppose that the flask contained instead of the meshwork of sponge material a very intricate system of branching elastic tubes. It is obvious that we could increase the diameter of some of the tubes if we reduced the capacity of the same number of others to the same degree.

---

[1] Though the adult skull is a rigid unyielding encasement, it must be remembered that its cavity is continuous with the spinal canal and that fluid—the **cerebrospinal fluid**—fills the space that is not occupied by the brain and spinal cord. Also, the joints between the vertebrae are closed by structures that are not entirely rigid. Small changes in the quantity of blood within the skull may, therefore, occur by the displacement into the spinal canal of cerebrospinal fluid, room for which is made by some bulging at the vertebral joints.

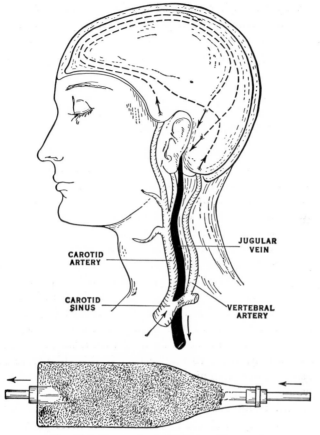

Fig. 18.3. The cerebral circulation. (See text.)

So it is with the blood supply to the brain. Though the total quantity of blood within the skull can alter to only a small extent, a shift of blood from one part of the brain to another can occur. The vessels are furnished with both constrictor and dilator nerves. The caliber of the vessels of the brain is also profoundly influenced by the composition of the blood. In those regions of the cerebral cortex that have been observed in experimental animals, an excess of carbon dioxide or a lack of oxygen causes vasodilatation.

The pressure of blood in the cerebral circulation alters from time to time, as does also the swiftness of the blood stream. The pressure of blood within the skull changes with the blood pressure in the rest of the body. Headache is not infrequently the result of increased pressure of blood within the cranial cavity. The rupture of a small artery in the brain causes what is known as a *stroke,* or *apoplexy.* This occurs more frequently in old people with brittle arteries, or in hypertension. The hemorrhage, by destroying some of the brain tissue that controls the movements of the muscles, causes paralysis—usually one half of the body (Ch. 37).

The more important arteries and veins of the brain are described in Chapter 13.

CIRCULATION THROUGH THE LUNGS— PULMONARY CIRCULATION

The circulation through the lungs is known as the **pulmonary, or lesser, circulation.** The blood leaves the right ventricle by the great **pulmonary artery,** which divides into a right and a left branch for the corresponding lungs. Each branch breaks up within the lung into small arteries and arterioles, which deliver the blood into the rich meshwork of capillaries. These delicate vessels surround the myriads (700 million) of air spaces (alveoli) of the lungs and so expose the blood to the air in these spaces, freshening the blood at each breath. Each drop of blood, in its journey through the capillary, gives up a load of carbon dioxide and takes on a load of oxygen, and like a spark in the wind, the red cell instantly flashes from a dull red to a brilliant scarlet (Fig. 12.7).

If the capillaries of the lungs were joined end to end, they would form a minute tube some 3000 miles long with a wall almost inconceivably thin. It is easy, then, to realize that if this tube were filled with blood and surrounded with air, the respiratory gases (oxygen and carbon dioxide) would pass freely to and from the fluid within its walls. This is essentially what happens in the lungs; the capillaries, along which the red cells move slowly in single file, are, for the most part, entirely surrounded by air. Though each red cell is small, together they present an enormous area to the lung air. Were all these cells placed flat and edge to edge, they would cover the floor of an ordinary classroom (50 × 30 feet). Thus the blood is afforded every facility to rid itself of carbon dioxide in exchange for a load of oxygen.

The blood pressure is very much lower in the pulmonary circulation than in the systemic, amounting to only 20 or 25 mm Hg.

Having passed through the capillaries of the lungs, the blood flows into the left auricle through the four **pulmonary veins.** The arterioles of the lungs, like those of other regions of the body, are under the control of constrictor and dilator nerves.

The bronchi and bronchioles, connective tissue, lymph nodes, and other tissue of the lungs not essentially respiratory in function do not depend for their oxygen supply and nourishment upon blood carried to them by the pulmonary artery, which, of course, has a low content of oxygen. They receive blood from the systemic circulation through the **bronchial arteries,** which are branches of the aorta, and are thus assured of an adequate oxygen supply.

EFFECT OF GRAVITY UPON THE CIRCULATION

The heart chambers must be supplied regularly with blood. If sufficient blood is not carried to the right side of the heart by the great veins, the arterial blood pressure falls, for the simple reason that, like the pump of a well gone dry, the left ventricle is not properly filled and so has not enough fluid to force into the arteries. As a result, the brain is deprived of its usual supply of blood, and unconsciousness follows. A large proportion of the blood supply to the right ventricle comes from below the level of the heart—that is, from the feet, legs, thighs, and abdomen. When a person is standing upright, this mass of blood must be lifted 4 or 5 feet in order to reach the heart. If for any reason the blood is not raised to the heart, unconsciousness, or *fainting,* as it is called, results. Man and the higher apes differ from four-footed animals in that their bodies are in the upright position for a great part of the time. Their circulatory systems have developed a way to overcome the effect of gravity upon the blood in the great veins of the lower part of the body. But a rabbit, if it is held for long by the ears, will die, for its blood simply of its own weight collects in the great veins of the abdomen and seeps into the smaller vessels, capillaries, and arterioles, and little is left to feed the heart. Sheep also often die if held in an upright position for too long during shearing, and the heart of a snake becomes almost empty when the reptile is suspended vertically. The dog, however, can accommodate itself for some time, though imperfectly, when held upon its hind legs.

The circulation of man overcomes the effect of gravity in the following way. Firstly, when the body rises to the upright position nerve impulses are discharged along the vasoconstrictor nerves, especially to the vessels of the abdominal organs. This is a reflex effect in which the aortic and sinus nerves play an important part. It reduces very materially the capacity of the peripheral vessels, and the blood, instead of collecting in the abdominal region under the force of gravity, flows upward to the heart.

Secondly, the muscles of the abdominal wall contract and offer a firm support to the great veins within the abdominal cavity. Thus the great veins of the abdomen, which have a large capacity, are not permitted to become distended under the weight of blood and so deprive the heart.

Thirdly, the veins possess valves that open upward but not downward. In this way the fluid column receives further support.

Fourthly, the contraction of the muscles of the lower limbs exerts a squeezing pressure on the veins lying between them, and on account of the valves the blood is driven toward the heart.

Fifthly, the respiratory movements aid the upward flow of blood. They act in such a way as to draw the blood upward, just as water is drawn from a well by a pump. The blood is literally sucked upward toward the heart every time we take a breath. The pressure within the thorax is at all times lower than that of the atmosphere to which the rest of the body is exposed. With each descent of the diaphragm (inspiration, Ch. 19) this intrathoracic pressure is lowered further. The blood, then, receives an impetus that urges it toward the heart at each inspiration. Furthermore, the descent of the diaphragm increases the intraabdominal pressure. Thus the blood, as well as being drawn upward, is also forced along the inferior vena cava into the thorax. It must be remembered that though the inferior vena cava contains no valve, the external iliac and femoral veins possess them. Therefore, when the intraabdominal pressure rises the blood cannot go downward; it must go upward.

Fainting. A person loses consciousness because the brain no longer receives its proper supply of blood. In most instances the failure of the left side of the heart to give the brain the blood it requires is due to the fact that the right ventricle does not receive enough from the vessels below its own level. Fainting very frequently follows a sudden shock or some intense emotion. We know that the caliber of the vessels in regions of the body exposed to view, such as the face, is changed by nervous impulses traveling from the brain. The face will flush with blood or blanch from emotional causes. The vessels of the abdomen may also constrict or dilate from similar causes. If they constrict, the blood pressure is likely to rise, but if great numbers of them dilate, a large proportion of the blood, instead of flowing to the heart, collects of its own weight in these vessels as in a pool. The capacity of this blood pool of the abdomen when the vessels are dilated to their widest diameter is so great that almost all the blood of the body can be held within it. It is very probable, however, that widespread dilatation of the small vessels of the abdomen is not such an important factor as has been thought. Recent research indicates that vasodilatation in the skeletal muscles occurs promptly in a faint, and is responsible largely for the diversion of blood from the great veins feeding the heart. Ordinary fainting is no indication whatever of disease or weakness of the heart; it is not *primarily* cardiac.

Fainting may be caused by fatigue. Or a patient for a long time confined to bed may feel giddy and even fall in a faint when he rises too suddenly, for the nerves to the vessels become, from lack of practice, less responsive and do not react quickly enough to a change from the recumbent to the upright position.

The foregoing description leaves little to be said with regard to the treatment of a person in a faint. He should be kept in a horizontal position in order that the effect of gravity upon circulation may be abolished and the blood permitted to flow to the heart and be pumped to the brain. This, indeed, is nature's own method—a person who has fainted cures himself, for when consciousness is lost, he no longer remains in the upright position but immediately topples over and thus annuls the effect of gravity. It is very unwise, if not actually dangerous, to support a person in the standing or sitting position during a faint, for were his heart deprived of its due supply of blood for some time, he might die, as does the rabbit held up by its ears.

The effect of centrifugal force upon the circulation. "Blackout." Everyone knows that it is possible to swing a pail of water at arm's length in a horizontal circle without spilling a drop. As a result of the circular motion, a force, known as **centrifugal force,** is developed that drives the water against the bottom or outermost part of the pail. In a similar manner, when the body is moved at high speed in a circle with the feet directed toward the circumference and the head toward the center of the circle, the blood is driven by centrifugal force toward the lower part of the body, where the vessels become distended with blood. The brain is thus deprived of its blood supply; temporary blindness and then loss of consciousness result. These effects, which are generally referred to as *blackout,* are likely to occur in an airman who, when flying at high velocity, makes a sharp turn with his head directed toward the center of the circular movement. A similar movement with the head directed toward the circumference drives the blood to the head; severe pain in the head and signs of concussion may be caused by this dangerous maneuver.

Space flight. Flight into outer space poses several physiological problems, but they can be touched upon only lightly here. The astronaut must take an imitation of his earthly environment with him into orbit. He must be supplied with oxygen, for he will pass beyond the earth's atmosphere; and the oxygen must be under pressure—otherwise it would not enter his lungs (Ch. 20). The temperature of his cabinet must be regulated, for he will enter a region marked by periods of the most intense cold. He will also pass beyond the pull of gravity—the attractive force of the earth. This gravity-free, or nearly free, state will suspend or reduce the normal circulatory reflexes elicited by the stimulation of pressoreceptors in the carotid sinus and other vascular areas. The blood will have no weight, so the work of the heart will be reduced and the skeletal muscles will not be called upon to expend energy upon ponderable objects. These effects of the absence of weight would be of little importance during a short period, but would lead to atrophic changes **if extended over long periods.**

THE PHYSIOLOGY OF BREATHING

PART V

19
The Physiology of Breathing

To the men of the ancient civilizations—Greece and Rome—the rising and falling of the chest, which we call breathing, were full of mystery and awakened within their minds strange thoughts, rich in imaginative beauty and tinged with their inborn sense of the supernatural. The ceaseless motion in waking hours and in sleep, its commencement at birth and its departure at death, its changing rate and rhythm during excitement and fear and other emotions, led the ancients, in their search for an explanation, to indulge in what today we look upon as mystical fancies. The air, which to us is but a mixture of the gases **oxygen, nitrogen,** and **carbon dioxide,** was to them something more. To them it contained an intangible, invisible something, a divine spirit, the psyche, or soul, which they called the **pneuma,** and which, having entered the body at birth, was not to leave it again until death. This old belief has become immortalized in such words of our language as "pneumatic," "inspire," and "expire." The last two words, consequently, came to have double meanings. To the physiologist **inspire** means to draw in the breath, **expire** to breath out. **Inspiration** is the act of breathing in, **expiration** the act of breathing out. **Respiration** is the term

Fig. 19.1. Mayow's experiment. As the candle burned, the water rose in the small flask above the level in the surrounding water, since a part of the air (oxygen) was used up. The candle became extinguished from lack of oxygen. *(After an old drawing.)*

278

used to include all the processes concerned with breathing. In every-day language the words "inspire" and "inspiration" refer to the mind or feelings, and breathing is never thought of. So also the words "expire" and "expiring"—literally, "giving up the spirit"—today are sometimes used meaning "to die" or "dying."

The term *respiration* in its broadest sense applies not only to the obvious act of animals possessing lungs or gills; it also embraces those processes carried on in nearly all living cells whereby food materials are oxidized to carbon dioxide and water. This function of the respiratory mechanism in higher animals—that is, the use of oxygen by the tissue cells and the formation of carbon dioxide and water, with the liberation of energy from the food for the performance of work and the produc-tion of heat—is called **internal, or tissue, respiration.** The acts involved in ventilating the lungs and in the exchanging of gases between the atmosphere and the blood—that is, the absorption of oxygen and the elimination of carbon dioxide—comprise **external respiration.**

It was not possible to gain any real knowledge of breathing until the sixteenth century, after the circulation of the blood through the lungs had been discovered and become known to the scientists of the day. Further knowledge came with the invention of the microscope and the

Fig. 19.2. A similar experiment to that shown in Fig. 19.1, but in this case the candle was re-placed by a mouse. The animal died when it had used up a large part of the oxygen con-tained in the air.

Fig. 19.3. An experiment similar to that shown in Fig. 19.2, performed by the Swedish chemist Scheele on the respira-tion of bees. The insects were placed in a glass vessel, which was inverted and its open end immersed in a larger vessel of limewater. As the bees con-tinued to live within the flask, the vol-ume of the air within it shrank and the water rose above the level in the sur-rounding vessel, for the bees had re-moved oxygen from the air, and the carbon dioxide that they exhaled was absorbed by the limewater.

Fig. 19.4. Lavoisier, the French chemist, performing experiments on respiration. Madame Lavoisier is seen taking notes. *(After a drawing by Madame Lavoisier.)*

ability to study the structure of the lung, and also with the experiments of the Englishmen Mayow and Boyle (1665). These experiments and those of the Swedish chemist Scheele (1770) showed that air contained an invisible, impalpable material (later called oxygen) essential both to the life of animals and to the burning of a flame (Figs. 19.1, 19.2, 19.3). Finally, the discovery of carbon dioxide by Black, and of oxygen by Priestley and Lavoisier (1785) completed the foundations upon which our modern knowledge of respiration has been built (Fig. 19.4). The pulmonary circulation has already been described (Ch. 18). The structure of the air passages and lungs, and the manner in which the gases of the air (oxygen and carbon dioxide) interchange with these same gases in the blood, will now be discussed.

THE AIR PASSAGES

The inspired air, in order to reach the lungs, passes normally through the **nose, pharynx, larynx, trachea,** and **bronchi** (Fig. 19.5).

The nasal cavities. The interior of the nose is divided into right and left halves by a partition called the **nasal septum,** which is formed by the perpendicular plate of the ethmoid above and posteriorly, the vomer below and posteriorly, and by a quadrilateral plate of hyaline cartilage in front (Fig. 19.6). The nasal septum is not infrequently deviated to one or the other side, one nasal cavity being then narrowed and the other widened. Each lateral half of the nose is further incompletely divided into four regions by the nasal conchae (Ch. 3) which raise the lateral wall of the nose into longitudinal mounds (Fig. 19.7). The horizontal furrows separating the elevations are called the **superior, middle,** and **inferior meatuses** (passages) of the nose. These passages run backwards and lead into the **nasopharynx,** which is the space situated between the nasal cavities and the pharynx proper, and above the soft palate.

The part of the nasal cavity just within the **nostril**, or **naris** (pl. *nares*), is called the **vestibule;** it is lined by skin containing coarse hairs. The rest of the interior of the nose is lined by mucous membrane, the covering epithelium being for the most part of the columnar ciliated type. The mucosa covering the superior concha and the adjacent part of the septum contains the organ of smell. The mucous membrane covering the septum and the middle and inferior conchae is thick and very vascular; its surface epithelium is of the ciliated epithelial type containing many goblet (mucus secreting) cells. The veins form a rich network (plexus) of sinuslike spaces that dilate widely when the mucous membrane becomes inflamed, and often also if the atmosphere is hot and "stuffy." The mucosa then swells and may block the

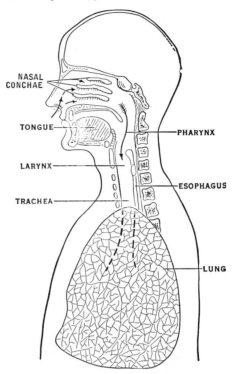

Fig. 19.5. Diagram of the respiratory passages and the lungs.

nasal passages. This vascular tissue is also affected by influences emanating from the organs of sex which appear to be hormonal as well as nervous in origin. Bleeding from the nose sometimes occurs at the time of menstruation; in both sexes this occurrence is most frequent at the time of puberty. In young women it is sometimes called, erroneously, "vicarious menstruation."

The meatuses are airways through which the air is carried to and from the lungs, and warmed as it is inspired. The hairs about the nostrils and the cilia (Ch. 2) covering the nasal mucosa serve to remove dust and other solid impurities from the air during its passage. For these reasons, if for no other, breathing through the nose is normal and healthful. The habit of mouth breathing should never be acquired.

The structure of the soft (nonbony) part of the nose is shown in Figure 19.7.

The paranasal sinuses. A system of air spaces situated within the maxillae and the frontal, sphenoid, and ethmoid bones (Fig. 19.8) communicate by narrow channels with the nasal cavities. The **frontal sinuses** are the air spaces situated between the tables of the frontal bone behind the superciliary arches and extending toward the mid-line above the root

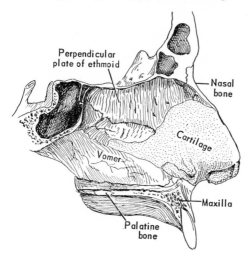

Fig. 19.6. The nasal septum, right lateral aspect.

of the nose. They communicate on each side with the middle meatus of the nose. The **ethmoidal sinuses** are a number of thin-walled air chambers within the labyrinth of the ethmoid bone; they open into the superior and middle meatuses of the nose. The **sphenoidal sinuses** are contained in the body of the sphenoid bone; they open into the nasal cavity above the superior nasal concha. The **maxillary sinus** (old term *antrum of Highmore*) is the largest of the paranasal sinuses. It is pyramidal in shape and is situated one in the body of each maxilla. It communicates with the middle meatus of the nose. The paranasal sinuses are lined by mucous membrane continuous with that of the nose, and are not infrequently inflamed by the extension of infection from the nasal cavities. The maxillary sinus may also become infected from a decayed molar tooth; the roots of the first and second molars are in close relation

Fig. 19.7. A, the interior of the left lateral wall of the nose; B, the exterior of the nose.

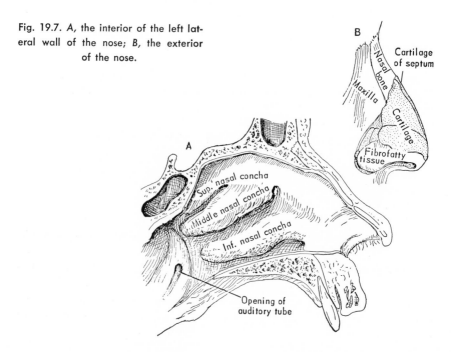

to, and may perforate, its floor. The communication of this sinus with the nasal cavity is higher than the floor. When suppuration occurs, it is therefore often necessary to make an artificial opening in order to provide drainage.

The larynx. The larynx is situated in front of the pharynx, and is continued below into the upper end of the trachea. It will be described in Chapter 22.

The trachea, or windpipe. The trachea commences at the lower border of the larynx, and passes behind the sternum into the thorax. It is a wide, flexible, membranous tube, stiffened by regularly spaced incomplete rings of cartilage. The gaps in the cartilage are on the posterior wall. The tube is lined by mucous membrane, the surface epithelium being ciliated columnar in character (Fig. 19.9).

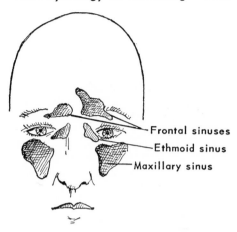

Fig. 19.8. The paranasal sinuses.

Frontal sinuses
Ethmoid sinus
Maxillary sinus

The bronchi and bronchioles. Soon after entering the thorax the trachea divides into a **right** and a **left bronchus** (pl. *bronchi*). Each bronchus divides into several branches that, after a short course, plunge into the substance of a lung. The cartilage, now less evenly spaced, is continued into the bronchi as far as their entrance into the pulmonary tissue, but then disappears. Within the substance of the lung the bronchi divide into innumerable branches of progressively diminishing calibers, like the roots of a tree, until divisions of very narrow diameter are reached, called **bronchioles.** The bronchi and bronchioles are lined by mucous membrane surmounted by ciliated columnar epithelium continuous with that lining the trachea. The smooth muscle, which in the larger bronchi and trachea is disposed longitudinally and confined to the posterior wall, has

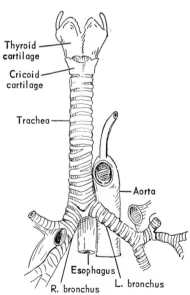

Thyroid cartilage
Cricoid cartilage
Trachea
Aorta
Esophagus
R. bronchus   L. bronchus

Fig. 19.9. The thyroid and cricoid cartilages; the trachea and bronchi with related structures.

a latticelike arrangement in the smaller bronchi and bronchioles. The whole extent of the bronchial tree is richly supplied with elastic fibers, a fact of great importance in respiration.

THE LUNGS

A lung (Fig. 19.10) occupies each half or so of the thorax. They are cone-shaped organs with their apices directed toward the root of the neck and their bases molded to the convex surface of the diaphragm. They overlap the greater part of the heart. The right lung is divided into three parts called **lobes** by two fissures. The left lung is divided into two lobes by a single fissure. On the medial surface of each lung is a depression called the **hilum,** where structures composing the root of the lung enter and leave the organ. These structures are a bronchus, a main branch of the pulmonary artery, two pulmonary veins, bronchial arteries

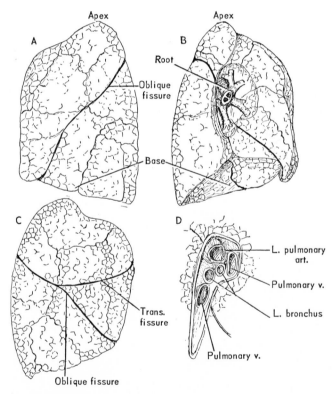

Fig. 19.10. The lungs. A, the outer surface of the left lung; B, the medial surface of the left lung, vessels not shown; C, the outer surface of the right lung; D, enlarged sketch of the root of the left lung.

and veins, nerves, lymphatics, and lymph nodes. Through the medium of the root of the lung (pulmonary vessels), the heart is connected to the trachea.

The respiratory part of the lung. The bronchi and bronchioles, having relatively thick walls composed of muscle and mucous membrane, do not permit the interchange of the respiratory gases (oxygen and carbon dioxide) between the air in the lungs and the blood. The finest branches of the bronchioles, the **terminal bronchioles,** are continued each into a delicate and short tube called a **respiratory bronchiole.** The latter is the first part of the truly respiratory tissue of the lung. It is succeeded by a cluster of air passages or chambers whose walls consist of a single layer of flat epithelium. The respiratory bronchiole and the spaces into which it leads are called a **lobule of the lung,** or a **lung unit.** A lobule is shown in Figure 19.11. The respiratory bronchiole gives rise to a number of short passages called **alveolar ducts,** each of which opens into several passages, called **atria.** Each atrium, in turn, leads into spaces called **air saccules,** or **air sacs,** which show several shallow pouches in their walls; these are the **pulmonary alveoli.** The pulmonary alveoli are in contact with a rich plexus of capillaries. Only through the walls of the spaces composing a lung unit does any interchange of respiratory gases occur. Smooth

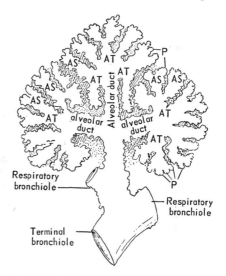

Fig. 19.11. A lobule of the lung. AT, atria; AS, air sacs; P, pulmonary aveoli.

muscle can be traced into the lung unit as far as the walls of the atria. Spasm of this muscle occurs in asthma, and by strongly constricting the airway at this point, impedes the outflow of air from the air saccules.

By far the greater part of the lung is made up of these air chambers. One might almost say that the lungs were formed of a "frothed" tissue. By virtue of the large volume of air that these spaces contain the lungs float in water, and for this reason are commonly known in popular language as the "lights." This buoyancy of the lungs is of medicolegal importance; before birth or in stillborn infants, the air spaces, not having been expanded by air, sink in water like liver or any other tissue.

The pulmonary alveoli, being in communication through the bronchial tree with the atmosphere, are always filled with air. The walls of the alveoli are extremely thin and incomplete, for they are composed

of flat cells with many gaps between them.[1] Since each alveolus is surrounded by capillaries, the red cells, as they pass slowly along these
vessels, are separated from the air at the most by only two membranes of
the greatest possible thinness.

The pleura. Each lung is covered by a membrane composed of a single
layer of endothelial cells lying on a stratum of areolar and elastic tissue.

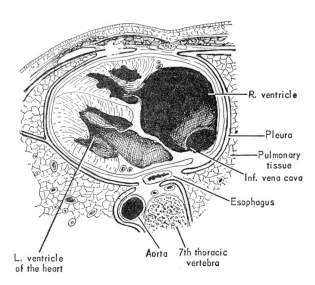

R. ventricle

Pleura

Pulmonary
tissue

Inf. vena cava

Esophagus

L. ventricle
of the heart

Aorta

7th thoracic
vertebra

Fig. 19.12. Transverse
section through the
thorax to show the
structures in the me-
diastinum, superior
aspect; heavy lines
indicate the layers of
the pleura.

This membrane, called the **pleura** (pl. *pleurae*), is adherent to the lung
and dips into the fissures separating the lobes. Traced toward the root
of the lung it is found to fall short of reaching that structure. Instead, it

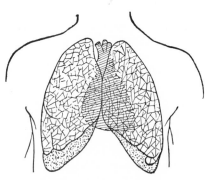

leaves the pulmonary surface, and
passing to the walls of the thorax,
lines the sternum and ribs. Below
it passes to the upper surface of
the diaphragm, which it covers,
and then, turning upwards, runs
through the thorax where it comes
into relation with the pericardium
and the great vessels. Turning
again in the upper part of the
thorax, it returns to the lung near
its root and becomes continuous
again with the pleura on the pulmonary surface. Thus, the lung in
its relation to the pleura may be

Fig. 19.13. The relation of the lungs to
the heart and to the front of the chest
wall.

[1] Owing to the gaps in the alveolar walls the capillaries are in many places directly
exposed to the lung air.

imagined as having been pushed into the side (not into the interior) of a closed membranous sac, which results in its being covered by two layers of the membrane. One layer, called the **pulmonary pleura,** is adherent to the lung, as mentioned above. The other layer that lines the thorax is called the **parietal pleura.** The two layers, which are in contact except for a thin film of serous fluid, can be separated when the chest is opened after death. The "space" between the two layers, which during life and in health is in reality nonexistent, is called the **pleural cavity** (see also p. 295). Inflammation of the pleural membrane is called *pleurisy,* or *pleuritis.* In this condition a large quantity of fluid may form, and separating the two layers of the pleura, convert the potential space into an actual one. Air in the pleural cavity is called *pneumothorax* (see below). The space between the pleurae of the two sides of the body is called the **mediastinum;** it contains the heart and pericardium, the great vessels, trachea, esophagus, the thoracic duct, the phrenic and other nerves, and several lymph nodes (Figs. 19.12, 19.13).

MUSCLES OF RESPIRATION

The chief muscles of respiration are the **diaphragm** and the **external intercostal muscles.** Other muscles of the thorax and those of the abdominal wall play a minor part in normal respiration, but may become important in difficult breathing.

The diaphragm. A large muscular sheet called the diaphragm completely separates the thorax from the abdomen (see Fig. 5.24). It is dome shaped with the convexity directed toward the thorax. This surface in its central part is in relation to the heart within the pericardium, and on either side to the pleura covering the bases of the lungs. It consists of a central leaflike aponeurotic tendon and a broad circumferential band of muscle. The muscle arises from (a) the xiphoid of the sternum, (b) the costal cartilages of the lower six ribs on each side, and (c) the lumbar vertebrae by two fleshy pillars called the **crura** (sing. *crus*). The muscle fibers converge from these three origins to the edge of the **central tendon,** into which they are inserted. There are three large openings in the diaphragm for the passage of the aorta, inferior vena cava, and the esophagus. The diaphragm is supplied by the **phrenic nerve.**

The intercostal muscles. These are two sets of muscles, **external** and **internal,** that run obliquely from rib to rib and fill up the spaces between them (see Fig. 5.25).

The external intercostal muscles arise from the lower borders of the ribs over a distance extending from the tubercle of each behind to near the costal cartilage in front. On the back of the thorax the fibers of the external intercostals run downward and laterally; on the front they are directed downward and medially; each muscle is inserted into the upper border of the next rib below.

The internal intercostal muscles extend from the sternum anteriorly to the angles of the ribs, taking their origins from the costal cartilage and the groove on the inner aspect of the rib near its lower border. The fibers run in a direction at right angles to that of the external intercostals, and are inserted into the upper border of the rib below. The actions of the diaphragm and intercostals will be described with the mechanics of respiration.

INSPIRATION AND EXPIRATION

The entrance of air into the lungs is called **inspiration, or inhalation.** The exit of air is called **expiration, or exhalation.** A double respiratory movement—inspiration and expiration—occurs from 16 to 18 times per minute in adults. The respirations are more rapid in young children. Since the air sacs are so small and so numerous, it is evident that some special means must be employed to force air into them all during the short time occupied by an ordinary breath. In order to understand the way in which this is accomplished, the structure of the chest and the relation of the lungs to the outside air must be described.

The thorax is a completely closed box. The diaphragm bounds it below, and separates it from the abdominal cavity. Its walls are formed by the ribs and the intercostal muscles, vertebrae, and the sternum. It is also completely closed above by the structures at the root of the neck. We have seen that on each side of the chest is a closed membranous sac whose walls are two membranous layers that envelop the lungs, and that between the layers (the interior of the sac) is a *potential* space called the pleural cavity. The layers, lubricated by a film of fluid, glide upon one another during the respiratory movements. They are held together partly by the fluid film but mainly because of a "suction"—that is, a pressure less than that of the atmosphere—that exists between them. This "suction" or subatmospheric pressure is created when the first breath is taken at birth (see below). Should the chest wall be punctured and a pleural sac opened, air enters through the opening, the suction pressure is abolished, and an actual space between the two layers is produced. The manner in which the two layers of the pleura are held together under normal circumstances may be compared to the way in which two wet glass slides adhere to one another. When they are pressed together so as to express the air from between their surfaces, the pressure of the atmosphere upon their outer surfaces holds the slides firmly together. They can be made to glide over one another, but only by permitting a little air to pass between them can one be lifted from the other.

Thus we see that while a pressure less than that of the atmosphere exists upon the pleural surfaces of the lungs, the interior of the lungs—that is, the air sacs—is in communication through the air passages with the atmosphere. During inspiration the thoracic cavity is increased in all its diameters; it resumes its previous size during expiration.

Whenever any cavity is increased in size, something—air, gas, or liquid—always tries to fill it. That is, the pressure within the enlarging cavity falls (see below) and the higher pressure surrounding it causes the air, gas, or liquid to enter it, until in the end the pressures within and without are equal. The cavity, as it enlarges, is said to suck air or fluid in, but actually it is the higher outside pressure that fills it to its new capacity.

The only way in which the extra space created within the thorax during inspiration can be filled is by air rushing through the trachea into the lungs and expanding them. That is actually what happens when one draws in a breath—air at the higher pressure of the atmosphere is forced in. To put the problem in another way, let it be supposed that the upper part of the thorax is open to the outside air simply through the trachea, the lungs being absent. Were the thorax completely closed everywhere else, then, when its capacity increased, air would rush in from the outside through the trachea. When the size of the thorax became reduced again, the air would be forced out. The thoracic box would be a kind of bellows, the trachea representing the nozzle, the thoracic walls the sides of the bellows. If the trachea ended below in an empty bag within the thorax, the general principle would not be altered. When the thorax increased in size, air would rush in as before, but would then fill the attached bag. The lungs essentially are no more than millions of tiny sacs, opening through the smaller tubes into the windpipe; therefore, the entrance of air when the chest expands (inspiration) and the expulsion of air when the chest collapses again (expiration) can be similarly explained.

The lungs contain a large amount of tissue that is highly elastic. During inspiration, when the lungs are inflated, this tissue is stretched; and the lungs, offering a certain resistance to this stretching force, strive, as it were, to return to their uninflated state. This causes a pull between the two layers of the pleura; but the pull is not sufficiently strong to tear them apart. When, however, a communication is made with the atmosphere by puncturing the chest wall, and suction is thus abolished, the elastic lungs recoil to their unexpanded, or collapsed, state. The layer of the pleura covering the lung is then drawn away from the layer lining the thorax. The actual space now created between the thoracic wall and the lung is filled with air. This condition, as previously mentioned, is called *pneumothorax*. It may result from disease or from an accident. The collapsed lung cannot, so long as the opening exists or air is present in the thorax, become inflated. Sometimes, therefore, in pulmonary tuberculosis a pneumothorax is produced intentionally, usually by injecting air into the pleural cavity, the object being to bring about a cure of the diseased lung by putting it at rest.

The model in Figure 19.14 will serve to illustrate some of the principles given in the foregoing paragraphs. The glass jar is completely sealed from the air, and a Y tube in imitation of the trachea and main bronchi passes through the cork. To each branch is attached an empty elastic bag, representing a lung. The floor is a flexible diaphragm, which can be drawn down to increase the flask's capacity. When the size of the space is increased in this way, the air pressure in the flask must tend to fall, but atmospheric air at once flows in (or, one might say, is sucked in) through the tube to equalize the pressure. The bags are expanded by the inrush of air and continue to distend until the greater space created by the descent of the chamber's floor is filled.

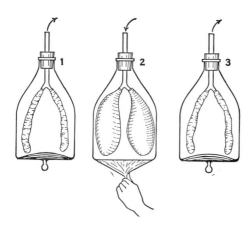

Fig. 19.14. Model to illustrate the manner in which air is taken into and expelled from the lungs. 1 and 3 represent expiration, 2 inspiration. The arrows indicate the directions of the air currents. (See text.)

How the changes in the capacity of the thorax are brought about. We must now study the means by which the changes in thoracic capacity are produced. The thorax is a chamber with jointed walls composed largely of bones and cartilage held together by muscles and ligaments; it has a movable floor of muscle called the diaphragm. Like bars of a cage, the ribs, twelve on each side, form the greater part of the chest's framework. In front the ribs (except the lower two on each side) are attached to the breastbone by cartilage. Behind they are connected to the thoracic vertebrae by movable joints. From these connections they run in a curved and slanting direction forward and for the most part slightly downward.

During inspiration the dimensions of the thoracic cavity are increased mainly by three movements.

1. The external intercostals contract. The contraction of these muscles, which lie between and are attached to each pair of ribs on either

side of the chest, raises the front ends of the ribs into a more horizontal position; thus the front to back diameter of the thorax is increased (Fig. 19.15, 1).

2. The transverse diameter of the chest is increased by a rotation of the ribs upward and outward. This movement has been compared to that of a bucket handle as it is raised from the side of the bucket (Fig. 19.15, 2).

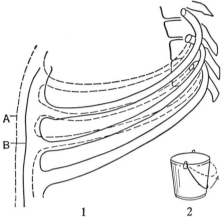
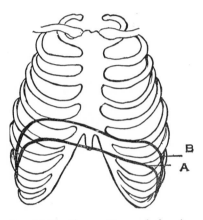

Fig. 19.15. 1, The positions of the ribs during A, inspiration, and B, expiration, lateral view. This movement increases the anteroposterior diameter of the thorax. 2, the bucket-handle movement (see text).

Fig. 19.16. The positions of the diaphragm during A, inspiration, and B, expiration.

3. The diaphragm moves downward with a pistonlike action (Fig. 19.16); thus the vertical dimension of the thorax is increased. The diaphragm in its descent presses the abdominal contents downwards and causes an outward movement of the abdominal wall. About 60 percent of the air drawn into the lungs during inspiration is accounted for by the downward movement of the diaphragm.

During expiration all these movements are reversed, the external intercostals relax, the ribs resume their more oblique direction, and the diaphragm rises to its previous position. Air is forced out of the lungs. The movement of inspiration involves a definite though usually unconscious effort on the part of the individual—a contraction of muscles. In expiration, on the contrary, the thorax returns to its former size with little or no effort, simply as a result of muscular relaxation. The bony cage falls largely of its own weight to resume its previous size. The elasticity of the ligaments and cartilages, of the lungs (the highly elastic bronchial tree) themselves, and of the abdominal muscles also aids the return movement, which is therefore rather in the nature of a recoil.

The expansion of the lungs at birth. Before birth the lungs are, of course, quite airless. The air spaces are small and contain only a little fluid. The pulmonary tissue receives just sufficient blood to ensure its nutrition. When the cord is tied and the newborn thus deprived of its oxygen supply received from the maternal blood, as well as the means of eliminating carbon dioxide, the respiratory mechanism is stimulated; the muscles of respiration contract, which means that the capacity of the thorax is increased. This tends to reduce the pressure on the pleural surfaces of the lungs. So, if the airways are clear the higher pressure of the atmosphere causes a flow of air through the trachea and into the fine air channels. The lung is therefore expanded to fill the enlarged capacity of the thorax. Were lungs made of a plastic but inelastic material, such as perished rubber, they would be pressed against the thoracic walls, but the pressure in the pleural cavity would be the same as that of the atmosphere. The lungs, however, are highly elastic, owing mainly to the elastic tissue in the bronchial tree. They are always tending to recoil to their prenatal state like stretched live rubber, thus striving, as it were, to pull the layers of the pleura apart. It is this elastic pull that creates the "suction" or subatmospheric pressure within the pleural cavity, and that persists, with variations due to the respiratory movements, throughout life.

20
The Physiology of Breathing (continued). Gas Exchanges

ATMOSPHERIC PRESSURE

The pressure of the air at the level of the sea, as at New York, Halifax, or San Francisco, is around 760 mm Hg. That is, the pressure of the atmosphere will support a vertical column of mercury (which is 13.6 times heavier than water) 760 mm high. The pressure of the atmosphere becomes progressively lower at increasing distances above the level of the sea. The reason for this difference is that at sea level the molecules of the gases (nitrogen, oxygen, and carbon dioxide) composing the air are more closely packed and their combined weights therefore greater than at higher altitudes.

The pressure of the atmosphere is measured by means of an instrument called a *barometer*. It consists essentially of a graduated vertical glass tube, closed at its upper end, exhausted of air and filled, except for a short length above, with mercury (Fig. 20.1). The barometer was invented as an outcome of a simple experiment by the Italian physicist Torricelli (1643) which proved that the atmosphere exerted a constant pressure upon the earth. He took a glass tube, closed one end, and filled it with mercury. The air, in this way, was driven out. The tube was then blocked at its open end with a finger and inverted. The blocked end was placed beneath the surface of some mercury in a small basin (Fig. 20.2). When the finger was withdrawn the mercury column fell until its upper surface was about 760 mm above the level of the mercury in the basin. Torricelli concluded that its further fall was prevented by the pressure (or weight) of the atmosphere upon the surface of the mercury

293

in the basin, for since the space in the closed end of the tube was free of air, there was no counterbalancing pressure upon the upper surface of the mercury column.

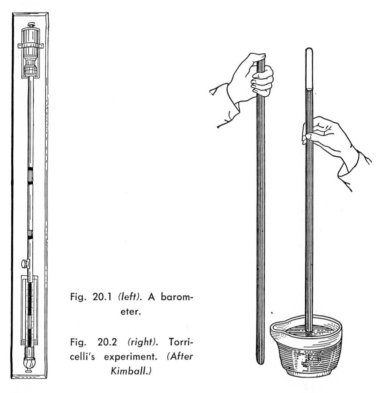

Fig. 20.1 *(left).* A barometer.

Fig. 20.2 *(right).* Torricelli's experiment. *(After
Kimball.)*

Some space has been given to a description of atmospheric pressure because many persons find it difficult to understand. Its effects are taken so for granted that their nature is not fully realized. For example, we speak of "drawing" water from a well or of the pump "sucking up" the water. But the pump merely creates a partial vacuum in the pipe; it is the pressure of the atmosphere upon the surface of the water in the well that forces the water up the pipe.[1] Similarly, because our bodies have become adapted to withstand it, we are unaware that the atmosphere exerts a tremendous pressure upon our bodies (about 1 ton to the square foot). Indeed, were the air as weightless as it seems to be, many physiological processes would have to be quite different. Were there no atmospheric pressure, air could not enter the lungs. Moreover, since there would be no counterbalancing pressure upon the body, the blood (at a

---

[1] Therefore, as is well known, a pump, however perfectly constructed, cannot "draw" water to a greater height than about 34 feet (or 10,336 mm), which is the equivalent of 760 mm Hg.

pressure of 120 mm Hg) would burst the vessels; the intestinal gases would expand and enormously distend the abdomen.

THE COMPOSITION OF THE AIR

The percentages of the three gases in ordinary, fresh, dry air are as follows:

Nitrogen .... 79.02[2]
Oxygen 20.94
Carbon dioxide 0.04

This is the composition of the air we inhale (inspired air). The air we breathe out (expired air) has a lower percentage of oxygen and a higher percentage of carbon dioxide, since the air, during its stay in the lungs, has had some of the oxygen removed from it and some carbon dioxide added to it.

The table below shows the composition of expired air and of the air in the pulmonary alveoli (alveolar air). Both these airs are saturated with water vapor.

TABLE 20.1
COMPOSITION OF EXPIRED AND ALVEOLAR AIRS
IN PERCENT

Gas	Expired air	Alveolar air
Nitrogen	79.2	80.3
Oxygen	16.3	14.2
Carbon dioxide	4.5	5.5

A gas or a mixture of gases, such as air, moves from a point of higher to one of lower pressure until the pressure throughout the entire body of the gas is equal. When two or more samples of a gas at different pressures are brought together, the equalization of pressure throughout the whole body of the gas is brought about by the diffusion and intermingling of the molecules until they are evenly distributed (Fig. 20.3). It is the incessant bombardment by the gas molecules on the walls of the containing vessel that is responsible for the pressure of the gas. Therefore, if the number of molecules within a given space is doubled—that is, if the gas is compressed to half its previous volume—the bombardment upon the walls of the vessel will increase proportionately, and provided that the temperature remains the same, the gas pressure will be doubled.

[2] This percentage includes 0.94 percent argon and other rare gases; they are of no physiological importance.

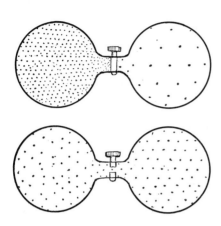

Fig. 20.3. The diffusion of a gas from a point of higher to one of lower pressure. The dots represent gas molecules. Two vessels are shown connected by tubing provided with a tap. In the upper pair the tap is closed: a high gas pressure is created in the left-hand vessel and a low pressure in the right-hand one. In the lower pair the tap has been turned so that there is free communication between them: the gas molecules pass from the region of high pressure to the region of low pressure until the number of the molecules in each chamber, and so the gas pressures in the two vessels, become equal.

Reducing the concentration of the molecules within the space to half—that is, doubling the volume of the gas—halves its pressure. These facts are embodied in *Boyle's law*.

Altering the temperature of a gas also affects the movements of its molecules (Ch. 1) and, consequently, its pressure. *Charles' law*[3] states that if the volume of a gas is kept constant its pressure increases by a certain ratio of the rise in temperature.

Each of the three gases—oxygen, nitrogen, and carbon dioxide—composing the atmosphere (or the individual gases in any mixture of gases) *exerts its own pressure in proportion to its percentage in the mixture and quite regardless of the presence of the other two gases.* This is *Dalton's law of partial pressures.* For example, the pressure of oxygen in the atmosphere, since it constitutes approximately 21 percent of the air,

TABLE 20.2

PARTIAL PRESSURES OF INSPIRED, EXPIRED, AND ALVEOLAR AIR IN MM HG

(Barometer 760 mm Hg)

Gas	Inspired air	Expired air	Alveolar air
Nitrogen	596.4	568.3	571.8
Oxygen	158.3	116.2	101.2
Carbon dioxide	0.3	28.5	40.0
Water vapor	5.0	47.0	47.0
Total	760.0	760.0	760.0

[3] This is also known as the *law of Gay-Lussac.*

is about 21 percent of the total pressure—that is, $^{21}/_{100} \times 760 = 160$ mm Hg at sea level. At a higher altitude—say where the atmospheric pressure is only 600 mm Hg—the pressure of oxygen would be only about 126 mm Hg. At sea level nitrogen exerts a pressure nearly four times greater than that of oxygen (approximately 79 percent of 760), and carbon dioxide (0.04 percent of 760) only about 0.30 mm Hg.

The partial pressures of nitrogen, oxygen, carbon dioxide, and water vapor in inspired (atmospheric), expired, and alveolar airs are given in Table 20.2.

GAS EXCHANGES

Nearly all living cells, of the highest to the lowest organisms, require oxygen, for in order to obtain the necessary energy for their various activities, they must burn (oxidize) the carbon of food materials. The burning of carbon, whether within the cells of the body or in a fire outside the body, consists in the combination of carbon (C) with oxygen (O_2); that is, the oxidation of carbon. Carbon dioxide (CO_2), therefore, is formed, which is exhaled in the breath, or which ascends in the smoke of the fire (Fig. 20.4).

The respiratory and circulatory systems of animals have entered into a partnership for supplying the tissues of the body with oxygen and for removing the carbon dioxide of which the cells must be rid. The blood removes oxygen from the air in the lungs, and to the air the blood in turn gives carbon dioxide. It will be necessary, in order that the reader may understand the manner in which these gas exchanges occur, to give an account of the principles underlying the absorption of gases by liquids.

As we already know, the pressure of a gas is high or low according to whether its molecules are in high or low concentration—that is, whether there are many or few within a given volume. Clearly, then, if a liquid and a gas are in contact, the greater the number of gas molecules that are bombarding the liquid's surface, the greater will be the number that enter it and become dissolved. It is true, therefore, that *the greater the pressure of any gas in contact with a liquid, the greater will be the amount of gas that the liquid will dissolve.* This is *Henry's law* of the solution of gases.

It also follows that what has been said elsewhere with regard to a gas flowing from a point of higher to one of lower pressure must apply also to the passage of gases between liquids and the atmosphere. For example, water in an open vessel dissolves, or as we sometimes say, absorbs oxygen and other gases from the atmosphere. The amount of oxygen that it will dissolve depends, as just stated, upon the pressure of oxygen in the atmosphere. For this reason water at sea level will dissolve more oxygen than at a higher altitude. The pressure of oxygen at sea level is about 160 mm Hg; on a high mountain top it is much lower. At any pressure the gas molecules pass into or out of a liquid until they are evenly distributed between the gas and the liquid. In other words, the pressure of oxygen or other gas to which a liquid is exposed becomes exactly the same inside the liquid as outside of it. By means of a compressing force—that is, a force that will pack the gas molecules more closely together—water and other liquids can be made to dissolve much greater quantities of oxygen and carbon dioxide than they will dissolve at the ordinary pressure of the atmosphere.

In this way such beverages as ginger ale and soda water are charged with carbon dioxide; they are exposed to a high pressure of the gas. An

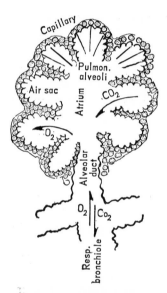

Fig. 20.4. External respiration. A respiratory bronchiole and alveolar duct shown going to a group of air sacs.

airtight cap is afterwards applied to the bottle to prevent the closely crowded molecules of gas within the liquid from escaping. Upon the removal of the cap, the imprisoned gas rushes out as bubbles until the pressure in the liquid and in the atmosphere are the same; bubbling then ceases. The ginger ale charged in this way is said to have a high pressure of CO_2, but its pressure of O_2 will be no higher than the pressure of the latter gas in ordinary air, for oxygen was not forced into it under pressure. Yet oxygen also could be forced into a liquid by exposing the liquid to a high oxygen pressure. When the fluid was exposed again to the outside air, the oxygen would escape until its pressure equaled the oxygen pressure in the atmosphere.

The exchange of gases between the atmosphere and the body. The exchange of gasses between alveolar air aid blood (*external respiration*) and between tissues and blood (*internal respiration*) is carried out according to the principles just described. The air, when it fills the air sacs of the lungs, comes into contact with the blood surrounding these spaces (Figs. 12.7 and 20.4). The venous blood coming to the lungs has a high pressure of CO_2, which it has absorbed from the tissues, but since it has at the same time as it received CO_2 given up some of its O_2, the pressure of the latter gas in the venous blood is low. The alveolar air, on the other hand, has a lower pressure of CO_2 but a high pressure of O_2, since the air sacs are being continually ventilated by the inspired air. As a result of these differences of pressure, CO_2 passes into the alveolar air, and O_2 passes from the alveolar air into the blood. The blood becomes

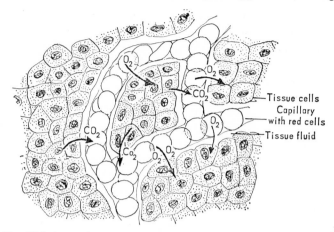

Fig. 20.5. Internal respiration. Capillaries between tissue cells shown filled with red cells.

bright and arterial in character because it has a higher pressure of O_2 and a lower pressure of CO_2 than when it entered the lungs. The arterial blood is carried to the tissues, where the process is reversed. The O_2 pressure of the tissues is low, since O_2 is being continuously used, and the CO_2 pressure is high, since this gas is being continuously formed. Thus O_2 passes from arterial blood to the tissues, and CO_2 passes from the tissues into the blood (Fig. 20.5). This exchange of gases in the tissues produces the alteration in the blood that gives its venous character.

The partial pressures in arterial and venous blood are given in Table 20.3.

TABLE 20.3
PARTIAL PRESSURES IN ARTERIAL AND VENOUS BLOOD
IN MM HG

(Barometer 760 mm Hg)

Gas	Arterial blood	Venous blood
Nitrogen	570	570
Oxygen	100	40
Carbon dioxide	40	46
Water vapor	47	47

The carriage of oxygen and its delivery to the tissues. Were the blood a simple fluid—no more than plasma (Ch. 6)—the exchange of gases between it and the alveolar air and tissues would be fully described by the account given in the preceding paragraphs. The quantity of O_2, however, that could be forced into a cell-free fluid such as plasma by the pressure of this gas in the lungs would be very small indeed—about 0.38 part to every 100 parts of plasma—a little less than pure water can carry. The quantity of oxygen carried in this way would not suffice for the maintenance of life for a second. The body, even at rest, requires each minute 50 times more oxygen than could be supplied by the *fluid portion* of the blood. But as we know, the blood contains red cells, and they hold hemoglobin, which can absorb relatively enormous amounts of oxygen—19 or 20 parts for each 100 parts of blood. The red cells, therefore, serve for the storage and transportation of oxygen. Oxygen, then, is held in the blood in two ways—a small quantity is dissolved in the plasma and a much greater part is combined chemically with the hemoglobin (Ch. 7).

The quantity of O_2 with which the hemoglobin can combine depends upon the pressure of the gas; that is, the quantity dissolved in the plasma which, in turn, is dependent upon the pressure of oxygen in the alveolar air (Fig. 20.6). When the pressure of oxygen is high, as in

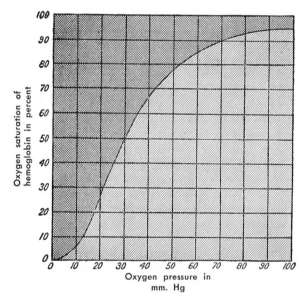

Fig. 20.6. Curve to show the degree of saturation of hemoglobin with oxygen at different pressures of oxygen. This is called the *oxygen dissociation curve of hemoglobin*. Note that as the oxygen pressure increases, the hemoglobin becomes more saturated. A glance at the curve shows that at an O_2 pressure of 100 mm Hg the hemoglobin is 95 to 98 percent saturated (the pressure of oxygen in the lungs is about 100 mm Hg). Also note that the curve is somewhat S-shaped. Dark shading, reduced hemoglobin; light shading, oxyhemoglobin. *(After Barcroft.)*

arterial plasma, the red cells hold nearly all (98 percent) the oxygen with which the hemoglobin can possibly combine—that is, the hemoglobin is 98 percent saturated with oxygen. Reaching the capillaries, the hemoglobin gives up about one third of its oxygen store owing to the low pressure of oxygen in the tissue fluids. The pressure of oxygen in the cells of the tissues is always low, for here it is being used up. These cells draw their supply from the fluids that bathe them; the tissue fluids replenish their oxygen supply from the plasma, and the plasma receives its oxygen from the hemoglobin. So, as the blood flows through the capillaries, the pressure of oxygen in the plasma falls; consequently, the hemoglobin unloads a part of its oxygen again to the plasma, which in turn delivers it to the tissue fluids. These finally deliver it to the cells, where the oxygen pressure is lower still. (See also pp. 149 and 155)

The carriage and exchange of carbon dioxide. The passage of carbon dioxide into and from the blood is, as in the case of oxygen, simply a matter of differences between the partial pressures of carbon dioxide in air, blood, and tissues. But the fall in pressure is reversed, namely, from the tissues to the lungs. Only a very small quantity of carbon dioxide is in ordinary or *simple solution* in the plasma; by far the greater part is stored and carried in *chemical combination*. Of the latter, 10 percent or less is loosely united to hemoglobin to produce a compound called **carbhemoglobin**. The remainder of the carbon dioxide entering the capillaries from the tissues is combined with sodium as *sodium bicarbonate*.[4]

The quantity of carbon dioxide present as sodium bicarbonate increases when the partial pressure of the gas in the plasma rises, and diminishes when the pressure in the plasma falls. So, the venous blood coming from the tissues, since its CO_2 pressure is higher—that is, it contains more of the gas in solution—also holds a greater quantity in the combined form than does the arterial blood. The blood in the capillaries of the lungs "bubbles" off some of its CO_2 in simple solution. As a result of this, the CO_2 pressure of the plasma falls; part of the gas carried as bicarbonate is then released from combination and diffuses into the alveolar air. The arterial plasma must then have a lower pressure of carbon dioxide and a smaller quantity of sodium bicarbonate.

The carriage of the respiratory gases reminds one of a well-organized transportation system. The blood, having delivered its freight of gas, always takes on a return load. Carbon dioxide is delivered into alveolar

[4] Carbon dioxide, when it enters the plasma from the tissue fluids, penetrates the red blood cells, where it is acted upon by an enzyme known as *carbonic anhydrase* and converted to carbonic acid $(CO_2 + H_2O \xrightarrow{\text{carbonic anhydrase}} H_2CO_3)$. In the capillaries of the lungs this enzyme brings about the reverse change—namely, the breakdown of carbonic acid to carbon dioxide and water $(H_2CO_3 \xrightarrow{\text{carbonic anhydrase}} CO_2 + H_2O)$. The gas is eliminated in the expired air.

air, while an oxygen load is taken on. Oxygen is later unloaded in the tissues, and a return load of carbon dioxide is received. The unloading of oxygen in the tissues is facilitated by the loading of carbon dioxide, and the loading of oxygen in the lungs encourages the unloading of carbon dioxide.

THE EFFECTS OF EXCESSIVELY HIGH OR LOW ATMOSPHERIC PRESSURES

Low atmospheric pressures. Mountain sickness. The pressure of the atmosphere at mountain heights may be less than half that at sea level. An expedition to scale Mount Everest in the Himalayas was undertaken in 1924, and a height of some 28,000 feet above sea level was reached. At this height the pressure of the atmosphere is only about 250 mm Hg. The *proportion* of oxygen in mountain air is, however, the same as that at sea level—namely, about 21 percent. So the *oxygen* pressure at 28,000 feet is no more than $(^{21}/_{100} \times 250) = 52.5$ mm Hg (see p. 297). It is clear that at this pressure the blood could take up only a fraction of the amount of oxygen that it could take up at the pressure existing at sea level (about 160 mm). The lack of oxygen, or *anoxia* (Ch. 21), has very serious effects. Vomiting, headache, distress in breathing, and blueness of the face and hands result, and finally unconsciousness and death. This condition, known as *mountain sickness,* increases in severity as higher and higher altitudes are reached. At levels of 10,000 feet or so the symptoms are mild, but in the Mount Everest expedition, in which nearly three times this height was reached, certain members of the party suffered severely. The rate at which the ascent is made also influences the severity of the effects. If a person makes the ascent slowly, he may reach a height of 28,000 feet or perhaps more without the aid of oxygen, because the body becomes acclimated to the rarefied air.

It is evident, then, that in order to enable a person to climb to a very high altitude or to ascend to a great height in an airplane, some means—such as a storage tank of pure oxygen, tubing, and a suitably constructed face mask—must be provided for supplying oxygen and thus preventing anoxia. Flights without oxygen to heights greater than 12,000 or 13,000 feet are decidedly risky. At altitudes of 30,000 feet or more a storage tank and mask are quite inadequate to prevent oxygen lack. Some form of airtight cabinet that can be filled with air under a pressure equivalent to that at a height of about 8000 feet must then be used. Should the aviator, as a result of some accident, be exposed to the rarefied air at 35,000 feet or more, the acute anoxia would cause unconsciousness within a few seconds.

High atmospheric pressures. Caisson sickness. Equally serious effects may result from exposure to high barometric pressures. In laying the foundations for bridge or quay piers, large steel chambers called *caissons* are constructed and lowered beneath the water to the river's bed. In order to expel and keep out the water from the interior of the caisson so that men can work inside, air is pumped into it under high pressure. The workmen draw this compressed air into their lungs, and the gases nitrogen, oxygen, and carbon dioxide are forced into their blood under high pressures and in a manner comparable to that whereby beverages are charged with carbon dioxide. So long as the workman remains in the caisson no ill effects, as a rule, are produced; but should he suddenly be brought to the surface and exposed to the ordinary atmospheric pressure, the gases (mostly nitrogen) that have been dissolved at high pressure in his plasma and tissue fluids escape and form bubbles for the same reason that bubbles of carbon dioxide gas appear in ginger ale when the bottle cap is removed. The bubbles of nitrogen in the capillaries of the nervous system cause paralysis of various regions of the body. The gas bubbles may form in and actually tear the soft nervous tissue. If a vital area in the medulla is involved, death results. The cause of the serious effects has not always been clearly understood, and several deaths have occurred in the past. Now, however, the men, after their shift in the caisson, are raised to the surface but are not permitted to enter a lower barometric pressure immediately. On the contrary, they are kept in an airtight chamber in which the pressure, to start with, is the same or only a little lower than that within the caisson that they have left. The pressure is then slowly reduced. The long period of *gradual decompression* avoids any violent discharge of gases from the blood or tissue fluids and so prevents the formation of bubbles and the occurrence of the serious effects mentioned above.

The severe pains in the muscles and joints that caisson workers suffer when *rapidly* decompressed are known as *the bends*. They are due to the bubbles of nitrogen pressing upon sensitive structures. Rapid ascents, such as those often made by military aviators, from sea level to a very high altitude—that is, to where the barometric pressure is considerably lower than 760 mm Hg—may cause effects similar to those suffered by caisson workers, though much less severe. In such instances the decompression is from a normal to a subnormal pressure, whereas in caisson sickness it is from a high to a normal pressure.

Another effect of rapid airplane ascents is the expansion of gases in the intestine (Ch. 27) which, though not dangerous, may cause much discomfort and pain. In rapid descents the sharp rise in barometric pressure may cause rupture of the eardrum.

21

The Control of the Respirations. Artificial Respiration. Anoxia

CONTROL OF THE RESPIRATIONS

For the control of many functions of the body two means are employed. The heart and blood vessels, and the intestines and stomach, for example, are controlled by nerves as well as by chemical substances carried to them in the blood stream. The respiratory movements also are governed by these two means. It is usual, therefore, to speak of the **nervous control** of respiration and the **chemical control.**

Nervous control. It is a matter of common knowledge that by an effort of the will we can modify the respiratory movements. The breath can be held, or one can, within limits, breathe quickly or slowly, lightly or deeply. In singing or talking the respirations are modified voluntarily to suit our purpose. Yet during sleep, as well as most of the time we are awake, the respirations are continued automatically and unconsciously. In the lowest part of the brain—the medulla oblongata (Ch. 37)—there lies a collection of nerve cells that transmits impulses in a ceaseless stream. The impulses pass along nerves to the various muscles of respiration to cause the rhythmical contractions and relaxations responsible for the alternate enlargement and reduction in capacity of the thoracic cavity. The phrenic nerve, which supplies the diaphragm, has already been mentioned (Ch. 19). The collection of nerve cells in the medulla is called the **respiratory center.** Should this center be seriously injured, as by a fracture of the skull or by a bullet wound, or become paralyzed by pressure or by poisons, such as morphine, anesthetics, etc., it can no longer send impulses to the respiratory muscles, and death results.

The expression *respiratory center* is an oversimplified term for three

304

interrelated centers. Groups of nerve cells in the medulla oblongata discharge impulses that cause inspiration; another group causes expiration. They are called, respectively, the *inspiratory* and *expiratory* centers. At a higher level of the central nervous system (pons) is an area named the *pneumotaxic center* which exerts an alternating inhibiting action on the lower centers, thus giving rhythmicity to the respiratory movements. The respiratory center is readily influenced by the rate at which it receives impulses from neighboring or distant parts of the body along various afferent nerves. That is, the respiratory movements are to a large extent under reflex (Ch. 34) control. Stimulation of the nerves of the nose, as by some pungent odor, may cause sudden suspension of the breath. This suspensory effect serves to prevent further inhalation of the irritant gas. Dropping water on the bill of a duck causes a similar response; when the bird dives and its bill touches the water, the breath is held without the need of any conscious effort upon the part of the animal itself. Irritating substances, such as pepper, etc., also stimulate the nerves of the nasal mucosa and cause sneezing (see below) which clears the nose of the irritant.

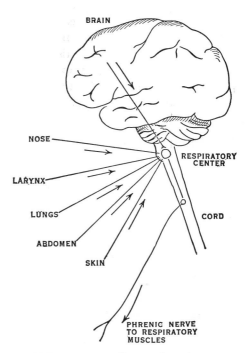

Fig. 21.1. Diagram to illustrate how the respiratory movements may be influenced by reflexes carried out through the respiratory center. The phrenic nerve supplies the diaphragm. The line passing from the cerebrum to the respiratory center represents the course of impulses from intellectual and emotional parts of the brain that have an influence upon the respiratory movements.

The respirations are also altered in rate and depth as a result of impulses reaching the respiratory center along the vagus nerve endings within the lungs themselves or in the abdominal organs. Heat or cold applied to the skin, as by a hot bath or a cold plunge, stimulates the nerve endings upon the body's surface and causes a reflex change in the rate of breathing. As a matter of fact, the stimulation of almost any sensory nerve in the body, if intense enough, will cause reflex changes in respiration (Fig. 21.1).

Coughing, sneezing, and *hiccuping* are modifications of the respiratory act brought about reflexly.

Coughing is caused, as a rule, by stimulation of sensory nerves in the larynx or trachea by an irritant—a vapor, mucus, or a small foreign particle. Or it may be the result of some inflammatory condition of the lower respiratory passages causing irritation of the sensitive nerve endings. A reflex through the respiratory center follows. A cough consists first of a quick inspiration; this is immediately followed by a forcible expiration with the laryngeal opening closed, resulting in the production of a high pressure within the lungs. The larynx is then suddenly opened, and the compressed air escapes explosively; the air blast, rushing through the air passages, sweeps any offending material away.

Sneezing consists of a deep inspiration followed by an explosive expiration that drives a blast of air through the nose and mouth.

Hiccuping results from some irritation of the diaphragm that causes it to contract spasmodically at irregular intervals. It is usually of little concern and arises from some temporary gastric disturbance, but occasionally it is a symptom of serious disease.

Laughing, crying, sobbing, and *yawning* are types of respiration modified by nervous impulses passing from the higher (conscious) regions of the brain to the respiratory center. Emotions other than amusement or grief, such as anger, excitement, and fear, also influence the activity of the center.

Control by the carotid body. Near the carotid sinus, the importance of which in the control of the circulation has been discussed (Ch. 17), there is to be found a small glandlike structure known as the **carotid body**. The carotid body is provided with small branches of the sinus nerve. The cells of which it is composed are stimulated by carbon dioxide when this gas is in high concentration in the arterial blood. They are also excited by a low content of oxygen in the blood. Impulses are set up in the sinus nerve by the stimulation of these peculiar cells when either of these extremes in blood composition exists. The impulses are conveyed to the respiratory center and increase its activity—that is, the respirations are increased in rate and depth. Since it requires a rather large excess of carbon dioxide or a severe oxygen lack in the blood to increase the respirations, it is doubtful whether the carotid body plays an important part in the control of respiration under ordinary physiological conditions.

Direct chemical control. The carbon dioxide in the blood flowing through the respiratory center provides the stimulus upon which the ceaseless flow of impulses to the diaphragm and other muscles of respiration largely depends. Even a slight increase in the amount of carbon dioxide in the blood increases the rate and depth of breathing. A reduction in the carbon dioxide of the blood slows the rate and reduces the depth of breathing, and if there is a great reduction, the respirations may cease entirely for a time. For these reasons the quantity of carbon dioxide in the blood in health is kept practically the same at all times. It is on this account that one cannot hold the breath for very long. Carbon dioxide accumulates in the blood and stimulates the center so forcibly that no effort of the will can prevent an inspiration or an expiration. On the other hand, should a person breathe rapidly and deeply (*forced breathing*) for some minutes and then stop breathing, he may have no desire to breathe for several minutes, since large quantities of carbon dioxide have been removed from the blood by the forced breathing, and the quantity that remains does not suffice to stimulate the respiratory center. Not until carbon dioxide reaccumulates do the respirations recommence. This state, in which the respirations are temporarily suspended, is spoken of as *apnea* (literally, no breathing). If oxygen is breathed before and during the period of forced breathing, the period of apnea may persist for 8 minutes. Even a short period of forced breathing alone before a dive will permit one to remain under water for a much longer time than usual. The reader, however, should be warned that breathing forcibly for more than a few seconds is risky, for in some persons it produces cramps or even convulsions (see tetany, Ch. 40).

We may conclude, then, that in the action of carbon dioxide the body possesses an efficiently adjusted mechanism for the control of the rate and depth of breathing—a regulation more delicate than that possessed by the most precisely regulated machine. When it is remembered that carbon dioxide is a waste gas, which must be removed from the body, we cannot but be overwhelmed with admiration for the ingenuity of the chemical control of breathing. Through the power of carbon dioxide to stimulate the respiratory center and through this the respiratory movements, it calls into play the means for its own removal. A much higher level of carbon dioxide in the blood is required to stimulate the carotid bodies.

Though seldom called into play, acids, such as lactic acid, if in excess in the blood, stimulate the respiratory center, both directly and through the carotid body. Oxygen lack does not stimulate the respiratory center directly; its effect upon the nerve cells is depressant, and severe damage to the center is caused by lack of oxygen.

ARTIFICIAL RESPIRATION

When the respiratory mechanism has failed, as in the apparently drowned or as a result of carbon monoxide poisoning, electrocution, or other cause, some artificial means must be employed to bring air into the lungs until natural breathing is resumed or until all hope of this occurring has been abandoned.

In any method of artificial respiration, promptness in starting the treatment is of first importance. So long as the heart beats, the tissues for a time are able to gain a small amount of oxygen from the circulating blood. But the heart is peculiarly susceptible to oxygen deprivation, and unless the air in the lungs can be renewed and the blood oxygenated, it will soon cease to beat. Nervous tissue also, especially the higher centers of the brain, does not survive for more than a few minutes after its oxygen supply has been arrested. When the heart ceases to beat and can no longer maintain the circulation, methods of resuscitation are usually of no avail. However, it is often impossible for one who is not medically qualified to detect the beat of the heart when it is very weak. For this reason artificial respiration should be continued until natural breathing has been restored or until a physician has pronounced the death of the patient. Until then efforts at resuscitation should be continued.[1]

Most methods of artificial respiration are designed to increase and reduce alternately the capacity of the thorax in such a way as to *draw* air into the lungs and expel it again. Thus the blood is oxygenated and carbon dioxide removed. Several methods have been devised for this purpose.

The Schafer method. Until recently the Schafer method of artificial respiration has been most widely used, but either the *Holger-Nielsen method* or the *mouth to mouth method,* both of which give better ventilation of the lungs, is now recommended. Whatever the procedure used,

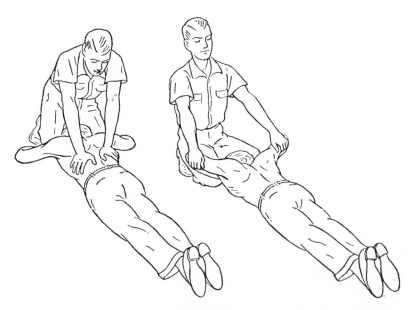

Fig. 21.2. The Holger-Nielsen method of resuscitation. *(After First Aid. Metropolitan Life Insurance Co.)*

[1] If a physician is not available, efforts at resuscitation should be persisted in until *rigor mortis* (stiffness of the muscles after death) is clearly evident.

water, mucus, or any other obstruction to the free passage of air is first removed from the mouth and throat; the tongue is drawn forward, and all clothing about the neck, waist, and chest loosened.

The Holger-Nielsen method. In the Holger-Nielsen or *back-pressure arm-lift method* the patient is in the prone position, with one cheek resting on his hands. The operator kneels in front of and facing the patient's head; he places his hands, with thumbs near the mid-line and fingers spread apart, on the patient's back below the shoulder blades. The operator then bends forward with elbows extended, and brings his weight to bear steadily on the patient's thorax (Fig. 21.2). He then slowly brings his trunk again into the erect position; at the same time he grasps the patient's arms just above the elbows, and draws them forward, that is, toward the patient's head. This movement expands the chest. The movements are repeated 10 or 12 times per minute.

The mouth to mouth method. In this procedure the subject's lungs are distended by the operator's breath as shown in Figure 21.3. It is claimed to be the most efficient of all types of resuscitation. The subject is laid on his back with neck extended. The operator draws the patient's lower jaw upward and forward with his left hand while his right hand presses steadily on the upper abdomen. Then the operator, applying his mouth to the subject's, exhales into it while he watches the rise of the chest. At the end of this "inspiratory" movement, the operator withdraws his mouth a

Fig. 21.3. Mouth to mouth method of resuscitation. *(After Henderson.)*

little while he himself takes a breath and then reapplies his lips to the patient's. These movements are repeated at the rate of about 15 per minute and continued until spontaneous breathing occurs, or until the subject is pronounced dead by a physician.

Care should be taken to keep the patient warm throughout the entire procedure. When consciousness returns a hot drink may be given.

Mechanical devices, such as the pulmotor, that *force* air into the lungs and draw it out again, though less exacting upon the endurance of rescue workers, are not so satisfactory, because unless the degree of ventilation of the lungs is carefully controlled the carbon dioxide of the blood may be reduced to a dangerous level and collapse of the circulation result. Rupture of lung tissue may also be caused.

When artificial respiration must be continued for long periods— days, weeks, or longer—the apparatus originally devised by Dr. Thunberg, the Swedish physiologist, and improved by Philip Drinker must be used. This apparatus, which is popularly known as the "iron lung," consists of an airtight cabinet in which the patient is placed except for his head, which protrudes from an opening hermetically sealed around his neck. By means of a motor the air pressure within the chamber is alternately lowered and raised at the rate of normal respiration. When the pressure is reduced below that of the atmosphere (Ch. 19) the chest expands and air enters the lungs. Air is expelled from the lungs when at the next moment the pressure is increased again. Thus, inspiration and expiration can be induced rhythmically for indefinite periods. It is only in exceptional circumstances, such as in hospital cases, that an apparatus of the kind described is available. A great many lives have been saved by prompt application of manual methods of respiration.

OXYGEN DEFICIENCY, ANOXIA, HYPOXIA

When for any reason the tissues do not receive an adequate supply of oxygen, the condition is called *anoxia* (no oxygen) or, more correctly, *hypoxia*[2] (low oxygen). The tissues may be prevented from getting enough oxygen through (a) failure of the blood to be properly oxygenated in the lungs, as a result of disease or of a low percentage of oxygen in the atmosphere such as at high altitudes (mountain sickness)— this is called *anoxic anoxia, or anoxemia;* (b) reduced oxygen-carrying capacity of the blood, as in severe anemia—called *anemic anoxia*—or in carbon monoxide poisoning; (c) slowing of the circulation, as in heart disease, as a result of which the blood in its passage through the capillaries gives up a larger than usual proportion of its oxygen load; the venous blood therefore has a lower oxygen content, that is, it contains more reduced hemoglobin than normally—this type is called *stagnant anoxia;* (d) poisoning by cyanide or a narcotic, when the tissues abstract less than the usual quantity of oxygen from the blood—this failure of the tissues to use the oxygen brought to them is called *histotoxic anoxia;* the venous blood is unusually bright in color since it contains more than the normal quantity of oxygen, that is, less reduced hemoglobin. In both the stagnant and histotoxic forms, the *arterial* blood carries the normal quantity of oxygen (Fig. 21.4).

Cyanosis (Gk. *kyanos,* blue). Cyanosis is the term applied to the blueness of the skin and mucous membranes of patients suffering from the types of hypoxia under headings (a) and (c) above. Cyanosis does not occur in severe anemia or in the histotoxic type. The blue color is caused by the abnormally high concentration of *reduced* hemoglobin in the capillary blood. There is a very definite concentration of reduced hemoglobin in the capillary blood at which cyanosis first appears, namely 5 grams per 100 cc (the total hemoglobin is around 15 grams per 100 cc of blood). For this reason cyanosis does not appear in severe anemia even though anoxia from other causes is present as well, nor in the histotoxic

[2] It is only quite recently that the more correct term *hypoxia* has come into general use. The terms *anoxic anoxia,* etc., are still the more common usage and are used here.

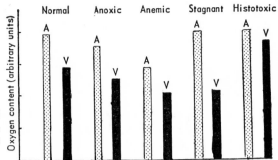

Fig. 21.4. Diagram illustrating the different types of anoxia. A, arterial blood; V, venous blood.

type. In the first instance, there is not the necessary amount of hemoglobin present in the blood to provide 5 grams of reduced hemoglobin; in the histotoxic form, since the tissues do not remove the oxygen from the capillary blood in the usual amount, little reduced hemoglobin, certainly much less than 5 grams per 100 cc, is formed.

Dyspnea, or difficult breathing. Dyspnea has been defined as breathing that requires a conscious effort. It may therefore be quite normal, as during and following strenuous exercise. Dyspnea is, however, a common symptom of disease and occurs when some slight muscular effort is undertaken that would cause no distress in a healthy person, or it may be present in the absence of any exertion, as in a patient lying quietly in bed. It is most frequently seen in heart disease or acute respiratory disease, in both conditions there being usually anoxia. Or it may be caused by an increased metabolism, as in hyperthyroidism or fever. Again, the respiratory mechanism may be stimulated by the accumulation of abnormal acids, as in diabetic coma. In anemia there is dyspnea during even mild exertion, but not during rest. This is because during exertion the circulation, which is speeded up during rest to compensate for the reduced oxygen-carrying capacity of the blood, cannot be further quickened sufficiently to supply the extra oxygen required for the exercise.

Oxygen administration. In certain acute respiratory conditions accompanied by hypoxia, the administration of oxygen in high concentration (50 to 100 percent) is of great value. Also in heart disease in which the stagnant type of anoxia may exist, oxygen inhalations are of benefit. It must be remembered, however, that there is a limit to the amount of oxygen that the blood will take up from the lungs. In health, blood coming from the lungs is nearly 98 percent saturated with oxygen, so increasing the oxygen in inspired air 5 times does not mean that the blood will take up 5 times as much oxygen as when ordinary air is breathed. The most that can be effected is to increase the oxygen saturation of the blood to 100 percent. In the stagnant type of anoxia when the *arterial* blood is at the normal of about 98 percent, this would mean an increase of only 2 percent or so. Nevertheless, this extra 2 percent in heart disease is often highly salutary.

22
The Larynx, the Organ of the Voice

THE ANATOMY OF THE LARYNX

The larynx is situated in front of the pharynx and above the commencement of the trachea. Its framework is entirely cartilaginous, consisting mainly of the *thyroid* and *cricoid cartilages*.

The thyroid cartilage (Fig. 22.1) is formed by two lateral plates called the **laminae,** which meet in the mid-line in front at an angle to form a prominence like the prow of a boat. In males after the age of puberty it is an obvious projection, especially if the neck is thin, which moves up and down during swallowing; it is popularly known as the "Adam's apple."[1] The laminae are widely separated behind; the gap is bridged by the tissues of the anterior wall of the pharynx. The posterior border of each lamina shows an upper and lower projecting bar at its superior and inferior ends, called the *horns,* or *cornua.* The upper horns are much the longer and are directed upward; the lower ones point downward. The upper part of the thyroid gland lies in close relation to the sides of the thyroid cartilage though separated from it by muscles to which the laminae give attachment.

The cricoid cartilage is shaped like a signet ring, the shield of the ring, called the *lamina,* forming the lower part of the posterior wall of the larynx. The cricoid cartilage lies below the thyroid cartilage and above the trachea, to the first ring of which it is joined by membrane.

---

[1] The prominence of the larynx in the male is a secondary sex character (Ch. 49). The adult male larynx is not only more prominent but is larger in all its diameters than the female organ. This accounts for the difference in vocal pitch between men and women. The size of the larynx in the male bears no relation to stature, for we have all known large men with high-pitched voices, and small men whose voices were a deep bass.

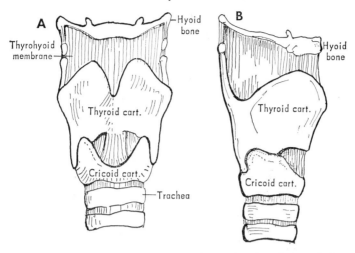

Fig. 22.1. The cartilages of the larynx. *A,* anterior view; *B,* lateral view.

It is also united to the lower border of the thyroid cartilage by a membrane and a central ligament.

The larynx has seven other cartilages: an *arytenoid,* a *corniculate,* and a *cuneiform* on each side, and an unpaired cartilage called the *epiglottis.*

The **arytenoid cartilage** is pyramidal in form and rests upon the lamina of the cricoid cartilage close to its fellow at the mid-line posteriorly. A small synovial joint is interposed between each arytenoid cartilage and the lamina of the cricoid.

The **corniculate cartilage** on each side surmounts an arytenoid cartilage, and is joined to it by a synovial joint.

The **cuneiform cartilage** lies in a fold of mucous membrane running from the corresponding arytenoid to the side of the epiglottis (*aryepiglottic fold*). The two last mentioned cartilages are quite small nodules (Fig. 22.2).

The **epiglottis** is a leaf of fibroelastic cartilage that lies behind the tongue and the hyoid bone; its free, rounded end projects upwards behind the back of the tongue. Its slender, stemlike lower end is attached by a ligament to the upper part of the thyroid cartilage in the angle between the two laminae. In man it does not appear to have any important function, and does not serve as a lid to the entrance into the larynx during swallowing as was thought at one time. Food does not enter the larynx after the epiglottis has been destroyed.

The interior of the larynx. Two pale folds of mucous membrane stretch across the cavity of the larynx from the middle of the thyroid cartilage near the angle made by the laminae, to the arytenoid cartilages on the posterior laryngeal wall. These structures, the organs of phonation, are called the **vocal cords** (or **folds**). They are separated by an interval that

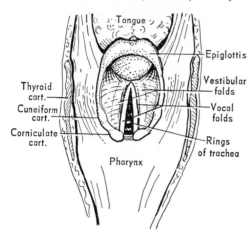

Fig. 22.2. The interior of the larynx as seen with the laryngoscope.

together with that between the arytenoid cartilages is called the **rima glottidis**, or simply the **glottis** (Fig. 22.2). The part of the larynx extending from its opening into the pharynx to a little above the vocal cords is known as the **vestibule.** In the "neutral" position of the vocal cords—that is, during ordinary breathing—the part of the rima glottidis between them is relatively wide and triangular, the apex of the triangle being in front (Fig. 22.2).

The interior of the larynx is lined with mucous membrane, covered, for the most part, by ciliated columnar epithelium; over the vocal cords and the epiglottis the epithelium is of the stratified squamous type.

PHONATION, VOICE PRODUCTION

The mode of production of the human voice, with its varied tones, its range of pitch, and its volume, has long aroused the interest of physiologists. As an instrument of sound, the voice box, or larynx, together with the cavities of the mouth, throat, trachea, and lungs may be compared to the pipes of an organ. Certain notes can be played by the organist that imitate the human voice in a truly remarkable way. A reed and the column of air in the organ pipe are set into vibration by an air blast. In a somewhat similar manner the vocal cords within the larynx are thrown into vibration by air expelled from the lungs. The nose, mouth, throat, and chest serve as resonating chambers.

Movements of the vocal cords. As mentioned above, during ordinary breathing the vocal cords lie at some distance from the mid-line; they are also relaxed; the respired air passes freely between them without setting them into vibration. In deep and forcible inspiration they are drawn still farther away from the mid-line (abducted) (Fig. 22.3). In speaking or singing the vocal cords are adducted, and in the emission of high-pitched sounds the interval between them may be a mere slit; their tension is also increased. These changes in the position and tension of the vocal cords are effected by miniature muscles[2] that rotate the arytenoid cartilages to which the vocal cords are attached. Rotation of the arytenoid cartilages laterally abducts (separates) the vocal cords; rotation medially adducts (approximates) them (Fig. 22.3).

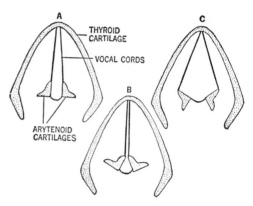

Fig. 22.3. The vocal cords, viewed from above, in different degrees of approximation. Diagrammatic. A, in mid-position; B, in full adduction; C, in full abduction.

Sound possesses three properties: loudness; pitch; and quality, or timbre.

The *loudness* of the voice depends upon the energy with which the vocal cords vibrate; the greater the pressure under which the air is expired and the greater the movements made by the cords, the louder will be the sound.

The *pitch* depends upon the length and tightness of the cords, which, in turn, determines the frequency of their vibrations. In children and women the cords are short, and the voice is high pitched. In men the cords are longer, and the voice is deeper. All of us can adjust the tension and to some extent the length of our vocal cords and so alter the pitch of the voice, but trained singers have developed this ability to the greatest degree.

The *quality*, or *timbre*, of our voices depends on the number and intensity of the overtones or harmonics that are produced, and these in turn depend upon the shape and capacity of the resonating chambers—

[2] The chief of these intrinsic muscles of the larynx are the **posterior** and **lateral cricoarytenoids**, running from the laminae and the lateral surfaces of the cricoid cartilage, respectively, to the arytenoid cartilage; the **transverse arytenoid** muscles, traversing the interval between the arytenoids; and the **oblique arytenoid** muscles, running diagonally from the upper part of one arytenoid cartilage to the lower part of the other and crossing each other in the mid-line behind (see Fig. 5.26). The adductor muscles of the larynx may enter into spasm as a result of a foreign body lodging between or on the vocal cords; if the glottis is completely closed asphyxia follows unless an opening is made into the trachea (*tracheotomy*). In tetany, also, adductor laryngeal spasm sometimes occurs (Ch. 40). Edema of the glottis due to inflammation of the laryngeal mucosa or of structures of the throat or neck may cause such swelling as to completely close the glottis.

the mouth, the trachea, and the chest. Training of the voice consists very largely in modification of the mouth and throat cavities so that the sound produced in the larynx receives the greatest possible number of these harmonics or supplementary tones.

In speech the sounds produced by the vibration of the vocal cords are modified by the numerous changes that may be made in the size and shape of the air passages—the pharynx and the mouth. In pronouncing vowel sounds (*a, e, i, o, oo, u, ow*) the air moves freely through the air passages without interruption, whereas in the sounding of consonants the issuing breath is stopped (stop consonants) at some point or impeded (continuing consonants) by a narrowed channel. The type and quality of vowel sounds is determined by the shape of the mouth and the nasal cavities; by the position—elevated, depressed, backward, forward—of the tongue, and its tenseness or laxness; by the position of the lips; and to some extent, by the degree of tension of the vocal cords. In the pronunciation of *who* or *oo*, for example, the lips are pursed or pouted and the tongue lax or depressed, whereas in the sounding of *ah* the lips are open; in the formation of *he* the lips are stretched with the tongue tense against the teeth, but in forming *i* the tongue is relaxed and the lips partly open (Fig. 22.4).

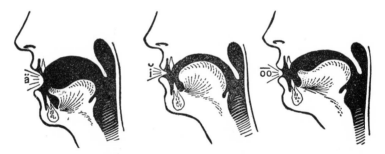

Fig. 22.4. Showing the positions of the lips and tongue and the shape of the mouth cavity when pronouncing ä, ĭ, and o͞o.

Consonants, besides being stopped or continuing, may be *voiced* or *unvoiced*. In a voiced consonant, such as *b, g,* and *k,* the vocal cords vibrate; in a voiceless one, such as *l, p,* and *f,* they do not. The difference can be demonstrated by blocking the ears with the fingers—the vibrations of the vocal cords will be heard as the voiced, but not the unvoiced, consonant is spoken.

The consonants *m* and *n* are sounded partly through the nose and are therefore called *nasals;* the nose passages remain open, but when they are blocked, as by a cold in the head, *m* becomes *b,* and *empty* is pronounced as though it were spelled *ebty.*

Whispered sounds are produced by putting the appropriate part into position and breathing through the aperture without causing the cords to vibrate. The air then passes through that part of the rima glottidis lying between the arytenoid cartilages, the part between the vocal cords themselves being completely closed.

The function of speech involves neuromuscular mechanisms of the utmost complexity; it is truly amazing that the intricate nervous pathways and the coordination of the many muscles of the larynx, tongue, and lips required to form words can be established within a few months after birth. The child first learns to form vowels, and consonants somewhat later.

23
Muscular Exercise and Physical Training

MUSCULAR EXERCISE

When a person contemplates strenuous muscular exercise, nervous impulses are sent out from the brain to various parts of the body. The heart beats faster, and more blood is pumped around the circulation. Breathing is more rapid, and more oxygen is taken into the lungs. The muscles become more tense. In these and in many other ways, the body is prepared for exertion even before the exercise begins. As soon as the active contraction of muscles commences, the mechanisms mentioned above are set in motion more vigorously. During extreme muscular effort the adrenal medulla (Ch. 40) discharges its hormones—*adrenaline* and *noradrenaline*—and thus helps to bring the muscles, circulation, and respiration to the highest state of proficiency.

In strenuous muscular exercise the body may use from 15 to 20 times as much oxygen as at rest. The body temperature may rise to 103 or 104° F as a result of the heat produced by muscular exertion. The heart in a strong healthy man is capable of pumping over 30 liters of blood each minute during the height of the exercise, and the skeletal muscles may develop energy at the rate of half a horsepower per minute. The readily available food reserves in the body are very rapidly used up during vigorous muscular work.

The fuel of muscular exercise. The type of food used as fuel by the muscles during exercise may be ascertained by analysis of the inspired and expired airs during and after the conclusion of the work. Information can also be gained from studies of the changes in the composition of the blood and urine. These studies have shown that sugars are the principal but not the only fuel used. Sugar is capable of providing

318

energy very quickly. As a result of very prolonged strenuous exercise, the amount of sugar available in the body may be lowered to a level at which various characteristic symptoms appear. Feeding sugar helps to correct this condition. In marathon races it is now common practice for the contestants to eat sugar in some form or other at regular intervals during the race. There is no depletion of sugar as a result of short periods of strenuous exercise, and no good effects can be expected from administering it. The fact that sugar is used in very large amounts during muscular exercise does not indicate that the carbohydrate in the diet of athletes should be increased. The body is able to form sufficient sugar from the adequate diet discussed under nutrition, except during very prolonged violent exertion, when the store of quickly available sugar is used up.

Recovery after exercise. Oxygen debt. During muscular exercise the respirations are increased in rate and depth and the total volume of air breathed greatly enlarged. Thus the excess CO_2 is eliminated and the lactic acid produced from the breakdown of carbohydrate (Ch. 30) is oxidized, minimizing the tendency toward a reduction in the alkalinity of the blood. The amount of oxygen taken into the body *during* the exercise is never sufficient to meet the requirement. Therefore, after the exercise stops, oxygen is consumed at a rate in excess of the normal resting consumption until the deficiency is made good. This oxygen intake may be determined by means of the apparatus described in Chapter 28. It may be said that during exercise the body goes into debt for oxygen, and that this debt is repaid during the recovery period that follows the exercise. The amount of the debt varies with the physical condition of the individual, with his state of training for the particular exercise, and with the intensity and extent of the exercise taken.

It is surprising that in so far as the oxygen consumption is concerned, an hour may be necessary for recovery from a 100-yard sprint. After prolonged violent exertion, the recovery period may be two hours or longer.

No attempt will be made here to discuss methods of physical training. We are interested only in the physiological mechanisms by which an individual is able to increase his ability to perform various muscular exercises. The fact that practice enables a person to perform a given exercise more efficiently, and for longer periods of time, needs no illustration. The remarkable endurance and efficiency of the trained runner or oarsman is, however, worthy of comment. The marathon runner may travel 25 miles in two and a half hours.

PHYSICAL TRAINING AND ITS EFFECT ON THE BODY

Various changes take place in the body as a result of graded physical exercise.

The lungs. The volume of air that can be forced out of the lungs after they have been fully inflated—that is, after a maximum inspiration —is termed the **vital capacity.** If the vital capacity of a sedentary individual is determined by having him expire through an air meter, and the individual then takes a series of exercises that are carefully graded so that respiratory processes are stimulated unduly, the vital capacity over a period of time will be found to have increased. That is, training increases the quantity of air that the lungs can hold.

The heart. The healthy heart of an athlete is able to increase enormously its output of blood when the demands of the contracting muscles for oxygen are increased. It has been stated elsewhere that the output of the heart is usually increased both by increasing the quantity of blood ejected at each beat and by increasing the number of beats per minute. The heart of a sedentary person depends, as a rule, more upon cardiac acceleration than does the heart of the athlete. Some famous athletes increase their heart rate surprisingly little, during even strenuous exercise, the great increase in cardiac output of which they are capable being brought about by the ejection of a much larger amount of blood at each heart beat. The heart rate returns to the resting level much more quickly in the trained than in the untrained individual after the same amount of exercise. The same is true of the respiratory rate.

As a result of physical training the healthy heart becomes only slightly larger—a purely physiological increase in bulk commensurate with the greater development of the skeletal muscles. No great enlargement ever occurs unless the heart is diseased. Furthermore, heart disease is never caused by athletics. If the heart shows great enlargement or other signs of disease during athletic training, it may be taken for granted that some cardiac abnormality existed before training was started, or developed during its course from some other cause.

The blood. The number of red blood cells may be slightly increased. The increase in the amount of hemoglobin enables the blood to carry greater amounts of oxygen. Apart from the effect of physical training upon the manufacture of red cells, the spleen contracts during effort and forces an extra quantity of blood rich in red cells into the circulation (Ch. 8).

The muscles. Although there is no change in the number of muscle fibers as a result of training, the size and strength of each fiber is greatly increased. It is an interesting fact that the maximum improvement is obtained within two or three weeks from the beginning of training in some muscle groups, and that the muscles return to their previous condition within three weeks of the cessation of the special exercise. The carbohydrate reserve in muscle increases as a result of training.

Elimination of superfluous muscular movements. A very great improvement in physical efficiency may be secured by the strict elimination of muscular movements that are not essential for the specific exercise involved. For example, unnecessary movement of the arms or shoulders may help to exhaust a runner. Even the main muscle groups may not be utilized to the greatest advantage, and it is often possible to correct this defect and thus to improve the performance. When superfluous movements are eliminated, the available energy may be expended much more profitably.

Nerve pathways. The factors referred to previously are not sufficient entirely to account for the increased efficiency with which certain muscular exercises are performed as a result of practice. We say that such and such a movement has become automatic, or that one is expert in it. This phenomenon is referred to by physiologists as **facilitation.** The various nerve pathways that are traveled by the several messages—brain to hand, brain to foot, etc.—become better fitted to carry these messages as a result of each experience, and the particular act or series of acts is performed with greater precision and ease.

THE PHYSIOLOGY
OF DIGESTION
PART VI

24
General Principles Involved in the Digestion of Food

The walls of the digestive tract from the lower part of the esophagus to the lower end of the large intestine are composed of smooth muscle lined by mucous membrane. Many glands discharge their secretions into the lumen of the digestive tract. These three types of tissue— *smooth muscle, mucous membrane,* and *glandular epithelium*—though found in many other situations, are appropriately and conveniently described here.

SMOOTH MUSCLE

Smooth muscle, also called **unstriated, plain,** or **involuntary** muscle, though showing no cross striations, possesses faint longitudinal linear markings. Its cells or fibers are long and slender with tapering or branched ends that often interlace with one another. The nucleus is usually single, and unlike skeletal muscle there is no distinct membrane (**sarcolemma**) enclosing the cell (see Fig. 4.1). But this type of muscle differs from the skeletal variety not only in structure but in physiological properties as well. The ways in which smooth muscle differs functionally from skeletal muscle are (a) slower, more sluggish contraction, (b) greater extensibility, (c) the exhibition of a sustained contraction, or tonus, for long periods without fatigue, even though separated from the central nervous system, (d) the power of rhythmical contraction, (e) the possession of a double autonomic innervation (parasympathetic and sympathetic), and (f) greater sensitivity to thermal and chemical influences and to certain types of mechanical stimulation, such as stretching, but a lower excitability to electrical stimulation.

Muscular tonus. **Tonus** of smooth muscle may be defined as the steady sustained contraction through which the muscle offers resistance to a stretching force. The rhythmical contractions are superimposed upon the tonus state, which may vary independently of the rhythmical contractions themselves. The tonic contraction of smooth muscle is associated with a negligible expenditure of energy. It is relatively insusceptible to fatigue; heat production and electrical changes are not detectable; and a rise or fall in the degree of tonus is not accompanied by a corresponding change in oxygen consumption.

Enlargement of hollow organs. Certain hollow organs such as the stomach and urinary bladder and, to a less degree, the intestines, have the remarkable ability to enlarge when their contents are considerably increased without showing any rise in internal pressure. The tone of the muscle composing the walls of these organs becomes adjusted automatically to the distending force. This adjustment in tone and change of capacity is very difficult to explain. It is possible that in the stomach at any rate, the individual fibers, which are disposed in layers, instead of being lengthened by the stretching force, simply slide over one another, the wall of the organ thus being increased in area but reduced in thickness. This could occur with little strain being placed upon the fibers themselves. In Figure 24.1 is a diagram illustrating how this might occur. In the case of the stomach, relaxation of the gastric walls occurs as soon as food passes through the cardiac orifice. This response was named *receptive relaxation* by Professor Common. The lowering of gastric tone may even occur while the food is in the esophagus and none has yet passed into the stomach. The tone of the urinary bladder also falls and its capacity increases as the organ fills. The same phenomenon is seen in other hollow organs.

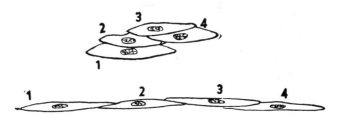

Fig. 24.1. Diagram to illustrate the manner in which muscle fibers may slide over one another and increase the capacity of a hollow organ. The upper group of four muscle cells (1 to 4) is from a hollow organ whose walls are contracted and its cavity almost obliterated; the lower group are the same muscle fibers when the organ is full. *(After Grützner.)*

MUCOUS MEMBRANE (MUCOSA)

A brief reference to the structure of mucous membranes has been made in Chapter 2; they will now be described in greater detail. Mucous membranes form linings for hollow structures that communicate with the exterior, such as the respiratory and digestive organs, the genito-urinary tract (ureters, bladder, urethra, and vagina), the eyelids, the lacrimal sacs and canals, the paranasal sinuses, and the middle ear. The surface epithelium of mucous membranes varies in type with the structures they line. We have seen that it is mostly of the ciliated columnar type in the respiratory passages. But it is a modified stratified type, known as *transitional,* in the urinary bladder and part of the urethra, and ordinary stratified squamous in the rest of the urethra and in the vagina. The epithelium of the digestive canal from the mouth to the lower part of the esophagus is also of the stratified squamous variety. But that lining the stomach and intestines is simple columnar with an abundance of mucus-secreting (goblet) cells. The epithelial covering is laid upon tissue made up of the following strata: immediately beneath the epithelium is (a) a thin, structureless layer of connective tissue called the *basement membrane,* or **membrana propria**; the basement membrane lies upon (b) a thicker cellular layer of connective tissue called the **lamina propria**; and (c) a deeper stratum of connective tissue named the **submucosa.** In the esophagus, stomach, and intestines the mucous membrane has a thin layer of smooth muscle not found in other situations; it lies between the lamina propria and the submucosa, and is called the **muscularis mucosae** (Fig. 24.2).

The mucous membranes serve protective and lubricating functions. From the epithelium of the mouth, the salivary glands and the dental enamel are developed.[1]

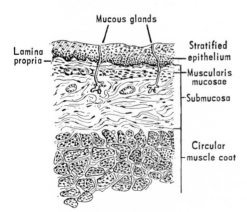

Mucous glands

Lamina propria —

Stratified epithelium

Muscularis mucosae

Submucosa

Circular muscle coat

Fig. 24.2. Perpendicular section through the wall of the esophagus to show mucous membrane. Only half or so of the muscular coat is shown.

[1] The epithelium of the mouth (exclusive of that covering the tongue) is derived from the ectoderm (p. 667), whereas the epithelium lining the stomach and intestines takes origin from the entoderm, and from it the secreting cells of the pancreas and the liver are developed.

Serous membrane. The serous membranes form linings for the closed cavities of the body, such as the peritoneal and pleural cavities and the pericardial sac. These membranes are composed of a single layer of flat endothelial cells laid upon a stratum of loose connective tissue.

GLANDULAR EPITHELIUM

The structure of externally secreting glands. Glands are composed of epithelial cells arranged around a cavity called an **alveolus,** or **acinus,** into which the product, or **secretion,** of the cells is discharged. The secretion is drained from the acinus by a fine tube called a **duct,** or by a more or less complicated system of ducts. Glands are classified according to the character and arrangement of their alveoli and ducts. The simplest gland, such as the mucous secreting glands in the mucosa of the mouth (Fig. 24.3*D*) is a single tubule or hollow sphere lined by cells one layer deep. It discharges its secretion, which is mainly moistening and lubricating in function, directly on to the mucosal surface without the intermediary of a definite duct. Such glands are called *simple tubular* or *simple alveolar,* respectively. In some glands the tubule is branched;

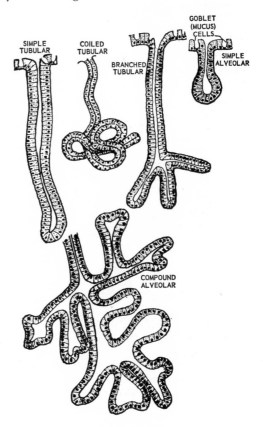

Fig. 24.3. Types of externally secreting gland.

in this case they are called *branched tubular glands*. When the ducts of a tubular or alveolar gland form a complicated system of many branches the gland is termed *compound tubular* or *compound alveolar glands,* respectively. The latter are also called **racemose glands,** from their fancied resemblance to a bunch of grapes (L. *racemus,* a bunch of grapes). A gland may contain both tubules and globular alveoli; it is then called *tubuloalveolar* or *tubuloacinar* (Fig. 24.3).

Glandular secretions. The secretions of gland cells vary widely, both chemically and functionally. Some contain substances called *enzymes* which act as catalysts (p. 337), and are capable of digesting the different foodstuffs; others secrete mucus, sweat, bile, etc., and in lower animals, poisons and other substances for purposes of defense. In some glands the enzyme or other gland product is present in the form of granules. When the product is an enzyme, this mother substance is called a *proenzyme,* or *zymogen* (enzyme former), or a *mucinogen* if the secretion is chiefly mucus. The granules become reduced in number when the gland secretes, and if the secretion is prolonged, may almost disappear; they re-form again during a period of rest. Glands, such as the salivary, that secrete only a part of their secretion in this way are called *merocrine* (Gk. *meros,* a part). Other glands, such as the mammary, form their secretion in pretty much the same way as those of the merocrine type but lose a part of their cytoplasm in the process; they are called *apocrine glands.* In a third type of gland, called *holocrine* (Gk. *holos,* whole), the cytoplasm after it has become loaded with its product undergoes complete disintegration and is discharged into the alveolus.

The *endocrine glands* (Gk. *endo,* within + *k(c)rino,* I separate), which have no ducts but secrete directly into the blood stream, are described in Chapter 38.

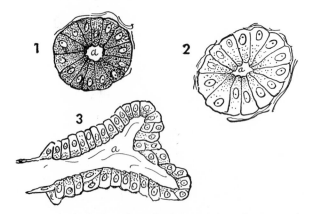

Fig. 24.4. Microscopic appearance of a typical gland. 1, the alveolus of a resting gland; the cells are loaded with granules from which the essential organic material of the secretion is derived. 2, an alveolus after a period of secretory activity; note that the granules are sparse and are completely lacking from the bases of the cells. 3, an alveolus sectioned lengthwise; the commencement of a fine duct is shown at the left. *a,* cavity of the alveolus into which the cells discharge their secretion.

TYPES OF FOOD; GENERAL DESCRIPTION

It scarcely seems necessary to explain what is meant by the word *food*. Yet science likes to be very precise and is not satisfied with merely saying that food is something we eat. The scientific description of a food is that it is a substance that furnishes the body with *energy*, gives the body material for its *growth*, or enables the body to *replace tissue* that has been worn out. Some foods do only one or another of these things; others do all three. These latter are complete and perfect foods.

Though there are a great many kinds of food—bread, cheese, butter, eggs, meat, potatoes, etc.—there are only three materials that go into the making of all foods, no matter of what type they may be. A great many different kinds of buildings can be made from the three materials wood, stone, and iron; so a great variety of foods are built from the three basic materials *carbohydrates, fats, and proteins* (see also Ch. 30). Other substances, such as vitamins (Ch. 31) and various salts of lime, iron, iodine, etc., though not foods in the strictest sense, are also essential to a wholesome diet.

Carbohydrates. There are two main classes of carbohydrates used as food—the *sugars* and the *starches*. Among the edible sugars are *glucose, fructose,* and *galactose; sucrose* (cane sugar), *maltose* (malt sugar), and *lactose* (milk sugar). Glucose, fructose, and galactose belong to the group of sugars known as *monosaccharides.* Their molecules are composed of 6 atoms of carbon and 6 molecules of water $(C_6H_{12}O_6)$; they are, therefore, also called *hexoses* (Gk. *hex,* six). The molecules of the other three sugars—sucrose, maltose, and lactose—consist of two hexose molecules joined together. They are therefore called *disaccharides.* The molecules of the starches are composed of large groups of hexose molecules. They belong to the great class of carbohydrates known as *polysaccharides* (Gk. *poly,* many). *Potatoes, bread, cakes,* and other foods made from *flour, rice, tapioca,* and *cassava* are composed largely of starch (Fig. 24.5). All starchy or sugary materials are merely different types of carbohydrate food. Carbohydrates come mainly from the vegetable kingdom.[2] The plant builds them up from the carbon dioxide of the air, and water drawn from the ground. They are, therefore, simply carbon and water; hence their name (Gk. *carbo,* charcoal (carbon) + *hydor,* water). It is perhaps hard to realize that such dry substances as sugar and flour contain large amounts of water. This is because the water is bound up so very closely with the carbon that only by the application of great heat can it be separated. If a carbohydrate, such as sugar or flour, were put into a hot oven and left until it had become completely charred to a

---

[2] A small amount of a type of starch (glycogen, or animal starch), is also found in the muscles and livers of animals (Chs. 27, 30).

Fig. 24.5. The appearance of several food materials beneath the microscope. A, starch grains; B, milk, showing droplets of fat; C, crystals of cane sugar; D, crystals of glucose.

black mass, we would then have separated it into its two chief constituents. The black mass is almost pure carbon; the water has been driven off as steam.

Fats. It is scarcely necessary to describe a fat. It too is largely carbon in combination with hydrogen and a small proportion of oxygen. There are animal fats, such as *lard, butter, suet, cream,* and fat of *egg yolk.* There are also vegetable fats, such as *olive oil, cottonseed oil, peanut oil,* etc.

The molecule of an ordinary fat consists of one molecule of glycerol combined with three molecules of a fatty acid, as shown in the following diagram:

$$\text{glycerol} \begin{cases} \text{fatty acid [3]} \\ \text{fatty acid} \\ \text{fatty acid} \end{cases}$$

The fatty acids in the common fats (or *triglycerides,* as they may also be called) are *stearic, oleic,* and *palmitic.* According to the fatty acid with which the glycerol is combined, the corresponding fats are called, respectively, *tristearin, triolein,* and *tripalmitin.* Animal and vegetable fats are a mixture mainly of these three fats. Tristearin predominates in beef fat, triolein in olive oil and other vegetable fats. Human fat is chiefly triolein and tripalmitin.

The absence of certain fatty acids from the food causes nutritional

[3] The following is the molecular structure of a fat (tristearin) :

$$\text{glycerol} \begin{cases} CH_2O—CH_{18}H_{35}O \quad \text{(stearic acid)} \\ CH_2O—CH_{18}H_{35}O \quad \text{(stearic acid)} \\ CH_2O—CH_{18}H_{35}O \quad \text{(stearic acid)} \end{cases}$$

defects that are relieved by adding to the diet the missing acids in very small amounts (Ch. 31).

A LIST OF SEVERAL FOODS CLASSIFIED ACCORDING TO THEIR COMPOSITION

Cane sugar Maple sugar and syrup Corn syrup Cornstarch Honey	Carbohydrates
Beef fat Lard Butter Olive and peanut oils	Fats
Lean meat Fish	Proteins
Eggs Cheese	Contain fats and proteins
Bread White and brown flour Porridge, shredded wheat Potatoes, cabbage, rice	Contain carbohydrates and proteins
Nuts Milk Beans	Contain carbohydrates, fats, and proteins

Proteins. It is a more difficult task to describe clearly just what is meant by a protein. In Chapter 2, it was said that protoplasm—the basis of all vegetable and animal life—is composed mostly of protein, salts, and water. Muscle or meat is very largely protoplasm; so, then, it is mostly protein. The white of egg also is almost pure protein and water. Anything living must be composed, in part at least, of protoplasm; many foods derived from the vegetable kingdom, therefore, also contain protein material. A grain of wheat, for instance, from which we get our flour, contains about 12 percent of protein. The potato, though largely starch, also contains a certain amount of protein. Other vegetable substances, such as peas and beans, are very rich in protein materials. Cow's milk, as well as containing fat, sugar, and water, is over 3 percent protein, and since it contains all three of the food materials, is an excellent food. Cheese is the protein and the fat of milk. Bread (chiefly carbohydrate) and cheese (protein and fat), then, should make a fairly complete diet, provided the necessary vitamins and salts are present, and indeed these foods form the diet of many peoples in different parts of the world.

Protein, like the other two food materials—carbohydrates and fats—contains a large proportion of carbon. Protein, however, also contains large amounts of nitrogen—an element that is absent from the other two. We can understand how very important it is that the body should obtain a certain amount of protein in one way or another. How else could we obtain the nitrogen to build up the protein in our muscles, brain, sinews, and bone? The air is about 80 percent nitrogen, but unfortunately the body is unable to take nitrogen from the air and make any use of it. Protein also contains sulfur and usually phosphorus—elements that are necessary for building protoplasm. Carbohydrate and fat may serve as fuel for the body to burn and so provide energy, but since these substances do not contain any nitrogen whatsoever, they cannot build up the protoplasm of which our bodies are largely composed. Protein of the food alone can build protein within the body. (See also Ch. 30.)

An automobile engine takes in gasoline and burns it to obtain the energy for driving its wheels. It uses oil to prevent wearing of the engine parts. But it would be absurd to think that either the gasoline or the oil could replace a worn part of the engine. It is just as impossible for carbohydrate and fat to replace worn parts of the body;[4] much less can they support body growth. Protein alone can do these things. How superior, then, as a machine is the body to the automobile! How wonderful we would think it, could we put something into the gasoline tank that would not only help to drive the engine but would also replace the steel as it became old and worn. Yet that is the part played by the protein in our food.

Protein material is made up of a large number of small units bound together into larger particles. The constituent units are slightly different from one another, though in general they are all very much alike. As a class they are called *amino acids*, but each kind has been given a special name. The simplest is glycocoll (or glycine). As we shall see presently, it is the function of the digestive juices secreted into the stomach and intestine to break down the large molecule of protein into the individual amino acids of which it is composed. Until this has been done, protein cannot be used by the body. The amino acids must pass individually into the blood and be carried to the cells of the body, where they are combined again into molecules of protein. A list of some of the commoner articles of diet with their compositions in carbohydrate, fat, and protein is given above.

THE GENERAL PLAN OF THE DIGESTIVE SYSTEM

The digestive tract, or alimentary canal as it is also called, consists of the mouth, the pharynx, the esophagus or gullet, the stomach, and the intestines. The human alimentary canal, from lips to anus, is from 30 to 32 feet long.

---

[4] Fatty acids in small amounts are required, however, for the construction and repair of the essential fatty envelopes and frameworks of cells.

Throughout most of its length, the work of the alimentary canal is directed toward the splitting of the molecules of the food into simpler compounds that, being absorbed into the blood, are carried to the tissues. Here they are oxidized to furnish energy, stored as fat or starch (glycogen), or built into living tissue. The reader should study Figures 24.6 and 24.7 in order to become familiar with the different parts of the digestive system.

The nature of the digestive process

Very little of our food, whether carbohydrate, fat, or protein, is capable in its unaltered form of nourishing the body. It must first be digested. This means that it must undergo certain chemical changes. The large molecules of proteins, carbohydrates, and fats are much too large to be absorbed into the blood through the mucous membrane of the stomach and intestine (see *colloids,* Ch. 1). Even should they pass through, they would be too large for use by the cells of the tissues.[5] The digestive juices must act upon the large molecules of the food and split them up into smaller ones that can pass through the intestinal wall and be carried to the tissue cells, where they are disposed of.

Food lying in the digestive tract cannot truly be said to have entered the body. It is only in a tube surrounded by the body. Not until the food has been changed so that it is able to enter the blood and be used by the tissue cells can the body be said to have accepted it. The digestive tube — the stomach and intestines — are, as it were, the kitchens of the

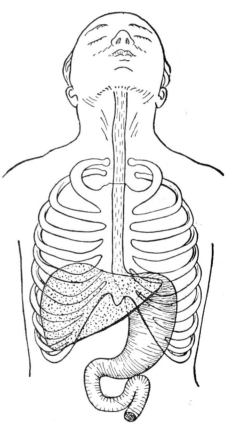

Fig. 24.6. Diagram to show the positions of the esophagus, liver, stomach, and duodenum in relation to the surface of the body.

body's household, where food is prepared for the tissues.

[5] Sometimes undigested protein, such as raw egg white, passes in very small amounts into the blood; it is excreted almost unchanged in the urine.

334 - The Physiology of Digestion

The chemical changes in the food that the digestive juices accomplish consist mainly of splitting each molecule of the disaccharides and starches into their constituent glucose molecules, of breaking up the fat molecules into one molecule of glycerol and three molecules of fatty acid, and as mentioned above, of disrupting the protein molecule into its several amino acids.[6] Only in these simple forms can the food be absorbed and assimilated. (See also Ch. 27.)

Let us for a moment enter a world that lies beyond our senses and try to form in our "mind's eye" a picture of what our knowledge tells us

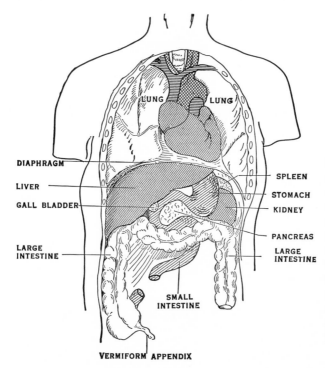

DIAPHRAGM

LIVER

GALL BLADDER

LARGE INTESTINE

VERMIFORM APPENDIX

SMALL INTESTINE

SPLEEN

STOMACH

KIDNEY

PANCREAS

LARGE INTESTINE

Fig. 24.7. The thoracic and abdominal organs. All but the upper part of the small intestine and the lower 3 inches or so where it empties into the large intestine have been omitted; the lower part of the large bowel including the rectum has also been removed.

---

[6] Some 25 different amino acids have so far been discovered. The more complex proteins contain nearly all of these different types. Others, such as gelatin, are called incomplete because they lack some of the amino acids that are essential for the promotion of growth or even for sustaining life. The amino acids are linked together in the protein molecule in the following way:

$$CH_3 \cdot CHNH_2 \cdot CO—HN \cdot CH_2 \cdot COOH$$
alanine   glycine

The size and weight of the protein molecule depends upon the total number of amino acids of all types that compose it. The weights of some proteins are relatively small; others have weights over 1000 times greater. The shapes of the molecules of different proteins are also variable; some are globular in form, others are long and slender and fiberlike in shape. (See Appendix for a list of amino acids.)

must be so. The lining of the digestive tract, though apparently free from any gaps or pores, is in reality thought to be pierced by millions upon millions of fine openings, like a sieve, though with a mesh beyond the power of any ordinary microscope to discover.

Molecules of food materials such as those of glucose or water, which are smaller in diameter than the intestinal "mesh," can pass through with little hindrance. Larger molecules are barred. Here and there we may see these larger molecules in the contents of the bowel being shattered by the chemical processes of digestion into smaller ones, no larger than the mesh of the enclosing intestinal screen. If we should take a sausage skin, made from the intestinal wall of a pig, and tied one end, filled it with salt and water, and submerged the little sac in a glass of pure water (Fig. 24.8), we should find that after a time the water in the glass had a salty taste. If we had filled the sausage skin with a solution of glucose instead of salt, we should have found that after a time the water in the glass had a faintly sweet taste. Evidently, then, the small molecules of salt or of glucose passed through the sausage skin into the surrounding water. If we were to fill the sac with white of egg, starch, or fat and repeat the experiment, we should not find white of egg or starch or fat in the surrounding water. (See also Ch. 1.)

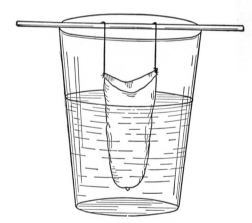

Fig. 24.8. Sausage skin containing sugar or salt solution and immersed in water. (See explanation in the text.)

Though a mechanical conception has been used here, in which minute pores in the intestinal membranes have been visualized, the true nature of the absorptive process is not clearly understood. It must not be thought that amino acids and other products of digestion pass through the intestinal wall by purely physical forces—for example, diffusion and osmosis—as through a dead membrane. Absorption from the intestine is the result of living processes. The mucous membrane of the intestine, like the tubules of the kidney, shows a selective power that is lost after its death. Glucose, for example, which is utilized by the body, is absorbed much more readily than are other sugars that have no nutritional value, but after the tissue of the intestinal wall has been severely injured so as to abolish its selective function, all sugars pass through it at about the same rate.

The digested food is absorbed almost entirely from the small intestine. Neither food nor water is absorbed from the stomach, though alcohol can enter the blood from this part of the alimentary tract. Water, but little or no food material, is absorbed from the large intestine.

The changes that digestion produces in the food are shown diagrammatically in Figure 24.9.

The reader may realize how wonderful is the digestion of food if he is told that a chemist, in order to carry out similar changes by the ordinary methods of chemistry, is forced to use powerful agents, such as strong acids, or great heat. The food in the stomach and intestines undergoes chemical changes—that is, digestion—with the greatest ease. No great heat is required, and the chemicals used by the body in its laboratories—

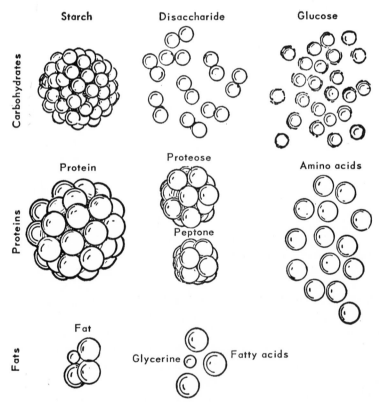

Fig. 24.9. Diagram to illustrate the constitution of the three foodstuffs—carbohydrates, proteins, and fats.

stomach and intestines—are comparatively mild. Yet even pieces of bone, if not too large, are digested in a dog's stomach.

When we eat a meal of roast beef, potatoes, bread and butter, and a glass of milk, we give little thought to the miracles that the laboratories of the stomach and the rest of the alimentary tract perform. We impose a task upon the digestive glands and their secretions that one skilled in the ways of chemistry and furnished with the facilities of a modern laboratory could not perform so quickly or so well, if at all.

How food is prepared for absorption into the blood; enzymes

What then enables the body to do things that the chemist can do only very clumsily? The answer is that the cells of the digestive glands elaborate substances called **enzymes,** which act, each in its own way, upon the various foods. The glands also form water in which the enzymes and various mineral salts are dissolved. When a gland forms a juice and discharges it into the mouth, stomach, or intestine, it is said to *secrete.* Secretion is a very complex process, and is far from being fully understood. The cells of which a gland is composed select from the blood, which flows through its fine vessels, the materials required for the manufacture of the several constituents of its juice. The enzymes, or the mother substances from which these active principles of the juice are finally produced, often may be seen microscopically in the cells of a resting gland as fine droplets or *granules* (Figs. 24.4 and 25.3). In this form the enzyme material is stored until required.

Enzymes, or **ferments,** as they are sometimes called, are responsible for the chemical changes in the food that take place during digestion. The various digestive juices—salivary, gastric, and pancreatic secretions—contain different kinds of enzymes, each of which acts upon a particular type of food—carbohydrate, fat, or protein. The nature of enzymes and their actions have been problems of long standing.

Enzymes are responsible for many chemical reactions other than those of digestion. The work of the great Pasteur showed that several hitherto unexplained chemical processes were in truth due to their actions. The conversion of sugar and water into alcohol and carbon dioxide —alcoholic fermentation—is brought about by enzymes formed by the cells of yeast. An enzyme, also formed by living organisms, converts alcohol to acetic acid. The formation of lactic acid in the souring of milk is produced by a germ—the lactic acid bacillus. Microorganisms are also used in industry to produce, through enzyme action, chemicals that cannot be made in any other way.

These examples show that enzymes are not peculiar to the digestive systems of animals but belong to a class of substances known widely throughout nature. Like the cell of the yeast plant, certain cells of the animal body have learned the trick of manufacturing them. Such enzyme-producing cells constitute the tissue of the digestive glands mentioned above. In their general nature the enzymes of the animal body are essentially the same as the yeast or lactic acid ferments. It is only in detail—in the particular chemical changes that they accomplish—that the digestive enzymes are different from these.

Many theories have been advanced in attempts to explain enzyme action. No theory is entirely satisfactory; yet several facts have been discovered. We know many things about the way an enzyme acts but not a great deal of the underlying causes of its action. Some of the characteristic features of this action may be described. Just as a lever can move an object many times its own weight, so an enzyme can act upon and produce chemical changes in a mass of substance many, many times its own size and weight. "A little leaven leaveneth the whole lump." Another peculiarity of an enzyme is that it does not form part of the final product of the chemical reaction. It can be recovered virtually unchanged after the chemical process for which it is responsible has come to an end. A digestive enzyme can act upon a food substance only when water and a certain amount of acid or alkali is present. Other enzymes require the presence of certain minerals—calcium, magnesium, potassium, etc. Such accessory substances are called **coenzymes.** The material upon which an enzyme acts—sugar, fat, protein, etc.—is called its **substrate.**

During digestion, the enzymes in some way bring together the molecules of water and the molecules of the foodstuff. The molecules of the food then break up into smaller ones. This process in which a substance takes up water and then splits into simpler compounds is called **hydrolysis.**

If the reader has studied chemistry, he will recall that certain inorganic substances in very small amounts act to speed up chemical reactions that without such action would proceed very slowly and sometimes almost imperceptibly. Substances of this nature are called *catalysts.* Thus, if a solution of cane sugar is left undisturbed for a long time, a certain small amount of the disaccharide will be found to have become converted into glucose (Ch. 30). If, however, a little hydrochloric acid is added to the solution, splitting of the cane sugar molecules proceeds much more rapidly. Only a small amount of the catalyst (hydrochloric acid in this case) is required and it remains itself unchanged by the reaction. Enzymes, since they act in very much the same way, might be called **organic catalysts**—that is, catalysts formed by living organisms.

The action of an enzyme is speeded up when the temperature is raised and is slowed down when the temperature is lowered. Enzymes are destroyed by very high temperatures. The digestive enzymes, as might be expected, do their work best at the temperature of the body. Each enzyme is a specialist. In its own particular field it does its work well, but it is unable to take on any other duty. Its action, that is to say, is highly specific. For instance, if it can digest starch, it is unable to digest protein or fat; if it can cause chemical changes in protein, it is worthless for splitting the molecule of fat or sugar, and so on. This characteristic makes one think of each enzyme as a key that will fit but one lock—a particular type of molecule.

Though the old names for certain of the digestive enzymes are still often used, such as *ptyalin* for the enzyme of the saliva, *pepsin* for the chief enzyme of the gastric juice, and *trypsin* for the enzyme of the pancreatic juice that acts upon protein, it has become more customary to coin a name for a particular enzyme by adding the suffix "ase" to the name of the substrate upon which the enzyme exerts its specific action. Thus: ptyalin acts upon starch—*salivary amylase* (L. *amylum,* starch) is therefore another name for this enzyme; an enzyme that acts upon protein is called a *protease*—so we have a *gastric* (pepsin) and a *pancreatic* (trypsin) *protease;* an enzyme that splits fat is called a *lipase.* On the other hand, some enzymes are given names that indicate their type of action instead of their substrates. One, for example, that hastens oxidation may be called an *oxidase.*

25

Preparation of Food
in the Mouth; Its Passage
into the Stomach

ANATOMICAL OUTLINE FROM MOUTH TO STOMACH

The cavity of the mouth (cavum oris, oral or baccal cavity)

The oral cavity, the first part of the digestive tract, commences at the lips and is continued behind into the pharynx through an opening called the *isthmus of the fauces,* or the **oropharyngeal isthmus.** The lateral boundaries of this opening are two fleshy columns on each side, called the *anterior* and *posterior pillars* of the fauces. The anterior pillar is also known as the *palatoglossal arch,* and the posterior as the *palatopharyngeal arch.* The part of the mouth cavity lying between the lips, and the gums and teeth is known as the **vestibule,** and that part behind the teeth as the **mouth cavity proper.** The **gums** (*gingivae*) consist of fibrous tissue attached to the periosteum of the alveolar processes of the jaw bones and covered by mucous membrane (Fig. 25.1).

The **mouth cavity proper** is bounded laterally by the cheeks formed by the buccinator muscles; its roof is the palate, which separates it from the nose and upper part of the pharynx; the greater part of its floor is formed by the tongue. The mucous membrane lining the mouth is covered by stratified squamous epithelium.

The **palate** consists of an anterior hard, or bony, part and a posterior part of soft tissue (Fig. 25.1). The **hard palate,** which is the anterior three fifths or so of the palate, is formed of the palatine processes of the maxillae and the horizontal plates of the palatine bones. A strong membrane called the **palatine aponeurosis** is attached to the posterior border

340

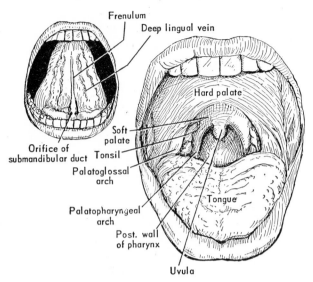

Frenulum

Deep lingual vein

Hard palate

Soft palate

Orifice of submandibular duct

Tonsil

Palatoglossal arch

Palatopharyngeal arch

Post. wall of pharynx

Tongue

Uvula

Fig. 25.1. The interior of the mouth; the smaller figure on the left shows the under surface of the tongue, which has been turned upwards.

and under surface of the hard palate; it gives attachment to the palatine muscles. The **soft palate** is a movable fold composed of fibrous tissue and muscle covered by mucous membrane; it is attached to and hangs from the posterior border of the hard palate. It separates the upper part of the pharynx (nasopharynx) from the mouth and, when raised, from the lower, or oral, part of the pharynx. Hanging from the middle of its lower border is a nipplelike projection called the **uvula.**

Five muscles are inserted into or arise from the soft palate—the *levator palati, tensor palati, musculus uvulae, palatoglossus,* and *palatopharyngeus.* The **levator** and **tensor palati** take origin, respectively, from the temporal and sphenoid bones at the base of the skull. The former muscle raises the soft palate, the latter one tightens it. The **musculus uvulae** arises from the palatine bones, and is inserted into the mucous membrane of the uvula. The **palatoglossus** arises from the palatine aponeurosis, and is inserted into the side of the tongue. The **palatopharyngeus** arises from the hard palate and the palatine aponeurosis, and is inserted into the posterior border of the lamina of the thyroid cartilage and into the fibrous tissue on the lateral wall of the pharynx. The palatoglossus muscles form the anterior pillars of the fauces, or the palatoglossal arch; the palatopharyngeus muscles form the posterior pillars of the fauces, or the palatopharyngeal arch. The triangular interval between the pillars on each side is occupied by the **tonsil** (see Fig. 25.10) . When the muscles contract, the pillars of the fauces are approximated and the oropharyngeal isthmus narrowed; the palatoglossus also draws the root of the tongue upwards; the palatopharyngeus draws the walls of the pharynx upwards.

The tongue *(lingua)* is a movable organ that performs the important functions concerned with taste, mastication, swallowing, and speech. It is composed of muscle and covered by mucous membrane; the surface epithelium is of the stratified squamous type. Its upper surface shows many elevations called *papillae* (Ch. 32). The tongue is attached to the mandible and the hyoid bone; these attachments constitute its **root.** The fold of mucous membrane running forward in the mid-line from the under surface of the tongue to the floor of the mouth is called the **frenulum;** on each side of the latter a vein—the *deep lingual*—can be seen shining through the mucous membrane. The posterior part of the tongue projects backwards into the isthmus of the fauces.

The muscles of the tongue are both intrinsic and extrinsic (see Fig. 5.27). The *intrinsic muscles* compose the substance of the organ, and consist of bundles of striated muscle fibers that run both longitudinally and transversely, and at the free anterior border, vertically. These bundles have been given different names, which need not be mentioned here. The *extrinsic muscles* pass between the tongue and the hyoid bone, the mandible and the styloid processes of the temporal bone, and are called, respectively, the **hyoglossus, genioglossus,** and **styloglossus.** The hyoglossus depresses the tongue; the genioglossus draws it forward and protrudes it between the lips; the styloglossus pulls the tongue upwards and backwards.

The **salivary glands** number three on each side, and are named the *parotid, submandibular,* and *sublingual,* respectively (Fig. 25.2).

The **parotid** is the largest of the three salivary glands. It is situated below the opening of the ear (external auditory meatus), and extends forward over the masseter muscle. It discharges its secretion into the

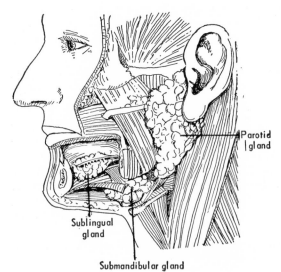

Parotid gland

Sublingual gland

Submandibular gland

Fig. 25.2. The salivary glands.

mouth through the **parotid duct** which pierces the buccinator muscle and opens on the oral surface of the cheek opposite the second upper molar tooth.

The **submandibular gland** lies below the mandible behind the anterior belly of the diagastric muscle. Its secretion is delivered into the mouth by the **submandibular duct** whose orifice opens beside the frenulum of the tongue.

The **sublingual gland** lies below the mucous membrane covering the floor of the mouth and against the inner surface of the mandible near the symphysis. It is the smallest of the salivary glands. Its secretion escapes through a number of fine ducts—8 to 20—that open on each side at the summit of a fold of mucous membrane running transversely in the floor of the mouth.

The structure of the salivary glands. The cells of the salivary glands are of two types, **serous** and **mucous.** The secretion of the former type is thin and watery; that of the latter type contains *mucin,*[1] and is therefore thicker, and more slimy and viscous. The parotid gland is composed entirely of serous cells, whereas the cells of the sublingual gland are predominantly of the mucous type, serous cells being scarce. The submandibular gland contains both serous and mucous cells in about equal proportions, the two types being seen in many instances in the wall of the same alveolus. The serous cells are then found on the outer side of the mucous cells which, therefore, abut upon the alveolar cavity. The serous cells form crescentic bodies known as the *demilunes of Gianuzzi* situated on the outer aspect of the mucous cells (Fig. 25.3).

Nerve supply. The secretory fibers of the salivary glands are derived from the autonomic nervous system. The secretion of the glands is brought about reflexly through centers in the brain stem. The parotid gland receives parasympathetic fibers from the *superior salivary center,* or *nucleus,* which leave the brain in the glossopharyngeal nerve. The submandibular and sublingual glands are supplied with parasympathetic fibers from the *inferior salivary nucleus* which pass to the gland in the chorda tympani nerve, a branch of the facial nerve. All three glands also receive sympathetic fibers.

The composition of saliva. The mixed saliva as collected from the mouth varies in its water content according to the proportions of the different secretions, but is usually over 99 percent water. Of the solid material the most important are mucin and the enzyme *ptyalin.* It also contains a number of substances found in other body fluids, such as the salts of sodium, potassium, calcium, and magnesium, as well as a variety of excretory products including urea and uric acid. An antibacterial

---

[1] Mucin is a compound of protein with a carbohydrate, and known chemically as a glycoprotein. It forms a sticky, slimy substance in aqueous solution as secreted by the salivary and other glands. Such a secretion is called *mucus,* or a *mucous secretion.*

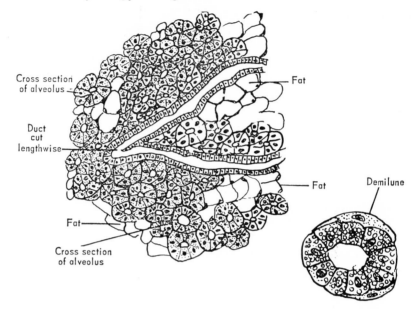

Cross section of alveolus

Duct cut lengthwise

Fat

Fat

Demilune

Fat

Cross section of alveolus

Fig. 25.3. Microscopic appearance of a section of a salivary gland; an enlarged drawing of an alveolus on the right.

substance known as *lysozyme* is an important constituent. Saliva is very faintly acid having a pH of about 6.8.

The secretion of saliva. The secretion of saliva is normally brought about through reflex action. The reflex may be one of two types. For instance, saliva is secreted when food or other material enters the mouth and is tasted. The material may be pleasant to the taste or disagreeable; saliva is secreted in either case. Even materials with little or no taste may cause secretion. Irritation or injury to the lining membrane of the mouth may also cause a flow of juice. The drilling of a tooth by the dentist often causes profuse salivation. This type of reflex, which results from direct stimulation of the organs of taste or of the mucous membrane of the mouth, is called an *unconditioned,* or *inborn, reflex,* and is the response to an *unconditioned stimulus.* The unconditioned reflex is the same in nature as the ordinary reflexes with which we are all familiar and that are described in Chapter 34; the nerves of taste or other nerves in the mouth are stimulated and the reflex brought about through the salivary centers and the secretory nerves supplying the glands. But in other instances a secretion of saliva occurs though no food or other material enters the mouth and no stimulus whatever has been applied directly to the lining of the mouth. For instance, the smell, the sight, the mention, or even the thought of food may, as we all know, "make the mouth water," especially when one is hungry. This type, which depends upon any one of the other senses—sight, smell, hearing, etc.—as well as upon previous taste sensations, is called a *conditioned, acquired,* or *learned, reflex.*

Conditioned reflexes. At the beginning of this century the Russian physiologist Ivan Pavlov carried out some interesting experiments upon dogs (Fig. 25.4), from which we have learned a great deal about the conditioned reflex. Pavlov performed his experiments in the following fashion. A dog was fed with appetizing food, and at the same time a bright white or colored light was flashed within the animal's view. The light was shown for several days each time the animal was fed. After a

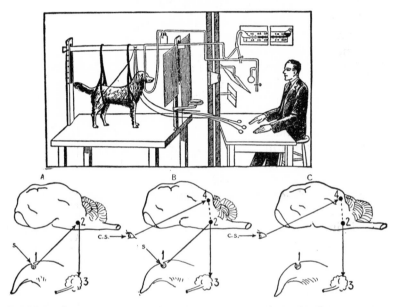

Fig. 25.4. *Above,* arrangement for carrying out a conditioned reflex experiment. The opening of the parotid duct has been transplanted to the skin of the cheek so that the saliva as it is secreted may be collected and measured. The animal is separated from the experimenter by a partition in order that extraneous types of stimulation (e.g., movements or sounds made by the experimenter) shall not arouse the animal's interest and thereby interfere with the conditioning process. *(After Pavlov, Lectures on Conditional Reflexes. International Publishers, N. Y.) Below,* diagram to illustrate the theory of the mechanism underlying conditioned reflexes. 1, taste buds; 2, salivary center; 3, salivary gland; 4, occipital (visual) cortex; S, unconditioned stimulus; C.S., conditioned stimulus. In *A,* the animal is fed and a stimulus thus applied to the taste buds. In *B,* a conditioned visual stimulus (e.g., a flash of light) is applied at the same time as the unconditioned stimulus; a pathway from the occipital cortex to the salivary center is thus established. In *C,* the conditioned stimulus is applied alone; impulses pass from the visual cortex to the salivary center and evoke salivary secretion. The center for taste and its connections with the visual and salivary centers are not shown.

certain number of such trials, or lessons, as they might be called, the light was shown, but the animal was not fed. Nevertheless a profuse secretion of saliva occurred. The same remarkable result was obtained when, instead of a light being shown at the time of feeding, a note was sounded upon a horn, or a bell rung, or the skin stimulated by a weak electric shock. After the preliminary period of training, the sound of the horn or the bell or the sensation of the electric shock was sufficient alone to cause secretion. Conditioned reflexes and Pavlov's experiments are discussed at greater length in Chapter 37.

The results described in the above experiments are actually not greatly different from the conditioned reflex that causes the mouth to water when we ourselves see or smell appetizing food. We too, though we do not remember it, have been trained to associate in our minds the sight or smell of an article of food, its color, shape, etc., with its taste. Having formed this association, the smell or sight of the food alone is enough to cause secretion. Had we been blind and but recently regained our sight, or had we just acquired the sense of smell, the sight or smell of the most tempting morsels would not make the mouth water.

The digestion of starch by saliva. The ptyalin (Ch. 24) of the saliva converts cooked starch into *malt sugar,* or *maltose.* It has no action upon fats or proteins. It therefore belongs to the class of enzymes called amylases (Ch. 24). Most starchy foods, before they can be attacked by the saliva or the other digestive juices of man, must be cooked. The potato, for instance, is made up of cells having an envelope of *cellulose,* and this material is indigestible. So long as the cellulose envelope remains unbroken, the enzymes cannot reach the starch in the interior of the cell. Raw potatoes, apples, wheat kernels, oats, etc., for this reason possess little nutritive value for man. Yet, as we know, raw vegetable food is the sole source of nourishment for herbivorous animals. These species possess means for the digestion of cellulose. Man, on the other hand, must rely upon heat to rupture the cellulose envelope before he can assimilate foods composed mainly of starch. Steaming, boiling, roasting, etc., burst the cellulose envelopes of the cells and allow the enzymes to come into contact with the starch within.

The digestion of starch by ptyalin is carried out in a series of steps that can be detected by suitable chemical means. If a little boiled starch and water is mixed with saliva in a test tube and the mixture kept warm, after a short time the starch will be found to have become more freely soluble. It then is called *soluble starch.* This, like the unchanged starch, gives a blue color when a drop of iodine is added to it. Later the soluble starch is converted into *dextrins,* which are *polysaccharides* possessing a smaller number of glucose molecules than the original starch. The dextrins are of two kinds. The one formed first gives a brownish-red color with iodine. It is therefore called *erythrodextrin* (Gk. *erythros,* red) . The second gives no color with iodine. This colorless dextrin is called *achroö-dextrin* (Gk. *a,* not + *chrōma,* color). Later the dextrin turns to **maltose,** a sugar belonging to the class of *disaccharides* (Ch. 24). The ptyalin has little or no power to carry the digestion of starch beyond the maltose stage. The steps in the digestion of starch by ptyalin are shown in the following table:

Boiled starch	blue color with iodine
↓	
Soluble starch	blue color with iodine
↓	
Erythrodextrin	red color with iodine
↓	
Achroödextrin	no color with iodine
↓	
Maltose	

Since the food is but a very short time in the mouth before it is swallowed, the enzyme of the saliva has little or no action upon it there. If, however, the food has been well chewed and thoroughly moistened with saliva, conversion of a large part of the starch into maltose may occur while the food lies in the stomach. But even so, maltose cannot be absorbed into the blood. Its molecule must first be split into its two glucose constituents before the digestion of starch can be said to be complete. The maltose, as well as any starch that has not been converted to maltose, must remain to be digested by the digestive juices of the intestine (Ch. 27).

Other functions of the saliva. The digestive action of the saliva, though described first, is probably of much less value than some of its other functions. Of greater importance is its use for moistening the food, rendering it plastic, and so enabling it to be easily swallowed. The saliva permits perfectly dry food to be eaten. We all know that even though our salivary glands secrete freely, it is not always easy to swallow a dry biscuit, and sometimes it is necessary to drink water or other fluid in order to aid the passage of other dry food into the pharynx and esophagus. Without saliva or some fluid to take its place, it would be impossible to swallow food that is perfectly dry. A man, in the course of a day, secretes a surprising amount of saliva. Something like a pint and a half of fluid is poured into the mouth by the salivary glands in this time. A cow eating dry fodder secretes 2 to 3 quarts in 24 hours.

Saliva also helps to keep the mouth clean and fresh. Food particles that otherwise would lodge upon the teeth, gums, and tongue are being constantly flushed away by the saliva, which is kept in motion by the actions of the tongue, lips, and cheeks. In keeping the soft parts of the mouth moist and pliable the saliva plays a very important role in the mechanisms of speech. It is almost impossible to speak plainly if the mouth is dry. Many public speakers must sip water occasionally during a speech or lecture, because sometimes evaporation of moisture from the mouth is so great that the saliva alone is insufficient to keep the parts soft and freely movable. In certain fevers, notably typhoid, the salivary secretion is suppressed, with the result that the mouth becomes very dry and the tongue and lips become hard and cracked. Food tends to collect upon the tongue and teeth and in the folds and crevices of the mouth. The mouth would soon become very foul unless measures were taken to prevent it. To overcome this unhygienic state, the nurse cleans the interior of the mouth frequently with a swab of gauze soaked in a mild antiseptic solution, such as boric acid. Drying of the mouth arouses the sensation of thirst, so that anything that tends to reduce or suppress the secretion of saliva will make one thirsty. Acid-tasting materials, such as lemons, oranges, and grapefruit, stimulate the secretion. Fruits and fruit-flavored drinks owe their refreshing and thirst-quenching qualities largely to this fact. The action of the saliva in dissolving various substances is also almost essential to the sense of taste. Sugar, salt, and many other substances must be in solution before they can be tasted.

Many substances are excreted from the blood into the saliva; among these are certain drugs, such as mercury, iodides, and lead. The germs of several diseases, such as rabies (hydrophobia), infantile paralysis, and mumps, also pass from the blood into the saliva. Infantile paralysis has been reproduced in monkeys by injecting them with the saliva of an infected person. It is apparent, then, that diseases may be easily transmitted from one person to another through particles of saliva clinging to eating and drinking utensils, by kissing, from dried saliva that has been expectorated and blown about as dust, or even by talking to a person infected with influenza or other diseases. During the act of speaking, saliva, in the form of fine invisible particles, is cast from the mouth for a distance of several inches.

The pharynx

The pharynx is that part of the alimentary canal lying anteriorly in relation to the nasal cavities, mouth, and larynx, with all three of which it communicates. It is continuous with the esophagus below, and is separated behind from the cervical vertebrae only by fasciae and muscles (Figs. 25.1 and 5.28).

The part of the pharynx above the soft palate is called the **nasal part,** or the **nasopharynx.** The auditory tube, through which a communication is established with the middle ear, opens into this portion. The remaining part of the pharynx is divided into an upper **oral portion** behind the mouth, and a **laryngeal portion** behind and communicating with the larynx. The lateral walls of the oral part of the pharynx are formed by the palatopharyngeus muscles and constitute the posterior pillars of the fauces. In the triangular interval on each side between the anterior and posterior pillars of the fauces the *tonsil,* a prominent mass of lymphoid tissue, is situated. The pharyngeal walls are composed of three coats—mucous, fibrous, and muscular, from within outwards. The nasal part of the pharynx, being part of the respiratory passages, is lined by mucous membrane whose surface epithelium is of the ciliated columnar variety. In the rest of the pharynx the epithelium is stratified squamous in type. The fibrous coat is thick above where it is attached to the basilar part of the occipital bone, but becomes thin below where it is represented mainly by the **posterior median raphe**—a narrow, central, vertically-running band—which gives attachment to the constrictor muscles of the pharynx. The muscles of the outer coat of the pharynx are the three *constrictor muscles—superior, middle,* and *inferior*—and the *stylopharyngeus, salpingopharyngeus,* and *palatopharyngeus.*

The superior constrictor of the pharynx takes origin from the medial pterygoid plate of the sphenoid bone at the base of the skull and from the inner surface of the mandible (Fig. 5.28). The fibers sweep backwards and are inserted in series with the other two constrictors into the posterior median raphe mentioned above.

The middle constrictor of the pharynx arises from the greater horn of the hyoid bone and the stylohyoid ligament. The fibers fan out as they pass backwards around the pharynx and are inserted into the posterior median raphe.

The inferior constrictor of the pharynx arises from the side of the cricoid cartilage and from the lamina of the thyroid cartilage.

The stylopharyngeus and the salpingopharyngeus are slender muscles that arise, respectively, from the styloid process of the temporal bone and the lower part of the cartilage of the auditory (pharyngotympanic, or Eustachian) tube, and are inserted into the side of the pharynx; the stylopharyngeus has an additional insertion into the posterior border of the lamina of the thyroid cartilage. The *palatopharyngeus* muscle has been described with the muscles of the soft palate.

The coordinated actions of the pharyngeal muscles constitute the act of swallowing and will be described under that heading.

The esophagus, or gullet

The esophagus is a muscular tube about 24 cm long, continuous above with the pharynx and opening below into the stomach. It descends through the lower part of the neck behind the trachea, passes through the posterior part of the mediastinum, and enters the abdominal cavity through an opening in the diaphragm (**esophageal hiatus**). After an abdominal course of about ½ inch it opens into the stomach through the **cardiac orifice.** The esophageal muscle consists of an outer layer of longitudinal fibers and an inner one of circular fibers. The mucous membrane of the esophagus is covered by stratified squamous epithelium, except near the lower end of the tube where it is similar to that in the adjacent part of the stomach; the mucosa here contains tubular glands that secrete an alkaline fluid. In man the upper fifth to third of the esophagus is composed of striated muscle, the remainder of smooth muscle. Just above where the esophagus enters the stomach, the circular layer of muscle is thickened to form the **cardiac sphincter**[2] which is capable of strong contraction, and sometimes enters into spasm; this abnormal state is called *cardiospasm.*

PREPARATION OF FOOD IN THE MOUTH

The teeth

Teeth are of different sizes and shapes, but in any tooth three parts, common to all, may be distinguished (Fig. 25.5) —namely, the **crown,** visible above the gum; the **neck,** covered by gum and extending a little beyond the bone of the jaw; and the **root** or **roots,** held in the socket of the bone (the maxilla or mandible) .

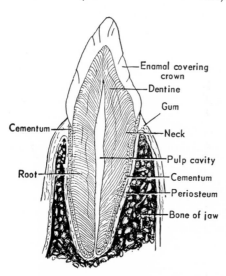

Enamal covering crown
Dentine
Gum
Cementum
Neck
Root
Pulp cavity
Cementum
Periosteum
Bone of jaw

Fig. 25.5. Section vertically through a tooth.

If a tooth is sectioned, it is found to be composed of an outer layer of very hard white material —the **enamel.** This layer covers only the crown. Beneath the enamel of the crown, and covering the neck and root is a less dense material resembling very hard bone and called the **dentine.** The center or core of the tooth is tunneled to hold delicate nerve filaments and blood vessels, which together are called the **pulp.** Between the dentine of the root and the bone of the jaw is a thin layer of modified bone called the **cementum.** Fine parallel tubules run outward from the pulp cavity through the dentine to end just beneath the enamel or the cementum. The teeth develop within the bony substance of the jaws. Their enamel covering is derived from the

[2] A sphincter is a band of circular muscle fibers surrounding one end or some part of a tube or other hollow structure, which can when it contracts narrow or completely close the opening of the hollow organ.

epithelium of the oral mucous membrane, and is, therefore, of ectodermal origin. The rest of the tooth is derived from mesoderm. As the teeth grow they gradually force their way into position.

Man receives two sets of teeth. The first set, called the **temporary, milk,** or **deciduous, teeth,** does not appear as a rule until after birth. On very rare occasions one or more teeth are already cut when a baby is born. It was formerly a common superstition that the child so born would grow up ill natured. The first tooth to cut the gum is usually a lower incisor, which does so between the sixth and the ninth month.

The **permanent teeth** are present within the jaw, though not fully formed, some years before the milk teeth fall out. X-rays show them lying all in a row beyond the roots of the temporary teeth (Fig. 25.6). As the permanent teeth grow, they press upon the roots of the milk teeth and cause them to become smaller and smaller. That is the reason why a milk tooth comes out so easily at the proper time. The first permanent tooth, usually a molar, appears about the sixth or seventh year. The milk teeth number twenty, the permanent teeth thirty-two.

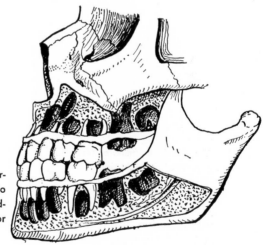

Fig. 25.6. Jawbones of a six-year-old child with bone removed to show permanent teeth (dark shading) and roots of deciduous, or milk, teeth (no shading).

There are four kinds of permanent teeth—**incisors, canines, bicuspids** (or **premolars**), and **molars** (Figs. 25.7, 25.8). The first two types lie in the front of the jaws and are used for cutting and tearing the food. The bicuspids and molars, on either side of the mouth, serve to grind and crush the food into very fine fragments.

In the following table are given the approximate ages for the eruption of the deciduous and the permanent teeth.

Deciduous Teeth

Lower central incisors.................... 6 to 9 months
Upper incisors .... 8 to 10 months
Lateral incisors and first molars........... 15 to 21 months
Canines .... 16 to 20 months
Second molars .... 20 to 24 months

Permanent Teeth

First molars ....   6 years
Central incisors ....   7 years
Lateral incisors ....   8 years
First premolars ....   9 years
Second premolars ....   10 years
Canines .... 11 to 12 years
Second molars .... 12 to 13 years
Third molars .... 17 to 25 years

Decay of the teeth, or dental caries. The teeth always decay from without inward. Once the protective enamel is broken, the less resistant dentine falls an easy prey to the bacteria of decay. Microorganisms travel along the fine tubules of the dentine, and breaking down the comparatively soft material, form a cavity, which sooner or later involves the pulp with its very sensitive nerves. Toothache is the result. Chemically the dentine resembles bone, being composed largely of the minerals calcium (lime) and phosphorus. Calcium is very quickly attacked and dissolved by acids. Acidity of the mouth, for this reason, is looked upon as an important cause of tooth decay. Carbohydrate food (starches and sugars) lying in the crevices between the teeth, and between the teeth and the gum furnishes food for germs, which through a fermentationlike action produce acid substances. The acid then attacks the enamel and later the dentine of the teeth. It is scarcely necessary, therefore, to point out how important it is to brush the teeth thoroughly night and morning.

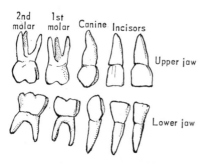

Fig. 25.7. The deciduous (milk, or temporary) teeth of the right side.

Though the dentist may tell us, we ourselves rarely know when the protective enamel has been broken and the underlying dentine exposed to the microorganisms of decay. Usually it is only after decay has extended into the sensitive dentine or pulp that we are aware that the tooth is diseased. Conditions in the mouth probably have been given an exaggerated importance as factors in tooth decay. Though brushing the teeth regularly is essential for hygienic reasons, it alone will not prevent dental caries. One person may have good teeth though he gives them little care in this regard, whereas another, though he cleans them regularly, suffers from carious teeth. It is likely that diet and general health play primary roles in the breakdown of tooth structure. An adequate supply of minerals—calcium, phosphorus, and fluorine—and of vitamins —especially D and C—as well as not too great a proportion of carbohydrate food appears to be conducive to dental health.

Salts of fluorine, an element belonging to the same class as iodine, have been found to be protective against tooth decay, especially in children. In localities where compounds of fluorine are present in drinking water in a concentration of one part in a million or more, dental caries is much less common than in other districts where the fluoride concentration of the water is unusually low. In some communities fluoride is added artificially to the municipal water supply in a concentration of one part or less in a million. This measure has proved successful as a preventive. Excessive concentrations of fluoride are, however, injurious to the teeth, causing mottling of the enamel.

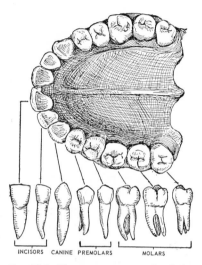

Fig. 25.8. The permanent teeth of the upper jaw (maxilla).

Tooth decay is not a modern disease. Evidence of it may be found in Egyptian mummies, but it is only within comparatively recent years that the serious consequences that follow in the train of decayed teeth have been realized. Indigestion, blood poisoning, infections of the heart valves, arthritis, and kidney disease are some of the evils that may result.

Mastication

In order that the tasks of the digestive glands may be accomplished with the least effort, the food must be thoroughly broken up into small fragments by the teeth. For instance, if we were to take a small lump of meat and drop it into a glass tube filled with pepsin and hydrochloric acid and leave it for an hour or two, we should find that only the surface of the meat had been digested into proteoses and peptones. On the other hand, if we should divide the same quantity of meat into fine pieces and repeat the experiment, it would be found that nearly the whole of the meat had undergone digestion by the pepsin. The incisors of the upper and lower jaws seize, tear, and cut the food. The molars grind and crush it. The jaws are brought together with tremendous force by powerful muscles attached to the skull bones above and to the jaw below. The force exerted by the human jaws was estimated 300 years ago by an Italian

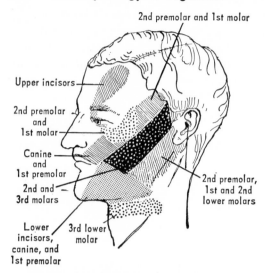

Fig. 25.9. Areas of radiated pain
in toothache.

physiologist and found to be equal to a pressure of over a hundred pounds. The jaws also perform a side to side movement by which the food is ground as well as crushed. As grist is passed into a mill, the muscles of the tongue, lips, and cheeks continually force the larger fragments of the food between the jaws for division into smaller and smaller pieces. All the while, saliva is pouring into the mouth to soak the food and turn it finally into a smooth pasty mass, which can be molded into a shape suitable for swallowing. Birds, of course, possess no teeth. Defenseless creatures on the whole, they must snatch as much food as possible in a short time. This they store in their crops and fly from danger. Nevertheless, they possess that which mammals have not—a gizzard. This has strong muscular walls that by the aid of swallowed pebbles, grind and crush the food much as the food of higher animals is masticated by the teeth.

The muscles of mastication and their actions are described in Chapter 5.

DEGLUTITION, THE ACT OF SWALLOWING

In the first movement of swallowing, the mass of masticated food is brought on to the upper surface of the tongue by the actions of the lips, cheeks, and the tongue itself; the food is then pressed against the palate and carried by the tongue to the posterior part of the mouth. The hyoid bone is immediately raised and carried forward by muscles attached to it—geniohyoid, mylohyoid, digastric, and stylohyoid—and fixed in this position. The posterior part of the tongue is then suddenly elevated and drawn backwards by the contraction of the stylohyoid muscles, and the food projected through the isthmus of the fauces. The swallowing act up to this point is called the first stage and is entirely voluntary. Once the food has entered the pharynx, however, it has started upon a journey over which we have no control. The subsequent stages of swallowing are purely reflex in nature.

The pharynx is like a city square where two important lines of traffic cross (Fig. 25.10). Air passes from the nose into the upper part of the pharynx and through it to the larynx and lungs. The pharynx also communicates in front and above with the mouth, and below with the esophagus. Other traffic must be held up to allow the food to pass from the mouth through the pharynx and down the esophagus. The opening from the nose into the pharynx is closed by raising the soft palate.[3] The food is prevented from returning to the mouth because the posterior part of the tongue is raised to block the way, and the pillars of the fauces approximated. The larynx is raised behind the hyoid bone, and its opening closed by pressing the posterior laryngeal wall against the root of the epiglottis. At this time a short inspiration occurs, and for an instant the breath is held. So the food does not enter the larynx, except

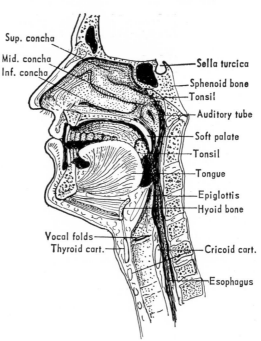

Sup. concha
Mid. concha
Inf. concha
Sella turcica
Sphenoid bone
Tonsil
Auditory tube
Soft palate
Tonsil
Tongue
Epiglottis
Hyoid bone
Vocal folds
Thyroid cart.
Cricoid cart.
Esophagus

Fig. 25.10. Sagittal section through the head and neck to show structures involved in the act of swallowing.

sometimes when, as is said, it "goes the wrong way." Having passed through the fauces, the food is seized and gripped by the muscular walls of the pharynx and forced down the only passage left open—the esophagus. The walls of this tube are muscular, and the stimulus of the food causes a wormlike wave of contraction—the **peristaltic wave**—to run through the muscle. This wave sweeps the swallowed material downward and carries it into the stomach.

As the food approaches the lower end of the esophagus the muscle that guards the opening into the stomach (**cardiac sphincter**), which is ordinarily contracted to prevent food from re-entering the esophagus from the stomach, relaxes and allows the food to enter.

---

[3] When the soft palate is paralyzed, as sometimes occurs following diphtheria and in other conditions, the palate cannot be raised and fluids pass into the nose during swallowing.

26
Digestion in the Stomach

FORM AND GENERAL STRUCTURE OF THE HUMAN STOMACH

The human stomach when empty of food, is a long, collapsed tube (except for its upper end) lying almost vertically in the upper part of the abdomen, or sometimes inclined down and to the right at an angle of about 45 degrees. Its upper blind end is dome shaped and lies below the apex of the heart, separated from it by a part of the liver and the diaphragm. This part of the stomach contains a few ounces of trapped air or gas which inflates it. A little below and to the right of the upper end of the stomach is the opening of the gullet or esophagus. The lower part of the stomach has usually the shape of the letter J or of a fishhook, and lies partly to the right of the midline of the body at about the level of the navel (**umbilicus**). If a person is given a mixture of barium and his abdomen then x-rayed, the stomach will cast a shadow picture upon a sensitive film because barium is opaque to the x rays. Such pictures have shown that the older descriptions of the position and shape of the stomach as a rounded, somewhat pear-shaped bag lying more or less hori-

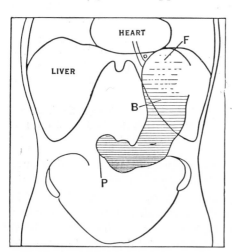

Fig. 26.1. Appearance of the stomach by x-rays. F, fundus; B, body; P, pylorus. (After Starling.)

356

zontally across the abdomen were wrong. Of course, the shape of the stomach and the position of its lower part changes from time to time with the degree to which it is filled with food.

The lower part of the stomach—that portion corresponding to the hook of the J—is called the **pyloric part.** The opening through which the food passes from this part into the intestine is called the **pyloric orifice,** or simply the **pylorus.** The rounded upper part of the stomach is known as the **fundus.** The opening of the esophagus into the stomach is called the **cardiac orifice.** The middle or main part of the stomach is called the **body.** The left border of the stomach forms a large curve called the **greater curvature.** The right border—from the entrance of the esophagus to the pylorus—is much shorter and is named the **lesser curvature.**

The wall of the stomach is composed of three layers of smooth muscle, lined by mucous membrane and covered by peritoneum. The latter is called its *serous coat.* The fibers of the outermost layer of muscle run longitudinally and are continuous with those of the esophagus. This layer is very thin on the anterior and posterior surfaces of the body of the stomach and relatively thick along the curvatures. The middle layer is composed of circular fibers that encircle the stomach. In the innermost layer the fibers run obliquely and do not form a complete coat, being confined largely to the fundus. The circular fibers are much thickened at the junction of the stomach with the duodenum where they form the **pyloric sphincter.** The muscle of the stomach is supplied by the vagus and sympathetic nerves (Ch. 37). The mucous membrane of the stomach is covered with nonciliated columnar epithelium many cells of which secrete mucus; its cells are continuous with those lining the gastric glands. Strands of involuntary muscle (*muscularis mucosae*) are present deep to the blind ends of the glands. A layer of areolar tissue—the *submucosa*—separates the mucous membrane from the innermost layer of the muscular coat of the stomach.

The glands of the stomach. The cells that secrete saliva, we have seen, are massed together into six large glands that deliver their secretions into the

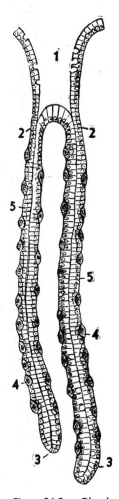

Fig. 26.2. Glands from the fundus of the stomach. 1. pit, or foveola, on mucous surface of stomach; 2, neck of gland containing mucin-secreting cells; 3, bottom (fundus) of gland; 4, parietal cells; 5, chief cells.

mouth along a few relatively large ducts. The **gastric glands,** on the other hand, are innumerable simple or branched tubular glands in the mucous membrane (Fig. 26.2). Each gland opens separately into a minute pit called the **foveola.** The slightly narrowed part of the gland a little below its opening into the foveola is called the *neck.* The main part of the gland has been named the *body,* and the deep blind end the *fundus.* The cells of the gland are of four types: (a) *chief cells of the neck,* which secrete mucin, (b) *chief cells of the body,* which secrete *pepsin,* (c) *parietal,* or *oxyntic, cells,* which form hydrochloric acid, and (d) *argentaffine cells* of the fundus (which stain with silver nitrate).

COMPOSITION OF THE GASTRIC JUICE

The digestive juice secreted by the gastric glands is called the **gastric juice.** It contains the following substances:

Hydrochloric acid

Enzymes $\begin{cases} \text{Pepsin (gastric protease)} \\ \text{Rennin} \\ \text{Lipase} \end{cases}$

Pepsin. Pepsin is an enzyme formed by the chief cells of the body of the gastric glands (*b,* above). It has the power to carry the digestion of protein food through the first stages toward its final breakdown. The large groups of amino acid molecules of which protein is composed are broken into smaller groups (see Fig. 24.9). These smaller groups of amino acids are called *proteoses* and *peptones.* The proteoses are composed of larger groups of amino acids than the peptones, and are the first fragments into which the protein molecule is broken by pepsin. Peptones are formed at a somewhat later stage of gastric digestion. These substances are quite different from the original protein. They can, for instance, be dissolved in water, and since the molecules are somewhat smaller, they can pass through some animal membranes. Nevertheless, they cannot nourish the body unless further digested.

When the action of enzymes was described (Ch. 24), it was stated that some of them required to be activated by acid, others by alkali or certain neutral salts. Pepsin as secreted and coming fresh from the gland cells is inactive, but is immediately activated by the hydrochloric acid secreted at the same time. The inactive form of the enzyme is called *pepsinogen.*

Hydrochloric acid. Hydrochloric is a strong mineral acid, which in full strength will dissolve small particles of iron, zinc, and other metals. If dropped upon the skin, it will burn painfully. It came as a great surprise, then, when this powerful chemical, which under ordinary circumstances is so injurious to living tissues, was discovered to be a constituent of the gastric juice. It is an extraordinary fact that such an acid should be manufactured by living cells. The only other instances of a strong mineral acid being formed by living processes is the production of sulfuric acid, probably for defense purposes, by certain mollusks, and the presence of acid within the vacuoles of some one-celled animal forms (Protozoa). The idea was so novel that for a time many could not believe that hydrochloric acid was actually formed by the cells of the gastric glands, and several experiments were performed to ascertain whether or not it was true. The fact now is established beyond dispute. Pure gastric juice contains from 0.4 to 0.5 percent of hydrochloric acid.

If a piece of meat is placed in a test tube with gastric juice or a solution of pepsin and hydrochloric acid, after a short time the meat will be found to have been dissolved. Conversion of the protein to proteoses and peptones has occurred. Yet the wall of the living stomach, which is composed chiefly of protein, is unaffected by the pepsin and hydrochloric acid of the gastric juice it secretes. Why is the stomach not digested like any other meat? This question for a long time went unanswered; but it now appears that the mucous membrane of the stomach produces ammonia (alkaline) from urea, which neutralizes the acid and thus protects the stomach from digestion. If, however, as a result of injury or through the cutting off of its blood supply, a small area of the stomach loses its vitality, then this part of the gastric tissue may undergo digestion by the mixture of pepsin and hydrochloric acid secreted by the rest of the stomach. This is the way in which an ulcer forms in the stomach.

Gastric and duodenal ulcer. The most common occurrence of a gastric ulcer is at the lesser curvature along which food first passes after it has been swallowed. The mucous membrane in this region is most likely to be injured by rough, coarse food. A duodenal ulcer is also caused by the digestive action of the gastric juice; it forms where the acid juice after issuing from the stomach first impinges upon the duodenal mucous membrane. Because they are caused in this way ulcers of the stomach and duodenum are called *peptic* ulcers. In their treatment rough food, and foods that tend to stimulate gastric secretion, as well as alcohol and coffee, are avoided. Milk, cream, and other bland items of diet are prescribed, and measures are taken to neutralize the hydrochloric acid or to suppress its secretion, such as the administration of *antacids, mucin,* or *enterogastrone* (p. 363).

Rennin, or rennet. This enzyme clots or curdles milk; it is secreted by the same cells that secrete the pepsin. Rennin is used a great deal commercially to curdle milk in the manufacture of cheese. It is obtained for this purpose by grinding up the lining of calf's stomach and extracting the ferment with glycerine and water. The same ferment is employed for making junket.

Lipase. This is a general term applied to ferments that digest fats (ch. 27) . The lipase of the gastric juice—*gastric lipase*—is very weak, and ordinary fats and oils cannot be digested at all in the stomach. Certain fatty materials, such as the yolk of egg, or cream, that are in the form of very fine emulsions undergo a certain amount of digestion by the gastric juice, but the great bulk of the fat in the food is digested in the intestine. It passes through the stomach unchanged chemically, though physically it is liquefied to a larger extent into oil as a result of the heat of the body, the separation of the fat cells by the digestion of the fibers binding them together, and the churning movements of the stomach.

It may be concluded from the foregoing account of the action of the gastric juice that the chemical changes that the food undergoes in the stomach are chiefly concerned with the digestion of protein. However, as a result of the movements of the stomach (see below) and the addition of fluids secreted by the gastric glands, swallowed as beverages, and secreted as saliva, all foods, whatever their nature, also undergo certain physical changes. Softening, liquefaction, or solution of the food occurs until, at the end of gastric digestion, the contents of the stomach are semifluid, having the consistency of gruel or thick cream. The food in this state is spoken of as *chyme*.

SECRETION OF GASTRIC JUICE

Food stimulates the gastric glands to secrete juice. Yet it has been known for many years that it is not necessary for the food to enter the stomach in order for the glands to be stimulated. The mere presence of food in the mouth will alone cause a very abundant secretion of gastric juice. The glands anticipate, as it were, the arrival of the food. The flow of juice that occurs under these circumstances is brought about reflexly, specifically through afferent impulses from the organs of taste to the medulla, and from the medulla by the vagus nerves to the gastric glands. The flow of juice produced in this way is called the *psychic secretion*. It is also well known that gastric juice is secreted by means other than through nerve impulses, for the stomach secretes juice even though all communication with the nervous system has been abolished; all nerves to the stomach may be cut yet it continues to secrete juice when it receives food. This type of secretion that occurs only if the food actually enters the stomach is termed, for the lack of a better designation, the *secondary secretion*, the *gastric phase*, or the *chemical phase* of gastric secretion. The secretion of gastric juice is also influenced by the food after it has passed from the stomach; this is called the *intestinal phase*.

The psychic, or cephalic, phase of gastric secretion. The psychic phase has been studied in animals by Pavlov. From the foregoing paragraph it is clear that in order to study the psychic secretion, food must be given for the animal to chew, but the stomach should not receive it. If the food entered the stomach, it would be impossible to distinguish the psychic from the gastric phase. The animal is accordingly "sham fed," that is, the esophagus is divided in the neck. The part above the division is then brought out through the neck wound and stitched into position. An animal prepared in this way can eat and enjoy its food (Fig. 26.3), but no food enters the stomach after being swallowed; it escapes from the opening in the neck. The animal eats with relish, yet it never becomes satisfied, and so "sham feeding" can be continued for any length of time, and large quantities of gastric juice are secreted into the stomach when the animal is fed in this way. Even five minutes of sham feeding will cause the production of several ounces of strong gastric juice. The greatest quantity of juice is secreted for meat and other foods for which the animal is eager, because the essential quality of the food that causes the secretion is its palatability—not its chemical or physical properties. A greater

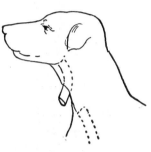

Fig. 26.3. A dog with an esophageal fistula made for sham-feeding experiments.

secretion occurs if the animal is hungry. In contrast to salivary secretion (Ch. 25), disagreeable substances, such as acids, pepper, or inedible materials, do not cause a psychic secretion of juice. Indeed, if juice is already being secreted, it may cease when some unpleasant substance is placed in the mouth.

These observations point to the involvement of mental processes in the reflex mechanism. The pleasure of eating, the agreeable stimulation of the organs of taste, and the gratification of appetite are essential conditions. It is not even necessary that the food enter the mouth in order to cause the glands to respond. Provided the food is sufficiently appetizing, the mere sight or smell of it will cause secretion. In other words, a conditioned reflex occurs for the secretion of gastric juice as for the secretion of saliva. The stomach "waters" as well as the mouth at the sight or smell of food (Ch. 25).

Experiments similar to those described above have been carried out upon man. A man, of course, cannot be "sham fed" in precisely the same manner, but occasionally a person is found who has a closed esophagus. Usually this is the result of his having swallowed an acid or other destructive substance in childhood, which has so injured the gullet that a scar has formed during healing and completely closed the tube. No food can then pass into the stomach. It is necessary, therefore, for the person to be operated upon and an opening made through the abdominal wall into the stomach through which he can be fed. Experiments upon such human subjects have shown that the principles discovered by Pavlov from his studies upon animals also hold true for man. Chewing food, or the sight or smell of an appetizing meal, causes a secretion of juice. The quantity of secretion is decidedly less if the food is unappetizing or if the appearance and environment of the meal are unttractive. Offensive odors, worry, and anxiety are especially likely to depress secretion.

All these facts have their obvious applications to dietetics. Food agreeable to the palate and attractive in appearance, impressions received from a meal that has been prepared in a pleasing way, and also, probably, sensations aroused by the surroundings yet not directly concerned with the food itself (music, good lighting, flowers on the table, etc.), all have an effect upon gastric secretion. The impulse that guides the gourmet is sounder physiologically than that which impels the glutton. In planning a meal, the question of calories and of the relative digestibility of the different foodstuffs should not be allowed to obscure entirely the psychic elements in digestion, for the "delights of the table" have true digestive value. These facts are expressed in the phrase of Pavlov, "Appetite spells gastric juice," or in the hospitable words of Macbeth, "Now, good digestion wait on appetite, and health on both!" Custom seems to have recognized this truth, for it is usual for a meal to commence and end with the more strongly flavored and appetizing morsels. For these reasons it is not always wise to force a child to eat something that is "good for him" but that he detests. Pleasant surroundings and an attractive appearance of the table are also valuable aids to digestion.

The gastric, or chemical, phase. The psychic secretion ceases within 30 minutes or so after the last morsel of food has been swallowed. There has never been any question, however, that gastric secretion continues for a much longer period than this under ordinary circumstances—that is, when the food enters the stomach and undergoes digestion. How is this secondary secretion brought about? It is not governed by nerves, since it occurs after all the nerves of the stomach have been severed. The glands are stimulated to a mild degree by distention of the stomach— that is, by the stretching of the stomach wall by the food. But the chief mode of stimulation is chemical. The chemical substance, or *hormone* (Ch. 38), is formed in the wall of the stomach and carried to the glands in the blood stream. Certain materials in the food stimulate the stomach wall to produce the hormone. These materials are present in meat and in many vegetables; since they can be extracted with cold or hot water, they are called *extractives*. When meat is boiled, the water or broth is rich in extractives. Soups, beef teas, etc., consequently contain large quantities of these substances. Extractives possess no nutritive value; but since they cause the formation of the gastric hormone that stimulates the gastric glands, they are important aids to digestion. For this reason the wisdom of starting the meal with a broth or a soup is self-evident.

Much experimental work has been undertaken in efforts to discover the nature of the gastric hormone. When it was first shown that an extract of the stomach wall caused a secretion of gastric juice when injected into the blood stream of an animal, the unknown stimulating substance was called *gastrin*. For a time many physiologists believed that the stimulating substance was simply *histamine* (Ch. 18) and not a specific hormone. Histamine is well known to be a powerful excitant of the gastric glands. It can be obtained in relatively large amounts from gastric mucous membrane and in variable amounts from many other tissues. But there is evidence that a chemical substance—a true secretory hormone—quite apart from histamine is formed in the gastric mucosa, but its nature is unknown.

The intestinal phase. Food in the intestine also exerts an effect upon the secretion of gastric juice. This action is especially notable in the case of fat, which inhibits the gastric glands. The mechanism is hormonal, for it continues to operate after all nerves to the stomach and intestine have been severed. The chemical material concerned has been named **enterogastrone.** It is formed in the intestinal mucosa by the action of the products of fat digestion—fatty acids; absorbed into the circulation and carried therein to the gastric gland, it suppresses their secretion. Enterogastrone also exerts an inhibitory action upon the *movements* of the stomach.

Some other products of gastric digestion (for example, peptones) acting upon the intestinal mucosa stimulate gastric secretion, but many details of the intestinal phase are vague and not clearly understood.

THE MOVEMENTS OF THE STOMACH

Within an hour or two after a meal the lower half of the stomach becomes very active. It appears under x-ray observation to be continually changing its shape. This appearance is given by rings or waves of contraction (peristaltic waves) that start a little below the center of the stomach and run downward in quick succession. After digestion has advanced to the point where the food is of such a consistency as to be received by the duodenum, these waves sweep it through the outlet from the stomach (**pyloric orifice**). The upper half of the stomach remains quiet; no movements are seen. The stomach, so far as its movements are concerned, consists, therefore, of two distinct parts. The upper, larger region, which includes the fundus and the upper part of the stomach body (p. 356), serves as a reservoir to hold the food for a time after it has been swallowed. The lower, pyloric part churns the food as it is mixed with gastric juice and passes it through the pyloric orifice into the intestine. As digestion proceeds, the food becomes thoroughly mixed and more uniform in consistency. The pyloric opening, which up to this time has been closed and has offered a barrier to the food carried to it by the peristaltic waves, now opens each time that a wave of contraction approaches, and the chyme is swept into the intestine.

Rhythmical contractions start in the lower half of the stomach shortly after it has emptied, and become progressively stronger and more frequent during a fasting period. If the next meal is long delayed they may become quite painful and are responsible for what are generally known as "hunger pangs." They were studied very thoroughly by Professor Carlson of Chicago and named by him *hunger contractions*.

It should be remembered that the movements of the stomach, and the physical changes these movements bring about in the food are of as great or perhaps of greater importance than the chemical transformations caused by pepsin and hydrochloric acid (p. 358). Persons in whom the gastric juice is entirely absent appear to suffer little or no difficulty in the digestion of food. The stomach may be removed, and provided the consistency of the food is made suitable, little digestive inconvenience results. Disturbances in the movements of the stomach on the other hand —the too rapid entrance of, or the interference with the passage of, material into the duodenum—will induce ill effects. A prime function of the stomach is to prepare the food for intestinal digestion—to break it up, to add fluid to it, and after reducing the entire mass to a semifluid consistency, to pass it on to the duodenum.

Vomiting. Vomiting is usually preceded by nausea. The ejection of the stomach contents is accomplished in the following manner. A strong contraction occurs in the pyloric part of the stomach, together with relaxation of the body of the stomach and the cardiac sphincter. Accompanying or immediately following these movements the abdominal muscles contract forcibly, and the diaphragm descends. Thus the stomach is compressed and its contents, being prevented from passing downward by the firm contraction of the pyloric region, are forced through the relaxed cardia into the esophagus. The latter relaxes throughout its length, which permits the free passage upward of the stomach contents. The larynx is raised at the same time and its opening closed, thus preventing the passage of material into the air passages. The stomach, it will be noted, is emptied *passively*, that is, from pressure applied from without. There is no evidence, in the adult at any rate, that an ascending peristaltic contraction of the gastric wall is instrumental in ejecting the stomach contents into the esophagus.[1] In the young infant, however, a reverse peristaltic movement of this nature probably does occur.

Vomiting is a reflex act and may follow irritation of nerve endings (vagus or sympathetic) in the stomach or duodenum. But the stimulation of afferent fibers, especially those transmitting pain impulses, in almost any organ of the body may induce vomiting. The vomiting due to disease of the appendix or gall bladder, or to some painful injury, is well known.

---

[1] That vomiting can occur without active participation of the stomach itself was shown many years ago by Francois Magendie, a French physiologist. He replaced the stomach of a laboratory animal with a pig's bladder and found that an emetic caused vomiting in the usual way.

Afferent impulses arising in a failing heart may also cause vomiting, or the act may be induced by psychic influences—anxiety, fear, or disgust. Seasickness and other forms of motion sickness are due to the stimulation of nerve endings in the labyrinths (utricles) of the ear (Ch. 46). Nausea or vomiting not uncommonly results from eye strain, the afferent impulses initiating the reflex arising in the eye muscles.

Drugs and other substances used in medicine for the induction of vomiting are called *emetics*. Among those that act upon the nerve endings in the gastric or duodenal wall are *antimony tartrate* (tartar emetic), *copper* and *zinc sulphates,* and *salt or mustard and water.* Certain other emetics, such as *apomorphine,* act upon the *vomiting center* in the medulla oblongata. It is probable, however, that the vomiting that follows the administration of emetics of the latter type is also essentially reflex in nature. The drug acts, apparently, by raising the excitability of the center—that is, the threshold of the center to stimulation is lowered, so that impulses from various parts of the body, which normally make no impression upon it, or even upon consciousness, become effective. The vomiting resulting from metabolic disturbances, for example, in pregnancy or nephritis, or that associated with general bodily fatigue, is explained in a similar way.

27
Digestion in the Intestines

For convenience of anatomical description or the indication of the site of an abdominal lesion, the abdomen is marked off into *regions* by a number of intersecting vertical and horizontal lines. The blocked-off areas on the surface with their names are shown in Figure 27.1.

Before describing the intestines and the digestive glands that secrete into their lumen, an account must be given of the peritoneum.

THE PERITONEUM

The peritoneum is the serous membrane lining the abdominal and pelvic cavities, and enclosing the viscera, or covering them only on their abdominal or pelvic surfaces. The membrane lining the walls of the abdominal and pelvic cavities is called the **parietal peritoneum,** and that enclosing the viscera, the **visceral peritoneum.** Those structures lying against the walls of the abdomen or pelvis, or in any position that permits the peritoneum merely to cover but not to envelop them are said to be **extraperitoneal** (Fig. 27.2). Such organs are the duodenum, pancreas, kidney, ureter and urinary bladder, and a good part of the large intestine and the uterus. The peritoneum completely or nearly completely encloses the liver, stomach, small intestine, transverse and pelvic colons, the spleen, and the uterine tubes. The parietal and visceral layers of the peritoneum are, like the corresponding layers of the pleura, everywhere in contact. But the space between the layers, though only a potential one, is called the **peritoneal cavity.** In enclosing a viscus the peritoneum gives off from the abdominal wall a fold, or reduplication, in which the organ is held and suspended as in a sling. The fold enveloping the small intestine springs from the posterior abdominal wall, and

366

spreads out enormously from its origin, as it must do to accommodate the twenty-odd feet of the bowel. Since it follows the coils of the intestine, it is thrown into turns and curves like the flounces in the hem of a very wide skirt. This fold of the peritoneum is called the **mesentery.** It, like the other peritoneal folds, carries the blood vessels, lymphatics, and nerves to or from the bowel. The transverse colon is slung in the **transverse mesocolon,** and the pelvic colon in a much shorter **mesocolon.**

The arrangement of the peritoneum is much more complicated in the upper part of the abdomen than in the lower part and in the pelvis. Starting from the level of the umbilicus on the anterior abdominal wall and tracing it upwards, the peritoneum is found to cover the under surface of the diaphragm and then to turn down on to the upper surface of the right lobe of the liver, which it invests.

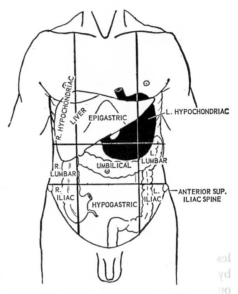

Fig. 27.1. The regions of the abdomen and their contents. The stomach is shown in solid black.

On the under surface of the liver it ascends in the great transverse fissure, or **porta hepatis,** where it folds downward upon itself, and meeting the peritoneum from the left side, descends to the lesser curvature of the stomach. This double-layered fold is called the **lesser omentum.** Its layers separate and enclose the stomach. The two layers rejoin along the greater curvature of the stomach, and extend below it. This double layer of peritoneum after descending for a short distance turns upward again upon itself and then passes backward, enclosing on its way the transverse colon, to the posterior abdominal wall, where its layers separate once again. One layer turns upward over the pancreas, aorta and vena cava, and the duodenum to the inferior surface of the diaphragm, the left part of which it covers. It then turns down to the left lobe of the liver, on the under surface of which it turns into the porta hepatis, and meeing the layer from the right side, descends with it to form the lesser omentum as just described.

The two closely applied layers of peritoneum depending from the greater curvature of the stomach obviously form four layers as they double back upon themselves. This fourfold apronlike structure is called the **greater omentum.**

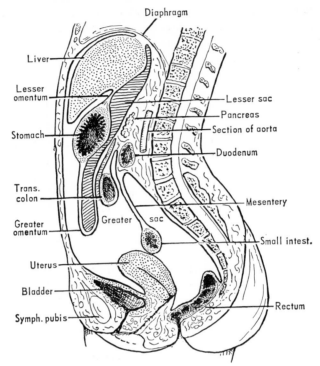

Fig. 27.2. Sagittal section through the female abdomen and pelvis to show the disposition of the peritoneum.

The main part of the peritoneal cavity is called the **greater sac.** The **lesser sac** lies behind the stomach. The greater sac is bounded in front by the anterior two layers of the great omentum, the stomach, the lesser omentum, and the left part of the liver. The posterior boundary is formed by the posterior double layer of the great omentum, the transverse colon and its mesocolon, and the peritoneum covering the upper part of the posterior abdominal wall. The greater and lesser sacs, which are potential cavities only, are separated from one another except for a slitlike opening called the **epiploic foramen,** through which they communicate. This is situated in the upper part of the lesser omentum near its right border. The greater omentum covers the coils of the small intestine like an apron. It contains an abundance of fat, especially in obese persons. The potential space bounded by its anterior and posterior double layers is called the **recess** of the lesser sac.

The greater omentum possesses a most valuable protective function, for it has the remarkable faculty of "finding" an inflamed area such as an acute appendix or a perforated ulcer, surrounding it, and "walling it off" from the general peritoneal cavity. It contains many macrophages in the areolar tissue between its layers.

The layer of peritoneum that descends on the posterior abdominal wall gives off a fold known as the mesentery, which has already been described. The peritoneum lines the pelvic walls for a variable distance but most usually to a point about 3 inches above the anus. It encloses the pelvic colon, to which it supplies a short mesentery. The pelvic peritoneum covers the upper parts of the uterus, bladder, seminal vesicles, and rectum. In the male the peritoneal cavity as a whole is completely sealed from the exterior. In the female the ovaries and uterine tubes are completely covered by peritoneum. The uterine tubes, however, open into the peritoneal cavity. Since these tubes are continuous with the uterine cavity, and it in turn leads into the vagina, a communication is established between the pelvic cavity and the outside world. Under certain unusual circumstances infection may spread along this route and cause inflammation of the peritoneum—*peritonitis.*

ANATOMY AND PHYSIOLOGY OF THE PANCREAS AND LIVER

The pancreas

This large gland secretes the pancreatic juice. It lies on the posterior wall of the abdomen, its right expanded portion, or *head,* occupying the concavity of the curve formed by the duodenum. The portion to the left of the head is called the *neck,* and the succeeding part the *body;* the slender extremity which running well to the left comes into relation with the spleen, is called the *tail* (Fig. 27.3). The pancreas is a racemose gland, resembling the salivary gland in its microscopic appearance; it is sometimes called the "salivary gland of the abdomen." The gland discharges its secretion through a long duct—the **pancreatic duct**— into the duodenum. This duct usually opens upon the duodenal mucosa through an orifice common to it and the common bile duct; the two ducts joining within the duodenal wall to form a short, wide passage called the **ampulla of Vater,** or the *ampulla of the bile duct.* Besides the important role that it plays in digestion, the pancreas produces *insulin,* the carbohydrate hormone (Ch. 30). Insulin is not formed by the same cells that secrete pancreatic juice, but by groups of special cells—the **islets, or islands, of Langerhans**—lying here and there throughout the ordinary glandular (acinar) tissue (Fig. 27.4).

The composition of pancreatic juice. Pancreatic juice is composed of the following:

Enzymes
- Trypsin (pancreatic protease)
- Amylopsin (pancreatic amylase)
- Steapsin (pancreatic lipase)
- Rennin

Sodium carbonate and sodium bicarbonate

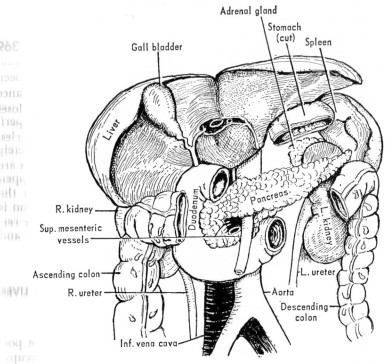

Fig. 27.3. Showing the relation of the pancreas to the duodenum and other abdominal viscera. The liver has been raised to expose underlying organs.

All the enzymes of pancreatic juice require alkali for their actions. This is provided by the sodium carbonate and bicarbonate that it contains.

Trypsin, or pancreatic protease, like pepsin, acts only upon proteins but carries the digestion of these a stage further, splitting the proteose and peptone molecules into still smaller groups of amino acids, called *peptids;* these, after complete tryptic digestion, may consist of only two

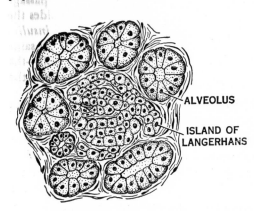

ALVEOLUS

ISLAND OF LANGERHANS

Fig. 27.4. Microscopic appearance of a section of the pancreas. An island of Langerhans is depicted surrounded by the alveoli that secrete jancreatic juice. Certain cells of the islands are the source of insulin.

or three amino acids. This enzyme is secreted as an inactive precursor, *trypsinogen*, but is converted in the intestine to trypsin by an enzyme called *enterokinase*.

Amylopsin, or pancreatic amylase, resembles the ptyalin of saliva in its action; that is, it breaks the large molecules of starch into the smaller molecules of maltose (Ch. 30). But it is many times more powerful than ptyalin. As a matter of fact, it is not until starch reaches the intestine and is acted upon by the amylopsin of the pancreatic juice that it is effectively attacked. Maltose, we have already seen, is not absorbed, since its molecule is composed of two molecules of glucose. The pancreatic juice contains a weak ferment, *maltase,* that effects the final splitting of a small proportion of the maltose. The great mass of this disaccharide, however, is converted into glucose by a ferment in the intestinal juice.

Steapsin splits fat into fatty acids and glycerol (see Fig. 24.9). In this action it is aided, as we shall see, by the bile.

Rennin has the same action as the rennin of the gastric juice—it curdles milk.

The secretion of pancreatic juice. The vagus nerve sends branches to the pancreas, and along these nerves messages flow from the autonomic nervous system (Ch. 37) to the gland and cause it to secrete. This, however, is only one means by which the secretion of the pancreas is governed. It is also stimulated by a hormone manufactured in the mucous membrane of the intestine and then carried by the blood to the gland. This hormone is called *secretin*. If the wall of the intestine of any animal is ground up with water and then filtered so as to free it of solid particles, the clear fluid so obtained will be found to contain large amounts of secretin; for when the fluid is injected into the blood of another animal, a very abundant secretion of pancreatic juice results.

Another hormone that stimulates the secretion of pancreatic juice has been discovered more recently. It is called *pancreozymin*. Whereas secretin induces mainly the secretion of the water and salts of the pancreatic juice, pancreozymin stimulates chiefly the secretion of the enzymes.

The liver (hepar)

This is a large gland—the largest in the body—of a dark chocolate color, situated in the right half and part of the left half of the upper end of the abdominal cavity. It lies to a large extent under the shelter of the lower ribs, its upper surface being molded to the under surface of the diaphragm, the central tendon of which alone separates it from the heart and pericardium. Its anterior surface is triangular with its apex toward the left. A deep transverse fissure called the portal of the liver, or the **porta hepatis,** marks its inferior surface, and through this the portal vein, hepatic artery, lymphatics, bile ducts, and nerves enter or leave the

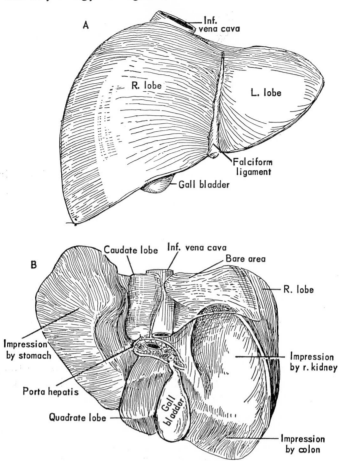

Fig. 27.5. A, the liver, anterior view; B, liver turned to left to show inferior and posterior surfaces.

organ. These structures reach or leave the liver by passing between the layers of the lesser omentum. The liver is divided into a large right and a smaller left lobe by the fold of peritoneum called the **falciform ligament,** turned down from the under surface of the diaphragm and the anterior abdominal wall onto its superior and anterior surfaces (Figs. 27.5 and 24.7). Two smaller lobes are marked off on the posterior and inferior surfaces of the right lobe, called the *quadrate* and *caudate lobes.*

The **quadrate lobe,** situated on the under surface, is marked off on the right by the impression made by the gall bladder, on the left by a fissure that lodges a fetal remnant known as the *ligamentum teres,* behind by the porta hepatis, and in front by the lower border of the liver (Fig. 27.5).

The caudate (Spigelian) lobe lies on the posterior surface between a fissure on the left that lodges the remains of the ductus venosus, another fetal vestige, on the right by a groove occupied by the upper part of the inferior vena cava, and below by the porta hepatis which separates it from the quadrate lobe. The caudate lobe is continuous above with the superior hepatic surface.

The liver is covered by peritoneum except for a *bare area* on the posterior surface of the right lobe.

The minute structure of the liver. The liver is composed of rows, or *cords,* of cubical cells that radiate from a *central vein.* On one side of each cord lies a blood vessel considerably wider than a capillary and known as a **sinusoid,** into which blood from both the portal vein and the hepatic artery is delivered; it empties into the central vein. On the other side of the single row of cells is a **bile capillary.** Bile pigment derived from the hemoglobin of disintegrated red cells, together with other materials, are taken from the blood by the hepatic cells and passed into the bile capillaries as bile (Fig. 27.6). The central vein, its tributary sinusoids, together with the liver cords and bile capillaries constitute a *unit,* or **lobule,** of the liver. The blood received by the central veins of a number of neighboring lobules empty into a larger vein running between them called a **sublobular,** or an **intercalated vein.** The latter unite to form two or more **hepatic veins** which drain the blood into the inferior vena cava. (See also Ch. 13.)

Outline of hepatic function. The liver is the great chemical laboratory of the body. In this organ glucose brought to it from the intestine by the portal vein is converted to glycogen, which is deposited in the hepatic cells. Upon demand the glycogen is reconverted to glucose and discharged into the circulation for use as fuel. The liver is also the seat of the fundamental processes concerned in the metabolism of protein and fat. Most of its manifold functions have been touched upon in other parts of this book. Here will be described its function in secreting bile.

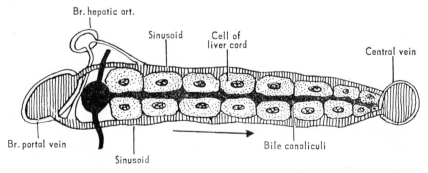

Fig. 27.6. Showing two liver cords and their relation to the blood and bile vessels.

The bile ducts and the bile flow. The bile is an excretory as well as a secretory product of the liver. It passes to its destination through a system of channels called the **bile ducts** (Fig. 27.7). We have seen that the bile is formed by the cells of an hepatic lobule and that the fine canals in which it first appears lie between the liver cords, and are called bile capillaries. These channels unite at the periphery of the lobule to form *interlobular bile ducts* which unite into large vessels until eventually at the porta hepatis the two *hepatic ducts,* one from each lobe, are formed; these join to form the *common hepatic duct* which after being joined at an angle by the *cystic duct* is called the *common bile duct.* The common bile duct opens with the pancreatic duct into the *ampulla of Vater* situated in the wall of the duodenum. The ampulla communicates with the interior of the duodenum by a small orifice.

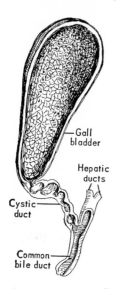

The bile is secreted continuously by the liver, but enters the duodenum only at intervals. This is because it can be stored in the gall bladder.

The gall bladder. This is a small sac, somewhat greenish in color from contained bile, and resembling a pear upon its stem. Its walls are thin; they possess a stratum of smooth muscle and a lining of mucous membrane. Its duct, the cystic duct, mentioned above, represents the stem of the pear; the interior of this duct shows a series of spiral folds in the mucous membrane called the **valves of Heister.** The gall bladder is situated on the under

Fig. 27.7. The gall bladder, opened to show mucous lining, and bile ducts; note valves of Heister in cystic duct.

surface of the liver to which it is held by the peritoneum passing over it. Its blind end, called the **fundus,** points downwards and peeps from beneath the lower border of the liver.

The functions of the gall bladder are to store the bile, to concentrate it by absorbing water and salts, and to discharge it from time to time into the duodenum. The stimulus to the contraction of the gall bladder is food in the duodenum, especially fatty food, such as cream or egg yolk. The contraction of the gall bladder caused by fat is not a nervous reflex, but is caused by a hormone formed in and released from the mucosa of the intestine; it has been named *cholecystokinin.*

The composition of bile. The principal constituents of the bile are the *pigments,* the *bile salts,* and fatlike or waxlike substances, *lecithin* and *cholesterol.* The percentages of these constituents are given in the following table.

Bile Constituent   Percent

Water 97.48

Solids 2.52

    Mucin and pigments 0.53

    Bile salts 0.93

    Fatty acids from soaps............ 0.12

    Cholesterol 0.06

    Lecithin ⎫
            ⎬ 0.02
    Fat   ⎭

    Inorganic salts 0.83

The bile pigments are *bilirubin* and *biliverdin*. Bilirubin has a golden-red color; biliverdin is yellow-green. The pigment of human bile is mostly bilirubin, whereas the bile of cattle and birds is chiefly biliverdin. Both pigments have the same origin. When bilirubin becomes oxidized, it passes through a series of color changes, and the first change is to green—that is, to biliverdin.

The bile pigments are derived from the hemoglobin of the red cells. We have already seen (Ch. 7) that each day millions of red cells die and are replaced by fresh ones turned out by the bone marrow. The dead or dying cells are seized by huge cells (*macrophages*) found in the spleen and in other places—the liver, bone marrow, and the general connective tissues. These cells, which belong to the reticulo-endothelial system, "mine" the hemoglobin for the valuable iron in its molecule. The hemoglobin, thus deprived of its iron, is passed on to the liver cells, where it is excreted in the bile as bilirubin, or as the latter's oxidation product, biliverdin. The iron is stored in the liver and spleen and used later from time to time for the manufacture of new hemoglobin.[1]

We have all seen the successive color changes of a bruise, which is caused by the escape of blood from small vessels into the subcutaneous tissues or deep layers of the skin. At first the skin appears a dark red color or almost black. After a few days the bruise becomes lighter and acquires a greenish-blue hue, later a yellowish green, then a yellow, which gradually disappears. The color sequence is due to bilirubin and its oxidation products. This is what happens: An injury to the surface of the body, particularly where the tissues are soft and loose, causes the rupture of some small veins lying perhaps at some little depth from the surface. Blood escapes and after a time makes its way to the surface and shows through the semitransparent skin. The blood at first is dark because the reduced hemoglobin has not yet been changed by the large cells of the tissues mentioned above; but after a time the iron is removed, and bili-

[1] When the bile reaches the intestine, the bilirubin and biliverdin are acted on by bacteria and undergo reduction again. Their color changes to a yellowish brown. This pigment colors the feces and is called *stercobilin*.

rubin is formed. Oxidation of the pigment and its gradual removal account for the changes in the tint and depth of the color that result as time goes on. In a bruise, then, we can see before our eyes the formation of bile pigment. From the hemoglobin of millions of red cells that break up every minute in the healthy body, small amounts of bilirubin are formed in the spleen and liver and are excreted in the bile.

Jaundice. This is the term given to the yellow color of the skin, mucous membranes, and whites of the eyes that is seen when the blood contains too much bile pigment. Should the duct that carries the bile into the intestine (common bile duct) become completely blocked, as by a gallstone, then the pigment, which should be removed from the blood in the bile, will of course accumulate within the body and stain the tissues yellow. Furthermore, since bile cannot now reach the intestine, the stools are unpigmented; they are usually described as "clay colored." But bile pigment is excreted by the kidney and stains the urine a deep yellow, or even brown or green.

It should be emphasized that jaundice is only a sign, or symptom, of disease, not a disease in itself. Jaundice also results from disease that injures the liver and interferes with its function of excreting bile pigment. Or jaundice of a milder type may be caused by the excessive destruction of red cells, as in certain types of anemia. The large quantity of bile pigment produced from the released hemoglobin cannot then be all excreted even though liver function is normal.

Thus, three types of jaundice are recognized according to the manner by which they are caused—whether by obstruction of the flow of bile, by insufficiency of liver function, or by an excessive liberation of hemoglobin from the red blood cells. They are termed *obstructive, hepatogenous* and *hematogenous,* respectively.

The bile salts are *sodium glycocholate* and *sodium taurocholate.* Strictly speaking the bile is not a digestive secretion, for it contains no enzyme that acts upon food. But through the action of the bile salts it plays a prominent role in the splitting of fat and the absorption of the split products. The bile salts exert their effect upon fat digestion by virtue of their property of lowering surface tension and of facilitating the solution of fatty substances in the aqueous fluids of the intestine. They thus enable the fat to undergo division into small globules, and as a result of this, to form a finer emulsion with the intestinal secretions. Thus the total surface of the fat exposed to the action of the fat-splitting enzymes—lipases—is increased manyfold, and the digestive action of the enzymes correspondingly augmented. When bile is absent from the intestine, as in obstruction of the common bile duct, a considerable proportion of the fat remains undigested and unabsorbed; undigested fat as well as unabsorbed products of its digestion appear in the feces, which are pale and bulky. The manner in which the bile salts favor the absorption of fat is not connected directly with their property of lowering surface tension, but is owing to the fact that they form compounds with the fatty acids. Such compounds are more readily absorbed than the fatty acids themselves.

Lecithin and cholesterol are greasy or waxy substances belonging to the class of compounds known as lipids.[2] They have a widespread distribution in the body, being found in many tissues, especially nervous structures and the erythrocytes. They are of interest in connection with the bile because their concentration in this fluid, or rather their concentration in relation to the concentration of the bile salts, is an important factor in the production of gallstones. If they are in high concentration as compared with that of the bile salts, these lipids, especially cholesterol, are likely to come out of solution and form a gallstone. Some gallstones are almost pure cholesterol, though others are composed mainly of precipitated bile pigment. Most stones are formed in the gall bladder, and in this situation may give rise to no symptoms. But severe colicky pain is caused should the stone be expelled from the gall bladder and passed along the cystic or the common bile duct. If the stone lodges in the latter situation and blocks the flow of bile into the intestine, jaundice will result.

THE INTESTINES (OR BOWELS)

The intestinal tract is divided for purposes of description into the *small* and the *large intestine* (see Fig. 24.7).

The small intestine

The length of the small intestine of man is about 21 feet (6.5 meters). When the abdomen is opened and the greater omentum lifted up, the small intestine appears as a tube a little over 1½ inches in diameter, thrown into a mass of glistening coils (see Fig. 24.9). This part of the intestinal tract extends from the pylorus of the stomach to the ileocolic valve, through which it empties into the first part of the large intestine. The small intestine is described in three parts—*duodenum, jejunum,* and *ileum*.

The duodenum (L. *duodeni,* twelve) is the first and widest (5 cm) part of the small intestine. It is about 10 inches (12 fingerbreadths) long, and in larger anatomical texts is described in three parts: first, second, and third. It forms a C-shaped curve with the concavity to the left, embracing the head of the pancreas (Fig. 27.3). The duodenum is covered only on its anterior aspect by peritoneum, and there-

Fig. 27.8. Section of small intestine, opened to show the circular folds, or valvulae conniventes.

---

[2] Cholesterol belongs to a subclass of the lipids called the sterols, and lecithin to a subclass known as the phospholipids because it contains phosphorus.

fore, unlike the rest of the small intestine, does not possess a mesentery. The duodenum receives the chyme from the stomach; the pancreatic duct and the common bile duct open into it, usually by a single orifice.

The jejunum (L., empty) succeeds the duodenum; it is about 8 feet long and therefore constitutes about two fifths of the entire small intestine. The junction of the duodenum with the jejunum is called the **duodenojejunal flexure.** It forms a sharp bend forward.

The ileum is the remainder of the small intestine; it is the narrowest part, being only about 1 inch wide toward its lower end where it opens into the commencement of the large bowel.

Structure of the walls of the small intestine. The intestinal wall consists of a *mucous, submucous, muscular,* and a *serous* (peritoneal) coat.

The surface epithelium of the **mucous membrane** is of the tall columnar type and contains an abundance of goblet cells. There is a well-marked muscularis mucosae. The **submucosa** is a layer of loose connective tissue lying beneath the mucous membrane and uniting it to the muscular coat; it carries plexuses of blood vessels and lymphatics, and a network of nerve fibers and ganglion cells called the *submucous plexus of Meissner.*

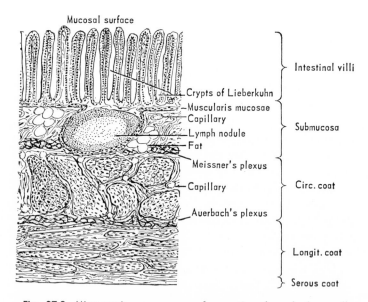

Fig. 27.9. Microscopic appearance of a section through the small intestine. The bundles of circular muscle are cut at right angles to their course, the longitudinal fibers along their length. A nerve plexus (Meissner's) is situated in the submucosa; another (myenteric plexus of Auerbach) lies in the connective tissue between the circular and longitudinal muscle coats.

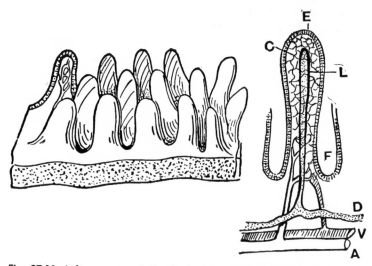

Fig. 27.10. *Left,* a group of intestinal villi (magnified). *Right,* section of a villus: *A,* small artery; *C,* capillary network; *D,* lymphatic; *E,* surface epithelium; *F,* crypt of Lieberkühn; *L,* lacteal; *V,* small vein.

The following structures of the mucosa should be particularly noted: (a) circular folds, (b) intestinal villi and glands, and (c) lymphatic nodules. The **circular folds,** or **valvulae conniventes,** are folds of mucous membrane that run partially or completely around the interior of the small intestine (Fig. 27.8). Commencing near the middle of the duodenum they become particularly prominent in the jejunum, but are much less conspicuous in the ileum, in the lower part of which they are few or absent. They serve to increase the absorbing surface of the intestine. The **villi** are minute fingerlike processes of the mucous membrane, just visible to the naked eye, that project from the inner surface of the intestine (Fig. 27.10). They give the mucosa its characteristic velvety appearance. Each villus is covered by epithelium and contains in its core a few smooth muscle fibers, a lymph vessel called a **lacteal,** and a plexus of blood vessels fed by an arteriole. The vessels arise from or join larger vessels in the submucosa. The villi are larger and more numerous in the duodenum and jejunum than in the ileum. In the intervals between the villi the mouths of minute tubular glands are to be found. These are the **intestinal glands,** or *crypts of Lieberkühn;* they secrete the intestinal juice. Patches of lymphoid tissue, known as **Peyers patches,** or **aggregated lymphatic nodules,** are found in the mucosa.

The villi are the absorbing units of the intestine. The muscularis mucosae is ceaselessly contracting and relaxing rhythmically during digestion and causes corresponding shortening and lengthening or swaying movements of the villi. Such movements have the effect of stirring the intestinal fluids and of constantly bringing them into contact with fresh surfaces. The absorption of digestive products is thereby facilitated.

The glands of the first half or so of the duodenum are different from those of the rest of the intestine. They are tubuloalveolar in type and known as **Brunner's glands;** each discharges its secretion into the duodenum through a single duct.

The **muscular coat** is composed of two layers of smooth muscle, an inner one of circular fibers and an outer one of longitudinal fibers. Between the two is the **myenteric** (nerve) **plexus of Auerbach.**

The large intestine

The large intestine commences at the ileocolic valve and ends at the anus. It consists of the *cecum, colon, rectum,* and *anal canal* (see Fig. 24.7).

The **ileocolic valve** guards the opening between the ileum and the first part of the large intestine, namely, the cecum. It is formed of two folds of mucous membrane that, like lips, close the opening, except when material is discharged through it from the ileum. It blocks the passage of fluid in the reverse direction, and thus prevents contamination of the small intestine from the large.

The **cecum** commences on the right side of the lower part of the abdomen. It is a saclike structure about 2½ iches long and about 3 inches wide; the ileum joins the upper part of its medial side. From it the large intestine is continued upwards as the ascending colon. The lower end of the cecum is blind, and about midway between this end and the entrance of the ileum it gives rise to a slender, worm-shaped tubular structure called the **vermiform appendix.** This little organ that so often is an abdominal storm center, its inflammation being known as *appendicitis,* has an average length of about 3½ inches, but may be 8 inches long. It is lined by mucous membrane and has a circular and a longitudinal coat of smooth muscle. A triangular fold of peritoneum called the **mesoappendix** runs

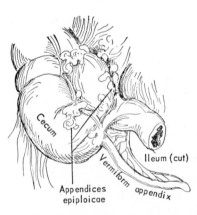

lleum (cut)

Appendices
epiploicae

appendix

Fig. 27.11. The cecum and vermiform appendix.

from the mesentery at the lower end of the ileum and encloses the appendix. It carries a small artery that may become occluded in acute appendicitis. When this occurs, death (gangrene or necrosis) of the appendix results. The cecum is usually completely enveloped by peritoneum.

The colon forms roughly three sides of a square with the open side below, and appears to enclose the coils of small intestine. It commences on the lower right side of the abdomen, where it is continuous with the cecum. Ascending to the region of the liver, it turns abruptly and crosses the abdominal cavity, at about the level of the umbilicus, to the left side in the region of the spleen; from here it descends in the left flank and enters the pelvis. The colon is therefore conveniently divided for descriptive purposes into four parts—the *ascending, transverse, descending,* and *pelvic* colons. The **ascending** and **descending colons** are covered but not enveloped by peritoneum; they have no mesentery and are therefore fixed to the posterior abdominal wall. The **transverse colon** on the other hand having a long mesocolon is freely movable between its attachments on either side where it joins the ascending and descending colons. It therefore sags in the middle like a festoon. The junctions of the transverse colon with the other parts of the colon in the region of the liver and the spleen are called, respectively, the **right** and **left colic flexures.** The **pelvic colon,** the continuation into the pelvis of the descending colon, commences at the brim of the true pelvis (Fig. 27.12). After making a curve that has in form been compared to the letter S, it becomes continuous with the rectum at the level of the third sacral vertebra. It is about 16 inches long and is attached to the pelvic wall by the **pelvic mesocolon.**

The **rectum,** which is continuous above with the pelvic colon, lies at first in the concavity formed by the sacrum and coccyx. But a little in front and below the coccyx it bends backwards to the anal canal.

The **anal canal** is a short passage about 1 inch long (2 to 3 cm) that opens to the exterior through the **anus,** or **anal orifice.** It is surrounded

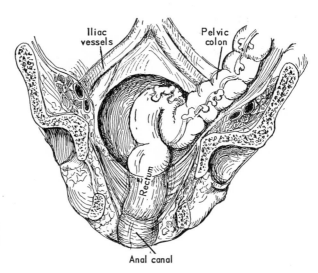

Iliac vessels

Pelvic colon

Rectum

Fig. 27.12. The pelvic colon, rectum, and anal canal.

Anal canal

by the internal and external anal sphincter muscles (sphincter ani internus, sphincter ani externus, Ch. 5).

The structure of the wall of the large intestine. Like that of the small intestine, the wall of the large intestine has four coats—*mucous, submucous, muscular,* and *serous.* The **serous coat** is, of course, the peritoneum, which, as we have seen, forms a complete covering only for certain parts—cecum, and the transverse and pelvic colons. The peritoneum covering the large intestine shows a number of small pouches filled with fatty tissue that appear as pear-shaped, oval, or round bodies about the size of large beans clinging to the surface; they are called **appendices epiploicae.**

The **mucous membrane** differs in several respects from that of the small intestine. It is covered with columnar epithelium, but there are no villi; the glands are longer, contain large numbers of goblet cells, but do not secrete digestive enzymes. Solitary lymph nodules are present but not the aggregated variety. The muscularis mucosae is well developed. The upper half of the anal canal is lined by mucous membrane, but the lower half by skin; the mucous membrane is raised into several (6 to 10) vertical columns called the **anal columns of Morgagni** (Fig. 27.13). The veins in the mucosa of the anal canal not infrequently become dilated (varicose), and form small pendulous swellings known as *internal hemorrhoids* or *piles.* Similar varicose swellings of the veins of the skin-lined lower part of the anal canal occurs less frequently; they are called *external hemorrhoids* or *piles.*

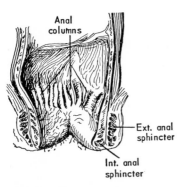

Anal columns

Ext. anal sphincter

Int. anal sphincter

Fig. 27.13. The anal canal, opened.

The **muscular coat** of the large intestine consists of an inner layer of circular fibers and an outer one of longitudinal fibers as in the small intestine, but the longitudinal layer is thickened to form three bands, called **taeniae,** which appear to be too short for the intestine and draw it into puckers and pouches known as **haustra** (Fig. 27.11).

The secretion of the intestinal glands

Two main types of cell are to be found in the intestinal glands, or crypts of Lieberkühn. Those lining the greater part of the crypts are low columnar in type and secrete mucus. But those in the deeper parts of the glands are of a special type; they contain numerous granules that stain selectively with acid dyes (such as the red dye eosin). They are believed to produce the enzymes of the intestinal juice, and are known as **the cells** of Paneth (Fig. 27.14). It should be mentioned that the term **intestinal juice** is applied specifically to the secretion of the intestinal glands, and is not used in a general sense to mean simply the fluids in the intestinal canal. The Latin name *succus entericus* is also sometimes applied to the secretion.

The intestinal juice contains the following enzymes:

Maltase
Erepsin
Lactase
Sucrase
Lipase

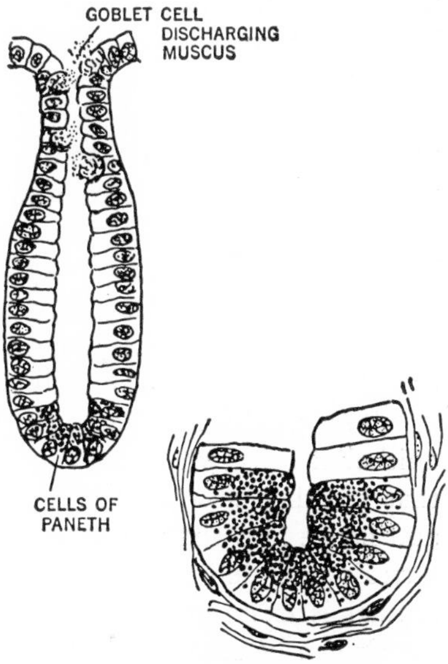

Erepsin is a very powerful enzyme that attacks the fragments (groups of amino acids) of the protein molecule after its digestion by the trypsin of the pancreatic juice. Erepsin separates the individual amino acids from one another and so carries the digestion of protein to its final stage. The separate amino acids are absorbed into the blood and are carried to the many cells of the body, where they may be built up into protoplasm to repair the "wear and tear" of the tissues or for growth.

Maltase splits the sugar maltose into two glucose molecules.

Lactase, in the same way, splits lactose into two hexose molecules (Ch. 30)—glucose and galactose.

Sucrase acts upon cane sugar (sucrose), breaking the molecule of this disaccharide into its constituent hexose molecules—glucose and fructose. No digestion of this sugar occurs until it reaches the intestine and comes into contact with the sucrase of the intestinal juice.

Lipase splits the molecules of fat into its constituents—glycerol and fatty acids.

In Figure 24.9 the digestion of protein, carbohydrates, and fats is summarized diagrammatically.

Fig. 27.14. *Left,* a crypt of Lieberkühn with goblet cells. *Right,* an enlarged sketch of bottom of crypt to show cells of Paneth loaded with granules.

ABSORPTION OF FOOD

Absorption from the digestive tract has been dealt with in a general way in Chapter 24.

Food, whether carbohydrate, fat, or protein, if thoroughly digested, is virtually all absorbed. Little, if any, is excreted in the feces (stools). Absorption of food occurs entirely through the small intestine, though water under certain circumstances, but probably not ordinarily, may be absorbed from the stomach. Large quantities of water are absorbed from the large intestine. Alcohol is absorbed from the stomach and even, in small amounts, from the mouth. Glucose solution, if in high concentration, may undergo some absorption through the gastric mucosa. Water and the soluble amino acids and glucose pass into the small veins of the villi and are carried first to the liver (Ch. 30). Here the amino acids may undergo chemical changes or may pass unchanged into the general blood stream. Of the glucose, part passes through the liver into the general circulation, but any excess that the body does not require at the moment is stored in the liver as *glycogen* (Ch. 30). From time to time the glycogen is changed again to glucose, which is delivered into the blood stream to satisfy the needs of the body's cells for carbohydrate food.

The products of fat digestion—fatty acids and glycerol—enter the epithelial cells, where they are recombined to form fine globules of fat that are then absorbed in part (60 percent) into the veins of the villi and hence into the portal circulation, and in part (40 percent) into the lacteals and delivered into the thoracic duct.[3] If the mesentery of an animal is examined during the digestion of a meal of fat, the lymph vessels can be seen as pearly strands, because they are filled with a milky fluid consisting of a fine emulsion of fat. This fluid as well as that in the thoracic duct is called *chyle*.

The material in the small bowel is much more fluid than that in the colon, for though water is absorbed from the small intestine, large quantities of digestive juices and bile are secreted into its lumen. Relatively little fluid, on the other hand, is secreted into the large bowel, but as just mentioned, a large volume of water is absorbed.

It should be pointed out that absorption from the intestine cannot be explained by simple physical laws; it is the result of physiological processes and as such requires the expenditure of energy by the living cells of the intestinal wall.

The movements of the intestines

The small intestine. Though ordinarily we are unaware of the fact, the small intestine is in almost constant motion. Contractions of the mus-

---

[3] This is the classical theory of fat absorption, according to which all fat must first be split into its constituents before it can be absorbed. But certain observations within recent years have led to the belief that only a part of the fact is treated in this way, and that a large proportion passes unchanged in the form of microscopic droplets through the intestinal lining. Minute canals in the intestinal cells have been described through which such particles could readily pass. It may well be that only this unsplit fat passes into the lacteals.

cular walls are incessantly changing the diameter of the tube, moving the food from place to place, churning it up, and mixing it with the digestive juices. There are three types of movement in the small intestine: (1) segmenting, (2) pendular, and (3) peristaltic.

The *segmenting* movements are simple constricting contractions that pinch the tube and its contents sharply several times a minute. Their purpose is to knead the food and thoroughly mix it with the intestinal juices. They do not move material along the tube. The *pendular* movements are also simple constricting bands of contraction; but they travel a few inches up and down the intestinal tube and churn the food back and forth. The *peristaltic* wave is a contraction that may travel long distances along the intestinal wall. It requires some special notice, since this type of contraction is found not only in the intestine but also in practically all muscular tubes of the body—esophagus, bile ducts, etc. We have already noticed it in the esophagus and in the stomach. A band of contraction is seen to seize the whole circumference of the tube with considerable force. The bowel may become blanched as a result of the compression of its blood vessels by the grip of the intestinal muscle. The contracting ring normally travels downward—rarely, if ever, upward. Progressing immediately in front of it is a circular band of completely relaxed muscle. It is apparent that if the constricting band arises behind a mass of material and travels downward, the tube in the region over which it passes will be cleared. The relaxed or dilated region that precedes the constriction must, of course, by removing any resistance to the passage of the material, aid its movement onward.

The large intestine. The principal movement in the colon is a peristaltic wave that occurs at intervals of several hours and sweeps the intestinal contents from the ascending colon, through the transverse colon, and into the descending and pelvic colons. This is referred to as the *mass movement.* It is initiated reflexly, most frequently by the entrance of food into the stomach. This is called the *gastrocolic reflex,* and is most likely to occur after breakfast. Peristaltic waves at other times are infrequent in the large bowel. The cecum often shows reverse peristalsis; that is, waves that move toward its blind end, as well as occasional ones running toward the ascending colon. This combination has a churning effect upon the contained fluids.

By the time they have reached the lower part of the descending colon and the pelvic colon, the intestinal contents have, from the absorption of water, a pasty consistency. They are now called *feces.* This part of the intestinal tract serves as a storehouse for the feces awaiting evacuation.

Evacuation of the bowel, or *defecation,* is initiated by a peristaltic contraction of the lower part of the colon that forces some feces into the rectum. This usually follows a mass movement that carries material into and distends the pelvic colon. The entrance of feces into the rectum, by stretching its walls, stimulates nerve endings therein and sets up the *defecation reflex*. This consists of a strong peristaltic contraction of the rectum and pelvic colon, accompanied by relaxation of the anal sphincters. The reflex is aided by voluntary contraction of the abdominal muscles while the diaphragm is held in position of nearly full inspiration. The intra-abdominal pressure is thus raised and a compressing force exerted upon the loaded bowel. Normally, the rectum, except during defecation, is empty.

Bacterial digestion in the large intestine. Though no digestive enzymes are secreted by the glands of the large intestine, putrefactive bacteria in this part of the intestine break any amino acids that have escaped absorption into simpler compounds, many of which have a strong odor and are highly toxic. Among these compounds are, *histamine* (from histidine), *indole* and *skatole* (from tryptophan), and *tyramine* (from tyrosine). Odorous gases, such as *hydrogen sulfide* (H_2S), are also produced from sulfur-containing amino acids (cystine and methionine). The odor of the feces is due mainly to indole and skatole and to these gases; the color of the stools is caused by the reducing action of bacteria on the bile pigment; this fecal pigment is called *stercobilin*. As well as these effects of bacterial action, the flora of the intestine perform an important function in nutrition. They synthesize certain vitamins of the vitamin B complex, vitamin C in some species (though not in man or the guinea pig), and vitamin K in man and several other species.

The reaction of the intestinal contents. The formation and nature of feces. The reaction of the duodenal fluids is usually slightly acid but it depends upon the stage of gastric digestion at which a sample is taken, upon the degree of acidity of the gastric contents, upon the quantity of alkaline juices, pancreatic juice, and mucus secreted into the duodenum, and upon the nature of the food. It may be definitely alkaline. The contents of the remainder of the small intestine and of the entire large intestine have a reaction a little on the acid side (a pH of about 6.8). The feces are very faintly acid as a rule.

The feces are not simply and solely unabsorbed residues of the food, but are made up largely of materials *excreted* from the blood. During starvation, for example, the bulk of the feces may not be greatly less than at ordinary times, and a loop of intestine isolated from the rest of the intestine becomes filled after a few days with a pasty mass indistinguishable in consistency and composition from ordinary feces except that, of course, being isolated from the rest of the intestinal tract, it contains no bile and is therefore pale. Bacteria make up about 9 percent of the feces; the other main solid constituents are food residues, which vary considerably in amount with the proportion of indigestible material (chiefly cellulose) in the diet, and fats, nitrogenous substances, and minerals eliminated from the blood, together with epithelial cells and leucocytes shed from the intestinal mucosa. Little if any digestible food appears in the feces. In other words, practically all the protein, fat, and carbohydrate that is eaten is absorbed, the food residues of the feces consisting almost entirely of indigestible substances. Vegetable material, since its framework is composed of cellulose, contributes more to the feces than do other foods. This indigestible material or "roughage," as it is commonly termed, serves a useful purpose in that it acts as a mechanical stimulus, increasing the motility as well as the secretions of the intestinal wall.

Control of the movements of the stomach and intestines

The movements of the alimentary tract from the pharynx to the large bowel are carried on automatically. They are beyond the control of our wills and, in perfect health, beneath our consciousness. Impulses are ceaselessly traveling from the stomach and intestine along afferent fibers to the spinal cord and brain. Impulses are discharged in turn along fibers of the autonomic nervous system to the musculature of the alimentary tract, which controls its movements.

The **vagus nerve** carries excitor or motor impulses—that is, impulses that increase the movements—to the stomach, small intestine, and upper half or so of the colon. These impulses arise in the medulla oblongata. Motor impulses to the lower half of the large intestine are conveyed from the lower part (*sacral region*) of the spinal cord by the **pelvic nerve.** Through it peristaltic waves are set up that empty the lower colon. The sympathetic nerves carry impulses that depress or inhibit the movements of the stomach and of the entire intestinal tract.

The natural excitants of the intestinal movements. The intestine is excited to activity by the food within its lumen. Some foods are more stimulating than others to the sensory nerves in the bowel wall. The intestinal muscle is most responsive to mechanical types of stimulus, especially stretching of the bowel wall by masses of undigested or semi-digested material, or the rubbing of food residues against the mucosa; the responses of the bowel to such stimuli are carried out through nerve plexuses in the intestinal wall. Solid particles in the food are particularly effective in exciting the peristaltic waves. Some foods, for instance, contain a large proportion of material that cannot be digested by the various ferments. This material is left as a residue, which, accumulating within the intestine, excites it to contraction. Green foods, which contain large amounts of the nondigestible material cellulose, for this reason are valuable for maintaining regular movements of the digestive tract. Fruits such as grapes, raisins, and figs, since the seeds and skins are not digested, act in the same way. Other fruits and vegetables contain certain **chemical**

materials that are stimulating to the bowel. On the other hand, concentrated foods, such as cheese, eggs, meat, and bread, which are almost completely absorbed, have a depressing effect upon the bowel movements. Milk, since it contains a large proportion of calcium, tends to depress the movements. Sluggishness of the intestinal tract, particularly of the large intestine, resulting in infrequent evacuations, is called *constipation*.

Constipation is caused most commonly by bad habits. As mentioned above, the desire to empty the bowel is aroused by the passage of feces into the rectum and the stimulation of afferent nerve endings in the intestinal wall. The act can, however, be voluntarily restrained, and when this is practiced, the tone of the rectal wall is reduced, and the rectum thus accommodates its capacity to the bulk of the feces (postural tone, Ch. 24) ; the afferent nerve endings are no longer adequately stimulated, or at any rate, are unresponsive, and the desire to defecate passes. As a result of the absorption of water the retained feces become dry and hard. When the habit of postponing defecation in this way is persisted in, the rectum, which normally is empty, contains feces most of the time; it becomes permanently less sensitive to distention, and its muscle, as well as that of the pelvic colon, loses tone. It is well known that the reflex mechanisms governing the emptying of the bowel are amenable to "training." A type of conditioned reflex becomes established. When the habit of emptying the bowels at a certain hour each day is practiced for a while, the desire to do so tends to recur regularly at this time.

Other causes of constipation are (a) a *diet* that leaves too little unabsorbed residue or one that contains too little fluid—the contents of the large intestine are, therefore, of small bulk and fail to furnish a sufficiently strong stimulus (stretching of the intestinal wall) to set up vigorous peristaltic contractions, (b) *colon* that *absorbs too readily* and thus causes undue drying of the feces, and (c) hypertonic state of the muscle of the colon—*spastic constipation*—the transverse and descending colons are the seat of a strong tonic contraction that impedes the progress of the feces.

We hear a great deal these days of ill health resulting supposedly from the accumulation of poisonous substances within the intestines. We are told to keep the digestive tract clean by irrigation, "internal flushings," etc., in order that these substances shall not be absorbed. This advice usually emanates either from ignorant but well-meaning persons obsessed by a theory of the way to health, or from patent-medicine manufacturers eager to promote the sale of their products. The lower intestinal tract is normally swarming with bacteria, and powerful poisons are always present. It is the cesspool of the body, and there is no use in denying the fact. It is designed to be a refuse pit and is quite capable of taking care of the poisons that are formed within it. Experimental work of recent years goes to show that we need no longer be frightened by the bogy of intestinal intoxication. The toxic products do not reach the general circulation, for they are detoxicated (combined with sulfuric and glycuronic acids to form innocuous compounds) in the liver. In the natural way, evacuation of the bowel once or twice a day is quite sufficient to keep the body healthy and fit. The discomfort, headache, and other unpleasant symptoms of constipation are well known. Yet even these are due, not to the absorption of poisons from the intestinal tract, but to quite a different cause—namely, the mechanical effect of the overloaded bowel upon the intestinal nerves and the reflex effects brought about through these nerves and the central nervous system.

Substances that cause evacuation of the bowels: laxatives, cathartics, and purgatives.[4] The manifold drugs and other substances employed to stimulate the intestinal movements and cause evacuation of the bowels do not bring about their effect all after the same fashion. Some, such as *Epsom salts* (magnesium sulfate), being not absorbable, cause a flow of water into the small intestine through their osmotic effect which, by increasing the bulk of the intestinal contents, causes distention and consequent stretching of the bowel wall; this, we have seen above, acts as a powerful stimulus to peristalsis. Other cathartics, such as *castor oil,* contain an irritant principle that serves to excite intestinal motility. *Croton oil* is an especially powerful irritant that in very small dosage causes profuse purgation and, in larger amounts, may induce acute inflammation of the intestinal mucosa. Undigested material of any sort within the bowel, for example, the *skins of fresh fruit,* the *cellulose of raw vegetables, whole wheat,* and *bran* all serve, as already pointed out, as intestinal excitants by increasing the bulk of the feces and consequently the stretch of the bowel wall. *Agar* (a gelatinous material prepared from seaweed) and *paraffin oil,* which are not absorbed in significant amounts, act similarly. There are a host of other laxatives and cathartics, many of them used from time immemorial, of which little is known definitely concerning their mode of action. Vitamin B_1 and other factors of the B complex tend to increase the tone of the intestinal musculature, and thus favor natural movements of evacuation.

Reliance upon medicines to ensure regular bowel movements should be avoided, for the intestinal musculature tends to become tolerant to their use and requires a gradual increase in dosage. Hygienic measures, diet, exercise, and habit should be depended upon whenever possible.

---

[4] The term *laxative* implies an agent with a milder stimulating action than either a *cathartic* or a *purgative.*

METABOLISM AND NUTRITION. RENAL AND CUTANEOUS FUNCTIONS

PART VII

28
Metabolism

GENERAL PRINCIPLES

Metabolism is a general term employed to embrace all the chemical processes carried on within the cells of the body (Ch. 2). Chief among these processes is the oxidation (combustion) of the food materials with the production of energy. The body bears a resemblance to a furnace or a gasoline engine; but, whereas the furnace oxidizes the carbon and hydrogen of coal or wood, and the engine the carbon and hydrogen of gasoline, the body obtains these elements from the food, and from their "burning," or oxidation, derives mechanical energy and heat. Oxidation of the carbon of the food produces carbon dioxide (CO_2); water (H_2O) is formed by the oxidation of the hydrogen. Heat is a form of energy; and all other forms—mechanical, electrical, chemical, etc.—can be reduced to heat. By measuring the heat produced by a fuel when it is completely burned, the total amount of energy that the fuel contained can be ascertained. We can, therefore, express food energy in terms of heat. The body's total heat production is called *general metabolism.*

The Calorie. Fluid is measured by the quart or by some smaller or larger measure of the English system, or in cubic millimeters, cubic centimeters, or liters of the metric system; length is measured in inches, feet, etc., or in millimeters, centimeters, etc.; and weight in such units as ounces and pounds, or grams and kilograms. So, too, we must have some unit for the measurement of a quantity of heat. The heat measure is called the *Calorie* (L. *calor*, heat). In physiological heat measurements a Calorie is the quantity of heat required to raise the temperature of 1 kg (about 2 pounds or a quart) of water 1 centigrade degree.[1]

---

[1] From 15° to 16° C. It is important that the terms *heat* and *temperature* should not be confused. The sense of touch tells us of any difference in temperature—whether an object is hot or cold, whether its temperature is high or low. Heat is a quantity, and the sense of touch will not inform us of how much heat any substance contains,

When 1 gram of sugar or starch (carbohydrate) is burned outside the body, about 4 Calories are produced. One gram of fat when burned in the same way generates approximately 9 Calories. When these substances are used for food and "burned" by the cells of the body, each produces the same quantity of heat as when an equivalent amount is burned outside the body. So we speak of one or another sample of food having a certain *heat,* or *caloric, value*—a certain fuel value—meaning by this that it is capable of furnishing so much heat, or energy, to the body. On the other hand, only a proportion of protein food is burned within the body; a part (the nitrogen-containing portion) is incombustible. Protein can be completely burned outside the body; hence it must furnish more heat in the latter instance than when used as food. A gram of pure protein furnishes only 4 Calories in the body as against 5.3 Calories outside. A list of some of the commoner foods with their composition and approximate number of Calories per pound is given in Table 28.1.

TABLE 28.1

Food	Composition, in percent				Calories per pound
	Protein	Fat	Carbo-hydrate	Water and salts	
Beef (lean)	20	12	. . .	68	886
Pork	17	30	. . .	53	1500
Eggs	13	11	. . .	76	755
Butter	1	85	. . .	14	3500
Cheese	30	38	. . .	32	2000
Milk	3	4	5	88	314
Sugar	. . . .	. . . .	100	. .	1790
Bread	9	2	53	36	1200
Potatoes	2	. . . .	18	80	350
Apples	0.4	0.5	11	88	200
Oranges	0.8	. . . .	12	87	175
Lettuce	1	. . . .	3	96	87
Tomatoes	7	. . . .	4	95	100

for the quantity of heat held by any material depends upon the mass of the material as well as upon its temperature. Thus a gallon of water may have a lower temperature than a single drop, but the *quantity* of heat held by the gallon may be immensely greater.

The physiological, or large, Calorie is a thousand times greater than the small calorie employed in physical heat measurements, which is the quantity of heat required to raise the temperature of 1 *gram* of water 1 centigrade degree. In order to distinguish it from the small calorie, the large Calorie is written with a capital or by C. alone.

The average man, during the course of the day, generates about 3000 Calories. This quantity of heat is sufficient to raise nearly 10 gallons of water to the boiling point. In order, then, to maintain this level of metabolism, the diet of the average healthy man should have an energy value of about 3000 Calories. (See also pp. 402, 424.)

Heat production under different physiological conditions. Several conditions influence the quantity of heat produced by the body. Obviously more energy is expended and more heat produced when work is done than during rest. The heat production may be increased 10 or even 20 times during strenuous muscular exercise. The temperature of the air is another important factor. In cold weather out of doors the body produces more heat than on a warm day in summer. The body tends to cool more quickly on a cold day—that is, it loses more heat; therefore, in order to maintain the body temperature at the normal level, more fuel must be burned and more heat produced by the tissues. During sleep the metabolism is reduced below the waking level. The ingestion of food, especially protein, causes an increase in metabolism above that during fasting.

BASAL METABOLISM AND ITS MEASUREMENT

There are two main methods of measuring the body's heat production—the *direct* and the *indirect*. In the *direct* method the subject occupies a chamber the size of a small room called a *calorimeter*. Through pipes in the walls and ceiling, water at a known temperature is circulated, which absorbs the heat given off from the body. The chamber is perfectly insulated so that no heat can escape or enter. At the end of the experiment the quantity of water that has circulated through the pipes is calculated, and its temperature is ascertained by means of delicate thermometers. The number of Calories produced can then be calculated. For example, if the quantity of water is 40 kg and its temperature rise during one hour is 2° C, then $(40 \times 2 =)$ 80 Calories of heat have been produced in the subject's body. The determination of the heat production in this way is quite simple in principle, but it involves a number of additional factors and is very difficult in practice. This method of *direct calorimetry*, as it is called, also requires extremely expensive apparatus and is employed only in large institutions.

Indirect calorimetry requires no very expensive equipment. It is based upon the following principles: The combustion of any food material involves the consumption of oxygen and the formation of carbon dioxide. Furthermore, when a given type of food is oxidized in the body, the quantity of oxygen used (and of carbon dioxide produced) is always the same for equal amounts of that particular foodstuff. These quantities are definitely known for the three different types of food. It is known, for example, that, when 1 gram of fat is burned, 2 liters of oxygen are consumed. We have already seen that this gram of fat produces at the same time 9 Calories of heat. Therefore, if one knows the quantity of oxygen that the body uses in a given time, and the type of food (fat, carbohydrate, or protein) that was being oxidized during that time, one could ascertain the quantity of foodstuff burned. The number of Calories that this amount of fuel produced could then be easily calculated. In short, the consumption of a certain quantity of oxygen by the body when it burns a given food or mixture of foods always corresponds to the production of a certain quantity of heat.[2]

Since the value of the heat production in different persons must be capable of being compared, some standard set of conditions must be followed in making the measurements. Otherwise it would be impossible to tell whether a person's heat production were greater or less than it should be. During muscular effort, for example, or after a meal, a person would produce more heat than at rest or on an empty stomach. On this account, measurements of the heat production are made with the patient lying down[3] and several hours after a meal (without breakfast shortly after arising in the morning) and at a room temperature of about 20° C. The value of the heat production under these specified conditions is called the *basal metabolic rate* (BMR).

Determination of the heat production from the oxygen consumption. The oxygen consumption of any person can be ascertained by a variety of methods. The *Benedict-Roth apparatus* (Fig. 28.1) or some modification of it is most frequently used. The instrument consists mainly of a bell-type spirometer, two wide-bored tubes (inspiratory and expiratory), and

---

[2] Since a given quantity of carbohydrate, fat, or protein, when it undergoes combustion, uses a known volume of oxygen and produces a known volume of carbon dioxide, the type of food being oxidized by the body can be ascertained from the ratio of the volumes of these gases consumed and produced, respectively. This ratio is called the *respiratory quotient*, or, briefly, the RQ. Thus,

$$\frac{\text{Volume carbon dioxide produced (expired)}}{\text{Volume oxygen consumed (inspired and retained)}} = \text{RQ}$$

When 100 grams of carbohydrate are oxidized, 75 liters of oxygen are consumed and the same volume of carbon dioxide is produced. The respiratory quotient is, therefore, ($^{75}\!/_{75} =$) 1.00. When 100 grams of fat are oxidized, 142 liters of carbon dioxide are produced and 200 liters of oxygen used. The respiratory quotient is ($^{142}\!/_{200} =$) 0.71. The respiratory quotient of protein is 0.80. For mixtures of the three types of food the respiratory quotient will lie anywhere between the two extremes, depending upon the proportions of each in the mixture. On an ordinary mixed diet it is around 0.85. The heat equivalent of oxygen at different respiratory quotients is obtained from a table.

Except for very precise experimental work the respiratory quotient is not determined in measuring the metabolism of any individual subject. After several hours of fasting, when the measurements are made, the body uses its fuel reserves and such a food mixture gives a respiratory quotient of 0.82. The heat equivalent of oxygen at this RQ is 4.825 Calories. This figure is therefore used in the calculations. That is, every liter of oxygen consumed at an assumed RQ of 0.82 corresponds to a heat production of 4.825 Calories.

[3] He should be lying quietly for at least 30 minutes before the measurement is taken.

a mouthpiece. The spirometer itself is a cylindrical vessel with two walls separated by a narrow space and an inverted single-walled vessel, or "bell." The wall of this second vessel fits between the walls of the first and is counterpoised by means of a weight and pulley as shown in the figure. Water fills the annular space between the walls of the first vessel and acts as a seal. Before the observation is started, oxygen is run into the bell until the pointer is raised to the zero mark on the graduated scale covering the rotating drum.

A clip closes the patient's nostrils while he breathes quietly into the apparatus through the mouthpiece and tubing. The carbon dioxide is absorbed from his expired air by soda lime. The heat production is arrived at from the oxygen consumption alone. The bell falls as the volume of oxygen is reduced; the quantity consumed by the patient is calculated from the descending curve drawn by the writing point on the graduated scale.

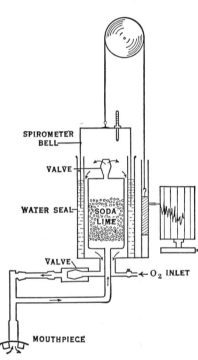

SPIROMETER BELL

VALVE

WATER SEAL

SODA LIME

VALVE

← O_2 INLET

MOUTHPIECE

Heat production and surface area. The heat loss of the body, as of any other hot object, is related to its surface—the greater the surface, the more rapid the heat loss. The more heat is lost from the animal body, the greater, automatically, becomes the heat production. In brief, then, the body of a person with a large surface area produces more heat than one with a smaller area.[4] Since the surface areas of different persons vary considerably, it is not customary to express the metabolic rate as so many Calories per person

Fig. 28.1. Diagram of the Benedict-Roth apparatus, used for the determination of the basal metabolic rate from the oxygen consumption.

[4] Of two objects having approximately the same shape but differing considerably in size, the smaller one will have a greater surface area in proportion to its mass than the larger one, and because the heat loss is proportional to the surface area, a small animal, such as a mouse, loses much more heat for its size than a larger one, such as a dog. The heat production of the mouse, that is, its metabolism, in proportion to its weight must be correspondingly greater in order that heat loss and heat production shall balance. (Of course the *total* heat production of the dog will be enormously greater than that of the mouse.) It will be found, however, that if the heat production is calculated in relation to surface area it will be about the same (per square meter) for both animals. This is true for all mammalian species.

TABLE 28.2

OXYGEN CONSUMPTION UNDER STANDARD CONDITIONS (IN LITERS) AND THE HEAT PRODUCTION (IN CALORIES PER SQUARE METER OF BODY SURFACE) PER HOUR FOR VARIOUS AGE GROUPS

Ages	Male		Female	
	O_2	Calories	O_2	Calories
14-15	9.53	45.9	8.91	42.9
16-17	8.91	42.9	8.29	39.9
18-19	8.50	40.9	7.88	37.9
20-29	8.19	39.4	7.67	36.9
30-39	8.19	39.4	7.57	36.4
40-49	7.98	38.4	7.46	35.9
50-59	7.77	37.4	7.25	34.9
60-69	7.57	36.4	7.05	33.9
70-79	7.36	35.4	6.84	32.9

Note the gradual diminution in heat production with advancing years.

per hour, or even as so many Calories per pound of person per hour. Instead, a square meter of body surface is used as the standard unit for comparison. The surface area of a person can be calculated from his height and weight. That for a man of average size is 1.8 square meters. The normal metabolic rate of an adult man is about 40 Calories per

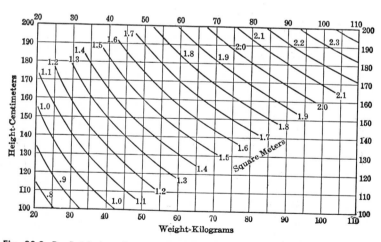

Fig. 28.2. Du Bois' chart for obtaining the surface area of the body in square meters (as indicated by the slanting lines) from a subject's height and weight. For example, a person 170 centimeters (approximately 5 feet 8 inches) tall and weighing 70 kilograms (154 pounds) has a surface area of 1.8 square meters.

square meter per hour. In young persons it is greater than this, and in older persons it is less. The rate is also less in females than in males of the same age (see Table 28.2 and Fig. 28.2).

Variations in the basal metabolic rate from the normal. If the basal metabolic rate is the same as that in a large number of people of the same race, age, and sex, the figure is said to be normal. If, however, the rate is less than that of the average for normal people, the rate is said to be lowered. Overactivity of the thyroid gland (hyperthyroidism, Ch. 39) causes a great increase in the basal metabolic rate, whereas decrease in the activity of the thyroid gland (hypothyroidism) results in a lower rate. It is raised in fever. The basal metabolic rate has been determined in virtually all diseased conditions, and the determination of this value is of great assistance to the physician in making a diagnosis or in following the progress of his patient.

29
The Regulation of
the Body Temperature

The temperature of the human body is about 98.4° F. It varies slightly above or below this level in different persons but remains practically unchanged from day to day or week to week in the same person, provided that it is taken at about the same hour of the day. The temperature in the axilla is about a degree lower than the mouth temperature, and the rectal temperature about a degree higher. Even in health, the body temperature does not remain at a constant level throughout the twenty-four hours, but is from 1° to 2° F lower in the early morning than in the late afternoon. The normal body temperature of infants and young children is somewhat higher and much less stable than that of adults, tending to rise from trivial causes, and to a higher level in infections.

The body temperature represents the balance struck between the heat generated by the active tissues, mainly the muscles and liver, and that lost from the body to the environment. It is remarkable how steady the body temperature remains under widely varying conditions. Little change in body temperature occurs though the air temperature rises to 100° F or falls below zero, nor does the extra heat produced during light work occasion a rise in temperature. Strenuous muscular exercise may, however, cause a temporary rise in temperature of from 1° to 4° F.

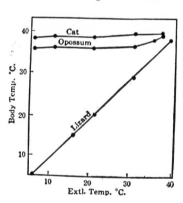

Fig. 29.1. Variation in body temperature of different types of animals by exposure for 2 hours in an environment rising from 5° to 35° C. (After Martin.)

399

Animals such as mammals and birds (warm-blooded animals) which can maintain a constant body temperature against variations in the temperature of their environment are called *homeothermic*. Those species, for example, fish, frogs, and reptiles (cold-blooded animals), that are unable to regulate their body temperature are called *poikilothermic*. Their body temperature is that of the environment (see Fig. 29.1).

Heat balance. It is obvious that the quantity of heat produced in the body (Ch. 28) must just balance the quantity lost to the environment. If the body produced more heat than it gave off, the retained heat would cause a rise in temperature; if it lost more than it generated, its temperature would fall. The average daily heat production—that is, the metabolism—of a man following a light occupation is around 3000 Calories. This quantity of heat is dissipated in the ways described in the following section.

PHYSICAL FACTORS IN TEMPERATURE CONTROL

Of the total heat lost from the body, about 95 percent is eliminated through radiation and convection, and the evaporation of water from the lungs and skin. The remaining 5 percent or so is lost in the urine and feces, and in raising the inspired air to body temperature.

Radiation and convection.[1] Through these two physical processes the body, like any other warm object, loses heat to the cooler air surrounding it, and to any cooler objects in contact with it or in its immediate neighborhood. The heat lost in this way can be increased or diminished through variations in the quantity of blood flowing through the skin. On a hot day, for example, the vessels of the skin dilate; more blood is therefore brought from the deeper parts of the body to the surface, and heat loss is accordingly increased. In cool weather the vessels of the skin constrict, and a greater proportion of the total blood volume is distributed to the internal structures; heat loss is thereby reduced. When the cold is extreme, the cutaneous vessels of covered parts of the body, such as the trunks and limbs, are constricted, but in the skin of the ears, nose, cheeks, etc., anastomosing vessels existing between the arterioles on the one hand and small veins on the other, dilate to permit a free flow of warm blood from deeper parts to the skin of the exposed regions; thus their temperature is prevented from falling too low. The anastomosing vessels lie beneath the subpapillary venous plexus, from which they divert a considerable proportion of the swiftly flowing blood (Fig. 29.2). The skin is kept warm more effectively in this way. Thus, the skin may appear pale or even of a bluish tint though quite warm, for it is the

---

[1] Ordinarily the loss of heat from the body by *conduction* is negligible. Air is a very poor conductor, and unless a person is in contact with cold ground or immersed in water below body temperature he does not lose much heat through conduction.

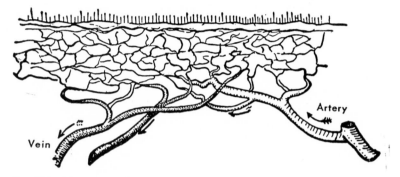

Fig. 29.2. Diagram to illustrate how the blood is carried through the vessels of the skin, which constitute the body's heat-radiating system.

amount of blood flowing through the venous plexus and not that in the deeper cutaneous vessels that gives the skin its color (see Ch. 32).

Another important factor is the variation in blood volume that results from changes in environmental temperature. The blood volume is increased by a rise in environmental temperature, the great volume being the result of the passage of tissue fluid into the circulation. Obviously, a greater quantity of heat will be absorbed from deeper structures and dissipated from the dilated vessels of the skin.

Evaporation of water from the lungs and skin. The latent heat of evaporation of water is about 0.6 Calorie[2]—that is, this quantity of heat is absorbed in the vaporization of 1 cubic centimeter (cc) of water. Under ordinary atmospheric conditions about 350 cc of water are vaporized from the lungs daily, and about 550 cc from the skin. This represents a heat loss of about $(900 \times 0.6 =)$ 540 Calories.

But it should be understood that the evaporation of water from the surface of the body occurs constantly in the absence of any visible sweating, even though the sweat glands are quite inactive or, as in some rare instances, when they are entirely lacking. Like any other moist mass, the body is continually losing weight by evaporation. The water "seeps" (diffuses) into the skin from the underlying tissues and is vaporized from the surface. This water loss together with that from the lungs was first observed and studied by an Italian physician, Santorio Santorio (1561-1636), upon himself and called by him *insensible perspiration*. The quantity of body water lost from the skin surface as visible sweat and as insensible perspiration varies with the degree to which the atmosphere is saturated with moisture, that is, with the relative humidity. If this is very high, a large part of the sweat may simply drip from the skin, and such unevaporated sweat exerts no cooling effect. The relative humidity is, therefore, of great importance with respect to our comfort on a hot day. Heat loss by both convection and evaporation is increased by wind.

[2] The latent heat of the evaporation of sweat is 0.59 Calorie.

It is clear that when the environmental temperature is higher than that of the body, heat cannot be dissipated by radiation, convection, or conduction; the body would gain rather than lose heat were it entirely dependent upon these processes. At such temperatures, evaporation of water from the skin and lungs plays the leading role in the regulation of body temperature. The sweat glands are stimulated, and visible sweating appears when a rise of from $0.5°$ to $1°$ F in blood temperature occurs. The rise in blood temperature may result from an increase in the temperature of the environment or from increased heat production, as in muscular exercise.

The effect upon the sweat glands is brought about through a center in the brain from which they receive impulses through the sympathetic nerves. A rise in temperature of the blood supplying the center is the most potent factor in causing the secretion of sweat. This is shown by the fact that heating the carotid artery in the cat causes sweat secretion from the toe pads, though the paws themselves are kept cool. Sweating may also be induced reflexly—that is, from the stimulation of afferent nerves in the peripheral tissues, skin, muscles, etc.

In dogs and cats functional sweat glands are absent from the body surface, being confined to the skin of the pads of the paws. In these animals rapid breathing (panting) and, in consequence, increased vaporization of water from the lungs is relied upon to increase heat loss at high temperatures.

Summary. The quantities of heat lost daily in each of the several ways are given (in round numbers) in the following table.

	Calories
(a) Radiation and convection	1950
(b) Evaporation of water from the skin	550
(c) Evaporation of water from the lungs	350
(d) Warming inspired air to body temperature	90
(e) Urine and feces (i.e., heat of these excreta over that of the food)	60
Total daily heat loss	3000

Variations in the quantity of heat lost through these physical factors are capable, under ordinary circumstances, of maintaining the body temperature at the normal level, but at very high environmental temperatures or when, as in strenuous muscular effort, heat production is very greatly increased, the mechanisms of temperature control may be inadequate; the body temperature then rises.

CHEMICAL FACTORS IN TEMPERATURE CONTROL

At low environmental temperatures the physical mechanisms alone are incapable of reducing heat loss sufficiently to prevent a fall in body temperature. Chemical regulation then comes into play, that is, heat production increases. The body's fires, so to speak, are fanned. The point in the temperature scale where physical factors are aided by chemical means in the control of body temperature is called the *critical temperature*. It varies of course with the nature and thickness of the clothing, but for the naked human body it is around 28° C (82° F). Cold therefore acts as a powerful stimulus to metabolism. The greater heat production in response to cold is brought about mainly by increased tone and, in some instances, by involuntary contractions of the skeletal muscles (shivering) and the smooth muscle of the skin (gooseflesh). A person when cold usually indulges, also, in some form of muscular activity— walking, swinging his arms, or stamping his feet—which very materially increases his heat production (see Fig. 29.3).

At temperatures between 28° and 30° C the body (naked) is able to establish a balance between heat production and heat elimination without calling accessory mechanisms into play—sweating on the one hand and muscular contraction (shivering or voluntary muscular movements) on the other—and one therefore feels quite comfortable. This temperature range, or correspondingly lower temperatures for the clothed body, is for this reason called the *comfort zone*.

In cold climates protein food, owing to its specific stimulating effect upon metabolism (Ch. 31, footnote 1), gives valuable assistance to the chemical mechanism of temperature control. On the other hand, a high protein diet is unsuitable in hot weather, since the greater heat produc-

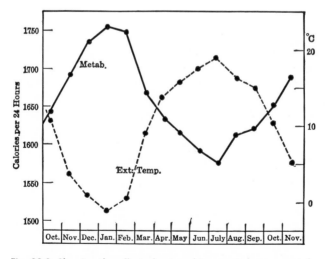

Fig. 29.3. Showing the effect of external temperature upon metabolism. (Redrawn from Martin after Gessler from observations upon himself.)

tion it induces throws an additional burden upon the mechanisms responsible for heat dissipation.

HEAT-CONTROLLING CENTERS

The main center for the control of body temperature is situated in the fore part of the **hypothalamus**—that region at the base of the brain near the origin of the pituitary stalk (Ch. 37). Isolation of this region by section of the brain stem or upper spinal cord renders an animal poikilothermic—that is, incapable of maintaining the height of its temperature independently of the temperature of its environment. This operation also paralyzes the skeletal muscles; the power to increase heat production is therefore largely lost. Stimulation of the center causes a rise in temperature. The center exerts its influence upon body temperature through the autonomic nervous system, causing vasoconstriction or vasodilatation, sweating, contraction of smooth muscle in the skin (shivering), and the liberation of adrenaline from the adrenal medulla which, as mentioned below, stimulates heat production.

These effects upon the sweat glands, vessels, and the adrenal gland are largely reflex in nature, the center being influenced by afferent impulses initiated in the temperature receptors of the skin. But such effects are also induced, as already mentioned, by a rise in the temperature of the blood supplying this region of the brain.

The endocrines and heat regulation. The secretions of both the thyroid and adrenal glands stimulate heat production. This effect, known as the *calorigenic action* of these hormones, enables an animal to withstand a greater degree of cold than is possible for one that has been deprived of either or both of these endocrines; the temperature of such animals is usually subnormal. Prolonged exposure to cold (over a period of weeks) causes an overproduction of the thyroid hormone, or, at any rate, the thyroid glands of rats who have been so treated show pronounced indications of increased activity and a rise in heat production. The latter effect does not appear in thyroidectomized animals similarly treated.

The hypersensitivity of hypothyroid patients to cold and of hyperthyroid patients to a warm environment are well known.

Fever, or pyrexia. A rise in body temperature above the normal level, unless of a temporary nature, as in strenuous exercise or as a result of exposure to a high air temperature, is called fever, or pyrexia. The highest body temperature compatible with life is between 111° and 112° F. The rise in temperature is due primarily to an *impairment of the mechanisms for heat elimination*, for example, increased blood volume, vasodilatation, and sweat secretion; and not to increased heat production. At the commencement of a fever, for example, the skin is pale and dry; the metabolism is not increased. Heat elimination is reduced; heat is therefore retained in the body and the temperature rises. Having reached a certain height, the temperature remains fairly steady, for now heat elimination keeps pace with heat production; a balance is struck, but at a higher level than in health. Though, as just mentioned, increased heat production is not responsible for the *onset* of the fever, the higher temperature induced through heat retention causes, in turn, greater heat production, for the heat generated in the body is the result of chemical reactions, mainly oxidative in nature, and like chemical reactions in general, they are accelerated by a rise in temperature. Also, as described below, if a chill occurs heat production is increased reflexly.

In acute infectious diseases and in bacterial infections generally, the accompanying fever is due to an action of the bacterial toxin upon the heat-regulating centers, for in animals whose brain has been cut across below the centers, the injection of a toxin, which in a normal animal would cause a sharp rise in temperature, does not cause fever. In some instances the bacterial toxin may act *directly* upon the heat-regulating centers, but probably its action is, as a rule, an *indirect* one, the first effect being to produce in the tissues chemical changes that alter the osmotic pressure of the tissue fluids, causing the withdrawal of water from the vascular system and, as a consequence, a reduction in the dissipation of heat by radiation. The reduced blood volume also causes the drainage of warm blood from the skin, and, as would a cold bath, stimulates cold receptors. A response from the heat centers is evoked leading to a great increase in heat production caused by involuntary contractions of muscles—that is, to shivering and shaking. One of the first symptoms at the onset of an acute infectious fever is often a feeling of intense cold, frequently with shivering, shaking of the limbs, and chattering of the teeth. The temperature taken in the mouth at this time of the "chill" is found to be high, though the skin may feel cold even to the hand of another person. The patient's lips and nose appear pinched, pale or even bluish. The mechanism of a "chill" and the subsequent increase in heat production by shivering, etc., may be compared, for the sake of illustration, to that controlling the temperature of a room isolated from a temperature-sensitive instrument (thermostat) connected by wires with a device controlling the fire in the furnace heating the room. When the instrument is exposed to a cold draft, the furnace blazes up and the room is overheated. The thermostat is analogous to the cold receptors (Ch. 32) of the skin. These sense organs are stimulated because the constricted vessels deprive them of warm blood from the deeper tissues. The heat centers in the brain connected through sensory nerves with the cold receptors and the muscles are comparable, respectively, to the mechanism controlling the fire in the furnace and to the furnace itself.

Heat stroke, heat exhaustion, and sunstroke. After a person has been exposed to a high temperature for a time, his heat-regulating mechanism may fail, and very serious symptoms, even death, may result. The effects of extreme heat fall into two categories known, respectively, as *heat stroke* and *heat exhaustion*. In the former, a person exposed to great heat, often while undergoing some physical exertion, suddenly becomes unconscious. The body temperature is found to be very high, and in a severe case may reach 108° or 110° F. Sweat secretion is suppressed; both blood volume and urine volume are increased. In heat exhaustion, the symptoms develop more gradually and consist of abdominal cramps, rapid pulse, low systolic blood pressure, and sometimes dizziness and dyspnea. The blood and urine volumes are reduced, and the chloride of the blood and urine is much below normal (due to loss of chloride in the sweat). Sunstroke is merely a form of heat stroke or heat exhaustion, the body absorbing heat from the direct rays of the sun. There is no special effect of the sun's rays apart from their heat, in causing the symptoms of so-called sunstroke.

Heat cramps. Painful muscular spasms occur if the sodium chloride of the body fluids falls to a low level, as may result from prolonged and excessive sweating. The condition is quickly corrected by the administration of salt.

30

The Metabolism of Carbohydrate, Fat, Protein, and Purines. DNA and RNA

CARBOHYDRATE METABOLISM

Classification of the carbohydrates. Carbohydrates (sugars, starches, etc.) are composed of *carbon, hydrogen,* and *oxygen.* The last two elements are present in the same proportions as in water (H_2O). Thus, the three sugars **glucose** (or *dextrose*), **fructose** (or *levulose*), and **galactose** contain 6 molecules of water and 6 atoms of carbon, as shown by their formula, $C_6H_{12}O_6$. These sugars are, therefore called **hexoses** (Gr. *hex,* six). Though they have a common formula—that is, the same number of each type of atom—the positions of the atoms in the molecules of each differ.

Glucose is found in fruits and in the blood and tissues of animals. Fructose is the chief sugar of honey. Galactose is present as a component of the disaccharide **lactose,** in milk, being combined in the molecule with glucose. It is also found as a constituent of certain fatty compounds in brain tissue. Other much less common sugars have molecules containing 7, 5, 4, 3, or 2 carbon atoms and a corresponding number of water molecules. Employing Greek prefixes, they are called heptoses, pentoses, tetroses, trioses, and dioses, respectively. Thus a heptose is represented by the formula $C_7H_{14}O_7$, a pentose by $C_5H_{10}O_5$, a tetrose by $C_4H_8O_4$, and so on. Octoses, nonoses, and decoses, though not known in nature, have been prepared in the laboratory.

Sugars belonging to the class just outlined are called **monosaccharides,** and may be represented by the general formula $C_n(H_2O)_n$, in which n has the value 2, 3, 4, 5, 6, 7, and so forth.

Disaccharides are sugars composed of two monosaccharide molecules less a molecule of water. **Sucrose** (cane, beet, and maple sugars), **maltose** (sugar of malt), and **lactose** (sugar of milk) belong to this group. Though a disaccharide may be made up of other monosaccharides, these three, which are important food elements and therefore of physiological interest, consist of hexoses either of the same or of different kinds. Their formula is $C_{12}H_{22}O_{11}$. They are split (hydrolyzed) into their constituent monosaccharides by the actions of specific enzymes in the intestine. Thus,

$$C_{12}H_{22}O_{11} + H_2O = 2C_6H_{12}O_6$$

Sucrose can be broken by the action of enzymes or strong acids into a molecule each of glucose and fructose, maltose into two molecules of glucose, and lactose into glucose and galactose.

Polysaccharides are made up of a large number of monosaccharides that may be either pentoses or hexoses, less a molecule of water. The polysaccharides of physiological importance, namely, the **vegetable starches, glycogen** ("animal starch"), **cellulose**, and **dextrins** are constituted of hexose molecules, and are therefore given the general formula $(C_6H_{10}O_5)_n$. They yield glucose.

Glycogen, which was discovered by the great French physiologist Claude Bernard, is found in traces in most tissues of the body and in fairly large amounts in liver and muscle. Muscle, including the myocardium, may contain any amount of glycogen between 0.10 and 1.0 percent of fresh tissue. Since approximately one half the total weight of our bodies is muscle, it will be appreciated that the total quantity of muscle glycogen is very considerable. The liver often contains as much as 10 or 15 percent of its wet weight of glycogen, and though it makes up only about 3 percent of the body weight, its total glycogen content is comparable with that of the muscular tissues.

Glucose is found in all body tissues; blood contains approximately 0.1 percent, but there is considerable variation in the amount in health as well as in disease. It is the most important single carbohydrate with which we have to deal in physiology. As such it can be used as food, passing unchanged from the small intestine into the blood, while complex carbohydrates, such as the disaccharides and polysaccharides (starches and glycogen), must first be hydrolyzed into glucose or other hexoses before they can be absorbed.

Glucose (as well as fructose and galactose) passes from the intestine into the blood of the portal vein to the liver. It may (1) pass through the liver unchanged and be oxidized in the tissues, thus providing an immediate source of energy, (2) be converted to glycogen and as such, stored in the liver, or (3) be deposited in the connective tissues of various parts of the body as fat, especially in the subcutaneous tissues, omentum, and around the internal organs.

The conversion of glucose to glycogen is a specific function of the liver cells, and is termed **glycogenesis** (literally, glycogen formation). The glucose in the blood is maintained at a fairly constant level by the reconversion of glycogen to glucose, which is then discharged into the general circulation. This process is termed **glycogenolysis** (literally, glycogen breakdown).

Muscle glycogen is derived from the glucose of the blood. During muscular contraction energy is furnished mainly by carbohydrates; the muscle glycogen breaks down into its constituent glucose molecules. Lactic acid, which is ultimately produced, is in part resynthesized to glycogen and in part oxidized.

Insulin—the carbohydrate hormone. Insulin is a hormone secreted by certain groups of cells in the pancreas called the *islets of Langerhans* (see Fig. 27.3).

Insulin promotes the combustion of glucose by the tissue cells, as well as the conversion of glucose to glycogen and the storage of the latter in the liver and muscles. If given in overdosage, this hormone causes a profound fall in the blood sugar of a normal person or of a diabetic patient. The subnormal level of the blood glucose, which is called *hypoglycemia,* causes an abnormal excitability of the nervous centers; disturbances in locomotion and other muscular movements, or generalized convulsions and loss of consciousness may result. A diabetic who has received an overdose of insulin may show such effects. His muscular incoordination and his mental vagueness may lead people to think him drunk, and the police are called to take him in charge. Of course, if he is thrown into a cell to recover from his "drunkenness" he will not improbably die.

Hypoglycemia stimulates the medulla of the adrenal glands. This is beneficial, for **adrenaline,** the secretion of these glands, has an effect on the blood glucose the reverse of that caused by insulin. The hypoglycemia therefore tends to moderate. But the effect of adrenaline liberation is not capable of raising the blood sugar to normal. Nor will an injection of this hormone abolish the convulsions. The surest way to do this is by an injection of a glucose solution; even sugar by mouth in the form of candies (which usually contain glucose) is effective.

Diabetes mellitus. This is a disease caused by an insufficient supply of insulin, resulting in turn from disease that destroys the cells of the islets of Langerhans in the pancreas or depresses their function.

When the pancreas is removed from an animal, a condition known as pancreatic diabetes rapidly develops. This is characterized by an abnormally high blood sugar (*hyperglycemia*), and the excretion of sugar in the urine. The extent of the increase of blood glucose and of the loss of glucose in the urine (*glucosuria,* or *glycosuria*) is proportional to the carbohydrate content of the diet, but even on a diet composed entirely of protein, or during fasting, the depancreatized animal excretes a considerable amount of sugar. The glucose reserves of the body, for example, liver glycogen, are rapidly lost. Sugar is then made from tissue protein, the animal losing weight as a result. The fat depots are also called upon; the fat may be oxidized directly or first converted to glucose. At any rate, the increased rate of breakdown of fat results in the accumulation of ketone bodies in the blood (*ketosis*) and urine (*ketonuria*).

The ketone bodies are β-hydroxybutyric and acetoacetic acids, and acetone. The two organic acids are normal intermediate products in the metabolism of fat, β-hydroxybutyric acid being derived through oxidation from acetoacetic acid. Both are present in the body in health though only in small amounts, acetoacetic acid undergoing almost complete oxidation to carbon dioxide and water. When, on the other hand, the metabolism of carbohydrate is defective, as in diabetes, for some reason not altogether clear, excessive quantities of fat are metabolized; acetoacetic acid is formed in such large amounts that it cannot be completely oxidized. It and β-hydroxybutyric acid accumulate in the blood and tissues, and are responsible for the acidosis and coma of diabetes. Acetoacetic acid is believed to be an especially toxic product. In diabetes, it is converted, through the loss of a molecule of carbon dioxide, to acetone, a volatile substance that often gives the breath of the diabetic a characteristic odor. It is also excreted in the urine.

All the signs and symptoms seen in animals following removal of the pancreas are seen in human diabetes mellitus. The chief symptoms are excessive thirst and hunger, and loss of weight. Large amounts of glucose are passed in the urine even though carbohydrate is excluded from the diet (p. 415).

The discovery of insulin has not solved the problem of the primary cause of diabetes, but has provided an effective means of treating the disease. It has also furnished a most valuable "tool" for studying carbohydrate metabolism. Insulin administered subcutaneously or intravenously eliminates all the signs of diabetes in experimental animals or in human patients. Its action is to promote the storage of glycogen in muscles and liver, to depress the wasteful new production of sugar in the liver, and to increase the oxidation of carbohydrate. The hyperglycemia and glucosuria disappear. Ketosis is eliminated. The rapid loss of body tissues is checked.

Insulin has now been prepared in crystalline form; it is a protein containing eight or more amino acids. The highly purified insulin is absorbed quickly when administered subcutaneously, and efforts have been made to lengthen the period of absorption, that is to prolong its action. The most satisfactory preparation thus far developed for this purpose is protomine zinc insulin, which is made by adding protamine and zinc to insulin. Protamine is a simple protein obtained from fish sperm.

While a deficiency of insulin causes diabetes, overproduction is responsible for a clinical condition called *hyperinsulinism*. The outstanding features of this disease are a low blood sugar (*hypoglycemia*), and the symptoms incident thereto (see above).

Other hormones and carbohydrate metabolism. The influence upon carbohydrate metabolism of certain hormones of the anterior lobe of the pituitary is described in Chapter 38, and of thyroxine and the hormones of the adrenal gland in Chapters 39 and 40, respectively.

These several hormones constitute a complex but delicately balanced mechanism whereby the metabolism of carbohydrate is regulated. The various phases of, and the ceaseless changes in carbohydrate metabolism —the utilization of glucose by the tissues, the formation and storage of glycogen and its breakdown to glucose, and the new formation of glucose from protein and fat—all come under the influence of one or more of the hormones mentioned. Due to their reciprocal actions the sugar of the blood and other body fluids is maintained at an approximately constant concentration.

The nervous system and carbohydrate metabolism. In 1855 Claude Bernard showed that injury to the brain that involved the pons and the cerebellum as well as the floor of the fourth ventricle produced hyperglycemia and glucosuria. It appears probable that these lesions set up nerve impulses that cause the breakdown of liver glycogen. This may be due to the conduction of the impulses directly to the liver or may be an indirect result of adrenaline liberation. It will be appreciated that interference with the nerve supply of any of the glands whose secretions affect carbohydrates may exert a profound influence on the metabolism of these substances.

FAT METABOLISM

The neutral fats. The common fats of vegetable and animal tissues are compounds of the higher fatty acids **palmitic** ($C_{16}H_{32}O_2$), **stearic** ($C_{18}H_{36}O_2$), and **oleic** ($C_{18}H_{34}O_2$) with the triatomic alcohol **glycerol** ($C_3H_5(OH)_3$). Each molecule of glycerol (or glycerin) is combined with three molecules of one or another of these fatty acids. The resulting compound (or ester) is called a *neutral fat,* or **triglyceride.** Depending upon the particular fatty acids in the triglyceride molecule, the three chief fats are named **tripalmitin, tristearin,** and **triolein,** respectively.

The fatty tissues of animals consist of connective tissue in which is deposited a mixture of neutral fats, triolein being in the greatest proportion. Tripalmitin is present in smaller and tristearin in least amount.

The triglycerides are hydrolyzed by the intestinal enzymes (lipases) into their constituents—fatty acids and glycerol. In the presence of alkali, fat is decomposed, the fatty acid then reacting to form soap. Thus,

$$C_3H_5(C_{18}H_{35}O_2)_3 + 3NaOH = 3CH_3(CH_2)_{16}COONa + C_3H_5(OH)_3$$

| tristearin | sodium hydroxide | sodium stearate (a soap) | glycerol |

Fatlike and waxy substances—the lipids. The two most important subdivisions of the lipids are the **sterols** and the **phospholipids.**

Cholesterol is a waxy substance belonging to the sterols. It is very widely distributed throughout animal tissues, especially in nerve sheaths and skin. Irradiation of a form of cholesterol in the skin by ultraviolet light gives rise to vitamin D. Cholesterol is closely related to the bile salts, and to the sex and the adrenal cortical hormones.

Ergosterol, a sterol found in plant tissues, also acquires antirachitic properties upon irradiation with ultraviolet light (Ch. 31).

The **phospholipids,** or **phosphatides,** are essential constituents of animal and vegetable cells. Brain, muscle, liver, bile, milk, and eggs contain these substances in especially large amounts. To this class of substance **lecithin, cephalin,** and **sphingomyelin** belong. Upon hydrolysis they yield fatty acids, phosphoric acid, and a nitrogenous base. The nitrogenous element in lecithin is **choline.**

The storage of fat. Every tissue in the body contains at least some fat or fatlike material, but the great store houses—the fat depots, as they are sometimes called—are the subcutaneous tissues, the abdomen (in the omentum and surrounding the extraperitoneal viscera such as the kidney), and the connective tissue between the muscles. The liver also contains considerable quantities of fat. In fat the body possesses the most compact material for the storage of energy, for over twice as much heat is produced when a gram of it is burned as when sugar or protein undergoes combustion in the "fires" of our bodies. It is very interesting, also, that fat is the only one of the three major classes of food material that is stored free of water. Carbohydrate and protein are stored in combination with water, which forms more than half the total weight of these stored materials. This means that at least four times as much energy is stored in an ounce of fat as in the same weight of stored carbohydrate or protein. All types of food—carbohydrate, the carbon part of the amino acids composing protein, and fat itself—are stored as fat when they are consumed in excess of the energy requirements of the body at the time. Every farmer knows that he can fatten his stock by feeding them wheat, oats, and other carbohydrate material and reducing their activity to a minimum.

The function of the liver in the metabolism of fat. Fat, when required to furnish energy, is liberated from the body's stores and conveyed to the liver in the blood stream. Having reached the liver, it apparently must first be converted to phospholipid (lecithin). The fatty acids are then oxidized, and compounds with only 4 carbon atoms, acetoacetic acid $(C_4H_6O_3)$ and betahydroxybutyric acid $(C_4H_8O_3)$, are produced. We have seen that these ketone bodies are formed greatly in excess in diabetes. These 4-carbon-atom compounds are finally oxidized in the cells of the general tissues.

Disturbances of fat metabolism. In certain abnormal states of the endocrine organs, for example, defective thyroid or pituitary function, or of the hypothalamus, the deposition of fat may greatly exceed the normal (Chs. 37, 38). On the other hand, overactivity of the thyroid gland (Ch. 39) causes depletion of the fat stores. Persons with such overactive glands are usually underweight.

Obesity. Overweight of the body due to the excessive accumulation of fat is called *obesity*, or *adiposity*. Though a very common state, it must, unless of very moderate degree, be considered an abnormality. Obesity is a definite hazard to the general health, and in several ways puts the physiological processes at a disadvantage. It places a greater than necessary burden upon the heart at all times, but especially in the performance of muscular work. Diabetes, arterial hypertension, degenerative changes in the arteries, and gallstones are among the conditions much more common in the obese than in persons of normal or subnormal weight. These are some of the penalties paid by the fat man for his fatness. Diabetes has been called the "fat man's folly." Obesity tends to reduce the body's resistance to infection, and the extremely obese person is looked upon as a poor risk by the surgeon, as well as by the insurance examiner. Someone has stated the case of the overweight person of middle age in respect to life expectancy in the epigram "the longer the belt the shorter the life." this is well borne out by insurance statistics. In persons over 45 years of age, the death rate for those who are overweight is considerably above the average, while that of lean persons is below average.

The cause of obesity. Though, as mentioned above, obesity is sometimes due to an endocrine disorder or other specific disease, this is rare. The common type of obesity, which is usually referred to as *simple* obesity, is due to an intake of energy (food) in excess of the energy output (work). That is to say, the subject eats too much for the physical work he does, or he prefers foods of higher caloric value than does a person of normal weight. The excess food is deposited as fat. This conclusion has been frequently questioned, but experiments upon human subjects have failed repeatedly to prove it false.

PROTEIN METABOLISM

The distribution of protein. Protein material enters largely into the composition of all types of protoplasm, both of animal and vegetable origin. Among foods, meat (muscle), cheese, eggs, beans, and peas (legumes) are the richest sources. Its basic elements are *carbon, hydrogen, oxygen, nitrogen,* and *sulfur,* and usually *phosphorus.* Its content of the latter three elements distinguishes it from either fats or carbohydrates, which contain only carbon, hydrogen, and oxygen. The body is dependent almost entirely upon protein for its supplies of nitrogen and sulfur, and mainly for its phosphorus.

The structure of the protein molecule—amino acids. It was stated in Chapter 24 that the protein molecule was built up from amino acids. For this reason the amino acids are often referred to as the "building stones" of protein. During digestion the protein building is placed in the hands of the "wreckers"—the enzymes of the alimentary tract. The building stones are torn apart, and after passing through the intestinal mucosa, are conveyed by the blood to various tissues of the body, where they are reunited in the building of new tissue (as during growth) or used in repairing dilapidations sustained by the protein fabrics composing muscle, brain, liver, kidney, etc.

Some twenty-five kinds of amino acids have been discovered. A partial list is given in the following table (see also Appendix). The simplest

A PARTIAL LIST OF THE AMINO ACIDS[1]

Glycine (or glycocoll), $C_2H_5NO_2$, or aminoacetic acid
Alanine, $C_3H_7NO_2$, or α-aminopropionic acid
*Threonine, $C_4H_9NO_3$, or α-amino-β-hydroxybutyric acid
*Valine, $C_5H_{11}NO_2$, or α-aminoisovaleric acid
*Leucine, $C_6H_{13}NO_2$, or α-aminoisocaproic acid
*Isoleucine, $C_6H_{13}NO_2$, or α-amino-β-ethyl-β-methylpropionic acid
Aspartic acid, $C_4H_7NO_4$, or aminosuccinic acid
Glutamic acid, $C_5H_9NO_4$, or α-aminoglutaric acid
*Arginine, $C_6H_{14}N_4O_2$, or δ-guanidin-α-aminovalerianic acid
*Lysine, $C_6H_{14}N_2O_2$, or α-ε-diaminocaproic acid
Cystine, $C_6H_{12}N_2S_2O_4$, or dicysteine, or di(β-thio-α-aminopropionic acid)
*Methionine, $C_5H_{11}SNO_2$, or α-amino-γ-methylthiobutyric acid
*Phenylalanine, $C_9H_{11}NO_2$, or β-phenyl-α-aminopropionic acid
Tyrosine, $C_9H_{11}NO_3$, or β-parahydroxyphenyl-α-aminopropionic acid
*Tryptophan, $C_{11}H_{12}N_2O_2$, or β-indole-α-aminopropionic acid
*Histidine, $C_6H_9N_3O_2$, or α-amino-β-imidazolepropionic acid

amino acid is **glycine,** or **glycocoll,** which consists of acetic acid in which a hydrogen atom has been replaced by an NH_2 group. Thus,

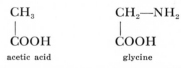

It is therefore also called aminoacetic acid. The majority of the other amino acids are constructed upon the same general plan. They contain a fatty acid, for example, propionic, valerianic, caproic, succinic, etc., and one or two NH_2 (amino) groups. They are combined in the protein molecule by the linking together of COOH (carboxyl) groups with NH_2

---

[1] The asterisk indicates an essential amino acid; see discussion below.

groups. This is called *peptid linkage*. When the amino acids are separated, as by enzyme action, it is here also that the split occurs, a molecule of water being first taken up. This is another example of the process known as *hydrolysis* or *hydrolytic cleavage* described elsewhere.

Several proteins contain more than 15 *varieties* of amino acids, but the assortment varies between different types of protein. The *total number* of amino acids in a protein molecule may be 200 or more. Such proteins are composed, therefore, of molecules of relatively enormous size. The molecules of certain other proteins, such as the protamines, contain much fewer amino acids and are correspondingly smaller. There is thus a very wide variation in the size and weight of the molecules of the different types of protein. The shape of the protein molecule also varies. The molecules of some proteins, such as the myosin of muscle and of that forming tendons and ligaments (collagen), are long and fiberlike in shape, while others, such as those of serum albumin, are globular. Some of the commoner food proteins are given in Table 30.1.

The growth of body tissue in the young animal and the repair of protein structure in the adult body are dependent upon the protein (amino acid) content of the diet. But since the tissue protein of a given animal is different in constitution from the protein of its food, the latter must be completely broken down into its separate amino acids before it can be utilized for building body tissue.

Those amino acids that cannot be built into body tissue are broken up; the carbon part of the molecule (that is, the fatty acid group) is oxidized to carbon dioxide and water, thus furnishing energy to the body, or is converted to body fat; the nitrogen goes to form urea which is excreted in the urine. The removal of the nitrogen (amino) group from the amino acid molecule is called *deamination;* this process and the production thereby of urea occurs chiefly in the liver. Certain amino acids not used for the construction of body protein may, after undergoing deamination, be converted to glucose which is then either oxidized or stored in the liver as glycogen (p. 408). In diabetes the glucose formed from amino acids is largely excreted in the urine. The diabetic subject, therefore, continues to excrete sugar though he receives no sugar or other carbohydrate; even during fasting he continues to excrete glucose, which is then derived from the protein of his own tissues (see Ch. 30).

The **urea** in the urine is formed mainly as a result of the deamination of amino acids composing the protein of the food. Raising the protein content of the diet, therefore, increases the output of urea in the urine and vice versa. But the urea is not entirely derived from the diet; a small part is formed from the nitrogen released by the breakdown of body protein, for the tissues are constantly undergoing disintegration and repair. A small quantity of nitrogen, combined in various ways, is also eliminated from the body by passing through the wall of the intestine from the blood into the feces.

During starvation or upon a protein-poor diet, the breakdown of body protein of course continues. The body loses nitrogen through the so-called "wear and tear" of tissue protein, but receives none to make good the loss. That is to say, the output of nitrogen in the urine and feces exceeds that of the food; the body is then said to be in *negative nitrogen balance*. Similarly, the nitrogen output will exceed the intake and the body will be in negative nitrogen balance if the food protein is inadequate in amount or of poor quality (that is, if its assortment of amino acids is unsuitable for repairing body protein, the nonutilizable amino acids being excreted in the urine). In the healthy adult receiving an adequate diet, the nitrogen excreted just balances the nitrogen taken in the food—that is, the nitrogen lost as a result of the breakdown of tissue protein is replaced from the food; the remainder of the food nitrogen is excreted. The body is then said to be in *nitrogen equilibrium*.

During growth, after a period of starvation, in pregnancy, in muscular training, or in convalescence from some disease that has caused the excessive destruction of body protein, the quantity of nitrogen excreted is *less* than that taken in the food, provided the protein intake is adequate. The body is then in *positive nitrogen balance*. In other words, nitrogen is retained for the construction of body tissue.

The essential amino acids and the relative nutritional values of different proteins. An *essential,* or *indispensable,* amino acid may be defined as one that must be present in the diet in order that the growth of young animals may proceed normally, and that the health of both young and old animals be maintained. In a sense, probably all or at least most of the amino acids are essential in one way or another for nutrition, but some can be synthesized in the body, for example, *glycine,* or formed from others furnished in the diet. It is not necessary, therefore, that such amino acids shall themselves be present in the food. There are 10 essential amino acids; they are marked with an asterisk in the table on page 414.

Proteins are not all of equal value in nutrition, for the reason that the various types differ widely in their amino acid constitution. Those that possess an amino acid assortment most closely resembling that of the body's proteins have the highest nutritive value. Generally speaking, and as might be expected, these are of animal origin—for instance, the proteins of milk, eggs, and meat. Some proteins, such as *gelatin* and *zein* (in maize), are incomplete—that is, they lack certain amino acids that are essential for growth and the maintenance of nitrogen equilibrium in the adult. Others, such as *gliadin* (in wheat), *hordein* (in barley), and *legumin* (in peas), will serve to repair body protein in the adult but will not support growth, since they lack certain essential amino acids or contain them in insufficient amounts. Young animals that receive one or another of these as their sole protein fail to grow. Wheat, peas, and barley, however, contain other proteins that make good the amino acid deficiencies of those that are incomplete (see Table 30.1). *Lactalbumin* of milk, *ovalbumin* of egg white and *ovoitellin* of egg yolk, *albumin* and *myosin* of meat, and *glutenin* of wheat contain all the essential amino acids. (See also RNA and protein synthesis, p. 419.)

TABLE 30.1

CHARACTER OF PROTEINS IN SOME COMMON FOODS

Food	Chief proteins present	Amino acid constitution
Milk and cheese	Casein	Complete but low in cystine
	Lactalbumin	Complete
Corn (maize)	Zein	Incomplete, lacks lysine and tryptophan; low in cystine
Eggs	Ovalbumin	Complete
	Ovovitellin	Complete
Meat	Albumin	Complete
	Myosin	Complete
Peas	Legumin	Incomplete, low in cystine
Wheat	Gliadin	Incomplete, lacks lysine
	Glutenin	Complete
Gelatin	Gelatin	Incomplete, lacks tryptophan and tyrosine; very low in cystine

In part from M. S. Rose, *Foundations of Nutrition.*

PURINE METABOLISM; DNA AND RNA

Many years ago a Swiss scientist discovered a nitrogenous compound in the nuclei of cells which he named **nucleic acid.** Nucleic acid combined with protein—**nucleoprotein**—or closely associated with protein is found in the nucleus and cytoplasm of all cells, both animal and plant, and in viruses. Viruses are virtually pure nucleoprotein, but their infectivity resides in the nucleic acid alone for it is not abolished by removal of the protein. When a bacterial virus (bacteriophage), for example, attacks a bacterium the nucleic acid enters the cell and leaves the protein behind.

The nucleic acid molecule consists of four compounds called **nucleotides,** which in turn are composed of *phosphoric acid,* a *pentose* (a 5-carbon sugar), and a *nitrogenous base.* There are five principal forms of the latter—*adenine* and *guanine,* called *purines;* and *cytosine, thymine,* and *uracil,* known as *pyrimidines*—any one of which may combine with the phosphoric acid and pentose groups to form a nucleotide. The phosphoric acid group of one nucleotide is linked to the pentose group of the next, forming polynucleotide chains.

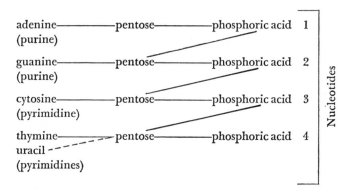

There are two kinds of nucleic acid, which differ in the type of pentose they contain. In one the 5-carbon sugar is *deoxyribose,* in the other it is *ribose;* and the former sugar contains one less oxygen atom than does the latter. The nucleic acid containing deoxyribose is named **deoxyribonucleic acid,** abbreviated **DNA;** that formed with ribose is **ribonucleic acid,** or **RNA.** DNA and RNA also differ in one of their pyrimidine bases: the fourth nucleotide of DNA contains thymine whereas the corresponding pyrimidine in RNA is uracil. The chief chemical differences between the two kinds of nucleic acid are summarized below.

	DNA	RNA
Sugar	Deoxyribose	Ribose
Bases	Adenine	Adenine
	Guanine	Guanine
	Cytosine	Cytosine
	Thymine	Uracil

DNA is found only in the nucleus; it forms about 40 percent of the substance of the chromatin, the remaining 60 percent being made up of 59 percent protein and 1 percent RNA. Ribonucleic acid is present in all parts of the cell—nucleus and cytoplasm. But most of the RNA is concentrated in ultramicroscopic[2] bodies called *microsomes,* or *ribosomes,* scattered throughout the cytoplasm, where it is associated with an equal amount of protein. RNA is synthesized in the nucleus and passes to the nucleolus; here it is temporarily stored to be gradually released and taken up by the ribosomes. RNA is also present in relatively low concentra-

[2] Ultramicroscopic refers to the ordinary light microscope, not to the electron microscope.

tion in the mitochondria. These threadlike or rod-shaped bodies are rich in enzymes and have a high metabolism. They appear to be the power-houses of the cell wherein the potential energy of food is harnessed for the performance of work.

A great mass of experimental evidence has been accumulated within recent years that points to DNA as the ultimate genetic material—the basic substance constituting the units of heredity, the *genes*—and indeed the essence of life itself. The high concentration of DNA in the chromo-somes is presumptive of this, but more direct evidence has been obtained from experiments upon two strains of pneumococcus.[3]

Except in the case of plant viruses (for example, the virus of tobacco mosaic) and certain animal viruses (of influenza and poliomyelitis) RNA seems to play no primary genetic role. There is convincing evi-dence, however, that this nucleic acid is an essential agent in protein synthesis within the cell, the short segments of the RNA helix (see below) in the ribosomes serving as platforms, or "templates," on which are arranged sites, or "stalls," in a definite pattern. RNA in solution out-side the ribosomes attaches itself to an amino acid in the cytoplasm and leads it into its appropriate stall on the ribosome template. These leaders are termed *transfer RNA*, of which a specific one exists for each of the twenty-odd amino acids. The protein when formed from a selection of amino acids passes from the ribosome into the surrounding cytoplasm.

Model of a nucleic acid molecule. The nucleotides—many hundreds or even thousands of them—are strung together in long parallel chains or strands to form huge molecules. From the data of many experiments and observations a model of such a molecule has been constructed (Fig. 30.1). In this model the chains are paired and twisted into a spiral or helix. The strands consist of alternate phosphoric acid and pentose groups from which the nitrogenous bases are given off at right angles; the latter connect and hold the strands together. The purine base of one strand is always linked to a pyrimidine base of the other. The purine-pyrimidine links are almost invariably guanine to cytosine, and, in the case of DNA, adenine to thymine.[4] A mutation, it is thought, may be the result of a "mistake" in this linkage, for example, guanine to thymine,

[3] There are a large number of pneumococcal types; normally all have capsules composed of carbohydrate, which differs in the various strains. Occasionally mutants arise that lack a capsule. When this happens rough, dull colonies are formed that can easily be distinguished from the smooth, glistening colonies of the capsulated form. In rare instances the "rough" mutants revert to the "smooth" form, but the reversion is always to the original type; that is to say, if the rough variety arose from smooth forms of Type II, when they again become smooth their capsules identify them as belonging to this same type (Type II). Now if these bacteria are cultured in a medium containing the ground-up bacteria of another type, say Type III, they acquire the characteristics of the latter. The material in the ground-up cells that exerts this effect has been shown to be DNA.

[4] In the RNA molecule, as mentioned above, uracil takes the place of thymine and therefore pairs with adenine.

AXIS OF ROTATION

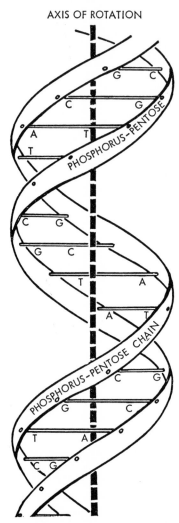

Fig. 30.1. Diagram of a DNA model. A = adenine; C = cytosine; G = guanine; T = thymine.

or adenine to cytosine. Such a construction of the nucleic acid molecule might be compared to a spiral staircase in which the handrails are the phosphate-pentose strands, and the treads, the purine-pyrimidine cross links. A gene is probably a segment of such a double helix.

The reader may ask, How with only four variables, the nucleotides, could such an immense number of species, which must differ by at least one gene, have come into being? But upon reflection he may recall that any word of the millions in all the languages of the world can be transmitted by a particular combination of only two symbols, a dot and a dash, with a maximum sequence of six per letter. The "code" by which a gene's "message"—*genetic information*—is transmitted is a four-symbol one—the *nucleotides.* The possible combinations and permutations are illimitable.

The fate and excretion of nucleic acid. The purine of the nucleic acid molecule is broken down to **uric acid,** which is excreted by the kidneys. Uric acid is the end product of purine metabolism in man and other mammals, just as urea is the end product of protein metabolism in these species. But in birds and reptiles uric acid is the end product of *both* protein and purine metabolism. Uric acid is of especial medical interest because in the arthritic disease known as *gout* its concentration in the blood is increased and its excretion in the urine reduced. Chalky deposits of compounds of uric acid (urates) are found in the soft tissues, such as the lobes of the ears or around the joints; they are called *tophi.* In this disease foods rich in nuclear material, especially the glandular tissues, liver, sweetbreads (thymus or pancreas), etc., should be avoided, and non-nucleated items, such as milk and eggs, to a large extent substituted.

31
Nutrition. Minerals and Vitamins

The body derives its energy solely from food (chiefly fat and carbohydrate). It receives the materials necessary for growth and repair largely from protein. Lean meat, which is from 20 to 25 percent protein and the remainder water, glycogen, and salts, possesses insufficient energy value as the sole food for man. The particular value of meat is that it furnishes protein for growth, for the repair of body tissue, or for the manufacture of essential secretions (Ch. 30).

We have already seen how the digestive processes prepare the foodstuffs for absorption into the blood and for their utilization by the tissue cells. But materials other than these three food principles are necessary in order that the efficiency of certain vital functions shall be maintained. A certain quantity of water must be taken into the body daily, since moisture is lost in the breath, urine, and feces, and from the surface of the body. Certain substances—salts and vitamins, in small amounts—are also absolutely essential.

The processes whereby the body makes use of these various substances and achieves that state which we all recognize as normal and healthy are embraced in the word *nutrition*. The production of energy and the processes of tissue growth and repair have been spoken of in the preceding chapter. Other phases of nutrition may now be considered.

THE NEED FOR MINERALS AND WATER

Minerals—inorganic salts. Numerous minerals in the form of their salts are found in small amounts in our diets. Calcium and phosphorus are necessary in quite large amounts to provide calcium phosphate—the important salt of which the bones are mainly formed. Iron is necessary for the formation of hemoglobin and the pigment of muscle, and for certain enzymes essential for tissue respiration. Iodine is an essential component of the active substance made by the thyroid gland—thyroxine. Calcium and phosphorus are found in milk and meat. Iron is obtained from vegetables such as spinach, from fruits, and from meat. Iodine is present in abundant amounts in the foods grown on certain soils, but in other regions the soil is deficient in this element and cannot supply it to the plant life. The significance of iodine is also discussed under the thyroid gland (Ch. 39). Common salt (sodium chloride) and other soluble salts must be supplied to the blood and tissue fluids in order that a suitable environment may be maintained for the cells bathed by these fluids. Zinc, copper, cobalt, manganese, fluorine, and certain other elements that are required in minute amounts are called "trace elements."

Water. From 75 to 80 percent of the soft tissues of animals is water. Water is lost from the body in the breath, in the perspiration, and through the kidneys. The water content of the body must be maintained at a constant level, since excessive loss of water may cause great damage. We obtain water in our food and drink, and in addition, water is formed in our bodies by the oxidation of the hydrogen of the food. This is called the water of metabolism (see Ch. 28).

PLANNING A BALANCED DIET

In planning a diet the following must be taken into account:

1. The total energy requirement—that is, the heat, or caloric, value of the food.

2. The proportions of the three main foodstuffs—carbohydrates, fats, and proteins.

3. Essential minerals.

4. Vitamins.

The diet of a healthy adult must have an energy value that will just balance the energy his body expends. If his food yields more Calories than he expends in work, in maintaining his body temperature, and in other vital functions, the excess will be stored as fat and he will gain weight. If he consumes food that provides less energy than is required, he will lose weight. The total energy requirement varies, of course, with the size and occupation of the individual, with the climate and season, and with age and sex. A man doing heavy outdoor work, for example, may require a daily diet of 4000 or 5000 Calories or even more, whereas 3000 Calories or less would be ample for an office worker.

In order, then, to arrive at the Calorie requirement of any individual the number of Calories required for work must be determined and (allowances having been made for climate or any other modifying condition) added to the value for his basal metabolism (Ch. 28). Now, the metabolism during sleep is less than the basal metabolism by at least 10 percent. The basal heat production during waking hours (16 hours)

Top, mice on diet containing poor quality protein; *bottom,* mice of same age receiving high quality protein. *(From Mendel.)*

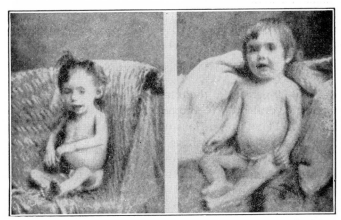

Left, improper diet; *right,* same child after diet corrected. *(From Greuenberg.)*

Cow eating bone to obtain phosphorus absent from pasture. *(From R. A. McIntosh.)*

Fig. 31.1. Effects of improper diet.

and the metabolism during sleep (8 hours) must for this reason be calculated separately for the 24 hours.

The Calorie value of the diet of a young man of average size who expends a total of about 3300 Calories daily is, therefore, made up from the following items:

		Calories
1. Basal metabolism (70 Calories per hour during the waking state of 16 hours)		$70 \times 16 = 1120$
2. Metabolism during sleep (63 Calories for 8 hours)		504
3. Allowance for work		1500
		3124
4. Specific dynamic action of food[1] (6 percent of 3124)		187
		3311

From 45 to 50 percent of the total Calories of the diet should be furnished by carbohydrates, 35 to 40 percent by fat, and from 12 to 15 percent by protein. These proportions of the three foods vary considerably under different conditions—such as age, sex, climate, and occupation. A much higher allowance of fat, for example, is required in northern climates than in tropical or subtropical zones. A larger proportion of protein is also an advantage in cold weather. The diet of laborers, growing children, and persons who have lost weight as a result of illness or from some other cause should contain a more liberal amount of protein than is required for healthy adults doing light work. The daily allowance of protein for the average adult is usually placed at 70 to 80 grams.

Apart from their value in furnishing energy, fats contain certain fatty acids (*linoleic, linolenic,* and *arachidonic*) that are absolutely essential in nutrition; severe nutritional defects result when they are absent from the diet.

The importance of various minerals in the diet has been mentioned above. The vitamin requirements will be discussed in the next section.

THE VITAMINS

The essential importance for nutrition of minute quantities of certain substances in food has been generally recognized only within comparatively recent years. When these indispensable materials were discovered very little was known of their chemical nature, but since they were thought, in error, to belong to a class of nitrogenous substances known as amines, they were called *vitamines* (L. *vita,* life). This name

---

[1] This item is an allowance for the increased metabolism caused by the food itself—an effect called its *specific dynamic action.* Food, especially protein, has a stimulating action on heat production quite apart and in excess of its Caloric value. The phenomenon has never been given an entirely satisfactory explanation.

has been retained but the spelling has been modified to **vitamins.** As new kinds were discovered and added to the list, each was designated by a letter—A, B, C, etc.

Vitamins have become very popular, and many commercial concerns try to increase their sales by advertising that their particular product contains this or that vitamin. This is too often simply "sales talk." Even in the case of vitamin preparations offered for sale in tablet form, the only assurance the public has that a particular tablet contains the vitamins as stated is the reputation of the manufacturer.

The following is a list of the better known vitamins:

Vitamin A (antixerophthalmic)
Vitamin B complex—thiamine (antineuritic), riboflavin, nicotinic
  acid, pyridoxine, B_{12}, etc.
Vitamin C (antiscorbutic)
Vitamin D (antirachitic)
Vitamin E (antisterility)
Vitamin K (antihemorrhagic)

Vitamin A. Vitamin A is present in largest amounts in cod-liver oil and in the liver oils of the various marine and fresh-water fish. The livers of mammals are also rich in this vitamin. The reason that the liver is

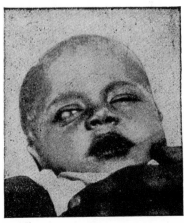

A   B

Fig. 31.2. A, a rat with abnormalities of the eyes and conjunctivae as a result of vitamin A deficiency. *(From* Therapeutic Notes, *Parke, Davis and Co.)* B, xerophthalmia in a child caused by vitamin A deficiency. *(From Bloch.)*

such a rich source of vitamin A is that the vitamin is produced in this organ from **carotene** absorbed from the intestine. Carotene is a yellow pigment found in many green and yellow plants used as food by both man and animals. Carotene, since it is converted in the body to vitamin A, is called **provitamin A.** We can, therefore, obtain a supply of vitamin A either from the carotene of such vegetables as carrots, yellow corn, and lettuce, and many fruits; or already formed from animal products such as fish oils and dairy products—cream, milk, butter, and eggs. The vitamin A content of dairy products depends upon the amount of carotene in the cow's food.

A well-balanced and liberal diet usually contains sufficient amounts of carotene of or vitamin A for normal nutrition. But when dairy products, vegetables, and fruits are absent from the diet or are present in meager amounts, serious nutritional defects result. The chief effects of vitamin A deficiency are seen in the skin, eyes, and nervous system. The disorders of the skin take the form of dryness, roughness, and a pimply rash. The membrane covering the surface of the eyes and lining the lids (*conjunctivae*) becomes dry owing to the suppression of the flow of tears that ordinarily lubricates them. Since vitamin A is required for the light-sensitive visual purple of the retina, night blindness may well result if this vitamin is lacking from the diet. Various degenerative changes in the nerves and nerve tracts of the central nervous system are produced by very severe deficiency of vitamin A (Fig. 31.2).

The vitamin B complex. Certain nutritional defects observed in experimental animals fed deficient diets were attributed by earlier investigators to the lack of a single dietary essential. It has since been shown that the defects were not due to the absence of one substance and that vitamin B, so called, consisted of a group of closely associated vitamins. These are now referred to as the B complex. They are sometimes designated by numbers placed after the letter B—B_1, B_2, etc., but more usually they are distinguished by special names.

The members of the vitamin B complex are as follows:

Thiamine (B_1)	Pantothenic acid
Riboflavin (B_2)	Inositol
Nicotinic acid	Biotin
Pyridoxine (B_6)	Para-aminobenzoic acid
Folic acid	Choline
Antipernicious anemia factor (B_{12})	

Only the first three will be dealt with here. Vitamin B_{12} and folic acid have been considered in Chapter 7. The others have been studied by creating deficiencies mainly in laboratory animals, and though there is little doubt that they are important in human nutrition, little or nothing is known of abnormalities in man resulting from their lack.

Thiamine, the antineuritic vitamin, or B_1, is essential for the normal nutrition and functioning of the nervous system. In its absence the metabolism of carbohydrates does not proceed normally. When the diet is lacking in the antineuritic vitamin a condition of the nerves develops leading to paralysis of the limbs. There also may be edema and dilatation of the heart. This deficiency disease, known as *beriberi,* is seen most commonly in Eastern countries—China, Japan, India, the Malay States, etc. —where the natives subsist mainly upon polished rice, that is, rice from which the outer coverings of the kernel have been removed in the milling process. In birds, thiamine deficiency causes retraction of the head (Fig. 31.3); in rats, pronounced slowing of the heart (bradycardia) occurs.

Beriberi is cured by feeding whole rice or the outer coverings of the rice grain (rice polishings), or any other good source of the vitamin. The richest sources of this vitamin are whole-grain cereals, milk, liver, and kidney. Pure thiamine, which is now made synthetically, is today more usually employed.

Fig. 31.3. *Top,* pigeon suffering from polyneuritis, the equivalent of beriberi in man. *Bottom,* the same bird an hour after treatment with vitamin B_1. *(After Funk.)*

Riboflavin belongs to a class of yellow fluorescent pigments known as *flavins.* It is found in largest amounts in milk, liver, kidney, and lean meats, especially lean pork. Severe abnormalities of the eyes result when it is absent from the diet or present in very small amounts. The chief eye defects are opacities over the pupil and the growth of fine vessels into the cornea, which normally is bloodless and perfectly transparent (Fig. 31.4). The eyes become extremely sensitive to light, being unable to tolerate an illumination of even ordinary intensity. Another effect of riboflavin deficiency is the appearance of deep creases or fissures surrounded by an inflammatory red area in the skin around the angles of the mouth. In the absence of this vitamin growth is retarded (Fig. 31.5).

Nicotinic acid, or niacin, is related chemically to nicotine present in tobacco leaf but has little or no toxic action. Liver, kidney, brewer's yeast, wheat germ, soybean, and peanuts are the chief sources of this member of the B complex.

The lack of adequate amounts of nicotinic acid in the diet is the

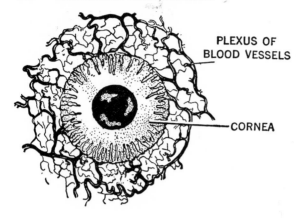

PLEXUS OF
BLOOD VESSELS

CORNEA

Fig. 31.4. Vascularization of the cornea due to severe riboflavin deficiency. Note the opaque areas over the pupil and the growth of vascular loops into the cornea, which normally is bloodless, from the vessels at the periphery (limbic plexus).

cause of pellagra, or of the main symptoms, at least, of this disease. Pellagra is a disease of the poor in southern districts of this continent and of Europe, whose diet consists principally of maize. Its chief features are red, inflamed patches on the skin (especially of parts exposed to the sun), gastric and intestinal disorders, and mental symptoms, sometimes culminating in mania.

Vitamin C, the antiscorbutic vitamin. Deficiency of vitamin C is the cause of scurvy (scorbutus), a disease characterized by hemorrhages from the gums and other mucous membranes and into the bones and joints. This disease caused many deaths on the early voyages of discovery and was often a reason for the failure of exploring parties. Captain Cook has told of its ravages. Jacques Cartier (1535), on one of his voyages to Canada, lost many men from scurvy until he was told by the Indians that a tea made from the young tips of evergreen branches was an effective remedy. James Lind (1747) deplored the prevalence of scurvy among British sailors and believed that it was due to the lack of fresh food, especially fruits and vegetables. His recommendation to the government

Fig. 31.5. The effect of riboflavin deficiency on growth. A, a rat fed a diet deficient in riboflavin and certain other factors of the vitamin B complex. Rat B received a normal diet.

of the day that lime juice be supplied to all ships of the Royal Navy was eventually adopted with excellent results. Thus the sobriquet "lime-juicer," or "limey," for the British sailor had its origin. Even today scurvy makes its appearance on exploration parties and during wars or in times of famine, when it is impossible to obtain foods containing adequate amounts of the antiscorbutic vitamin. The chemical name for this vita-min is **ascorbic acid.** It is also known by the etymologically objectionable name of *cevitamic acid.* The richest natural sources are lemons, limes, oranges, apples, and other fresh fruit, turnips, tomatoes, and green vege-tables. Ascorbic acid has been synthesized.

Vitamin D, the antirachitic vitamin. Deficiency of this vitamin is the cause of rickets (rachitis), a disease of young children in which the bones have not the normal rigidity and strength because they contain less than the required amount of mineral—calcium and phosphorus. Vitamin D is necessary for the concentration of these minerals as calcium phosphate in the growing bone. Deformities of the skeleton result (Figs. 31.6, 31.7). Rickets is more likely to appear during the winter months than during the summer, because certain rays of the sun produce the vitamin in the

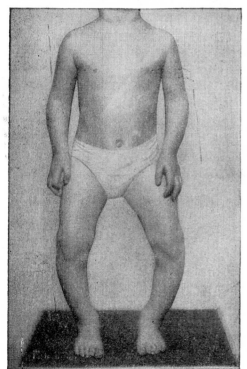

Fig. 31.6. The deformity of the leg bones in rickets.

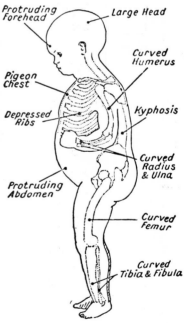

Fig. 31.7. Diagram showing the chief features of infantile rickets. (After Harris.)

TABLE 31.1 THE VITAMINS AND THEIR FUNCTIONS

Vitamin	Effects produced by deficiency of the vitamin	Human requirements per day	Food sources	Effects of cooking	For 1 day's requirement use all these foods or their equivalent
VITAMIN A	Retarded growth Keratinization and drying of the cornea (xeropthalmia) Poor vision in dim light Degeneration of nerves	Children: 50 units per pound of body weight Adults: 6000 units	Butter Milk Green-leaf and yellow vegetables Liver Fish liver oils (such as cod or halibut)	Very slight	3 glasses milk 3 servings butter 1 serving green-leaf or yellow vegetables
MEMBERS OF VITAMIN B COMPLEX Thiamine (Vitamin B_1, or antineuritic vitamin)	Deceased growth Failure to use carbohydrates properly Nerve disease leading to paralysis Mental depression	Infants: 100 units, or 0.3 mg Children and Adults: 500 units, or 1.5 mg	Whole-grain cereal products Milk Potatoes Meat (especially pork) Eggs Wheat germ Yeast	10 to 25% loss due to heat Up to 50% loss in cooking water	3 glasses milk 6 slices vitamin-rich bread 1 serving meat 1 serving oatmeal or whole-wheat cereal 1 egg 1 serving potatoes
Riboflavin (Vitamin B_2, or G)	Retarded growth Loss of appetite Eye lesions (vascularization and opacities of cornea) with photophobia	Children: 1.5 mg Adults: 3 mg	Milk Eggs Meat (especially liver) Green-leaf vegetables	No loss due to heat May be serious loss in cooking water	3 glasses milk 6 slices vitamin-rich bread 1 egg 1 serving meat 1 serving green vegetable
Nicotinic acid	Pellagra: skin rash, sore and inflamed tongue Mental symptoms	Children: 10 mg Adults: 20 mg	Meat Fish Milk Green-leaf vegetables Eggs Whole-grain cereal products Yeast	No loss due to heat May be serious loss in cooking water	3 glasses milk 1 serving meat 6 slices vitamin-rich bread 1 egg

	Deficiency symptoms	Daily requirement	Sources	Effect of heat and cooking	Remarks
Pantothenic acid	Deficiency symptoms in humans not known. In animals: decreased growth, graying of black hair in rats and foxes	Not known	Milk Liver and other meats Eggs Whole-grain cereal products Peas Potatoes	No loss due to heat May be serious loss in cooking water	Cannot be stated because requirement unknown
Pyridoxine (Vitamin B$_6$)	Deficiency symptoms in humans not known. In animals: decreased growth, failure to use proteins properly	Not known	Meats (particularly liver) Whole-grain cereal products	No loss due to heat May be serious loss in cooking water	Cannot be stated because requirement unknown
Folic acid	Not known; but cures pernicious anemia	Not known	Liver Green leaves	Not known	Not known
VITAMIN C (Ascorbic acid, or antiscorbutic vitamin)	Scurvy: hemorrhages due to weakening of blood vessel walls Poor formation of bones and teeth	Children: 800 units, or 40 mg Adults: 1200 units, or 60 mg	Tomatoes Potatoes Turnips Green-leaf vegetables Most fruits Citrus fruits	Heavy loss if food is exposed to air In commercial canning loss is slight Serious loss in cooking water	1 glass tomato juice (or 1 large serving canned or fresh tomatoes) 1 serving potatoes 1 serving other vegetables
VITAMIN D (Antirachitic vitamin)	Rickets Osteomalacia Poor utilization of calcium and phosphorus (bone salts)	Children: 500 units Adults: Not known	Vitamin D milk Eggs Fresh and can sea fish Fish-liver oils (cod or halibut)	No effect	In winter months particularly, children should have one teaspoon fish-liver oil daily
VITAMIN E	Possible habitual abortion and muscular dystrophy In animals: sterility in males and failure to complete pregnancy in females	Not known	Whole-grain cereal products (especially wheat germ oil) Corn oil Eggs Meat Green-leaf vegetables	No effect	Cannot be stated because requirement unknown
VITAMIN K (Antihemorrhagic vitamin)	Hemorrhages due to defective prothrombin production	Not known	Green-leaf vegetables Tomatoes	No effect	Cannot be stated because requirement unknown

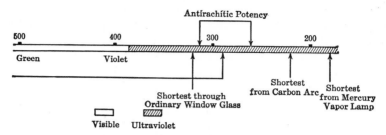

Fig. 31.8. Scheme of wavelengths of the spectrum, showing the ranges of those possessing antirachitic power. Figures in millimicrons (mμ). *(Modified from Blunt and Cowan.)*

skin of human subjects or of animals (Fig. 31.8). Also, the best food sources—fresh fish, eggs, and milk from cows that are receiving the vitamin in their diet—are more generally available in the summer months. This vitamin should be supplied in adequate amounts to infants and very young children if proper bone development is to take place. It is available in concentrated form in cod-liver oil or as *calciferol,* which is produced by the ultraviolet irradiation of ergosterol. The latter substance is also known as vitamin D_2, whereas that produced by the action of ultraviolet light upon the skin and in cod liver and milk is called vitamin D_3. (There is no vitamin D_1.) The substance in the skin that upon exposure to ultraviolet light is converted to vitamin D_3 is a sterol closely related to ordinary cholesterol and associated with it in minute amounts. It is called 7-dehydrocholesterol.

Only the shorter ultraviolet rays are capable of producing vitamin D from ergosterol or from 7-dehydrocholesterol. The active rays will not pass through ordinary window glass.

Vitamin E, the antisterility vitamin. Vitamin E has been shown in animal experiments to be essential for the normal functioning of the reproductive system. Female rats fail to give birth to living offspring if they are deprived of this vitamin. On a similar diet male rats become sterile. Vitamin E is found most abundantly in leafy vegetables and wheat germ.

Vitamin K, the antihemorrhagic vitamin. When the body lacks this vitamin the prothrombin of the blood (Ch. 7) becomes reduced, and as a consequence, the coagulation of the blood is greatly delayed. Serious hemorrhages, therefore, may follow otherwise trivial wounds. Vitamin K is synthesized in the intestine of many animals as well as of man. This means that it may be lacking from the diet with no ill effects. But the presence of bile in the intestine is necessary for its absorption. As a consequence, in jaundice due to obstruction of the bile passages, vitamin K is not absorbed, the blood-clotting mechanism is defective, and severe hemorrhage may result. Owing to this risk surgeons were reluctant to operate upon a severely jaundiced patient. Now the prothrombin concentration of the blood of such patients can be raised to normal before operation by injection of the vitamin or by giving an absorbable (water soluble) synthetic preparation of it by mouth.

A serious hemorrhagic disease of the newborn is caused by a lack of this vitamin; the prothrombin level is greatly reduced. But if the baby can be tided over the first day or two after birth by the administration of the vitamin, the condition corrects itself, for the vitamin is synthesized by bacteria introduced into the intestine with the food.

Vitamin K is present in greatest amount in green plants—for example, clover and spinach—and in cauliflower and cabbage.

32
The Kidneys and Skin

THE KIDNEYS

Each human kidney is about 4½ inches (11 cm) long, 2½ inches (6 cm) broad, and a little over 1 inch (3 cm) thick. The kidneys are bean-shaped organs lying posterior to the peritoneum, one on each side of the vertebral column, and sheltered behind by the eleventh and twelfth ribs. The convex border of each kidney is directed laterally, the concave border medially, that is, toward the vertebral column (Fig. 32.1). The left organ is a little higher than the right. A large branch of the aorta—the **renal artery**—enters the center of the kidney's concave border and breaks up within its substance into short branches, and finally into arterioles and capillaries. The blood is collected again by numerous small veins. These join together to form a single large vein—the **renal**

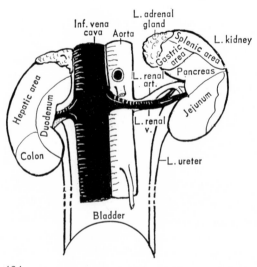

Fig. 32.1. Anterior view of the kidneys and the areas on their surfaces covered by overlying structures.

vein—which leaves the kidney close to the point where the artery entered. This part of the kidney at the middle of its concave border is called the **hilum.** It consists of a vertical fissure that leads into a cavity called the **renal sinus.**

The ureter is the muscular tube that conveys the urine to the urinary bladder. Its upper, expanded end fills the renal sinus, and is called the **pelvis of the ureter;** it divides within the sinus into a number of smaller cavities called **calyces** (sing. *calyx*).

The internal structure of the kidney. If a kidney is sliced lengthwise through its center, two zones, an outer and an inner, will be evident. The inner zone, called the **medulla,** is pale and consists of a number of pyramidal masses with their apices projecting into the calyces of the pelvis of the ureter. They are known as the **renal pyramids,** and their apices in the calyces as the **renal papillae.** The outer zone of the sectioned kidney is dark red in color and is called the **renal cortex.** It dips into the intervals between the pyramids. The pyramids when examined with a hand lens show fine alternating light and dark lines. The lighter of these striations are continued outwards through the more granular cortex; they are called the **medullary rays** (Fig. 32.2).

The nephron. The kidney contains great numbers of microscopic filters called **glomeruli** (sing. *glomerulus*). There are about a million of these structures in each human kidney. Blood is carried to each glomerulus by a single **afferent arteriole,** one of the numerous minute branches of the renal artery. The afferent arteriole gives rise to about 50 capillaries that are bent into short loops; but the separate loops cannot be easily

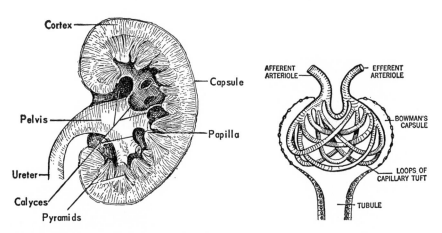

Fig. 32.2 *(left)*. A section lengthwise through the kidney.
Fig. 32.3 *(right)*. Diagram of a glomerulus of the kidney. Note that capillaries pass from the afferent to the efferent arteriole in separate loops. There are many more capillary loops than are shown here; each glomerulus contains 50 or more.

distinguished, the whole appearing as a tangled, red, skeinlike structure called the **glomerular tuft.** The capillary loops converge into a second fine vessel—the **efferent arteriole**—which carries the blood from the glomerulus. The glomerular tuft of capillaries is invaginated into a small membranous sac called **Bowman's capsule** (Fig. 32.3). Into the cavity of the capsule, water, salts, glucose, urea, uric acid, creatinine, etc., are

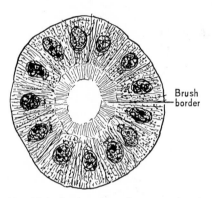

filtered from the blood flowing through the capillaries of the tuft. Bowman's capsule is drained by a fine tube called the **renal tubule.** From its commencement at Bowman's capsule, the renal tubule runs a tortuous course for some distance; this portion is called the **proximal convoluted tubule.** It then straightens and descends toward the medulla, but turns back again to form a hairpin bend called the **loop of Henle.** This ascending limb is continued into a second coiled segment called the **distal convoluted tubule** (Fig. 32.5).

Fig. 32.4. Section through a convoluted tubule.

Each glomerulus and the tubule as far as the end of the distal convoluted tubule is the essential urine-forming unit of the kidney. This set of structures with their vessels is called a **nephron.** The distal convoluted tubules drain to a system of wide tubes called **collecting tubules.** The nephrons lie, for the most part (renal corpuscles and convoluted tubules), in the cortex. Henle's loops and the collecting tubules are situated mainly in the medulla. The collecting tubules are merely conduits; they perform no specific renal function. These channels, by a series of unions, form tubes of ever-increasing caliber as they descend through the medulla. They end as a few relatively large tubes—the **ducts of Bellini**—which open into the pelvis of the ureter at the summits of the renal papillae.

A microscopic section of renal tissue is shown in Figure 32.6.

Significant features of the renal circulation. (1) The renal artery is a short, wide branch of the aorta that breaks up into its branches immediately upon entering the kidney. This ensures delivery of the blood at relatively high pressure. (2) The efferent glomerular arteriole is considerably narrower than the afferent vessel, another fact that provides for a high glomerular pressure and adequate filtration. Furthermore, the glomerular pressure can be readily increased by dilatation of the afferent arteriole or constriction of the efferent vessel, or the pressure can be reduced by contrary changes in the calibers of these vessels. (3) The tubules are supplied with blood that has first traversed the glomerular

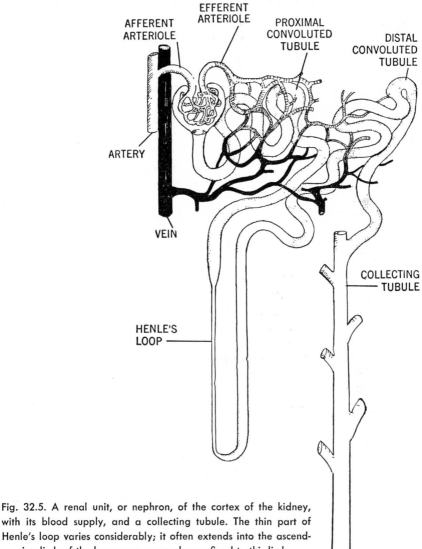

EFFERENT
ARTERIOLE

AFFERENT
ARTERIOLE

PROXIMAL
CONVOLUTED
TUBULE

DISTAL
CONVOLUTED
TUBULE

ARTERY

VEIN

COLLECTING
TUBULE

HENLE'S
LOOP

Fig. 32.5. A renal unit, or nephron, of the cortex of the kidney, with its blood supply, and a collecting tubule. The thin part of Henle's loop varies considerably; it often extends into the ascending limb of the loop or may even be confined to this limb.

capillaries. Disease that destroys the latter will, therefore, interfere with the blood supply to the lower parts of the nephron.

Filtration through the glomerulus. In the structure of the glomerulus are all the requirements of a perfect filter. A fluid containing solid material can be filtered off from such material by pouring it into a funnel lined by a cone of special paper (filter paper) that is permeable to the clear fluid itself but holds back the solids. The weight of the fluid itself forces it through and thus brings about the separation. More elaborate filters have been devised in which a membrane is used instead of paper and the pressure on one of its surfaces is much greater than on the other. The glomerulus is such a filter. The fluid to be filtered is the blood, and the walls of the glomerular capillaries together with the layer of Bowman's capsule that covers them constitute the filtering membrane. The pressure of blood in the glomerular capillaries is much higher than that in any other capillary of the body. It amounts to 60 or 70 mm Hg. The pressure on the other side of the membrane—that is, in Bowman's capsule—is only about 5 mm Hg. The glomerular membrane offers a complete barrier to the passage of the blood cells. The membrane also prevents the large molecules of the colloids, that is, the proteins, of the

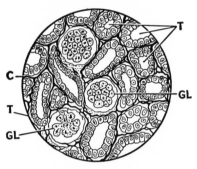

Fig. 32.6. Microscopic appearance of the kidney. C, dark lines representing capillaries; Gl, glomeruli; T, tubules.

plasma from escaping into Bowman's capsule. The filtered fluid contains all the other constituents of the plasma and in the same concentrations as in the plasma. The fluid filtered into Bowman's capsule is therefore identical in composition with plasma that has been freed of its proteins.[1]

Though each glomerulus filters a very small quantity of fluid in 24 hours, the volume filtered by all combined may amount to 150 liters or more daily.

The concentration of the filtered fluid and the kidney's function in the formation of urine. The fluid filtered through the glomerular capillaries is *not* urine. The function of the kidney involves more than a simple process of filtration. The volume of the urine is only one $\frac{1}{100}$ or so of the volume of the fluid that enters Bowman's capsule. The urine is also much more concentrated than the filtered fluid—that is, it contains more solids in solution, and the proportions of its various constituents are different (Table 32.2). It contains no sugar, for example, but its concentration in such nitrogenous waste substances as urea, uric acid, and creatinine is many times greater than that of the fluid filtered from the blood. The conversion of this dilute fluid into the concentrated urine is brought about by the reabsorption into the blood, from the tubules, of water and of those essential materials that the body cannot afford to lose in unlimited amounts—namely, calcium, sodium, potassium, magnesium, and sugar. Though each tubule is only about 2 inches long and less than $\frac{1}{50}$ inch in diameter, the combined length of all the tubules of one human kidney is about 40 miles and the total absorbing surface more

[1] This statement has been proved conclusively by analyzing a sample of fluid withdrawn under the microscope from Bowman's capsule by means of a very fine pipette.

than 6 square yards. Water and those substances that the tubules reabsorb and return to the blood in relatively large amounts—namely, sugar and the essential minerals—are called *high-threshold* substances, which means that they are excreted in the urine in small amounts or not at all unless they are in abnormally high concentration in the blood. Those substances that the body discards and that are concentrated in the urine— that is, waste materials such as urea and uric acid—are called *low-* or *non-threshold* materials (Fig. 32.7).

The quantity of water reabsorbed from the tubules amounts to 98 or 99 percent of the total volume of fluid filtered from the plasma. Thus, in man, some 150 liters of fluid are filtered into Bowman's capsule in 24 hours, but only between 1 and 2 liters of urine are produced in this time. The balance of the filtrate has been reabsorbed. The ability to concentrate the urine is one of the most important functions of the kidney. It is lost in the more advanced stages of renal disease. It is not possessed by lower orders, such as frogs, and is not acquired by the human kidney until several months after birth. This is the principal reason for the large volume of urine passed by infants.

Other functions of the kidney. The formation of urine is, of course, very closely bound up with the kidney's really essential function of regulating the composition of the blood and other body fluids. By excreting acid and preventing the excessive loss of base, the kidney is of paramount importance in maintaining the alkalinity of the tissues. The fluid filtered

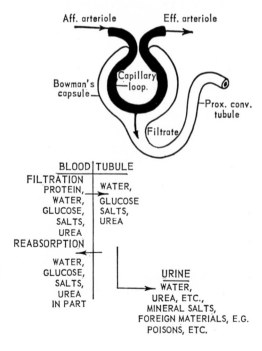

Fig. 32.7. Diagram to illustrate the filtration and reabsorption processes in the formation of urine by the kidney. The constituents of plasma, filtrate, reabsorbed fluid, and urine are represented in tabular form. The arrows indicate the directions of their movements.

into Bowman's capsule is alkaline in reaction like the plasma, but in passing through the tubules, base is returned to the blood and the urine becomes acid. The kidney also serves to render certain toxic substances innocuous. Finally, it produces and excretes ammonia combined with acids. Thus, by the use of ammonia for the neutralization of acids, valuable base, for example, sodium, is conserved. The ammonia is produced from glutamine by the renal cells.

In **kidney disease** and **acute** or **chronic nephritis,** the kidney performs its functions very imperfectly, and finally fails. The composition of the body fluids is greatly altered from the normal. Nitrogenous substances, such as urea and uric acid, accumulate in the body and the concentrations of the various salts in the blood are abnormal. The alkali reserve is reduced and the urine volume declines. **Uremia,** as a result of which the patient usually dies, follows these changes. The principal signs and symptoms of uremia are physical and mental fatigue, muscular spasm, exaggerated tendon reflexes, urinary odor of breath, and drowsiness merging into coma. Complete failure of renal function is called **suppression of urine,** or **anuria.**

The quantity and composition of the urine. The adult human body excretes on the average from 1 to 2 liters of urine in 24 hours. More urine is formed during the waking hours than during an equivalent period of sleep, though the total quantity of waste products excreted during the two periods is about the same, the night urine being merely more concentrated. The greater volume of urine formed by infants has been mentioned. The amount of urine produced varies, of course, with the amount of fluid drunk and that lost through the skin and intestines. A rise in blood pressure in the vessels of the kidney, since it increases the filtration force in the glomerulus, increases the amount of urine formed. Dilatation of the capillaries in the glomerulus also increases urine production, because the total filtering surface is then increased. That is one reason why certain substances such as coffee and tea increase the urinary flow. They contain caffeine, which dilates the renal vessels. Cold constricts the vessels of the skin and causes more blood in consequence to flow through the kidney. In these circumstances the urine is also increased in amount (see also *diuresis,* below).

The urine is slightly acid; its specific gravity is 1002 to 1030. The chief substances it contains are given in Table 32.1.

The degree to which the various constituents of the plasma are concentrated by the kidney is shown in Table 32.2.

Drugs and other substances taken into the body and not required are promptly excreted in the urine. Certain dyes pass from the body in the urine, staining it various colors. Patent-medicine manufacturers make use of this fact and put dyes into their pills to impress and fool the unwary public. Another practice of the patent-medicine advertiser is to

TABLE 32.1

COMPOSITION OF THE URINE

I. *Inorganic constituents*

	Grams per liter
Chloride expressed as NaCl............	9.0
Phosphorus expressed as P_2O_5...........	2.0
Total sulfur expressed as SO_3............	1.5
Sodium expressed as Na_2O..............	4.0
Potassium expressed as K_2O.............	2.0
Calcium expressed as CaO..............	0.2
Magnesium expressed as MgO...........	0.2
Iron	0.003

II. *Nitrogenous constituents*

	Grams per liter		Nitrogen, grams per liter
Urea	25.0	containing approximately	10.0
Ammonia	0.6	containing approximately	0.4
Uric acid	0.6	containing approximately	0.2
Creatinine	1.5	containing approximately	0.5
Undertermined nitrogen	0.6	containing approximately	0.6
Total			11.7

TABLE 32.2

(After Cushny)

Plasma constituent	Concentration; grams per 100 cc		Change in concentration in kidney
	Blood plasma	Urine	
Water	90-93	95	
Proteins, fats, and other colloids	7-9	0	
Glucose	0.1	0	
Na	0.30	0.35	1
Cl	0.37	0.6	2
Urea	0.03	2	60
Uric acid	0.004	0.05	12
K	0.020	0.15	7
NH_4	0.001	0.04	40
Ca	0.008	0.015	2
Mg	0.0025	0.006	2
PO_4	0.009	0.15	16
SO_4	0.002	0.18	90
Creatinine	0.001	0.075	75

try to convince the public that pain in the back is a sign of kidney disease. The kidney when diseased very rarely gives such a sign. We all at some time or other have suffered from back pain, but this usually arises from the muscles attached to the spine and is not due to any abnormal condition of the kidney.

Though, as mentioned above, the protein of the blood does not in health appear in the urine, in kidney disease the membranes of the kidney may have become so deteriorated that protein material (usually albumin) and sometimes red cells "leak" into Bowman's capsule. These abnormal constituents can be detected by special means. In diabetes the amount of sugar (glucose) in the blood is much greater than normal. The kidney tries to remove the excess, and large quantities of glucose are passed in the urine. As mentioned above, the urine of a healthy person is practically free from sugar. It is all reabsorbed in the proximal convoluted tubule.

Diuresis. Increased flow of urine is called diuresis, and drugs that cause such an effect are known as *diuretics*. The group of drugs includes *caffeine* (of coffee), *theobromine* (of cocoa), *theophylline* (of tea), *urea,* and various salts, for example, *potassium nitrate, potassium citrate, ammonium chloride, sodium sulphate,* and certain *mercury compounds.*

It is evident from the outline of the mechanism of renal excretion just given that there are two ways by which a greater flow of urine could be produced—namely, by increasing glomerular filtration or by diminishing tubular reabsorption.

In some species both methods are employed, but in man, increased urinary production is brought about nearly always by reducing reabsorption.

Diuresis caused by water drinking. The drinking of a large quantity (1 to 3 pints) of water is followed within 60 minutes or so by the passage of a large volume of very dilute urine (sp. gr. around 1.001). The renal effect lasts for 2 or 3 hours. The resemblance of this response, as well as the very dilute nature of the urine, to the characteristic renal features of diabetes insipidus (due to the lack of the antidiuretic principle of the pituitary body) has long been recognized. The suspicion grew that in the mechanism of water diuresis the antidiuretic hormone of the pituitary was in some way involved. The results of recent experiments have shown how well founded was this suspicion. Without going into details the course of events will be briefly described. The ingested water after absorption from the intestine causes, through dilution, a slight fall in the osmotic pressure of the blood. The blood dilution exerts an effect upon certain nerve cells of the brain (their exact location is unknown) that are extremely sensitive to any change in the osmotic pressure of the blood with which they are supplied. The nerve cells—a type of receptor organ (Ch. 33)—are called **osmoreceptors.** Through nervous connections with the cells of the posterior lobe of the pituitary gland the osmoreceptors, in response to a lowering of plasma osmotic pressure, exert an inhibitory action upon the output of the antidiuretic hormone which, under ordinary conditions, is being continually secreted into the blood stream, and therefore constantly exercising its characteristic action upon the function of the kidney (Ch. 38). The withdrawal of its influence results in an increase in urine volume, that is, diuresis.

During a period of water deprivation, the kidney conserves its water stores. The volume of urine is reduced due to the liberation of an excess of the antidiuretic hormone. Again, the effect upon the pituitary is brought about by a change in the osmotic pressure of the blood but now the effect upon the osmoreceptors is in the opposite direction, for the deprivation of water has caused some slight increase in blood concentration and, consequently, a rise in its osmotic pressure.

The reduction in urine volume caused by the injection of a small quantity (0.001 cc) of pituitary extract into the internal carotid artery can be duplicated exactly by 10 cc of a 2.5 percent (hypertonic) solution of sodium chloride or of sugar, introduced in the same manner into the cerebral circulation, for such hypertonic solutions cause a rise in the osmotic pressure of the plasma of sufficient magnitude to affect the osmoreceptors.

The role played by the adrenal cortex in renal function is touched on in Chapter 40.

The anatomy and physiology of the structures concerned in the collection and voiding of the urine

The ureters (Fig. 32.1) are two muscular tubes about 10 inches (25 cm) long that extend, one from each kidney, to the bladder. They are excretory ducts of the kidney. They lie behind the peritoneum and are composed of an outer circular and an inner longitudinal coat of smooth muscle. They are lined by mucous membrane; like that of the bladder the surface epithelium is of the transitional type (see below). The ureters pierce the bladder wall obliquely, so that when the latter contracts to expel its contents the ureteral openings are blocked, and thus any reflux of urine prevented. The upper expanded part of the ureter has been described. Peristaltic waves descend the walls of the ureters at regular intervals and carry the urine into the bladder.

The bladder is the receptacle and reservoir for the urine. It has an average capacity of 220 cc (see Fig. 49.11). It lies in the pelvis and is covered only on its upper surface and the upper part of its lateral walls by peritoneum. Its muscular coat, generally known as the **detrusor mus**cle, consists of three layers, an outer and an inner of longitudinal fibers and a middle one of circular fibers. It possesses a mucous and a submucous coat. The surface epithelium of the former is *transitional* in type; it resembles the stratified squamous type, but its most superficial cells are round rather than scalelike (Ch. 2). The triangular area of the bladder marked off by the orifices of the ureters and the urethra is called the **trigone.**

The circular layer of muscle fibers is thickened at the neck of the bladder, which is the most dependent part of the organ, where it opens into the urethra. This thickening of the circular layer constitutes the **internal sphincter,** or **sphincter vesicae;** it extends beyond the bladder to surround the commencement of the urethra.

The urethra is a tube leading from the bladder to the exterior. The length of the male urethra is about 8 inches (18 to 20 cm), that of the female only about 2 inches. In the male the first inch or so of the urethra is surrounded by the prostate; the remaining part, except for a short length (2 cm) below the prostate called the **membranous urethra,** is surrounded by a mass of erectile tissue (Ch. 49) known as the **corpus spongiosum.** A band of circular muscle fibers surrounds the membranous urethra; it is known as the **external sphincter,** or the **sphincter urethrae.**

The evacuation of the bladder. The voiding of urine, or micturition. As urine gradually collects within the bladder, the pressure within the viscus shows very little change for a time, the tone of the detrusor muscle adapting readily to the increased volume (see postural tone, Ch. 24). Not until the urine volume is between 200 and 300 cc does any noticeable rise in internal pressure occur. Rhythmical contractions of the detrusor muscle then follow in response to the tension exerted upon the muscle fibers. The contractions are weak at first, but, gradually gaining strength as the urine volume increases, culminate in a strong reflex contraction of the bladder wall, accompanied by relaxation of the internal sphincter.

The act of micturition, though dependent upon reflex mechanisms, is, in the adult, very largely under voluntary control. The reflex contractions of the detrusor can be inhibited and contractions of the internal sphincter induced by an effort of the will. Thus, the reflex mechanisms can be restrained until an opportunity for voiding the urine presents itself. The restraint is then removed, and the contractions of the bladder wall that ensue are reinforced by voluntary nerve impulses transmitted along the motor nerves supplying the detrusor muscle. A rise in intra-abdominal pressure, due to contractions of the abdominal muscles and fixation of the diaphragm in the inspiratory position, usually precedes and accompanies the act of micturition. However, a voluntary movement of this character is not essential, the bladder mechanism being capable itself of expelling the urine.

The motor fibers to the detrusor muscle, and the inhibitory fibers to the internal sphincter and trigone are derived from the parasympathetic division of the autonomic nervous system through the *pelvic nerves* (second, third, and fourth sacral segments). These fibers are peculiar in that, as indicated above, they transmit voluntary as well as involuntary impulses to the detrusor muscle.

The sympathetic division of the autonomic nervous system exerts an opposite effect upon the movements of the bladder. Through the *hypogastric nerves* it transmits inhibitory impulses to the detrusor muscle and motor impulses to the internal sphincter and trigone.

The external sphincter of the male, which is composed of striated muscle, is supplied with motor fibers through the pudendal nerves. The afferent nerves of the reflex arc governing micturition run mainly in the *pelvic nerves*.

The centers of the micturition reflex are situated in the midbrain, pons, and sacral part of the spinal cord (second, third, and fourth sacral segments). Micturition is carried out through the spinal center when the cord is severed above the sacral region. Even after destruction of the spinal center, the bladder empties automatically, its movements being then brought about through the nerve plexuses in close relation to the bladder wall.

The nervous mechanisms through which restraint is exercised in the control of micturition—that is, the inhibition of the micturition reflex— is late in developing to the state of efficiency where, as in a healthy adult, the urine can be retained in even an uncomfortably distended bladder. In infants, urine is voided involuntarily, apparently no effort being made at restraint. In young children, though there may be complete control of the act of urination during the day, the emptying of the bladder during sleep, *"bed wetting,"* or *nocturnal enuresis,* as it is called, is of common occurrence. The age at which restraint is fully developed—at night as well as during the day—varies with the nervous constitution of the child and with his training, but is usually established, except for an occasional lapse under unusual circumstances, at 3 or 4 years. In persons of neurotic disposition nocturnal enuresis may persist into adult life, and in the feeble-minded restaint may fail to be exercised either during sleep or in the waking hours.

THE SKIN

Whereas the skin forms a complete covering for the outer surface of the body, the digestive and respiratory tracts, and other tubes or cavities that open into the digestive tract or to the outside world are lined by a soft, dark red, velvety tissue called mucous membrane; this latter membrane has been described in Chapter 24.

Next to the bones, the skin and the structures that grow from it, such as the nails of man and the claws, horns, and hoofs of animals, are the firmest and toughest tissues of the body.

The layers of the skin. If a very thin section of skin is made perpendicular to the surface and examined under the microscope, several layers of closely packed cells (stratified epithelium) will be seen (Fig. 32.8). The outer layers of cells are flat and resemble scales (squamous epithelium). They are resistant and relatively hard (horny layer). The cells of the underlying layers are more rounded and become massed together to form tongues that project into the true skin below. They contain a dark pigment. The deepest layer is composed of a single row of columnar cells. The skin pigment is greater in amount in some persons than in others and also varies greatly in different races. The Negro's skin has a high concentration of pigment; the skins of American and East Indians, Chinese, and Japanese have less, and the white races least. All the layers of cells described above are together called the epidermis, cuticle, or scarf skin. No blood vessels or nerves are found in any of these layers. The superficial cells are being continually shed and replaced by others that move up from below. The thickness of the epidermis is different in the various regions of the body; on the eyelids, for instance, it is no more than $\frac{1}{100}$ inch thick. On the soles of the feet or palms of the hands, especially in one who performs hard manual labor, it may be $\frac{1}{10}$ inch thick or more.

Beneath the cuticle is a meshwork of connective tissue fibers, which are very elastic. For this reason the skin, as we know, can be stretched very easily, and when released it quickly springs back again into place. This deep part of the skin is called the corium, dermis, or true skin. It is heaped up into mounds or hillocks (papillae), which lie between

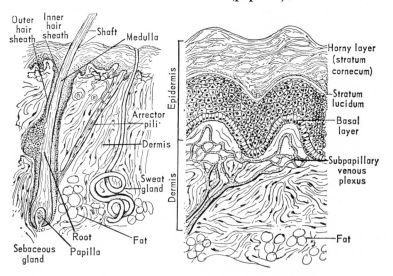

Fig. 32.8. Vertical sections through the skin. *Left,* low power of microscope showing appendages of skin. *Right,* high power of magnification.

projecting tongues of the overlying cuticle. In it are found blood vessels, nerves, and sweat glands. Beneath the true skin is a layer of connective tissue containing a variable quantity of fat; it is called **subcutaneous tissue.** The subcutaneous tissue is much thicker in some parts of the body than in others and serves as a padding to round out certain unevennesses in the body surface or to cushion its bony parts. The amount of fat also varies in different people, and is thicker, usually, in women than in men.

The hairs. The skin over all regions of the body, with very few exceptions, such as the palms of the hands and soles of the feet, is covered with hairs. Except in certain regions, such as the scalp and the faces of men, they are very fine and short. The part of the hair we see above the skin is called the **shaft;** the part lying below the skin surface is called a **root.** Each hair has its root planted deeply in the true skin or in the layer of fat beneath this. The

root runs obliquely upward through the cuticle and is completely enclosed in a little tube called the **hair follicle** (Figs. 32.8, 32.9). The shaft, or visible part of the hair, does not rise straight up from the surface of the skin, but is slanting, like a blade of grass blown by a breeze. The hairs in any one part of the body all slant in the same direction. A network of fine nerves surrounds the hair follicle where it lies in the true skin, and that is why pulling the hairs is so painful. The organs of touch (Ch. 47) lie in

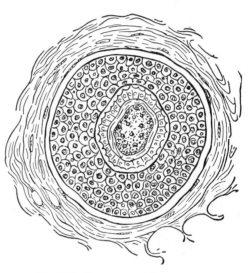

Fig. 32.9. Cross section of a hair root.

the true skin close to the hair follicle—just beneath that region of cuticle that lies on the "windward" side of the hair shaft. Hence, a slight movement of the tips of the hairs causes a sensation of touch, because the movement stimulates the neighboring touch organ. Small glands (**sebaceous glands**) in the true skin pour an oily material into the hair follicles, which lubricates the hairs and oozes out on the surface of the skin.

The sweat glands. These are tiny coiled tubes lined with cells that draw fluid from the blood to form a secretion, called *sweat*, or *perspiration*. The little gland lies in the true skin, but it sends its secretion along a spiral tube that passes through the cuticle and opens by a small mouth upon the surface of the skin. The mouths of the sweat glands are often called the "pores" of the skin.

The nails. The human nails, the claws, horns, and hoofs of animals, the antlers of stags, and the horns of rhinoceros are simply the cuticle of the skin that has been hardened and otherwise changed in character. The nails and the hard structures just mentioned grow from the true skin. The **root** of the nail is the buried part covered by ordinary cuticle (Fig. 32.10). In the root, the cells forming the soft deeper layers of the skin, as they grow outward, are turned into the stiff and hardened type so characteristic of the horny material of well-formed nails. The claws and hoofs of animals also each have a root where this change takes place.

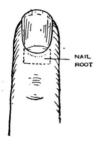

Fig. 32.10. The fingernail.

The functions of the skin and mucous membranes. The skin has four important functions to perform. These are (1) protection, (2) excretion, (3) the regulation of body temperature, and (4) the production of vitamin D upon exposure to sunshine (Ch. 31). The firm, insensitive cuticle protects the underlying delicate tissues with their sensitive nerves and important blood vessels. How exquisitely sensitive the flesh is when the outer layers of skin have been removed after a burn or blister is known to us all. The hard, resisting outer layer of skin and the mucous membranes also serve as barriers against most microorganisms. Once one of these barriers is broken down by some injury, such as a cut or a burn, bacteria, which are everywhere about us, find the weakened spot in the body's defenses. It is of the greatest importance, therefore, that any opening in the skin be thoroughly cleansed to rid it of any infection that may have found a foothold. A dressing must then be put on to prevent any other bacteria from getting in. Infection of the denuded surface is probably the most serious danger of an extensive burn.

The body excretes its waste material chiefly through the lungs (carbon dioxide), the kidneys (urea, uric acid, etc.), and the bowels; but the skin, though much less important as an excretory organ than these three, nevertheless does excrete small amounts of waste materials in the sweat. When, for any reason, the other organs fail in their excretory powers, the excretory functions of the skin increase. But even in health small quantities of carbon dioxide are given off by the blood through the skin, and the sweat carries away a little of the urea and uric acid. The mucous membrane of the bowel is a very important pathway along which many substances are excreted from the blood. Its absorptive functions have been spoken of elsewhere. The important part played by the skin in regulating the temperature of the body has also been described (Ch. 29).

Skin, when its vessels are constricted together with the layer of fat lying beneath, possesses insulating qualities of a high order. It is comparable in this regard to a layer of cork of the same thickness. Thus heat is conserved in cold weather. In hot weather the cutaneous vessels dilate and heat is radiated from the blood to the surroundings. The evaporation of water secreted by the sweat glands is an additional means whereby heat is dissipated (Ch. 29).

The color and temperature of the skin. The color of the skin apart from that due to pigment—that is, its pinkness, blueness, or pallor—is due to the quantity and the state of the blood in a plexus of small veins lying in the corium just beneath the papillae, and known as the *subpapillary venous plexus.* The temperature of the skin is dependent in part upon the blood flow in this plexus and also upon the blood in more deeply lying vessels, the heat being then conducted to the surface through the overlying skin. When the vessels of the subpapillary venous plexus are dilated and the blood flow through them is rapid, the skin is red and hot; if the vessels of the plexus are constricted, the skin is pale, though not necessarily cold, for the blood in the deeper vessels may be filled with warm, rapidly flowing blood even though giving no color to the skin. When the arterial blood is not fully oxygenated or the blood flow through the plexus slow, as in heart failure, and the vessels of the plexus are dilated or at least not strongly constricted, the skin has a bluish tint owing to the high proportion of reduced hemoglobin in the blood of the subpapillary venous plexuses (see *anoxia* and *cyanosis,* Ch. 21).

THE NERVOUS SYSTEM
PART VIII

33
The Microscopic Structure of the Nervous System. The Nerve Impulse. Receptors. The Nature of Sensation

Not until the microscope had been discovered could even the faintest idea of the texture of the nervous tissue be formed. And not, of course, until the structure of nervous tissue was known could any clear knowledge of the functions of the nervous system be gained. The central nervous system (brain and spinal cord) is made up of a vast number of nerve cells, bound together by a special kind of connective tissue called **neuroglia.**

The nerve cell

The nerve cell (Fig. 33.1) is also called a **neuron.** It has a **body,** which may be rounded, pyramidal, oval, or star shaped. The shapes and sizes may vary in different regions of the central nervous system. Some nerve cell bodies are quite large; others are small. The outstanding feature of nerve cells is their possession of two or more extensions of their protoplasm known as **processes.** The processes are of two kinds. One kind in its most typical, but by no means invariable, form is short with many branching like the limbs of a tree. For this reason it is called a **dendron, dendrite,** or the *dendritic process* (Gk. *dendron,* a tree). The dendron may be single, but more commonly the nerve cell possesses two or more. The other kind of process, which as a rule springs from the

452

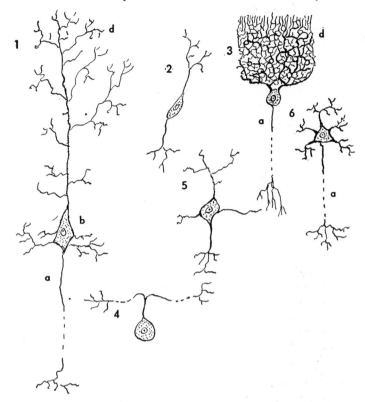

Fig. 33.1. Some of the commoner types of nerve cell. 1, pyramidal cell from the motor area of the cerebral cortex with long axon that connects with cells of the spinal cord; 2, fusiform cell with short axon; 3, cell from the cerebellar cortex (Purkinje cell); 4, unipolar cell from a ganglion of a posterior spinal nerve root; 5, cell with short axon from the cerebral cortex; 6, motor cell from the anterior horn of the spinal cord, its long axon constitutes a fiber of a peripheral nerve trunk. a, axon; b, body; d, dendrite.

opposite pole of the cell, is called the **axon,** or the *axis cylinder process.* In its most common form it is long and slender, but it may be short with many branches. The axon is always single. The two processes—dendron and axon—are "one-way" lines. The dendron carries impulses to the cell body; the axon carries impulses from the cell body. Neither process normally transmits both ways (see Ch. 35) . The nerve processes—axon and dendron—though often quite short, may be very long—several feet, indeed. The nerves of the body are simply great numbers of these long processes—now called **fibers**—bound together into cablelike bundles.

The adjective **afferent** (L. *ad,* to + *ferre,* to bear) is applied to those processes of nerve cells, that is, the dendrites, that conduct impulses or "messages" toward the body of the cell, whether they are in the central nervous system or in a peripheral nerve. The adjective is also applied to the impulses themselves. One may therefore speak of afferent fibers or of afferent impulses. The word **efferent** means conduction in the reverse direction, as occurs in the axons. *Centripetal* and *centrifugal* are corresponding terms used to denote incoming and outgoing impulses, respectively. Thus, sensory nerves—for example, nerves of touch, pain, sight, etc.—are composed of afferent fibers, or dendrons. Nerves that carry impulses to muscles and glands are called efferent; they are composed of axons.

The terms *afferent* and *sensory* are sometimes used as though they were synonymous, but this is not strictly correct. Only those afferent fibers that transmit impulses to consciousness are truly sensory; other afferent fibers that carry impulses to the centers of the spinal cord or the brain, such as the cerebellum, pons, and medulla oblongata, and that give rise to no sensation cannot properly be called *sensory*. Therefore, though all sensory fibers are afferent, not all afferent fibers are sensory.

Minute structure of the nerve cell body. Like almost all cells in the animal body the nerve cell possesses a nucleus, situated usually at or near its center. The surrounding protoplasm when stained with certain dyes shows numerous small, dark, angular flecks of granular material. They are known as *Nissl bodies.* They are arranged roughly in rows that give a striped tiger-skin appearance to the body of the cell and on this account are sometimes referred to collectively as the *tigroid substance.* The Nissl bodies are most pronounced in the resting cell; during activity they become reduced in number and in the fatigued or exhausted cell may disappear entirely for a time. Very fine lines are to be seen streaming into the body of the cell from the axon and dendrons. They are known as **neurofibrils** and are seen as fine lines in the cytoplasm along which the tigroid substance appears to be disposed (Fig. 33.2).

Gray and white matter. The grayish color of certain areas—gray **matter**—of the brain and spinal cord is due to the presence of great numbers of nerve cell bodies. The **white matter** consists of the processes (fibers) of nerve cells massed into compact bundles that conduct impulses to or from the gray matter. In a cross section of the brain or spinal cord, these two types of nervous tissue are quite distinct to the naked eye. A collection of nerve fibers within the central nervous system that forms a definite strand or bundle connecting remote groups of nerve cells is called a **tract,** or **fasciculus.**

A more or less circumscribed group of nerve cells with common functions, such as those that give rise to the fibers composing one or another of the cranial nerves, is called a **nucleus,** or **center.**

The nerve fiber. Each fiber in a nerve trunk, which as mentioned above is a process of a nerve cell, consists of a central core called the **axis**

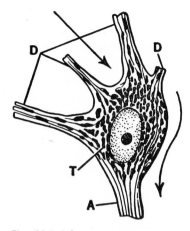

Fig. 33.2 (above). Minute structure of the body of a nerve cell. A, axon; D, dendrites, cut across; T, tigroid substance, or Nissl bodies.

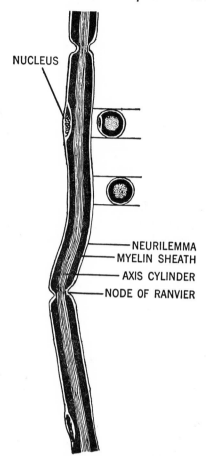

NUCLEUS

NEURILEMMA
MYELIN SHEATH
AXIS CYLINDER
NODE OF RANVIER

Fig. 33.3 (right). Diagram to show the structure of a nerve fiber, in longitudinal section and in cross section at two levels.

cylinder and, usually, a sheath of fatty material called the **myelin sheath,** which serves to insulate the fiber from its neighbors. The outermost covering of the nerve is a thin membrane called the **neurilemma** which shows constrictions at regular intervals (*nodes of Ranvier*) (Fig. 33.3).

THE NERVE IMPULSE

The changes that take place in and travel along a stimulated nerve are referred to as the **nerve impulse.** Much remains to be learned concerning the impulse, but we do know that it is invariably accompanied by an electrical effect—a change in electrical potential. If a nerve is connected with an instrument (such as a galvanometer) that will record small electrical changes, the currents set up in the nerve when it is stimulated can be picked up and recorded photographically. The curve shown in Figure 33.4 is such a record from the sciatic nerve of a frog. If the pas-

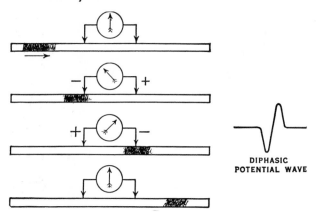

DIPHASIC
POTENTIAL WAVE

Fig. 33.4. A record of the electrical change that accompanies the nerve impulse. Electrical contacts are placed upon the nerve and connected through a galvanometer (as represented by the circle with the arrow). The movement of the indicator of the galvanometer (as represented by the arrow) is recorded photographically. The double (diphasic) curve on the right is the type of record obtained. The dark area on the nerve represents the nerve impulse; i.e., the excited part of the nerve at successive intervals of time.

sage of the impulse between two points on a nerve is timed, its speed can be calculated. In the large nerves going to the skeletal muscles of mammals—the **motor nerves**—and in the nerves conveying impulses to consciousness, the impulse velocity is about 120 meters per second; the velocity of the impulse is much lower in the nerves of the frog and other cold-blooded animals.

The frequency of the impulses—that is, the number of impulses that travel along the nerve per second—varies widely, from 10 to 1000, according to the particular nerve that is stimulated and the strength of the stimulus. The impulse frequency rises with increasing strength of stimulus. *No change in the magnitude of the impulse, as indicated by the electrical response, results from varying the strength of the stimulus* (see "all or none" law, below). There is a definite upper limit to the rate at which the nerve fiber can conduct impulses, because for a brief time after the impulse has passed, the nerve will not transmit a second impulse. This period of unresponsiveness is called the *absolute refractory period*.[1] It has a duration of only $\frac{1}{1000}$ second or less in mammalian nerve. One thousand per second is, therefore, the theoretically maximal rate at which impulses can be transmitted along the nerve (Fig. 33.5).

The reader may have gained the impression that the nerve impulse

[1] Following the absolute refractory period is a brief interval of time during which the nerve, though it will respond to a stimulus, is less excitable than normally, as is shown by the relatively small magnitude of the electrical record. This interval is called the *relative refractory period*.

is simply an electric current and the nerve fiber an inert conductor. But though the impulse is invariably accompanied by an electrical change and much information has been gained from the study of electrical records, it is not merely an electric current; it is propagated at a much slower rate. An electric current travels at the speed of light. Nor is the nerve fiber an inert conductor. Not only is it a living structure, but it shows metabolic changes during activity, and the transmission of the nerve impulse is dependent upon these changes. The nerve consumes more oxygen and produces more carbon dioxide during activity—that is, during the passage of the impulse—than during rest.

In the mode of its propagation the nerve impulse is more like a spark traveling along a fuse of gunpowder than an electric current, for it and the spark both *derive the energy for their transmission from the path along which they travel.* An electric current is generated, not in the conducting wire, but in a battery or dynamo, and merely conducted by the wire. If a small section of a fuse of gunpowder is slightly dampened somewhere along its course and one end of the fuse then lighted, a spark or flame is started that travels rapidly until it reaches the dampened portion. It progresses more slowly and with difficulty through this region, burning feebly, perhaps spluttering, and may become almost extinguished. But if not completely extinguished, the spark flares up to its original brilliance upon reaching the dry powder beyond the damp section. The nerve impulse behaves in a way essentially similar. It too

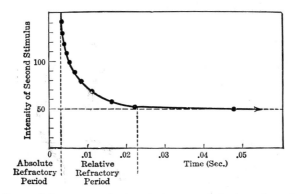

Fig. 33.5. Curve of the recovery in the sciatic nerve of the frog. Two stimuli were applied to the nerve in a series of tests, the second stimulus in each instance being separated from the first by various time intervals and of just sufficient strength to excite. Intensity of the second stimulus is plotted along the vertical axis, time along the horizontal. The interrupted horizontal line indicates the strength of current required to excite the *resting* nerve. During the absolute refractory period (about 0.003 second in this instance) a stimulus, however strong, will not excite. The excitability returns gradually during the next 0.02 second (relative refractory period). *(After Adrian.)*

depends for its propagation upon energy-yielding materials in its path—the nerve fiber. If a section of nerve is treated with a chemical that depresses its metabolic processes, such as chloroform, ether, or alcohol, but does not cause a complete block, the impulse upon arriving at this section is impeded. It travels more slowly and its magnitude, as indicated by the electrical record, is greatly reduced. When it reaches the untreated part of the nerve beyond the depressed region, which is comparable to the dampened section of the gunpowder fuse, its original strength and velocity are regained. Now, a wire transmits an electric current in an entirely different way, for if some resistance is placed in its path its strength is reduced but is not restored after the resistance has been passed (Fig. 33.6).

Other comparisons can be drawn with profit between the fuse of gunpower and the nerve fiber. The spark progresses because it is able to heat and then ignite successively the sections of fuse immediately ahead of it. So too the electrical current accompanying the nerve impulse serves to stimulate the part of the nerve just in front. Thus both the spark and the nerve impulse are self-propagating. After the spark has passed nothing remains but a trail of ash, which, of course, is incombustible. Fresh powder must be laid before another spark can be started on its way. This after state of the fuse corresponds to the refractory period of the nerve fiber; but, unlike the fuse of gunpowder, the nerve fiber itself restores within a small fraction of a second the materials necessary for the propagation of another impulse. Again, the size of the spark, the speed at which it travels, and the amount of heat generated are not influenced at all by the size or heat of the flame used to light the fuse. So long as the heat applied is sufficient to ignite the powder it is immaterial whether an electric spark, an ordinary match, or a blowtorch is used. So it is with the nerve fiber; any stimulus strong enough to excite the nerve at all,

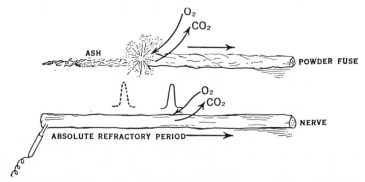

Fig. 33.6. Comparison of a spark traveling along a fuse of gunpowder with the nerve impulse. The horizontal arrows indicate the direction of transmission. The curves in the lower figure represent the electrical response at two points on the nerve.

under the conditions existing at the moment, causes a maximal impulse to be set up. This is known as the *all or none law;* its application is not confined to the excitation of nerve but holds true for other excitable tissues as well—for example, muscle (Ch. 4) .

RECEPTORS. HOW THE NERVES PICK UP MESSAGES FROM THE WORLD AROUND US

The sensory cranial nerves carry to the brain messages (nerve impulses) that, upon reaching our consciousness, give information concerning the outside world. The nerves of sight (optic nerve) carry messages from the eye, and the nerves of hearing (auditory) messages from the ear. The nerves of smell (olfactory) bring information from the nose; and the nerves of taste, information from the mouth. All these nerves run directly to the brain and for the greater part of their courses run within the skull or cranium. Many other sensory nerves (spinal sensory nerves) , such as those coming from the skin and causing sensations of pain, heat and cold, and touch—that is, the nerves through which we feel—do not run to the brain directly. They run into the spinal cord (Ch. 35) . Some of their fibers then separate and run upward in the cord by different routes to reach the brain.

But the sensory nerves, even those to the skin, do not end simply as bare branches. Each fine terminal of a sensory nerve is surrounded by a tiny structure, sometimes a single cell, that is especially designed to receive stimuli and to set up impulses in the nerve fiber to which it is attached. These specialized "end organs" are called **receptors.** Each type of sensory nerve has its own particular type of receptor,[2] which differs in structure from all other types and responds effectively to but one form of stimulation. For example, the receptors of sight—the rods and cones of the retina—are stimulated by light (Ch. 41) ; those of hearing, which are contained in the basilar membrane of the internal ear, respond to sound vibrations (Ch. 46) ; and those of pain, touch, and heat and cold, situated in the deeper layers of the skin, are excited by mechanical forms of stimulation, or changes in temperature (Ch. 47) . The receptors of smell and of taste are especially designed for the reception of chemical forms of stimulation—that is, when odorous substances (in gaseous form) or substances possessing taste come into contact with them.

It should be pointed out, however, that a receptor, though it possesses a very special ability to respond by the creation of nerve impulses to only one type of stimulus, will respond in an imperfect way to other forms of stimulation for which it is not especially adapted. For example, although the receptors in the retina respond most effectively to the

---

[2] Nerve fibers that conduct impulses causing pain appear to be an exception, for their endings are bare—that is, no organized structure surrounds the ends.

waves of light, they may in addition be stimulated mechanically, as by a blow upon the eyeball, or electrically, when flashes of light are experienced. A blow upon the ear will cause ringing, humming, or other auditory sensations, and an electric current applied to the tongue arouses a metallic taste. Stimulation of the bare optic nerve itself or of the nerve of hearing (acoustic nerve) will also cause a sensation that is a crude imitation of that produced by the corresponding receptors. These facts are exemplified by the behavior of an electrical instrument such as the telephone. The transmitter is especially designed to receive and respond to sound waves, but rubbing or tapping the diaphragm will also produce electrical impulses, which travel along the wire and produce harsh and meaningless sounds in the receiver at the other end.

Receptors such as those mentioned, which receive stimuli from the outside world, are called **exteroceptors.** But there is another type that is stimulated by changes within our bodies. These are called **proprioceptors** and are situated in the walls of the stomach and intestines, in the heart and large blood vessels, in the muscles, tendons, and joints, and in the internal ear (Ch. 46). Many proprioceptors give rise to impulses that make no impression upon our consciousness (nonsensory impulses); they give secret information to the central nervous system. Through them many reflex acts are brought about. Those in the muscles, tendons, and joints, and in the internal ear are stimulated by movements of the structures in which they lie. Through them both sensory and nonsensory impulses are discharged along the nerves that they serve. Thus, the central nervous system is constantly informed of the movements or positions of the different parts of the body, and of the body as a whole in space.

The impulses carried to the central nervous system along the various sensory nerves do not all have the same destination, but each type of nerve—whether of sight, hearing, touch, etc.—conveys its impulses to some particular part of the cerebral cortex. These cortical regions are called **areas,** or **centers.**

THE NATURE OF OUR SENSATIONS

Should we examine the different nerves very closely, we would find that they all looked very much the same. Even if we took a thin slice from each and compared these slices under the microscope, we should find that each was made of a number of fibers that appeared almost identical, no matter what nerve was being examined. Furthermore, when we study the electrical currents associated with the impulses of each kind of sensory nerve—optic, acoustic, etc.—no essential difference can be found between them. From every test that can be applied there is no reason to believe that the impulses are not the same in all nerves, including the motor nerves. How is it then that there are several very different sensations? We have seen that the differences do not depend upon the receptors, for stimulation of a bare nerve causes a sensation that though crude and disorganized (a flash of light for example, rather than a visual pattern) is nevertheless characteristic. From these facts the conclusion is forced upon us that the quality of any sensation depends upon the area, or center, of the cerebral cortex where the impulses arrive. The nerve cells in each of these areas interpret, in their own way, and quite beyond our understanding, the impulses they receive. Indeed, in disease one of these cortical areas may be stimulated *directly*, not by impulses arriving by the usual pathways. Flashes of light, noises, or other hallucinations may then be experienced by the patient.[3] Therefore, the sensation we know as sight or hearing is not created in the eye or ear. These organs merely set up effective impulses. Impulses arriving in the center for sight (*occipital lobe*) are perceived as visual sensations, those in the auditory center (*temporal lobe*) as sensations of sound, and so on. It may, then, with truth be said that sight is a special function, not of the eye, but of the occipital lobe of the brain. Sound, likewise, is the sensation that the cells of the temporal lobe make of impulses, no matter how produced, arriving there. Our other sensations—taste, smell, and touch—are also due to different interpretations that other centers of the brain put upon the nerve impulses they receive. Just as a bell, a glass jar, an iron bar, or a gong produces each its different tone when struck in turn by the same object, so the different centers of the brain give rise to different sensations, though the nerve impulses that each receives are similar. If, therefore, it were possible to connect the *eye* with the *temporal lobe*, and the *ear* with the *occipital lobe*, we would, as someone has expressed it, "hear the lightning and see the thunder."

It is, therefore, not strictly correct, though convenient, to say that the nerve fiber carries "messages" to the brain. The nerve fibers are rather like the electric wires of an annunciator system; the wires carry identical electrical impulses upon pressing a certain button, which actuate a *particular indicator* in the annunciator box (brain). Of course, in the annunciator system the buttons (receptors) differ from one another only in being in different situations (but see theory of hearing, Ch. 46). Now, in a telephone system messages are really carried over the wire, for the sound waves are converted to electrical impulses of the same frequency and reconverted to sound waves at the other end.

The **intensity** of a sensation, for example, the brightness of a light, the loudness of a sound, the sharpness of pain, etc., depends upon the *frequency* of the nerve impulses. A strong stimulus causes a higher impulse frequency than does a weak one and consequently a more intense sensation.

[3] By the electrical stimulation of different regions of the exposed brain of a conscious subject, various sensations can be produced, depending upon the area stimulated.

34

The Functional Organization of the Nervous System. Reflex Action. Reciprocal Innervation

THE FUNCTIONAL ORGANIZATION OF THE CENTRAL NERVOUS SYSTEM

There are something like 12 billion nerve cells in the human brain. We have seen that each nerve cell has two processes that connect with cells in other parts of the brain or in the spinal cord. Also many processes of cells in the spinal cord ascend to the brain. The white matter of the nervous system is, then, composed of an immense number of nerve fibers. Some of these fibers are very long, for as we know, many pass from the central nervous system into the various cranial and spinal nerves to reach parts of the body more or less remotely situated. A nerve fiber in a large animal, such as a horse, may have a length of 4 or 5 feet, and one going to a remote part of a man's body, say to the sole of the foot, is 3 feet or more in length. Other fibers are no more than a fraction of an inch long. Upon a rough calculation it may be said that if it were possible to join all the fibers in the nervous system end to end they would form a thread that could be wound several times around the earth at the equator. It should again be impressed upon the reader that the fibers (both axons and dendrons) composing the various nerves of the body are processes of nerve cells whose bodies lie in the brain, spinal cord, or spinal ganglia (Ch. 35).

Communications between nerve cells are carried out through their

462

processes. The terminals of an axon of one nerve cell make contact with the dendrons of another, or with the surface of the other cell body. Contact is made through small terminal swellings called **synaptic knobs,** or *end feet* (Fig. 34.1). An axon never makes contact with another axon; and a dendron never connects with the dendron of another nerve cell. In the central nervous system several nerve cells, and often great numbers, are connected together in this way to form long "nerve chains." In Figure 34.1*B*, there is not true union between the two nerve cells. Their processes merely touch or are separated by a slight gap like leaves of adjacent trees. This relation of the two processes to each other is called a **synapse.** The nerve impulse travels from one process to the other at this point.[1] Most nerve cells in the brain and cord are connected with all the other nerve cells, and so any one nerve cell can send impulses to almost any other cell of the central nervous system. All these communications, of course, cannot be direct ones—that would be an utter impossibility. Since there are 12 billion cells, each cell, in order to send impulses to and receive impulses from every other cell, would need to have 24 billion fibers. The difficulty is overcome by having the impulses from large numbers of cells brought to central exchanges or stations, which are composed of smaller groups of nerve cells connected together. These central stations are connected with other stations, which in turn are connected with and receive impulses from many other nerve cell groups.

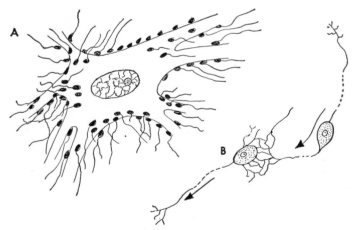

Fig. 34.1. Showing synaptic connections between neurons. *A,* synaptic knobs; there are usually many more than shown here to each nerve cell. *B,* synapse; the arrows indicate the direction taken by the nerve impulses.

---

[1] It is more likely that a fresh impulse is created at the junction rather than that the impulse passes from one neuron to the other across the synapse.

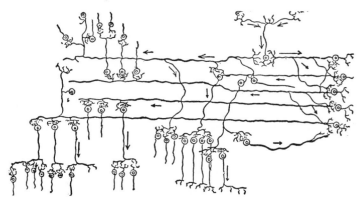

Fig. 34.2. Diagram to show how a few nerve cells may communicate with a great number of others in different parts of the central nervous system.

We have all experienced the long train of thought that may be started in our minds by perhaps some very trivial thing—the sight of a familiar object, the smell of some well-known flower, or the sound of some old tune. A number (perhaps comparatively small) of nerve cells have been excited by the sight, smell, or sound. They send impulses with lightning speed to vast hosts of other cells to create the pictures and thoughts in our minds. As these words are being written, some nerve cells are awakened at the seat of memory in the writer's brain. Others are being excited through the eyes as he sees the word he has written; still more are directing the movements of his fingers as he writes, while others are forming the thoughts and ideas he endeavors to put upon the paper. Other cells are receiving impulses through the nerves of hearing and the nerves of touch. All these myriads of cells are linked into a communicating system of the utmost intricacy. The cells in the central "exchanges" never give the "wrong number"—that is, discharge impulses over the wrong fiber. Not only must nerve impulses be transmitted along the right path, but they must be very accurately timed. They must not be even a thousandth of a second early or late in arriving at their destination. All must be dispatched in perfectly regular order. Sometimes, though seldom, a mistake in timing is made. While eating, for example, the tongue may be bitten. This unpleasant experience results from the messages to the tongue arriving a little too late or the messages to the jaw muscles arriving too early, so that the tongue does not get out of the way of the teeth quickly enough. Again, food sometimes "goes the wrong way"; that is, a little food slips into the larynx at the upper end of the windpipe (trachea), and we cough and splutter. The messages from the brain that should close the entrance to the larynx when we swallow have not arrived on time, and the food has passed into the forbidden region (Ch. 25).

REFLEX ACTION

Anyone who has fished with worms for bait knows how the worm twists and coils as though in agony when the hook transfixes it. Very tender-hearted persons are inclined to pity the squirming worm, and in their minds compare it with some higher animal and think the movements mean that the creature is suffering. But the worm has no brain; therefore it cannot feel in the sense that a horse or a dog or a human being feels. The antics of the transfixed worm are performed unconsciously and are a form of *reflex action*. Merely touching or pricking the worm will produce the coiling and twisting motions that seem expressive of resentment—for even a "worm will turn." Also, when a person accidentally touches a hot object that causes pain, or pricks a finger, he quickly draws the injured part away (Plate IV*a*). As we know, this is a purely involuntary movement, and though we feel pain at the time, the sensation is not absolutely necessary for the action to occur. For example, a frog with its brain destroyed will quickly pull its foot away when touched with something hot. Even if the toes are pinched, it will withdraw its foot. Obviously, the animal cannot feel in the ordinary sense of the word. These are all examples of reflex action.

Reflex action (also simply called a **reflex**) is an automatic, involuntary, and often unconscious act, brought about when certain nerves are stimulated. Of all the duties or functions performed by nervous tissue, reflex action is the most elementary. The movements of such simple animals as jellyfish, clams, worms, and snails are purely reflex in nature. Many of our everyday acts, also, are simply reflexes. The winking of the eye when a particle of dust touches an eyelid; coughing when some material finds its way into the larynx; sneezing when something irritates the inside of the nose; the quick recovery of the body's balance when we trip and nearly fall; the pulling away of the hand or other member when it is hurt, are all examples of reflexes. These actions occur apart from our wills or intelligence. Nevertheless we can often, through the exercise of higher faculties, to some extent control them. Some people have greater control than others. Children usually have less control than older persons. For instance, when one is in the dentist's chair and is suddenly hurt, the first impulse is to jump or jerk the head away, but one manages, through the exercise of his will power, or, as it is often called, his self-control, to prevent the reflex from coming into effect.

A sudden, intense pain may start a reflex that comes into action so quickly that it is impossible to check it. A motorist, for example, driving along the highway in the summer is sometimes stung by an insect. The acute pain causes a reflex movement of the hands and body to occur so suddenly that it cannot be checked. The control of the car may be lost for an instant and a serious accident occur. Besides such obvious reflex actions as those just mentioned and of which we are conscious, a very great many of the functions of our bodies are carried out reflexly and unconsciously. The action of the heart, the secretion of saliva and of gastric juice, swallowing, the movements of the stomach and intestines, as well as many other vital actions, are quite automatic, unconscious, and involuntary. Most of these are carried out through the autonomic nervous system (Ch. 37).

How the stimulation of a nerve causes a reflex. It was mentioned in Chapter 33 that a nerve cell has two fibers, or processes. One, the dendron, carries impulses to the nerve cell body; the other, the axon, carries impulses from the cell body. At least two nerve cells are required to carry out a reflex. The axon of one cell is brought into contact with the body or the dendron of the other, as shown in Figure 34.3. The dendron of cell 2 is simply one of the fibers of a sensory nerve. It is a nerve, let us say, that goes to the skin and ends in a receptor. The axon of cell 1 goes to a muscle. When the ending of the sensory nerve is stimulated— as when the skin is pricked or burned—a message passes in the direction of the arrows to the central nervous system and then to the muscle. In other words, the message is turned back, or *reflected,* to a point near the one from which it started; hence the name *reflex.* Now we may see how the hand almost inevitably must be jerked away when the finger is hurt.

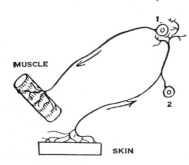

MUSCLE

SKIN

Fig. 34.3. Diagram of a reflex arc, showing a connection between two nerve cells; axon (1) to muscle, dendron (2) from skin.

Reflexes may be carried out through the nerves of the brain (cerebral reflexes), as in the winking reflex; or they may occur through the spinal nerves (spinal reflexes), as when the finger is burned or pricked. Figure 34.3 may be taken to represent two nerve cells in a spinal reflex. Of the two, the body of cell 1 lies within the cord itself. The body of cell 2 lies close to but not actually in the cord (Ch. 35). So we may represent these two nerves lying in their proper positions in the body as in Plate IV*a.*

Figure 34.3 shows the simplest possible kind of reflex since the pathway is composed of but two neurons. Only one such pathway is shown in the diagram. Only one reflex (knee jerk) as simple as this can be demonstrated in higher animals. Usually the reflex path consists of three neurons, and impulses are discharged over hundreds or thousands of such three-neuron linkages when a reflex act occurs. For example, many fine nerves end in a very small area of skin, and many motor nerve branches go to even the smallest muscle. Indeed, every motor nerve fiber divides into a number of minute branches each one of which is received by a single muscle fiber of the group (Fig. 34.4).[2] So, then, when the arm muscles suddenly draw the hand away as a result of some painful stimulation of the skin, messages travel along many sensory fibers and are reflected along a very great number of motor nerve fibers to the various muscles of the arm. The nerve cells that furnish the dendrons to skin and the axons to muscle may also communicate with many other cells within the central nervous system, and so during the performance of a complicated reflex act enormous numbers of nerve cells may be involved.

Fig. 34.4. The ending of a motor nerve in a muscle fiber.

Definition of terms. The complete pathway along which an impulse passes to produce a reflex act—that is, from skin to spinal cord, for example, and from cord to muscle—is called the **reflex arc.** The ingoing "leg" of the journey is called the **afferent limb** of the arc; the outgoing—that is, from cord or brain to muscle (or gland)—is called the **efferent limb.** In Plate IV*b* is depicted a reflex arc composed of three nerve cells; one lies entirely within the cord and connects the fibers of the other two. Nearly all reflexes of man and higher animals involve these three types of nerve cells. The one carrying the impulse to the central nervous system is also frequently referred to as the **receptor neuron,** and the one leading from cord to muscle (or gland) as the **effector neuron.** The connecting link within the cord is called the **connector neuron.**

RECIPROCAL ACTION OF THE MUSCLES

When the forearm is moved, as, for example, when the hand is raised to the face, the muscle on the front of the arm (*biceps*) shortens (contracts) and pulls upon the forearm to bend the elbow. When the arm is straightened again, the muscle on the back of the arm (*triceps*) contracts and pulls upon the forearm to bring it into a straight line with the upper arm. It must be quite clear that both muscles, biceps and triceps, should not shorten at the same time. One must lengthen (relax) when the other contracts. Otherwise, the two muscles would pull against each other and the arm could not be bent, or if it had been bent, it could not be straightened. No matter how quickly a person bends and straightens his arms, as in boxing or rowing, or bends and straightens his legs, as in running or jumping, the muscles on the fronts and backs of

[2] The group of muscle fibers supplied by a single fiber is called a *motor unit.*

the limbs under normal circumstances always act in the proper way—one set contracting, the other set relaxing. Sometimes, however, one set of muscles does not relax as it should, and the arm or leg cannot be bent if it is straight, or straightened if it is bent. The limb is held set and rigid, as when a person develops cramps in his arms or legs. When the muscles are acting normally, impulses are discharged to one set of muscles, say the flexors, and cause them to contract at the same instant that the opposing set, the extensors, are made to relax. The latter muscles are said to be *inhibited.* At the next instant the movements may be reversed, the muscles that were contracting now relax, and those that were relaxed contract. The arrival of the impulses must be timed with an accuracy measured by small fractions of a second. This give-and-take, this "seesaw" of contraction and relaxation brought about by the accurate timing of the impulses arriving along the nerves to the muscles, is called **reciprocal innervation,** or **reciprocal inhibition**[3] (Fig. 34.5).

Usually a great number of muscles of various sizes and shapes act in a regular and orderly way to bring about a muscular act. Each muscle,

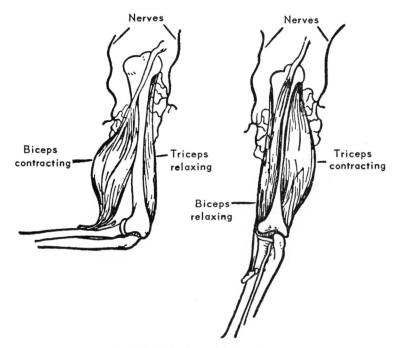

Fig. 34.5. Reciprocal innervation.

[3] The arrangement of nerves whereby the messages (of contraction or relaxation) are conveyed to the alternating muscles (for example, biceps and triceps) is termed *reciprocal innervations;* the term *reciprocal inhibition* refers to the relaxation of the antagonistic (contracting) muscle.

in turn, is made up of an immense number of separate fibers (Ch. 4), and each fiber must receive a separate series of impulses from the central nervous system before it will contract. In carrying out any voluntary or willed act, the impulses arise in and are discharged from the **motor area** of the cerebral cortex (Ch. 37).

In order to realize with what wonderful precision the human machine of brain, nerves, and muscles does its work, one needs only to think, for example, of a pianist reading and playing a difficult piece of music. The musician's brain is interpreting the notes of the music, which he sees through impulses received from the eyes. Impulses are sent in turn, at a speed of 120 meters per second, along the trunk lines and innumerable "wires" of his nervous system. The muscles of the shoulders, arms, wrists, and forearms are contracting and relaxing with the exactness of a complex machine. His fingers move rapidly over the keyboard; each small muscle pulls upon the finger bones at the right instant and relaxes at the next to allow another muscle to contract. A similar give-and-take is seen in other muscles of the body. In speaking, for instance, muscles of the tongue, lips, cheeks, throat, and chest all act with one accord. No muscle interferes with the action of another.

35
The Spinal Cord and Nerve Trunks. Degeneration and Regeneration of Nerve

The nervous system consists of (1) the **brain,** (2) the **spinal cord,** and (3) the **peripheral nerves** (Fig. 35.1). The brain and cord together are called the **central nervous system.** The system of nerves and ganglia lying for the most part outside the central nervous system though in communication with it is called the **autonomic, involuntary,** or **vegetative, nervous system** (Ch. 37).

THE SPINAL CORD

The spinal cord is white and soft like marrow and about ½ inch in diameter. It lies within the vertebral foramina formed by the arches and bodies of the vertebrae, and is thus protected from shocks and other mechanical injuries. Many nerves leave and enter the cord and serve to carry impulses to and from various parts of the body and the central nervous system (Fig. 35.2). When the spinal cord is sectioned transversely, it is found that its center, or core, has a darker color than its peripheral portion (Figs. 35.2, 35.6). This central part, which has a shape resembling that of the letter H or of a butterfly, is, like the cerebral cortex (Ch. 37), composed of **gray matter**—that is, nerve cell bodies and nerve fibers. The latter, both axons and dendrites, are derived from the contained nerve cells as well as from nerve cells in more remote parts of the nervous system. The wings of gray matter are inclined forward and backward. The former are broad and are called the **anterior** (or **ventral) horns;** the more slender hind parts of the wings are called the

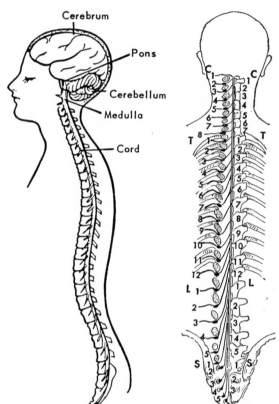

Cerebrum

Pons

Cerebellum

Medulla

Cord

Fig. 35.1 *(left).* Outline sketch of the central nervous system.

Fig. 35.2 *(right).* Showing the emergence of the posterior spinal nerve roots from the spinal canal. Numbers on the right refer to the vertebrae, on the left to the nerve roots (heavy black lines with swellings representing the ganglia); C, cervical; T̄, thoracic; L, lumbar; S, sacral; Coc., coccygeal.

posterior (or dorsal) horns. The nerve cells of the anterior horns give rise to fibers (axons) that leave the cord by the anterior roots of the spinal nerves (p. 476). The cells of the posterior horns receive fibers from the posterior roots. The part of the cord surrounding the central gray area is composed entire of white matter—that is, bundles of nerve fibers. The spinal cord is ensheathed by three membranes—dura mater, arachnoid, and pia mater—which are continuous with those of the same names covering the brain (Ch. 37). Cerebrospinal fluid also fills the space between the arachnoid and the pia mater.

As well as being a *reflex center* (Ch. 34), the spinal cord is a two-way conducting pathway. Like a great cable whose wires carry messages in both directions, the fibers of its white matter carry impulses up and down. It transmits voluntary impulses from the motor area of the cerebral cortex (Ch. 37) to groups of cells in the anterior horns of the spinal gray matter. Many of its afferent (ascending) messages are secret, reaching only unconscious centers of the brain (cerebellum, medulla oblongata, and pons), and many of its efferent (descending) fibers carry orders of which we are unaware, to blood vessels, glands, and other structures which, therefore, appear to act automatically.

The white matter of each half of the cord is divided into three columns—*anterior, lateral,* and *posterior*—by the gray matter of the anterior and posterior horns, and the emergence of the fibers of the spinal nerve roots (Fig. 35.3). The fibers of these columns are gathered into groups called **tracts,** or **fasciculi** (L., sing. *fasciculus,* a small bundle). Those that transmit impulses upward are called **ascending tracts;** those that carry impulses in the reverse direction are called **descending tracts.** Each column of the cord contains two or more tracts, or fasciculi, that have been given names to indicate the origins and destinations of their constituent fibers.

The **anterior columns** contain the **anterior corticospinal** (or **direct pyramidal**) **tracts,** which transmit voluntary motor impulses. Impulses that give rise to the sensation of touch are transmitted by the **anterior spinothalamic tracts** contained in the anterior columns.

The **lateral columns** contain both ascending and descending tracts. The former, through the **lateral spinothalamic tract,** transmits impulses that give rise to *pain,* and to sensations of *heat* and *cold;* and through the **spinocerebellar tracts,** nonsensory (subconscious) impulses from the muscles and joints to the cerebellum. The most important descending tract is the **lateral corticospinal** (or **crossed pyramidal**) **tract** which occupies the posterior part of each lateral column. The fibers of this tract are the axons of cells in the motor area of the cerebral cortex; they form connections with the anterior horn cells and transmit impulses that are relayed by the axons of the latter cells (and which form the motor nerves) to the skeletal muscles (see also p. 504).

The **posterior columns** are composed entirely of ascending fibers that form two tracts named the **fasciculus gracilis** and the **fasciculus cuneatus.** These tracts are purely sensory; they carry impulses giving rise to sensations of touch, and to sensations from the muscles and joints. Our knowledge of the movements and positions of our limbs is conveyed through these tracts of the posterior columns.

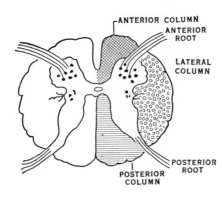

ANTERIOR COLUMN
ANTERIOR ROOT
LATERAL COLUMN
POSTERIOR ROOT
POSTERIOR COLUMN

Fig. 35.3. Diagram showing the cross section of the spinal cord and the fibers leaving and entering by the anterior and the posterior nerve roots. The left half of the cord is left blank; on the right side the three main columns of the cord are marked by distinctive shading. The small dots in the anterior horns represent the anterior horn cells.

The principal tracts of the spinal cord are given in Table 35.1.

TABLE 35.1

THE PRINCIPAL TRACTS OF THE SPINAL CORD

	Ascending	*Descending*
Anterior column	Anterior spinothalamic Sensation of touch	Anterior corticospinal

Lateral column	Lateral spinothalamic
	  Sensations of pain, heat and cold
	Spinocerebellar (dorsal and ventral tracts)
	  Transmits nonsensory impulses to the cerebellum
		Lateral corticospinal
		  Transmits impulses from the cerebral cortex to the motor cells of the anterior horns of the spinal cord

Posterior column	Fasciculus gracilis Fasciculus cuneatus Sensations of touch, and sensations from the bones and joints	

THE NERVE TRUNKS

The nerves are long, tough cords that connect the muscles, skin, sense organs, and practically every tissue of the body with the spinal cord and brain. Each nerve is simply a great number of nerve fibers bound together side by side like fine wires in an electric cable. If one takes a piece of ordinary electric extension cord and cuts off the cloth cover, a rubber insulating material will be found underneath. When the rubber is removed, a large number of fine copper wires are seen within, bound closely together. A nerve is made up in somewhat the same way. The nerve is covered on the outside by an insulation of fatty material. Within this are a great number of fine fibers, but in ordinary nerves each fiber is insulated from its neighbor. The nerve fibers are also very much finer and a great deal more numerous than the fine copper wires in the electric cord. They are too fine to be seen with the naked eye, and a large nerve may contain many thousands of them (Fig. 35.4). *Each fiber is a process of a nerve cell of the central nervous system* (Ch. 33) *or of a cell in the ganglion of a posterior spinal nerve root.* Some nerves, such as the **motor nerves** that supply the voluntary muscles, are composed entirely of efferent fibers. Others contain only afferent fibers and are called **sensory nerves**. Other nerves again contain both efferent and afferent fibers and are called **mixed nerves**. Many afferent nerves, however, carry secret information, that is, impulses that are beneath consciousness. Impulses from the stomach and heart, for example, are usually of this type. The efferent fibers that cause contraction of the smooth muscle of these organs, or secretion of their glands belong to the autonomic nervous system (Ch. 37).

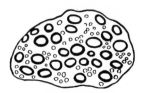

Fig. 35.4. Cross section of a small mixed nerve. The very fine circles are sympathetic nerve fibers (see Ch. 37).

As well as the general terms afferent, efferent, sensory, motor, etc., nerves also are given names to indicate their origins. For instance, the afferent nerves of sight, hearing, smell, and taste, the nerves of the teeth and of the skin of the face, and the motor nerves (efferent) to the facial muscles, since their fibers pass directly to or from the brain and therefore enter or issue from the cranial cavity, are all called **cranial nerves** (Ch. 37).

The spinal nerves. The nerves that enter (afferent) or leave (efferent) the cord are called **spinal nerves.** There are 31 pairs of these (Fig. 35.2). When the spinal canal, formed by the vertebrae, is opened up, the nerves can be seen leaving the cord at intervals throughout nearly its entire length. The nerves leave the spinal canal by passing through the intervertebral foramina which are situated between the bodies of the vertebrae. Each spinal nerve has an *anterior* and a *posterior root,* which emerge in vertical series from the longitudinal grooves between the columns of the cord (Fig. 35.5). The **anterior roots** are composed entirely of efferent fibers, most of which are motor; they enter into the formation of one or another of the various nerves, and relay impulses received by the anterior horn cells via the corticospinal tracts to the voluntary muscles. Fibers of the autonomic nervous system (Ch. 37) also leave the cord by the anterior roots in the thoracic and upper part of the lumbar region of the spinal cord.

The **posterior roots** contain only afferent fibers, many of which are sensory, but there are many also that carry impulses destined for the cerebellum and other parts of the brain concerned with subconscious

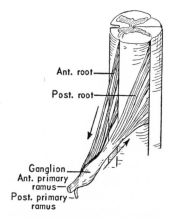

Ant. root

Post. root

Ganglion

Ant. primary ramus

Post. primary ramus

Fig. 35.5. The spinal nerve roots of one segment of the spinal cord; the arrows indicate the direction taken by the nerve impulses.

functions. The purely efferent nature of the anterior roots was shown by a Scottish surgeon, Sir Charles Bell; that the posterior roots were entirely afferent was demonstrated by a French physiologist, François Magendie. The statement of these two facts is called the *Bell-Magendie law.*

The two spinal nerve roots join a short distance from the cord to form the complete **nerve trunk,** which, being composed of both afferent and efferent fibers, is therefore a *mixed nerve.* But at variable distances along their course from the cord to their destination, motor sensory, and autonomic fibers become separated from one another to form smaller nerves composed purely of one or the other type (Ch. 36).

A small swelling is seen on the posterior root of each spinal nerve. This enlargement, called a **ganglion,** is made up of a mass of nerve cells. It is these cells that supply the afferent or sensory fibers of the mixed nerve (Figs. 35.2, 35.5). The cells are *unipolar*—that is, only one process is given off by the cell; but this process after a very short course divides into two. One branch of the T- or Y-shaped fiber thus formed enters the spinal cord; the other passes to the periphery as a fiber of a peripheral afferent nerve.

Should a *sensory* nerve be cut or destroyed by disease, no impulses can reach the brain from the organ—whether eye, ear, or skin—in which this nerve had its ending. Blindness, deafness, or loss of sensation in the skin, according to the nerve injured, would be the consequence. When a *motor* nerve is cut through or seriously injured, no impulses can reach the muscle in which the nerve ends; so the muscle cannot be made to contract—it is paralyzed.

DEGENERATION AND REGENERATION OF NERVE

The fibers of any nerve are dependent for their nourishment and integrity upon the nerve cell body of which they are merely extensions. When, therefore, the nerve fiber is interrupted in any way, as by crushing or cutting, the part of the fiber farther from the body of the cell undergoes degeneration. This consists of a breakdown of the structure of the fiber while the fatty material of the myelin sheath breaks up into droplets of oil (Fig. 35.6). These changes were studied by Augustus Waller, an English physiologist, and hence are known as *Wallerian degeneration.* The fibers lose all power to conduct. The body of the nerve cell itself also shows changes *(retrograde degeneration)*, namely, dissolution of the tigroid substance. If the nerve possesses a neurilemma, the nerve fibers after a time undergo regeneration which may result in complete restoration of function. This process consists of the growth of fibers from the nerve above the injury into the neurilemma sheaths of the fibers below. Regeneration is more readily effected if the nerve has been only crushed so that the fibers have been interrupted but the continuity of the neurilemma left intact. The degeneration of a nerve after section is a most valuable experimental method for determining the direction in which the bodies of the nerve cells of any tract in the central nervous system lie, or for tracing the course of the fibers. Thus, if part of the motor area of the cerebral cortex is destroyed, fibers can be detected

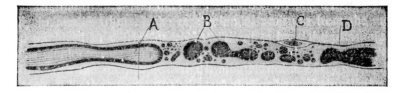

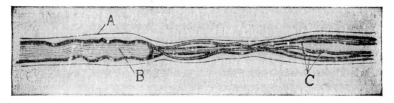

Fig. 35.6. *Above,* degenerating nerve fiber two days after section. *A,* end of proximal segment of nerve; *B,* drops of myelin derived from the myelin sheath; *C,* nucleus of neurilemma; *D,* neurilemma. *Below,* regenerating nerve fiber. *A,* neurilemma; *B,* proximal segment of nerve fiber showing bulbous end; *C,* neurofibrils which have sprouted from the end of the original fiber. *After Ranvier.)*

microscopically extending down the lateral columns of the spinal cord (lateral corticospinal tract). Again, if an anterior spinal nerve root is divided, the fibers on the distal side of the cut degenerate but not those on the proximal side; the cell bodies, then, must lie in the cord. But if a posterior root is sectioned close to its origin from the cord, only those on the proximal side of the cut degenerate (Fig. 35.7); the cells that give origin to the fibers must lie, therefore, on the distal side of the section, namely, in the ganglion of the root.

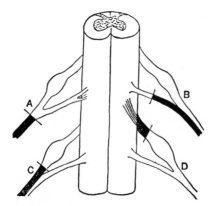

Fig. 35.7. Diagram to illustrate Wallerian degeneration. Section at A causes degeneration of all motor and sensory fibers of the peripheral nerve beyond the point of section (black area). In B, section of the anterior root causes degeneration of the motor fibers because the motor cell bodies lie within the spinal cord; in C, section of the posterior root is followed by degeneration of the sensory fibers of the peripheral nerve because the cell bodies of the sensory fibers lie in the ganglion; in D, section of the posterior root between the ganglion and the cord causes degeneration of the sensory fibers of the spinal stump of the root and of ascending fibers within the cord as far as the next cell station. *(After Halliburton.)*

36
The Distribution of the Spinal Nerves

The spinal nerve trunks, as already noted, are mixed in type; each receives motor and sensory fibers through its two roots—fibers that carry voluntary impulses to the muscles, and those that convey afferent impulses from skin, mucous membranes, muscles, joints, etc., to conscious or to subconscious parts of the brain, such as the cerebellum. The nerves from the thoracic and upper part of the lumbar region of the spinal cord also receive fibers of the autonomic nervous system (Ch. 37).

It has also been explained how the first two types of fiber arise and how they form a motor and a sensory root that join within the spinal canal to form the mixed nerve trunk (Ch. 35). In this chapter the course

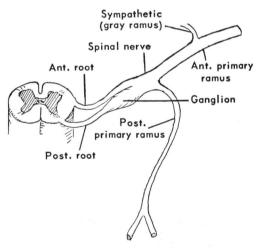

Fig. 36.1. Showing a spinal nerve dividing into anterior and posterior primary rami.

477

and distribution of the nerve trunks so formed will be described from their emergence through the intervertebral foramina to their distribution to muscles, skin, etc.

Each nerve after it leaves the intervertebral foramen gives off a small twig that returns again to the spinal canal and supplies the membranes of the spinal cord. The mixed nerve trunk then immediately splits into two branches called the *posterior* and *anterior primary rami* (Fig. 36.1).

THE POSTERIOR PRIMARY RAMI OF THE SPINAL NERVES

The posterior primary rami supply the muscles and skin of the posterior aspect of the trunk and the scalp over the posterior half or so of the skull. These primary rami of the spinal nerves run in series down the back, piercing the overlying muscles and reaching the skin, in which their finest branches terminate.

THE ANTERIOR PRIMARY RAMI OF THE SPINAL NERVES

The anterior primary rami supply the limbs, but most of them first join to form complicated nerve patterns called **plexuses** (Figs. 36.2, 36.4, 36.7). These are four in number and are named the *cervical, brachial, lumbar,* and *sacral plexuses.* A rearrangement of the fibers of the anterior primary rami takes place within the plexuses so that in the nerves that finally emerge (that is, the branches of the plexus) the grouping of the fibers is different from that in the spinal roots themselves.

The cervical plexus

This plexus lies deep in the neck, opposite the upper four cervical vertebrae. It is formed by the anterior rami of the upper four cervical nerves. Each of the lower three nerves divides into two branches (upper and lower) that, uniting, form three loops that give off branches for distribution to the muscles and skin of the neck and posterior part of the scalp (Figs. 36.2, 36.3); and each sends, as well, communicating branches to the tenth, eleventh, and twelfth cranial nerves. The main branches of the cervical plexus are as follows:

Superficial	Lesser occipital	Anterior cutaneous
	Great auricular	Supraclavicular
Muscular	Phrenic to diaphragm	To sternomastoid
	To rectus capitis lateralis	To trapezius
	To rectus capitis anterior	To levator scapulae
	To longus capitis	To scalenus medius
	To longus cervicis	
Communicating	To vagus, accessory, and hypoglossal nerves	

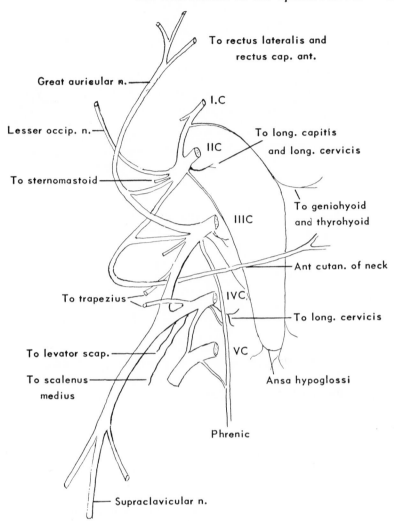

To rectus lateralis and
rectus cap. ant.

Great auricular n.

I.C

Lesser occip. n.

IIC

To long. capitis
and long. cervicis

To sternomastoid

To geniohyoid
and thyrohyoid

IIIC

Ant cutan. of neck

To trapezius

IVC

To long. cervicis

To levator scap.

VC

To scalenus
medius

Ansa hypoglossi

Phrenic

Supraclavicular n.

Fig. 36.2. The cervical plexus; IC to VC indicate anterior primary rami of cervical nerves.

The brachial plexus

The brachial plexus (Fig. 36.4) lies in the lower part of the neck and in the region of the clavicle and axilla. The anterior primary divisions of the lower four cervical nerves and most of the fibers of the anterior primary rami of the first thoracic nerve enter into its formation. Fibers are also, as a rule, received from the fourth cervical nerve, which descend to join the fifth cervical nerve. The anterior primary rami of these spinal nerves are called the **roots** of the plexus. The roots form three short **trunks**—*upper, middle,* and *lower.* The upper trunk is formed

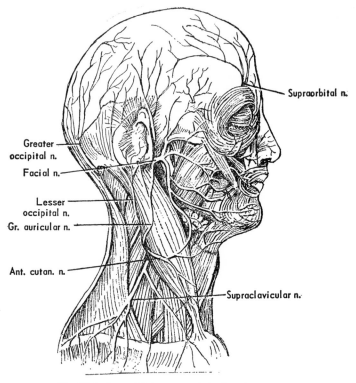

Supraorbital n.

Greater occipital n.

Facial n.

Lesser occipital n.

Gr. auricular n.

Ant. cutan. n.

Supraclavicular n.

Fig. 36.3. Superficial nerves of the head and neck.

by the union of the fifth and sixth cervical nerves; the seventh cervical nerve alone forms the middle trunk; the eighth cervical and first thoracic nerves form the lower trunk.

These trunks pass downwards and laterally; just above or behind the clavicle, each divides into an anterior and a posterior division. There are thus three anterior and three posterior divisions. Next, by reunions of these divisions, three **cords**—*lateral, medial,* and *posterior*—are formed. The outer two anterior divisions form the lateral cord, the inner anterior division by itself forms the middle cord, while the three posterior divisions unite to form the posterior cord. From these the four principal nerves of the upper limb—*musculocutaneous, radial, median,* and *ulnar*—are derived.

Branches of the brachial plexus. A number of muscles of the neck (rhomboids, scaleni, serratus anterior, subclavius, supraspinatus, and infraspinatus) receive small branches from the roots or the trunks of the plexus. The pectoralis major and minor are supplied by branches, the **pectoral nerves,** from the lateral and medial cords. The **nerve to the latissimus dorsi** is a branch of the posterior cord and supplies the muscle

Branches	Cords	Divisions	Trunks	Roots	Spinal segments

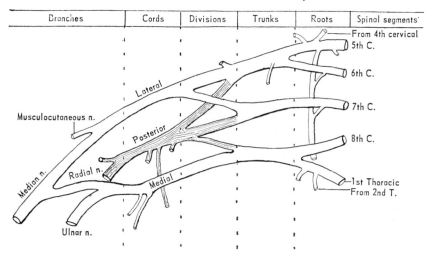

Fig. 36.4. The left brachial plexus.

of the same name. A branch of the posterior cord, called the **circumflex nerve,** supplies the deltoid muscle and the shoulder joint. The large nerves springing from the cords of the brachial plexus and supplying the arm are given in the following table.

Lateral cord { Musculocutaneous / Lateral root of median

Medial cord { Medial root of median / Ulnar

Posterior cord   Radial

The musculocutaneous nerve is the smaller of the two terminal branches of the lateral cord of the plexus. It runs down the arm between the biceps and the brachialis muscles to reach the outer side of the biceps tendon on the front of the elbow joint; it is continued into the forearm as the **lateral cutaneous nerve of the forearm.** This latter nerve runs along the outer border of the front of the forearm to the wrist and ends in the skin over the ball of the thumb (thenar eminence). The musculocutaneous nerve sends branches to the coracobrachialis, biceps, and brachialis muscles, and a twig to the elbow joint. The lateral cutaneous nerve supplies the skin over the lateral surface of the forearm and, as just stated, over the thenar eminence of the hand (Fig. 36.5).

The median nerve arises by two roots, one from the lateral, the other from the medial cord, which unite on the front of the axillary artery. It descends the arm, lying first on the outer side of the brachial artery but later crossing the front of the artery to its medial side. It sends branches to all the superficial muscles on the front of the forearm, excepting the flexor carpi ulnaris. In the palmar aspect of the hand it supplies the muscles of the thenar eminence, the skin over the palm, the thumb, the first and second fingers, and the lateral half of the ring finger, as shown in Figure 36.6 (right). It also supplies the skin on the back of the thumb and outer three fingers as shown in this figure (left).

The ulnar nerve arises from the medial cord of the brachial plexus and runs down the inner side of the axillary and brachial arteries to the middle of the arm, then inclines medially and backwards to the interval between the olecranon of the ulna and the medial epicondyle of the humerus, where it lies just beneath the skin. It is often struck here, and a tingling sensation is felt, which is spoken of as "knocking the funny bone." It inclines forwards again, and entering the forearm, descends on the medial side of its anterior surface, where it is covered in its upper

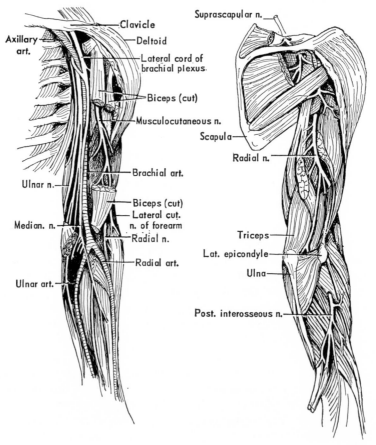

Fig. 36.5. Nerves of the upper limb. *Left,* anterior aspect; *right,* posterior aspect.

half by the flexor carpi ulnaris. Its lower half is covered only by skin and fascia. In the palm, it ends by dividing into a *superficial* and a *deep* branch.

The ulnar nerve supplies the flexor carpi ulnaris muscle and the medial half of the flexor digitorum profundus; it also supplies the skin on the medial parts of the dorsal and palmar surfaces of the hand, and on the adjacent parts of the fingers, as shown in Figure 36.6.

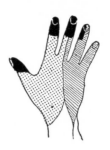

Fig. 36.6. Distribution of the cutaneous nerves to the hands. *Left,* dorsal aspect; *right,* palmar aspect. Hatched area, ulnar nerve; black, median nerve; stippled, radial nerve.

The **radial nerve** (old term *musculospiral*) is the continuation of the posterior cord of the brachial plexus, and is the largest nerve of the upper limb. As it enters the upper arm from the axilla, it runs backwards between the long and medial heads of the triceps muscle, and behind the humerus. Descending obliquely in the spiral groove of the bone, and covered by the lateral head of the triceps, it reaches the outer side of the humerus and comes to the front of the arm. It then descends in the furrow between the brachialis and brachioradialis to the front of the lateral epicondyle. Here it gives off its *posterior interosseous branch.* It then runs down the other side of the anterior surface of the forearm and lateral to the radial artery. Lower in the forearm, it turns around the outer side of the radius and divides into branches that supply the skin over the radial half of the back of the hand, the base of the thumb, the proximal and middle phalanges of the index finger, and the part of the middle finger not supplied by the median and ulnar nerves.

The radial nerve has been called the great "extensor" nerve of the upper limb. Before giving off its large posterior interosseous branch, it supplies the triceps, anconeus, brachioradialis, extensor carpi ulnaris, brachialis, and extensor carpi radialis.

The radial nerve may be injured in the arm in fractures of the humerus, or from pressure, as when a person falls asleep with the arm hanging over the back of a chair, especially during a drunken stupor. The nerve may be injured in a similar way in an anesthetized patient if the arm hangs down over the edge of the operating table. It is also sometimes injured in the axilla by the pressure of a crutch ("crutch palsy"). When the nerve is paralyzed the wrist cannot be raised (extended), the condition being termed *dropped wrist.*

The **posterior interosseous nerve,** the terminal branch of the radial nerve, turns backwards through the supinator muscle and around the lateral side of the radius to gain the back of the forearm. It sends branches to the supinator, extensor carpi radialis brevis, extensor digitorum, extensor digiti minimi, extensor indicis, abductor pollicis longus, and extensor pollicis brevis, in which it terminates.

The anterior primary rami of the thoracic nerves

The anterior primary rami of the thoracic nerves enter the thorax and run forward along the lower borders of the ribs, where they are known as the **intercostal nerves,** except the twelfth of the series which is called the **subcostal nerve;** the latter runs below the last rib and not in an intercostal space. The intercostal nerves supply the internal and external intercostal muscles. The upper six nerves pierce the thoracic wall near the sternum and supply the skin over the front of the thorax. These terminal branches are called the **anterior cutaneous nerves of the thorax.** The lower intercostal nerves (seventh to twelfth, inclusive) pass forward from the intercostal spaces and supply the muscles and skin of the abdominal wall.

The lumbar plexus

The anterior primary rami of the lumbar nerves curve downward and outward behind or within the psoas major muscle. The anterior primary rami of the first, second, and third lumbar nerves, and most of the fibers of the anterior primary ramus of the fourth enter into the formation of this plexus (Fig. 36.7).

The primary ramus of the first lumbar nerve divides into an upper and a lower branch. The former divides into the *iliohypogastric* and *ilio-inguinal nerves.* The lower branch of the anterior primary ramus of the first lumbar nerve joins a branch of the anterior primary ramus of the second lumbar nerve to form the *genitofemoral nerve.* Parts of the anterior primary rami of the second and third lumbar nerves give rise to the *lateral cutaneous nerve of the thigh.* The *obturator* and *femoral nerves* are formed by parts of the second, third, and fourth lumbar nerves (Fig. 36.7).

The **iliohypogastric nerve** is distributed to the skin of the anterior part of the buttock and of the skin above the pubic region.

The **ilio-inguinal nerve** supplies the skin over the upper and inner part of the thigh at the root of the penis and upper part of the scrotum, or over the pubis and labium majus in the female.

The **genitofemoral nerve** supplies the skin of the scrotum (or labium majus in the female) and the upper part of the anterior surface of the thigh.

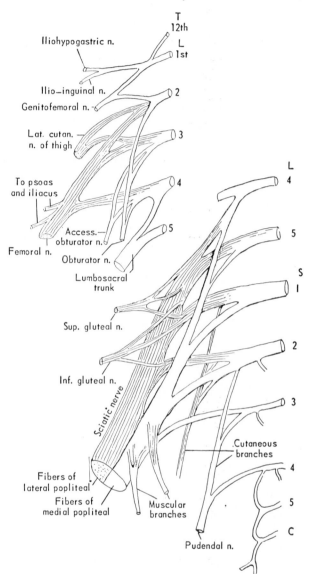

Fig. 36.7. Above, the lumbar plexus; *below*, sacral and coccygeal plexuses. *T, L, S,* and *C* refer to thoracic, lumbar, sacral, and coccygeal segments of the spinal cord.

The lateral cutaneous nerve of the thigh supplies the lateral part of the anterior surface of the thigh from the hip to the knee.

The obturator nerve enters the thigh through the obturator foramen; it supplies the obturator externus, gracilis, and adductor muscles.

The femoral nerve is a much larger nerve than any of the preceding. It enters the thigh by descending behind the inguinal ligament, and in the upper part of the limb lies in close relation to the femoral artery. Within the pelvis it gives branches to the iliacus and pectineus muscles.

A little below the inguinal ligament it gives off a number of muscular and cutaneous branches. The former supply the rectur femoris and the three vasti (medius, lateralis, and intermedius), and the skin over the anterior and medial parts of the thigh.

The **saphenous nerve** is a large cutaneous branch of the femoral nerve that lies, at first, in close relation to the femoral artery, but leaving this vessel in the lower part of the thigh, descends on the medial side of the knee and enters the leg. It runs down the medial side of the leg beside the long saphenous vein. In the lower part of the leg it divides into two branches, one of which is continued in front of the ankle into the foot to supply the skin on its medial side.

The sacral plexus

From the sacral plexus the large sciatic nerve and a number of smaller muscular nerves are derived. It is formed by the lumbosacral trunk and the anterior primary rami of the first three sacral nerves and part of the anterior primary ramus of the fourth (Fig. 36.7). The *lumbo-sacral trunk* is composed of a part of the anterior primary ramus of the fourth and all of the anterior primary ramus of the fifth lumbar nerves. The fourth lumbar nerve thus contributes to both lumbar and sacral plexuses and connects the two.

The sacral plexus lies in the pelvis on the piriformis muscle and behind the internal iliac vessels.

The anterior primary rami of the sacral nerves that enter into the formation of the plexus give off branches, mostly muscular, and then converging toward the greater sciatic foramen, join to form a large trunk called the *sciatic nerve*—the largest nerve of the body.

The branches of the sacral plexus are as follows:

Superior gluteal nerve
Inferior gluteal nerve
Nerve to pyriformis
Nerve to quadratus femoris and gemellus inferior
Nerve to obturator internus and gemellus superior
Posterior femoral cutaneous, or posterior cutaneous nerve of thigh
Perforating cutaneous nerve
Pudendal nerve
Sciatic nerve

The **posterior femoral cutaneous nerve** is distributed to the skin of the gluteal region, perineum, back of the thigh, and upper half of the calf of the leg. The **perforating cutaneous nerve** supplies the skin of the lower gluteal region. The **pudendal nerve** is distributed to the skin of the perineum, scrotum (labium majus in the female), and about the anus. A branch supplies the skin and substance of the penis (or clitoris in the female). Branches are given to the muscles of the perineum, and to the external anal sphincter and the sphincter of the urethra (Fig. 36.8).

The sciatic nerve. The sciatic nerve emerges from the pelvis through the greater sciatic foramen to occupy the interval between the greater trochanter and the tuberosity of the ischium. It descends in the middle of the back of the thigh. In this part of its course it lies upon the adductor magnus muscle and under cover of the long head of the biceps femoris. It divides in the lower part of the thigh into the *medial* and *lateral popliteal branches*. Before its division it sends branches to the biceps femoris, semitendinosus, semimembranosus, and adductor magnus muscles, and to the hip joint.

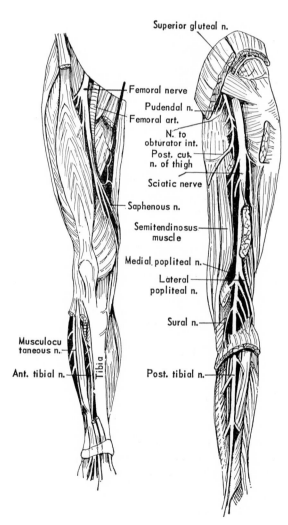

Fig. 36.8. Nerves of the lower limb. *Left,* anterior aspect; *right,* posterior aspect.

The medial popliteal nerve descends behind the knee joint and between the two heads of the gastrocnemius muscle, and is continued as the *posterior tibial nerve* into the leg. In its course behind the knee the medial popliteal nerve gives branches to the gastrocnemius, popliteus, plantaris, and soleus muscles, and supplies twigs to the knee joint. A long, cutaneous branch called the **sural nerve** arises from the medial popliteal nerve behind the knee and descends in the middle of the calf and along the outer border of the tendo calcaneus to the ankle. Here it turns forward below the lateral malleolus and then runs along the lateral part of the foot and side of the little toe.

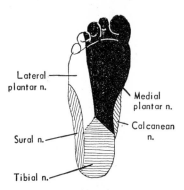

Lateral plantar n.

Medial plantar n.

Calcanean n.

Sural n.

Tibial n.

Fig. 36.9. Distribution of the cutaneous nerves to the sole of the foot.

The posterior tibial nerve, the continuation of the medial popliteal nerve, descends the middle of the back of the leg and turns beneath the medial malleolus. Here it divides into the **medial** and **lateral plantar nerves,** which supply the muscles and skin of the sole and toes. The distribution of the medial plantar nerve simulates that of the median nerve in the hand, while the lateral plantar nerve corresponds in its distribution to the ulnar nerve.

The lateral popliteal nerve is much the smaller of the two terminal branches of the sciatic nerve. It descends just behind the head of the fibula, where it can be felt with the finger. It gives off articular branches to the knee joint, and two cutaneous branches near the head of the fibula. One of these, known as the **lateral cutaneous nerve of the calf,** supplies the upper part of the leg on its anterior, posterior and outer sides. The other communicates with the sural branch of the medial popliteal nerve and is called the **sural communicating branch.** On the outer side of the neck of the fibula, the lateral popliteal nerve ends by dividing into the *musculocutaneous* and *anterior tibial nerves.*

The musculocutaneous nerve descends in close relation to the front of the fibula to the lower part of the leg, where it pierces the deep fascia and appears on the front of the limb. Here it divides into a *medial* and a *lateral branch.* The former supplies the skin over the dorsum of the foot, the inner side of the great toe, and the adjacent sides of the second and third toes. The lateral branch sends twigs to the cleft between the third and fourth, and the fourth and fifth toes, twigs going to their adjacent sides. The musculocutaneous nerve, before it divides into its terminals, sends branches to the peroneus longus and peroneus brevis muscles.

The anterior tibial nerve, the other terminal branch of the lateral popliteal, passes forwards and descends on the anterior surface of the interosseous membrane (Fig. 36.8); it supplies the tibialis anterior, extensor hallucis longus, extensor digitorum longus, and peroneus tertius, and sends a twig to the ankle joint. It divides into a *lateral* and a *medial terminal branch.* The former supplies the extensor digitorum longus and several joints of the foot. The medial terminal branch sends branches to the other joints of the foot and to the cleft between the great and second toes, the adjacent sides of which it supplies (Fig. 36.9).

37
The Brain, or Encephalon. Cranial Nerves. Autonomic Nervous System

THE BRAIN, OR ENCEPHALON

The brain is a mass of nervous tissue weighing in man about 3 pounds. Its under surface, which rests upon the floor of the skull, is very irregularly shaped. Its upper surface is curved into an oval dome and lies just beneath the roof of the skull.

There is probably no organ in the body that shows such great differences in shape, weight, size, and degree of development in various animals as does the brain. The brain of a rabbit or of a rat, or even a cat or a dog, resembles the brain of a man only in a very general way. By comparison with the human brain, the brain of even the highest sub-

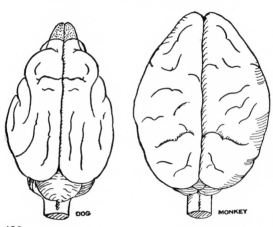

Fig. 37.1. Brains of a dog and a monkey. Compare the monkey's brain with the human brain.

490

human species appears as a very rudimentary structure, and is, of course, much smaller in relation to the weight of the body. The fore part of the animal brain is more sloping and narrower, not high and filled out like the brain of man. The vertex also in lower animals is much flatter and does not rise in the rounded swelling so characteristic of the human brain. In animals still lower in the scale, such as fish, snakes, and frogs, the brain is by comparison a very simple affair. The parts that have to do with the senses of smell (olfactory lobes) and of sight (optic lobes) form a large part of these primitive brains. In man the olfactory lobes are of an almost insignificant size. No definite optic lobes are seen, and the great development of that part of the brain concerned with the higher faculties (the cerebrum) completely overshadows those primitive parts so prominent in the brains of the lower animals (Figs. 37.1, 37.2).

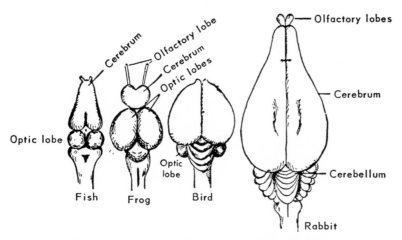

Fig. 37.2. Comparison of the brains of different animals.

All that part of the nervous system lying within the cranium is spoken of in general terms as the brain. It comprises four primary divisions which can be separately described. From below upwards they are the *brain stem* (medulla oblongata, pons, and midbrain), the *interbrain* (thalamus and hypothalamus), and the *cerebrum;* behind the brain stem and under the shelter of the posterior part of the cerebrum lies the *cerebellum,* or little brain (Fig. 37.3).

The brain stem

The cerebrum, like a blossom upon its stock, appears poised upon the comparatively slender column of nervous tissue known as the brain stem. Below, the latter is continuous through the foramen magnum of the occipital bone with the still more slender spinal cord. From above downwards the brain stem comprises the *midbrain* (or *mesencephalon*), the *pons,* and the *medulla oblongata* (Fig. 37.3).

The midbrain, or mesencephalon. This is the uppermost part of the brain stem; it lies below the relatively small part of the brain called the interbrain, or diencephalon, which is interposed between it and the cerebrum. The midbrain consists of a *ventral* and a *dorsal* part. The ventral part, called the **cerebral peduncles** or **crura,** is divided again into a ventral (or anterior) and a dorsal (or posterior) portion. The former comprises two stout arms each of which is called the **base** of the corresponding peduncle. These arms issue from the upper surface of the pons and plunge into the cerebrum, diverging as they ascend. The dorsal, or posterior, portions of the cerebral peduncles are fused along the mid-line to form a continuous mass known as the **tegmentum.** When sectioned (Figs. 37.4, 37.5), the base of each peduncle is seen to be separated from the adjacent part of the tegmentum by a crescentic band of pigmented nervous tissue called the **substantia nigra.** The bases of the peduncles are occupied mainly by efferent (descending) fibers, such as the corticospinal. The tegmentum transmits sensory (ascending) fibers and contains circumscribed masses of gray matter (for example, the *red nucleus*) as well.

The dorsal portion of the midbrain is marked off from the cerebral peduncles by a canal called the **cerebral aqueduct;** it is called the **tectum,** and is composed of four hemispherical elevations known as the **corpora quadrigemina,** two on each side, a superior and an inferior. These structures are reflex centers through which appropriate muscular movements, such as turning the head and eyes, are brought about by visual and audi-

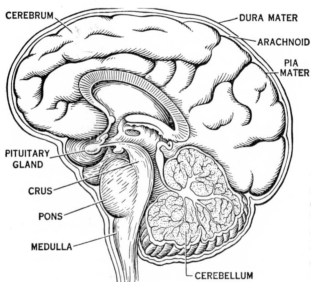

CEREBRUM
DURA MATER
ARACHNOID
PIA MATER
PITUITARY GLAND
CRUS
PONS
MEDULLA
CEREBELLUM

Fig. 37.3. The brain divided by a sagittal section between the cerebral hemispheres. The brain stem includes the crura (sing. *crus*), or cerebral peduncles, pons, and medulla oblongata.

Fig. 37.4. Section through the midbrain (mesencephalon). The serrated mass of gray matter (shaded)
between the tegmentum and the
base of the peduncle (crus) on
each side is the *substantia nigra*.
The red nuclei are not shown in
the figure; they are two rounded
masses of gray matter lying in the
tegmentum, one on each side of
the mid-line, and through which

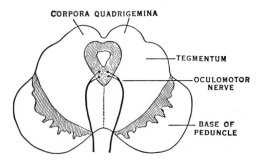

pass the fibers of the oculomotor nerve. The small triangular area surrounded by gray
matter and lying near the dorsal part of the midbrain is the cross section of a short
canal—the *cerebral aqueduct*—which connects the third and fourth ventricles.

tory stimulation. The walls of the cerebral aqueduct are composed of
gray matter. From cells in this gray mass the fibers composing the third
cranial (oculomotor) nerve arise.

The pons. The pons is made up to a large extent of the ascending
and descending fibers mentioned above. It also contains bundles of fibers
that run transversely and appear partly to surround and clasp the brain
stem. Behind, the two open ends of the horseshoelike clasp plunge into
the cerebellum, and constitute its middle peduncles. The fibers composing these peduncles carry impulses from the cerebrum to the cerebellum.
Some of the cranial nerves (p. 510) arise from the pons.

The medulla oblongata. The medulla oblongata lies just below the
pons and rests upon the floor of the skull. It is continuous, below and
just outside the skull, with the spinal cord. This part of the brain also
transmits the bundles of ascending and descending fibers mentioned in
previous sections, and contains as well many groups of nerve cells. The
activities of the vital organs—the rate of the heart, the calibers of the
blood vessels, and the respiratory movements—are governed by cells in
the gray matter of the medulla oblongata. The motor fibers form two
well-defined columns called the *pyramids* (p. 503) on its ventral (anterior) aspect. Many of the cranial nerves also arise from its nuclei—for
example, nucleus ambiguus, and nuclei of VIII, IX, X, and XI nerves
(p. 510).

The interbrain, or diencephalon

The interbrain, or diencephalon, is situated between the midbrain
and cerebrum, and comprises the *thalamus* and the *hypothalamus.*

The thalamus. The thalamus, the more dorsal part of the interbrain,
is a large gray mass lying in the depth of the brain and completely covered by the cerebrum. It lies close to the mid-line, the third ventricle
alone being interposed between it and its fellow of the opposite side

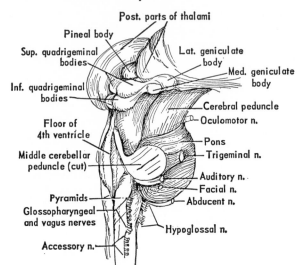

Post. parts of thalami

Pineal body

Sup. quadrigeminal bodies

Lat. geniculate body

Med. geniculate body

Inf. quadrigeminal bodies

Cerebral peduncle

Floor of 4th ventricle

Oculomotor n.

Pons

Trigeminal n.

Middle cerebellar peduncle (cut)

Auditory n.

Facial n.

Pyramids

Abducent n.

Glossopharyngeal and vagus nerves

Hypoglossal n.

Accessory n.

Fig. 37.5. The thalami and brain stem viewed from a point behind and a little to the right.

(Figs. 37.5, 37.6). The lateral ventricle, part of whose floor it forms, lies above. The thalamus is composed of a large number of cell groups (called nuclei), through the efferent and afferent fibers of which it is connected with many parts of the brain. It is a great receiving center. Sensory impulses—of touch, muscle sense, etc.—are relayed to the cerebral cortex (Fig. 37.15), but impulses serving the sensation of pain end in the thalamus. It is therefore a center for the appreciation of pain, and also of certain other sensations and "feelings" (p. 502); it is thought to be the seat of consciousness. The evidence for these statements is both experi-

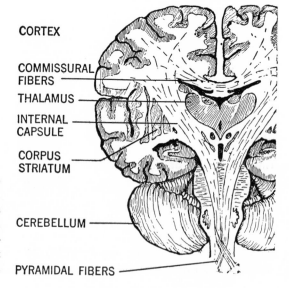

CORTEX

COMMISSURAL FIBERS

THALAMUS

INTERNAL CAPSULE

CORPUS STRIATUM

CEREBELLUM

PYRAMIDAL FIBERS

Fig. 37.6. Vertical (coronal) section through the brain to show its internal structure. Note the commissural fibers forming the corpus callosum and the projection fibers descending from the cortex through the internal capsule.

mental and clinical. Disease of the thalamus is associated with severe pain and great magnification of certain other sensations and feelings. In operations upon the brains of conscious patients, slight manipulation in the region of the thalamus may cause sudden unconsciousness. As well as being a relay station or a terminal for sensory impulses, the thalamus receives nonsensory impulses from the cerebellum and transmits them to the cortex of the cerebrum.

The hypothalamus. This is the region at the base of the brain lying behind the optic chiasma (Ch. 41) and beneath the floor of the third ventricle. It contains several groups of nerve cells—the **hypothalamic nuclei**—that constitute centers controlling the sympathetic and parasympathetic functions. Axons from three groups of nerve cells—the **supraoptic, paraventricular,** and **tuberal nuclei**—form a bundle of nerve fibers known as the **hypothalamico-hypophyseal tract.** This tract enters the neural lobe of the hypophysis (pituitary body), and governs the liberation of the hormones of this part of the pituitary (Fig. 37.7). Injury or stimulation of this region of the brain affects one or more of the fundamental processes of the body, for example, vasomotor control; temperature regulation; fat, carbohydrate, and water metabolism; the development of the sex functions; as well as gastrointestinal motility. It has been reported that electrical stimulation of the hypothalamus in animals induces a sleeplike state. It also appears to be a center from which the reactions expressing the primitive emotions are controlled, for when, in an experimental animal, all restraint of the higher centers of the brain is withdrawn by removal of the entire cerebral cortex, the reactions of an enraged fighting animal are exhibited. Thus, a cat that before the operation was a placid, friendly animal, spits and bares its claws when approached; its fur bristles and its tail becomes bushy, as when a normal

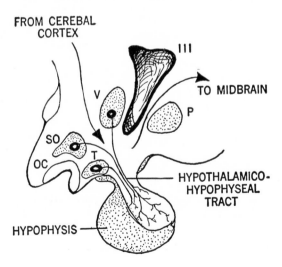

FROM CEREBAL CORTEX

III

TO MIDBRAIN

V

P

SO

OC

T

HYPOTHALAMICO-HYPOPHYSEAL TRACT

HYPOPHYSIS

Fig. 37.7. Diagram of the hypothalamic region and the hypophysis. OC, optic chiasma; P, posterior hypothalamic nuclei; SO, supraoptic nuclei; T, tuberal nuclei; V, paraventricular nuclei; III, third ventricle of the brain.

cat is attacked by a dog. This state of the decorticated animal has been appropriately termed "sham rage." When, on the other hand, a tract of fibers connecting the frontal lobe with the hypothalamus is severed, a naturally wild and unfriendly animal becomes docile and affectionate. This latter observation has been put to practical advantage in the treatment of certain mental states in man. Section of this connecting nerve tract is often followed by improvement of the mental condition.

The cerebrum, or telencephalon

The cerebrum is the dome-shaped mass of brain substance that lies just beneath the skull roof and fills the greater part of the cranial cavity. In man it weighs nearly 2 pounds. It is this part that makes the human brain so different both in appearance and in capability from the brains of animals. The general form and structure of the human cerebrum reminds one of the kernel of a walnut. The kernel of the walnut is protected by a shell, just as the brain is protected by the skull bone. The walnut's kernel is divided lengthwise into two halves; so also is the cerebrum, each half of which is called a **cerebral hemisphere**. The surface of the nut's kernel is covered with many wrinkles—mounds and furrows. The surface of the cerebral hemispheres is wrinkled or grooved in an irregular and somewhat similar way. The mounds upon the surface of the brain are very important and are called **convolutions** (Figs. 37.8, 37.10). The furrow between any two mounds, if small and shallow, is called a **sulcus** (pl. *sulci*). If it is long and deep, it is called a **fissure**.

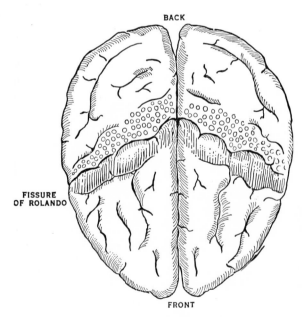

BACK

FISSURE
OF ROLANDO

FRONT

Fig. 37.8. The human brain from above. A longitudinal fissure divides the cerebrum into two hemispheres, each of which is marked off near its center, but not divided, by the fissure of Rolando. The shaded area in front of this is the motor area. The band behind marked by small circles is the somesthetic area. The fissure of Rolando separates the frontal from the parietal lobe.

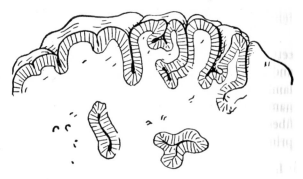

Fig. 37.9. A vertical section through the cortex to show how the gray matter dips into the white matter around the fissures and sulci. This indicates that the convolutions have been formed by an infolding process.

Were we to slice the kernel of the walnut with a sharp knife, we should find that the cut surface was a creamy color through and through. But if we were to section one of the cerebral hemispheres in the same way, the cut surface would be found to have a pale grayish or brownish color near the outside of the brain and a lighter creamy color toward the center. The darker substance at the surface of the brain—*gray matter*—is called the **cerebral cortex.** It should be observed that the cortex dips into the fissures and sulci; indeed, in the human brain as much cortex is buried in this way as covers the surface of the convolutions. Thus, there is an obvious advantage in the convoluted arrangement of the brain surface; it allows for an increase of cortical gray matter with a minimal increase in the volume of the brain (Figs. 37.10, 37.11). The amount of gray matter of the highly convoluted human cerebrum is immensely greater than that of the brains of subhuman species without there being a proportional increase in skull capacity.

The cream-colored substance beneath the cortex is called the *white*

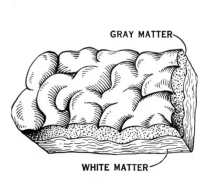

GRAY MATTER

WHITE MATTER

Fig. 37.10. A section of the superficial part of the cerebrum to show the gray matter of the cortex and the underlying white matter.

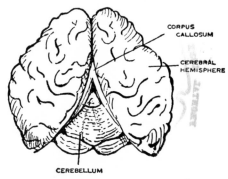

CORPUS CALLOSUM

CEREBRAL HEMISPHERE

CEREBELLUM

Fig. 37.11. The hemispheres have been spread apart to show the connecting mass of white matter—the corpus callosum—which is also partially divided lengthwise to show the cerebellum.

matter; it is composed of countless numbers of nerve fibers with immensely varied destinations.

The cerebral hemispheres are joined across the mid-line by a solid felted mass of nerve fibers called the **corpus callosum** (Fig. 37.11).

The microscopic structure of the cerebral cortex. When a section of the cerebral cortex is made perpendicular to the surface of the hemisphere and a thin slice examined under the microscope, it is found to have a laminated structure. Six layers have been distinguished and given special names based upon the type of nerve cell and the proportion of cells and fibers that they contain. The layers from without inwards with their principal characteristics are as follows:

I. Molecular (or plexiform) layer	Small cells and a dense feltwork of fibers
II. Outer granular layer	Closely packed small cells; relatively few fibers
III. Pyramidal cell layer	Pyramidal cells varying from medium to large
IV. Inner granular layer	Small star-shaped cells and many fibers
V. Ganglionic layer (or inner pyramidal layer)	Giant pyramidal cells (cells of Betz). This layer is especially well developed in the motor area of the cortex (p. 497, and Figs. 37.14, 37.15)
VI. Fusiform cell layer	Closely packed small spindle-shaped cells

Most of the axons of the nerve cells leave the cortical layer in which they originate and travel longer or shorter distances before reaching

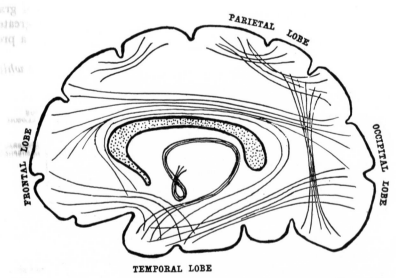

TEMPORAL LOBE

Fig. 37.12. Diagram to show the general course of the association fibers of the right cerebral hemisphere. The stippled area is the *corpus callosum* which is composed of commissural fibers.

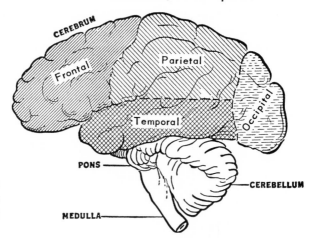

Fig. 37.13. The human
brain; cerebral lobes
marked by different
shading.

their destinations. These fibers are of three classes, called respectively **projection, association,** and **commissural.** The projection fibers are those, such as the corticospinal, that pass to other parts of the nervous system; the association fibers connect different parts of the cortex of the same hemisphere (Fig. 37.11) ; the commissural fibers cross in the corpus callosum to the opposite hemisphere (Fig. 37.12) .

The lobes of the cerebrum. The cerebrum has been marked off into a number of masses called **lobes.** Four of these are shown in Figures 37.13 and 37.15. Two main fissures, an oblique and a horizontal, will be seen on the lateral aspect of the hemisphere; the first is called the **central fissure,** or **fissure of Rolando.** The part of the hemisphere lying anterior to it is called the **frontal lobe** and the part behind it, the **parietal lobe.** At the lower part of the hemisphere a shoulder will be seen. This is the anterior extremity of the **temporal lobe** which extends backwards below the parietal lobe. The deep horizontal furrow separating this lobe from the frontal and parietal lobes is known as the **lateral cerebral sulcus,** or **fissure of Sylvius.** The portion of the cerebrum lying behind the parietal and temporal lobes is called the **occipital lobe.**

Functions of the cerebrum. The cerebrum is undoubtedly the seat of the mind; it is the "organ" of thought. Intelligence, memory, reason, and all those mental endowments in which man excels so greatly the rest of animal creation are dependent upon this part of the brain.

In the posterior part of the frontal lobe immediately in front of the fissure of Rolando is a long tapering band of cortex called the **motor area** (Figs. 37.14, 37.15) . It is the center for voluntary movement, its cells giving rise to the corticospinal, or pyramidal, tracts, which, as we have seen, descend in the lateral and anterior columns of the spinal cord. The motor area is continued over the upper border of the hemisphere on to the medial surface. The cells in the upper part of the motor area occupying the lateral surface of the hemisphere generate impulses causing movements of muscles that extend or flex the knee joint, while the lower end of this area discharges impulses that cause movements of the face, tongue, and throat. From the regions in between are discharged impulses to the muscles moving the knee, hip, trunk, shoulder, arm, and hand, in this order from above downwards. Movements of the ankle and toes are governed from the part of the motor area that is continued on to the medial surface of the hemisphere.

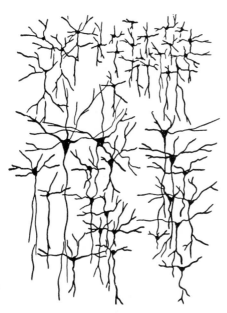

Immediately behind the fissure of Rolando—that is, in the anterior part of the parietal lobe —is an area of similar extent that receives impulses from the various receptors of the body— receptors of touch, heat and cold, and of movement in the muscles and joints (*kinesthetic sense*). This part of the parietal lobe is called the **somesthetic area**. The center for *taste* lies at its lower end. The center for *hearing* is located in the upper part of the temporal lobe and in the depth of the fissure of Sylvius; that for *smell* lies in a deeper part of the brain called the **uncus** which is in close relation to the anterior pole of the temporal lobe. The center for *vision* is situated on the medial surface of the occipital lobe.

Fig. 37.14. A section of the motor area of the cerebral cortex, showing the large pyramidal cells.

Destruction of this area in both occipital lobes would cause total blindness. If it were destroyed on only one side blindness of one half of each eye would result (see Ch. 41 and Fig. 43.1).

The identification of the parts of the motor area governing the various muscle groups was first shown by experiments upon animals, especially apes and monkeys, whose brains resemble most the human brain. When the motor area of an ape's brain is exposed under an anesthetic and its different parts stimulated successively with a weak electric current, the muscles governed by the nerve cells in the stimulated part contract. Thus, flexion or extension of a limb can be readily induced. Similar observations have been made on man during operations upon the brain. In this way the motor area of the human cerebral cortex has been accurately mapped out. Sometimes an injury to the head causes a piece

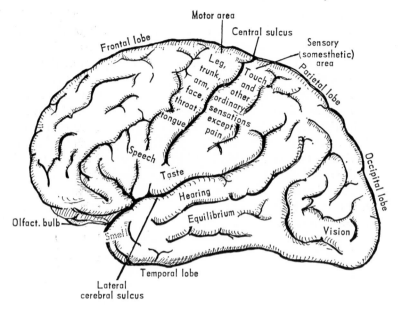

Fig. 37.15. Showing the functions of the different areas of the cerebral cortex.

of the skull bone to press upon and irritate some part of this area and cause uncontrolled muscular contractions. The contractions, which at first are usually confined to a small group of muscles—arm, leg, etc.— quickly spread to involve other muscles, until generalized convulsions may develop. This disease is called *Jacksonian epilepsy*. By observing in which muscles the contractions start the surgeon knows where to look for the irritated nerve cells.

It was once thought that the mental processes were carried on mainly in the fore parts of the frontal lobes. But modern experiments upon higher animals—for example, monkeys and apes—and observations upon human subjects who have had the frontal lobes severely damaged by accident or removed by operation have required a revision of this belief. A man deprived of his frontal lobes, though upon close examination will show some mental and moral defects, may appear quite normal to a casual observer and be able to perform ordinary mental tasks.[1] No region of the cerebral cortex can be singled out as being especially concerned

---

[1] The classical example of a severe injury to the fore part of the brain that resulted in surprisingly little mental defects in the case of the American Phineas Gage (1848), who suffered extensive damage of his frontal lobes from a tamping bar driven through his head by an explosion. The bar penetrated the left orbit and emerged from the midline of the head just anterior to the coronal suture. He was stunned for only an hour and was able with assistance to walk to a surgeon's office. He lived for 12 years after the accident and showed only minor mental and moral changes.

with intellect. If we think for a moment it will be evident why this should be so. Our intelligence has been developed as a result of the manifold and various impressions from the world around us. Our various experiences are imprinted as memory pictures in various parts of the cerebral cortex, where the impulses received through the sensory nerves—sight, hearing, touch, etc.—are interpreted. These several areas, as already stated, are connected with one another by great numbers of nerve fibers running in the white substance beneath the gray matter of the cortex (Fig. 37.11). Intellectual capacity is determined by the sum of all those past experiences that can be recalled in consciousness, and by the abundance of the association fibers through which the different sensory areas are in communication with one another. Destruction of any one area of the cortex, therefore, may reduce but will not destroy the intellect.

It has also been the general belief that the cerebral cortex was the seat of consciousness. But it is very probable that the conscious state, the essential feeling of "awareness," depends rather upon the activity of other deeper (subcortical) parts of the brain, the principal one being the thalamus, and that sensory impulses received in these regions after being synthesized into more complex sensations or feelings are passed on to the cerebral cortex. The cortex elaborates such impressions received from subcortical levels into the complex mental product that we speak of as thought, intellect, or the mind. Pain, for example, and other sensations both pleasant and unpleasant, it appears from the evidence, are felt not in the cortex, but in these deeper parts of the brain. An animal, such as a dog or cat, reacts to circumstances arising in its environment by expressions of fear, rage, or pleasure after complete removal of its cerebral cortex, but it displays nothing that might be called intelligence. Though it will eat its food, avoid obstacles in its way, and respond to a bright light or a loud sound, it is little better than a reflex machine.

The corpus striatum and the internal capsule (Figs. 37.6, 37.16, 37.18). The corpus striatum is a collection of gray matter buried in the white substance of the cerebrum. It is composed of two principal nuclear masses, the **caudate nucleus** and a larger lens-shaped body called the **lenticular, or lentiform, nucleus.** The caudate nucleus lies in front of and lateral to the thalamus; the lentiform nucleus is situated in a more posterior and lateral position.

Little is known of the functions of the corpus striatum, though it is associated in some way with the tone of the muscles. In certain chronic nervous diseases in which muscular rigidity is a prominent feature, this part of the brain shows pathological changes.

In a horizontal section through the cerebrum, a strip of white matter is seen to intervene between the caudate nucleus and thalamus on the medial side and the lentiform nucleus laterally. This band of fibers is called the **internal capsule.** It is bent to form an anterior and a posterior limb, the angle (or knee) between the two opening outwards. It is

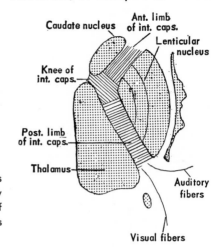

Fig. 37.16. Diagram of the right corpus striatum. The corticospinal fibers (voluntary movement) descend in the posterior limb of the internal capsule; the internal capsule is the bent structure in hatched shading.

composed of fibers that convey various sensory impulses—touch, heat and cold, muscle sense, visual, and auditory—to the cerebral cortex, and motor (corticospinal) and other efferent impulses from the cortex to lower levels of the nervous system. The internal capsule is a region of the brain where a small lesion will cause the greatest damage to the conducting pathways (Fig. 37.18).

The pathway for voluntary motor impulses. The pathway for impulses that govern the movements of the skeletal muscles consists of an upper and a lower link—the corticospinal tract and the neurons whose axons form the peripheral motor nerves (Figs. 37.17, 37.18). These two links, which are known as the **upper** and **lower motor neurons** respectively, are connected in the spinal cord, that is, at the synapse between the termination of the corticospinal fiber and the cells of the anterior horns of gray matter. The axons of the latter cells leave the spinal cord by the anterior nerve roots. The corticospinal fibers, which constitute the upper link, are, as already stated, the axons of cells situated in the motor area of the cerebral cortex. The corticospinal tract in its course through the brain descends through the internal capsule (above), the base of the cerebral peduncle, the pons, and medulla oblongata. These tracts form two well-marked columns called the **pyramids** on the anterior surface of the medulla (p. 493). At the lower border of the medulla each column or pyramid divides into a smaller and a larger bundle of fibers. The former descends in the anterior column of the spinal cord and has already been met with (Ch. 35) as the anterior corticospinal, or direct pyramidal, tract. The larger bundle of fibers crosses with its fellow of the opposite side of the medulla, and descends in the lateral column of the spinal cord as the lateral corticospinal, or crossed pyramidal, tract. This crossing is called the **decussation of the pyramids.**

It is clear that an injury that interrupts the motor pathway any

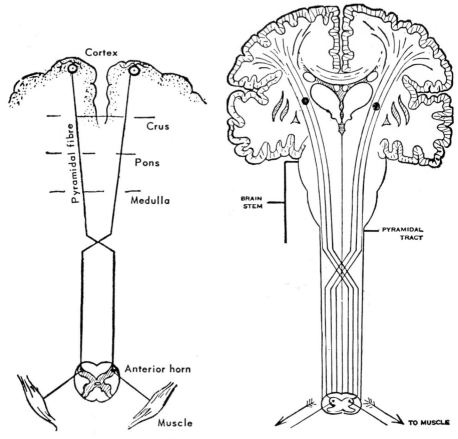

Fig. 37.17 *(left)*. Diagram to show the course taken by impulses from the motor area of the cerebral cortex to a voluntary muscle. The horizontal lines indicate the levels of the different parts of the brain stem.

Fig. 37.18 *(right)*. A more detailed drawing than that shown in Figure 37.17. The black dots mark usual sites (internal capsules) of cerebral hemorrhage. It is clear that the fibers are massed together at these points in order to pass through narrow channels. Hemorrhage in either of these situations is therefore likely to cause destruction of a large number of fibers and so produce a widespread paralysis.

where along its course will prevent the impulses from reaching the muscles just as surely as a telephone message would fail to be transmitted should the conducting wire be broken. Paralysis of the muscles for which the impulses are destined will therefore result should disease or other injury destroy (1) the motor cells in the cortex, (2) the fibers anywhere in their course to the anterior horn cells, (3) the anterior horn cells themselves, or (4) the motor nerves going to the muscles.

An injury to the brain may destroy some of the cells in the motor area of the cortex. Apoplexy, or *cerebral hemorrhage,* is due to the rupture of a small blood vessel in the white matter of the cerebrum where the pyramidal fibers pass through that narrow gap or "bottle-neck" known as the *internal capsule* (Figs. 37.6, 37.16, 37.18). The escaping blood therefore destroys fibers of the corticospinal tracts, and in this way paralyzes the muscles of one half of the body—a type of paralysis called *hemiplegia.* Since the pyramidal fibers cross at the lower border of the medulla or in the spinal cord, the paralysis that results from apoplexy is on the side of the body opposite to that in which the cerebral hemorrhage occurs. In *infantile paralysis (anterior poliomyelitis)* some of the anterior horn cells are attacked and destroyed.

The type of paralysis caused by interruption of the upper motor neuron is different from that caused by injury to the lower. Loss of continuity of the upper neuron is caused by cerebral hemorrhage, and of the lower by anterior poliomyelitis (anterior horn cells destroyed) or by an injury to the peripheral motor nerves. In an upper motor neuron injury, the muscles are stiff and the limbs rigid and difficult for an examiner to bend, a state generally referred to as *spastic.* The knee jerk or other tendon reflex, depending upon the muscles that are paralyzed, is exaggerated, and atrophy of the paralyzed muscles is not a pronounced feature. When the lower neuron is interrupted the paralysis is of the *flaccid* type, that is, the muscles are flabby; the limbs "flop" about, a condition that has suggested the term flaillike. The knee jerk or other tendon jerk is absent, and the wasting of the paralyzed muscles is often extreme.

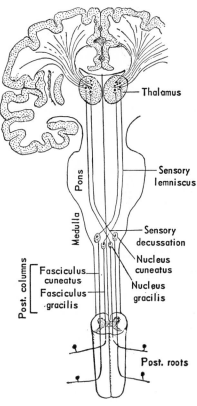

Fig. 37.19. The sensory pathways.

The sensory pathways. The sensory fibers, which enter the spinal cord by the posterior spinal nerve roots and ascend in the posterior columns, end by forming connections (synapses) with nerve cells in the nucleus gracilis and nucleus cuneatus situated in the lower part of the medulla (Fig. 37.19). These nuclei receive, respectively, the similarly named fasciculi. The axons of the cells in the nuclei cross to the opposite side of the medulla (*sensory decussation*) and ascend through the pons and midbrain to the thalamus as a compact bundle called the *sensory lemniscus* or *fillet*. In the thalamus the sensory fibers synapse with neurons whose axons relay the impulses to the somesthetic area of the cerebral cortex. Thus, the sensory pathway for impulses ascending in the posterior columns is constituted of three neuron links, the first having its cell body in a posterior root ganglion, the second in the nucleus gracilis or nucleus cuneatus, and the third in the thalamus.

The spinothalamic tracts (anterior and lateral) ascend through the medulla without interruption and join the sensory lemniscus to reach the thalamus. From here the impulses, *except those for pain* which end in the thalamus, are relayed to the somesthetic area of the cortex.

Brain waves; the electroencephalogram. The electroencephalogram is a record of the electrical changes occurring in the brain which is obtained through electrodes applied to the shaved scalp. From the analysis of these records three types of waves differing in frequency and height have been distinguished and designated *alpha, beta,* and *delta.* The alpha waves occur at a rate of about 10 per second. The beta waves have a higher frequency and a greater amplitude. The alpha waves are obtained best from the occipital region of the scalp when the eyes are closed, or looking at a blank or a uniform surface; they disappear when the eyes are opened and the attention directed to any object, or when any mental effort is made, such as working at a problem in arithmetic (Fig. 37.20). These waves are therefore characteristic of the inattentive brain. The beta waves are most readily obtained when the electrodes are on the scalp over the somesthetic area of the brain. The delta waves are the slowest, and are rarely seen normally during wakefulness, but are usual during sleep.

Fig. 37.20. A normal electroencephalogram taken from the occipital region of the skull. At O the eyes are opened, and closed at C.

When these "brain waves" were first discovered (in 1929) they were looked upon as little more than interesting physiological curiosities, but have since been found to give valuable aid to the physician. In epilepsy, for example, waves of abnormal size, shape, and rhythm appear that show special and distinguishing features for the three types of the disease; also, brain tissue in the neighborhood of a tumor generates characteristically slow waves that enable an examiner to locate the position of the growth.

The cerebellum, or little brain

The cerebellum, which is much smaller than the cerebrum, lies under the shelter of the back part of the latter. The cerebellum is connected to the rest of the brain by three bundles of nerve fibers called *cerebellar penduncles*. It consists of two lateral halves called **hemispheres.** These are joined together by a central, somewhat elongated structure that resembles a worm or caterpillar or the body of a butterfly. It is therefore called the **vermis** (L. *vermis,* worm) (Figs. 37.3, 37.21).

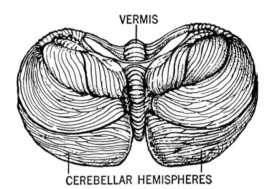

Fig. 37.21. The cerebellar hemispheres and vermis from below.

The surface of the cerebellum is quite different in appearance from the surface of the cerebrum. The irregular convolutions so typical of the cerebral surface are not seen; several fairly regular and nearly parallel linear grooves or wrinkles mark its surface. Like the cerebrum, the cerebellum is composed of gray and white matter. A large part of the gray matter is on the surface and is called the **cerebellar cortex.** Masses of gray matter are also found in its center; the largest of these is called the **dentate nucleus** (Fig. 37.22).

The cerebellar peduncles. Three pairs of compact bundles of fibers constitute the sole paths of communication between the cerebellum and the rest of the nervous system; these are the *superior, middle,* and *inferior peduncles.* The **superior peduncles** are composed mainly of axons of nerve cells situated in the cerebellum. These fibers connect with nerve cells in the midbrain, from which fibers course upward to the thalamus

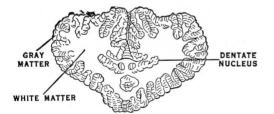

Fig. 37.22. A section through the center of the cerebellum.

and are relayed to the cerebrum and downward to form connections with cells in the pons (**pontine nuclei**), medulla, or spinal cord. These peduncles also carry a smaller number of fibers in the opposite direction—that is, from the spinal cord through the medulla and pons to the cerebellum. The fibers from the spinal cord, like those that travel by the inferior peduncles, convey subconscious impulses from the muscles, tendons, bones, and joints, and thus bring to the cerebellum information concerning the movements and positions of the different parts of the body.

The **middle peduncles** unite the cerebellum to the pons. They are composed of those transverse fibers mentioned before that are the axons of cells of the pontine nuclei. These cells are connected in turn with the cerebrum. Thus, through the middle peduncles and pons, the cerebrum is in communication with the cerebellum.

The **inferior peduncles** bring the cerebellum into communication with the spinal cord. These peduncles are composed mainly of nerve fibers carrying impulses from the muscles, tendons, bones, and joints. They also contain fibers that carry impulses to the cerebellum from the semicircular canals of the internal ear (Ch. 46). The complicated connections between the cerebellum and the rest of the nervous system through the three pairs of cerebellar peduncles will be best understood from a study of Figures 37.23 and 37.24. The cerebellum is connected with the spinal cord by all three peduncles, but only through the superior and middle peduncles does it communicate with the cerebrum.

Functions of the cerebellum. This part of the brain carries out its very important functions beneath consciousness. Nonsensory impulses are being received ceaselessly by the cerebellum from various parts of the body—the muscles and joints of the limbs, neck, and trunk; the eyes; and the organs of equilibrium in the internal ear (Ch. 46). The impulses received from these various parts inform the cerebellum of the

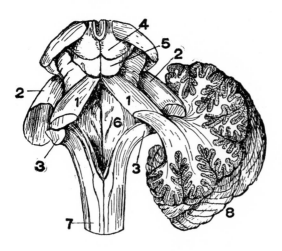

Fig. 37.23. Showing the three pairs of cerebellar peduncles. 1, superior peduncle; 2, middle peduncle; 3, inferior peduncle; 4, superior corpus quadrigeminum; 5, inferior corpus quadrigeminum; 6, floor of fourth ventricle forming posterior aspect of pons and medulla oblongata; 7, spinal cord; 8, cerebellum (cut).

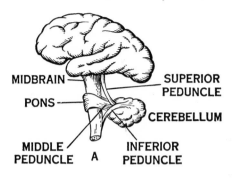

MIDBRAIN

PONS

SUPERIOR
PEDUNCLE

CEREBELLUM

MIDDLE
PEDUNCLE   A

INFERIOR
PEDUNCLE

Fig. 37.24. The peduncles of the
cerebellum. A, general view. The
different parts of the brain have
been separated to show the cerebellar peduncles more clearly. B,
showing how nerve cells of the cerebellum connect with cells in the
pons, medulla, and cord.

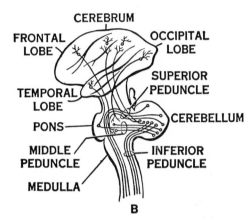

CEREBRUM

FRONTAL
LOBE

OCCIPITAL
LOBE

SUPERIOR
PEDUNCLE

TEMPORAL
LOBE

CEREBELLUM

PONS

MIDDLE
PEDUNCLE

INFERIOR
PEDUNCLE

MEDULLA

B

positions and movements of the body and its members. The cerebellum
sends messages in turn through the cerebrum and midbrain to the muscles and keeps them in a certain degree of tension, or tautness, necessary
for the execution of muscular acts in a smooth and coordinated manner.
Precise movements of the fingers or of the limbs, for example, would be
impossible in the absence of the cerebellum. In experimental animals
deprived of this part of the brain, or in patients suffering from cerebellar
damage (tumor or gunshot wound), the movements lack smoothness and
precision; trembling and jerkiness of action result. The tension of the
muscles necessary for standing or for walking or for holding the limbs
firm and steady is lost. Normally, messages from the cerebellum dispatched to the neck muscles keep the head poised at the correct angle,
no matter what change is made in the body's position.

The information transmitted to the cerebellum from the equilibrat-
ing apparatus of the internal ear and the impulses that it, in turn, discharges are probably of greatest importance with regard to maintaining
the correct position of the head in space, but afferent impulses received
from the eyes and the neck muscles are also essential. Falling backward

or to one side or the other is a common manifestation of disordered cerebellar function. The impulses that the cerebellum transmits to the muscles do not themselves induce movements, but by contributing to the maintenance of tone, the cerebellum conditions the muscles for the reception of motor impulses from the cerebral cortex, and thereby renders voluntary movements surer, more precise, and more forceful.

The functions of the cerebellum may be summed up as follows:

1. To keep the muscles in a normal state of tension or tautness
2. To reinforce the action of the motor area of the cerebral cortex
3. The two foregoing functions allow muscular movements to be nicely gauged and to be carried out with the usual smoothness, precision, and strength.

THE CRANIAL NERVES

The nerves arising from the brain are twelve in number on each side. They are designated by number in the order of their origin, from before backward. Roman numerals I to XII are usually employed in referring to them, or the words *first, second, third,* and so on (Figs. 37.25, 37.26). Each nerve also receives a name descriptive of its function or distribution. The numbers and the corresponding names of the cranial nerves are given in the following list:

I. Olfactory	VII. Facial
II. Optic	VIII. Acoustic (or auditory)
III. Oculomotor	IX. Glossopharyngeal
IV. Trochlear	X. Vagus
V. Trigeminal	XI. Accessory
VI. Abducent	XII. Hypoglossal

The olfactory nerves, or nerves of smell, are a number of short slender nerves that are distributed to the olfactory mucous membrane covering the roof of the nose. They will be described in the section on the sense of smell (Ch. 47).

The optic nerve, or nerve of sight, is composed of the axons of the ganglion cells of the retina. The central connections of the fibers of the optic nerve will be described in the section on vision (Ch. 41).

The oculomotor nerve arises from the group of nerve cells, the *nucleus* of the oculomotor nerve, situated in the gray matter of the floor of the cerebral aqueduct (p. 492). The fibers course forward through the midbrain, emerging from the medial aspect of the cerebral peduncle. The oculomotor nerve supplies all the eye muscles with the exception of the superior oblique and external rectus, which are innervated, respectively, by the trochlear and abducent nerves. It also conveys parasympathetic fibers to the constrictor muscle of the iris, and to the ciliary muscle.

The trochlear nerve has its nucleus in the floor of the cerebral aqueduct, a little behind the oculomotor nucleus. It emerges from the brain at the lateral border of the pons. The trochlear nerve supplies the superior oblique muscle of the eyeball.

The trigeminal nerve contains both *sensory* and *motor* fibers. Its motor fibers are the axons of a group of cells situated in the upper part of the pons. This collection of gray matter is called the *motor nucleus* of the trigeminal. The sensory fibers originate in the *trigeminal (semilunar) ganglion* which lies upon the floor of the skull and is homologous with the posterior root ganglia of the spinal nerves. The central processes (axons) of the ganglion cells form a short trunk, the sensory root of the trigeminal, which enters the brain with the motor root. Within the brain, the fibers of the sensory root divide into ascending and descending groups. The former end in a collection of gray matter, the *superior sensory nucleus* of the trigeminal, situated in the pons close to the motor nucleus. These fibers mediate the discriminative qualities of sensation—such as light touch, localization, and kinesthetic sense—from the face. The descending fibers terminate in the *spinal nucleus* of the trigeminal nerve, an elongated mass of gray substance extending from the lower part of the pons to the upper part of the spinal cord. The fibers entering the spinal nucleus transmit impulses of the crude forms of sensation from the face—namely, pain and extremes of temperature. The peripheral

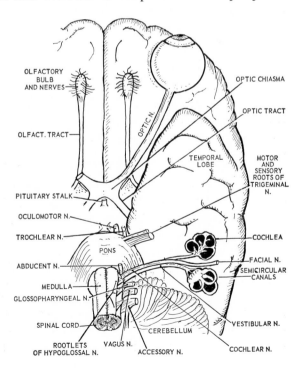

Fig. 37.25. The base of the brain to show the relation of the cranial nerves. Semidiagrammatic; the eyeball and structures of the internal ear are enlarged unnaturally.

OLFACTORY BULB AND NERVES

OPTIC CHIASMA

OPTIC TRACT

OLFACT. TRACT

OPTIC N.

TEMPORAL LOBE

MOTOR AND SENSORY ROOTS OF TRIGEMINAL N.

PITUITARY STALK

OCULOMOTOR N.

TROCHLEAR N.

PONS

COCHLEA

ABDUCENT N.

FACIAL N.

SEMICIRCULAR CANALS

MEDULLA

GLOSSOPHARYNGEAL N.

SPINAL CORD

CEREBELLUM

VESTIBULAR N.

ROOTLETS OF HYPOGLOSSAL N.

VAGUS N.

ACCESSORY N.

COCHLEAR N.

processes of the cells of the trigeminal ganglion form three nerve trunks or *divisions* named, respectively, the **ophthalmic, maxillary,** and **mandibular nerves,** which are distributed to the skin of the face, forehead, and anterior half or more of the scalp, to the eyeball and conjunctiva, to the mucous membrane of the nasal cavities, to the teeth and gums, and to the anterior two thirds of the tongue. The motor fibers of the trigeminal supply the muscles of mastication. The skin areas supplied by the three divisions of the trigeminal nerve are shown in Figure 37.25; see also Figure 37.26.

The **abducent nerve** arises from the abducent nucleus situated in the lower part of the pons beneath the floor of the fourth ventricle. The nerve emerges from the anterior aspect of the brain in the groove lying between the pons and the upper end of the pyramid of the medulla oblongata. It supplies the external rectus muscle of the eyeball.

The **facial nerve** has a large *motor* and a small *sensory* root. The fibers forming the motor root arise from the *motor nucleus,* which lies in the lower part of the pons. This root also transmits *secretory* and *vasodilator* (parasympathetic) fibers to the submaxillary and sublingual glands; these fibers arise from a separate group of nerve cells—the **superior salivatory nucleus**—lying in close proximity to the motor nucleus. The motor root of the nerve leaves the anterior aspect of the brain at the lower border of the pons. The fibers of the sensory root (also called the **nervus intermedius**) are the axons of cells situated in the *facial*

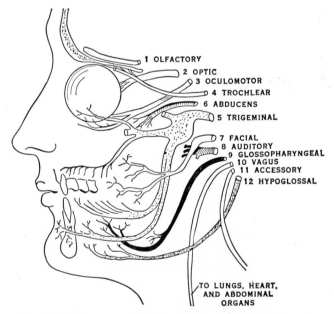

Fig. 37.26. The twelve cranial nerves on one side of the head.

(*geniculate*) *ganglion* which lies within a canal in the temporal bone. The sensory root enters the brain in close association with the motor root. The peripheral processes of the ganglion cells are distributed to the anterior two thirds of the surface of the tongue. They transmit impulses of taste to a nucleus in the medulla oblongata named the **tractus solitarius.** From the latter the impulses are relayed to the thalamus and thence by tertiary neurons to the center for taste in the cerebral cortex (p. 500). Both taste and parasympathetic fibers (secretory and vasodilator) leave the facial trunk in its **chorda tympani** branch. The motor fibers of the facial nerve form a stout trunk that leaves the cranial cavity through a small opening in the floor of the skull. The nerve curves forward below the ear to reach the face, where it breaks up into numerous branches. These supply the muscles of the face, lips, eyelids, forehead, and anterior part of the scalp.

The **acoustic, or auditory, nerve** is entirely *sensory* in function. It consists of two distinct sets of fibers, the **cochlear** and **vestibular nerves.** The terminations of these nerves are described in Chapter 46.

The **glossopharyngeal nerve** contains *motor, sensory, secretory,* and *vasodilator* fibers. The motor fibers issue from the upper part of the **nucleus ambiguus** situated in the medulla oblongata, and are distributed to a single muscle (the stylopharyngeus). The sensory fibers conduct impulses of taste from the posterior third of the tongue to the lower part of the tractus solitarius. The taste impulses are relayed to the optic thalamus, and thence to the cerebral center for taste. Sensory fibers are also distributed to the mucous membranes of the pharynx, tonsil, and palate; they convey impulses of ordinary sensation—touch, temperature, etc. The secretory and vasodilator (parasympathetic) fibers leave the glossopharyngeal nerve in the **tympanic** branch and are distributed to the parotid gland. The secretory and vasodilator fibers have their origins in the **inferior salivatory nucleus,** which lies below the superior salivatory nucleus. The glossopharyngeal nerve also sends a fine branch composed of afferent fibers to the carotid sinus; it is called the **sinus nerve** (Ch. 17).

The **vagus nerve** contains *motor, sensory, secretory,* and *vasodilator* fibers. The motor fibers are of two types—voluntary and autonomic. The fibers to voluntary muscle originate in the lower part of the nucleus ambiguus. These fibers are, actually, derived from the cranial root of the accessory (eleventh cranial) nerve; they supply the cricothyroid muscle of the larynx, and the inferior constrictor muscle of the pharynx. The autonomic motor fibers are distributed to the muscles of the bronchi, heart, esophagus, stomach, gall bladder, pancreas, small intestine, and first third or so of the large intestine; inhibitory fibers pass to the heart (Ch. 17). The involuntary motor fibers, the secretory fibers (to the gastric glands and pancreas), the cardiac inhibitory fibers, and the vasodilator fibers belong to the parasympathetic division of the autonomic system. They arise from the *dorsal nucleus* of the vagus. This nucleus is a mixed one, for it is also a terminal for sensory fibers. Some of the latter connect with motor autonomic neurons within the dorsal nucleus, which thus functions as a reflex center.

The vagus emerges from the lateral aspect of the medulla oblongata as a series of rootlets that soon join to form a stout trunk. This leaves the skull through the jugular foramen, and passes down the neck in close relation to the internal and common carotid arteries. Two ganglia are situated upon the vagus trunk; the upper one lies within the jugular foramen at the base of the skull; the other just below the point where the nerve issues from the skull. The afferent fibers of the vagus have their origin within these ganglia.

The accessory nerve is entirely *motor* in function, and consists of a *cranial* and a *spinal* root. The cranial fibers arise from a nucleus lying below and continuous with the lower end of the nucleus ambiguus. They leave the side of the medulla oblongata as four or five delicate strands that after uniting pass from the skull through the jugular foramen. The spinal fibers are the axons of anterior horn cells situated in the upper five cervical segments of the spinal cord. This part of the nerve enters the cranial cavity through the foramen magnum and re-enters the neck through the jugular foramen. Within the latter foramen it joins the cranial part, but becomes separate again almost immediately.

Most of the muscles of the pharynx, larynx, and soft palate are supplied by the cranial part of the accessory nerve. The fibers pass into the pharyngeal and laryngeal branches of the vagus, through which they are distributed to voluntary muscles in these structures (cricothyroid and pharyngeal constrictors). The spinal part sends fibers to certain muscles of the neck and shoulder (sternomastoid and trapezius).

The hypoglossal nerve is distributed entirely to the muscles, intrinsic and extrinsic, of the tongue. Its fibers arise from the hypoglossal nucleus in the medulla oblongata, and appear as a series of rootlets in the groove situated on the anterolateral aspect of the pyramid. The rootlets leave the skull through the hypoglossal canal and unite just below the base of the skull. The trunk so formed curves forward in the upper part of the neck to reach the cavity of the mouth.

THE MEMBRANOUS COVERINGS (MENINGES) OF THE BRAIN AND SPINAL CORD

The brain and spinal cord are ensheathed by three membranes called, from without inwards, the *dura mater, arachnoid mater,* and *pia mater.*

The dura mater is a strong fibrous and relatively thick membrane that serves as a periosteal lining for the skull as well as a covering for the brain. It consists of an outer and an inner layer and gives off four processes, or *septa*, that extend between parts of the brain. The two largest of these are the **falx cerebri**, a sickle-shaped process that descends vertically between the cerebral hemispheres, and the **tentorium cerebelli**, a crescentic partition running horizontally forward between the cerebellum and the occipital lobes of the cerebrum (Fig. 37.27). A third process, the **falx cerebelli**, also sickle-shaped, projects forward from the under surface of the tentorium cerebelli into the notch between the posterior parts of the hemispheres. The fourth process of the dura mater is a small sheet called the **diaphragma sellae;** it forms the roof of the *sella turcica*, of the sphenoid bone, which lodges the pituitary body. An opening in the center of the diaphragma sellae gives passage to the stalk of the pituitary. The spinal part of the dura mater is continued downwards to form a loose investment for the spinal cord. It sends tubular sheaths to enclose the spinal nerve roots and the commencements of the spinal nerves.

The **arachnoid mater** is a more delicate membrane consisting of fibrous and elastic tissue covered by endothelium. It forms a loose invest-

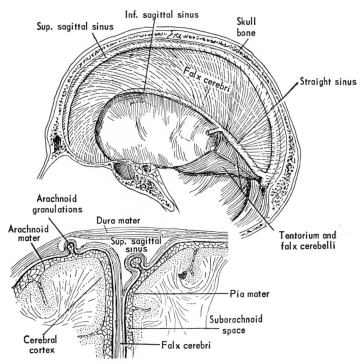

Fig. 37.27. The membranes (meninges) of the brain. *Above,* sagittal section through the skull. *Below,* coronal section.

ment for the brain, and is separated from the dura mater by a space (the **subdural space**) crisscrossed by a network of connective tissue strands (Fig. 37.27). The arachnoid mater is continued downwards to ensheath the spinal cord. This membrane does not dip into the fissures and sulci of the cerebrum but bridges them, thus leaving small spaces filled with cerebrospinal fluid. In certain regions the interval between the arachnoid and pia maters, which is known as the **subarachnoid space**, becomes expanded to form much larger containers for the cerebrospinal fluid; they are called the **subarachnoid cisternae**. They are created by the arachnoid stretching over the depressions in the contour of the brain (Fig. 37.28). The largest of these spaces is called the **cisterna magna**, or **cisterna cerebellomedullaris**. As the latter term indicates this space lies in the angle formed by the medulla oblongata and the cerebellum. Fingerlike processes of the arachnoid, known as the **arachnoid granulations**, project into the superior sagittal, transverse, and other intracranial sinuses.

The pia mater is a delicate, very vascular membrane that adheres closely to the surface of the brain and is extended into the fissures and sulci of the cerebral hemispheres. It, like the other membranes, is continued over the surfaces of the spinal cord.

The ventricular system. Four spaces filled with cerebrospinal fluid are to be found within the brain itself. They are called the *lateral* (paired), *third,* and *fourth ventricles.* The **lateral ventricle** is the largest of the three (Fig. 37.29), and is situated one in each cerebral hemisphere. It consists of a *central* portion and three prolongations called *horns—anterior, inferior,* and *posterior*—which extend, respectively, into the frontal, temporal, and occipital lobes. The lateral part of the upper surface of the thalamus and the caudate nucleus lie in the floor of the central portion. The corpus callosum forms its roof. The **third ventricle** is a narrow cleft between the two thalami; its floor is formed mainly by the hypothalamus. The **fourth ventricle** is a diamond-shaped space between the cerebellum behind and the pons and upper half of the medulla

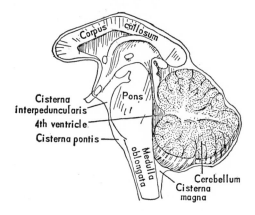

Fig. 37.28. Sagittal section showing the cisternae of the subarachnoid space.

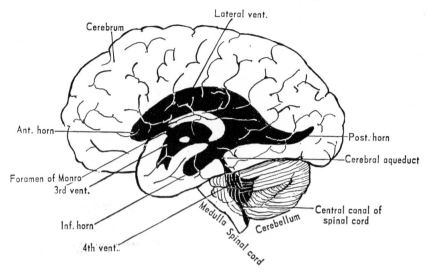

Fig. 37.29. The ventricular system of the brain.

oblongata in front. The latter two structures, which really form its anterior wall, are more usually referred to as its floor.

Richly vascular folds of the pia mater project into the cavities of the ventricles. They are known as the **choroid plexuses.**

All the ventricles communicate with one another, with the central canal of the spinal cord, and with the subarachnoid space of both brain and cord. Each lateral ventricle communicates with the third through the interventricular foramen (*foramen of Monro*). The third ventricle is connected with the fourth through the cerebral aqueduct (*aqueduct of Sylvius*). The fourth ventricle is continued from its inferior angle into the central canal of the spinal cord (Fig. 37.28); it communicates with the subarachnoid space through a foramen in each lateral angle, and an aperture in its roof (*foramen of Magendie*). Hence the ventricles of the brain, the central canal of the spinal cord, and the subarachnoid space constitute a continuous system filled with cerebrospinal fluid.

The properties and composition of the cerebrospinal fluid. The cerebrospinal fluid is perfectly clear, about as pale as water, and has a specific gravity of 1.008 to 1.010. It contains very few cells, and they are of the lymphocyte variety. Its protein concentration is only a small fraction of that of plasma or tissue fluid; it also contains much less calcium, potassium, magnesium, phosphorus, and glucose, but the concentration of sodium chloride is higher than in plasma.

An examination of the cerebrospinal fluid is a most valuable diagnostic aid in diseases of the central nervous system, especially in the various forms of meningitis, brain abscess or tumor, or in neurosyphilis.

Pronounced changes from the normal are found in these conditions, such as a high concentration of protein and the presence of granular leucocytes. A sample of cerebrospinal fluid is obtained for examination by *lumbar puncture,* which consists in introducing a specially designed hollow needle between the third and fourth lumbar vertebrae and into the subarachnoid space. The fluid escapes drop by drop under its own pressure. Sometimes a sample of cerebrospinal fluid is withdrawn from the cisterna magna through a needle inserted between the atlas vertebra and the occipital bone; or a sample can be obtained from a lateral ventricle.

The cerebrospinal fluid is produced by the choroid plexuses chiefly by a process of secretion, but to a small extent also by filtration from the vessels. The fluid is reabsorbed by the arachnoid granulations, the total volume of fluid being kept constant by the fine balance set between production and reabsorption.

Hydrocephalus. This condition consists of a great increase in the volume of cerebrospinal fluid. It is usually congenital. The accumulation of fluid causes separation of the bones of the skull with consequent expansion of the fontanelles and enlargement of the head. This form of the disease is called *internal hydrocephalus* because it is caused by blockage of the circulation of the fluid at some point in the ventricular system, such as the foramen of Munro or where the fourth ventricle communicates with the subarachnoid space. Since cerebrospinal fluid continues to be produced by the choroid plexuses but cannot reach the arachnoid granulations to be reabsorbed, the ventricles become greatly distended by the fluid. Blockage may also occur in older persons, but is then usually due to meningitis or tumor. The fontanelles being closed, there is little or no enlargement of the head, but the rise in intracranial pressure damages nervous structures. Increase in fluid in the subarachnoid space is called *external hydrocephalus,* and is due, usually, to some obstruction in the region of one or another of the cisternae.

CONDITIONED REFLEXES

The **unconditioned reflex,** which has been considered in connection with the secretion of saliva (Ch. 25) and with reflex action (Ch. 34), is carried out entirely through centers situated in the spinal cord or lower (subcortical) levels of the brain. Unconditioned reflexes are inborn; they are not dependent upon past experience, education, or training. In **conditioned reflexes,** on the other hand, the activity of the cerebral cortex plays an essential role. Conditioned reflexes were first demonstrated and studied by Pavlov, the Russian physiologist, and most of the knowledge which we possess of this type of response is the outcome of his investigations. An understanding of the conditioned response can best be gained by giving a few examples of the results of Professor Pavlov's experiments (see also Ch. 25).

When a newborn puppy is given milk to drink there is a secretion of saliva, due to the stimulation of the taste buds in the mouth. The reflex arc in this instance is constituted of the nerves of taste, the salivary centers in the medulla, and the secretory fibers (chorda tympani or glossopharyngeal) to the salivary glands. This is a simple, or unconditioned, reflex, and, as just stated, is quite independent of previous experience gained through any of the organs of special sense. Now, as the puppy grows older it associates the appearance or smell of the milk, or both, with its taste and the pleasure of gratifying the appetite. The mere sight or smell of the milk will then elicit a secretion of saliva; such a response is called a *conditioned reflex*. Pathways have become established in the brain between the cortical center for sight or for smell, and the salivary center. In other words, the visual and olfactory stimuli—*conditioned stimuli*—set up impulses that, impinging upon the salivary centers, are capable alone (that is, without stimulating the nerves in the mouth) of exciting them (see Fig. 25.4). If, on the other hand, a puppy that has never tasted meat is offered some (but is not allowed to taste it), there is no secretion of saliva. The association paths between the higher centers of the brain and the secretory centers have not been developed. Conditioned reflexes become established not only with respect to feeding and the secretion of saliva, but in many other similar ways in the everyday life of the growing animal. Such processes are essentially psychic in character and dependent upon experience. They therefore form the basis of training, and are of the greatest biological importance. The animal through the conditioning process reacts appropriately to the various stimuli—beneficial or injurious—in the environment; responses, excitatory or inhibitory, may be evoked.

The Pavlov school has shown that conditioned responses can be developed experimentally to an extraordinary degree. For example, if a bell is rung within a dog's hearing and a moment later the animal is fed, a secretion of saliva occurs. After a few experiences of this sequence of events—sound of bell following by feeding—an association between the two is established in the animal's brain, and the mere ringing of the bell causes a secretion of saliva. Of course saliva would have been secreted if the animal's taste organs had been stimulated by food, though no bell had previously been rung; this is an *unconditioned reflex,* and direct stimulation of the taste organs an *unconditioned stimulus* (Ch. 25). Now, the experimenter will not be able indefinitely to bring about a response by the sound of the bell alone. If the animal is not "rewarded" from time to time by food, such as an appetizing chunk of meat, the conditioned reflex becomes weaker and weaker with repetition, and finally dies out—it is *inhibited* or suppressed. Its maintenance, by feeding, is called **reinforcement.**

The flash of a light, the sound of a buzzer, horn, or ticking metronome, a particular odor, a touch upon the skin, or the passive movement of a limb into a certain position, and many other types of stimulus may serve for the establishment of the conditioned response—that is, may act as conditioned stimuli. The conditioning process can be so developed that stimuli closely similar in character can be *differentiated* with astonishing precision. A dog in which a conditioned salivary reflex has been established to a sound of a certain pitch (*auditory* stimulus) will not respond to a sound of the same quality and intensity but varying in pitch from the original by only two or three double vibrations per second.

Differentiation of *visual* stimuli can also be developed to a phenomenal degree. Figures of various shapes—a cross, a square, or circle—are readily differentiated (see. Fig. 37.30). A circle can be differentiated by the dog from an ellipse, whose diameters have a ratio no greater than 9 to 10. That is, if a salivary conditioned reflex has been established to a circular object, such as an unilluminated disc, it alone evokes a response. A disc precisely the same in all respects except that it is not quite circular but has diameters in the ratio of 9 to 10 will not cause a secretion of saliva. Olfactory, tactile, and proprioceptive stimuli can likewise be differentiated with remarkable precision.

These are all typical examples of conditioned reflexes. They are brought about through associations formed in the brain between sight, smell, hearing, touch, or certain other sensations and the sense of taste. This implies that those parts of the brain where the sensations of sight, smell, hearing, etc., are recorded, are connected by nerve fibers with that part where are seated the memories of taste. This latter region of the brain must also be connected with those nerve cells that send secretory fibers to the salivary glands. Unquestionably the higher parts of the brain play an essential part and intelligence and education are necessary for the elicitation of the reflex.

The precise pathways taken by the nerve impulses when, for example, a secretion of saliva occurs as a conditioned reflex are not known.

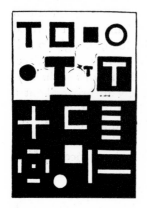

Fig. 37.30. Examples of different figures that were successfully differentiated in experiments upon a dog. The letter T shown in the upper left-hand corner of the figure served for the positive stimulus; the other black figures and the white letter T were differentiated from the positive stimulus. In another dog the white cross was the positive stimulus from which the other white figures were differentiated. *(From Pavlov, Conditioned Reflexes. Oxford University Press.)*

But we may imagine, in a general way, their course. Let us say that secretion has been caused by the sight of some appetizing food, or merely by a visual stimulus (such as a flash of light) that previously has been associated, during a period of "learning," with an agreeable taste. The impulses set up in the retinas are transmitted along the nerves of the eyes (optic nerves) to those parts of the brain where visual sensations are interpreted and recorded. They then pass (actually fresh impulses are set up), as in a groove or channel established by previous experience, along nerve fibers to the region where memories of taste are stored and from there to nerve cells (salivary center) in the hindbrain (medulla) from which the nerves to the salivary glands arise; or the impulses may take a more direct course, as shown in Figure 25.4, from the visual to the salivary center.

It is evident that conditioned reflexes afford a valuable means for studying perception in animals. It has been established, for example, that the dog possesses the ability of discriminating between slight variations in the intensity, quality, and pitch of a musical note, between various odors, and by sight between objects of different sizes and shapes, and between lights of different intensities. Colors, on the contrary, cannot be differentiated, nor can a colored object be distinguished from a colorless one of the same size and shape. It is concluded, therefore, that the dog is totally color blind, its surroundings being perceived only in white, gray, and black.

THE PHYSIOLOGY OF SLEEP

During sleep most of the functions of the body are carried on at the lowest levels possible in health. Heat production is from 10 to 15 percent below the so-called basal level. The mechanisms regulating the body temperature are less sensitive than in the waking state and the temperature is depressed by $1°$ or $2°$ F; the rate of the heart is reduced in frequency by from 10 to 30 beats per minute, and a decline in blood pressure of about 20 mm occurs in quiet, restful sleep. The urine volume is considerably reduced, but its concentration in solids is increased. The cutaneous vessels are usually dilated and the secretion of sweat is stimulated. The tone of all the skeletal muscles is lessened, the deep tendon reflexes are depressed or abolished, and there may be a Babinski (extensor) response of the great toe (glossary). The eyes are usually rolled upward and the pupils constricted. Gastric motility and secretion have a tendency to be greater during sleep than in the waking state.

Seriously detrimental effects may be exerted upon the nervous system by lack of sleep. Experiments upon human subjects in which wakefulness was enforced for long periods caused profound psychological changes. In one series of experiments the volunteers went without sleep for periods of a duration up to 112 hours. Loss of memory, irritability, hallucinations, and even schizophrenic manifestations were observed within from 30 to 60 hours of sleeplessness.

The required hours of sleep; depth of sleep. The amount of sleep required at different ages is given in the table below. Adults vary greatly in the hours of sleep that they find necessary to "knit up the ravelled sleeve of care."

	Hours
New born	18-20
Growing children	10-12
Adults	6-9
Aged persons	5-7

The depth of ordinary restful sleep fluctuates throughout the sleeping period. In most adults, sleep deepens through the first hour, after which it lightens rather sharply, and then more gradually until morning, or until the usual time of wakening. In growing children, however, sleep deepens a second time for a little while in the eighth or ninth hour. In these observations the depth of sleep was judged by the amount of movement of the subjects.

Theories of sleep. Many theories have been advanced to explain the temporary loss of consciousness that we know as sleep. Their very multiplicity emphasizes the difficulty of finding a satisfactory explanation of the physiological processes underlying the phenomenon. Probably the oldest theory is that sleep is induced by a reduction in the blood supply to the brain, or at least to the conscious centers. This is the so-called ischemic theory. Even the ancient Greek physicians had an idea that the carotid artery was in some way concerned with the onset of sleep. The name itself embodies this belief (Gk. karotides, carotid arteries, from karoō, to put to sleep). In modern times the drowsiness after a meal (the blood being diverted presumably from the brain to the digestive organs) was pointed to in support of the ischemic theory.

Some have favored a chemical theory, in one form or another. Chemicals such as lactic acid, acetylcholine, bromide, or a specific "fatigue toxin" were supposed to accumulate during the waking hours that acted like a drug upon the nerve cells of the higher centers of the brain. But no sound evidence can be cited in confirmation of this theory.

It would carry us too far afield to discuss all the various theories, nor would it be of much profit to do so. However, three theories will be briefly reviewed.

The first of these places a sleep center in the hypothalamus (p. 495). A state at least closely resembling sleep has been induced in animals by the electrical stimulation of this region of the brain. It is also true that many of the bodily changes in sleep—such as constriction of the pupil, vasodilatation, reduced frequency of the heartbeat, increased gastric tone and secretion—are manifestations of activity of hypothalamic nuclei (especially of parasympathetic centers).

The second theory to be outlined is that which has as its chief basis the reduction in the discharge of the afferent impulses from the periphery to the conscious centers. During waking hours, these centers are being continually "bombarded" by impulses from the organs of special sense as well as from the skeletal muscles (impulses of kinesthetic sense) and semicircular canals. The centers are being constantly "alerted." But when the sum of these impulses is reduced to a minimum, consciousness becomes dulled and sleep is induced. That muscular relaxation and freedom from visual, auditory, and cutaneous stimulation are conducive to sleep needs no emphasis. We require a dark and quiet room, a soft bed, and an even, comfortable temperature in order to sleep. But the reduction in the flow of afferent impulses to the brain can be no more than a contributory factor in the onset of sleep, for the presence of all the desirable conditions mentioned will not always bring sleep. On the other hand, sleep may supervene in the face of the most adverse conditions, in a bright light and noisy surroundings, and even on hard ground.

Pavlov, as a result of his study of conditioned reflexes in dogs, proposed a theory of sleep based on conditioned inhibition caused by the repeated elicitation of a conditioned response without reinforcement (see *conditioned reflexes,* above). The conditioned inhibition thus established in one area of the cerebral cortex may spread to associated areas and finally involve the entire cortex. Such widespread cortical inhibition is sleep, according to Pavlov. It may be induced by various types of conditioned stimulation, if repeatedly applied. It is a familiar experience that a monotonous sound, an uninteresting, unchanging view, a boring lecture or speech, or any recurring event for which our interest flags, is conducive to drowsiness. Counting sheep, the least exciting of animals, is a well-known device resorted to by those suffering from insomnia. Pavlov described some experiments in which the animal subject would fall into a sleeplike state standing in its harness and even while it was being stimulated. All attempts to elicit the conditioned response failed. On later occasions, it would fall asleep when merely brought into the room where the previous experiments had been conducted. The well-known surroundings had themselves acted as conditioned inhibitory stimuli. There is little doubt but that the familiar appointments of our bedroom (we know very well that it is more difficult to go to sleep in a strange room), the preparation for bed, the feel of the bedclothes, and even the time of retiring act in a similar way upon ourselves. Having been associated innumerable times with sleep, they act as inhibitory conditioned stimuli and induce in the cerebral cortex an inhibitory influence that gradually diffuses over broad areas.

All three of the theories that have been briefly sketched have in them each a degree of truth, but no one alone is entirely satisfactory.

THE AUTONOMIC NERVOUS SYSTEM

The **autonomic** (Gk. *autos,* self + *nomos,* law, that is, self-governing) , or **involuntary,**[2] nervous system governs those functions that are carried out automatically, and that under ordinary circumstances do not obtrude upon consciousness. These functions include the control of the rate of the heart, the movements of the gastrointestinal tract, the caliber of the small blood vessels, the contraction or inhibition of smooth muscle in various other structures (for example, skin, urinary bladder, gall bladder, and bronchi) , and the secretion of the sweat glands and of various digestive glands.

The nerves of the autonomic nervous system arise from groups of cells situated at different levels of the central nervous system, from the midbrain to the sacral region of the spinal cord. The fibers, after issuing from the brain or cord, make connections with nerve cells situated either in a ganglion or in the innervated organ itself (smooth muscle or gland) . The impulses are transmitted to the structure to be activated by the axons of the outlying nerve cells. These fibers are called *postganglionic;* those arising from cells within the central nervous system are termed *preganglionic.*

The autonomic nervous system is divided upon an anatomical as well as upon a physiological basis into two parts, called the *sympathetic* and the *parasympathetic* divisions (Plate Va) .

The parasympathetic division. The parasympathetic division is subdivided into a *cranial* and a *sacral outflow.* The preganglionic fibers of the **cranial outflow** arise from groups of cells situated in the midbrain, pons, and medulla oblongata. The midbrain fibers originate in the oculomotor nucleus and connect with cells in the ciliary ganglion; postganglionic fibers are distributed to the iris, and transmit impulses that constrict the pupil. The cells in the pons are in close association with the nucleus of the facial nerve; the preganglionic fibers are conveyed in the chorda tympani branch of the facial nerve to ganglion cells situated in, or in close relation to, the submaxillary and sublingual (salivary) glands. From here the impulses are transmitted by postganglionic fibers to the gland cells. The fibers in the chorda tympani nerve are vasodilator as well as secretory in function.

In the medulla, the cells giving rise to the parasympathetic fibers are situated in the glossopharyngeal and vagus nuclei. The former enter

---

[2] The name *autonomic,* though now most commonly used, is misleading, for this system cannot act independently of the central nervous system. As will be seen, the governing cells lie within the spinal cord and brain. The autonomic system cannot function after its connections with the central nervous system have been severed. *Involuntary* nervous system is therefore a better name.

the glossopharyngeal nerve and pass to the otic ganglion; from here postganglionic fibers conveying vasodilator and secretory impulses are relayed to the parotid gland.

The vagus nerve is composed in the main of parasympathetic fibers; these have a very wide distribution—to the heart, bronchioles, esophagus, stomach, small intestine and first third of the large intestine, pancreas, liver, gall bladder, and bile ducts. The preganglionic fibers of the vagus may, therefore, be 2 feet or more in length, whereas the postganglionic fibers are very short. The latter form a rich plexus—**Auerbach's plexus**—in the walls of the gastrointestinal tract, bronchioles, and biliary ducts. Groups of (ganglionic) nerve cells are scattered throughout the plexus of fibers.

The cells of the **sacral outflow** are situated in the second, third, and fourth sacral segments of the spinal cord. The fibers leave the cord by the anterior spinal nerve roots. Separating again from the other anterior root fibers, they combine to form the *pelvic nerve*. This nerve supplies motor fibers to the distal two thirds of the large bowel and to the wall of the urinary bladder, and vasodilator fibers to the penis and clitoris. It also contains inhibitory fibers to the internal anal sphincter and to the internal sphincter of the bladder. The postganglionic fibers of the sacral outflow arise from small ganglia situated in close proximity to or in the walls of the innervated organ.

The sympathetic division. The preganglionic fibers of the sympathetic nerves are the axons of cells in the spinal gray matter between the anterior and posterior horns, from the first thoracic to the second or third lumbar segments, inclusive. The sympathetic is, therefore, commonly referred to as the **thoracicolumbar outflow** of the autonomic nervous system. The preganglionic fibers leave the cord by the anterior roots of the corresponding spinal nerves (Fig. 37.31). The ganglia of the sympathetic are in two main groups, the *vertebral* and the *prevertebral*. The vertebral ganglia are situated on either side of the vertebral column (Plate V*a*). They appear as a series of 22 swellings on each side, connected together to form a long, beaded cord. This extends from the base of the skull to the coccyx, and is called the **gangliated cord of the sympathetic.** The prevertebral ganglia are larger than the vertebral; they lie in front of the spinal column and in close relation to the aorta and its branches.

The sympathetic fibers destined for the supply of the limbs (blood vessels, sweat glands, and smooth muscle of the skin) soon separate from the anterior nerve roots and enter the vertebral ganglia. These fibers (preganglionic) are seen issuing as slender glistening white strands, one from each anterior spinal nerve root from the first thoracic to the second or third lumbar segment. They are called the **white rami communicantes** (sing. *ramus communicans*). The fibers of which each of these strands is composed enter the vertebral ganglion corresponding to the segment of the spinal cord from which they arise; here synapses are usually made by at least a small portion of the fibers, with nerve cells (Fig. 37.31). But the fibers of the white rami communicantes do not necessarily terminate around the nerve cells in the ganglion that they first enter; they may pass up or down the gangliated cord to synapse with ganglion cells at a higher or lower level. The axons of the cells in the ganglia (*post-ganglionic fibers*) leave the ganglia as short yellowish-pink filaments known as the **gray rami communicantes,** which join the spinal nerves. The sympathetic fibers are thus distributed to the periphery with the ordinary motor and sensory fibers. All the spinal nerves (limbs, head, and neck) receive postganglionic fibers, though the anterior roots of only a proportion of the spinal nerves (first thoracic to second or third lumbar) give rise to white rami (preganglionic fibers). That is to say, the spinal nerves above the first thoracic segment or below the third lumbar have gray rami (postganglionic fibers) but no white rami. The sympathetic fibers above or below these levels must travel up or down the gangliated cord to the appropriate vertebral ganglion and then pass as gray rami to the spinal nerves (see Plate V*a*).

The sympathetic fibers to the viscera and blood vessels of the abdomen do not connect with the vertebral chain of ganglia, but pass to the prevertebral ganglia—**celiac, superior mesenteric,** etc. The postganglionic fibers form plexuses around the branches of the abdominal aorta, from which the vessels and viscera receive their sympathetic supply. The fibers passing from the spinal cord to the prevertebral ganglia are collected on each side into three well-defined strands called the **greater, lesser,** and **least splanchnic nerves.**

Functions of the autonomic nervous system. The autonomic nervous

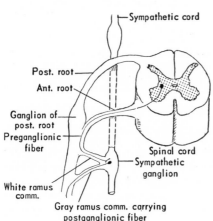

Sympathetic cord

Post. root
Ant. root
Ganglion of post. root
Preganglionic fiber
Spinal cord
Sympathetic ganglion
White ramus comm.
Gray ramus comm. carrying postganglionic fiber

Fig. 37.31. Origin and course of the sympathetic fibers to the limbs.

system exerts a regulating influence upon the functions of a great number of structures. Its sympathetic division through the cardiac accelerator nerves increases the rate of the heart; through the splanchnic nerves it inhibits the movements of the intestinal tract, maintains the tone of the arterioles of the abdomen, hastens the formation of glucose from glycogen by the liver, and causes the liberation of adrenaline from the adrenal medulla. Through the part of the sympathetic in the neck—the cervical sympathetic—impulses are conveyed to the pupil (causing dilatation), to the salivary glands, and to the blood vessels of the head and neck. Sympathetic impulses cause relaxation of the wall of the urinary bladder, but contraction of the internal sphincter of this organ. Sympathetic fibers in the cutaneous nerves transmit motor impulses to the smooth muscle of the skin, secretory impulses to the sweat glands, and both constrictor and dilator impulses to the blood vessels of the voluntary muscles.

Many structures, such as the iris, heart, intestines, urinary bladder, salivary glands, and pancreas, receive fibers from both divisions of the autonomic nervous system. The actions of the two upon a given organ are *antagonistic* and *balanced* one against the other, the activity shown by the organ at any moment being the resultant of the two opposing influences. The parasympathetic fibers (vagus) to the heart, for example, are inhibitory, the sympathetic excitatory. On the other hand, motor fibers (excitatory) to the wall of the intestine are derived from the parasympathetic, the inhibitory fibers from the sympathetic. The walls of the urinary bladder and intestine receive their motor innervation from the parasympathetic (pelvic and vagus nerves), whereas the sympathetic is inhibitory. The internal sphincters of the bladder and anus are innervated in a reverse manner; they are excited by the sympathetic and inhibited by the parasympathetic.

A summary of the actions of the parasympathetic and sympathetic fibers upon a number of structures is given in Table 37.1.

The sympathetic and the hormone of the adrenal medulla are closely similar in their actions. The two, acting in conjunction, constitute what is referred to as the **sympatho-adrenal system,** and play an important role in the regulation of the internal environment of the body, that is, the composition and temperature of the fluids bathing the cells of the tissues. Thus, through its effect upon the blood vessels, sweat glands, and smooth muscle of the skin, the sympathetic controls heat loss; and by its action upon the blood vessels it also varies the distribution of water between the vascular system and the tissues. Through an action upon the liver, either through sympathetic nerve impulses or the liberation of adrenaline, the sugar of the blood is raised. The sympatho-adrenal system through its various activities increases the body's efficiency in times of stress. Many manifestations of an animal when in danger or when its powers are being taxed to the utmost are those of sympathetic stimulation, for example, dilated pupils, rapid heart action, contraction of the spleen, and the erection of hair or the ruffling of feathers (due to contraction of cutaneous smooth muscle; see also Ch. 40).

The sympatho-adrenal system, highly important though it is, can nevertheless be dispensed with. It is not essential to life nor even to well-being, provided the animal is not exposed to some environmental hazard. Animals from which the entire sympathetic and the medulla of both adrenals have been excised live in perfect health in the sheltered surroundings of the laboratory. Such an animal cannot, however, withstand cold and is less well equipped than a normal animal to meet an emergency that demands the marshaling of its resources, either to defend itself or to fly from the threatened danger.

The transmission of autonomic effects by chemical substances. Research of recent years has disclosed the amazing fact that many sympathetic and parasympathetic effects are not brought about directly by the nerve impulses themselves, but by chemical substances that the impulses cause to be liberated from the nerve endings. In treating of the control of the heart, it has been mentioned that when the vagus is stimulated, *acetylcholine* is liberated, and is the direct cause of the inhibitory effect upon the heart muscle. Similarly, *adrenaline* or an *adrenalinelike substance* (*noradrenaline*, Ch. 40) is produced at the terminals of the cardiac accelerator nerves, and at the endings of other nerves of the sympathetic nervous system. These facts, which have led to a revolutionary change in our ideas of peripheral nervous action, have been supplemented within the last few years by a number of observations of great interest and importance.

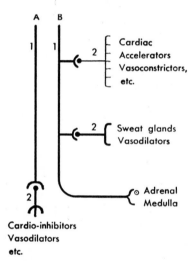

Fig. 37.32. Diagram showing the distribution of cholinergic and adrenergic fibers. A, parasympathetic; B, sympathetic; 1, preganglionic; 2, postganglionic; heavy lines, cholinergic; light lines, adrenergic.

It has been shown, for example, that acetylcholine is liberated at the terminals of such parasympathetic nerves as those going to the iris (in the oculomotor nerve), to the salivary glands (in the chorda tympani), to the stomach and intestines (in the vagus), and to the bladder (in the pelvic); it is liberated as well from certain sympathetic nerves, for example those going to the sweat glands and those that cause dilatation of the vessels of the skeletal muscles.

TABLE 37.1

Organ	Parasympathetic effects[3]	Origin of sympathetic postganglionic fibers	Sympathetic effects
Heart	Inhibition	Superior middle and inferior cervical ganglia	Acceleration
Vessels			
Cutaneous		Various vertebral ganglia	Constriction
Muscular		Various vertebral ganglia	Dilatation
Coronary	Constriction	Cervical ganglia	Dilatation
Salivary glands	Dilatation	Superior cervical ganglion	Constriction
Pulmonary	Constriction	Thoracic vertebral ganglia	Constriction and dilatation
Cerebral	Dilatation	Superior cervical ganglion	Constriction
Abdominal and pelvic viscera	Dilatation	Prevertebral ganglia	Constriction
External genitalia	Dilatation	Prevertebral ganglia	Constriction
Eye			
Iris	Constriction	Superior cervical ganglion	Dilatation
Ciliary muscle	Contraction	Superior cervical ganglion	Relaxation
Smooth muscle of orbit and upper lid		Superior cervical ganglion	Contraction
Bronchi	Constriction	Thoracic ganglia	Dilatation
Glands			
Sweat		Vertebral ganglia	Secretion
Salivary	Secretion	Superior cervical ganglion	Secretion
Gastric	Secretion	Celiac ganglion	Inhibition Secretion of mucus
Pancreas			
Acini	Secretion	Celiac ganglion	
Islets	Secretion	Celiac ganglion	
Liver		Celiac ganglion	Glycogenolysis
Adrenal medulla		No postganglionic fibers	Secretion
Smooth muscle			
Of skin		Vertebral ganglia	Contraction
Of stomach wall	Contraction or inhibition	Celiac ganglion	Contraction or inhibition
Of small intestine	Increased tone and motility	Celiac and superior mesenteric ganglia	Inhibition
Of large intestine	Increased tone and motility	Inferior mesenteric and hypogastric ganglia	Inhibition
Of bladder wall (detrusor muscle)	Contraction	Inferior mesenteric and hypogastric ganglia	Inhibition
Of trigone and sphincter	Inhibition	Inferior mesenteric and hypogastric ganglia	Contraction

[3] With certain exceptions, for example, those supplying the sublingual and parotid glands and the sphincter pupillae, the postganglionic fibers of the parasympathetic arise from cells situated in, or in close proximity to, the innervated organ itself.

Acetylcholine liberation also plays a part, though its exact nature is not altogether clear, in the transmission of nervous effects across sympathetic and parasympathetic synapses—that is, from preganglionic fibers to the ganglionic cell. Still more extraordinary is the discovery that acetylcholine liberation in the region of the motor-end plate is an essential event in the contraction of skeletal muscle.

Following the suggestion of Sir Henry Dale, the English physiologist, it is now customary to speak of those fibers that liberate an adrenaline-like substance as **adrenergic,** and those that liberate acetylcholine as **cholinergic** (Fig. 37.32). All preganglionic fibers (sympathetic or parasympathetic), all postganglionic parasympathetic fibers, and certain postganglionic sympathetic fibers (for example, to sweat glands), as well as the fibers of voluntary motor nerves are cholinergic. The remainder are adrenergic. Preganglionic sympathetic fibers (cholinergic) pass directly to the cells of the adrenal medulla, no ganglion cell being interposed.

ENDOCRINE, OR DUCTLESS, GLANDS

PART IX

38
General Description.
The Pituitary Gland, or Body

GENERAL DESCRIPTION

In the section dealing with the physiology of digestion, the general structure and actions of glands were described. All the glands there mentioned pour their secretions into the alimentary tract. The tear glands, the sweat glands, etc., deliver their secretions upon the surface of the body. All glands of this type have outlet tubes called ducts, along which the fluid that they manufacture is conducted to the surface or into one of the cavities of the body (Fig. 38.1). For this reason they are called **glands of external secretion.** The glands that we are about to consider are peculiar in that, as their name implies, they possess no ducts. The **ductless glands** pour their secretions directly into the blood stream. None of their secretions passes to the outside of the body (Fig. 38.2). They are, on this account, also called the **endocrine glands** (Gk. *endo,* within + *krino,* I separate), or, **glands of internal secretion.**[1] Their secretions are known as **hormones.**[2] From the many chemical substances in the blood, the cells of these glands manufacture secretions with very powerful effects. They take in their raw materials by the front door—the arteries—and turn the finished product out at the back door—the veins or lymph vessels. Thence the hormone is carried to all parts of the body (Plate VII*a*).

These glands are little chemical laboratories of marvelous ingenuity;

---

[1] In this section, only four endocrine glands are described—the pituitary, thyroid, adrenal, and parathyroid. The gastrointestinal hormones and those of the pancreas (insulin) and gonads are discussed in Chapters 26, 27, 30, and 49.

[2] Hormone is a general name given to any chemical substance that has been formed in one part of the body and is carried in the blood stream to another organ or tissue, and excites it to activity.

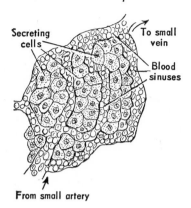

Fig. 38.2. Plan of a ductless gland —a gland of internal secretion. Note the rich blood supply, blood sinuses (filled with red cells) running between small groups of gland cells. In some glands the cells are arranged in cords, as in the anterior pituitary gland; in others the cells are in small groups or clumps; and in others, as in the thyroid, they are arranged in well-defined alveoli (Fig. 39.5).

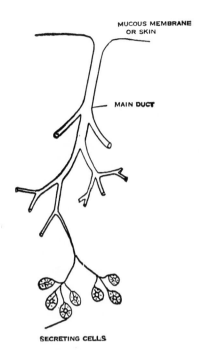

Fig. 38.1. Plan of an external secreting gland, such as the salivary.

the active principles of their secretions have most complex chemical structures. Though a number of hormones have been synthesized by the chemist, others have defied all attempts even to discover their chemical structure. It is the action of one of these secretions that paints the plumage of the male bird in such brilliant colors and also prompts its song. Others cause the growth of bone and direct the development of stature along normal lines—overactivity of this gland or underactivity of that one, and a giant or a dwarf is the result. Others influence various mental processes—instincts, emotions, and intelligence. In order that mind and body shall function normally, all the various ductless glands must pour their secretions into the blood stream in exactly the right amounts. None must produce too much or too little of its very potent chemical. If it does, abnormalities in growth and development or in behavior result (Fig. 38.3).

Some of the endocrines are of such a size and prominence that they did not escape the notice of the ancient philosophers. Their functions were pondered and speculated upon, and many fanciful ideas were suggested to account for their existence. The discovery of their true functions is comparatively recent. Previously, the central nervous system was

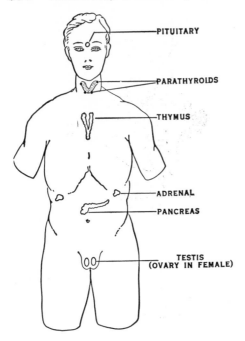

Fig. 38.3. Positions of the various endocrine organs. The thyroid, with which the parathyroids are closely associated, is shown but not labeled. The ovaries (not shown) are situated in the pelvis close to the uterus. The endocrine function of the thymus, if any, is unknown.

believed to play the dominant role in the control of bodily functions; its authority was thought to be supreme and undisputed. With the discovery of the endocrine glands an entirely new and quite unthought-of type of control was brought to light. The functions of these glands, though not so obvious as those of the nervous system, are of equal importance.

The internal secretions, with the exception of those formed by the adrenal medulla and the posterior lobe of the pituitary, govern slowly moving processes, such as the growth of the skeleton, the development of the sex organs, and the metabolism of food materials—processes measured by hours, months, or years; whereas the nervous system presides over those rapid processes of thought, muscular movement, and external secretion by glands—processes measured by fractions of seconds, or at the most, minutes.

THE PITUITARY GLAND, OR BODY

The **pituitary gland,** or **hypophysis cerebri,** is the most important endocrine gland in the body, for upon its activity the functions of most of the other endocrine glands depend. Yet in man this gland is scarcely larger than a cherry. It lies at the base of the brain, to which it is attached by a short stem or stalk (Figs. 38.4, 38.5).

The pituitary gland is made up of two main parts, or *lobes,* as they

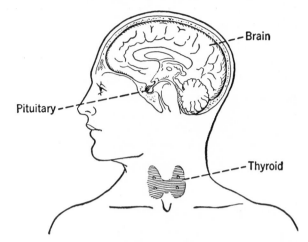

Fig. 38.4. Section of the brain between the hemispheres to show the position of the pituitary.

are usually called—*anterior* and *posterior*—that, though of quite different embryonic origins, have become fused together. The anterior lobe has developed from a pouch that has grown upward from the primitive mouth of the embryo, and the posterior lobe as a downgrowth from the base of the brain. A narrow band of tissue along the line of fusion of these two parts and of the same origin as the anterior lobe, is known as the *intermediate lobe*.

These three parts of the pituitary have entirely different endocrine functions and will therefore be described separately.

The anterior lobe, or adenohypophysis. The immense physiological importance of this part of the pituitary has been discovered only within recent years. Upon the hormones that it secretes the activities of most of the other endocrine glands—thyroid, adrenals, and ovaries or testes— depend. The growth of the skeleton is also under its control. It is with reason, therefore, that the anterior lobe of the pituitary has been called the *master gland* of the endocrine system.

The indispensability of the anterior lobe of the pituitary for many physiological processes can be shown in a striking manner by removing

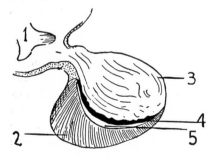

Fig. 38.5. Diagram of the pituitary. 1, third ventricle of the brain; 2, anterior lobe; 3, posterior lobe; 4, intermediate lobe (black); 5, cleft at line of fusion of embryonic parts.

it from an animal and studying the effects that follow. If this operation, which is called *hypophysectomy,* is performed upon a young animal, growth is arrested or greatly retarded (Fig. 38.6). The thyroid gland and the cortex of the adrenal glands shrink (*atrophy*) and fail to produce their hormones in sufficient amounts. The animal does not develop sexually,

because its sex glands—ovaries or testes—are not urged to produce their hormones; these glands also atrophy and become inactive. In adult animals the effects upon the thyroid, adrenal cortex, and sex glands, and the suppression of their secretions are also clearly evident. Removal of the anterior lobe at whatever age causes a profound fall in the blood sugar (glucose), and death may occur in generalized convulsions. These defects can be largely corrected by injections of the hormones extracted from the anterior lobe. Seven hormones or principles have been obtained from the anterior lobe in nearly pure form. Each hormone so prepared produces one effect predominantly and has little or no effect that could be attributed to any of the other six hormones.

Fig. 38.6. The effect of hypophysectomy upon the growth of a young animal. Two puppies of the same litter; the animal on the right was hypophysectomized a few weeks previously. *(From Dandy.)*

The hormone that stimulates the growth of the tissues generally—bones and soft parts—is called the **growth hormone**; the one that stimulates the thyroid and maintains this gland in a healthy and active state is called the **thyrotrophic hormone** (Ch. 39); the hormone that exerts a corresponding effect upon the adrenal cortex is termed the **adrenocorticotrophic hormone** (abbreviated ACTH), and those (two in number) that stimulate the gonads (testes or ovaries) are called **gonadotrophic**. The sixth hormone stimulates the production of milk and is called **prolactin**. The actions of the gonadotrophic hormones and of prolactin are described in Chapter 49.

The anterior lobe of the pituitary gland has a profound effect upon carbohydrate metabolism. As mentioned above, the blood sugar of an animal deprived of its pituitary falls to a low level, as if it had been given a large dose of insulin (Ch. 30). On the other hand, injection of an extract prepared from anterior lobe tissue causes hyperglycemia and the other signs and symptoms of diabetes. The internal secretion of the pancreas—that is, insulin—and a hormone produced by the anterior lobe of the pituitary are therefore antagonistic in their actions. In health, the two hormones. are perfectly balanced and the blood sugar is thus maintained at the normal level.

The actions of the other hormones prepared from the anterior lobe of the pituitary can also be demonstrated upon normal animals or upon those that have been deprived of their pituitary glands. Many of the defects already mentioned as following hypophysectomy can be corrected or the effects of any particular hormone exaggerated by injecting it into a normal animal, just as hyperthyroidism can be produced by means of the thyroid hormone. Thus, by the injection of the thyrotrophic hormone, the thyroid gland rendered inactive after hypophysectomy can be restored to normal appearance and function, or the normal thyroid can be stimulated to produce an excessive amount of its secretion. The effects of the growth and gonadotrophic hormones and of prolactin can be shown in a similar way. Young rats or puppies given daily doses of the growth hormone become of giant size as compared with untreated animals (Fig. 38.7).

Injections of the adrenocorticotrophic hormone (ACTH) causes cortisone and other hormones to be liberated from the adrenal cortex (Ch. 40).

The control of pituitary function. The anterior lobe of the pituitary body is not functionally independent of the central nervous system but is under the influence of humors secreted by groups of nerve cells (nuclei) in the hypothalamus (Ch. 37). The secretions of the thyroid and gonads, for example, are automatically controlled through this neurohumeral mechanism that, in turn, is affected by the level of these hor-

Fig. 38.7. The effect of an extract of the anterior lobe upon the growth of rats. The animal on the right has received daily injections for a period of several weeks. (*After Evans.*)

mones in the blood. Thus, when the level of one or the other hormone rises above or falls below the required concentration in the blood, the secretion of the thyrotrophic or of the gonadotrophic principle of the anterior lobe of the pituitary is reduced or increased reciprocally.

The posterior lobe, or neurohypophysis. The first recorded experiment upon the posterior lobe of the pituitary was performed in Edinburgh about seventy years ago. A rather crude extract of the pituitary was found to constrict the small blood vessels throughout the body, and thus to cause a sharp rise in blood pressure. This extract was later prepared commercially and sold under the name of *pituitrin*. Apart from its effect upon the circulation, which is called its *pressor action,* this extract has been found to have three other actions in mammals. It (a) stimulates the contraction of smooth muscle, for example, the uterus and intestine; its action upon the uterus is called its *oxytocic action*; (b) exerts an action upon the cells lining the renal tubules, increasing the reabsorption (that is, reducing excretion) of water and sodium and diminishing that of potassium; the reduction in the excretion of water and sodium constitutes the *antidiuretic effect* of the hormone, and (c) raises the blood sugar, thus antagonizing the action of insulin. To what extent these different effects of pituitrin are due to separate hormones is not fully known, but it seems that the pressor and oxytocic actions at least are caused by distinct principles.

The smooth muscle-stimulating action of pituitrin accounts for its *galactogogue action,* that is, for its causing a flow of milk from the nipple of the mammary gland. This is not a true secretory effect but is simply the result of the contraction of smooth muscle around the follicles and ducts of the gland, and the expression of milk already formed (Ch. 49).

Another of the main actions of pituitrin is not exerted upon higher animals; but in many cold-blooded animals a principle found in the posterior lobe, though as mentioned below it is actually produced by the intermediate lobe, causes changes in skin color. The skins of many lower forms—for example, fish, frogs, toads, snakes, and lizards—contain large numbers of irregularly shaped pigmented cells called **chromato-**

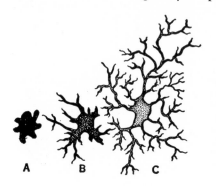

Fig. 38.8. Pigment cells (melanophores) of frog's skin, highly magnified. A and B, pigment granules confined to body of the cell or to the roots of the processes, when animal is in a bright light; C, in darkness, the granules have migrated into the many branching processes.

A B C

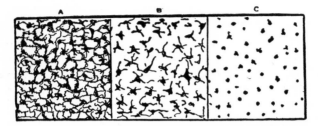

Fig. 38.9. Sections of a frog's skin (lower magnification than in Fig. 38.8), showing patterns formed by pigment cells in different degrees of illumination. A, when the animal is in a dim light; B, in a medium light; C, in a bright light. *(After Hogben.)*

phores. The irregular shape of these cells is due to their possessing many branching processes. The pigment is in the form of fine mobile granules and varies in color with the species (Fig. 38.8). In frogs it is dark brown, green, or black and the cells are called **melanophores, or melanocytes** (Gk. *melanos*, black). In the corresponding cells of some fish the pigment is red or yellow; they are therefore called **erythrophores** or **xanthophores**, respectively. By means of the color changes brought about by these cells the animals mentioned are enabled to make their bodies less conspicuous in their natural surroundings and can thus more easily elude their enemies. When the animal is in shade or upon a dark background, the mobile pigment granules stream outwards into the branching processes which, since they form a rich network darken the skin so that it blends more readily with surrounding objects (Fig. 38.9). In bright light or when the animal is against a light background, the granules gather near the center of the cell. The cell's processes are then poorly marked and the skin becomes correspondingly pale.

An injection of pituitrin into a frog causes a migration outwards of the pigment granules. The animal's skin becomes dark, as it does when in shade (Fig. 38.10). This action is brought about in the living animal by a hormone produced by the intermediate lobe that is probably distinct from the other pituitary hormones. It is called the **chromatophore-expanding hormone, melanocyte-stimulating hormone,** or **intermedin.** But there must be some means of controlling the secretion of this prin-

Fig. 38.10. A, the color of a normal frog. B, the same frog after the injection of an extract of the posterior lobe of the pituitary. *(After Hogben.)*

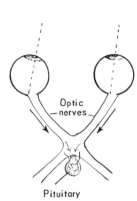

Optic
—nerves—

Pituitary

Fig. 38.11. Diagram to illustrate the manner in which light striking the retina controls the discharge of the posterior-lobe hormone of the pituitary.

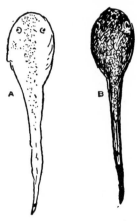

Fig. 38.12. Effects of the removal of the pituitary upon the color of tadpoles. A, the pituitary removed; B, a normal animal.

ciple in order that the skin shall change color in conformity with the animal's environment. The controlling mechanism is connected with the eyes. When the animal is in darkness, the hormone is secreted in small amounts into the blood stream; the pigment is then dispersed and fills the branching processes. But when the retina is stimulated by light, nerve impulses are set up and conducted by fine nerve twigs to the pituitary (Fig. 38.11). These impulses suppress the output of the chromatophore-expanding principle, and as it gradually disappears from the circulation the pigment granules gather near the center of the chromatophores. This nervous-hormonal mechanism can be proved experimentally step by step. That the control of this hormone of the pituitary is dependent upon nerve impulses from the retina is shown by temporarily blinding the animal, as by sealing its eyes with wax. No change in the color of its skin then occurs whether it is in darkness or in bright sunshine. Animals that have been hypophysectomized also lose the ability to alter the depth of the color of their skins, which are then uniformly pale (Fig. 38.12).

The well-known effect of light upon the sexual cycle of birds and of some mammals is also dependent upon the pituitary, but the hormone through which this action is brought about is unknown.

DISEASE OF THE PITUITARY IN MAN

Acromegaly. One of the main avenues of approach to an understanding of the glands of internal secretion has been through a study of their disorders in the human subject. The first step toward our present-day conceptions of pituitary function was made by the French physician, Pierre Marie. It was he who first described a condition characterized by overgrowth of the bones of the face, hands, and feet. The enlargement of the facial bones was seen particularly in the ridges above the eyes, in the nose, and in the lower jaw. The latter in some cases reported by Marie measured 18 inches from ear to ear, and the chin was some 4 inches deep (Figs. 38.13, 38.14). The soft tissues are also thickened, the combination of fleshy and bony overgrowth producing extreme coarsening of the features. The result in many cases amounts to grotesque ugliness. The bones of the hands and feet, especially the former, show a similar overgrowth. This is no moderate enlargement, for the hand of one of these individuals may be double the size of that of a normal person of the same height.

Marie ascribed this condition to disordered function of the pituitary and called it *acromegaly* (Gk. *akros,* extremity + *megas, megal,* big). It is due to the secretion of excessive amounts of the growth hormone.

Acromegaly develops gradually, but the changes in the facial features are very evident when a photograph of the subject taken some five or ten years previously is compared with his present appearance (Fig. 38.15). The disease, if it progresses, is invariably fatal.

Giantism, or gigantism. Acromegaly is a disease of the anterior lobe of the pituitary commencing in adult life—that is, after the normal period of growth. But the anterior lobe may produce an excessive amount of the growth hormone during the growing period. When it does, not only do the bones of the face and extremities overgrow, but all the bones of the body are urged into an extraordinary overdevelopment. In this way are giants made. Those men of tremendous stature who earn their livelihoods in circus sideshows are victims of overactive pituitary glands. Some of these giants reach the "altitude" of 8 or 9 feet. They would knock their heads against the ceilings in the modern American house, and would need to bend at the waist to pass through a doorway (Fig. 38.16). The tallest that has been reported was a Finn, standing 9 feet 5 inches. But a Chinese giant has been described who was 8 feet 1 inch, and an American has been recorded who was over 8 feet 2 inches. These are extreme cases, but there are many degrees of *gigantism,* or *giantism,* as the condition is called. A certain French baron some years ago sought, by encouraging the intermarriage of giants and giantesses of this type, to produce a race of supermen, but the experiment, for which a million francs were subscribed, was quite unsuccessful. The gigantic parents had averaged-sized offspring. This is a characteristic of pituitary giantism. The giants are usually the children of normal parents, and they themselves have normal children.

Dwarfism. Deficiency of the growth hormone of the pituitary results

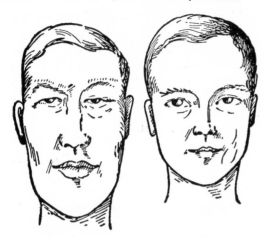

Fig. 38.13. The face of an acromegalic *(left)* and of a normal person *(right)*.

Fig. 38.14 *(below)*. Skulls of a normal person *(left)* and of an acromegalic *(right)*. *(From Cushing.)*

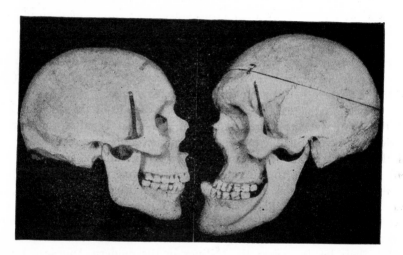

Fig. 38.15. Photographs of a victim of acromegaly taken *(left to right)* at the age of 24 before the onset of the disease, at 29 about the time of the commencement of the disease, at 37, and finally at 42, when the acromegalic changes are pronounced. *(From Cushing.)*

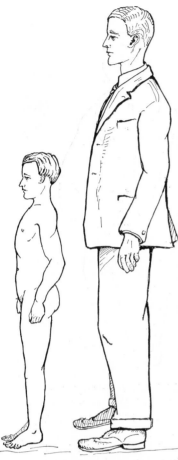

Fig. 38.16 *(above)*. An example of giantism. The boy in the center, 13 years of age, is 7 feet 4 inches tall and weighs 290 pounds. He is seen with his father and brother, who are of normal size.

Fig. 38.17 *(left)*. Midget type of dwarfism due to pituitary deficiency. Age 21 years. Bodily proportions, with relatively large head, are those of a 12-year-old boy; sexual and mental development normal. The man on the right is of about average height.

in a type of dwarf popularly known as a midget. Midgets are seen most commonly in circus sideshows. They are normally proportioned, of slight build, and usually not unattractive in appearance and personality (Fig. 38.17).

Another type of pituitary dwarf is due to failure of other hormones as well as of the growth principle. The posterior lobe or the hypothalamus (Ch. 37) may be involved as well as the anterior lobe. This type of dwarfism is marked by extreme obesity and lack of sexual develop-

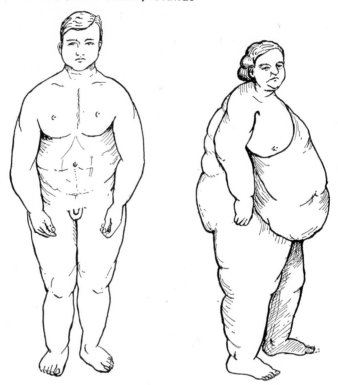

Fig. 38.18 *(left)*. Dwarfism, obesity, and sexual infantilism due to pituitary or hypothalamic disorder. Age 15 years. This type of dwarfism is known as the juvenile form of dystrophia adiposogenitalis and is associated with the name of Fröhlich.

Fig. 38.19 *(right)*. Extreme case of dystrophia adiposogenitalis developed in a woman reaching adult age. *(From a photograph.)*

ment. Fat metabolism and carbohydrate metabolism are both disturbed. Juveniles with this type of dwarfism often have voracious appetites and show an inordinate longing for sweets of all kinds, which of course add to their obesity. Not infrequently there are also excessive thirst and increased urine volume (which points to deficiency of the antidiuretic principle of the posterior lobe). Such children, as a rule, are below par mentally, progress slowly at school, and show an unchildlike lethargy. They are ready to sleep at any time. A subject of this type of pituitary disorder is shown in Figure 38.18. Great obesity without dwarfism may result from a similar disorder in adults. The fat woman of the circus is in most cases an example of this condition (Fig. 38.19).

Diabetes insipidus. Disease or injury of the posterior lobe of the pituitary or of the hypothalamus (Ch. 37) may prevent the production of the antidiuretic hormone. The reabsorption of water from the tubules of the kidney (Ch. 32) is then greatly reduced with the result that the volume of the urine is increased many fold. This disease is called *diabetes insipidus.*

Cushing's disease. Excessive stimulation of the adrenal cortex by overproduction of the adrenocorticotrophic hormone, as by a pituitary tumor, may cause Cushing's disease (Ch. 40).

39
The Thyroid Gland

A gland with which everyone, to some extent, is familiar is the **thyroid,** which lies beneath the muscles of the neck and embraces the sides of the larynx and upper part of the trachea (Fig. 39.1). When greatly enlarged, it constitutes the condition known as *goiter.*

The thyroid gland consists of two lateral masses called **lobes,** and a bar, or **isthmus,** that connects the lower poles of the lobes across the mid-line.

The minute structure of thyroid tissue. Viewed under the microscope, thyroid tissue appears as a mass of round or oval acini (Fig. 39.5). These acini, or follicles, are lined by a single layer of cuboidal epithelium and contain a structureless material called **colloid.** The colloid is the thyroid hormone in storage form, and is made up of a protein called thyroglobulin combined with the essential principle *thyroxine.* When required, the hormone is taken up by the cells lining the acini and passed into the blood stream.

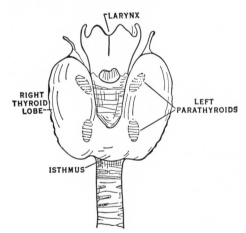

Fig. 39.1. Relationship of the thyroid to the larynx and trachea. The parathyroids lie behind the thyroid or are embedded in it.

Thyroxine, the thyroid hormone in pure crystalline form, is an amino acid containing iodine. It is formed by the thyroid gland from the amino acid, tyrosine by the addition of iodine; thyroid tissue has an ability above that of all other tissues of extracting iodine from the blood. It contains more iodine than the rest of the entire body though it is only a very small fraction of the body weight. Thyroxine has been synthesized in the chemical laboratory. The essential action of the thyroid hormone is to increase the rate of oxidation in the tissues—that is, to increase the metabolic rate—to fan, as it were, the "fires" in the cells.

The regulation of thyroid secretion. The growth and activity of the thyroid gland is under control of the anterior lobe of the pituitary body. Nerves apparently have no *direct* effect upon the output of the thyroid hormone. The pituitary exerts its influence upon the thyroid by discharging a hormone (thyrotrophic hormone, Ch. 38) into the blood stream that acts directly upon the thyroid cells. But the output of the pituitary hormone is regulated in turn by the concentration in the blood of the thyroid hormone. The output of the latter in health is therefore largely self-regulated. That is to say, if the blood concentration of thyroxine falls, the pituitary discharges more of its thyrotrophic hormone, and the thyroid responds by producing more of its hormone. When, on the other hand, the concentration of thyroxine is raised to a certain value the discharge of the thyrotrophic hormone is suppressed. The discharge of the thyrotrophic hormone, however, is influenced by the nervous system (through the hypothalamus). In this way the activity of the thyroid may be affected *indirectly* by impulses initiated in nervous centers.

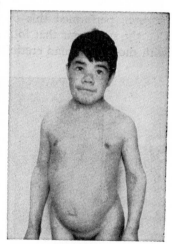

Fig. 39.2. A typical cretin. Age 28 years; mental age **4** to **5** years. *(From Selye's Endocrinology, after Mason.)*

Hypothyroidism. Cretinism and myxedema. In Switzerland, in the valleys of the Alps, there was commonly to be seen, until recent times, a type of dwarf known as a *cretin* (Figs. 39.2, 39.3A). A cretin is the direct result of the absence or the extreme deficiency of the thyroid hormone in infancy or childhood. These individuals are truly the most pitiable and grotesque parodies on mankind.

Cretins have a characteristic appearance that usually cannot be mistaken. Their growth is retarded or arrested at an early age. Their bodies are squat and flabby. They are mentally defective and often imbecile; many are deaf-mutes. Their low intelligence is usually quite evident from their facial expression. Their features are coarse and ugly, often goblin or gargoylelike. The forehead is low, the bridge of the nose depressed (saddle shaped), the lips large and loose, and the tongue, which appears larger than normal, protrudes from the partly open mouth. The skin of the face and of the body generally is thick, pale, and pasty. The hair is dry, coarse, and sparse. Cretins are sexually undeveloped. Their basal metabolism is much below the normal value. The word *cretin* is a corruption of the French word *chrétien,* meaning Christian, and was originally used in speaking of these unfortunates much in the same sense as the English words *innocent* and *simple* are applied to the feeble-minded.

Though cretins were more common in Switzerland than in other parts of Europe, they were by no means confined to that country. Cretinism was at one time not uncommon in England, especially in Derbyshire. It was seen occasionally on this continent, notably in districts bordering on the Great Lakes. But it was in the valleys of the Alps, of the Pyrenees, in the Tyrol, and in the Himalayas that it was seen most frequently.

It was not until the thyroid gland was removed from young animals that the cause of cretinism was revealed. Sir Victor Horsley, a London surgeon, performed this operation upon young monkeys, and showed that the symptoms that followed the operation were practically identical with those of human cretinism. Removal of the gland from other young

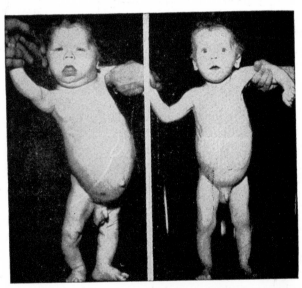

Fig. 39.3. Cretinism, showing the effect of thyroid treatment. *Left,* age 3½ years, before the commencement of treatment. *Right,* age 3 years, 11 months, after 3 months of treatment. *(From Selye's* Endocrinology, *after McCullagh.)*

Fig. 39.4. Three kids (triplets) of a horned goat. The middle one, which originally was smaller than the one on the right and about the same size as the one on the left, was kept as a control; the other two were thyroidectomized. (From Sutherland Simpson.)

animals causes arrested growth (Fig. 39.4). Through this work the responsibility for cretinism was definitely fastened upon the thyroid.

Several questions had still to be answered: Why is cretinism common in certain regions and virtually unknown in others? Why does the gland fail to perform its normal function? The usual answer given to these questions was that the drinking water was at fault. Even during the first two decades of the twentieth century authorities accepted his explanation. The specific thing that was supposed to depress thyroid function was unknown, though some thought it was an excess of calcium (lime), others that it was a microorganism.

Without going further into detail, it may be said that the question has at last been settled. It is not due to something in the water that should not be there, such as lime or germs, but to the absence of iodine from water and food. For this knowledge we are indebted to an American scientist, Dr. David Marine, who showed some 30 years ago that thyroid disease (goiter) in brook trout could be cured by the addition of very small amounts of iodine to the water in which they lived. He also showed that thyroid enlargement in children could be prevented by small doses of iodine.

This explains why cretins are rarely, if ever, seen on the seacoast. The sea is an inexhaustible storehouse for iodine, which finds its way into the food and the drinking water of the inhabitants along the coast. It is practically always in inland territories that thyroid deficiency is seen—particularly in the mountains and on the high land, since they, as a rule, are farther removed from the iodine supplies of the sea. Examination of the soils of goitrous districts has shown that they are poor in iodine.

The thyroid must have iodine in order to manufacture its secretion. Without this element it is unable to produce its hormone in sufficient amounts. The gland becomes enlarged, but the enlargement is made up to a large extent of worthless tissue, its follicles filled with a secretion of very low potency. The essential glandular tissue has degenerated, and though the gland is of greater size, it is a fraud, being made up largely of fibrous tissue and large irregular spaces instead of the small and regularly shaped follicles (Fig. 39.5). The tissue of such a gland has a very low content of iodine.

Cretinism is seen much less commonly today, and when it does occur it is rarely the result of goiter; it is usually seen in babies and is then due to defective development of the thyroid gland before and after birth. There are two reasons why the cretin is now a rarity. In the first place, the tendency to goiter in those parts of the world where it used to be prevalent has been greatly reduced by supplying iodine to the population, especially to growing children. On this continent as well as elsewhere it has become the custom to add minute amounts of iodine to table salt. The second reason why cretinism is now seen infrequently is that thyroid deficiency can be easily and quickly corrected by treatment with the thyroid hormone obtained from the glands of sheep. In 1894 Dr. George Murray, an English physician, first treated persons suffering from thyroid deficiency with injections of a glycerine extract of sheep's thyroid tissue. Of all the discoveries in the field of medicine this proved one of the most brilliant. Soon it was shown to be unnecessary to give the treatment by injection. Today sheep's glands are dried and powdered, compressed into tablets, and taken by mouth. If thyroid deficiency is recognized at an early age all the defects that have been described as characteristic of cretinism can be corrected. Growth and development— bodily, mental, and sexual—proceed in normal fashion, and if the treat-

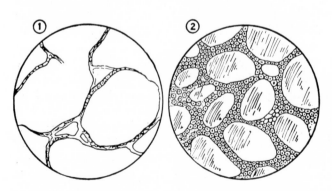

Fig. 39.5. The microscopic appearance of a goitrous thyroid, 1, compared with that of a normal thyroid, 2. Shaded areas in alveoli indicate colloid.

ment is maintained, as it should be to the end of life, no signs of thyroid deficiency recur (Fig. 39.3*B*).

Should the thyroid, as a result of disease, fail in its function after adult life has been reached—that is, after growth has ceased and mental and sexual development has attained maturity—a state develops that in its essentials is strictly comparable to cretinism. The effects upon growth and development, which are so prominent in the cretin, are, of course, absent. But the mental processes and sexual functions are depressed. The basal metabolism is below normal, the skin dry, thick, and puffy, and the hair sparse, dry, and brittle. This condition is called *myxedema*. It is promptly relieved by thyroid hormone in the form of tablets of dried thyroid tissue or by thyroxine, the chemically pure thyroid hormone.

Hyperthyroidism. Thyrotoxicosis. Like most of the other endocrine glands, the thyroid may secrete an excess of its powerful hormone. In some instances the excessive secretion is due to a tumor of the gland composed of actively functioning thyroid tissue. In other instances there is no definite tumor, but the entire gland is stimulated to increase its hormone production. The gland becomes considerably enlarged. What stimulates the thyroid in this way is not known with certainty, but it is very likely that the stimulant action is brought about through the thyrotrophic hormone produced by the pituitary gland (Ch. 38).

Fig. 39.6. Hyperthyroidism; exophthalmic goiter with moderately severe exophthalmos. *(From Bram.)*

When a normal animal is treated continuously with fairly large doses of the thyroid hormone, characteristic effects make their appearance within a few days. The same effects would follow if a normal person were given corresponding doses. The heart rate increases, the metabolism is raised, and there may be trembling of the limbs and extreme nervousness. These effects of overdosage with the thyroid hormone are precisely the symptoms from which a patient suffers when his thyroid gland becomes overactive. But, in addition, the eyes of patients suffering from hyperthyroidism, in many instances, bulge prominently (exophthalmos) and cause a staring or alarmed expression. The disease, for this reason, is called *exophthalmic goiter* (Fig. 39.6).[1]

[1] Exophthalmos, though frequently associated with hyperthyroidism, is *not* the result of an excess of the thyroid hormone, which is the cause of the other symptoms of the disease. The cause of the ophthalmic signs is not known for certain, but is believed to be increased secretion of the *thyrotrophic hormone* of the pituitary.

Within recent years a number of drugs (thiourea, thiouracil, etc.) have been discovered that depress the production of the thyroid hormone and are of great value in the treatment of hyperthyroidism. A radioactive isotope of iodine is also employed for the same purpose (Ch. 1), for it has been mentioned that the thyroid gland has the peculiar property of concentrating iodine. These drugs have to a large extent replaced surgical operation in the treatment of thyrotoxicosis.[2]

Thyroid experiments upon lower animals. The thyroid hormone has a remarkable effect upon the development (metamorphosis) of frog larvae—ordinarily known as tadpoles. When a number of these creatures that have just recently been hatched are divided into two groups and one group fed upon thyroid tissue, or thyroid extract is added to the water in which they live, they develop into frogs much more rapidly than the other group. The members of the latter group, which are not given treatment of any kind, develop in the usual way and in the usual time and therefore serve as *controls*—that is, as normal standards for comparison (Fig. 39.7).

If the thyroid glands are removed from the members of one group of tadpoles and they are thus deprived of thyroid hormone, they do not metamorphose, whereas the members of a control group develop into frogs in the usual time (Fig. 39.8). If, however, thyroid tissue is fed to the thyroidless larvae, metamorphosis proceeds in a normal fashion and at the usual rate.

Thyroid function has been put to the test on another close relative of the frog family. In Mexican waters there lives a strange creature known

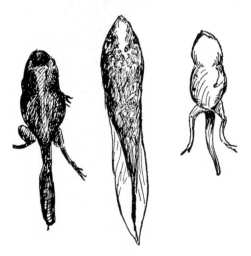

Fig. 39.7. The effect of thyroid extract upon the development of tadpoles. The three animals are of the same age. Those on the right and the left have received thyroid extract; the one in the center has not been treated. *(After Swingle.)*

[2] It might be thought that iodine administration would aggravate the thyrotoxicosis since the element is an essential constituent of the thyroxine molecule; that the reverse is true is a fact that has not been satisfactorily explained.

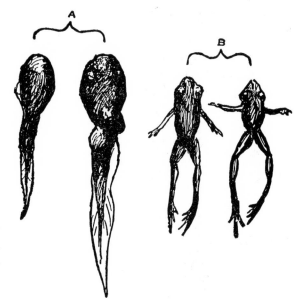

Fig. 39.8. The effect of the removal of the thyroids upon the development of tadpoles. A, thyroidless tadpoles; B, normal frogs of the same age as A. (After Allen.)

as the axolotl. The axolotl is a sort of halfway house along the evolutionary path between the fish and the frog. It looks like a huge tadpole—for it is several inches long—that had started out to be a frog but remained a grotesque-looking object with gills, a finned tail, a square head, and short fore and hind limbs. This is the usual adult form of these creatures; they breed in this form, most of them never developing into land animals, and a few others doing so very, very slowly. If an axolotl is fed upon beef thyroid, even one or two meals, it develops into a land animal. It loses its gills and tail and develops air-breathing organs. The head becomes oval and the eyes prominent. It comes out of the water and lives on land (Fig. 39.9).

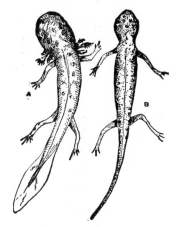

Fig. 39.9. Axolotls. A has not been treated; B has received thyroid extract. Note the disappearance of the gills and the fin from the tail.

Here is an instance in which an animal—forsaken, as it were, at a certain wayside station in the evolutionary journey—has been brought a step further by an internal secretion. These facts make one wonder just how important a part the ductless glands have played in the evolutionary process.

Summary of thyroid function. From the results of the many experiments upon animals and the innumerable observations on man, we are left with no doubt concerning the important functions of the thyroid gland. It absorbs iodine and other materials from the blood, producing from them a hormone that controls the growth and development of the body and stimulates oxidations in all the tissue cells. In excess, the hormone raises the metabolism above the normal level; if secreted in less than normal amounts heat production is depressed.

40
The Adrenal and Parathyroid Glands

THE ADRENAL GLANDS

The **adrenal** (or **suprarenal**) glands are two bodies shaped something like cocked hats, and in man are about the size of the last joint of the little finger. They are placed one on each side of the spinal column just above the kidneys (Fig. 40.1). When an adrenal gland is cut through the center, it is found to be composed of two parts—a central dark area and an outer rim of lighter-colored material. The central part is called the **medulla**. The outer rim, which reminds one of a skin or rind, is called the **cortex**. The duties of these two parts are entirely different.

The adrenal cortex. This part of the adrenal gland is absolutely essential to life. An animal lives for only two or three weeks after both adrenal cortices have been removed. Among the chief functions of the cortex are the regulation of the water content of the body, and the excretion of sodium and potassium. It is also concerned in the metabolism of sugar. When it fails in its functions, as it occasionally does in man, the volume of the blood and other body fluids becomes reduced, and the excretion of sodium chloride in the urine is increased. As a consequence of the latter effect, the sodium chloride of the blood and tissues falls to a dangerously low level. The excretion of potassium, on the other hand, is reduced, and its concentration in the blood rises. The sugar of the blood is diminished and its concentration may reach the level at which convulsions occur (Ch. 30).

Only within recent years has it been known that these important changes in the blood resulted from defective function of the adrenal cortex, but the general symptoms of the disease, which consist mainly of

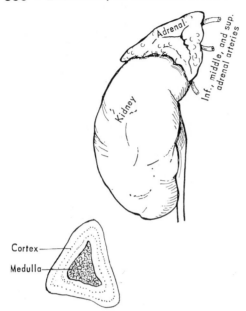

Cortex
Medulla

Fig. 40.1. Showing relation of the adrenal gland to the kidney. Lower figure is a cross section of the gland; semidiagrammatic. Note the concentric zones in the cortex. From without inwards they are named *zona glomerulosa, zona fasciculata,* and *zona reticularis.*

extreme weakness, low blood pressure, anemia, and a peculiar brown pigmentation of the skin, were described about 100 years ago by Thomas Addison, a physician of Guy's Hospital, London, England. Failure of the adrenal cortex (adrenal insufficiency) is, therefore, frequently referred to as *Addison's disease.* An extract of the adrenal cortex is effective in its treatment. A diet with a high content of sodium, but low in potassium, is also of great benefit.

Active principles of the adrenal cortex. The adrenal cortex is composed of lipid material from which several crystalline steroid principles (Table 40.1) have been isolated. Each of these exerts certain characteristic physiological effects. The cortical principles (sometimes called **corticoids**) are closely related chemically to cholesterol, the bile salts, and the sex hormones (Ch. 49); they are believed to be formed in the body from cholesterol. At least seven physiologically active crystalline principles have been isolated from the adrenal cortex or synthesized in the laboratory. They are very much alike in their general chemical structure, but differ both in kind and degree in their actions. Their names and principal actions are given in the following table.

These compounds, especially 11-deoxycorticosterone and 17-hydroxy-11-dehydrocorticosterone, correct the defects caused by cortical deficiency (Addison's disease). The last mentioned compound, which is known most commonly today as *cortisone,* has been found to exert a remarkably beneficial effect in acute rheumatism and rheumatoid arthritis. It has also

TABLE 40.1

Name	Principal actions
Corticosterone	On carbohydrate, protein, and fat metabolism; antagonizes the action of insulin
11-Deoxycorticosterone	On water and mineral metabolism, increases the retention of sodium and the excretion of potassium by the kidney
Aldosterone	Similar in action to deoxycorticosterone on sodium retention, but from 30 to 100 times more powerful in this respect
11-Dehydrocorticosterone	On carbohydrate metabolism
17-Hydroxycorticosterone (cortisone)	On carbohydrate metabolism; on connective tissues; antirheumatic
17-Hydroxy-11-dehydrocorticosterone (cortisone)	On carbohydrate metabolism; on connective tissues; antirheumatic
11-Deoxy-17-hydroxycorticosterone	On connective tissues; antirheumatic

been used in the treatment of a number of other diseases involving the connective tissues, but with less satisfactory results.

Both male and female sex hormones are contained in the adrenal cortex. One of those possessing male hormone action is called **adrenosterone**, or sometimes **andrenosterone**.

As in the case of the other endocrines, excessive secretion of the cortical principles also occurs, and is the cause of a disorder known as *Cushing's disease* (Fig. 40.2), in which there are overgrowth of hair over the general body surface and an increase in the fatty tissue of the face and trunk, but not of the limbs. The face is "puffed out" with fat, giving the appearance known as "moon face." Another abnormality caused presumably by hyperfunction of the adrenal cortex—the excessive production of adrenal sex hormones—is marked by precocious sexual development in young children, or when occurring in women by the growth of hair on the face and the appearance of other signs of masculinization. These conditions may arise from an adrenal tumor, or as a result of overstimulation of the adrenal cortex by the anterior lobe of the pituitary body (adrenocorticotrophic hormone).

The adrenal medulla. The medulla of the adrenal gland secretes into the blood stream a hormone most commonly known as **adrenaline**, though it also goes by the name of *epinephrine*, or *adrenin*. It produces another hormone, called **noradrenaline** or **norepinephrine**, which is closely allied chemically to adrenaline; its effects are very similar to, but not identical with, those of adrenaline.

The actions of adrenaline when injected into the body closely resemble those caused by stimulation of the sympathetic nervous system. This hormone increases the rate and force of the heart beat and con-

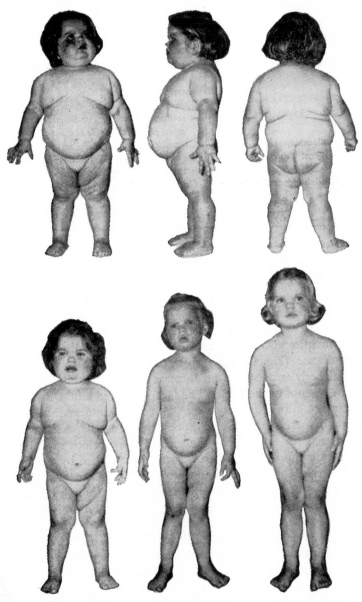

Fig. 40.2. Cushing's disease in a 4-year-old child due to a tumor of the adrenal cortex. *Above*, before operation. *Below*, 1, 7, and 14 months after operation, respectively. *(From Grobe.)*

stricts the blood vessels (except those of the coronary system and the muscles, which are dilated) ; thus the blood pressure is raised. It inhibits the movements of the intestines, dilates the bronchioles, stimulates the smooth muscle in the skin, widens the pupil, and increases the concentration of sugar in the blood. All of these effects can be duplicated by stimulating sympathetic nerves. The function of the secretion of the adrenal medulla in the living animal appears to be defensive or protective in character. It reinforces the action of the sympathetic nervous system in states of emergency or bodily stress, so that the animal is more capable of defending itself against its enemies or of adjusting itself to changes in the environment. Thus, the increase in the blood sugar provides an adequate supply of fuel for the contracting muscles. The muscles also fatigue less readily under the influence of adrenaline, and the blood clots more quickly. The latter effect is important in that it lessens the dangers of hemorrhage should the animal suffer a wound when defending itself or attacking its prey. The dilation of the bronchioles enables a greater volume of air to be breathed, and consequently permits the greater quantity of blood flowing through the lungs during the exertion required for fight or flight to be oxygenated to the greatest possible degree. The value of the effects upon the circulation—namely, the increased action of the heart, the rise in blood pressure, and the dilatation of the coronary vessels—is obvious. Ruffling of the feathers in birds and the bristling of the hairs in fur-bearing mammals are brought about by the contraction of smooth muscle in the skin. These are in many instances defense reactions. As mentioned above, the contraction of the skin muscles is stimulated by adrenaline. In some cold-blooded animals the hormone of the adrenal medulla has an action opposed to that of the chromatophore-expanding hormone of the pituitary (Ch. 38). It causes

Fig. 40.3. Showing the effect of an extract of the adrenal medulla upon the skin color of the horned toad. *Left,* a normal animal. *Right,* an animal injected with adrenaline; note the pallor. During excitement these animals become pale as a result apparently of the passage of adrenal secretion into the blood stream.

the pigment granules of the chromatophores to gather near the cell centers, thus causing pallor of the skin (Fig. 40.3) .

THE PARATHYROID GLANDS

The parathyroid glands are four little bodies about the size of peas, lying two on each side behind or within the thyroid. Though so small, they are nevertheless essential to health and, indeed, to life itself. Their name suggests a relationship with the thyroid, but the relationship is purely anatomical. So far as their functions go, they have nothing whatever in common with the thyroid. A close anatomical relationship between two ductless glands having entirely different functions is not unusual; we have already seen other examples of this—the anterior and posterior lobes of the pituitary, and the medulla and cortex of the adrenal gland.

The story of the parathyroids goes back to the end of the nineteenth century, when they were first discovered and described more as curiosities than anything else. Their important functions were then not even guessed. Their very existence was forgotten soon after their discovery. It was not until two surgeons in Switzerland, famous for their skill in removing goiters, reported that occasionally a patient upon whom they had operated developed convulsions, that attention was again directed toward these glands. With a view to discovering their functions, a French physiologist about this time carried out experiments upon animals. When he removed the parathyroid from rabbits, the animals went into violent convulsions and died. It was immediately realized that the cause of the convulsions in the surgeon's patients had been the unwitting removal of the parathyroids along with the thyroid. The utmost care is now exercised to avoid interfering with these tiny glands when the thyroid is removed by operation.

Hypoparathyroidism. Tetany. Tetany[1] is the name given to the type of convulsion that follows removal of, or injury to, the parathyroid glands. In human beings the hands and feet are drawn into characteristic attitudes that are readily recognized. In animals the jaws are tightly clamped together, and all the muscles of the body become rigid or show spasmodic contractions; death always occurs if all parathyroid tissue has been excised and the condition is not treated.

The calcium (lime) of the blood falls to a low level after the removal of the parathyroids, and it is quite evident that the low calcium is the cause of the convulsions. If calcium is injected so that its concentration in the blood is raised to the normal level, tetany is relieved. In 1925 an extract of the parathyroid glands was prepared by Dr. J. B. Collip. This,

[1] This should not be confused with *tetanus,* or "lockjaw," an entirely different disease that is due to the tetanus bacillus.

when injected into the body, raises the calcium of the blood to normal and thus quickly cures tetany. It has been named *parathormone*. When injected into a normal animal the calcium of the blood is raised well above the normal level. From this and other facts it has been concluded that the parathyroid glands manufacture a hormone that alters the quantity of calcium in the body. The greater amount of calcium found in the blood after the injection of parathormone evidently comes from the bones, which are largely composed of phosphate and carbonate of lime. After prolonged treatment of an animal with the extract, the bones become less hard and dense, showing that the minerals have been withdrawn from the skeleton. Just as in the case of other endocrines, defective function of the parathyroid glands sometimes, though very rarely, occurs spontaneously; that is, from some unknown cause. The low blood calcium that results leads to tetany. In other conditions associated with a low blood calcium, especially rickets, tetany also occurs. But there is no reason to believe that the low blood calcium in such conditions is caused by any deficiency of the parathyroid function (Fig. 40.4).

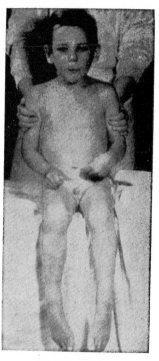

Hyperparathyroidism. In man, overactivity of the parathyroid glands sometimes occurs, usually as a result of the development of a tumor of parathyroid tissue within the gland. The parathyroid hormone is then discharged into the blood stream in excessive amounts and causes very serious effects. The calcium in the blood rises, for, as has just been said, the hormone dissolves calcium from the bones. These become softer and

Fig. 40.4. Tetany due to hypoparathyroidism. Note the positions of the hands and feet (carpopedal spasm). *(From Collins-Williams.)*

less rigid, and are therefore likely to be bent into unusual shapes. Cavities also develop within the bones where large quantities of mineral have been removed, and stones form in the kidneys as a result of the excretion of the excess calcium extracted from the skeleton.

INTERACTION OF THE DUCTLESS GLANDS

The endocrine glands have been described and dealt with as though they were quite independent one of the other. This method of treating them is unavoidable, because this is the way in which they have been studied, and this is the way in which most of the information regarding them has been gained. There is no doubt, however, that their actions are very closely related to one another, and that it is purely artificial to study them separately.

We should look upon the secretions of the ductless glands as forming, with the other constituents of the blood, a suitable environment—an appropriate fluid medium—to bathe the cells of the tissues. When all these secretions are present in their correct proportions, the cells are healthy and they flourish and grow normally. On the other hand, when one secretion in this nicely balanced mixture is present in reduced or excessive proportion, the environment becomes unsuitable, and the cells suffer. Their special functions can no longer be carried out. In order that there may be physiological harmony, each gland must play its part in tune with its fellows.

The constancy (steady state) in the composition of the blood and other body fluids as maintained by the various physiological processes, including the activities of the endocrine glands, was given the term **homeostasis** by the late Professor W. B. Cannon of Harvard. The fluids themselves that constitute the internal environment of the body (since they bathe the cells of the tissues) were called the *fluid matrix,* and by Claude Bernard, the great French physiologist of the nineteenth century, the *milieu interne.*

THE SPECIAL SENSES
PART X

41
The Physiology of
Vision

GENERAL DESCRIPTION OF THE ORGAN OF SIGHT

The eyes have developed from hollow outgrowths of the fore part of the brain. The adult human eye is almost spherical in shape and about 1 inch in diameter (Fig. 41.1). A clear, circular window about $\frac{1}{2}$ inch across and situated on its front (anterior) wall, and called the **cornea,** permits rays of light to pass into the interior of the eye and fall upon the **retina.** The retina is the sensitive tissue that lines most of its inner aspect. A compact, cylindrical bundle of nerve fibers—the **optic nerve**—issues from the posterior pole of the eyeball and carries nerve impulses to the brain. Upon arriving at their destination, these impulses give rise to the sensation we know as sight, or vision. In the protection of such a valuable organ as the eye, nature has taken every possible precaution. The eye, except for a small part of its circumference in front, is enclosed in a bony case—the eye socket, or **orbital cavity.** It is separated, however, from the unyielding bone by a thick layer of loose fat upon which it is cushioned, so that a force striking the delicately structured globe is less likely to damage it. The eyelids, as we know, are able at an instant's warning to close over the front part of the eye and protect it when injury threatens (Plate V*b*).

Small muscles stretch between the wall of the bony cavity and various points in the circumference of the globe, and by their contractions pull upon one or the other side of the eye to roll it about in its bed. The eyelids are lined by a delicate membrane called the **conjunctiva.** At the upper limit of the upper eyelid and at the lower limit of the lower lid, the membrane becomes folded over to pass from the inner surfaces of the lids on to the front of the eyeball, which it completely covers.

564

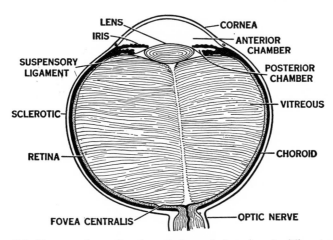

Fig. 41.1. Diagram of a section through the eyeball to show its different parts.

When the lids move up and down, these two folds of membranes slide over each other. The surfaces are kept lubricated by a small amount of tear fluid, which is continuously secreted by a gland—the **lacrimal gland** —lying under the shelter of the bone forming the upper and outer part of the eye socket. The tears, after flowing over the surface of the eye, are drained away from its inner angle by small tubes—the **lacrimal ducts**— and pass into the nose. If it were not for the constant washing and lubrication of the surface of the eyeball by the tears, the delicate covering membrane would soon become dry and inflamed, and destruction of the eye would result (Fig. 41.2). The tears contain *lysozyme* (p. 344).

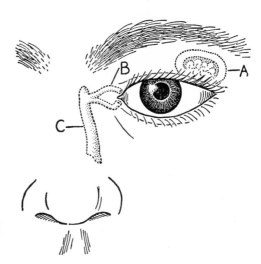

Fig. 41.2. The lacrimal apparatus. A, lacrimal gland; B, lacrimal ducts; C, nasolacrimal duct.

STRUCTURE OF THE WALL OF THE EYE

The wall of the eye is composed of three layers or coats—an *outer,* a *middle,* and an *inner* (Fig. 41.1).

The **outer layer, or sclerotic coat.** The outer layer is made of a tough and dense fibrous material, which preserves the form of the globe and protects the more delicate structures within. Part of this coat may be seen in the front of one's own eye, where it forms what we know as the *white of the eye.* In front, and in the very center of the sclerotic coat, is a circular window called the **cornea.** But this "window of the eye," though apparently as clear as glass, is not as homogeneous, for under the microscope it can be seen to be made up of several rows of flat cells laid one on top of the other and cemented together. Should the surface of the cornea be cut or seriously injured in any way, a scar will form, which, if large and in the line of sight, will cause blindness in the affected eye.

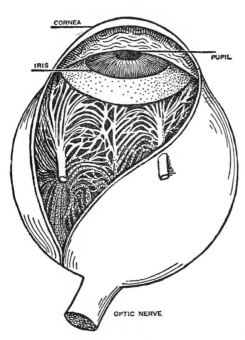

The **middle layer, or choroid coat.** The choroid coat carries the greatest number of blood vessels with which the eye is supplied. It shows a fine network of small arteries and veins (Fig. 41.3). Its weave of vessels, like a dark red carpet, completely sheathes the eyeball except in front, where a small punched-out hole is seen. The round opening, which lies behind the center of the cornea,

Fig. 41.3. The eyeball with part of the sclerotic coat cut away to show the choroid and its network of veins.

if, of course, familiar to everyone. It is known as the **pupil** of the eye. The circular band of the choroid coat surrounding the pupil is also familiar to all, for it is this that gives to the eye its brown, blue, black, or hazel color. This colored band has been named the **iris,** after the mythical goddess of the rainbow. If we think of a rainbow mirrored in a pool, the name perhaps is not inapt.

The **inner layer, or retina.** The retina lines the interior of the eyeball, and may be described as a layer of tissue highly specialized to convert the energy of light waves into nerve impulses that are transmitted by the optic nerve to the brain. If a section of the retina is examined under the microscope, several layers can be distinguished; but though the layers have each their own special features, they must be looked upon as being in close connection with one another and as forming together a single structure for receiving light and converting it into messages of sight.

As will be seen when its cell layers are described, the retina is essentially a nervous structure. Its origin from the brain has been mentioned.

THE MINUTE STRUCTURE OF THE RETINA

The chief layers to be distinguished in the retina are shown in Figure 41.4. In order from front to back, that is, from the inside of the eyeball outward, they are as follows:

1. Layer of nerve fibers
2. Layer of ganglion cells
3. Inner and outer nuclear (molecular) layers
4. Layer of rods and cones
5. Layer of pigment cells

The layer of nerve fibers. These fibers are the axons (Ch. 33) of the ganglion cells composing the layer (No. 2, above) lying just beneath. The ganglion cells give off these long fibers, which, after passing forward for a short distance, turn horizontally and form a felted layer above the cells from which they arose. The fibers, about 500,000 in number, converge to one point near the center of the back of the eyeball like streams of water into a vortex. Here they are collected into a rounded bundle to form the **optic nerve.**

The layer of ganglion cells. The ganglion cells forming the second layer of the retina are, for the most part, large, plump cells whose axons form the first layer, as just mentioned. Their dendritic processes are directed outward to form synaptic junctions (Ch. 34) with cells of the internal molecular layer.

The rods and cones. These curiously shaped cells, which are shown diagrammatically in Figures 41.4 and 41.5, form the outermost layer but one of the retina. They are the receptors (Ch. 33) of vision; when stimulated by light they cause impulses to be set up in the nerve cells, which are transmitted along the optic nerve to the brain. In most animals, the cones are in greatest number in the **fovea centralis** (see below), that part of the retina concerned with acute vision—that is, with the perception of the finer details of the visual image. In man, this region contains only cones. The cones are also responsible for the appreciation of color. In other parts of the human retina (**extrafoveal region**) the cones are intermingled with the rods but are found in progressively fewer numbers farther and farther from the fovea centralis; the rods increase

INTERIOR OF EYE

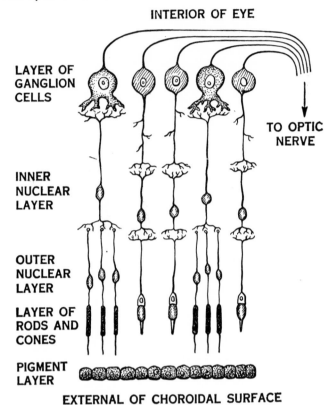

LAYER OF
GANGLION
CELLS

TO OPTIC
NERVE

INNER
NUCLEAR
LAYER

OUTER
NUCLEAR
LAYER

LAYER OF
RODS AND
CONES

PIGMENT
LAYER

EXTERNAL OF CHOROIDAL SURFACE

Fig. 41.4. Simplified diagram to show the chief layers of the retina.

in number as the cones decrease. These rod receptors are concerned only with the perception of light and shade. They give rise to no sensation of color, but they are very sensitive to light of low intensity. It is through the medium of the rods that objects can be seen in dim light. The threshold of the cones is much higher—that is, they require a stronger light to stimulate them. That is the reason why a faintly illuminated object, such as a small star, often cannot be seen if we look at it directly (foveal vision). Only when we turn our eyes a little to one side so that its image falls upon the extrafoveal region of the retina does it become visible; we see it "out of the corner of the eye."

The insensitivity of the cones to weak illumination and the inability to perceive color by means of the rods account for our blindness to color in twilight. Our surroundings are then seen only as light and shade, white or gray and black. The rods, though they give no sensation of color when an image of a green, blue, or yellow object falls upon them, are stimulated, nevertheless, and the object appears gray. But dark red

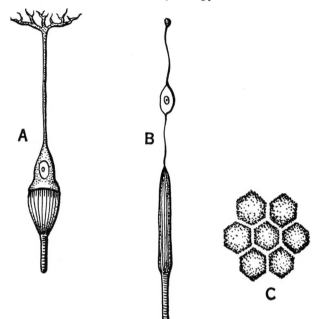

Fig. 41.5. Cells
from the outer two
layers of the retina.
A, a cone; *B,* a rod;
C, pigment cells.

light fails to stimulate the rods at all; the absence of any kind of visual stimulation then gives a sensation of black. In their sensitivity the rods thus resemble an ordinary photographic film.

The outer sections of the rods contain a red pigment called **visual purple,** or **rhodopsin.** This is decomposed by light into an orange-yellow substance[1] and upon further exposure into *vitamin A* and a *protein.* These latter products are colorless; it is usually said, therefore, that visual purple is "bleached" by light. Reconversion of vitamin A and protein to visual purple takes place in darkness. It is through this photochemical change that the rods serve as visual receptors. The changes in the light-sensitive substance in some way cause impulses to be set up in the nerve cells of the retina. A constant supply of vitamin A must be brought to the retina in the circulation in order for a rapid reformation of visual purple to occur, since a certain amount of the vitamin is inevitably destroyed in the bleaching process. This is the reason why persons whose diets are deficient in vitamin A are unable to see clearly in dim light. This visual defect is called *night blindness,* or *nyctalopia* (Ch. 31).

[1] This substance consists of a carotenelike pigment and protein, and has been called **retinene.** The cycle of changes is as follows:

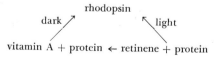

The bleaching of visual purple by light can be shown very strikingly in the excised eye of an animal. The animal is kept in the dark for a time to allow complete restoration of the visual purple, and the eye is removed in darkness. Then, as in taking a photograph, the eye is directed toward an object with strong contrasts of light and shade, such as a window sash against a bright sky. Thus an image is thrown upon the retina that can be seen when the eye is opened in a dim light. The picture, known as an *optogram*, was printed upon the retina because the visual purple was bleached only where the bright parts of the image fell (Fig. 41.6).

Fig. 41.6. Effects produced in a rabbit's eye by casting an image of a window upon the retina. The image of the bright panes bleaches the visual purple. A picture produced in this way is called an optogram. (After Howell.)

Though the existence of a light-sensitive pigment has not been proved for the cones of the retina, there is evidence that their function too is dependent upon a photochemical process.

The nuclear and pigment layers. Between the rods and cones on the one hand and the ganglion cells on the other are situated numerous nerve cells that form functional links between these two sets of retinal elements. Their bodies form a well-defined layer known as the **inner nuclear layer**. Their axons connect with the dendrons of the ganglion cells and their dendrons with the fibers of the rods and cones. Thus, impulses set up by stimulation of the visual receptors are transmitted to the ganglion cells and thence along the axons of the latter (optic nerve fibers) to the brain. The **outer nuclear layer** consists simply of the expansions (nuclei) on the rod fibers. The **pigment layer** is a single row of irregularly shaped cells containing granules of a dark pigment. They lie in contact with the outer ends of the rods and cones. They probably serve, like the black paint in the interior of the camera, to absorb light rays and prevent blurring of the retinal image by rays of reflected light. It will be noted that in order for light to reach and stimulate the rods and cones it must pass through all the other layers of the retina except the pigment layer.

The yellow spot and fovea centralis. The optic disc. During waking hours the eyes are incessantly making fine, often imperceptible, movements from side to side or up and down. The main purpose of these movements is to bring the images of objects onto that part of the retina that is capable of the most acute vision. If the reader will place some object and look directly at it, he will be able to describe it in detail. But other objects well to one side, above, or below his line of vision are seen only vaguely; he can scarcely tell their shapes or their colors. The part of the retina capable of acute vision, and upon which images are focused in order to see things clearly, is a very small depressed area called the **fovea centralis**. In man this area, since it contains only cones, is quite blind in very dim, light (see above). In man it is only about $\frac{1}{2}$ mm across. It is hard to realize that objects in the outside world cast images upon the retina so small as to fit upon such a tiny spot. Indeed, an object that casts an image whose diameter is measured in thousands of a millimeter is clearly visible.

The fovea centralis lies in the center of a larger yellow area—the **yellow spot**, or **macula lutea** (simply the Latin words for the same thing). The yellow spot, with its central pit, or fovea, lies to the outer side of the optic nerve (Fig. 41.7).

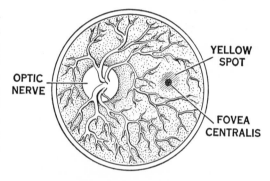

Fig. 41.7. The interior of the posterior wall of the left eyeball as seen from the front. The entrance of the optic nerve and the retinal blood vessels is clearly shown. This part of the eye can be seen in a living person by means of an instrument known as an *ophthalmoscope*, which throws a light through the pupil upon the retina.

OPTIC NERVE

YELLOW SPOT

FOVEA CENTRALIS

The fibers of the optic nerve where they enter the eyeball form a pale pink circular area known as the **optic disc** (Fig. 41.7) ; it lies a little to the inner (nasal) side of the posterior pole of the eyeball. The retinal vessels enter the eyeball near the center of the disc, and coursing over its surface, supply the surrounding retina. The opthalmologist examines the interior of the eyeball as a matter of routine by means of an instrument known as an *ophthalmoscope*. By such an examination much can also be learned of conditions other than those of the eye itself. In atrophy of the optic nerve, for example, as occurs in certain neurological conditions, the disc is glistening and pale; in raised intracranial pressure it appears swollen and congested (*optic neuritis*), and in arterial hypertension the retinal arteries are constricted and wiry in appearance.

Though the retina is stimulated most effectively by light rays, other types of stimulus will produce visual sensations. In whatever manner the retina is stimulated, the sensation experienced is always a visual one (Ch. 33). A blow on the eyeball (mechanical stimulus), for instance, causes one to see flashes of light in the form of circles, streaks, or "stars."

THE OPTIC NERVES, CHIASMA, AND TRACTS

The optic nerves converge behind the eye and appear to fuse in front of the pituitary body. Here the fibers from the inner (nasal) half of each retina, but not those from the outer retinal halves, cross to the opposite side (see Fig. 43.2). The structure formed by this partial crossing is called the **optic chiasma.** From the chiasma, the fibers, now called the **optic tract,** continue on each side of the midbrain, whence the visual impulses are relayed by fresh neurons to the occipital lobe. Thus, the right occipital lobe receives impulses from the nasal half of the left retina and the temporal half of the right, while impulses from the nasal half of the right retina and the temporal half of the left go to the left occipital lobe. It is evident that a lesion of one occipital lobe or optic tract will cause "half-blindness," or *hemianopia,* in the corresponding retinal halves.

42

The Physiology of Vision (continued)

GENERAL OPTICAL PRINCIPLES. THE CRYSTALLINE LENS. ACCOMMODATION OF THE EYE

Reflection and absorption of light. Light travels in waves at a speed of 186,000 miles per second. The waves or vibrations of light are of different lengths, but all are extremely short, being measured in millionths or ten millionths of a millimeter.[1] Since light waves travel at such an enormous speed, immense numbers must be reflected to our eyes each second from the various objects around us.

The color of any light depends upon the length of the waves of which it is composed (see also Ch. 45). The waves of red light are the longest (700 to 800 mμ) that cause a visual sensation. Waves longer than these are felt as heat, or are known as radio waves, which, as everyone knows, are measured in meters instead of millionths of millimeters. The waves of violet light are the shortest that stimulate the retina. Shorter waves than these—the ultraviolet—have powerful effects upon the body, but they do not excite the retina to produce the sensation of sight. Waves still shorter than the ultraviolet are the x rays. The waves of orange light are shorter (650 mμ) than the red rays, but are longer than those of yellow (600 mμ) or of green (500 to 550 mμ). The waves of blue light (about 450 mμ) and of violet (around 400 mμ) are shorter still. Therefore, starting at the red side of the rainbow—that is, at the left-hand end of the *spectrum* (Ch. 45)—the different colors are laid out side by side in the order of their wavelengths. The red is on the extreme left, violet

---

[1] A millionth of a millimeter is a millimicron (abbreviated mμ); a ten millionth of a millimeter is called an angstrom unit. Either unit may be used to express the wavelengths of light.

on the extreme right; orange, yellow, green, and blue, in this order, lie in-between (Plate VI*d,A*).

Waves of light continue to travel from their source until they strike some material through which they cannot pass. Some of the waves may then be reflected; the rest are absorbed. It is the reflected waves alone that enter the eye and through which the reflecting objects are seen. Light waves of different lengths are not always reflected to the same degree (Fig. 42.1). The surfaces of some objects reflect mainly the long

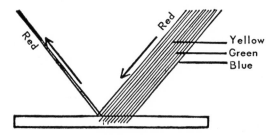

Yellow
Green
Blue

Fig. 42.1. Diagram to illustrate the absorption and reflection of light from the surface of a red object. Note that all the constituent rays of white light are absorbed except some of the red, which are reflected.

red waves and absorb the shorter waves of orange, yellow, blue, green, and violet. Such an object therefore appears red. If the reflected light consists mainly of the shorter waves—orange, yellow, and green—the object is of the corresponding color. If all wavelengths are reflected equally, the object appears white. A surface that absorbs completely, or nearly so, all the light that falls upon it, appears black, for there are no reflected waves to stimulate the retina, and the sensation of blackness is simply the absence of any retinal stimulation. A material through which

Fig. 42.2. The refraction of light.

light passes with little or no obstruction—that is, one that neither reflects nor absorbs light—is transparent. Some perfectly transparent materials, such as air, or clear glass placed at a certain angle, are invisible.

Refraction of light. Rays of light become bent from their straight paths when they pass from air into some other transparent material, such as glass or water, or, vice versa, when they pass through one of these materials into air. This blending of the rays of light is called *refraction*. We have all noticed that a stick partly submerged in water appears broken at the point where the air and water meet. The illusion is due to the fact that the rays of light reflected from the submerged portion of the stick become bent, or *refracted*, in passing from the water into the air to meet our eyes. Having no experience of the bending of light rays and therefore assuming that they come straight from the object to our eyes, we receive the impression that the stick is broken (Fig. 42.2).

A glass prism—that is, a wedge-shaped block of glass—refracts unequally the rays of light transmitted through its different parts. Those rays transmitted nearer the apex are refracted more strongly than those transmitted nearer the base. All rays are bent toward the base of the prism. Therefore, if two prisms are placed base to base, the light rays are converged, and at a certain distance from the glass surfaces, brought to one spot, or *focus*. A lens with two convex surfaces (Fig. 42.3) is in reality composed of two prisms placed in such a position. A lens with two concave surfaces (Fig. 42.4), on the other hand, bends the rays away from one another, acting like two prisms placed apex to apex.

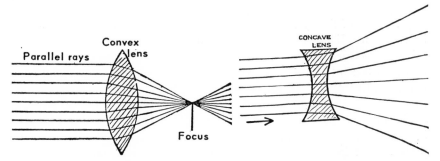

Fig. 42.3. The convergence of light by a convex lens.

Fig. 42.4 Diverging effect of a concave lens upon parallel rays. Radiating rays are made more divergent by a concave lens.

The converging action of a convex lens can be shown very simply by means of an ordinary "burning glass." The sun's rays travel in straight parallel lines, but in passing through the glass are refracted and can be brought to a focus as shown by a small spot of bright light. The heat rays are also concentrated, and the temperature of the object upon which they fall may be raised to the point at which it ignites. The more curved— that is, the more convex—the surface of any lens, the greater is its converging power, and, as a consequence, the shorter is the distance from the lens at which the rays are brought to a focus.

Not only sunlight, and rays from other sources a great distance away, but rays emitted from any source except those at very short distances travel in practically parallel lines. Rays from a near source are divergent, or radiating, and must therefore be refracted more strongly in order to bring them to a focus at the same distance from the lens as parallel rays (Fig. 42.5). In order to do this the lens must be more convex. The distance from the lens at which parallel rays are focused is called the *focal length* of the lens; the shorter its focal length the greater, therefore, is the converging power of a lens.

The eye as a camera. In the invention of the camera the main parts of the eye have been imitated very closely. A lens serves to focus the rays of light upon the sensitive film. The light coming from an object in front of the camera passes through the lens, and is brought to a focus and forms a small image of the object upon the film. In the eye also there is a lens that brings the rays of light from objects in the outside world to a focus upon the retina, which, like the photographic film, is sensitive to light. The camera has a diaphragm, or "stop," to increase or reduce the amount of light reaching the film. The eye also is able to control the amount of light entering it. The iris serves this purpose; its opening can be widened or narrowed. The globe of the eye corresponds to the box of the camera; the rays of light pass through this darkened chamber to reach the retina.

The lens of the eye. The **crystalline lens** is suspended within the eyeball a short distance behind the cornea in a hammocklike structure called the **suspensory ligament.** The lens and the structures surrounding it divide the interior of the eyeball into two compartments. The compartment in front of the lens is filled with a clear watery solution called the **aqueous humor;** the larger compartment behind is occupied by a semifluid material called the **vitreous body.** The crystalline lens is a biconvex disc, but the anterior surface is more strongly curved than the posterior. In health the lens is almost perfectly transparent. When, as sometimes occurs, it becomes semitransparent or opaque, the sight, of course, is lost. Such a condition is spoken of as *cataract.* The cornea also refracts the light, and so acts as an important aid to the lens. The eyes of insects are provided not, like man, with a single lens but with a large number of lenses placed side by side. An object casts a large number of images nearly, though not quite, the same upon the insect's retina.

Accommodation of the eye for near vision. As stated above, rays of light coming from a distant object are parallel, but those coming from a point close to the eyes are radiating, or divergent. The parallel rays obviously do not need to be bent so acutely as the radiating rays in order to bring them to a point at the same distance behind the lens. Consequently, if we take a lens that has a certain power to refract light rays, it will be

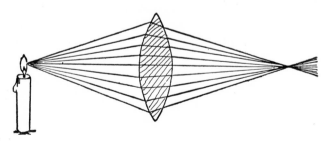

Fig. 42.5. The convergence of radiating (divergent) rays of light by a convex lens.

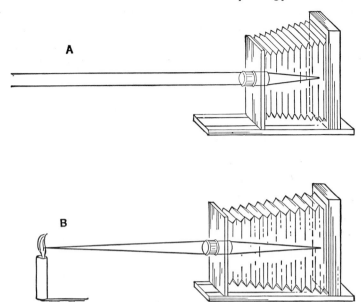

Fig. 42.6. Illustrating how parallel rays, A, and diverging rays, B, are focused upon the film in a camera of the bellows type. Since the power of the lens cannot be altered, the distance between lens and film for B must be increased; that is, the film is placed at the new point of focus.

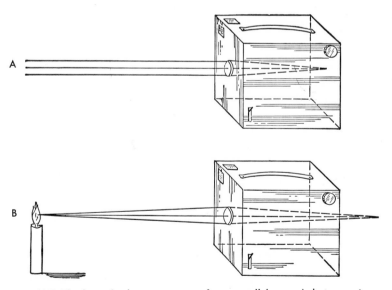

Fig. 42.7. The lens of a box camera can focus parallel rays, A, but cannot focus diverging rays, B, which are cast from a very near object; a blurred image is thrown upon the film.

found that the parallel rays from a distant object are brought to a focus at a shorter distance beyond the lens than the radiating rays from a near object (Figs. 42.3, 42.4).

When, with the bellows type of camera, we wish to take a photograph of an object only a few feet away from the camera front, the bellows must be drawn out so that the lens is farther from the film than when a more distant view is being photographed (Fig. 42.6). The reason for this is, of course, that, as just mentioned, the radiating rays from the near object are brought to a focus at a greater distance behind the lens than are parallel rays from a distance object. When the distance from the lens to the film is such that the rays of light are brought together to form a clear image, the camera is said to be "in focus." With the ordinary box camera, which is not provided with the means for moving the lens back and fourth, photographs of very near objects cannot be taken unless, in front of the original lens, another lens is placed that will bend the rays of light more acutely and bring them to a focus upon the film— that is, at the same distance—behind the lens. The addition of an extra lens is equivalent to using a more convex single lens (Figs. 42.7, 42.8).

Like the bellows camera, the eye can form clear images upon its sensitive surface—the retina—of either near or distant objects. Unless the eye were provided with some means of adjustment, the view of distant objects might be quite clear, but in reading, writing, or examining small objects the images upon the retina would be out of focus and blurred. In order that the reader may convince himself that the eye has this power, let him look at some object near the farther end of the room. While his eyes are focused for this object, let him bring this page in front of his eyes. The words will appear blurred and indistinct, for the letters are out of focus upon the retina. In an instant, however, he can direct his eyes to the letters, which are immediately seen clearly. This ability to bring

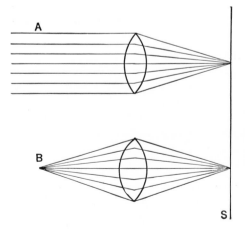

Fig. 42.8. The lens A can focus parallel rays to the surface S but could not focus diverging rays to the same point. The more convex lens B bends light rays more acutely and so can bring the diverging rays from a near object to a focus upon S. Compare with Fig. 42.9.

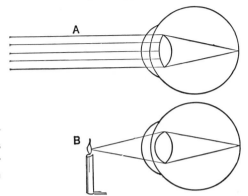

Fig. 42.9. Showing how the eye by increasing the convexity of its lens can focus rays of light from either distant, A, or near, B, objects upon the retina.

near objects into focus upon the retina is called the *accommodation of the eye*.

We must next consider how the accommodation is accomplished. The eye cannot, of course, like the bellows camera, move its lens forward or backward[2] and so increase or reduce the distance between the lens and the retina. It resembles more the box camera, in which the lens is placed at a fixed distance from the film. As mentioned above, a near object can be photographed with the box camera only by employing an extra lens, which will aid in bending the diverging rays of light. The eye, however, cannot obtain an extra lens, but it can accomplish the same effect in an instant by increasing the power of its lens. The lens becomes more convex when near objects are viewed, and so bends more strongly the radiating rays and brings them to a focus at the same distance behind the lens at is does the parallel rays. Thus, in viewing either near or distant objects, a clear image is thrown upon the retina (see Figs. 42.8 and 42.9).

The shape of the lens is changed in the following way. The lens is an elastic body and, ordinarily, it is slightly compressed by the **lens capsule** that encloses it, and blends with the **suspensory ligament** whose outer parts are connected indirectly to the interior of the eye. When one looks at a near object, the delicate **ciliary muscles** within the globe contract, and the tension on the ligament and capsule is reduced by drawing forward the attachments of the former to the wall of the eyeball (Fig. 42.10). This relieves the flattening pressure upon the lens, which springs into a more curved, or bulging, shape. This action is similar to the flattening and recoil of a rubber ball held between the finger and thumb, when the pressure upon it is increased or reduced (Fig. 42.11). The lens of the eye shares with the other tissues of the body the tendency to become less elastic with age. Its surface does not spring forward and

[2] In some classes of fish this method is actually employed, and in certain mollusks accommodation for near vision is brought about by a lengthening of the eyeball.

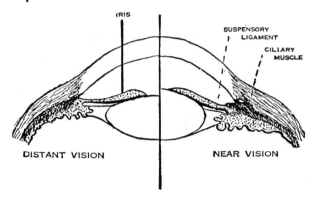

IRIS

SUSPENSORY LIGAMENT

CILIARY MUSCLE

DISTANT VISION   NEAR VISION

Fig. 42.10. Showing the shape of the crystalline lens for distant and for near vision, respectively. The suspensory ligament and ciliary muscles are shown. *(After Helmholtz.)*

become more convex in the usual way when the pressure is relieved. That is the reason why elderly persons have difficulty in accommodating their sight for near objects *(presbyopia,* see Ch. 44). They hold a printed page at arm's length in an effort to focus the letters upon the retina. They cannot increase the power of the lens at will. Convex glasses are employed for reading and other fine work. The eye of the elderly is like the box camera; it must seek the aid of an extra lens to bring the light rays from near objects to a focus upon the retina.

The act of accommodation includes two additional factors—*narrowing of the pupil* (contraction of the iris) and *convergence of the eyes* (the lines of sight thus meeting at the object).

The function of the iris. The iris (Ch. 41) is made of a delicate, ring-shaped sheet of muscle. The muscle consists of two sets of fibers, one of which is arranged circularly, the other radiating from the central opening —the **pupil** (Fig. 42.12). Each set of muscle fibers is supplied by fine nerves belonging to the autonomic nervous system—the constrictor muscle by parasympathetic, and the dilator muscle by sympathetic, nerve

A
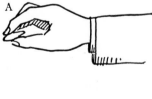

B

Fig. 42.11. Diagram of a small rubber ball held between finger and thumb to illustrate how the elasticity of the lens causes it to become more convex when the suspensory ligament is slackened. In A the ball is compressed by the fingers. In B the pressure has been released, and the ball springs back to a more rounded shape. It should be pointed out, however, that only the anterior surface of the lens becomes more convex during the accommodation of the eye. Little or no change occurs in the shape of the posterior surface. (See Fig. 42.10.)

Branches of ciliary arteries

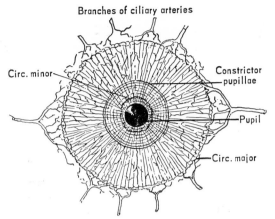

Fig. 42.12. The iris. The ciliary arteries, branches of the ophthalmic, form a circle (circulus major) around the circumference of the iris; from this, fine vessels, anastomosing freely, converge toward the pupil at whose margin a second vascular ring (circulus minor) is formed. The fibers (not shown) of the dilator pupillae muscle run in a direction roughly parallel with the converging vessels.

fibers. When the circular fibers contract, like a purse string, the pupil is narrowed. When the radiating fibers shorten, the pupil widens. The diameter of the pupil is larger in dim than in strong light. In darkness the pupils dilate widely. Thus, the iris serves the same purpose for the eye as the diaphragm, or "stop," does for the camera; it controls the amount of light entering the eye. The pupils are also narrowed when the eyes are directed to a near object, but dilate again when they are turned upon a distant view. The reader may verify these facts for himself by alternately shading and exposing the eyes of another person and noticing the changing size of his pupil, and also by having him direct his vision alternately to a near and a distant object. The pupil dilates with fear and narrows in anger. It becomes progressively smaller with age. Epithelial cells containing pigment, which gives the eye its blue, brown, black, or hazel color, cover the posterior surface of the iris.

The field of vision. We cannot see an object behind our heads, as we all know. Our field of vision—that is, the actual region in front of us in which we can see objects by turning the head (but not the body) to one or the other side—is about four fifths of a circle of which the head is the center. When the eyes are directed straight ahead the visual field is restricted to a little more than half a circle. If the reader will look straight ahead, hold his two forefingers at arms' length in front and level with his eyes, and then, separating the fingers, carry them circularly to right and left, he will find that they cannot be seen when they have been carried a little behind a point opposite either ear. The region behind this is spoken of as the *blind zone*. The bird has no blind zone; as its eyes are placed upon the side of its head, it can see objects behind almost as well as in front of its body.

The blind spot. A small object placed at a certain point in front of one eye while the other is closed in invisible, because its image falls

Fig. 42.13. The blind spot. Close the left eye, hold the figure about 6 inches in front of the right eye, and look steadily at the white disk. Move the book slowly toward the eye until the cross disappears. When this occurs the image of the cross has fallen upon the entrance of the optic nerve. At this spot rods and cones are absent, and it is therefore insensitive to light.

upon that part of the retina occupied by the commencement of the optic nerve (Fig. 42.8). Here the rods and cones are absent. Only the nerve fibers, as they stream together from different parts of the retina, are present in this area, and in consequence it is insensitive to light. The visual receptors—the rods and cones—alone are capable of creating nerve impulses when exposed to light. The reader is referred to Figure 42.13 for a demonstration of the blind spot in his own eye.

43
Interpretation by the Brain of Impulses Received from the Retina

We have seen that the eye is an instrument for the conversion of light energy into nerve impulses. But visual sensations have their seat in the occipital lobe (Ch. 37)—the cortex of that part of the brain lying at the back of the cranial cavity. Destruction of this part of the brain on both sides in man will cause blindness just as complete as if both eyes were destroyed. This region of consciousness interprets the messages received from the retina.

Position of the retinal image. In a camera, the image thrown by the lens upon the film or plate is upside down and reversed from side to side. Images are cast upon the retina in a similar way (Fig. 43.1). Yet we do not see things upside down nor as mirror images. Things are really as they seem. Through experience the brain has learned to interpret correctly the pictures cast upon the retina, so that we see objects in their true positions. This fact may be demonstrated by the reader upon himself. If he closes his eyes and presses upon the outer side of one eyeball so as to stimulate the retina, he will perceive a ring of light. The bright figure, however, does not appear to be in the region of the finger, but on the opposite side of the eye. Similarly, if the lower part of the globe is pressed, the ring of light appears to be above the eye. This simple experiment shows that the brain interprets impressions received from the outer or upper parts of the retina as being opposite the inner or lower parts, and vice versa. The brain, through experience and with the aid of other senses, especially of touch, in the forgotten earliest years of our lives, has learned that the inverted and reversed images that outside objects cast

584 - The Special Senses

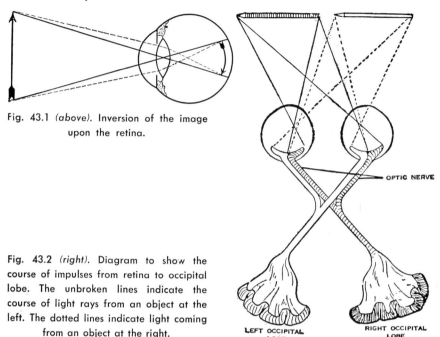

Fig. 43.1 *(above)*. Inversion of the image
upon the retina.

Fig. 43.2 *(right)*. Diagram to show the
course of impulses from retina to occipital
lobe. The unbroken lines indicate the
course of light rays from an object at the
left. The dotted lines indicate light coming
from an object at the right.

LEFT OCCIPITAL
LOBE

RIGHT OCCIPITAL
LOBE

OPTIC NERVE

upon the retina do not represent these objects in their true positions,
and without any conscious effort sees them upright as they are.

Binocular vision. It must also be remembered that an image is formed
upon *each* retina. Our vision for this reason is called **binocular.** Yet only
one image is seen so long as both eyes are maintained in their correct
positions by the eye muscles. If one eye, however, is pressed gently to one
side by the finger so that the direction of its sight is not correctly related
to that of the other eye, two images at once appear, one beside the other.
The reason that, normally, only one image is perceived though two are
formed—one in each eye—may be understood from Figure 43.2. Each
of the two images formed by any object falls upon one half of each
retina; but, as a result of the crossing and rearrangement of the optic
nerve fibers behind the eyes, the two images are recorded on only one
side of the brain. Thus, an object placed before our eyes throws images
simultaneously upon the left or the right halves of the two retinas, but
never, so long as the eyes are in their true positions and the object is not
too close to the eyes, do the images fall upon different retinal halves—
on the right half of one retina and on the left half of the other; if this
occurs we see double.

It seems then that any given point on one retina is paired with a
point in the same relative position on the corresponding half of the
opposite retina. Hence we may think of one or a group of receptors (rods
and cones) in the two retinas functioning together to form a double

receptor mechanism. But impulses set up by the stimulation of these paired receptors pass to the occipital cortex of one side of the brain and probably have their destination in a single nerve cell or a small group of nerve cells. This is known as the *theory of corresponding points,* advanced to account for the fusion of the separate retinal images. Figure 43.2 shows the fibers from the left halves of the retinas going to the left side of the brain, and those from the right halves going to the right side of the brain. The result is that a single impression is registered in consciousness. When the eyes are "out of line," the two images fall upon noncorresponding points in the retinal halves, and the impulses pass to both sides of the brain. As mentioned above, double vision (*diplopia*) then results.

Severe damage to the optic nerve of one side causes blindness to the nerve of that side (Fig. 43.2). But if the pathway has been injured after the fibers have crossed, or if the occipital region of only one side is destroyed, the blindness is confined to the halves of the retinas from which impulses are received. This is called *hemianopia* (literally, half-blindness) (Ch. 41).

Stereoscopic vision. The impression of distance and the solid substantial appearance of surrounding objects are also dependent upon processes having their seat in the brain. Our surroundings are not flat like a photographic scene; everything about us stands out clearly from its background. Objects appear to have depth and volume, as well as width and height. Our vision is three-dimensional, or **stereoscopic.** The stereoscopic effect is due chiefly to the fusion of the two retinal images, which are not precisely the same. If a cubical object placed directly in front of the reader is viewed with one eye (the other one being closed), and then with the other alone, it will be found that the image formed by the right eye is very slightly different from that formed by the left (Fig. 43.3). The right eye is in a position to see more of the right side of the object and the left eye to see more of the left side. The brain blends the two dissimilar images into one; but, just as when two colors are mixed together the resulting single color has some of the original two in its make-up, so the single fused image has hidden in it the slight differences of the two of which it is composed. It is this hidden difference that is largely responsible for objects standing out in relief with the appearance of solidity. A photograph or picture appears flat because the images in the two eyes are identical and their fusion by the brain produces no stereoscopic effect.

Fig. 43.3. Stereoscopic effect caused by the fusion of slightly dissimilar images. Hold the figure about 6 inches from the eyes and "stare through it." The images will become fused and produce an effect of solidity and depth in the drawing.

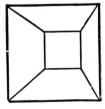
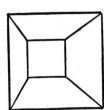

Even images quite unlike may be fused (Fig. 43.4). *Parallax* (see Glossary) is also of prime importance in stereoscopic vision.

Fig. 43.4. Fusion of dissimilar images. When the figure is held about 6 inches from the eyes and gazed at steadily, the mouse enters the glass vessel.

The ordinary stereoscope makes use of these principles. A camera with two lenses, set, like the eyes, a short distance apart, takes two views. The photographs are slightly different, because the angles at which they were taken are different. When viewed through the stereoscope, the pictures are directed one to each eye by means of special lenses. The brain fuses the images to produce a remarkable illusion of depth and solidity.[1]

The judgment of size. Our appreciation of the size of any object depends upon the size of the image that the object casts upon the retina. But the size of the retinal image is dependent not only upon the actual dimensions of the object itself but also upon the distance of the object from the eye. For instance, a church steeple a mile away throws an image upon the retina that is no larger—perhaps smaller—than the image cast by a needle a foot in front of the eyes. Yet we know that the steeple is immensely larger than the needle. The brain has estimated the difference in the distances of the steeple and the needle, and has made allowances in judging the size of the two objects. This sense of distance is caused to a large extent by impulses that arise from the muscles within the eyeball (ciliary muscles) when they contract or relax to accommodate the eye for near or distant objects (Ch. 42). For similar reasons, the moon when rising above the horizon appears to be twice or three times the size that it does when high in the sky. The image it forms upon the retina is, however, of the same size in both positions. It is our estimate of the distance that is at fault. When we look at the moon over the land the distance appears to be greater than when we look at it

[1] A very ingenious but simple stereoscope involving the same principal is one in which two slightly dissimilar pictures, one in blue and the other in red, are printed, one overlapping the other. When looked at with the unaided eyes, the pictures are no more than a confused jumble with a red-blue outline. If, however, the pictures are looked at through a pair of spectacles with a red glass on one side and a blue glass on the other, a remarkable stereoscopic effect is produced. The colored spectacles sort out the confused pictures and send one to each eye. The red picture is seen as black through the blue glass, since this absorbs the red rays; the blue picture is indistinct. The blue picture is seen as black through the red glass, since the blue rays are absorbed; the red picture is indistinct. So, the separate and slightly dissimilar images fall upon opposite retinas. The resulting sensation is a scene in black and white conveying the impression of depth and solidity. The stereoscope may be used for the detection of counterfeit notes. The suspected note is placed beside a genuine one. If one note is a copy of the other and not made from the same plate, it will inevitably differ in detail from the genuine, no matter how skillfully the work has been done, and the dissimilar images will give an appearance of depth in certain parts of the design that otherwise would not appear.

overhead. Consequently, since our judgment of an object's size from the size of its retinal image is influenced by our estimation of its distance from us, the rising moon appears much larger (Fig. 43.5).

We have all experienced the effect that is produced when, while our eyes are accommodated for a *distant* scene, a minute near object, such as a speck of dust, comes suddenly into view: the tiny object appears to be of huge proportions. The same effect is produced by afterimages (Ch. 45). If a small bright object placed close to the eyes is looked at steadily for a time and then the eyes are directed to a blank wall some distance away, the afterimage seems immensely larger than the object itself. The accommodation of our eyes to the more distant wall deceives the brain, for the nerve impulses it receives from the muscles of accommodation lead it to believe that the afterimage comes from a distant object; it consequently seems larger.

The judgment of distance. Not only does our appreciation of distance influence our judgment of size, but also our general knowledge of the size of objects of certain shapes influences our judgment of distance. For example, we know from previous experience that a steeple is much larger than a needle; therefore, if the retinal image of the steeple is no larger than that of the needle at a short distance, the former is judged to be much farther away. The relation of an object to other objects in front of and behind it, the stereoscopic effect of depth, and the effects of accommodation already referred to, all aid us in our appreciation of distance as well as of size. The air is not perfectly transparent; hence, when a distant view is seen it appears dimmer and takes on a bluish tint. For this reason visitors to climates where the air is unusually clear make mistakes in judging distances: objects appear closer than they really are. A hazy day makes scenes appear more distant (Ch. 44).

Optical illusions. The brain is sometimes deceived by imitations of certain effects upon which it bases its judgment of the size, shape, and color of objects in the outside world. Errors of judgment caused in this way are called optical illusions. The effect produced by the stereoscope (see above) and the misjudgment of size and distance have already been briefly referred to. The illusions of distance caused by blue and of nearness by red and yellow are discussed in Chapter 44. Other examples of optical illusions are shown in Figures 43.5 to 43.10.

Movements of the eyeballs. Each eye is furnished with six small muscles, which are attached by their outer ends to the circumference of the eye globe near its equator, and by their inner ends to the bony walls of the eye socket (see Fig. 5.29). One muscle (**external rectus**), attached to the outer side of the eye, turns the eye outward; another (**internal rectus**), on the inner side, rotates it inward. The eye is turned upward by a muscle (**superior rectus**) fixed to the upper part of its circumference; its rotation downward is effected by a corresponding muscle (**inferior rectus**) attached below. The remaining two muscles are directed

Fig. 43.5. Illusion of size. The figure of the man is actually smaller than that of the child, but the effect of distance produced by the converging lines causes it to appear larger.

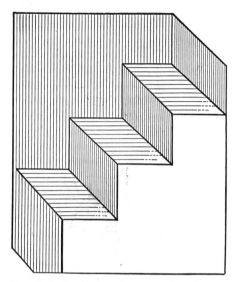

Fig. 43.6. The figure shows a series of steps which, when gazed at fixedly, appear as an overhanging wall. *(After Bernstein.)*

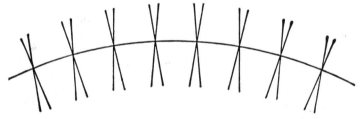

Fig. 43.7. Hold the page in a horizontal position a little below the level of the eyes and about 8 inches in front of the face. Look steadily at the curved line. A series of short vertical bars appear to pierce the paper. When the page is moved slowly from side to side, the bars appear to sway to and fro. *(Redrawn from Franklin after Howell.)*

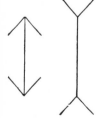

Fig. 43.8. Zollner's lines. The long diagonal lines are parallel, though they appear otherwise.

Fig. 43.9. Illusion of size. The vertical lines are both of the same length.

Fig. 43.10. Illusion of distance. The distance from A to B appears to be greater than that from B to C. They are both the same.

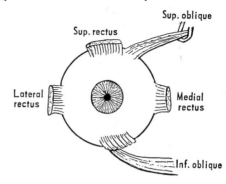

Fig. 43.11. The extrinsic muscles of the right eye.

obliquely, to be attached one to the upper and outer segment of the globe, the other to the lower and inner segment. The first mentioned of these oblique muscles (**superior oblique**) rotates the eyeball downward and outward; the other (**inferior oblique**) rotates it upward and outward toward the temple. Normally, the muscles of both eyes act in unison, so that the positions of the eyeballs are always kept in their proper relation to each other. When a muscle of one eye pulls more strongly than the corresponding muscle of the other eye, the lines of sight of the two eyes are not correctly directed. The person is said to be cross-eyed. The technical term for this condition is *strabismus*. Under these circumstances the images fall in different regions of the two retinas (p. 585), and it might be thought that such a person would suffer from double vision, but, as a matter of fact, he usually learns subconsciously to disregard the image in one eye.

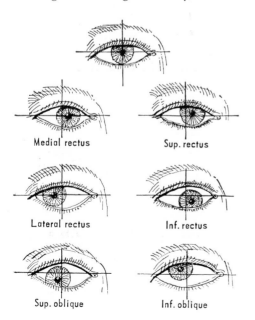

Fig. 43.12. Actions of the ocular muscles. The uppermost sketch indicates the normal forward-looking position of the eyes.

44
Optical Defects

LENS DEFECTS

Two defects, *spherical* and *chromatic aberration,* are possessed by all ordinary convex lenses.

Spherical aberration. Rays of light passing through a simple convex lens are not all brought to a focus at one point. The rays passing through the lens near its circumference are bent (refracted) more strongly than the rays transmitted nearer its center. The result is that the rays passing through the outer part of the lens cross those passing more centrally (Fig. 44.1). This defect of lenses is called *spherical aberration.* In the manufacture of expensive camera lenses special means are employed to correct the defect. Such lenses are made of several parts, cemented together. The central part of the lens is composed of a glass that refracts the light rays more in accordance with the refraction of the outer part. All rays, whether they pass through such a lens near its circumference or near its center, meet at the same point. On the other hand, clear images may be formed with a cheap lens if the outer interfering rays

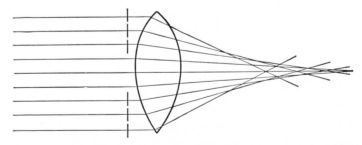

Fig. 44.1. Spherical aberration. Note that the outer rays come to a focus in front of the more central rays. The vertical broken lines in front of the lens show how a "stop" of a camera, or the iris of the eye, cuts off the outer rays.

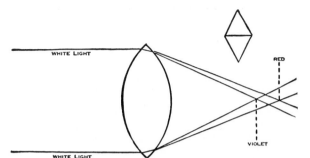

Fig. 44.2. Illustrating chromatic aberration. The small figure shows how a simple lens is essentially two prisms placed base to base.

are cut off by means of a diaphragm. For this reason, as we all know, the sharpest photograph can be taken when the small "stop" is used, and the rays of light are thereby restricted to the center of the lens. These devices, resorted to by the manufacturers of lenses for the correction of spherical aberration, are an imitation of the methods employed by nature to perfect the organ of sight. The central portion of the crystalline lens is composed of a material slightly different from that composing the outer part, with the result that the outer and inner rays are refracted to nearly the same degree. The iris, also, like the camera's diaphragm, cuts off any outer interfering rays.

Chromatic aberration. The waves of different lengths composing white light are not all refracted to the same degree by an ordinary simple lens (Fig. 44.2). When one attempts to focus the rays of light from the sun by means of a cheap convex lens, it is impossible to get a uniformly white light. A halo or fringe of colors—red, orange, yellow, green, and blue—appears. The ring of spectral colors is caused by the glass prisms of which the lens is composed[1] refracting the light rays to different degrees according to their wavelengths. The red rays are refracted less strongly than are the orange, the orange less than the yellow or green, and the green less than

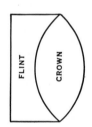

Fig. 44.3. The structure of an achromatic lens.

the blue. Thus the colors are separated and laid out in bands as in a rainbow. Chromatic aberration (Gk. *chromos,* color) is corrected in camera and microscope lenses by cementing a biconvex lens of crown glass to a concave block of flint glass (Fig. 44.3). A lens made in this way is called *achromatic,* that is, noncolor-forming. The lens of the eye is not corrected for chromatic aberration; yet we do not see objects surrounded by colored halos. The reason that we do not is that in looking at colored objects the eye alternates its focus rapidly for the different colors. At one instant the refracting power is slightly increased, at another

---

[1] A simple biconvex lens is in reality two glass prisms placed base to base. The splitting of white light by a prism is described in Chapter 45. A simple concave lens resembles two prisms placed apex to apex.

slightly diminished. At one instant red is in focus, at another instant blue or green. The different color impressions occur so rapidly that they become fused in the retina to produce the sensation of white (see Ch. 45). The adjustments of the lens are so slight and made with such little effort that we are unconscious of them.

These facts are used by the artist to produce the illusion of distance. As stated previously, our judgments of distance are dependent in part upon the efforts of accommodation that we make practically unconsciously (Ch. 42). For instance, when we look at a distant object, the suspensory ligament is taut, and the ciliary muscles are relaxed. When the eyes are focused upon a near object, the suspensory ligament is relaxed, and the ciliary muscles are contracted. The brain receives nerve impulses from these structures, and through long experience, has learned to judge the distance of an object by the changes in accommodation required to see it clearly. When the artist, therefore, paints a distant hill in blue or violet, the eye must, in order to bring the blue color into focus, counteract the greater bending of the blue rays. Its lens is therefore put into the shape in which its power is least (Ch. 42); that is, as though the eye were focused upon a far object. The brain is deceived to a certain extent, and an impression of distance is created. Yellows and reds when included in a picture produce the reverse impressions. They seem to bring objects closer. Yellow and red rays are bent less strongly; therefore, in order to bring these colors into focus, the crystalline lens must increase its power, just as though the eye were viewing a near object. These facts may be clearly demonstrated by placing a red and a blue lantern side by side. Though both lights are exactly the same distance from the eye, the blue one appears to be behind the red. Chromatic aberration is more pronounced toward the circumference of a lens; hence the iris, to a certain extent, by covering this part of the lens, diminishes this defect of the eye.

Presbyopia. This is a defect of the eye, already described in Chapter 42, in which the lens, having lost the resilience or elasticity of youth, is unable to increase its power sufficiently to focus images of near objects upon the retina.

DEFECTS OF VISION DUE TO
ABNORMAL SHAPES OF THE EYEBALL

The three defects described above may be considered natural, or physiological. The first two are present in all eyes. The third occurs as a natural consequence of age. The three defects to be described in the following paragraphs are present in some eyes only and are due usually to imperfections at birth. The normal eye, as mentioned elsewhere, is nearly spherical. The vertical and transverse diameters are almost the same and only ¹⁄₂₅ inch shorter than the diameter from front to back. In other words, the eyeball is normally very slightly longer than it is broad and high. A normally proportioned eye is called **emmetropic**. Sometimes, however, the eye is considerably longer than it is broad. A person with such an eye is nearsighted, and the condition is called *myopia*. On the other hand, the eye may be shorter than it is broad; this condition is known as *hyperopia* (Fig. 44.4). Again, the cornea or the lens or both may be distorted, and the condition known as *astigmatism* is produced.

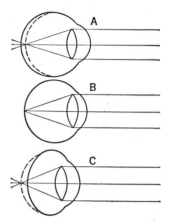

Fig. 44.4. Defects of vision due to abnormalities in length of the eyeball as compared with the normal. A, myopia; B, emmetropia (normal); C, hyperopia (or hypermetropia).

Myopia, or nearsightedness. In this condition the crystalline lens refracts the ray of light to the same degree as in a normal eye, but since the diameter of the eyeball from front to back is too great, the retina is a little beyond the point where the rays come to a focus. In other words, the lens is too strong for the length of the eyeball. After the rays come to a focus in front of the retina, they cross again, and upon reaching the retina, form a blurred image. It is just as though the film or plate of a camera were moved backward from the point where the rays entering through its lens would come to a focus and form a clear image. There is only one way in which the defect of nearsightedness may be overcome—by making the rays of light more radiating (divergent) before they enter the eye, so that the crystalline lens will be just strong enough to bring them to a focus upon the retina. The myopic person is therefore fitted with concave lenses, which diverge the rays, and so partly counteract the converging action of the crystalline lens (Fig. 44.4). The myopic person without glasses remedies the defect by bringing the book or other objects at which he is looking closer to the eyes, since the closer the object is, the more divergent are the rays reflected from its surface.

Hyperopia, or farsightedness. In this condition the diameter of the eye from front to back is too short. The crystalline lens is unable to converge the rays sufficiently to bring them to a focus upon the retina. The hyperopic person, to examine an object, holds it at arm's length, for then the rays are less divergent. Convex lenses are employed to aid the crystalline lens.

Astigmatism. This is probably the commonest of all defects of the eye. Indeed, practically all eyes possess it to a greater or less extent, but it is only when the condition is extreme that vision is impaired. The word itself means "without point" (Gk. *a,* not + *stigma,* point). That is, rays of light are not brought to sharp points upon the retina but form, instead, short lines. The stars, for instance, should appear as small bright dots; but as a result of the slight astigmatism of even the best of eyes, they seem to have short lines radiating from their centers; hence the expression "star-shaped." The constant rapid movements of our eyes cause the lines to shift slightly upon the retina, and the stars appear to twinkle. A light in darkness, for similar reasons, seems to emit radiating beams.

In order that rays coming from some point in the outside world shall all converge and come to a point upon the retina, they must all be converged to precisely the same degree. They must all stream together, like water in a funnel, toward a single point. If we should place a lens in the wall of a dark and dusty room and allow the sunlight to stream through, we would see, not a flat pennantlike beam of light, but one that was cone or funnel-shaped.

The rays passing through all diameters of a perfect lens come to a single point or focus. If, on the other hand, the curvature along one diameter (meridian) is greater than along another, the rays passing through the former will be bent more sharply and come to a focus at a shorter distance behind the lens than those passing through the latter.

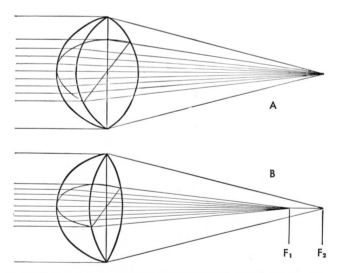

Fig. 44.5. In A the horizontal curvature of the lens is the same as the vertical; rays of light passing through the horizontal and vertical diameters are in consequence focused to the same point. In B the horizontal curvature is greater than the vertical; the rays passing through the horizontal diameter are focused at F_1 and those passing through the vertical diameter at F_2.

We know that a flaw in a lens—a raised area here, or a depressed area there—will cause distortions of the images it forms. Rays passing through a meridian having the raised or depressed region will not, of course, be bent to precisely the same extent as rays passing through elsewhere. When such blemishes exist, the rays passing through different diameters of the cornea or lens will not meet at one point as they should to form a clear-cut image (Fig. 44.5). Astigmatism is due to just such unevenness in the surface of the cornea or of the lens, a person with this defect being unable to focus perfectly the rays passing through the lens in all its diameters. Looking at the face of a clock, for example, the vertical numerals XII and VI may be clear, but the horizontal IX and III may be blurred, or vice versa. Again, the diagonal numerals may be out of focus, while the vertical and horizontal are clear. The person suffering from astigmatism wears glasses with the convexity of the lens increased or reduced, as the case may be, in certain diameters (meridians) to counteract the defects in corresponding diameters of the eye.

45
Color Vision

Theory of color vision. White light is in reality a combination or blend of several colors—a mixture of red, orange, yellow, green, and blue light rays. When white light is passed through a glass prism it is separated into its constituent wavelengths, and the colors of the rainbow are laid out in a row, from red to violet. The prism refracts the waves of red light less than it does the waves of orange light. The orange rays, though bent more than red, are bent less than yellow, and the waves of yellow less than those of green, and so on. The different kinds of waves in white light, therefore, when they pass through the prism, take different paths and fall upon different points of any surface situated beyond (Fig. 45.1). This array of colors is called the *spectrum* (see Plate VI*d, A*). The diamond owes its flashing beauty of spectral colors to the fact that its surface has been cut to form facets which split white light. The colors of the rainbow are formed by the raindrops, which act like prisms to split the sunlight and as tiny concave mirrors that reflect the spectral colors to our eyes. The sun's rays are refracted unequally as they enter the raindrop, and, after reflection, are refracted again as they leave (Fig. 45.2).

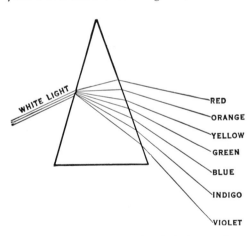

Fig. 45.1. The splitting of white light by a prism into its constituent colors. (See Plate VI*d*, A.)

The colors into which white light is split can be recombined to produce white. It is not necessary, however, to employ all the colors of

596

the rainbow or in the fires of the diamond to obtain a white light. It is a well-known fact that not only white light but all the colors in nature can be produced from the three colors *red, green,* and *blue* (or violet). These are called *primary colors.* If we were to set up three lanterns, one to throw a red, another a green, and a third a violet light, we should be able, by casting upon a screen one, two, or three of these colors blended in suitable combinations, to produce white light or any color we should desire. For example, by blending red, green, and violet light in proper proportions, white light would be produced. Red and green, together with a very little blue or violet, would produce yellow or orange; green and violet would give blue; red and violet, purple; and so on. Pure red, green, or violet would, of course, be produced by the corresponding single lights used alone.

According to the most widely accepted theory of color vision, the retina possesses three kinds of sensitive cells (cones). One type is stimulated by red, one by green, and the third by violet. When white light falls upon the retina, all these elements are stimulated nearly equally, and a sensation of white is experienced. When a yellow color is seen, the sensation is due to the stimulation of equal numbers of green and red, but very few of the violet, elements. If violet and green elements are stimulated, a sensation of blue results. When a large proportion of the elements of green, red, or violet are excited alone, we see green, red, or violet (Plate VI*a*).

Retinal areas sensitive to color. Color sensations are aroused through only a part of the retina. A large portion, namely that part lying more forward and toward the sides of the globe, is insensitive to color because it contains few or no cones. Images, whatever their colors, falling upon these regions are seen only in black and white. The area of the retina

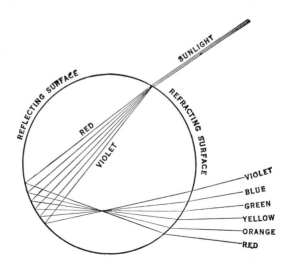

Fig. 45.2. The splitting of sunlight and the reflection of the
separated rays by a raindrop.

over which blue can be distinguished is larger than that over which either green or red can be seen. The area sensitive to green is smaller again than that sensitive to red and is restricted pretty well to the posterior wall of the globe (Plate VI*b*). The areas of the retina through which these three colors are perceived may be compared to three saucers of differently colored glass and of graded sizes, placed one inside the other. Light passing through the small green saucer will also pass through the red and blue saucers. Light striking the area of the retina represented by the green saucer will therefore be sensitive to green, red, and blue. This area supposedly contains all three types of cone. Light passing through the outer band of the red saucer will pass through the blue as well, but not through the green. The area of the retina represented is therefore sensitive to red and blue only. The rim of the largest—the blue —saucer transmits blue light only, and the retinal area it represents is sensitive only to blue. It possesses presumably only those cones that respond to blue light (Plate VI*c*).

The three qualities of color. The features of a color by which it can be distinguished from any other color are three—*hue, brilliance,* and *saturation.*

Hue simply means color in the sense in which this latter word is commonly used. Red and green, for instance, are different hues. Hue is determined by the length of the light waves. This quality, therefore, corresponds to the pitch of a sound (Ch. 46), the spectrum being compared to the scale in music. The hue (or pitch) varies from one end of the spectrum (or scale) to the other. The origins of the names of the fundamental hues can be traced to the language of civilization's infancy. It is of interest to recall that the adjectives red, blue, green, and yellow have been derived from the names of materials and objects having these colors. Thus, red comes from an ancient word for blood. Blue is derived from the color of the sky and from the same root as the verb *to blow.* Green, the characteristic color of young plant life, arose from the word *grow,* and yellow from *gold.*

Brilliance, or *brightness,* is that quality of a color that depends upon the proportion of blackness mixed with it. For instance, scarlet is brighter than cherry, since it contains less black. Brilliance of a color corresponds to the loudness of a sound. Indeed, "loud" is a word often applied to brilliant colors. A sound is loud because the ear is stimulated more strongly by the sound waves. An object has a brilliant color when it absorbs few of the waves of that color and so reflects them in larger proportion to stimulate the retina.

Saturation refers to the proportion of white light with which a color is mixed. If the proportion of white light is high, the saturation of the color is low, and vice versa. Thus pink is a paler—that is, a less saturated—color than red, which gives to the eye a deep rich sensation of color. An object has a color of low saturation when a large proportion of the light it reflects is white, and only a small proportion of the reflected light has the wavelength characteristic of the particular color. The color sensation is rich—that is, the saturation is high—when a small proportion of the light reflected from the object is white.

Color blindness. Some persons are blind to red or green or to both colors, and in rare instances to blue. It is thought that the retinas of these persons are lacking in the elements sensitive to these fundamental colors. The condition is usually hereditary and as a general rule affects only males—rarely females. Occasionally green blindness results from the excessive use of tobacco. A green object appears grayish to a green-blind person. A person who is red blind confuses red with green, and he cannot see a red square on a black background. He may choose a bright red tie and think that it is dark green or brown. Any color that contains a mixture of red, such as purple or orange, is perceived by the red-blind as though no red were present. So, to the red-blind person, purple appears a pure blue and orange a yellow. A color mixed with green, such as a greenish blue or a greenish yellow, appears a pale blue or yellow to the green-blind.

In certain occupations, such as navigation and railroad operation, color blindness may lead to serious accidents, and for this reason it is of the greatest importance that tests for color vision be made before men are accepted for employment in these occupations. Since about 9 percent of persons are color blind, and so many drive automobiles today, lights of more suitable colors than red and green might be chosen for traffic signals. Red and green, for the same reason, are poor colors to use for license plates. Red letters on a black background would be indistinct to the color blind and even to a normal person at dusk. In semidarkness we all lose the ability to perceive colors. Red is the first color that we fail to see. In the garden at dusk the poppies and geraniums appear as black blotches, while the cornflowers and delphiniums still retain their blue color. A flower that appears a mauve or bluish pink in daylight is seen as pure blue in the shadows of the evening, for the eye has become insensitive to the red blended with the blue.[1]

Contrast effects. Most persons have probably noticed that black letters look blacker upon a white than upon a colored background. But it is also true that blue letters look bluer upon a yellow ground than upon a ground of any other color, and yellow letters appear a brighter yellow upon a blue ground. Also, green letters look greener against red, and red letters redder against green. Cherries, for example, look brighter against the leaves of the tree than elsewhere. These phenomena are examples of what is termed *simultaneous contrast*.

[1] If the reader looks at Plate IV*d* in a fading light, he will find that the blue persists longer than the red.

If the color pairs mentioned above—blue and yellow, or red and green—were blended together in the form of lights, it would be found that they produced white light. Any pair of colors that, when fused, produce white are said to be *complementary* to one another.[2] Not only red and green and the other fundamental colors but every color and shade of color has some other with which it may be combined to produce white (see Table 45.1, below, and Plate VI*d,B*). There are consequently a large number of complementary colors, and the contrast effect is produced when any such color pairs are placed side by side. Briefly, each color makes its complementary appear more intense. Furthermore, if any two colors that are not complementary to each other are placed side by side, each will take on a tint that is the complementary of the other. For instance, if a lemon were placed upon a white surface in bright sunshine, the shadow it cast would not be a simple dull gray, but a gray tinged with blue—the complementary of yellow. The gray shadow cast by a red object would be tinged with green, or one thrown by a green object

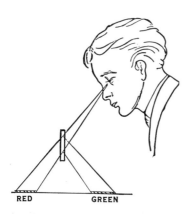

RED   GREEN

Fig. 45.3. Combining complementary colors to produce the sensation of white.

---

[2] These facts may be demonstrated very simply by employing a glass plate to blend two complementary colors upon the retina. A green book or other object of this color is placed in front of the person making the experiment. If the green has a bluish tinge, so much the better. A little in front of the green book a red one is placed. A clear glass plate is then held midway between and about 6 inches above the two books, so that the red book can be seen through the glass, and the image of the green book is reflected from the glass's surface (Fig. 45.3). When the two colors fall upon the same part of the retina and are blended, an almost white sensation is produced. Blue and yellow objects looked at in the same way would also produce white.

A top with vertical bands of red and bluish green, of blue and yellow, or of any two complementary colors, when spun rapidly, appears a uniform dirty white. The separate sensations produced by the complementary colors when the top is still become blended in the retina when the top is spinning, since they are repeated in such rapid succession (see *afterimage*, below). The reader may know by experience, however, that blue and yellow paints, when mixed together, do not give white—far from it, they give a vivid green. A distinction, however, should be drawn between lights and paints. A paint has a certain color because it reflects a certain light and absorbs others. Even the bluest paint is not pure blue; it absorbs all light but blue and a little green—these it reflects. A yellow paint is not pure yellow; it reflects a little green with the yellow. When the two paints are mixed, blue light is absorbed by the yellow paint, and yellow light is absorbed by the blue. So neither of these lights is reflected. On the other hand, green rays, of which a little is reflected by each separate paint, are doubly reflected when the two are mixed. If we could obtain an absolutely pure blue paint and mix it with a pure yellow, rays of all colors would be absorbed, and the result would be not green but black.

with red. The shadows upon the snow in the yellow sunlight are not gray but blue. The artist, by studying these effects and applying them to his work, gives brilliance, life, and beauty to his paintings. He makes a yellow flood of sunshine more dazzling by painting blue into the shadows, which, in turn, are given a depth and an appearance of reality that gray alone could not give.

Table 45.1 shows the effects produced by certain colors when they are placed side by side (see also Plate VI*d, B*).

TABLE 45.1

CONTRAST EFFECTS

I. Noncomplementary pairs of colors

Red with orange	Red becomes tinged with greenish blue (the complementary of orange) and so inclines to purple; orange becomes tinged with bluish green (the complementary of red) and so inclines to yellow.
Yellow with red	Yellow becomes tinged with green (complementary of red) and so inclines to green; red becomes tinged with blue and so inclines to purple
Blue with green	Blue becomes tinged with red (complementary of green) and so inclines to violet; green becomes tinged with yellow and so inclines to yellow-green
Violet with orange	Violet becomes more blue; orange becomes more yellow

II. Complementary pairs of colors

Red and bluish green	Both colors become more brilliant
Orange and greenish blue	Both colors become more brilliant
Green and purple	Both colors become more brilliant
Violet and yellow-green	Both colors become more brilliant

Gray becomes tinged with the complementary of any color placed beside it

Simultaneous contrast may be readily seen in Plate VI*d, D* and *E*. When the figures are looked at through a tissue paper as it is moved slowly up and down, the gray area on the green ground takes on a faintly red tint (complementary of green), while the gray area on the blue ground appears tinged with yellow (complementary of blue).

If the eyes are directed to a red surface for a short time and then to one colored in the complementary green, the green appears brighter than it would have if the retina had not first been stimulated by red. If these colors were viewed in reverse order—first green and then red—the red would appear more brilliant than usual. This effect is called *successive contrast,* and can be shown for other pairs of complementary colors. Successive contrast is believed to be due to fatigue of the cones of one type (for example, the red-responsive) and, as a consequence, the apparently more intense reaction of those sensitive to the complementary color (that is, the green-responsive).

Afterimages. If we look for a while at a bright object, an electric light, for example, and then close our eyes or direct them to a dark surface, an image of the lighted bulb appears before the eyes. This is called a *positive afterimage,* since it has the same appearance as the object seen with the eyes open. Again, if we look for a time at a light or a bright white object and then turn the eyes to a *white* surface, such as a blank sheet of white paper, a *black* image in the form of the light or of the object floats before the eyes. This is a *negative afterimage.* When the light or object is colored, the afterimage is in the complementary color of the original—blue if the original light was yellow, red if the original was green, and vice versa.

A positive afterimage is due, it is believed, to the persistence of nervous impulses arising in the retinal cells after the original stimulus has been removed, much in the same way as when the skin is struck sharply, pain sensations continue to be felt for a short time afterwards. A visual sensation is not instantaneous, like an explosion, but instead takes time to develop, persists for a measurable length of time, and then fades away. The sensation is more like the striking of a bell with a hammer; the metal continues to vibrate and give out sound for a time afterwards. In motion pictures the effect of movement is, as we know, produced by a succession of views showing objects in different positions. The rate at which these different views are shown must be carefully gauged. If the intervals are too short, the impression made by one view upon the retina will not have subsided before the next appears. Blurring is the result. If the interval is too long, the effect produced by one view has ceased some time before the next scene appears. Lack of smoothness and realism is the result. An example of a number of visual impressions overlapping is seen in the effect produced by the spokes of a wheel revolving rapidly (Fig. 45.4). The separate spokes follow one another so quickly that the sensations become fused upon the retina and the wheel appears solid.

Fig. 45.4. The black spokes of a wheel revolving against a white background appear as a solid gray disk owing to the fusion of the sensations (black and white) upon the retina. A disk marked in alternate segments of different colors would, when rotated, also cause a fusion of the separate color sensations. Thus red and blue would produce a purple, and red and yellow an orange sensation. Complementary color pairs would give a near white.

Negative afterimages are believed to be caused by fatigue of those receptors of the retina stimulated by the bright light. If the fatiguing light was white, then all three types of cone are fatigued, and when a second white image—the blank white surface—falls upon the retina there is no response from the receptors in the previously stimulated area, a sensation of black resulting. When the light is colored, only the cones sensitive to that particular color are fatigued. The subsequent white stimulus (which ordinarily excites all three types of cone) therefore calls forth a response from the other two types of cone alone and an afterimage in the complementary color appears (see Plate VId, C).

46
The Physiology of Hearing and Equilibrium

STRUCTURE OF THE EAR

The organ of hearing consists of three distinct compartments or regions, each of which has its own special part to play in the mechanism of hearing. These regions are termed the *outer (external)*, *middle,* and *inner (internal) ears* (Fig. 46.1).

The outer (external) ear. The outer ear consists of (1) the irregularly shaped but roughly semicircular shell of skin and cartilage projecting from the side of the head, called the **pinna, or auricle,** and (2) a short funnel-shaped canal called the **external auditory meatus.** The auditory meatus is somewhat tortuous and tunnels the bone of the skull; it is lined with skin. Its inner end is blind, being closed by a thin membrane covered with delicate skin and known as the **tympanic, or drum, membrane.** This membrane forms a flexible partition between the outer and middle ears and forms a part of the outer wall of the latter chamber.

The middle ear, or tympanum. The middle ear lies on the inner side of the tympanic membrane. It is a small chamber hollowed out of the temporal bone. Its walls, therefore, are composed of bone, except the outer one, which is partially formed by the tympanic membrane. A chain of three miniature bones, or **ossicles,** is slung from the drum membrane to the inner wall of the middle ear. The outermost ossicle is shaped like a hammer or club, and is therefore called the **malleus** (Fig. 46.2), the Latin word for hammer. It is attached firmly by its handle to the drum membrane. The middle bone looks something like a tiny bicuspid tooth. It was thought by some to resemble an anvil and so was named the **incus.** The innermost bone looks not unlike a stirrup, and has, therefore, been named the **stapes** (L., a stirrup). The longest of the ossicles

604

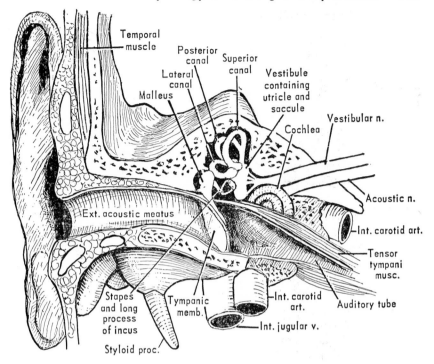

Fig. 46.1. Section through the temporal bone showing the auditory and equilibratory organs.

(the malleus) is only about a third of an inch long (8 to 9 mm); the incus and stapes are about 7 and 4 mm, respectively, in their longest diameters.

The inner wall of the tympanum is also the outer wall of the internal ear. A small oval opening is to be seen in it called the **oval window**, or **fenestra vestibuli.** It lodges the foot-plate of the stapes which is held in place by an annular ligament. Lower down on the inner wall is a second gap in the bone known as the **round window**, or **fenestra cochleae.** It is closed by a thin membrane. Through these two gaps in the bony wall the middle and internal ears are in functional communication (see also internal ear, below).

No doubt the reader has noticed the cords that run down the side of a bandsman's drum, by which the parchment can be stretched. The tympanic membrane is also furnished with the means for making it tighter for the perception of high-pitched sounds. A tiny muscle called the **tensor tympani** (drum stretcher), which runs from the wall of the tympanum to the malleus, serves this purpose (Fig. 46.2). This muscle also fulfills a protective function against loud sounds, serving to prevent a too violent movement of the tympanic membrane. A second muscle,

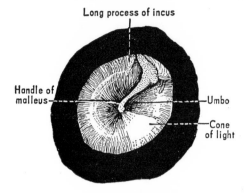

Long process of incus

Handle of malleus

Umbo

Cone of light

Fig. 46.2. The living tympanic membrane illuminated and viewed through a speculum. The depression in the region of attachment of the handle of the malleus is called the umbo, from which a triangular area of reflected light (cone of light) is directed downward and slightly forward. Prominence of the handle of malleus is somewhat exaggerated.

called the **stapedius,** stretches from the wall of the tympanum to the stapes. It prevents the foot-plate of the stapes from being driven too forcibly into the oval window.

A small tube—the **auditory tube**—runs from the middle ear to the back of the nose (Fig. 46.1). By means of this passage, air can pass into or out of the middle ear. The importance of the auditory (*Eustachian*) tube will be explained later.

The internal ear. The internal ear contains the essential organ of hearing, as well as the organ of bodily equilibrium. It comprises a system of passages tunnelled in the petrous part of the temporal bone and known as the *bony labyrinth.* The latter houses a series of membranous ducts and sacs called the *membranous labyrinth.* The outer wall of the internal ear forms the inner wall of the middle ear.

The **bony labyrinth** consists of three parts—the *cochlea,* the *vestibule,* and the *semicircular canals.* The **cochlea** lodges the organ of hearing. It is a spiral passage that has received this name from its resemblance to the shell of the common snail (L. *cochlea,* a snail shell). It is a short conical structure with its apex directed forward and outward. It makes $2\frac{3}{4}$ turns around a bony pillar called the **modiolus** (L., hub of a wheel). A spiral ledge of bone is given off by the modiolus, which projects into the cochlear passage and divides it incompletely into two. The division is completed by the *basilar membrane* (see below), which extends from

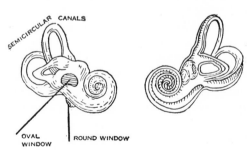

SEMICIRCULAR CANALS

OVAL WINDOW

ROUND WINDOW

Fig. 46.3. The cochlea and semicircular canals. In the right-hand figure both have been sectioned to show their interiors.

the tip of the bony ledge to the outer wall of the cochlea. The spiral passages are called *scalae* from their fancied resemblance to spiral staircase (pl. of L. *scala,* a staircase). The upper is known as the **scala vestibuli** (because it opens into the vestibule), and the lower one as the **scala tympani** (because its lower end is closed by the membrane of the round window that separates it from the middle ear). The two scalae communicate at the apex of the cochlea by an aperture called the **helicotrema** (Gk. *helix,* a spiral + *trema,* a hole).[1]

The **vestibule** is an oval chamber occupying the central part of the bony labyrinth. It is in communication in front with the scala vestibuli of the cochlea, behind with the three semicircular canals, and, through the fenestra vestibuli in its outer wall (see middle ear, above), with the tympanum. It contains the utricle and saccule of the membranous labyrinth.

The **semicircular canals** are three crescentic passages that house the semicircular ducts (p. 616) of the membranous labyrinth. Both ends of each canal communicate with the vestibule as shown in Figure 46.1.

The **membranous labyrinth** is considerably smaller than the bony labyrinth that it occupies. It comprises the *cochlear duct,* which serves the auditory function; the *semicircular ducts* and the *utricle,* which constitute the organs of equilibrium and orientation of the body in space; and the *saccule.* These nonauditory parts

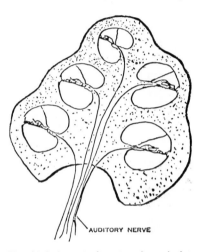

Fig. 46.4. A vertical section through the cochlea showing the three canals, **or** stairways; diagrammatic.

of the membranous labyrinth with their functions are described later in the chapter.

The **cochlear duct** is a spiral membranous tube that follows the turns of the cochlea. It occupies a position between the scala vestibuli and the scala tympani (Fig. 46.5) and for this reason is sometimes called by its older name, the *scala media.* A membranous partition, the **vestibular membrane,** separates it from the scala vestibuli, while the **basilar membrane,** which forms its floor, divides it from the scala tympani. The basilar membrane carries the **spiral organ,** or **organ of Corti,** which contains the *auditory receptors.* These cells bear fine hairlike processes and are therefore usually referred to as **hair cells.** Overlying the sensitive hairs is a very delicate membrane—a mere wisp of tissue—that is fastened

---

[1] In this account the usual practice has been followed of describing the cochlea, **not** in its true position (on its side), but as though resting on its base.

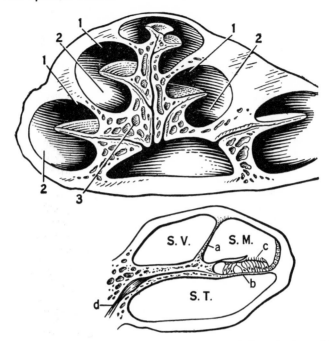

Fig. 46.5. *Above,* a view of the osseous cochlea divided through the middle. *(After Arnold.)* 1, scala vestibuli; 2, scala tympani; 3, modiolus, showing tunnels transmitting branches of auditory nerve. *Below,* enlarged sketch of one turn of the cochlea. *(After Quain.)* S.V., scala vestibuli; S.M., (scala media) cochlear duct; S.T., scala tympani; a, Reissner's membrane; b, basilar membrane; c, organ of Corti; d, auditory nerve.

by one end, but like a tag of seaweed clinging to a rock, has its other end free to move with every movement or vibration of the fluid in which it floats. It is called the **roof,** or **tectorial, membrane.**

The internal ear is supplied by the *eighth cerebral,* or *auditory,* nerve. It consists of two divisions, the *cochlear* (the nerve of hearing)

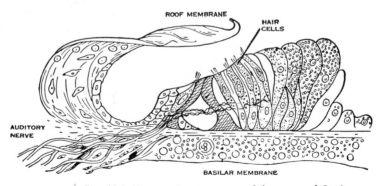

Fig. 46.6. Microscopic appearance of the organ of Corti.

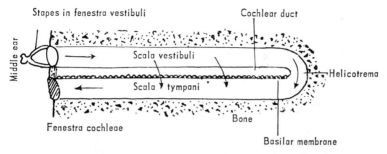

Fig. 46.7. Diagram of the passages of the cochlea unwound and straightened out to show how the vibrations (arrows) are transmitted from the fenestra vestibuli across the basilar membrane to the fenestra cochlea.

and the *vestibular* (the nerve serving the sense of equilibrium). The cochlear nerve enters the base of the modiolus and, ascending, breaks up into fine branches that pass at different levels into the basilar membrane. Each hair cell receives a nerve filament.

It is somewhat difficult to visualize the complicated structure of the internal ear, with its three spiral stairways, and the manner in which these communicate through the oval and round windows with the middle ear. For the sake of simplicity, the three compartments may be, as it were, unwound and shown in a straight line side by side, as drawn diagrammatically in Figure 46.7.

THE SENSE OF HEARING

The structure of the ear—outer, middle, and inner—having been sketched, we are in a position to understand how sound waves, sent out by a vibrating body and reaching the ear through the air, are converted into those sensations that we know and speak of as music, noise, and sounds of various kinds.

A few words must first be said concerning the physical nature of sound. Every sound we hear is due to waves of air beating upon our ears. The type of sound—its pitch, its loudness or its softness, its sweetness or its harshness—depends upon the *frequency, size,* and *form* of the air waves. Sound waves are transmitted through the air at a speed of about 1100 feet per second. As compared with the speed of light, this, of course, is but a snail's pace. That is why we see the puff of a steam whistle a mile away long before we hear it. The waves of sound, however, may be long, and only a few may reach the ear during each second. Or they may be very short, and then thousands may strike the ear in a second. When the waves are long and at a rate of only a few per second, we hear a deep booming or rumbling sound. When the waves are smaller and beat in

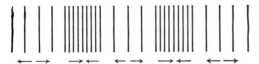

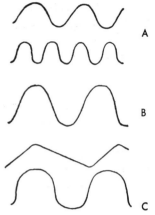

Fig. 46.8 *(above).* Diagrammatic representation of sound waves. The groups of lines separated by narrow spaces represent the compression phases of a wave; the more separated lines represent the phases of expansion or rarefaction. The arrows indicate the direction of movement of the air particles.

Fig. 46.9 *(right).* Sound waves. A, waves of different frequency, illustrating pitch. B, a wave of greater height than those shown in A or C, illustrating intensity, or loudness, of sound. C, waves of different forms to illustrate quality, or timbre.

more rapid succession upon our ears, the sound has a higher pitch. When a body such as a bell, a gong, or a tuning fork is struck, or a violin string is twanged, all the tiny particles of the object's substance are set into vibration. The vibrations are transmitted in all directions as a series of compression waves—that is, alternating compressions and rarefactions (or expansions) of the surrounding air. These motions of the air are called *sound waves, double vibrations,* or *cycles* (Figs. 46.8, 46.9).

Not all waves in the air cause a sensation of sound. Unless their frequency is within a certain range, nothing is heard. For example, waves are set up when a stick is moved slowly through the air, but they are too large and infrequent to make any impression upon our ears. But if the stick is swished rapidly through the air, the wood itself vibrates, smaller and more rapidly repeated waves are formed, and a sound is heard. On the other hand, we know that some animals, bats, and some insects have means (larynx, wings, etc.) for causing very rapid waves in the air that our ears are not sensitive enough to hear. The human ear does not register sound waves that are of very low or extremely high frequency. If the double vibrations are fewer than 16 or more than 30,000 per second, no sound is heard by the human ear. Cats are said to be able to detect sound waves of a higher rate than this; they can probably hear the high-pitched sounds made by a mouse, which are usually quite inaudible to human ears. The various musical instruments produce sound waves that range from 30 to 4000 cycles per second. The vibrations of the ordinary human voice range from about 90 to 800 cycles per second. Some famous bass singers can go as low as 50 cycles per second, and sopranos as high as 1500 per second or even higher.

The sound waves are caught by the pinna, or auricle, and directed down the funnel-shaped auditory meatus. The pinna is set so that it looks a little forward to catch sound waves coming from the front. But man cannot turn his ears in the direction of a sound without turning his head as well. Animals, however, have special muscles that move the ears. We have all seen dogs and horses "prick up their ears" and turn them to catch the sound waves coming from a certain direction. Though man has similar muscles, they are weak relics and of no use for this purpose.

The sound waves reaching the bottom of the auditory meatus set the drum membrane into vibration. The membrane beats in time with the air waves. The vibrations are carried across the middle ear by the chain of small bones to the oval window in the bony partition separating the middle and inner ears. We have seen that the foot-plate of the stapes fits into the oval window. This window, in turn, communicates with the fluid in the cochlea. Thus the vibrations of the tympanic membrane are transmitted to the inner ear, where the receptors of hearing are situated. The three ossicles of the middle ear of man and higher animals are joined together in such a way that they act as a lever that magnifies the movements of the drum membrane and thus increases the force exerted upon the foot-plate of the stapes in the oval window. Furthermore, since the area of the tympanic membrane is much greater than that of the oval window, the force of the sound waves is concentrated at the latter point.

As we have already noted, the scala vestibuli is separated from the cochlear duct by a thin membranous partition. It is easy then to understand that vibrations set up in the fluid of the scala vestibuli will be transmitted to the cochlear duct and thence to the scala tympani (Fig. 46.7). It follows, therefore, that the basilar membrane, which forms the partition between the cochlear duct and scala tympani, will vibrate in unison with the tympanic membrane. The hair cells of the organ of Corti, lying upon the basilar membrane, will be driven swiftly with each double vibration against the tectorial membrane, which floats above them. Thus a series of taps are applied to the processes of the hair cells, which serve as mechanical stimuli to the terminals of the acoustic nerve.[2] Nerve impulses are in this way transmitted to the center for hearing in the cortex.

The round window of the middle ear. The round window, which lies in the bony partition between the inner and middle chambers of the ear, is closed by a thin flexible membrane, which alone separates the scala tympani of the cochlea from the middle ear. The window, with its membranous covering, is for the purpose of allowing the fluid in the scala tympani to make an outward movement when the foot-plate of the stapes

---

[2] It may be, as some believe, that the hairs of the hair cells are not separated from the roof membrane but are actually attached to it. If this is so, a succession of pulls upon the hairs, rather than a series of taps, provides the stimulus when the basilar membrane vibrates up and down.

moves inward, and an inward movement when the foot-plate moves outward. Fluids, as we all know, cannot be compressed; therefore, if there were no round window, the foot-plate of the stapes could not make any movement, nor could any movement be transmitted to the fluid within the cochlea. The fluid would be bottled up in unyielding bone, and the sensitive hair cells immersed in it could not be moved by any force applied to the stapes. If a bottle is filled to its mouth with water, it is a foregone conclusion that the cork cannot be inserted. If, however, the bottom of the bottle were bored through and the opening covered with a rubber membrane, the cork could be slipped in without difficulty.

The function of the auditory tube. The auditory tube, as stated earlier, runs from the back of the nose (nasopharynx) to the middle ear. It therefore permits this part of the ear to communicate with the outside air. By this means the pressure of air on the two sides of the drum membrane is equalized. It must be remembered that the air around us has a great weight (Ch. 20). It presses upon every square foot of our bodies with a weight of 1 ton. If the pressure in the middle ear were not as great as the pressure of the atmosphere, the drum membrane would be pushed in and could not move freely in and out when sound waves struck it. It would be pushed in toward the cavity of the middle ear and be as rigid as a board and not sensitive to rapid vibrations. In sailing, for example, the sail is stiff and rigid when the wind is on our beam. When the boat is headed into the wind, however, the sail flaps to and fro, since the pressure on its two sides is practically equal. Probably all of us at one time or another have known the slight deafness that accompanies a cold in the head. This is caused by the Eustachian tube becoming blocked by the swelling of the mucous membrane around its lower opening (in the nasopharynx). The air within the middle chamber of the ear becomes partially absorbed into the blood, and the slightly greater pressure of the atmosphere then upon its outer surface prevents the drum membrane from moving freely. Blowing the nose or swallowing, by momentarily forcing air up the tube, will often restore the hearing, for a time at any rate, to its usual acuteness. It is not a wise practice, however, to open the tube by blowing the nose when it is closed as the result of a cold. Infection may be forced into the middle ear and cause inflammation, with earache and perhaps worse consequences.

The tube is not always open, but only during swallowing. This is sufficient to keep the air pressures equal. If it were open all the time, one's own voice would send sound waves up to the middle ear and cause an unnecessarily loud noise.

In rapid airplane descents from a high altitude, equalization of pressure between the middle ear and the atmosphere may not occur promptly enough. If the auditory tube does not open as the descent is made, the air pressure in the middle ear remains at that of the high alti-

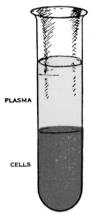

Plate 1a. Blood after centrifuging, shows separation of plasma (55%) from cells (45%).

Plate 1b. Red corpuscles in rouleaux.

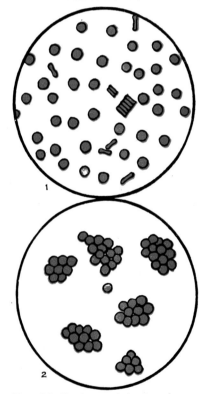

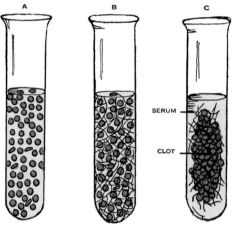

Plate 1c. Showing the microscopic changes which occur during the clotting of the blood. A, before clotting had set in; B, formation of threads of fibrin; C, contraction (shortening) of the fibrin threads and trapping of the blood cells in the mesh. Diagrammatic.

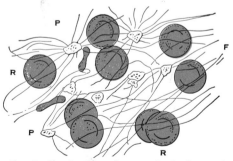

Plate 1d. Showing agglutination of corpuscles by incompatible blood. 1. Corpuscles of one subject mixed with compatible serum of another; 2. corpuscles mixed with incompatible serum; note agglutination.

Plate 1e. Showing R, erythrocytes; P, platelets; and F, fibrin threads formed in the clotting of blood. Note that the fibrin threads appear to radiate from the platelets.

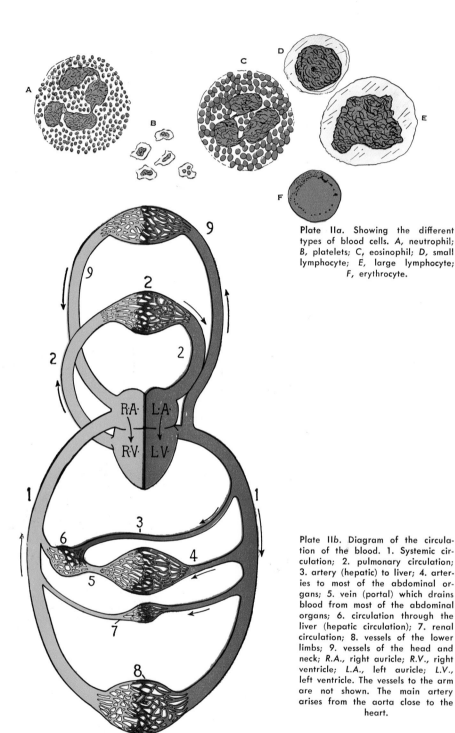

Plate IIa. Showing the different types of blood cells. A, neutrophil; B, platelets; C, eosinophil; D, small lymphocyte; E, large lymphocyte; F, erythrocyte.

Plate IIb. Diagram of the circulation of the blood. 1. Systemic circulation; 2. pulmonary circulation; 3. artery (hepatic) to liver; 4. arteries to most of the abdominal organs; 5. vein (portal) which drains blood from most of the abdominal organs; 6. circulation through the liver (hepatic circulation); 7. renal circulation; 8. vessels of the lower limbs; 9. vessels of the head and neck; R.A., right auricle; R.V., right ventricle; L.A., left auricle; L.V., left ventricle. The vessels to the arm are not shown. The main artery arises from the aorta close to the heart.

Plate IIIa. The large blood vessels. The pulmonary veins, four in number, which carry blood from the lungs to the left side of the heart, are hidden behind the aorta and pulmonary artery.

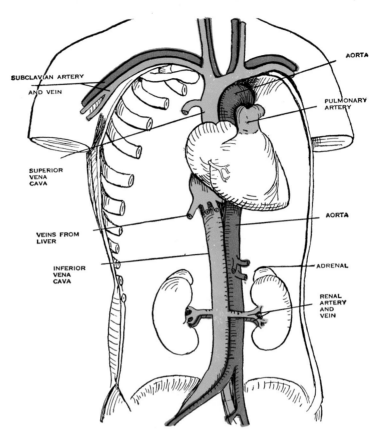

AORTA

SUBCLAVIAN ARTERY AND VEIN

PULMONARY ARTERY

SUPERIOR VENA CAVA

AORTA

VEINS FROM LIVER

ADRENAL

INFERIOR VENA CAVA

RENAL ARTERY AND VEIN

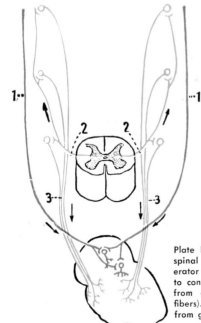

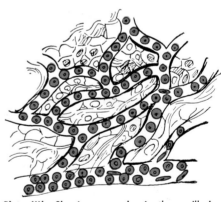

Plate IIIb. Showing corpuscles in the capillaries of the web of a frog's foot.

Plate IIIc. Diagram of the nerves that pass from the brain and spinal cord to the heart. 1. Vagus (of parasympathetic); 2. accelerator fibers leaving the cord (sympathetic preganglionic fibers) to connect with cells of sympathetic ganglia; 3. accelerator fibers from ganglia to the heart muscle (sympathetic postganglionic fibers). Note that the postganglionic fibers of the vagus arise from ganglion cells in the walls of the heart itself. Arrows indicate the course taken by the nerve impulses.

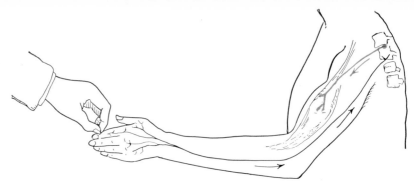

Plate IVa. Showing the manner in which a reflex movement is brought about. When the finger is pricked or stimulated painfully in any way, impulses pass to the spinal cord by sensory (afferent) nerves where fresh impulses are set up in the nerve cells of the spinal center and transmitted to the muscles by motor (efferent) nerves.

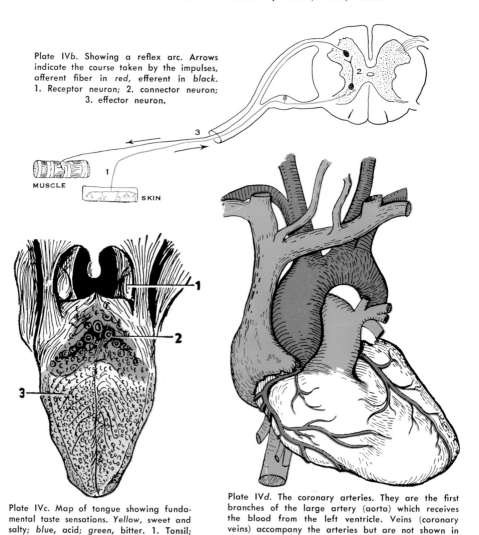

Plate IVb. Showing a reflex arc. Arrows indicate the course taken by the impulses, afferent fiber in *red,* efferent in *black.* 1. Receptor neuron; 2. connector neuron; 3. effector neuron.

Plate IVc. Map of tongue showing fundamental taste sensations. *Yellow,* sweet and salty; *blue,* acid; *green,* bitter. 1. Tonsil; 2. large papillae (circumvallate); 3. small papillae (fungiform) which give a velvety appearance to the surface of the tongue.

Plate IVd. The coronary arteries. They are the first branches of the large artery (aorta) which receives the blood from the left ventricle. Veins (coronary veins) accompany the arteries but are not shown in the figure.

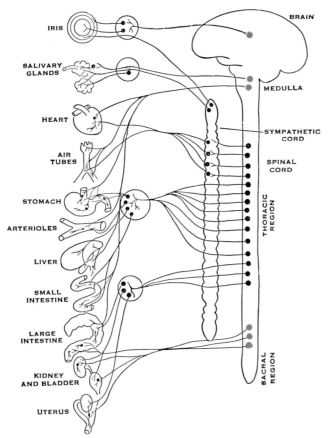

Plate V*a*. The autonomic nervous system. Sympathetic division in *black*, parasympathetic division in *red*.

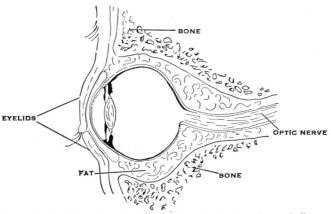

Plate V*b*. A section through the orbital cavity showing the eyeball, optic nerve, and surrounding parts. Conjunctiva in *red*.

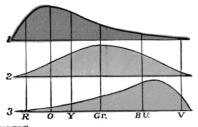

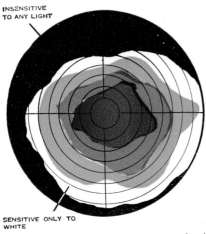

Plate VI*a*. Diagram of the three primary color sensations (Young-Helmholtz theory). 1. Represents the *red*; 2. the *green*; and 3. the *blue* color sensation. The lettering along the base line indicates the colors of the spectrum. The diagram indicates by the height of the curve at which it is cut by the vertical lines the extent to which the several primary sensations of color are excited by vibrations of different wave lengths. (*After Helmholtz.*)

INSENSITIVE TO ANY LIGHT

SENSITIVE ONLY TO WHITE

Plate VI*b*. Showing the distribution of color perception in the retina. Note that the area for *green* is the smallest, that for *blue*, the largest.

Plate VI*c*. Diagram of the color areas of the retina.

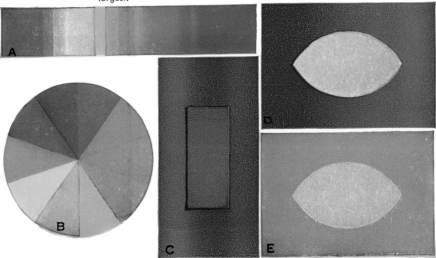

Plate VI*d*. A, the spectrum. The series of colors—*red, orange, yellow, green, blue,* and *violet*—produced when sunlight is split into its constituents by means of a prism. B, complementary colors arranged as segments of a disc. The color pairs that are directly opposite one another are complementary. C illustrates colored afterimage. If the figure is stared at for about a minute and the eyes are then directed to a sheet of white paper, the figure will float before the sight with the colors reversed, i.e., a green bar will be seen upon a red ground. D and E illustrate simultaneous contrast. The figures should be looked at through tissue paper. In D the gray ground takes on a *pink* tint (red is complementary to green). In E the gray takes on a faintly *yellow* tint (*yellow* is complementary to *blue*).

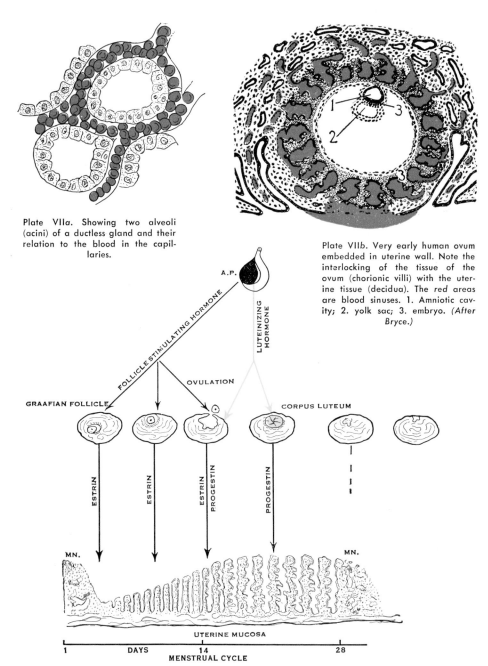

Plate VIIa. Showing two alveoli (acini) of a ductless gland and their relation to the blood in the capillaries.

Plate VIIb. Very early human ovum embedded in uterine wall. Note the interlocking of the tissue of the ovum (chorionic villi) with the uterine tissue (decidua). The red areas are blood sinuses. 1. Amniotic cavity; 2. yolk sac; 3. embryo. (After Bryce.)

A.P.

FOLLICLE STIMULATING HORMONE

LUTEINIZING HORMONE

OVULATION

GRAAFIAN FOLLICLE

CORPUS LUTEUM

ESTRIN

ESTRIN

ESTRIN
PROGESTIN

PROGESTIN

MN.

MN.

UTERINE MUCOSA

| 1 | DAYS | 14 | 28 |

MENSTRUAL CYCLE

Plate VIIc. Showing the direct control of ovarian activity (growth of Graafian follicle and production of hormones) by the anterior lobe of the pituitary (A.P.) and secondarily, through the liberation of the hormones of the ovary, upon the rhythmical changes in the uterus leading to menstruation (Mn). Note the thickening of the mucous membrane of the uterus and the growth of its glands. If the ovum after its escape from the ovary (ovulation) becomes fertilized, it embeds itself in the mucous membrane of the uterus and develops into the embryo; the corpus luteum then does not degenerate but continues to grow until it reaches a diameter in the human of nearly an inch. Such growth is essential for the continuance of pregnancy.

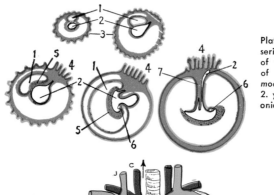

Plate VIIIa. Diagram showing a series of stages in the growth of the ovum and development of the embryo. (*Redrawn and modified from Gray.*) 1. Amnion; 2. yolk sac; 3. chorion; 4. chorionic villi; 5. embryo; 6. heart; 7. umbilical cord.

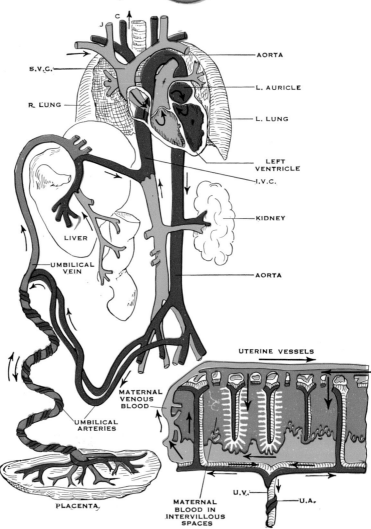

Plate VIIIb. Fetal circulation. *Red,* oxygenated blood; *blue,* reduced blood; *purple,* mixed blood; *C,* carotid artery; *I.V.C.,* inferior vena cava; *J,* jugular vein; *S.V.C.,* superior vena cava; *small diagram below* represents a section of the placenta; only two complete villi are shown; *red* indicates maternal blood delivered into intervillous spaces, and, after giving up oxygen, is returned by uterine veins (*blue*); *U.A.,* umbilical artery from the fetus to placenta; *U.V.,* umbilical vein to fetus.

tude, while the atmospheric pressure on the outer side of the tympanic membrane increases rapidly. The membrane is forced inward and may rupture. In order to avoid this accident the auditory tube is opened by swallowing a number of times in quick succession.

The three characteristics of sound. The ear can distinguish between the *pitch, quality,* and *intensity* of different sounds. (See also p. 610.)

Pitch. Little more need be said regarding pitch; it depends upon the *vibration frequency*—the greater the frequency the higher the pitch. We speak of a low or a high note, of the bass or treble of the piano, or of a bass or soprano voice, meaning that the sounds are of low or high pitch. The greater the number of waves per second the shorter, of course, they must be (Fig. 46.9*A*).

Quality, or *timbre.* This characteristic is what distinguishes harsh sounds or noises from musical notes, and the tones of different instruments from one another. The tone of a violin, for example, is quite different from the tone of a bugle, a piano, or a flute. The quality of a sound is not due to the frequency of the vibrations, but to the *form* of the sound waves. Sounds of the same vibration frequency—that is, of the same pitch—may differ greatly in quality. The form of the sound waves depends in turn upon the number and character of the simple harmonic waves of which it is composed (Fig. 46.9*C*).

Intensity, or *loudness.* The loudness of a sound depends upon the *amplitude* of the sound waves (Fig. 46.9*B*). The firing of a cannon causes a great commotion in the atmosphere; huge waves travel out from the point of the explosion to strike the drum membrane. We hear a loud report. A pin dropping upon the floor gently ruffles the air with tiny ripples. The very large waves will, of course, strike the air with greater force, cause the drum membrane to be forced in and out violently, and indeed may rupture it. The stapes is pushed in and out of the oval window more energetically. The stimulation of the hair cells is consequently more intense with a loud than with a soft sound, and the frequency of the impulses is higher.

How the ear distinguishes differences in pitch. Even animals can tell a high-pitched from a low-pitched tone. The human ear is very sensitive to differences in pitch. A person with a "good ear" can very accurately distinguish between two tones differing from each other by only one double vibration per second; that is, if 100 double vibrations strike the ear per second, the tone is perceived as being lower in pitch than one in which the vibrations are 101 per second.

At least two theories have been proposed to explain the pitch-discriminating faculty of the auditory mechanism. According to one theory the basilar membrane is set into vibration as a whole by the sound waves transmitted to it from the tympanic membrane through the ossicles of the middle ear and the fluid of the internal ear. Sound waves of, say,

10,000 double vibrations per second thus induce vibrations of the same frequency in the basilar membrane and cause a corresponding number of taps or pulls upon the processes of the hair cells. Ten thousand impulses per second would therefore be discharged along each fiber of the acoustic nerve. Impulses of this frequency would be interpreted by the brain in such a way as to give a sound sensation of a given pitch. A sound of, say 5000 double vibrations per second would be interpreted as one of lower pitch. This is known as the *telephone theory* because, like the operation of the telephone, sound waves striking the drum membrane and conveyed to the basilar membrane (corresponding to the telephone transmitter) set up nerve impulses (electrical impulses in the telephone wire) of exactly the same frequency and transmit them to the brain (the telephone receiver).

This theory, though it has the advantage of simplicity, can no longer be entertained, for it has been shown without question that a fiber of the acoustic nerve cannot transmit impulses at the high frequency that would be required for the appreciation of high-pitched sounds. The upper limit of frequency of impulses that a nerve fiber can transmit is about 1000 per second (see Ch. 33).

The theory that explains the known facts most satisfactorily is founded upon the principle of *sympathetic resonance*. It is known as the *harp, resonance,* or *place theory*. This theory, which was advanced by Helmholtz, the great German physicist and physiologist of the 19th century, has been amply supported by modern experimental work. The point that it emphasizes is that the basilar membrane does *not vibrate as a whole* but only at one part in response to a given sound frequency. That part of the membrane alone vibrates that is "in sympathy," or in tune, with the sound.

The essential part of this theory will be made clearer by an example. If close to a stringed instrument, such as a harp or a piano, a note is sounded upon a bugle, bell, or any other sounding body, that particular string of the harp or piano is set into vibration that, if it were plucked or struck, would itself give out the same note. The instrument gives out a faint sound, apparently of its own accord, in perfect tune with the bugle's note. In other words, the sound waves from the bugle pick out and set vibrating only that string of the harp or piano that can produce sound waves of the same frequency. This is a simple example of sympathetic resonance.

Now, the spirally twisted, ribbonlike basilar membrane contains a great number of fine cross fibers. These, like the strings of a piano or a harp, are of graded lengths and probably also of graded thicknesses and tensions. The numbers of fibers are, however, much greater than the number of strings in a piano or in any other stringed instrument. There are about 24,000 fibers. The longer fibers, which may be compared to the bass strings of the piano, lie near the top of the spiral; the shorter treble fibers are found at the bottom. When the basilar membrane is removed from its position, uncoiled, and laid flat, it is found to be only about 1½ inches long. It is $\frac{1}{125}$ inch wide at its narrow end but nearly double this width at its broad end. Hence, if we consider the 24,000 fibers that stretch across it as strings, then we have a tiny piano or harplike instrument, which may vibrate and show sympathetic resonance (Fig. 46.10).

Fig. 46.10. The basilar membrane. The cross lines indicate the fibers, of which there are some 20,000. The narrow part of the membrane is at the base, the wide end at the top of the cochlea.

We can now see how a note of a certain pitch will set, not all the fibers of the membrane into vibration, but only those that can vibrate at the same or nearly the same rate as the vibrating body that gave rise to the note. The vibrations of these particular fibers stimulate the hair cells immediately overlying them, and no others. Impulses travel along the nerve twigs, with which the cells are supplied, to reach certain cells in the brain.

Thus, we may conceive that the nerve fibers composing the acoustic nerve and arising in the hair cells in one or another part of the basilar membrane transmit impulses to nerve cells in a corresponding and definite part of the cortex of the temporal lobe. The situation in the cortex of the cells receiving these impulses is the basis upon which the pitch of a sound is appreciated. In the last analysis, therefore, pitch perception, like any other sensation, is a matter of *where* in the brain the impulses arrive (Ch. 33). The basilar membrane through its resonating property serves to localize the vibrations to hair cells at a certain *place* and to direct impulses to a limited region of the cerebral cortex. This view of the perception of pitch, therefore, is also known as the "place theory."

The following observations confirm our belief that this theory truly explains the way in which the ear distinguishes between notes of different pitch. (1) Boilermakers, who have for long periods been exposed to the clang of high-pitched noises, sometimes become quite deaf to high tones. Lower tones are heard clearly. Examination of the inner ears of men suffering from this form of deafness has shown that the fibers of the basilar membrane at the base of the cochlea—that is, the short, treble fibers—have been destroyed. (2) Destruction of these fibers has also been caused by experiments upon animals, in which they have been forced to listen for a long time to loud, shrill noises.

To solve the mystery of the mental process whereby an impulse arriving in the brain from the upper part of the cochlea gives the sensation of a low tone, whereas one arising in the lower cochlear region is heard as a high tone, seems as hopeless a task as to explain why stimulation of the retina within a limited range of wavelengths gives a sensation of light and color.

The sensitivity of the ear. The threshold of hearing. By reducing the intensity of a sound until it is just perceptible the extreme limit of the sensitivity of the ear can be determined. This is called the *threshold of hearing*. But the sensitivity of the ear varies widely with the pitch, being greatest (that is, the threshold is lowest) for sounds with frequencies between 500 and 5000 double vibrations per second. A sound wave of a frequency within this range arouses an audible sensation though it causes a pressure variation no greater than one twelve billionth of the pressure of the atmosphere at sea level, and a movement of the tympanic membrane of less than one ten millionth of a millimeter. The ear is found to be progressively less sensitive as the sound frequencies are increased or reduced beyond this range. Sounds of very high or of very low pitch, in order to be audible, must be increased in intensity several thousand times above the intensity required for sounds around 1000 double vibrations per second. Sounds with vibration frequencies above 30,000 or below 16 per second, no matter what their intensity, are inaudible to the human ear. Frequencies that cause no audible sensation may, however, be felt, the lowest frequencies giving a low rumbling sensation. Some vibrations, if very intense, may give rise to pain in the ear.

It has been stated that the intensity of a sound sensation—that is, the loudness of a sound of any given pitch—depends upon the rate of impulse discharge[3] along the fibers of the acoustic nerve. With respect to the relationship of impulse frequency to intensity of stimulation and sensation, the sense of hearing does not differ, therefore, from the other senses (Ch. 33). The greater the amplitude of the waves set up by a sounding body and transmitted to the internal ear, the more forcibly will the basilar membrane vibrate, the stronger will be the stimulus applied to the hair cells, and the higher will be the frequency of the impulses discharged.

THE ORGANS OF THE EQUILIBRATORY SENSE—THE SEMI-CIRCULAR DUCTS AND THE UTRICLE. THE SACCULE

The semicircular ducts. The semicircular ducts are three sickle-shaped tubes lying within the semicircular canals. They, with the utricle, comprise the organs of the equilibratory sense and are not concerned with the sense of hearing. One end of each duct shows an expansion

[3] This should not be confused with the frequency of the sound waves, which range up to 30,000 per second, whereas the nerve impulses have a maximum frequency of only 1000 per second.

called the **ampulla**. A ridge of connective tissue, the **crista**, projects from the wall of each ampulla well into its cavity. Each crista is covered by sensitive hair cells, surmounted by a gelatinous capping called the **cupula**, in which the hairlike processes of the sensitive cells are embedded (Fig. 46.11). The fibers of the *vestibular nerve* ramify within the cristae and send fine twigs into the hair cells. Both ends of the ducts communicate with the utricle, the ampullary ends opening individually. Of the opposite ends, that of one duct opens into the utricle separately, but those of the other two do so by a common stem (Fig. 46.11).

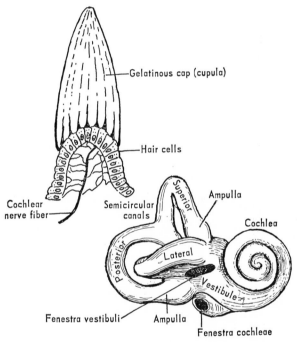

Gelatinous cap (cupula)

Hair cells

Cochlear
nerve fiber

Semicircular
canals

Superior

Ampulla

Cochlea

Posterior

Lateral

Vestibule

Fenestra vestibuli

Ampulla

Fenestra cochleae

Fig. 46.11. Drawing on the left shows crista and cupula (or cupola)[4]; the semicircular ducts, utricle, and cochlea are shown on the right.

The membranous labyrinth is filled with a fluid called **endolymph,** and is surrounded by a similar fluid known as **perilymph,** which occupies the space between it and the walls of the bony labryinth. (See also p. 606.)

Functions of the semicircular ducts. The receptors of the semicircular ducts are stimulated by a quick rotary movement of the body as a whole, or by a sudden turn of the head alone. Each duct is stimulated

---

[4] Though *cupula* (L., a tub) is the more usual word in America, *cupola* (L., a vault or dome) is more accurately descriptive and therefore more correct.

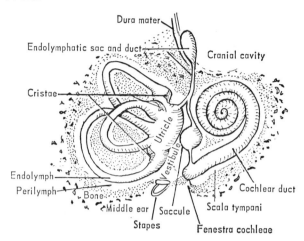

Dura mater

Endolymphatic sac and duct

Cranial cavity

Cristae

Utricle

Vestibule

Endolymph

Perilymph

Bone

Cochlear duct

Fig. 46.12. The membranous labyrinth within the bony canals.

Middle ear

Saccule

Scala tympani

Stapes

Fenestra cochleae

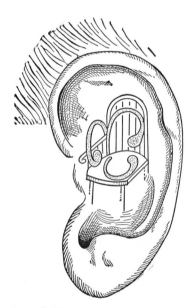

Fig. 46.13. Diagram to show the different plans of the semicircular ducts in relation to the head. The canals are at right angles to one another and in this are comparable to the arm, seat, and back of a chair.

most strongly when the rotary motion or the quick turn of the head is in the same plane as that of the duct itself. Thus, rotation around a vertical axis, as when a ballet dancer spins upon her toe (that is, pirouettes), stimulates most effectively the horizontal duct. The rotary motion causes the endolymph, owing to its inertia, to lag behind the movement of the wall of the duct. The endolymph thus presses upon and bends the sensitive hair cells, which results in a discharge of impulses along the fibers of the vestibular nerve. When the rotary movement ceases, the endolymph continues to move (owing now to its momentum) along the stationary duct in the same direction as it did during rotation. This bends the hair cells in a direction opposite to that at the beginning of the rotary movement. The brain interprets this in the usual way, and is deceived, with the result that the subject has a sensation, though standing still, of being spun in the opposite direction. It is only for a few seconds after the commencement of the rotation, and for about the same time after the movement has ceased, that any sensation of rotation is experienced, because the inertia of the endolymph is overcome soon after the

Fig. 46.15. A bird in which the semicircular ducts have been injured attempting to drink. It cannot bring its head into the correct position. *(Modified from Ewald.)*

Fig. 46.14. Position of the head and body of a frog during rotation to the left. *(After Ewald.)*

movement has started; the endolymph moves with the duct, and the hair cells, therefore, come back to their previous resting position. Rotation prolonged beyond the first few seconds, if perfectly smooth, arouses no sensation.[5]

As a result of stimulation of the receptors of the ducts by a rotary motion, reflexes are initiated that cause appropriate movements of the neck and limbs to maintain the body in proper balance (Fig. 46.14). When the ducts are destroyed or diseased, giddiness and disturbances of equilibrium occur. The brain has lost an important source of information with respect to the relation of the body to its surroundings.

The utricle. The utricle contains minute calcareous bodies called **otoliths** which rest upon and are attached to sensitive hair cells. The latter are stimulated when the head is in such a position that the otoliths, owing to their weight, pull upon them. The hair cells and otoliths of the utricle are therefore *gravity receptors,* whereas the sensitive cells of the semicircular ducts are *rotary receptors.* The receptors of the utricle cause, when stimulated, reflex muscular movements that enable an animal to bring its head and body into the normal upright position when placed upon its back or in any other abnormal position. These are called *righting reflexes.* If, for example, a kitten is held a few feet above the ground with its back downward and allowed to fall through the air, it turns in a flash to the back-upward position and lands in perfect balance upon its feet (Fig. 46.16). Seasickness and other forms of motion sickness are caused by repeated and unusual stimulation of the receptors of the utricle and not, as was previously thought, of the receptors of the semicircular ducts. The receptors of the utricle also respond to move-

[5] Though quick turns of the head are of very common occurrence, *continuous* rotation is a most unusual motion under ordinary and natural circumstances. The body has, therefore, not needed to develop any special means of recording it.

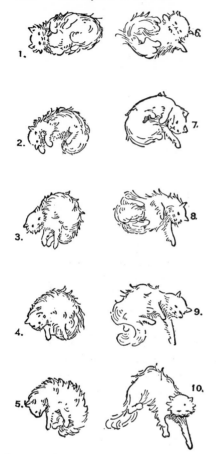

Fig. 46.16. Successive positions taken by a cat in falling from a height.

ments in a straight line, forwards or backwards, laterally, and possibly up or down, as in the ascent or descent of an elevator. These movements would tend to exert a pull upon the otoliths.

The saccule. The saccule is a much smaller sac than the utricle. Its functions are uncertain; it may also be concerned with the maintenance of equilibrium. But some believe that its function is auditory, and enables one to appreciate the sound of one's own voice through the bones of the skull. It communicates through two narrow ducts with both the utricle and the cochlea. The membranous labyrinth is thus a continuous series of fluid-filled chambers and passages.

47
The Senses of Smell and
Taste. Cutaneous Sensations

Taste and smell are alike in that they are both chemical senses; that is, the stimulus that excites the receptors of taste and those of smell is a chemical one, and it is upon the chemical nature of a material that its characteristic smell or taste depends. Salt has a different taste from sugar because these two substances are essentially different chemically. The perfume of the rose is distinguished from the smell of the violet because, as the chemist knows, the essences from which these scents arise are not the same chemically. The sense of smell, however, is apparently different from the sense of taste, for we can smell a substance without bringing it in contact with the interior of the nose—we can smell a thing at a distance.[1] In this regard the sense of smell and the senses of sight and hearing are similar. To taste a material, on the other hand, the sense organs of taste must be stimulated more directly. We must place the material in the mouth. In this respect the sense of taste and the sense of touch are alike.

THE SENSE OF SMELL—THE OLFACTORY SENSE

The sense of smell is almost incredibly acute in some animals, but is rudimentary in man. It is said, however, that certain tribes of South American Indians are aided by the sense of smell in tracking game. There are also instances on record of persons who, deprived of the sense of sight, have so developed the olfactory sense that they can recognize their acquaintances by smell alone.

An odorous material is continually throwing off particles of its sub-

[1] This is not an essential difference, for in order for a substance to be smelled, molecules or fine particles of it must come into actual contact with the olfactory receptors.

stance—molecules—to be carried to our noses. The molecules are relatively so sparse and widely separated that they are really the substance in gaseous form. Some materials, such as ether, gasoline, and turpentine, which throw off large numbers of molecules in a short time and, as we say, evaporate quickly or give off fumes, have a very strong smell. Other materials, such as the common metals, which do not cast their particles about so freely, have little or no odor, unless heated to a high temperature. Though the proportion of its substance that it gives off may be almost infinitesimal, a material, nevertheless, may have a very powerful odor. A small piece of musk, for instance, will show no change in its size or weight after a period of several years, though it has throughout the whole time permeated a large room with its scent.

Odor relationships. There appears to be some relationship between the colors of flowers and their smells. Generally speaking, white flowers are more strongly scented than colored ones. Of colored flowers, red are more likely to be highly perfumed than yellow varieties, and yellow flowers are usually more odorous than blue. Though smell is a chemical sense, the smell of a material and its chemical nature do not necessarily go hand in hand, for substances that differ greatly in their chemical composition may have very similar odors. For example, some compounds of arsenic smell like garlic; nitrobenzene and prussic acid, though chemically quite different, have similar odors. Yet, with certain substances, some relationship between smell and chemical nature appears to exist, their odors increasing in strength with their molecular weights. For example, propyl alcohol is faintly odorous; ethyl or grain alcohol, which has a higher molecular weight, has a distinct odor; and the smell becomes increasingly more powerful with each alcohol higher in the scale. Again, formic acid is inodorous; acetic acid has the characteristic odor of vinegar; butyric is more powerful-smelling; and valerianic is very offensive.

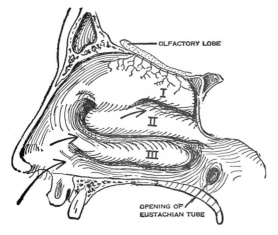

Fig. 47.1. The inner surface of the outer wall of the nose. I, upper turbinate bone; II, middle turbinate bone; III, lower turbinate bone. The olfactory area lies above the upper turbinate. The arrows indicate the course taken by the air in breathing. The area of mucosa above the upper turbinate contains the receptors of smell.

How we smell. The nasal mucous membrane is raised into three ridges, or hummocks, by three small bones (conchae) that spring from the outer wall of the nose. They divide each half of the nose incompletely into four chambers, or passages, placed one above the other and running from front to back (Fig. 47.1). The inspired air flows through the lower three passages but not through the upper-most one, which lies beneath the floor of the skull. The sense organs of smell are situated in the mucous membrane (olfactory mucous membrane) of this upper passage. Substances, in order that they may stimulate the sensitive cells in this chamber, must be carried there in a gaseous form mixed with the inspired air. Since the uppermost chambers of the nose are, as it were, blind alleys or pockets, through which the main air currents do not pass, the question arises as to how the odorous gases reach the sensitive cells. Experiments have shown that they are carried upward by eddies from the lower air currents. We have all noticed the air currents rising from a radiator, or wherever cold and warm air meet. Similar air movements occur in the nose when the cold outside air meets

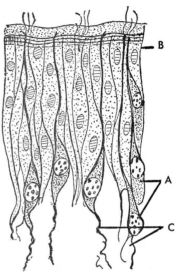

Fig. 47.2. A section of the mucosa from the olfactory area of the nose. A, sensitive cells (receptors of smell); B, supporting cells; C, nerve fibers.

the warmer air within the nasal passages. These upward-moving currents carry the molecules of the odorous substances to the *olfactory cells* (see below). In order to smell more acutely we purposely take a short breath or sniff, which draws in colder air and increases the number and force of the ascending currents.

Some individuals are incapable of smelling certain scents. Prussic acid, employed to kill vermin, though it has a strong odor of almonds to a person with a normal sense of smell, is inodorous to a few others. For this reason deaths occasionally result from breathing this highly poisonous gas, since those who cannot smell it may enter a room containing it in dangerous concentration and be quite unaware of its presence. The olfactory receptors after a short time become, as a rule, insensitive to any particular smell, though they remain quite sensitive to any other odor.

The olfactory cells—receptors of smell. The olfactory cells are elongated cells with plump, rounded nuclei, embedded in the mucous membrane of the uppermost passage of the nose. Each cell possesses a long thread of protoplasm that passes outward to the mucous membrane. From the other end of the cell a delicate nerve fiber proceeds upward, and passing through minute holes in the floor of the skull (cribriform plate of ethmoid), ends in the brain (olfactory lobe) (Figs. 47.1, 47.2). The sensitive cells are supported by other cells that surround them. These have tufts of minute hairs (cilia), which project from the mucosa.

THE SENSE OF TASTE

In order for a substance to be tasted, it must first be dissolved. If a solid material is placed in a perfectly dry mouth, it cannot be tasted. In ordinary circumstances the saliva dissolves materials taken into the mouth as food and arouses the sense of taste.

The organs of taste. The organs of taste are carried chiefly upon the tongue, though the mucous membranes of the soft palate, the tonsils, and the epiglottis also contain a few. If the reader examines the surface of his tongue in a mirror he will see tiny projections that give it an appearance resembling the pile of plush. These projections, called **papillae** (Plate IV*c*), are absent from the undersurface of the tongue. Farther back on the upper surface of the tongue the projections become much larger, and each is surrounded by a groove and outside the groove by a ridge, giving the resemblance of a little squat tower surrounded by a moat and a wall. Embedded here and there is the covering (epithelium) of both the small papillae at the tip and the larger ones toward the back of the tongue, are small collections of slender cells packed side by side in bundles.

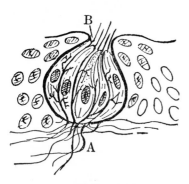

Fig. 47.3. A taste bud from the surface of the tongue. A, nerve fibers from taste receptors; B, taste pore.

These are the sensitive cells of taste, and the oval bundles they compose are called the **taste buds** (Fig. 47.3). Each cell is supplied with fine branches of the nerves of taste (chorda tympani and glossopharyngeal). The taste bud opens upon the surface of the papillae by a tiny pore, and all its cells, coming together here, end in a number of fine hairlike projections. Substances in solution enter these pores of the taste buds and stimulate the hairlike ends of the cells within.

The fundamental sensations of taste. There are only four fundamental taste sensations—**sweet, bitter, sour,** and **salty.** The various other tastes that we experience are due to a blending of these four in different proportions, and also to their combination with other sensations in the mouth besides those of taste proper. For instance, pepper and ginger are recognized more by the burning sensation that they arouse than by their actual tastes. They excite other nerves in the mouth besides those of taste. Oils are unpleasant to a large extent because of their feel. Acids are astringent, and soda water "nips." Alkalis have a bitter, soapy taste. Some of the finer flavors are in reality sensations of smell. The back of the nose communicates with the mouth, and as we eat or drink, aromas ascend to stimulate the olfactory cells. For that reason, when the nose is held or the mucous membrane of the nose is inflamed, as by an ordinary cold, the sense of taste is blunted. In certain fish the outer surface of the body is furnished with taste organs. In the catfish, for example, long processes containing taste buds are found upon the head and back and near the tail.

The fundamental taste sensations are not aroused equally well over all regions of the tongue's surface. Sweet substances, for instance, are tasted best by the tip and front part of the tongue. The small boy licking a stick of candy demonstrates this fact. Salty tastes are also best perceived by the tip, whereas the sides of the tongue are more sensitive to sour tastes. Bitterness is tasted most strongly at the back of the tongue and in the throat. A bittersweet substance tastes sweet when first taken into the mouth, the bitter element being most noticeable after the substance has passed over the back of the tongue and has been swallowed. The central area of the tongue is scarcely at all sensitive to taste.

CUTANEOUS SENSATIONS

The sensations that can be aroused by stimulating the skin are five in number—namely, **touch, pressure, pain, heat,** and **cold.** Touch may be defined as the sensation elicited by lightly brushing the skin with a wisp of cotton wool, or by pressing a stiff hair vertically upon the skin. The sensitivity to touch of a particular cutaneous area is tested by using hairs of graded thicknesses (von Frey's hairs), and finding the one that arouses a sensation when applied with just sufficient pressure to bend it.

If a more rigid object, such as a matchstick, is pressed against the skin the sensation aroused is one of pressure. Pressure, though usually classed as a cutaneous sensation and often confused with touch, is, in reality, due to the stimulation of receptors (Pacinian corpuscles) situated in the subcutaneous tissues. These sense organs are also found in other parts, for example, in the periosteum, beneath tendons, and in the mesentery. If the rigid object is pressed still more firmly into the skin, or if the skin is pricked with a sharp pointed instrument such as a pin, pain is experienced.

The cutaneous sense receptors. The sensations of touch, pressure, heat, and cold are each dependent upon a special type of sense organ in which the nerve fiber terminates after losing its neurilemma and myelin sheath. The sensation of pain, on the other hand, is transmitted by fibers that

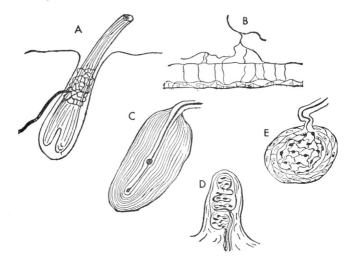

Fig. 47.4. The receptors of the skin. A, bare nerve fiber for pain surrounding the root of a hair; B, pain fiber in the cornea of the eye, similar fibers are found in the deeper layer of the skin; C, receptor (Pacini's corpuscle) that responds to pressure; D, receptor for light touch (Meissner's corpuscle); E, cold receptor (of Krause).

terminate as bare axis cylinders. That is, the nerve fiber mediating pain loses its neurilemma and myelin sheath, but does not end in a structure of special design. The receptors of touch, pressure, and temperature respond each to one type of stimulus, but the nerve endings giving rise to pain respond also to any other type of stimulation—mechanical, thermal, electrical, or chemical—provided it is intense enough. Thus the sensation of pain is protective in function, serving to signal a threat of injury to the body. The several types of cutaneous receptor are shown in Figure 47.4.

The localization of cutaneous sensations. The different types of cutaneous sense organ are separated from one another by measurable distances. By applying the appropriate stimulus to points upon the skin, the positions of the receptors can be determined. The small cutaneous areas mapped out in this way are referred to as "spots." Thus, when the sensitivity of the skin to touch is investigated with a von Frey hair, the sensation is elicited only from certain points; these are called touch spots, while those which respond to heat or cold or to pain are called, respectively, hot, cold, and pain spots. The touch spots are most numerous over the tips of the fingers and in the mucous membrane of the tip of the tongue. In cutaneous regions covered with hair—that is, almost the entire skin surface except the palms of the hands and the soles of the feet—the touch spots lie on the "windward" side of the hairs (the hairs slant in one or another direction like grass bent by a breeze). For this reason, light contact with the hair tips causes a sensation of touch. The hair when moved, acting as a tiny lever, transmits the movement to the skin at its base; thus the touch end organ is stimulated. Pain fibers form a rich network in the skin; they also ramify within the hair sockets around the hair roots.

The localization of cutaneous sensations is effected with remarkable accuracy. The localization of touch is tested by bringing a wisp of cotton wool or a von Frey hair in contact with the skin while the subject's eyes are closed, and then asking him to place a finger upon the spot touched. Pain and pressure are also very accurately localized, but the sensations aroused by heat and cold are more diffuse. Cutaneous localization is an *acquired* faculty, being developed through an association, previously established in the brain, between the point upon the skin and the muscular movement required to touch it. In other words, it is based upon memories of muscular movements resulting from conditioned responses to cutaneous stimuli.

Aristotle's experiment illustrates our dependence upon experience for the interpretation of tactile stimuli. A small object, such as a pea, held between the adjacent sides of the first and second fingers is felt as one, because a touch stimulus when applied simultaneously to both of these surfaces has always in our experience been associated with but a single object. But when the small object is held between the fingers, crossed as in Figure 47.5, the skin is stimulated at two points that experience tells us may be touched by two separate small objects but never by one alone. The single pea is, therefore, felt as two. Nerve cells in the sensory area of the cerebral cortex that receive impulses from the opposing sides of the fingers in their normal positions are probably very closely connected, whereas those receiving impulses from the other sides of the fingers are not in such intimate association.

Fig. 47.5. Illustrating Aristotle's experiment.

Spatial discrimination. This faculty is closely allied to the foregoing; it is the recognition of the separateness of two simultaneous stimuli. For example, if the points of a pair of compasses an inch apart are applied to the skin of the forearm, a single sensation is felt. If the distance between the compass points is increased to 1½ inches or more, and applied as before, two distinct sensations are experienced. *Two-point discrimination* is a faculty of essential importance. In acquiring information through the sense of touch, of the size, texture, and shape of various objects, it is indispensable. This faculty varies considerably in different regions, being most highly developed in the coverings of the more mobile parts of the body—that is, parts such as the fingers, lips, and tip of the tongue—which have received the most practice in investigating the immediate environment.

In the following table several different regions are compared with regard to the minimal distance by which two simultaneous stimuli must be separated in order to arouse a double sensation.

	Minimal distance, in millimeters
Tip of tongue............................	1.1
Palm side of finger tip....................	2.3
Red part of lips.........................	4.4
Tip of nose.............................	6.6
Palm of hand...........................	11.3
Heel	22.0
Back of hand	31.6
Forearm	39.6
Middle of back, upper arm, and thigh......	67.0

REPRODUCTION

PART XI

48
Fundamental Principles

Those several associated processes whereby a living thing perpetuates its kind are embraced within the term **reproduction.** The study of the physiology of reproduction must inevitably lead us to inquire into the related phenomena of heredity. No law of nature is more invariable than the one that decrees that the members of any species, whether of the animal or vegetable kingdom, shall create new individuals belonging to their own species alone. In its main features the younger generation always resembles the older. The one is almost the replica of the other. Briefly, "like begets like." These facts are common knowledge and are expressed in such well-known phrases as "a chip off the old block," "like father like son," and "as ye sow, so shall ye reap." Nevertheless, the principle of variation is just as unyielding; for though in their essential parts the progeny closely resemble the parents, there are always slight differences in form, structure, habits, temperament, etc. Even so-called identical twins are not cast in precisely the same mold. No two living things, since the world began, were ever exactly the same in all particulars. Upon this law of variation Darwin based his theory of the origin of the myriad species populating the globe.

THE ORIGIN OF LIFE

At one time it was almost universally believed that humble creatures such as snails, worms, and maggots were generated from inanimate materials. Maggots, as we all know, quickly appear upon a piece of meat when it becomes putrid. But everyone knows now that though they appear to form from the meat they are actually hatched from eggs laid by flies, and will soon develop into a younger generation of flies. Covering the meat with a wire screen was a very simple experiment that showed that the meat itself, no matter how decomposed it might become, did not give

630

rise to maggots. The flies, attracted by the putrid odor, laid their eggs upon the wire screen. Even mice were believed to come into being unbegotten and unborn. Indeed, one famous scientist[1] of the seventeenth century confidently offered a simple recipe for the creation of mice: some soiled linen and a few grains of wheat or a piece of cheese, placed in a closed container, were supposedly all that were required to perform this miracle. Ben Jonson's alchemist voices the belief of his times in these lines:

> Art can beget bees, hornets, beetles, wasps,
> Out of the carcasses and dung of creatures.

The discovery of the microscope permitted these beliefs to be carefully investigated. It was soon shown how untrue they were. **Spontaneous generation,** the term that was applied to this supposed creation of living organisms from nonliving material, commenced to pass into the realm of myths and superstition, to be believed in by only the ignorant and credulous. Not, however, until after the middle of the last century did the question cease entirely to trouble the scientific mind, for, with Pasteur's discovery of the germs of disease it was believed by some that bacteria, the most elementary of all living things, could arise from nonliving material. The great Frenchman soon convinced those whose minds were open to conviction that even a germ must have forebears. Even this mere speck of life can be created only from others of its kind.

Pasteur performed the following experiment: A fluid material in which germs will live and multiply freely was placed in flasks. The fluids and the flasks were then heated until all microscopic life had been destroyed. The flasks had long curved necks, which were each drawn out to a fine point; only a tiny opening directed downward was left for the entrance of air (Fig. 48.1). Consequently, it was practically impossible

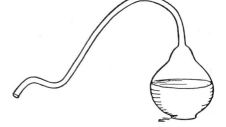

Fig. 48.1. Shape of the flask used by Pasteur in his experiments upon spontaneous generation.

for specks of dust that might carry microorganisms to reach the fluid in the flasks. After four years there were no signs of life in the fluid. Examination showed it to contain no living thing. Other flasks containing similar fluid, but left open for the free entrance of air, were soon teeming with microscopic life.

[1] Van Helmont.

REPRODUCTION IN PRIMITIVE FORMS OF LIFE

Bacteria (Ch. 11) belong to the vegetable kingdom and multiply by simply dividing into two individuals, each of which very soon divides again. Thus, starting with a single bacterium, the next generation would number 2 individuals, the next 4, the succeeding ones 8, 16, 32, 64, and so on. Should the conditions for continuous multiplication—such as food supply, warmth, and moisture—be suitable, multiplication would proceed in this way indefinitely; and, by the method of doubling the individuals in each succeeding generation, it requires only a simple calculation in arithmetic to show that enormous numbers would be created, which in a very short time would smother all other forms of life. Fortunately, conditions are not suitable for unrestricted bacterial growth. The food supply becomes inadequate, and the bacteria themselves produce substances that discourage their growth and destroy many already formed. Also, lack of moisture and other adverse circumstances stifle their productivity before it reaches the gruesome lengths that arithmetic seems to predict. But even so, at the end of a few hours millions of bacteria may have arisen from a few original individuals.

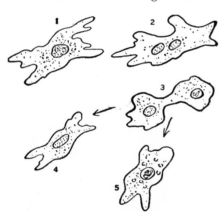

Primitive forms of animal life, such as the single-celled *amoeba* (Ch. 2), also reproduce their kind by simply dividing into two parts, each of which becomes a separate, free-living individual. This type of reproductive process is called **fission**. The nucleus of the amoeba first divides into two parts, each of which forms a separate nucleus. These separate from each other, the cytoplasm between them is severed, and two new cells are formed, which live apart (Fig. 48.2). This one-celled (*unicellular*) organism

Fig. 48.2. The reproduction of a primitive organism (e.g., an amoeba) by fission.

and similar ones of its class never age or die, in a sense, unless some accident befalls them.

Increase in size of the parent cell and failure of its protoplasm to receive sufficient nourishment appear to decide the time for its division. Nourishment, of course, can be received only from the water with which the organism is surrounded. Therefore, as the mass of the organism increases, the surface of its body, through which alone food materials can be supplied, must become in proportion to the volume progressively less.[2] By the division of the cell into two parts, the mass of protoplasm forming the original cell obtains a much greater surface area for exposure to the sources of food material. The processes of growth and reproduction are therefore closely related. In other forms of primitive animal life (for example, *volvox*) the newly formed cells do not live an independent existence, but cling together to form one large organized *colony*. Though in a colony like this the cells have practically all the same functions, there being no division of labor as in the bodies of higher forms of life, it is probable that it represents the first step in the creation of many-celled (*multicellular*) types.

Some other one-celled animals propagate their species by the process of **conjugation.** Two individuals come together side by side or end to end, and in some instances the part of one fits into the other, as a key

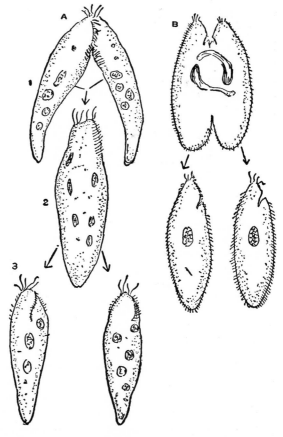

Fig. 48.3. Two types of conjugation. *A*, the animals shown in (1) have fused completely to produce an individual (2), which has then divided by fission to produce the two new individuals shown in (3). *B*, these animals (paramecia) do not fuse, but come together and exchange a part of the chromatin of their nuclei; they then separate again, and each individual divides by fission.

[2] It is scarcely necessary to point out that a small body has a greater surface area in proportion to its mass or volume than a larger body of the same shape. The surface area of a pebble, for instance, is much smaller than the sum of the surface areas of all the fine pieces that would result from crushing the pebble.

fits a lock. The two conjoined cells may then become fused into a single mass (Fig. 48.3), which later divides into two. These, in turn, divide into two by fission, and each of the progeny again into two, and so on. This process of conjugation in one-celled animals resembles very closely the junction of the male and female sex cells (see below), which is the first stage in the development of the offspring of higher animals and of man.

Still other animal forms reproduce by forming small buds that separate from the parent and later grow to adult individuals. In certain species of worm, for instance, a head develops near the center of the body. The head and front section of the body then separate from the hind portion, to swim away as a new individual. Some sponges also form small buds that, after reaching a certain size, separate from the parent and later develop to adult size and form. **Budding** is the term applied to such types of reproduction. In these lower forms of animal life the individuals all resemble one another very closely. There are no sex differences.

Two of the three types of reproduction described above—fission and budding—have no sexual basis and are consequently called **asexual** in type. Conjugation may be looked upon as the most primitive type of **sexual** reproduction. True, no structural difference between the two cells of the union can, as a rule, be detected, yet reproduction by the fusion of two separate cells is the essential feature of sexual reproduction. For this reason conjugation must be placed in the latter category.

SEXUAL REPRODUCTION

Animals of higher classes than those mentioned in the preceding section, such as many worms and insects, reptiles, frogs, birds, and mammals, are divided into two groups—the male and the female sexes. The ordinary cells composing the bodies of these animals do not enter into the formation of the offspring. These animals are furnished with special cells—the **sex cells**—to serve for the reproduction of their kind and the continuation of their species. Nature has provided animals with means for preserving their bodies against injury and premature death. The instinct of self-preservation is strong in all forms of animal life. But the perpetuation of the species is of greater importance in nature's scheme than the preservation of the individual. The sexual instincts, the protection of the female by the male and of the eggs or the young by the mother, are all part of life's plan to ensure that one generation shall hand on to the next the torch that it received at birth. The individual dies, but the cells of sex, which continue the existence of the race, are passed from parent to offspring through countless past ages, and, like the amoeba, in a sense never die so long as they divide and the parts redivide.

The material from which the sex cells arise and which, like a living stream, has flowed from generation to generation bearing the numberless individuals of our race has been called the **germ plasm.** The essential part of the germ plasm is the chromatin material of the cell nuclei (Chs. 2, 49). At an early stage in the development of the individual the germ plasm, it is believed, is set apart from those cells (the **body plasm**) that are destined to form the general structure of the animal's body.[3] It plays no part in the building up the various tissues—muscle, bone, nerve, etc.— but is concerned with the greater work of producing sex cells and ensuring immortality to the race (Fig. 48.4).

The cells of sex. The sex cells, or **gametes** as they are also called, are formed in suitably designed organs—the *essential,* or *primary, sex organs.* Individuals of each sex have their own special type of organ called the *ovary* in the female and the *testis* in the male (see Ch. 49). Each of these develops its own type of gamete or sex cell. The female gamete is called the **egg,** or **ovum,** and the male gamete the **spermatozoon,** or **sperm.**

The ovum is a single, usually spherical cell, which varies in size in different species but is usually many times larger than the spermatozoon

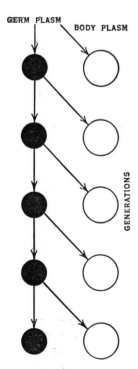

Fig. 48.4. Diagram to illustrate the continuity of the germ plasm.

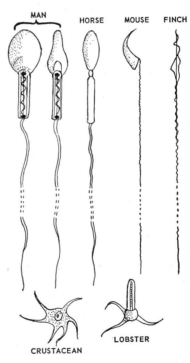

Fig. 48.5. Showing human and other spermatozoa.

[3] This separation into two types of cells, one of which goes to form sex cells, the other body cells, has actually been seen in some forms of life.

(Fig. 48.5). The ova (eggs) of reptiles and birds, as compared with the ova of most other animal classes, are of enormous size. The yellow part of the hen's egg, for instance, is a huge cell, containing a large store of nutritive material—the yolk—whereas the human ovum is so small (0.02 mm) as to be scarcely visible to the naked eye and contains only traces of yolk. The hen's egg is about $\frac{1}{50}$ of the adult bird's weight. The human body is millions of times larger than its ovum. The human spermatozoon is described in Chapter 49, and the spermatozoa of several species are shown in Figure 48.5.

In birds and most reptiles though fertilization (Ch. 49) takes place within the female body, the eggs are laid outside,[4] whereas in frogs and most fish the eggs are passed into the water. Upon these the male deposits a fluid containing the spermatozoa. This method of effecting the fertilization of the ova is termed **spawning.**

In most mammals the ovum, as well as being fertilized within the mother's body, is also developed therein, and the new individual is not born until almost or quite perfectly formed. During its development the unborn mammal receives its nourishment from the blood of the mother. The yolk of the mammalian egg is consequently very limited in quantity, large reserves of food material being unnecessary. The yolks of reptiles' and birds' eggs, on the other hand, must be large, since the developing animal enclosed within the shell is isolated from all other sources of nourishment, yet must be sustained until hatched and able to fend for itself.

These different modes by which fertilization of the ovum is brought about necessitate different types of reproductive apparatus. Those of mammals are considered in the next chapter.

Hermaphroditism. Some lower animal forms—certain worms, mollusks, crustacea, etc.—like most plants, contain both male and female reproductive tissue in the same body. Sometimes both testes and ovaries are functional, producing spermatozoa and ova; sometimes only the testes *or* ovaries produce sex cells. This combination of the sex organs (gonads) is called **hermaphroditism,** and the individual an *hermaphrodite* (Gk. god and goddess, *Hermes* and *Aphrodite*). An hermaphrodite may fertilize its own eggs or those of another.

In man, hermaphroditism occurs as a rather rare developmental abnormality. The two types of tissue, testicular or ovarian, may be present as separate organs (testes and ovaries) or fused to form *ovotestes.* The external sex organs—penis, clitoris, etc.—are indeterminate between male and female as a result of the double hormonal influence. Such a condition is called *true hermaphroditism.* It is of genetic origin. On the other hand, only one type of sex gland, testes *or* ovaries, may exist, though

---

[4] Some reptiles bear their young alive.

the external genital organs show both male and female features. This is called *pseudohermaphroditism*. It most frequently has an endocrine basis. Occasionally certain regions of the body, even an entire half, has male characteristics, while other regions or the opposite half are female. Such persons are called *gynandromorphs* (Gr. *gynē,* a woman + *anēr* (*and-*), a man + *morphē,* form). It is often difficult to decide in which sex a pseudohermaphrodite should be placed and, if a child, whether dress, education, training, etc., should be along male or female lines. Recently a means has been discovered whereby the dominant sex can be determined. There is present in the body cells of females, but not in those of males, a dot of chromatin within the nucleus in contact with or close to the nuclear membrane. It is called the **sex chromatin.** By excising a small piece of skin and examining it microscopically for the presence or absence of this body, the real sex of the individual can be ascertained (see also Ch. 49).

49
Reproduction in Mammals

The organs in which the sex cells of animals are produced —ova or spermatozoa—are called the **primary sex organs, or gonads.** The female gonads are also known as the **ovaries;** the male gonads are called **testes.** The other organs of sex, such as the uterus in the female and the external genital structures in both sexes, which are necessary for the completion of the reproductive process and which depend for their full development and growth upon the hormones secreted by the gonads, are called the **accessory organs of sex.** Those characteristic and generally recognized differences between the sexes—namely, the deep voice and the growth of hair upon the face in men, and the development of the mammary glands and hips of women—as well as the appearance of hair upon the pubes and in the axillae of both sexes are also dependent upon the action of the male or female hormones. These signs of sexual maturity are termed the **secondary sex characters.**

The human female organs of reproduction

The ovaries, or female gonads. The human ovaries are two bodies about the size and the shape of shelled almonds. They are situated, one on each side, in a shallow depression on the lateral wall of the pelvis (Fig. 49.1), and attached to the posterior layer of the broad ligament of the uterus by a short peritoneal fold called the **mesovarium.** A rounded cord runs between the layers of the broad ligament of the uterus (p. 643) from the ovary to the upper part of the lateral border of the uterus; it contains smooth muscle and is called the **ligament of the ovary** (Fig. 49.4). A fold of peritoneum (the **infundibulopelvic ligament**) passes from the pelvic wall to the ovary; it carries the ovarian vessels and nerves.

638

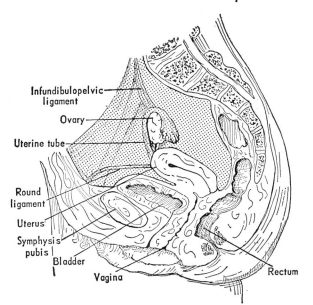

Fig. 49.1. The female reproductive organs.

Infundibulopelvic ligament
Ovary
Uterine tube
Round ligament
Uterus
Symphysis pubis
Bladder
Vagina
Rectum

Fig. 49.2. Successive stages in the development of the ovum within the Graafian follicle. *EP,* germinal epithelium covering the surface of the ovary; C, a cord of cells growing from the germinal epithelium into the substance of the ovary; G, the primordial ovum encircled by a single layer of cells which later develops into a Graafian follicle (sketches 2 to 4); F, the connective tissue stroma of the ovary which contains the interstitial cells.

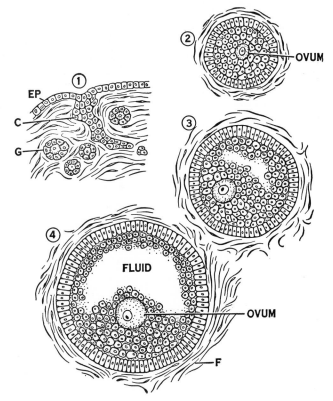

The ova are developed from cuboidal epithelial cells—the **germinal epithelium**—covering the surface of the ovary. Columns of these cells penetrate deeply into the connective tissue, or **stroma**, of the ovary. Small groups of cells separate from the columns and become arranged with a large cell in the center and others in a single layer around it. These structures are found in great numbers in the fetal ovary and in the ovaries of children. They are called *primary, primitive,* or **primordial, Graafian follicles** (Fig. 49.2). The central, somewhat larger cell is a *primitive,* or **primordial, ovum.** In the sexually mature female—that is, from the time of puberty to the menopause—some of the primitive follicles, under the influence of the follicle-stimulating hormone (FSH) of the hypophysis, become, from time to time, mature. Two more layers of cells derived from the ovarian stroma develop around the original one encircling the ovum. The outer of these is fibrous and is known as the **theca externa;** the inner layer, called the **theca interna,** is more vascular and cellular in character. The cells of the original layer surrounding the primitive ovum multiply to form a mass several strata deep. This cell mass is soon separated into two parts by the collection of fluid—the **liquor folliculi**—near its center. A heaped-up hillock of cells remains at one side of the follicle in which the ovum lies embedded. It is called the **discus proligerus** (L. *proles,* offspring + *gero,* I bear) or the **cumulus oöphorus** (L. *cumulus,* a heap + Gk. *oöphoros,* egg-bearing). The other group of cells separated off by the liquor folliculi is pressed against the wall of the follicle that it lines; it is known as the **membrana granulosa** (Fig. 49.3). The single layer of regularly arranged cells in immediate contact with the ovum is called the **corona radiata.**

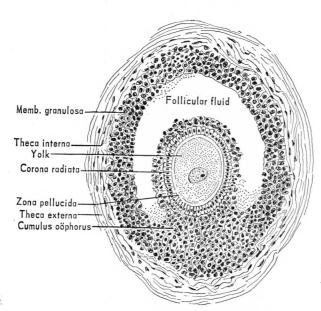

Fig. 49.3. A Graafian follicle containing a developing ovum.

The ovum itself when discharged from the ovary is immature. Maturation occurs during its progress along the uterine, or Fallopian, tube (see p. 642).

Ovarian hormones. The phenomena of the estrous and menstrual cycles, described later in this chapter, are dependent upon hormones produced in the ovary. The Graafian follicles of the ovary increase in size during proestrus (or, in the human subject, in the phase of the menstrual cycle immediately following menstruation) and become filled with fluid; the ova enlarge and approach maturity. A hormone called *estradiol*, or the *follicular hormone*,[1] is produced at this time by the cells lining the follicles. When a follicle reaches maturity, it ruptures and discharges the ovum. This event, called **ovulation**, occurs in animals during estrus, and in women midway between the menstrual periods. The cells lining the ruptured follicle then multiply and form a mass or body called the **corpus luteum** (yellow body), for the cells composing it contain a yellow, fatty material known as **lutein**. The yellow body, or corpus luteum, replaces the small blood clot that filled the follicle immediately after its rupture and the discharge of the ovum. The corpus luteum is virtually a small temporary ductless (endocrine) gland (Fig. 49.9), for it produces an internal secretion—the *hormone of the corpus luteum*. This is more commonly referred to as *progesterone*, which has been prepared in pure crystalline form.

Estradiol is responsible for the changes in the accessory organs of reproduction during proestrus and estrus, for the psychic phenomena of estrus, and for the development of the secondary sex characters of the mature female. It is therefore sometimes called the *female sex hormone*, and corresponds to the male hormone elaborated by the testes (p. 656). It has long been known that removal of the ovaries of a young animal prevents it from becoming sexually mature. The accessory organs fail to develop, estrus does not occur, the secondary sex characters do not appear, and the sex instinct is never manifested. Injections of the female sex hormone into such an animal correct all these effects of ovariectomy. On the other hand, young immature animals treated with estradiol show precocious sexual development. The role played by estradiol in pregnancy and parturition is described at the end of this chapter.

---

[1] Several substances closely similar chemically and possessing the physiological activity of the follicular hormone have been obtained from the ovaries, as well as from female urine and other body fluids and tissues. *Estrone* (also known as *theelin*), which differs from estradiol in chemical structure to a minor extent, was formerly thought to be the naturally occurring hormone produced by the maturing Graafian follicle. Estradiol has been synthesized and has also been isolated in crystalline form from the urine of pregnant women.

Estrin is an earlier term given to the follicular hormone before its chemical structure was fully known. It is still in use as a physiological term but carries no precise chemical meaning. *Estrogen* is another name with a purely physiological connotation; it is applied to any agent, whether of biological or other origin, which is capable of inducing estrus and often other effects of the follicular hormone.

Progesterone prepares the uterus for the reception of the fertilized ovum. It is responsible for the uterine changes characteristic of postestrus or pseudopregnancy, for one phase of menstruation in women, and for the development of the placenta—the organ that enables the embryo to receive nourishment from the mother during pregnancy (p. 668). For example, if a pregnant rabbit is castrated (ovariectomized) early in pregnancy or if the corpora lutea are excised, the embryo dies and is expelled from the uterus (*abortion*). Progesterone can be prepared most conveniently from hogs' ovaries. This preparation, when injected into ovariectomized animals after they have become pregnant, permits pregnancy to continue to full term. Normally if fertilization of the ovum occurs, the corpus luteum continues to increase in size until the later months of pregnancy, its hormone exerting a constant influence upon the growth and functional integrity of the placenta. On the other hand, if the ovum remains unfertilized the life of the corpus luteum is short. After exerting its hormonal influence for a time and causing the uterine changes characteristic of pseudopregnancy, it undergoes degeneration. In the human subject, changes in the uterine mucosa occur after ovulation analogous to those of pseudopregnancy, but again, failure of the ovum to become fertilized is followed by degeneration of the corpus luteum. The uterine mucosa then reverts to its resting state; it is at this time that menstruation occurs (Figs. 49.8, 49.9, 49.10).

Progesterone also brings the mammary glands to full maturity during pregnancy, induces multiplication of the uterine muscle fibers, and inhibits contractions of the uterus.

The uterine, or Fallopian, tubes. These tubes (called oviducts in animals) are two slender ducts, one on each side, possessing a trumpet-shaped mouth with a fringed rim—the **fimbriated extremity**—that lies in close relation to the ovary (Fig. 49.1). This expanded upper end of the Fallopian tube receives the ovum, which is then conveyed along the duct by the movement of the cilia in its mucosa, as well as by peristaltic contractions of its muscular wall. The Fallopian tubes open medially into the upper part of the *uterus* (womb). They are enclosed between the two layers of the broad ligament of the uterus; this part of the broad ligament is called the **mesosalpinx** (Gr. *salpinx,* a tube). Conjugation of the ovum with the male germ cell (*spermatozoon*), or **fertilization** of the ovum, as this event is usually termed, is thought to take place in the Fallopian tube. In birds, the oviducts transmit the fertilized ovum to the exterior, but in women and in most other mammals, it is delivered into the uterus.

The uterus. The uterus is a hollow pear-shaped organ though somewhat flattened from front to back (Fig. 49.4). Its walls are formed of smooth muscle and are lined by mucous membrane; the latter is called

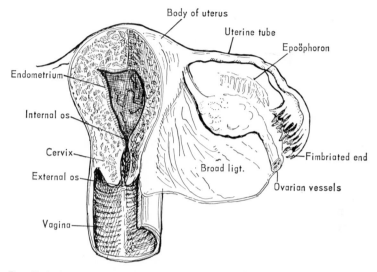

Fig. 49.4. The uterus, vagina, and broad ligament; uterus and vagina opened.

the **endometrium**. The small narrower end, the neck, or **cervix**, of the uterus, is directed downwards and backwards, opening by its mouth, or **os**, into the upper end of the *vagina*. The latter is a narrow sheathlike canal of muscle and mucous membrane that receives the male copulatory organ, or *penis*. The fertilized ovum upon reaching the cavity of the uterus establishes connections with the uterine mucosa and develops into the fetus (p. 667). The reaction of the endometrium will be described in greater detail later.

The **ligaments of the uterus.** The uterus is connected to the pelvic walls and to the rectum and bladder by six ligaments—an *anterior* and a *posterior* ligament, two *broad* ligaments, and a pair of *round* ligaments.

The **anterior ligament** is a fold of peritoneum stretching from the uterus near the cervix to the bladder. The **posterior ligament** passes from the upper part of the vagina to the rectum.

The **broad ligaments** are two wide folds of peritoneum that extend from the sides of the uterus to the lateral walls of the pelvis. They together with the uterus divide the pelvic cavity into an anterior and a posterior compartment, the former containing the urinary bladder, the latter the rectum. The upper border of the broad ligament encloses the uterine tube. A little below this, near the open end of the uterine tube, the ovary is attached to the posterior layer of the ligament by a fold called the *mesovarium* (see also the *ovaries,* above) .

The **round ligaments** are two narrow flat bands containing smooth muscle that run on each side from the upper part of the lateral border

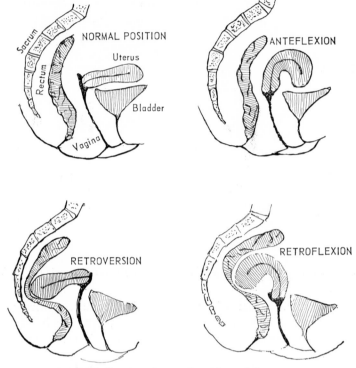

Fig. 49.5. Showing abnormal positions of the uterus.

of the uterus between the layers of the broad ligaments to the deep abdominal ring (Ch. 5). They traverse the inguinal canal on each side and end in the *labium majus.*

In addition to the ligaments just described, two folds of peritoneum that stretch from the uterus to the sacrum are sometimes called the **uterosacral ligaments.**

The growth of the uterus in the virgin state and during pregnancy. The virgin uterus reaches its full development at puberty as a result of the maturation of the Graafian follicles and the liberation of the follicular hormone, estradiol. At this time it weighs only 50 grams or less, but during pregnancy it shows phenomenal growth, reaching a weight exclusive of its contents, of some 1000 grams—a 20-fold increase. Almost immediately after impregnation of the ovum, before it has become attached to the endometrium, and even while it is still in the Fallopian tube, the uterine muscle shows very active *hyperplasia,* that is, a great increase in the number of fibers occurring through mitosis. Under microscopic examination thousands of mitotic figures are to be seen in a small sample of the uterine muscle. But this hyperplastic phase soon comes to an end. The growth of the uterus from this time on is confined entirely to thickening and lengthening of the existing muscle fibers. The increase in the *number* of fibers (mitosis) is due mainly to the action of progesterone. The enlargement of the individual fibers, and the consequent great increase in the size of the uterus, is the result of the distension caused by the progressive increase in bulk of the fetus, a stretch stimulus being thus applied to the uterine muscle. The effect of this stretch stimulus upon uterine growth is modified after a somewhat complicated fashion by both estradiol and progesterone. The growth of the uterine muscle ceases toward the end of the sixth month of pregnancy. But the fetus shows rapid growth from this time on, accompanied by a commensurate distension of the uterus. The stretch stimulus applied to the muscle fibers, though it elicits no growth response, induces other effects that lead eventually to the termination of pregnancy (p. 676).

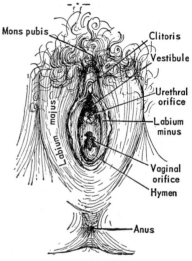

Fig. 49.6. The female external genital organs. The labia majora have been separated; normally their margins are in apposition.

Relaxin, the last female sex hormone to be discovered, is present in the blood of pregnant animals and women. It softens and relaxes the ligaments of the symphysis pubis and thus, by allowing expansion of the pelvis, facilitates the passage of the fetal head during the second stage of labor. It is formed in the uterus under the influence of estradiol and progesterone.

The external female genital organs. The several parts of the external genital structures are together called the **vulva,** or **pudendum;** they are the *mons pubis* (or *mons Veneris*), the *labia majora* and *labia minora,* the *vestibule,* and the *clitoris.*

The **mons pubis** is a cushionlike elevation overlying the symphysis, and that, after the age of puberty, is covered with hair.

The **labia majora** (sing. *labium majus*), which correspond to the scrotum of the male, are two longitudinal elevated folds of skin running backwards and downwards from the mons pubis to within an inch or so of the anus, where they merge (Fig. 49.6).

The **labia minora** (sing. *labium minus*) are two smaller cutaneous folds lying under cover of the labia majora, and extending backwards from the clitoris. The cleft between the labia minora is called the **vestibule of the vagina;** it contains the vaginal opening and just above the latter the orifice of the urethra.

The **clitoris** is placed between the anterior ends of the labia minora (Figs. 49.6 and 5.30). It corresponds to the penis in the male; it resembles a penis in miniature in that it consists of erectile tissue that forms two corpora cavernosa and a rudimentary glans. It possesses two crura that are attached to the ischial and pubic rami, and a diminutive prepuce. Each crus is covered by the bulbocavernosus muscle of the corresponding side. The function of this muscle is similar to that of the muscle in the male. The clitoris, however, is not traversed by the urethra. The bulb of the penis is represented in the female by the **bulb of the vestibule,** which consists of two oblong masses of erectile tissue situated one on either side of the vaginal opening.

The vagina. The vagina (L., a sheath) is a curved canal that leads downwards and forwards from the uterus to the external genital organs. Its posterior wall is somewhat longer (9.0 cm) than its anterior (7.5 cm). The vagina is composed of an inner circular and an outer longitudinal layer of smooth muscle, and is lined by mucous membrane, the epithelium of which is of the stratified squamous type. The opening of the vagina, which is situated between the labia minora, is partly closed in virgins by a lamina of mucous membrane called the **hymen.**

The structure and development of the mammary glands. The mammary glands of women, commonly known as the breasts, are composed of a mass of cells arranged to form follicles, or alveoli, that are drained by a branching system of ducts. The mammary tissue, capable of secreting milk under appropriate stimulation, is separated by means of partitions, or septa, of connective tissue into some twenty lobes in each breast (Fig. 49.7). Each lobe is divided again into a number of lobules. The breast is surmounted at its center by a small conical eminence composed of erectile tissue and covered by darkly pigmented skin; it is known as the **nipple,** and is surrounded by a circular area of similarly pigmented skin known as the **areola.** The whole mass of glandular tissue is embedded

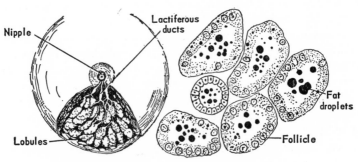

Fig. 49.7. *Left,* the human mammary gland, a segment of skin and subcutaneous tissue removed. *Right,* microscopic appearance of a group of alveoli containing newly formed fat.

and covered by a variable but often very abundant amount of fatty (adipose) tissue. In the active gland the milk is secreted into the centers of the follicles and drained away by the duct system. The milk is carried from each lobe by a single duct (**lactiferous duct**) to the nipple, from the apex of which it reaches the exterior through a minute pore.

The development of the mammary glands to the adult size and form commences at puberty. Their enlargement at this time is one of the chief secondary sex characteristics of the mammalian female. Before the age of puberty, the gland of the female shows little difference from that of the male either in the amount or in the histological appearance of the mammary tissue. In both sexes at this time, as well as in the adult male, the glands consist mainly of connective tissue with a limited number of rudimentary collapsed follicles and a few scattered sparsely branched ducts. With the onset of puberty, signs of cellular activity (hyperplasia) appear in the female gland. The duct system becomes more extensively branched, though the follicles remain rudimentary. Not unless pregnancy supervenes do the latter become fully developed and capable, under ordinary circumstances, of secreting milk. There are, therefore, two periods in the growth of the mammary glands, the first at puberty and confined to the duct system. This is brought about by the action of the follicular hormone (estradiol, see *ovarian hormones,* above). The very active growth of the follicles characteristic of the pregnant state is caused by progesterone. Due to the high concentration of estradiol in the blood during pregnancy the duct system also receives further stimulation at this time. Though milk is formed within the gland toward the end of pregnancy, none appears externally, as a rule, until the child or the young animal has been born. The mechanism underlying the *secretion* of milk (lactation) is described later.

The breasts do not form true milk at first, but for a couple of days or so after delivery secrete, instead, a sticky yellowish fluid called **colostrum.** Small quantities of colostrum can usually be expressed from the nipple as early as the third or fourth month of pregnancy. Colostrum is much richer in protein than milk and is coagulable by heat. It contains cells, *colostrum corpuscles,* filled with fat globules.

The composition of milk. Milk provides all the materials necessary for the growth of the infant up to the age of about 6 months. Human milk contains about 6.7 percent of *sugar* (lactose, or milk sugar), 1.5 percent of *protein* (mainly lactalbumin and casein), and about 4 percent of *fat.* Its main mineral is calcium (approximately 1 gram per quart of cow's milk). But it also contains adequate amounts of phosphorus, sodium, potassium, and magnesium. The chief difference between human and cow's milk is the higher concentration of protein (3.5 percent) in the latter. Both kinds of milk are poor in iron; it is for this reason that the infant after the age of about 6 months is likely to become anemic if fed upon milk alone. The baby comes into the world with a good supply of iron, but the stores of this mineral (derived from the hemoglobin freed by the disintegration of the excess of erythrocytes during the few days after birth) become exhausted after the first half year or so. The milk of healthy mothers usually contains the required amounts of vitamins A, B, and C, but tends to be low in vitamin D. This is also often true of cow's milk. Infants and young children should be given additional amounts of vitamin C for the prevention of scurvy, and of vitamin D to forestall the development of rickets.

The various constituents of the milk are derived from the blood flowing through the gland. In the secreting gland the fat can be seen as microscopic globules within the cells of the alveoli. As the globules collect and coalesce, the cells swell, and finally *bursting,* discharge their load of fat into the center of the alveolus (Fig. 49.7). This type of secretion, known as *apocrine,* is less common than that in which the cells extrude their product, saliva, for example, and remain intact.

The sexual phenomena of the mature female. The organs of sex in both the male and the female animal mature at a definite age that varies in different species. At this time, which is called **puberty,** the reproductive functions commence. Sex desire is aroused and mating occurs. The *reproductive period* extends throughout the greater part of the animal's life; it ends with atrophic changes in the sex organs and the gradual suppression of sexual activity. In the human species puberty occurs at from 13 to 15 years of age, being usually a little earlier in girls than in boys. The secondary sex characters already described now make their appearance.

In the majority of animal species, the female will receive the male only at a certain period or periods of the year. These so-called *mating seasons* are characterized by certain sexual phenomena that are generally referred to by animal breeders as "heat" and by physiologists as **estrus** (also spelled *oestrus*). Estrus and the sex phases immediately preceding and following it are together referred to as the **estrus cycle.** The phase preceding estrus is called **proestrus;** that following it, **postestrus.** The changes during proestrus consist of swelling and increased vascularity of the vulva and vagina. The uterus becomes enlarged and its glands hypertrophy. In some animals at this time, bleeding occurs from the uterus and appears externally. The changes of proestrus are preparatory in nature, the female organs being brought into a condition suitable for the reception of the male and the fertilization of the ovum. The Graafian follicles in the ovary (p. 640) are undergoing maturation. Estrus itself is the period during which ovulation occurs and the female will mate. The changes occurring during postestrus are anticipatory to the implantation of the fertilized ovum in the uterus. The uterine mucosa hypertrophies and its glands show increased secretory activity. During postestrus the corpus luteum is developing. The uterine changes in postestrus resemble those taking place during pregnancy which, indeed, are an extension or continuation of the former.

In a number of animals the postestrus preparation of the uterus for the implantation of the fertilized ovum, that is, for pregnancy, is a very prominent feature of the estrus cycle. Postestrus in such species is therefore called **pseudopregnancy.** If fertilization of the ovum by a sperm cell occurs, the uterine changes of postestrus merge into those of pregnancy. If fertilization does not result, the uterus returns to its resting state and all sexual activity subsides until the commencement (proestrus) of the next estrus cycle.

Some animals, such as the dog, are called *monestrous,* since a single estrus cycle occurs in each mating season. The term *anestrus* is applied to the quiescent periods intervening between the mating seasons. In other species, such as the cow, mouse, and rat, a series of estrus cycles occurs during each mating season; such animals are termed *polyestrous.* The interval elapsing between any two estrus cycles is then termed *diestrus,* and the period between mating seasons, as in the case of monestrous animals, is called anestrus.

The phases of the estrus cycle in a monestrous animal are shown in the following scheme and in Figure 49.8.

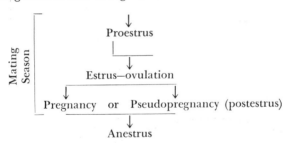

The menstrual cycle. The rhythmical series of changes in the sex organs that occurs about every 28 days throughout the reproductive life of women is analogous to the estrous cycle of lower animals. It is called the **menstrual cycle** (L. *mens,* month). In one phase of the menstrual cycle uterine bleeding occurs. This phase is referred to as **menstruation,** or the *menstrual period;* it has a duration of from 3 to 5 days. Ovulation occurs about midway between the menstrual periods—that is, some-

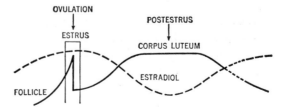

Fig. 49.8. Diagram of the estrus cycle in relation to hormone concentration. *(Modified from Corner.)*

where between the thirteenth and seventeenth days following the commencement of the bleeding (Fig. 49.9).

Though, as just mentioned, the menstrual cycle corresponds to the estrus cycle, the two differ in this respect, that bleeding, which is a prominent feature of the former, is absent or inconspicuous in the latter. It is not possible to say what phase of the estrus cycle (whether to proestrus or postestrus) menstruation itself corresponds. Since bleeding in certain species occurs in proestrus, it has been assumed by some that such bleeding is analogous to menstruation; others have thought that menstruation corresponds to the end of postestrus—that is, to the breakdown of the uterine mucosa built up during postestrus. There are objections to both these views.

Conspicuous histological changes occur in the uterine mucous membrane (*endometrium*) during the menstrual cycle. Though these changes have been very minutely described and divided into stages, it will suffice to give a brief outline here. The endometrium first becomes thicker and more vascular, the small arteries become tortuous and spirally coiled like springs; the surface epithelium hypertrophies. The glands of the mucous membrane elongate and show secretory activity. The hypertrophy of the epithelium and the vascular changes are due to the action of estradiol; the somewhat later glandular changes are caused by progesterone. Should fertilization and implantation of the ovum (p. 667) occur, the stimulating effects of the ovarian hormones become more pronounced, and merge with those of the pregnant state. If, on the other hand, the ovum is not

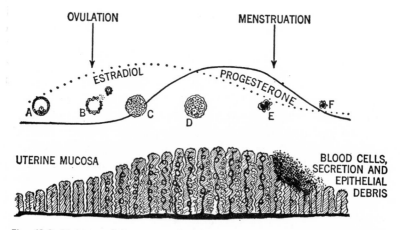

Fig. 49.9. Diagram of the menstrual cycle. The uterine mucosa is represented in the lower half of the figure. Note the thickening of the mucosa, the increasing tortuosity of the vessels and glands as progestin production increases. Breakdown of the mucosa with menstrual bleeding occurs as the corpus luteum degenerates or retrogresses. A, developing Graafian follicle; B, rupture of follicle and discharge of ovum; C and D, corpus luteum; E and F, degeneration of corpus luteum.

impregnated by a male sex cell spermatozoon, (p. 654), it degenerates, as does also the corpus luteum. The hypertrophied endometrium cannot be sustained in the absence of the latter; its epithelium is shed, and bleeding (menstruation) then occurs. Menstruation, therefore, is the sign that a fertilized ovum has not become implanted in the uterine mucous membrane, in other words, that pregnancy has not commenced. After from 3 to 5 days of menstrual bleeding, repair processes restore the surface epithelium, the vascular and glandular activities of the endometrium subside, and the uterus returns to the resting condition; the menstrual cycle has now been completed (Fig. 49.10).

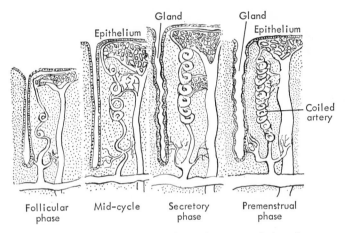

Fig. 49.10. Showing changes in the endometrium during the menstrual cycle.

The first menstrual cycle commences at puberty. Toward the end of the reproductive period, the cycles become irregular and finally cease at from 45 to 50 years of age; the suppression of the menstrual cycle at this time is called the **menopause.** This period is accompanied by atrophic changes in the ovaries and the accessory organs of reproduction. Psychic phenomena, depression, or irritability are common during this period. Instability of the vasomotor system, causing sudden flushing of the face, and a sensation of warmth—hot flushes—are of frequent occurrence.

The male reproductive organs

The testes. The testes are the gonads or sex organs of the male and, therefore, correspond to the ovaries of the female. They are two ovoid bodies that in such animals as fish, frogs, reptiles, and birds lie within the abdominal cavity. Even in the mammalian fetus they occupy this

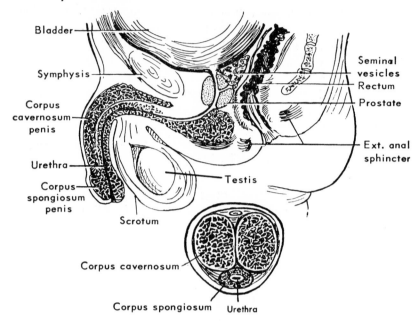

Bladder

Symphysis

Corpus
cavernosum
penis

Urethra

Corpus
spongiosum
penis

Scrotum

Seminal
vesicles

Rectum

Prostate

Ext. anal
sphincter

Testis

Corpus cavernosum

Corpus spongiosum   Urethra

Fig. 49.11. The male reproductive organs.

position. About two months before birth, in man, the testes leave the abdomen, and descending along the inguinal canal, enter the **scrotum.** The latter is a cutaneous pouch suspended from the pubic and perineal regions.

The interior of the testis is a compact mass of narrow and very tortuous tubules—the **convoluted seminiferous tubules.** Fibrous partitions divide the testicular substance into a great number of wedge-shaped lobes, each of which consists of from one to three convoluted tubules. The tubules of neighboring lobes unite to form a series of larger straight ducts that after a short course unite in a plexiform manner. The plexus —known as the **rete testis**—leads again into a number of ducts, small and straight at first, but that shortly become enlarged and tortuous (Fig. 49.12), and ultimately united into a single large convoluted duct. This is called the **epididymis;** it lies on the posterior aspect of the testis, its upper part, or *head,* being considerably larger than the lower part, or *tail.* From the tail a straight tube—the **vas deferens**—ascends along the posterior border of the testis to enter the abdomen, wherein it joins the duct of the seminal vesicle of the corresponding side (Fig. 49.13).

The seminiferous tubules are lined by several layers of cells. Those of the outermost layer—that is, the layer lying upon the basement membrane—are of two types; (a) cuboidal cells, supported by (b) columnar cells. The latter, which are known as the **cells of Sertoli,** extend inward

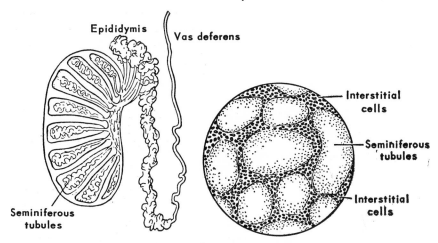

Fig. 49.12. *Left,* the internal structure of the testis. *Right,* microscopic appearance of the seminiferous tubules on cross section.

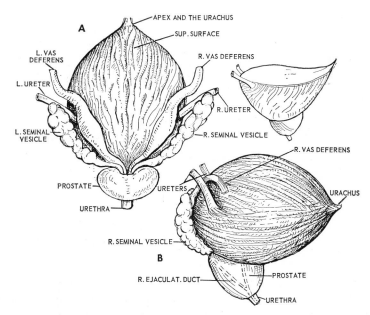

Fig. 49.13. The male bladder. A, the full viscus viewed from above and behind; B, lateral aspect. The urachus is a remnant of the urinary system of the fetus, which persists after birth and throughout adult life as a partly canalized fibrous cord extending enclosed in a fold of the peritoneum to the region of the umbilicus.

(that is, toward the lumen of the tubule) through the other layers. The former, called the **spermatogenic cells,** give rise through a series of divisions to the male sex cells, or **spermatozoa** (sing. *spermatozoon*). The inner cell layers forming the wall of the tubule consist of spermatogenic cells showing various stages in the maturation process, those most advanced in development lying nearer the lumen of the tubule. The cells, as they mature into spermatozoa, become detached from the tubule wall (Fig. 49.14). The spermatozoon is about 0.1 mm long; it has an oval flattened head and a long taillike process (see Fig. 48.5) by which it propels itself. The head is the essential part of the cell, consisting of a large nucleus surrounded by a narrow rim of protoplasm.

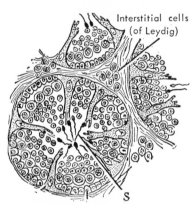

Fig. 49.14. Cross section of a seminiferous tubule of the testis showing the production of spermatozoa, *S,* from the lining cells.

The connective tissue lying between the convoluted tubules contains scattered cells with yellow granules in their cytoplasm. These are called **interstitial cells,** or the **cells of Leydig.** They are believed to furnish the male hormone, *testosterone* (p. 656).

The seminal vesicles. These are two coiled tubes with sacculated walls, situated between the lower part of the bladder and the rectum. The **ejaculatory ducts** are short tubes formed one on each side by the union of the duct of the seminal vesicle with the vas deferens; they open into the urethra (the canal of the penis) near the outlet from the bladder.

Ejaculation and the fertilization of the ovum. The spermatozoa are conveyed from the convoluted seminiferous tubules along the complex system of canals just described to the epididymis. The spermatozoa show no spontaneous movements in the convoluted tubules, but become actively motile in the epididymis. As coitus nears completion and the climax, or orgasm, of the act occurs, contractions of the epididymis and vasa deferentia propel the spermatozoa through the ejaculatory ducts into the urethra. At the same time, the seminal vesicles contract and expel a viscous secretion. The **semen,** which this fluid with its suspension of spermatozoa is now called, is ejected from the urethra with considerable force by the contractions of the urethral muscle and of striated muscle in the perineum. The ejection of the semen and the movements that bring it about constitute the *act of ejaculation.* It is a reflex act of which sensory nerves in the penis are its afferent limb, and sympathetic nerves its efferent limb. A thin secretion from the prostate gland and secretions of small urethral glands are added to the semen in the urethra. The secretion of the seminal vesicles appears to be essential for maintaining the life and motility of the spermatozoa, but the prostatic secretion and the secretions of the urethral glands are not of importance in this respect; they probably serve mainly as a lubricant.

The spermatozoa, deposited in the upper part of the vagina during coitus, propel themselves upward by lashing movements of their tails at the rate of about 6 inches per hour, and passing through the uterus, enter the Fallopian tube where *fertilization* occurs. It is probable that contractions of the uterus during coitus may draw the semen into the uterine cavity.

The head of the spermatozoon penetrates the ovum; in a short time its tail disappears and the changes described later in connection with fertilization follow. The semen contains an enzyme (hyaluronidase) that effects the removal of the mass cells (discus proligerus, p. 640) in which the ovum is embedded, thus facilitating its penetration by the spermatozoon.

The life of the spermatozoon after it has been deposited in the vagina is from 4 to 5 days. The ovum, on the other hand, if unfertilized, survives for only about 7 hours; after this it starts to degenerate.

The penis. The copulatory organ of the male, the penis, is composed of *erectile* tissue arranged as three longitudinal columns bound together by fibrous tissue, and covered with skin. Two of the columnar masses called the **corpora cavernosa penis,** lie side by side on the upper or anterior aspect of the organ. The third, called the **corpus spongiosum penis** (or *corpus cavernosum urethrae*) is under the other two, lodged in the groove between them; it is canalized by the urethra. The urinary bladder is evacuated through the urethra, which also transmits the semen during coitus. The extremity of the corpus cavernosum urethrae is expanded into a pyramidal structure called the **glans penis,** which is molded over the ends of the corpora cavernosa penis (Figs. 49.11 and 5.31). Near the base of the glans penis the skin of the penis forms a movable fold called the **foreskin,** or **prepuce.** It is common practice today to excise the prepuce a few days after birth; this operation is called *circumcision.*

The corpus spongiosum penis extends backwards into the perineum where it is expanded to form the **bulb of the penis** (see Fig. 5.31). The two corpora cavernosa diverge from one another posteriorly, and are attached to the ischial and pubic rami of the os coxae. These parts of the penis are called the **crura** (sing. *crus*). The bulb of the penis is covered by the **bulbospongiosus muscle.** This muscle consists of two lateral and symmetrical parts joined by a median raphe, its fibers arising from the latter and the perineal body. Running forwards, the fibers diverge and are inserted into the fascia covering the corpora cavernosa penis and the corpus spongiosum. The bulbospongiosus operates to expel urine from the urethra at the end of miturition, and by compressing the deep vein of the penis, to aid in producing erection of the organ. Each crus of the penis is covered by the **ischiocavernosus** muscle of the corresponding side; this muscle arises from the tuberosity and ramus of the ischium; by compressing the crus it aids in the erection of the penis.

Erectile tissue possesses a spongelike structure, showing a meshwork of wide blood spaces (cavernous spaces). These are fed by capillaries and arterioles, and drained by small veins. Smooth muscle fibers run in the walls of the blood spaces and surround their venous outlets. To this construction of erectile tissue is due its peculiar property, namely, the ability to alter in volume and consistency. Erection of the penis is brought about in the following way. The arterioles feeding the blood spaces dilate, and the muscle fibers in the walls of the latter relax. The muscle guarding the venous outlets contracts, thus tending to impede the outflow of blood. The spaces of the erectile tissue are expanded as the blood under high

pressure is driven through them. The organ, thus becoming turgid with blood, is rendered tense, hard, and erect.

The nerve fibers governing this mechanism are derived from the pelvic (parasympathetic) nerves. The sympathetic sends fibers that exert the reverse effect (contraction of the smooth muscle of the arterioles and in the walls of the blood spaces, accompanied by relaxation of that surrounding the venous outlets) with consequent relaxation of the penis.

Fig. 49.15. Left, the effect of castration upon the development of the comb and wattles of the cockerel. Right, the same bird after receiving a series of injections of male hormone.

The erectile organ of the female corresponding to the penis is called the *clitoris* (p. 646). It is situated above and just outside the entrance to the vagina. Erectile tissue is also present beneath the mucosa of the vagina.

The prostate. This is a body about the size of a chestnut and somewhat conical in shape. Its base is directed upward and lies in contact with the lowest part of the bladder. It embraces the first $1\frac{1}{2}$ inches of the urethra. The ejaculatory ducts pierce its upper and posterior part (Fig. 49.13). The prostate is composed of muscular and glandular tissues. It secretes a thin fluid into the urethra.

Prostatic enlargement, with consequent interference with the passage of urine, not uncommonly occurs in men past middle age. There has been much speculation as to the cause of enlargement of the prostate, but so far the problem has not been solved. Some hormonal imbalance is thought to be the fundamental cause.

The male hormone—testosterone. In 1929, McGee obtained the male hormone in crude form by the extraction of bulls' testes with acetone. This preparation was shown to cause the growth of the comb and wattles of the castrated cockerel (capon) (Fig. 49.15) and to bring about the normal development of the accessory organs (penis, seminal vesicles, and prostate) of castrated male rats. In immature rats treated with the extract, the accessory sex organs develop and sexual maturity is reached prematurely. The extract also stimulates the comb growth in hens and inhibits ovulation.

More recently, the hormone has been obtained in crystalline form from testicular tissue. This purified material is called **testosterone**, and has the empirical formula $C_{19}H_{30}O_2$. The hormone has also been obtained in crystalline form from male urine. Chemically, this latter material differs slightly from testosterone and has been designated **androsterone**; its activity is also much less (one seventh to one tenth) than that of testosterone. The male hormone does not appear in the urine of boys until after the tenth year, but oddly enough it is present in the urine of normal women. The male hormone belongs, with the ovarian hormones, to the class of substances known as *steroids*. Both testosterone and androsterone have been synthesized in the laboratory from cholesterol. This suggests the possibility that the male hormone is formed in the body from this substance, which is a constituent of nearly all animal tissues.

Cells in the interstitial tissue of the testes—the so-called *cells of Leydig*—are generally believed to manufacture the male hormone. That these cells and not the spermatogenic cells (p. 654) are responsible seems evident from the fact that castration effects do not follow irradiation of the testes with x rays, which destroys the spermatogenic cells but leaves the cells of Leydig unaffected.

The relation of the anterior lobe of the pituitary to the sexual functions

Gonadotrophic hormones. The anterior lobe of the pituitary of either male or female produces two hormones that act upon the gonads. In the female one of these **gonadotrophic hormones** stimulates the growth and maturation of the Graafian follicles in the ovary. Thus, indirectly, this hormone causes the production of the follicular hormone, *estradiol*. It is called the **follicle-stimulating hormone** (**FSH**) of the anterior pituitary. The other gonadotrophic hormone of the pituitary acts upon the second phase of the ovarian cycle, that is, it stimulates the growth of the corpus luteum. This hormone is known as the **lutein-stimulating hormone** (**LSH**). It, therefore, through its stimulating effect upon *progesterone* formation, indirectly causes the changes in the uterine mucosa characteristic of pseudopregnancy and of the corresponding phase of the menstrual cycle, or, if pregnancy ensues, of the development of the placenta (p. 668). Both gonadotrophic hormones, whether derived from female or male pituitaries, produce analogous effects upon the testes. The follicle-stimulating hormone acts upon the elements of the testes corresponding to the lining cells of the Graafian follicles, namely, the spermatogenic cells. The lutein-stimulating hormone acts upon the cells of Leydig and for this reason is also known as the **interstitial cell-stimulating hormone (ICSH)**.

Removal of the pituitary is followed by atrophy of the gonads and, secondarily, of the accessory sex organs (Fig. 49.16). Transplantation of tissue of the anterior lobe or injections of anterior lobe extracts prevent these otherwise inevitable results of hypophysectomy. The anterior lobe of the pituitary is therefore ultimately responsible for the sexual development of the male or female animal. The phenomena of puberty—namely, the development and maturation of the gonads and, through the intermediary of the hormones liberated by the latter, the growth of the accessory organs of sex and the development of the secondary sex characters—are dependent upon the gonadotrophic hormones.

Prolactin, the lactogenic hormone. The anterior lobe of the pituitary also liberates a hormone that stimulates milk secretion in the mother after the birth of the young. This hormone is called the **lactogenic principle,** or **prolactin.** It is obtained from the pituitary by extraction with an acid solution. If the pituitary is removed late in pregnancy, only a small quantity of milk is secreted after the young are born, and the secretion soon dries up. This hormone evidently also exerts an influence upon the maternal instinct, for hypophysectomized animals do not care for their young like normal mothers. Furthermore, injections of prolactin arouse the maternal instincts in young virgin rats; they commence to build a nest from straw, wool, or other soft material that they can gather.

The liberation of prolactin from the hypophysis and its stimulating action on the flow of milk coincide so closely with the termination of

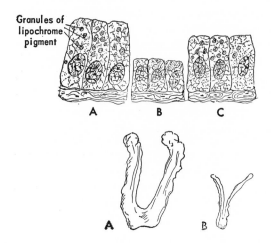

Granules of lipochrome pigment

A B C

A B

Fig. 49.16. *Above, the effect of removal of the pituitary body (or of the testes) on the epithelium of the seminal vesicles. A, normal epithelium; B, after hypophysectomy (or removal of the testes); note the disappearance of granules and reduced height of the cells; C, partial restoration to normal after treatment with male hormone. Below, A, normal uterus of rabbit; B, after hypophysectomy (or excision of the ovaries.)*

pregnancy that curiosity must naturally be aroused concerning the mechanism underlying such accurate timing.[2] Many details of the highly complex mechanism are obscure, but it appears from the great volume of experimental work carried out within recent years that the *immediate* or *direct* cause of the flow of milk from the breasts is hormonal rather than neural in nature. There is abundant evidence that prolactin is not concerned alone, but that the galactogogue principle (Ch. 38), estradiol and progesterone, a hormone of the adrenal cortex, and even the thyroid hormone also play their parts. However, the liberation of prolactin from the hypophysis is initiated by nervous impulses. The latter, set up in the nipple by the act of suckling and conveyed to the pituitary body (through autonomic nerves), constitute probably the most important single nervous factor in inducing the production and liberation of the lactogenic hormone. Suckling also causes the passage of the galactogogue principle into the circulation. But that there are other nervous influences affecting milk secretion can be attested to by any dairyman. Contentment of milking cows, and even music in the stable, facilitates the "letting down" of the milk, an effect that is believed to be due, at least in part, to the release of the galactogogue principle and the resulting stimulation of the smooth muscle in the walls of the milk follicles and ducts. During pregnancy progesterone is in high concentration in the blood, and according to some investigators, this depresses prolactin production, but when, toward the end of pregnancy, a rather abrupt reduction in the blood content of this hormone occurs, prolactin liberation follows automatically.[3]

THE PROCESSES OF REPRODUCTION

Maturation of the sex cells, or gametes (sperm and egg cells). The spermatogenic cells lining the seminiferous tubules undergo maturation as follows. First the chromatin within the nucleus loses its netlike arrangement and forms a few or many threads, bars, or rods, called **chromosomes;**

[2] Some secretion of milk into the follicles of the mammary gland occurs before the end of pregnancy, but as a rule, it is not until the uterus has been emptied that milk appears externally. This milk secreted before the birth of the offspring and retained by the gland is yellow in color and creamy in consistency; it is known as *colostrum* (see also p. 647).

[3] In certain abnormal states of the hypophysis associated with overactivity of the anterior lobe, such as acromegaly, milk may be secreted in the absence of pregnancy, or even in males. This is due presumably to the production and liberation of prolactin. Also the mammary glands of new-born infants of either sex sometimes secrete milk. This was long known as "witch's milk" and is now attributed to prolactin in the infant's circulation derived from the blood of the mother before birth.

The action of prolactin upon the crop glands of doves and pigeons is of especial interest. These glands secrete a creamy material with which the birds feed their young. The crop glands of virgin pigeons enlarge and secrete an abundance of crop milk when injected with a potent preparation of the lactogenic hormone.

the number (46 in man) varies with but is constant for the species (Figs. 49.17, 49.19). Soon fine lines are seen radiating from the centrioles into the surrounding cytoplasm. The starlike bodies thus formed soon separate from one another, and move one to either side of the nucleus. Each chromosome next divides lengthwise into two halves, while the rays from each star body are seen to stretch toward them, the whole nuclear structure being now referred to as the **spindle**. As the radiating strands of the spindle shorten, the chromosome halves are drawn apart and collect together at opposite sides of the cell to form two separate nuclei. Each

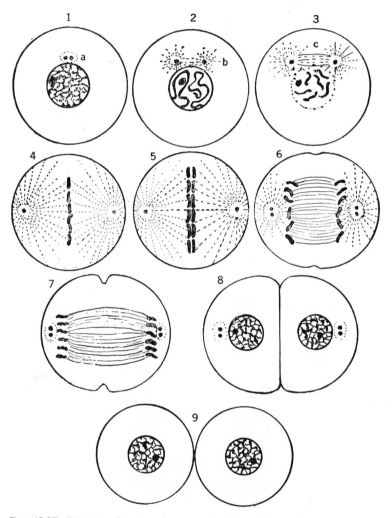

Fig. 49.17. Diagram showing phases or stages in the division of a cell by mitosis. 1, resting cell; 2, 3, and 4, prophase; 5, metaphase; 6, anaphase; 7 and 8, telophase; 9, two new cells (daughter cells).

half chromosome develops into a complete chromosome, so, obviously, each new nucleus must have the same number of chromosomes as the original one. The protoplasm between the two nuclei then divides to form two separate **daughter cells.** These redivide, and their daughter cells divide in turn. The divisions are repeated through several cell generations. The above description of cell division is termed **mitosis** and is typical of the division of body cells in general. From now on, the development of the sperm cells takes a characteristic course. For a time the cells of the last division cease to multiply, but they enter a growth period and form large cells called **spermatocytes.** Among these the division process recommences, but the chromatin follows a different course from that pursued in the previous divisions. The chromatin breaks into the same number of sections (chromosomes) as before, but these arrange themselves in pairs, and *do not divide lengthwise.* A spindle forms, the singles of the pairs are drawn apart, and two daughter cells are formed that are converted directly into mature spermatozoa. It is clear that each of these must have just half the number of chromosomes found in the original germ cell. This is spoken of as reduction division, or meiosis. Eggs are formed after a similar fashion from the germ cells of the female reproductive organ. Multiplication by mitosis occurs for a series of cell generations, full maturation being accompanied by reduction division (Fig. 49.18). In the case of the egg, however, some of the cells resulting from the final divisions are small in size and do not develop fully, but are discarded. The male and female sex cells after they have undergone reduction division are called **gametes** (Gk. *gametēs,* a husband; *gametē,* a wife).

Conjugation of the egg and sperm cells. The unfertilized ovum in some unknown way exerts an attractive force upon the spermatozoon, which, by means of the lashing movements of its tail, reaches the female gamete. The head of the sperm penetrates the ovum. A change in the boundary wall of the ovum then occurs that as a rule serves to prevent the entrance of other spermatozoa. The tail of the penetrating sperm soon disappears, leaving the head within the cytoplasm of the egg. The result is the formation of a single cell that has a power for growth not possessed by ovum or sperm cell alone. The compound cell commences at once to divide and redivide into 2, 4, 8, 16, 32, and so on. Thus is formed a compact mass of cells, which develop structurally and functionally along different lines to produce the various kinds of cells from which the different tissues and organs are built up. This process whereby the cells develop special structures and functions is called **differentiation.** Ultimately, a new and complete individual is created almost identical with others of its species. Whether plant or worm, fish, bird, or man, nearly all forms of life other than the very primitive have developed from a single cell resulting from the union of sperm and egg.

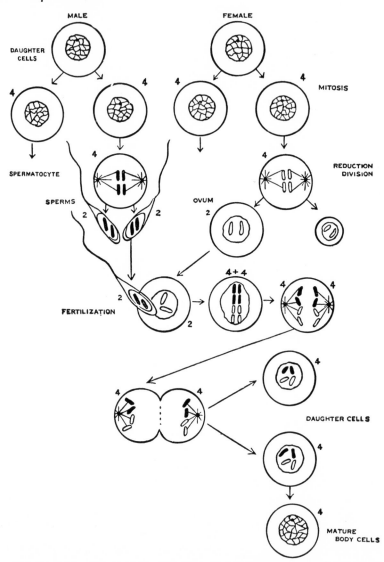

Fig. 49.18. Maturation of the germ cells and fertilization of the ovum. The numbers refer to the number of chromosomes (for simplicity only 2 in the gametes and 4 in the zygote).

The conjugation of the male and female gametes (ovum and spermatozoon) is termed the **fertilization, or impregnation, of the ovum.** The cell resulting from the union is then spoken of as the **fertilized ovum, oösperm, or zygote.**

Changes in the nuclei of the conjoined cells. Almost immediately after fertilization both nuclei commence to enlarge, move toward each other, come together, and finally fuse near the center of the ovum. Fusion is followed by the complicated changes already described as characteristic of mitosis. The chromatin of each nucleus is not broken up into sections at random or in any haphazard fashion, but is always divided into precisely the same number of pieces (chromosomes) as are found in the sperms and ova in the final stage of their maturation. Furthermore, the number of chromosomes in each nucleus, as in each original gamete nucleus, is always the same for a given species, and as a result of the reduction division already described, is precisely half the number of those in the body cells and in the original germ cells of the reproductive organs (Fig. 49.18). *The fused nucleus must therefore contain an equal number of maternal and paternal chromosomes, and the total number must be equal to that in each body cell of the species.*[4] By the division lengthwise of each chromosome into equal halves the number is straightway doubled. The halves lie in pairs near the center of the ovum and, as in ordinary mitosis, star bodies appear on either side, form a spindle, and soon draw them apart. The protoplasm divides and two daughter cells are formed. Each of these has therefore received maternal and paternal chromosomes, and the number is precisely the same as in a body cell but double the number in each original gamete. It is clear, then, that though each gamete contains just half the number of chromosomes characteristic of the body cells of the species, the latter number is restored by the fertilization of the ovum and segmentation of the zygote. This is a fundamental fact in the mechanism of reproduction.

Chromatin, of which the chromosomes are composed, is the essential procreative substance. Through it hereditary characters are transmitted, and upon it the perpetuation of the species depends. Yet it has been stated that the total quantity of chromatin contained in all the ova and sperms from which have been created the two billion-odd persons inhabiting the globe could have been no greater in size than a match head.

Parthenogenesis. In some animal forms, especially certain insects, the females, though themselves produced from a fertilized egg, may for some generations lay eggs that do not become fertilized. These spermless eggs, nevertheless, develop into the young of the species. In other words, the young of these generations have a mother but no father. To this mode of reproduction **parthenogenesis,** a term derived from the Greek word *parthenos* meaning a virgin, is applied. The drones of the honeybee, for instance, are developed from unfertilized eggs of the queen. The

---

[4] In some insects, such as the fruit fly, the number of chromosomes in the body cells is 8, which is reduced to 4 in the gametes. In certain species of worms there are 12 in the body cells and 6 in the ova and sperms. The mouse, the trout, and the lily have 24 in their body cells and 12 in their sex cells. Other forms of animals and plants have each a characteristic number, which may be as low as 4 or as high as 168. There are 23 chromosomes in the gametes of the human race and 46 in the body cells.

female workers of the hive arise from fertilized eggs, which have been laid about the same time as the unfertilized. A frog's egg, though under ordinary circumstances it must receive a spermatozoon before segmentation will ensue, may be induced to develop into a tadpole by artificial means. Pricking the wall of the ovum with a needle will start segmentation, which ultimately results in the production of a fatherless frog.

Twinning. There are two ways in which twins may be conceived: (1) by the fertilization of two separate ova, or (2) by the fertilization of a single ovum. When two ova are fertilized—and this is the commoner way—the offspring, known as **fraternal twins,** may be of the same or of different sexes and usually do not resemble each other more than might any two members of a family. When two individuals are formed from a single ovum, the twins are always of the same sex and are remarkably alike. They are called **identical twins** and are formed by the division of the cell mass within the ovum into two distinct parts, each of which develops into a separate child. Identical twins are contained within the same amniotic cavity and are on very rare occasions joined together, as in the case of the Siamese twins. Most animals produce their litters by the fertilization of several ova, but in some, such as the armadillo, only one ovum is fertilized, and the mass of cells within becomes divided into several smaller groups, each of which develops into a fetus.

Fig. 49.19. The chromosomes of man, 46 in number. Y indicates the unequal mate of the X chromosome in the male.

The determination of sex. It would be an inestimable boon to animal breeders if the sex of the offspring could be determined by artificial means, or even if it could be predicted. Man's ingenuity in this direction seems, however, to be forever checked. Had human interference been possible in the past, the history of nations no doubt would have run a different course. The sex of the newly created organism is fixed unalterably at the moment that the spermatozoon fertilizes the ovum. A pair of chromosomes (**sex chromosomes**) in the nuclei of the immature sex cells determines whether the zygote shall develop into a male or a female. None of the other chromosomes (**autosomes**) exercises this function. In the male, the sex chromosomes are dissimilar, one, called the **Y chromosome,** being usually smaller than the other (Fig. 49.19). The larger one is called the **X chromosome.** In the immature female sex cells, the sex chromosomes are identical and like the male X chromosomes. Now, when the male sex cells develop into mature spermatozoa and reduction division occurs—that is, when the pairs separate—half of the sperm cells receive Y chromosomes, half receive X chromosomes. If a spermatozoon possessing a Y chromosome conjugates with the egg, a male (XY) will be produced; if the sperm cell contains an X chromosome, a female (XX) results. Obviously it is all a matter of chance what the sex of the offspring will be.

When the gonads develop, the influence of the testicular or the ovarian hormone encourages development along male or female lines, respectively. This hormonal influence is sometimes seen in a striking way in cattle when as a result of a developmental anomaly in the circulation of twin embryos of opposite sexes the blood of the two fetuses is permitted to mix. The female embryo then comes under the influence of the male hormone and abnormalities in its generative organs are induced. The uterus remains undeveloped and masculinization of other reproductive structures occurs. The masculinized female is called a *freemartin;* it is sterile.

Comparative viability of males and females. Since spermatozoa containing an X chromosome and those bearing a Y are produced in equal numbers, and each apparently has the same chance of fertilizing an ovum, one would expect that in any large group of matings half the embryos be male and half female. But this does not occur; more males than females are conceived. Such a **primary sex ratio** in favor of males has been found in all mamalian species investigated. It is 130:100 for cattle. But owing to the higher mortality of male embryos the ratio at birth— the **secondary sex ratio**—is considerably lower than this; it is 106:100 for man (for obvious reasons the human primary sex ratio is almost impossible to determine). Deaths in infancy and childhood are also higher for males so that at adolescence the number of boys and girls is about equal. But from this time on females progressively outnumber males until at 85 years of age there are twice as many women in the popu-lation as men.

The sex chromatin. A few years ago it was discovered by Professor Murray Barr of the University of Western Ontario that there is a micro-scopic difference between the body cells of males and females. In female cells but not in the cells of males, the nucleus contains a dot of chromatin that is situated just beneath the nuclear membrane; it has been named the **sex chromatin.** In congenital abnormalities of sex (see *hermaph-roditism,* Ch. 48) in which doubt arises as to whether the subject should be classed as male or female, a histological examination of a section of tissue for the presence or absence of the sex chromatin enables the true sex to be determined.

Segmentation of the fertilized ovum and the development of the embryo. Each daughter cell formed immediately after fertilization divides into two and each of the four cells that result likewise divides. In this way groups of 2, 4, 8, 16, 32, 64, etc., are produced successively. So, by a process of division and redivision, large masses of cells are formed, which ultimately produce a new individual. This process whereby the fertilized ovum undergoes repeated divisions is called **segmentation,** or **cleavage.**

With each cell division the chromatin breaks up into chromosomes; as described above for mitosis, each chromosome splits into half, and an equal number of halves go to each new nucleus. All the cells resulting from the long series of divisions that occur in the development of the offspring must therefore contain the same number of chromosomes as did the original fused nucleus of the fertilized ovum, and each receives chromatin material from both parents, as previously described.

In the earlier stages of embryonic development of the various mammalian species, cell multiplication follows a common pattern. At first a rounded, mulberrylike mass of cells is formed, called the **morula** (L. diminutive of *morus,* a mulberry). The morula soon differentiates into an outer and an inner group of cells (Figs. 49.20, 49.21); fluid collects within it. The fertilized ovum at this stage is called the **blastocyst.** The outer group of cells now pressed eccentrically to form the wall of a sphere is called the **trophoblast** (Gk. *trophē,* nourishment + *blastos,* germ or primitive form), because through its agency the blastocyst receives nutriment from the mother. The trophoblast later develops numerous fringe-like processes that give the ovum a shaggy appearance. These processes grow larger and become branched and are then known as **chorionic villi** (Fig. 49.22); the outer covering of the ovum from which they arise is called the **chorion.** The more centrally situated mass of cells becomes so disposed as to form the walls of two sacs—the **amnion** and the **yolk sac** (see Plates VII*b*, VIII*a*, and Fig. 49.21). The cells of the area over which the amnion and the yolk sac come into contact multiply to form a plaque-like elevation called the **embryonic shield** or **disc,** from which the body of the embryo is developed. The cavity of the amnion enlarges and comes to enclose the embryo, the sac expanding until it comes into contact with the inner surface of the chorion. The yolk sac shrinks and gradually disappears.

When the embryonic shield is no more than 2 mm or so in diam-

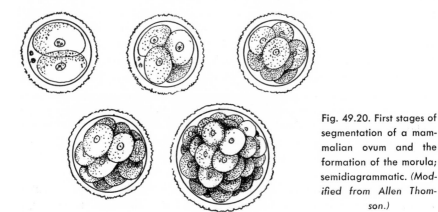

Fig. 49.20. First stages of segmentation of a mammalian ovum and the formation of the morula; semidiagrammatic. (Modified from Allen Thomson.)

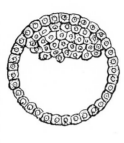
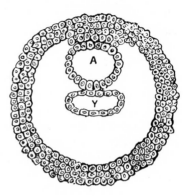

Fig. 49.21. The blasto-cyst. *Left,* diagram showing the segrega-tion of cells of the morula into an outer and an inner group. *(After Simon). Right,* formation of amnion, **A,** and yolk sac, **Y.** *(After Bryce)*

eter, its cells become arranged in two layers, separated by a narrow space. The outer of these layers is called the **ectoderm,** and the inner one the **entoderm.** A little later a third layer appears in the space between the other two; it is known as the **mesoderm.** From these three **germ layers,** to give them their collective name, all the structures of the body are ulti-mately formed (Fig. 49.25). The nervous system, the greater part of the eye, the salivary glands, the skin, the epithelial lining of the nose and part of the mouth, and the dental enamel originate from the *ectoderm.* The *mesoderm* gives rise to the skeleton and the muscles (both striated and nonstriated), the heart, blood vessels, and blood, the lymphatic sys-tem, the kidneys, the urinary bladder (with the excep-tion of its epithelial lining), and the connective tissues. From the *entoderm* are developed the epithelial linings of the alimentary and respiratory tracts (exclusive of those parts derived from the ectoderm), the epithelium lining the urinary bladder, and the secreting (epithelial) cells of the liver, pancreas, and of the parathyroid and thyroid glands.

Fig. 49.22. The human ovum at about the eighth day after fertili-zation.

The earlier of the changes just described—up to the stage of the blastocyst and the development of the trophoblast—take place in the Fallopian tube while the blastocyst is being propelled toward the uterus by ciliary action and peristaltic movements of the tubal walls. Between the third and the fifth days after fertilization of the ovum the blastocyst enters the cavity of the uterus. Through the destructive effect that the trophoblast exerts upon the uterine mucosa and the reaction set up in the latter, the ovum is enabled to embed itself and, like a parasite, obtain nourishment from the maternal tissue. The activity shown by the uterine mucosa at this time consists of multiplication of the surface epithelium and elongation and hyperplasia of its glands, together with dilatation and twisting of its vessels. A special type of uterine tissue is thus produced called the **decidua** because it is shed after the birth of the offspring

(Plate VII*b*). These changes in the endometrium commence before the blastocyst reaches the uterus, or after ovulation, even though fertilization has not occurred (see p. 648). They are dependent upon the action of progesterone. This hormone also diminishes the irritability of the muscle of the uterus; any contractions of the muscle that might occur to disturb the secure implantation of the blastocyst are suppressed. Hyperplasia of the uterine muscle, as mentioned on page 644, also occurs at this time. A photograph of a blastocyst in the uterus of a monkey is shown in Figure 49.23.

The placenta. In Figure 49.24 a fetus from about a month to eight weeks old is shown within the amnion. In the right-hand sketch the chorionic villi have disappeared except where the chorion is attached to the uterine wall, in which situation they have increased greatly in size and complexity. They are surrounded by spongy masses of decidual tissue consisting largely of blood spaces; thus the embryonic and the maternal tissues are intimately interlocked. The chorionic villi, which are supplied through a rich vascular system with fetal blood, are bathed by the mother's blood. The structure formed by the union of the maternal (decidua) and embryonic tissues is called the **placenta.** When fully grown, the placenta is a disc-shaped mass that occupies a third or so of the uterine wall (Figs. 49.24, 49.26, and Plates VII*b* and VIII*b*). Though the

Fig. 49.23. Photograph of an 8-day-old blastocyst of a monkey attached to the mucous membrane of the uterus. The lighter area within is the embryo itself. *(From Heuser and Streeter, Contributions to Embryology, 479. Carnegie Institute of Washington, 1937.)*

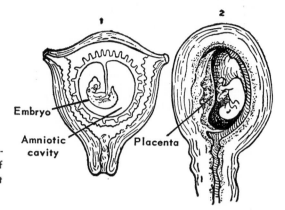

Fig. 49.24. Early human embryos. 1, embryo at the age of
about one month; 2, at about
2 months.

Embryo
Amniotic cavity
Placenta

fetal and maternal circulations come into the most intimate association in the placenta, the blood in the two sets of vessels does not mix, for the delicate walls of the capillaries in the chorionic villi are interposed. Oxygen and nutriment, hormones, antibodies, etc., are transferred across the walls of the chorionic vessels from the mother to the fetus, while carbon dioxide and other waste materials pass from the fetal to the maternal blood. Thus, the placenta serves the respiratory, nutritional, and excretory functions of the fetus.

The hormones of the placenta. The placenta contains four hormones— *estradiol, chorionic gonadotrophin, progesterone,* and *relaxin.* Chorionic gonadotrophin has a luteinizing action and for a time was thought to be LSH of the anterior lobe of the pituitary; when shown by Collip to be a different hormone produced by the placenta itself, it was given the rather cumbersome name of anterior-pituitary-like (abbr. APL) hormone. Chorionic gonadotrophin is found in the urine of pregnant women at a very early stages of gestation, and upon its detection the *Aschheim-Zondek test for pregnancy* depends. These German workers found that the injection of a small quantity of urine of a pregnant woman into a young (sexually immature) mouse caused within 100 hours the following effects:

1. Onset of estrus
2. Small hemorrhages into some of the Graafian follicles
3. Formation of corpora lutea

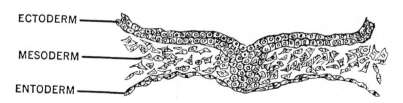

ECTODERM

MESODERM

ENTODERM

Fig. 49.25. The germ layers.

The Aschheim-Zondek test for pregnancy is almost infallible; its error is only about 1 percent.

The estradiol found in the placenta is apparently manufactured by this organ, and does not simply represent a store of the hormone produced by the ovary. This conclusion is justified by the observation that in pregnancy large quantities of the follicular hormone continue to appear in the urine though the ovaries have been removed.

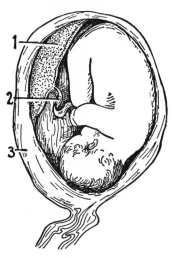

The fetal circulation. The fetal heart drives the blood to the placenta through two vessels—the **umbilical arteries.** The blood is returned from the placenta to the fetus by a single vessel—the **umbilical vein** (Plate VIII*b*). The umbilical vessels run together, coiled or twisted with one another and covered by a soft jellylike substance, to constitute the **umbilical cord.** This arises from the body of the fetus about the middle of the abdomen; its point of origin is marked in life by a circular, depressed, and puckered area of skin called the **navel,** or **umbilicus.**

The oxygenated blood of the umbilical vein passes in part through the liver to enter the **inferior vena cava** of the fetus, but the greater proportion pours directly into this vein, wherein it mixes with blood returning from the lower limbs

Fig. 49.26. Usual position of the fetus shortly before birth. 1, placenta; 2, umbilical cord; 3, uterus.

and abdomen. The mixed blood empties into the right auricle; most of it is then directed through an opening in the interauricular septum, called the **foramen ovale,** to the left side of the heart, and a much smaller part passes into the right ventricle. The blood that passes through the foramen ovale, upon reaching the left ventricle, is discharged into the aorta; a part is distributed to various parts of the body; the remainder is carried by the umbilical arteries to the placenta where it is reoxygenated from the mother's blood.

The blood returned from the upper part of the body (head and neck, upper limbs and thoracic walls) enters the right auricle through the **superior vena cava.** It then passes into the right ventricle (without mixing, apparently, with the stream from the inferior vena cava passing to the left auricle through the foramen ovale). Upon reaching the right ventricle it is pumped into the pulmonary artery, but only a small proportion is distributed to the lungs—an amount sufficient only for the nourishment of the pulmonary tissue. The greater part is short-circuited, through a vessel known as the **ductus arteriosus,** into the aorta. Thus, the great bulk of the blood delivered to the right side of the fetal heart is "shunted" to the arterial side by the short cuts provided by the foramen ovale and the ductus arteriosus.

With the first few respirations the lungs of the newborn child are expanded, and the course of the circulation becomes altered to meet the requirements of an air-breathing organism leading an independent existence. The foramen ovale closes and the channel afforded by the ductus arteriosus becomes obliterated. All the blood reaching the right auricle is now directed through the pulmonary circuit. The umbilical vessels shrink and are converted to solid cords. One or the other or both of the circulatory adjustments that direct the blood through the lungs at birth may fail to occur. Then, owing to the higher pressure of the arterial blood, a part of it is driven from the aorta into the pulmonary artery if the ductus arteriosus remains pervious; also, should the foramen ovale fail to close, blood passes from the left to the right auricle. These abnormalities cause, as a rule, little or no *cyanosis*. But in other types of cardiac defect, such as a large gap in the interventricular septum with narrowing of the pulmonary artery, there is intense cyanosis (so-called *blue babies*), for then venous blood passing through the gap mixes with arterial blood.

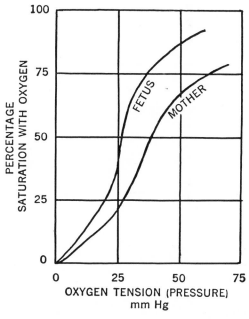

Fig. 49.27. A comparison of the dissociation curves of fetal and maternal hemoglobins.

If the reader has followed the rather intricate course of the fetal circulation he will have observed that the fetal tissues are never furnished with fully arterialized blood; the blood is always less saturated with oxygen than the arterial blood after birth. Yet, strange to say, the blood returning from the placenta—that is, the blood in the umbilical vein—has a higher oxygen saturation than the maternal blood in the placenta—the only source from which the fetal blood can obtain oxygen. This physiological paradox has been explained by the discovery that the oxygen dissociation curve of fetal hemoglobin is different from that of animals in postnatal life (see Fig. 20.6). The oxygen dissociation curve of the blood of the fetus is steeper than that of the mother—that is, it lies more to the left. This means that at a given oxygen pressure (tension) the fetal blood absorbs a greater volume of oxygen than can the mother's blood, or than the baby's blood will be able to absorb after birth (Fig. 49.27). Through such a provision the fetus is more adequately furnished with oxygen than would otherwise be possible.

The law of recapitulation, or biogenesis. The vertebrate embryo from the earliest stages of its development tends to recall, or *recapitulate,* in a more or less vague way the forms of its ancestors from a remote period in its evolutionary history. This is known as the law of *recapitulation,* or *biogenesis.* For example, the embryo of the human species or of any vertebrate commences its existence as two cells (ovum and sperm) fused into a single one. Some unicellular forms reproduce by a similar preliminary fusion of two cells. The segmentation of the fertilized ovum with the formation of the morula is identical with that seen in the development of many of the most primitive forms of life. Again, in the early vertebrate embryo, including the human, a series of five arched ridges appear in the entoderm of the primitive pharynx on each side. Corresponding elevations are to be seen on the surface (ectoderm) of the neck. The arched structures have a core of mesoderm, and are known as the **branchial, or visceral, arches;** the depressions or furrows between them on the outer aspect of the neck are called the **branchial clefts;** the furrows (entodermal) in the pharynx between the arches are referred to as the **pharyngeal pouches** (Fig. 49.28). The branchial structures are found in all vertebrate embryos. From them the respiratory apparatus of fish is developed, the tissue between the arches (branchial clefts and pharyngeal pouches) disappearing to leave slits that establish communications between the pharynx and the exterior. In the fish, the arches (with the exception of the most headward one, which goes to form the jaw) develop rich capillary plexuses that with the supporting tissue constitute the gills. Water taken into the mouth and pharynx is ejected through the slits, and passing swiftly over the gills, gives up oxygen to the blood in the capillary vessels and receives carbon dioxide in return. Obviously a respiratory apparatus of this nature would be quite useless to an air-breathing animal. But the branchial arches of mammalian embryos, which seemingly at first are designed for the development of gills, are devoted to other purposes. They enter into the formation of the lower jaw, the muscles and bones of the face, the structures of the neck, ears, mouth, pharynx, and the thyroid and laryngeal cartilages. The branchial clefts disappear almost entirely, but the entoderm of the pharyngeal pouches gives rise to the thymus, the parathyroid glands, and parts of the ear and the thyroid gland.

Other examples to illustrate the law of recapitulation, such as the persistence in the human adult of the useless ear and tail muscles and the outmoded vermiform appendix, may be mentioned. Again, the heart

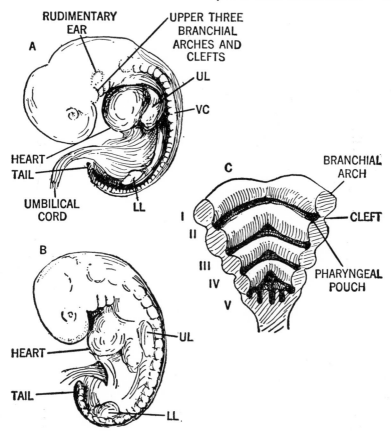

Fig. 49.28. Drawing of a human embryo, A, at the age of 5½ weeks (about 8 mm long), and of a monkey embryo, B, of about the same age. UL, upper limb; LL, lower limb; VC, vertebrae. C, enlarged drawing of the five branchial arches and clefts; the inner aspect of the throat region is exposed to show the pharyngeal pouches.

of the early embryo is a simple tubular structure as in fish; but later, it becomes bent upon itself and develops separate chambers. For a short time it closely resembles the heart of an amphibian, such as the frog, possessing a sinus venosus and other features of the cold-blooded heart.

As development proceeds, the human embryo ascends, as it were the evolutionary ladder, passing rapidly over the lower rungs, more slowly over the higher. For some time it resembles its mammalian kindred; not until about six weeks after fertilization of the ovum does it show distinctly human characteristics. The human embryo possesses a tail that only commences to disappear in the seventh week.[5]

---

[5] A child is sometimes born with a tail, but it is a developmental anomaly of extreme rarity.

Pregnancy and parturition. Pregnancy, or gestation, is the term applied to the period in the reproductive cycle occupied by the growth and development of the new organism within the body of the mother—that is, from the fertilization of the ovum (**conception**) to the birth of the young animal (**parturition**). Most of the structural and physiological adaptations of the pregnant state, such as the fertilization and implantation of the ovum, the enlargement of the uterus, and the growth and development of the mammary glands, have been touched upon elsewhere in this chapter. In a book of this scope little more remains to be written.

Pregnancy in the human race has a duration of about 280 days, or from 9 to 9½ months. From the fertilization and implantation of the ovum to the eighth week the product of conception is called the **embryo;** from this time until birth it is referred to as the **fetus.** From about the middle of pregnancy onward, movements of the fetus occur of which the mother is aware; they are referred to as *quickening.* Sucking and spasmodic movements of the chest resembling those of respiration have been observed in fetal animals. The unborn child lies within the sac formed by the amnionic and chorionic membranes, submerged in a fairly large body of fluid (**liquor amnii**) that serves to protect it from sudden jars or injuries from the outside world. The amniotic sac fills the uterus, and is considerably larger than the fetus itself, which is thus permitted a certain freedom of movement.

Toward the latter part of pregnancy, the unborn child usually assumes a position with its head directed downward and, most frequently, the posterior part of the head (occiput) pointing forward and to the left (Fig. 49.26). It is fitted in this position into the cavity of the pelvis.

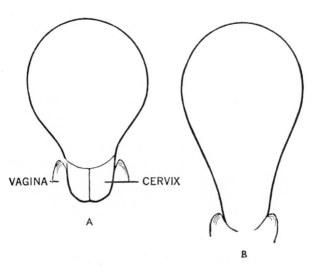

VAGINA — CERVIX

A

B

Fig. 49.29. Showing the thinning of the lower segment of the uterus and the dilatation of the outlet during the first stage of labor. A, before the commencement of labor; B, toward the end of the first stage.

The descent of the fetus is aided very materially by previous softening of the ligaments and capsules about the pelvic joints (action of relaxin), which are loosened thereby and rendered more pliable. Indeed, this is a process essential for normal childbirth. The birth of the child is brought about by strong contractions of the uterine muscle, aided in the later stages by voluntary contractions of the abdominal muscles. The contractions of the walls of the uterus, weak at first and of short duration, become stronger and more prolonged in an hour or two; they cause molding of the infant's head and gradual dilatation of the outlet of the uterus with drawing up and disappearance of its neck, or cervix; at the same time the vaginal walls become more pliable and distensible. Later, the membranous sac enveloping the fetus bulges into the vagina, and after a time ruptures, a part of the amniotic fluid then escaping. When the canal from the uterus to the exterior has enlarged sufficiently to allow the passage of the baby's head, the latter is expelled by powerful contractions of the uterus, accompanied usually by contractions of the abdominal muscles. The rest of the child's body follows almost immediately.

For a time the newborn babe still remains attached to the interior of the uterus through the umbilical cord and placenta. The physician ties the cord with tape close to the baby's body and divides it on the mother's side of the tape. Not until 15 or 30 minutes later is the placenta, and the attached sac composed of the chorionic and amniotic membranes, expelled. The placenta and membranes are commonly referred to as the **afterbirth. Labor,** or **parturition,** is the term given to the series of events bringing about the emptying of the uterus and the termination of pregnancy.

A consideration of the factors determining the onset of labor. The termination of pregnancy at the usual time is not due to a single factor, but to several. A sufficient number of these factors are known to enable us to draw in outline a picture of the mechanism leading to the precipitation of labor. The picture must of necessity be incomplete and many details left blank to be filled in when more knowledge has been gained.

It has been stated (p. 645) that the growth of the uterus ceases between the sixth and the seventh months of pregnancy; this is attributed to the rise, from this time onward, of the concentration in the blood of estradiol, which has an inhibitory effect upon the growth response of the uterus to distension. But the fetus is growing rapidly at this time, and the distension of the uterus now takes place in the long axis of the organ. The tension set up in the uterine tissues tends gradually to compress, narrow, and finally obliterate many vessels supplying blood to the placenta. Degenerative changes proceed in the latter, and the nutrition of the fetus suffers; it must be released and take on a new mode of existence if it is to survive. At the same time, the output of placental hormones is reduced and the corpus luteum undergoes degeneration. Thus, the depressing effect of progesterone upon the irritability of the uterine muscle —an effect very necessary in early pregnancy—is withdrawn. The high concentration in the blood of estradiol further increases uterine irritability and thus enhances the tendency of the uterus to contract under slight provocation. Estradiol also raises the sensitivity (lowers the threshold) of the uterus to the action of the oxytocic principle of the posterior lobe of the hypophysis. A further word should be said about this latter principle. Its liberation is apparently under nervous control, for in animals, stimulation of the vagina or uterine cervix causes contractions of the uterus, a response that does not occur if the stalk of the hypophysis, along which nerve fibers reach the posterior lobe, has been first divided. An oxytocic substance is found in the blood and urine of women in labor; though there is a strong suspicion that this substance is derived from the hypophysis, such has not been definitely established. For this reason, it is not possible to estimate accurately the importance of the oxytocic principle of the pituitary body in the mechanism that brings on labor. Furthermore, though labor is sometimes prolonged and difficult in animals after hypophysectomy, in other cases the young are born easily and within the usual time. It can therefore be said, at any rate, that the pituitary principle is not absolutely essential to the labor mechanism (see Fig. 49.30).

INCREASE IN ESTRADIOL CAUSING

1. CESSATION OF UTERINE GROWTH
2. INCREASED IRRITABILITY OF MUSCLE
3. INCREASE SENSITIVITY TO OXYTOCIC PRINCIPLE

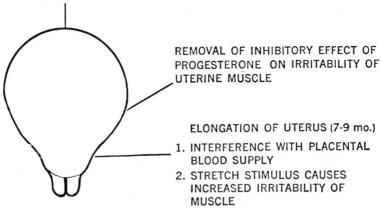

REMOVAL OF INHIBITORY EFFECT OF PROGESTERONE ON IRRITABILITY OF UTERINE MUSCLE

ELONGATION OF UTERUS (7-9 mo.)

1. INTERFERENCE WITH PLACENTAL BLOOD SUPPLY
2. STRETCH STIMULUS CAUSES INCREASED IRRITABILITY OF MUSCLE

Fig. 49.30. Diagram summarizing the factors leading to the onset of labor.

A few facts in the physiology of the fetus and the newborn child. The beating of the fetal heart can be heard in the later part of pregnancy by means of a stethoscope placed on the mother's abdominal wall over the uterus. The heart rate runs from 140 to 200 per minute. In the newborn it is around the former figure. The respirations of the newborn are from 30 to 35 per minute, as compared with the adult rate of from 18 to 20. The liver as well as the kidneys of the newborn are functionally immature. The infant's urine, like that of certain lower orders of animals (for example, the frog), is hypotonic, indicating that the ability possessed by the adult kidney to concentrate the glomerular filtrate has not yet been acquired (see Ch. 32). The high erythrocyte count with which the baby comes into the world, and the difference between the hemoglobin of the fetus and that of the newborn or of the adult have been mentioned elsewhere. The destruction of the excess of red cells shortly after birth, combined with the functional immaturity of the liver, accounts for the slight jaundiced tint of the skin sometimes seen in the newborn infant. The intestine of the newborn contains a dark brown or black tarry material known as **meconium;** it is quite sterile, and for this reason the baby, if it does not receive vitamin K from the mother in sufficient amounts before birth, may suffer from hemorrhages that are sometimes fatal (see p. 162). After the first day or so of the infant's life, the danger passes, for by this time bacteria capable of synthesizing the vitamin have reached the intestine in the food, or have been carried from the mouth in the saliva; the hemorrhagic tendency is thus corrected.

Most unconditioned reflexes are well developed at birth. The accommodation reflex of the eye, however, is usually in abeyance; and, since the corticospinal tracts of the brain and spinal cord are not fully developed, the plantar response is of the extensor type (Babinski response).

The puerperium, or puerperal period. This is the period following the third or final stage of labor, during which the mother is recuperating and the uterus with the other structures of the birth mechanism are being restored to the nonpregnant state. Immediately following the expulsion of the placenta and fetal membranes (afterbirth) the uterus contracts down to a firm rounded body that can be plainly felt by a hand pressed upon the mother's abdomen. This strong gripping contraction compresses the open mouths of blood vessels and vascular spaces in the uterus, and is essential to prevent excessive bleeding. Intermittent uterine contractions at this time may be distressingly painful ("after pains"). In the days that follow, the uterine muscle shrinks, the redundant tissue being absorbed, and the uterus returns nearly to its virgin size. This process, which is called the **involution of the uterus,** is accompanied by a gradually lessening vaginal discharge consisting chiefly of blood and endometrial debris. The completion of the process of involution, which takes from 6 to 10 weeks, marks the end of the puerperal period.

The secretion of milk becomes well established usually by the end of the first day or so, and if the baby is put to the breast, the act of suckling stimulates contractions of the uterus and encourages its involution.

The two chief dangers of the puerperal period are hemorrhage and infection.

Glossary

Pronunciation. The vowel sound of an accented syllable is indicated by the position of the accent mark; if the vowel is long, the mark immediately follows it; if short, the mark follows the consonant. Thus, in *ab'scess*, the *a* is short, whereas in *adeno'ma* the *o* is long. Vowel sounds in all unaccented syllables unless otherwise indicated are short. Further information or pronunciation is given by the mark ⁻ or ˘ above the vowel letter, or in parentheses following the word.

Plurals are given after the word.

Derivations are within brackets. The derivation of a word that has come into English unchanged from another language is indicated by the abbreviation for that language. The following abbreviations are used: F., *French;* Gk., *Greek;* Ger., *German;* L., *Latin;* ME., *middle English;* Med., *medieval;* OE., *old English;* fr., *from;* prec., *preceding* (item); foll., *following.*

Only words not described adequately in the text are listed.

a-; an- [privative, Gk. negative, meaning the absence or removal or something fr. L. *privatio,* deprive]. Used as a prefix (*a-* before a consonant and *an-* before a vowel) in words derived from the Greek, to indicate negation.

ab- [L. from]. A prefix meaning away from, off.

abdo'men [L.]. The large cavity below the diaphragm, the belly. *Ab'domen* is an incorrect pronunciation.

ab'scess [L. *abscessus,* going away]. A circumscribed area of tissue, usually accompanied by the signs of acute inflammation, and containing pus. *Cold abscess* is one not showing the ordinary signs of inflammation; it is usually tuberculous.

accessory food factors. Old term for vitamins.

acid'ophil, acid'ophile [*acid* + Gk. *philos,* fond]. Having an affinity for acid; oxyphil.

adaptation. The failure to respond to a stimulus that has been applied repeatedly for some time. Thus the ticking of a clock is after a time unperceived, and the pressure and rubbing of the clothes against the skin is disregarded.

adeno'ma [Gk. *adēn,* a gland + *ōma,* indicating a tumor]. A tumor of glandular tissue.

adrenalec'tomy [adrenal + Gk. *ektomē,* excision]. Removal of the adrenal glands.

adrenolyt'ic [*adreno (adrenal)* + Gk. *lysis (lyt-),* solution]. Referring to the action of certain agents that annul the effects of adrenaline.

679

adsorption [L. *ad,* to + L. *sorbeo,* to suck up]. The attraction and adhesion of minute particles to the surface of a solid.

ægoph'ony [Gk. *aix (aig),* a goat + *phōnē,* voice]. The sound like a goat bleating heard in auscultation of the chest in certain diseases of the lungs.

aero'bic [Gk. *aēr,* air + *bios,* life, manner of living]. Referring to respiration and other processes carried on in the presence of oxygen.

ag'minated [L. *agmen (agmin),* a multitude]. Aggregated, arranged in clusters.

agno'sia [Gk. ignorance, fr. *a,* privitive + *gnosis,* knowledge]. A condition allied to aphasia due to a cerebral lesion, in which the patient does not know the meaning of the sounds that he hears *(auditory agnosia),* or recognize the nature and use of ordinary things that he sees *(visual agnosia),* though his hearing and sight may be perfect.

agran'ulocyto'sis [Gk. *a,* privitive + *granulocyte* + *osis,* a state or condition]. A disease, often fatal, characterized by an almost complete absence of granulocytes from the circulation. Since these cells are of such importance in the defense of the body against the inroads of bacteria, severe uncontrollable infections may result. The disease is often caused by certain synthetic drugs or antibiotics that poison the bone marrow and suppress its function.

agraph'ia [Gk. *a,* privitive + *graphō,* to write]. A condition allied to aphasia in which the patient cannot express himself in writing, or write from dictation.

aldos'terone. A steroid hormone obtained from the adrenal cortex that has a more pronounced effect than has desoxycorticosterone upon the metabolism of water and salts (sodium and potassium).

al'lergy [Gk. *allos,* other + *ergon,* work]. Hypersensitivity to certain agents, e.g., pollen, in hay fever.

alve'olus of tooth [L. diminutive of *alveus,* a trough]. A tooth socket.

amne'sia [Gk. *a,* privitive + *mnēmē,* memory]. Loss of memory due to a cerebral lesion, or from any cause.

am'phi-; ampho- [Gk. on both sides, around, both]. A prefix in words of Greek origin, meaning on both sides, around, surrounding, both.

amphoter'ic [Gk. *ampho,* both]. Referring to compounds, such as the amino acids that can act either as an acid or a base, depending upon the pH of the medium in which they are dissolved.

ampul'la [Gk. a double-handled bottle]. A saclike dilatation of a tube or canal; e.g., a semicircular canal of the inner ear.

ana- [Gk. up]. A prefix in words of Greek origin, meaning up.

anab'olism [Gk. *anabolē,* a building up, fr. *ana,* up + *bolē,* to throw]. The metabolic processes involved in the synthesis of compounds, as in growth.

anaero'bic [Gk. *an,* privitive + *aerobic*]. Referring to respiration or other process carried on in the absence of oxygen.

an'alogue [fr. Gk. *ana-logus,* analogous]. An organ, or part, of one species that though differing more or less in structure from that of another species is similar in function; e.g., the hoof of a horse and the fore part of the human foot.

anastomo'sis [Gk. to furnish with a mouth *(stoma)*]. The junction between the branches of two nerves or arteries either produced naturally in development or by surgical operation, or the surgical union of two hollow organs; e.g., intestine to stomach, intestine to intestine, ureter to colon, etc.

an'drogen [Gk. *anēr (and),* a man + root *gen,* to produce]. Any compound that exerts an effect like that of the male hormone, testosterone.

an'eurysm [Gk. *aneurysma,* an *aneurysm,* fr. *eurys,* wide]. A localized, usually saccular or fusiform, dilatation of an artery with weakening of its wall. *Arterio-*

venous aneurysm, communication between a large vein and an artery, with a local dilatation of the former.

angi′na [L. a sore throat]. Sore throat or severe pain from any cause.

angi′na pec′toris [L. *pectus (pector)*, the chest]. Severe, often agonizing, pain in the chest radiating down the left arm, due to disease of the coronary arteries resulting in a deficiency in the oxygen supply to the heart muscle.

ankle clo′nus. A rhythmical contraction of the calf muscles in a subject of spastic nervous disease, caused by sudden dorsiflexion of the foot.

ankle jerk. A sharp plantar flexion of the foot following a tap on the tendo calcaneous.

an′nular [L. *annulus*, a ring]. Ring shaped.

anorex′ia [Gk. *an*, privitive + *orexia*, appetite]. Loss of appetite.

ante- [L. before]. A prefix in words of Latin derivation, meaning before, in front of.

anteflex′ion [L. *ante*, before, forward + *flexio*, bend]. A bending forward; anteflexion of the *uterus*, bending forward of the uterus upon itself at the junction of the cervix with the body.

antever′sion [L. *ante*, before, forward + *versio*, to turn]. Falling forward of the uterus as a whole without bending upon itself.

anti- [Gk. against]. A prefix meaning against, opposite, antagonistic.

antiketogen′ic [L. *anti*, against + *keto (-ne)* + root, *gen*, produce]. Indicating an action of certain foods, especially glucose, in antagonizing the tendency to ketogenesis.

apha′sia [Gk. *a*, privitive + *phasis*, speech]. A speech disorder due, not to any paralysis of the muscles normally involved in speech, but to a lesion of the part of the cerebral cortex concerned with the memory of words or of the motor mechanism of articulation. There are several types: *motor, visual, auditory*, etc. In motor aphasia, due to a lesion of the posterior and inferior part of the frontal lobe, the patient, though he may understand spoken and written words, cannot speak some or any words. In visual aphasia, the ability to recognize printed or written words is lost; and in auditory aphasia the patient does not understand what is said to him.

ap′o- [GK. from]. A prefix to words of Greek origin, meaning from, away from, off.

aprax′ia [Gk. *a*, privitive + *pratto*, to do]. The inability to perform a given act at will or when commanded to do so; this is *motor* apraxia. In *sensory* apraxia, the patient does not comprehend the use of an object; when given a pencil, for example, and asked to use it, he may attempt to brush his teeth with it, or to smoke it like a cigarette.

arboriza′tion [L. *arbor*, a tree]. Fibers arranged in a pattern like the branchings of a tree.

archen′teron (k) [Gk. *archē*, beginning + *enteron*, intestine]. The cavity of the gastrula.

arrect′or muscles [L. *arrector*, to raise]. Smooth muscle in the skin attached to the shafts of the hairs.

arthro′dia [Gk. a gliding joint]. A joint that permits a sliding or gliding movement only.

arth′us phenomenon. A localized anaphylactic reaction; when a sensitized rabbit is injected with the antigen, necrosis occurs and a sterile abscess forms at the site of the injection.

asci′tes [L. fr. Gk. *askos*, a bag]. An abnormal and excessive collection of serous fluid in the peritoneal cavity, as may occur in hepatic, renal, or cardiac disease.

atax′ia [Gk. *a*, privitive + *taxia*, order, arrangement]. Muscular incoordination.

atre′sia [Gk. *a*, privitive + *trēsis*, a hole]. Congenital absence of an opening (e.g., the anus), or pathological closure of a normal orifice.

at′rophy [Gk. *a*, privitive + *trophe*, nourishment]. Reduction in size of any organ or tissue due to shrinkage or wasting of its parenchyma which is largely, or at least in part, replaced by connective tissue.

aur′icle [diminutive of L. *auris*, ear]. The pinna of the ear or the older term for an atrium of the heart.

ausculta′tion [L. *auscultō (atus)*, listen to]. A method of examination in which the examiner listens, usually with a stethoscope, for sounds within the chest or any other part of the body.

aut′acoid [Gk. *autos (o)* + *akos*, a remedy]. An active principle secreted by one of the endocrine organs; it may be either a hormone or a chalone.

auto- [Gk. *autos*, self]. A prefix in words of Greek origin, meaning self.

autotransplanta′tion. The transplantation of an organ or the grafting of a tissue into another part of the same body. The transplanted structure has a good chance of surviving.

aux′ins [Gk. *auxō*, to increase, to cause growth]. Plant hormones that promote growth and development in plants.

avitamino′sis [Gk. *a*, privitive + *vitamin* + *osis*, a state or condition]. Deficiency of one or other of the several vitamins; thus, one may speak of avitaminosis A, avitaminosis B_1, etc.

az′ygos [Gk. *a*, privitive + *zygon*, a yoke]. Single, unpaired.

Babin′ski response. Extension of the great toe upon gently stroking the inner side of the sole with the finger or a pencil. It is seen in certain nervous diseases; e.g., interruption of the corticospinal tracts. The normal response to such a stimulus is plantar flexion of the great toe.

bacteriol′ysin [foll.]. An agent that causes bacteriolysis; some formed in the body act specifically upon the type of bacteria that causes a certain disease.

bacteriol′ysis [*bacteria* + Gk. *lysis*, solution]. Destruction of bacteria by breaking up or dissolving the cell.

bacteriostat′ic [*bacteria* + Gk. *statikos*, causing to stand]. Referring to agents; e.g., sulphonamide drugs and antibiotics that do not destroy bacteria or do so as a secondary effect, but interfere with some normal and essential process in the bacterial cell, and thus arrest or inhibit their multiplication.

bel [after Alex. Graham Bell, inventor of the telephone]. A unit of loudness.

bi-; bis- [L. twice]. A prefix meaning twice, double.

bīcip′ital [L. *biceps (cipitis)*, two-headed]. Relating to any structure with two heads; e.g., the biceps brachii or biceps femoris.

bīcip′ital groove. The groove on the anterior surface of the humerus between the tuberosities that lodges the tendon of the biceps brachii.

bicus′pid teeth. Premolar teeth.

bīliver′din [L. *bilis*, bile + F. *verd* (L. *viridis*), green]. A green pigment in bile derived from the oxidation of bilirubin.

bi′otin [Gk. *bios*, life]. A factor of the vitamin B complex that neutralizes the effects of a poisonous protein in egg white called *avidin*. Animals fed a diet with a high percentage of egg white, and deprived of biotin, develop a severe skin condition and other symptoms. Biotin deficiency in man apparently does not occur.

blas′tula. Blastocyst.

bleeding time. The interval, measured in minutes, elapsing between the moment that blood appears from a prick of the skin and when it clots, as determined by dabbing the wound with a scrap of filter paper.

Bohr effect. The action of carbon dioxide in causing a shift to the right of the oxygen dissociation curve of blood; that is, in reducing the affinity of hemoglobin for oxygen.

bo′lus [L. a throw, a choice morsel]. A masticated mass of food in the mouth ready for swallowing or in the esophagus or intestine that is moved along the tube by peristalsis.

brach′y [Gk. *brachys,* short]. A prefix in words of Greek origin meaning short.

bradycar′dia [Gk. *bradys,* slow + *kardia,* the heart]. Unusually slow action of the heart.

brain case. The part of the skull that encloses the brain.

bronchioli′tis (k). Inflammation of the bronchioles.

bronchi′tis (k). Inflammation of the bronchi.

cal′cify [L. *calx,* lime + *facio,* make]. To harden a tissue, such as the arterial wall in arteriosclerosis, by the pathological deposition of insoluble salts of calcium, or the incorporation of calcium into cartilage or membrane in the normal formation of bone.

cal′culus [L. a pebble]. A stone formed in any organ (usually hollow), such as the gall bladder, ureter, urinary bladder, salivary duct.

canalic′ulus [diminutive of L. *canalis,* a canal]. A minute canal.

can′thus [Gk. *kanthus*]. The junction of the eyelids at the outer and inner angles of the eye.

car′dia [Gk. *kardia*]. The cardiac orifice.

castra′tion [L. *castro (-atus),* to deprive of genital organs]. Excision of the gonads, either male or female.

catab′olism [Gk. *cata,* down + *bolē,* throw]. The metabolic processes involved in the breakdown of compounds to simpler ones; *see* anabolism.

catal′ysis [Gk. *cata,* down + *lysis,* solution, dissolution]. The process whereby certain agents (e.g., enzymes), while not entering intimately into a chemical reaction or forming part of the final product, increase the speed of the reaction.

celiac (se′liak) [Gk. *koilia,* belly]. Relating to the abdomen.

celluli′tis [L. *cellula,* a cell + *itis,* meaning inflammation]. Inflammation of connective tissue.

cerebroside (ser′ebrōsīd). A lipid containing the sugar galactose.

chalone (kal′ōn) [Gk. *chalāo,* to relax]. An internal secretion with an inhibitory action; e.g., enterogastrone.

chem′orecep′tor. A receptor, as in the carotid body, that responds to chemical stimuli.

Cheyne-Stokes respiration (chān-stōks). An abnormal type of breathing occurring in grave disease in which the respirations increase progressively in depth and vigor to a maximum, then diminish again and finally cease (apnea) for a time. The return of the breathing marks the beginning of another cycle.

chlor′ophyll [Gk. *chloros,* green + *phyllon,* a leaf]. The green pigment of plant life that functions in photosynthesis; it is allied to hemoglobin.

choana, -ae (ko′an-ah) [Gk. *choanē,* a funnel]. A funnellike passage, such as the posterior apertures of the nasal cavities.

choline (ko′lēn). A factor of the vitamin B complex; a deficiency results in fatty liver. Deficiency, however, does not appear to occur in man.

chorda tȳm′pani nerve (kor′da) [L. *chorda,* a chord or string + *tympani,* of the tympanum (fr. Gk. *tympanon,* a drum)]. A branch of the facial nerve that passes through the tympanum of the ear and supplies the submaxillary gland and the anterior part of the tongue (taste fibers).

chromaffin (kro'mafin) [*chrom* (-*ic* salts) + L. *affinis* (fr. *ad* + *finis*, boundary, end), meaning attraction]. Having an affinity for the salts of chromic acid; e.g., the cells of the adrenal medulla and of the carotid body that are stained yellowish brown.

chro'matid. One of the parts resulting from the longitudinal splitting of the chromosomes in the prophase of mitosis.

chro'moproteins [Gk. *chroma*, color + *protein*]. Proteins whose molecules contain a pigment group; e.g., hemoglobin.

chronaxia, chronaxie (krōn-ak'se-a, krōn-ak'sē) [Gk. *chronos*, time + *axia*, value]. The length of time, measured in thousandths of seconds, required for an electrical stimulus to act in order to excite a tissue, such as nerve or muscle, when the strength of the stimulus is twice that of the rheobase.

cicatrix, cicatres (sik'-a-tricks, sik'-a-trēz) [L. scar]. A scar.

cir'cum- [L. around]. A prefix meaning around, surrounding, circular.

clo'nus [Gk. *clonos*, a tumult]. Intermittent rapid contractions of a group of muscles, or generalized convulsions consisting of such contractions. Adjective, *clonic. See* Ankle clonus.

coagula'tion time. The time elapsing between the instant that a sample of blood is collected and the appearance of the first signs of clotting. There are a number of methods for determining this, but whatever method is used the conditions are standardized so that all results by that method are strictly comparable. The coagulation time of human blood is normally between 3 and 4 minutes.

coelom (se'lōm) [Gk. *koilōma*, a hollow]. The cavity of the embryo formed between the layers of the mesoderm, and from which the pericardial, pleural, and peritoneal cavities are developed. This is the *intra-embryonic coelom;* it communicates with the cavity of the chorion which is called the *extra-embryonic coelom.*

color index. An index employed in distinguishing between different types of anemia that expresses the relative quantity of hemoglobin in each red cell. It is a quotient derived from the following fraction:

$$\frac{\text{hemoglobin in percent of normal}}{\text{number of red cells per mm of blood in percent of normal}}$$

The index is 1.0 in normal blood, above this in hyperchromic anemias, and below in hypochromic anemias.

com'missure [L. *commissura*, a joining, a seam]. Any band of fibrous, nervous, or other tissue that joins two parts of (usually) similar structure.

complemental air. The volume of air that can be inspired above that of a normal ordinary inspiration.

congen'ital [L. *congenitus*, born with]. Relating to any disease, condition, structure, etc., present at birth.

con'jugated proteins [L. *con-jugo* (-*jugatus*), join together]. Any protein containing in its molecule a pigment, carbohydrate, lipid, nucleic acid, or other nonprotein group; e.g., hemoglobin, glycoprotein, nucleoprotein.

convection [L. *con-veho* (-*vectus*), carry or bring together]. The change in the positions of particles in a gas (e.g., air) or liquid caused by temperature, the heated particles rising while the cooler particles, being heavier, fall. Thus, convection currents are set up.

corpus, corpora [L. body]. A body.

cor'tex [L. bark]. The outer part of a structure that is distinguishable from the more centrally placed tissue—called the *medulla.*

crepita'tions [L. *crepo,* to rattle]. Fine grating, rattling, or crackling sounds characteristic of certain rales; or the gritty, grinding, or clicking sensation given to an examiner's fingers laid upon a fractured bone. They are caused by the fragments rubbing upon one another and can usually be felt by the patient himself.

crib'riform [L. *cribrum,* a sieve + *forma,* form]. Perforated, sievelike.

crossing over. The interchange of chromatids between the members of a chromosome pair that occurs in the prophase of mitosis.

cum-; com-; co- [L. with]. A prefix meaning with, combined, joined.

cūne'iform [L. *cuneus,* a wedge + *forma,* form]. Wedge shaped.

cȳst [Gk. *kystis,* a bladder]. Any saclike structure.

cȳsti'tis [Gk. *kystis,* bladder + *itis,* meaning inflammation]. Inflammation of the urinary bladder.

cȳtol'ogy [Gk. *kytos,* cell (hollow) + *logos,* word, discourse, treatise]. The study of cells, histology.

cȳtol'ysis [Gk. *kytos,* cell (a hollow) + *lysis,* breaking up, solution, dissolution]. Disintegration, solution of cells.

deamina'tion; deaminiza'tion [L. *de,* from + am (fr. ammonia)]. The splitting off of an amino group, as from an amino acid.

decibel (des'i-bel) [L. *deci* (abbrev. *decimus),* ten + *bel*]. One tenth of a bel.

deciduous (de-sid'ū-us) [L. *decido,* to fall down]. Pertaining to anything that falls off or is discarded; e.g., the first set of teeth, or the part of the endometrium that is shed with the placenta or during menstruation.

dehydration [L. *de,* from + Gk. *hydor,* water]. The removal of water from the body or from any structure or substance.

del'toid. Shaped like the Greek capital letter delta (Δ).

dermal [Gk. *derma,* the skin]. Pertaining to the skin.

dermal bones [prec.]. Bones forming vault of skull developed in membrane just beneath the skin.

dĕsquama'tion [L. *de,* from + *squama,* a scale]. The shedding of the superficial layers from the surface of the skin, or of any part covered by squamous epithelium.

deutoplasm; deuteroplasm (du'to-plazm) [Gk., *deutero,* second + *plasma,* a something formed]. The nutritive yolk of an egg. It is very small in the ova of mammals but relatively enormous in the eggs of birds. The rest of the yolk, from which the embryo is developed, is called the cytoplasm, or the *formative yolk.*

di-; dis- [L. apart, sundering into two parts, two]. A prefix meaning two or separating into two.

dia- [Gk. through]. A prefix meaning through, in different directions, or completely.

dīath'esis [Gk. an arrangement]. A constitution predisposed to some disease or abnormal state.

dīchot'omy [Gk. *dicha,* in two + *tomē,* a cutting]. A branching into two, hence, *dichotomous* in referring to such a division.

dicrot'ic pulse [Gk. *dicrotos,* fr. *di,* two + *crōtos,* a beating, a pulse]. A type of pulse occurring in typhoid fever and certain other conditions associated with low blood pressure and lax arterial walls, in which the dicrotic wave (ordinarily not palpable) can be felt as a distinct tap following the main pulse wave.

dip'loë [Gk. feminine of *diplous,* double]. The cancellous layer of bone lying between the two layers of compact bone of the cranium.

dip'loid [Gk. *diplous*, double + *eidos*, resembling]. The double number of chromosomes characteristic of the immature sex cells, the zygotes, and the body cells generally; *see* Haploid.

dominant [L. fr. *dominus*, a master]. (1) Relating to an hereditary character which appears in the offspring and masks another character called *recessive*, though the gene carrying the latter has also been transmitted. (2) Relating to the cerebral hemisphere which determines right or left "handedness." Thus, the left hemisphere is dominant in right-handed persons and the right hemisphere in those who are left-handed.

drop'sy [Gk. *hydrops*, an abnormal collection of fluid in a tissue or cavity]. An old term for edema or ascites and still in popular use; any abnormal and excessive collection of fluid in the tissues or a body cavity.

dȳne [Gk. *dynamis*, force]. A unit of force, defined as that which acting on a mass of 1 gram for 1 second causes an acceleration of 1 cm per second.

dȳs- [Gk. bad, difficult]. A prefix in words of Greek derivation meaning difficult, bad, abnormal, or distressing.

dȳsarth'ria [Gk. *dys*, bad + *arthrōo*, articulate]. Difficulty in speaking due to weakness or paralysis of the muscles of articulation, or to stuttering or stammering.

dȳspha'gia [Gk. *dys*, bad + *phagein*, to eat]. Difficulty in swallowing owing to pain or any other cause.

dȳspnea [Gk. *dys*, difficult, bad + *pnoē*, breathing]. Difficult, distressful, or painful breathing.

ec-, ex- [Gk. *ektos*, without, out of]. A prefix meaning out of, outside, removal of.

ectop'ic [Gk. *ek*, out + *topos*, a place]. Misplaced, not in the normal situation; e.g., *ectopic gestation*, pregnancy occurring in a uterine tube or in the peritoneal cavity.

edema [Gk. *oidēma*, a swelling]. An abnormal increase in tissue fluid, especially in the subcutaneous tissues, causing a puffy swelling of the part which, when pressed with a finger or thumb, shows a hollow imprint due to the temporary dispersal of the fluid.

elbow jerk. A sharp contraction of the triceps muscle caused by tapping its tendon of insertion.

elec'trocor'tin [*electro* (abbrev. electrolyte) + *cortin*]. Aldosterone.

em'bolus [Gk. a wedge or stopper]. A clot, mass of agglutinated cells, a piece of fibrin, etc., carried in the blood stream and blocking a vessel.

em'bryo [Gk. *embryon*, fr. *en*, in + *bryo*, be full, to swell]. The developing organism from the fertilization of the ovum to emergence from the egg, as in birds; in man, the product of conception from the second to the eighth week of pregnancy.

embryol'ogy [Gk. *embryon* (prec.) + *logos*, treatise, discussion, word]. The study of the development of the embryo and fetus.

empir'ical [Gk. *empeirikos*, experience]. Not based upon any known scientific fact but purely upon experience.

empȳe'ma [Gk. *empyema*, suppuration, fr. *en*, in + *pyon*, pus]. Pus in any cavity, but, especially in the pleural cavity.

endem'ic [Gk. *endemos*, a native, fr. *en*, in + *demos*, the people]. Relating to a disease of which one or more cases are always present in the particular district under consideration.

endo- [Gk. *endo*, within]. A prefix meaning in, within.

endog'enous (j) [Gk. *endon*, within + root *gen*, beget, produce]. Formed within the body.

en′terogastro′ne [Gk. *enteron*, intestine + *gaster*, belly]. A principle (chalone) formed in the mucosa of the duodenum which under the influence of fatty materials in the chyme passes into the blood stream and inhibits the secretion of gastric juice and the movements of the stomach.

ephēbiat′rics [Gk. *ephēbos*, a youth coming to manhood + *iatrikos*, medical treatment]. The branch of medicine concerned with matters relating to puberty and adolescence; *see* Geriatrics, Pediatrics.

ep′i- [Gk. upon]. A prefix meaning upon, above, on top of, the upper side.

ep′izo′ic [Gk. *epi*, on + *zōon*, an animal]. Living parastically on the body surface.

ep′izoot′ic [prec.]. Relating to an epidemic disease in animals.

erg [Gk. *ergon*, work]. A unit of work, defined as that performed in moving a mass against a force of 1 dyne.

es′trogen [Gk. *oistros*, mad desire + root, *gen*, produce]. Any substance that induces effects similar to those of estradiol.

ēvagina′tion [L. *e*, out + *vagina*, a sheath]. The protrusion of the wall or other part of any structure.

exfōlia′tion [L. *ex*, out + *folium*, a leaf]. The shedding of superficial parts of any structure, especially in layers or sheets; a form of desquamation.

ex′ocrine [Gk. *exo*, outside + *krino*, to separate (secrete)]. Relating to an external secretion; e.g., saliva, gastric juice, etc., that is secreted onto the surface of the body or into one of the body cavities.

exog′enous (j) [Gk. *exo*, outside root, *gen*, produce]. Formed or originating outside the body.

exophthal′mos [Gk. *ex*, out + *ophthalmos*, the eye]. Protrusion of the eyeballs beyond their normal positions.

ex′terocep′tor [L. *exterus*, outside, external + *ceptor*, a receiver]. One of the end organs, receptors (e.g., of touch) on the skin.

ex′terofec′tive [L. *exterus*, outside + *facio*, do]. Professor Cannon's term for the cerebrospinal nervous system, as opposed to the interofective (or autonomic) nervous system.

ex′udate [L. *ex*, out + *sudare*, to sweat]. A fluid or semifluid material; e.g., serum or pus, which flows or oozes from any part.

falciform (făl′si-form) [L. *falx* (*falc-*), a sickle + *forma*, form]. Shaped like a sickle.

fecunda′tion (k) [L. *fecundo* (*-atus*), make fruitful]. Fertilization.

fenes′tra [L. a window]. A window; e.g., fenestra ovale (fenestra vestibuli) of the internal ear.

fe′tus; foe′tus [L. offspring]. The unborn offspring from the eighth week to the termination of pregnancy.

fībril′la, -ae [L. *fibrilla*, diminutive of *fibra*, a fiber]. A minute fiber.

fībrilla′tion [prec.]. Fine contractions or twitchings of muscle due to independent activity of the separate fibers. It occurs in degenerating skeletal muscle, in cardiac muscle in electrocution, as a result of poisoning by certain drugs, and just preceding death from almost any cause.

fila′ment [fr. L. *filium*, a thread]. An extremely fine fiber or threadlike structure.

fi′lum termina′le [L. terminal thread]. A slender filament that descends from the end of the spinal cord to the termination of the vertebral canal.

fim′briated [L. *fimbria*, a fringe]. Fringed or like fringe.

fis′tula [L. a pipe, tube]. An abnormal passage leading from an abscess cavity, or any hollow organ or part, to the exterior.

foreign protein. A protein not naturally present in the body; e.g., a vegetable protein or one from another species; it acts as an antigen.

fos'sa [L. a trench or ditch]. A depression, usually in a bone and longitudinal in shape.

funic'ulus (k) [diminutive of L. *funis*, a cord]. A cord or cordlike structure, such as the umbilical or spermatic cord.

fu'siform [L. *fusus*, a spindle + *forma*, shape]. Spindleshaped.

Gasse'rian gang'lion. Semilunar ganglion.

gas'trula [fr. Gk. *gaster*, belly]. The embryo in the stage of development when it consists of a sac with a double-layered wall; the inner layer is the endoderm, the outer the ectoderm.

gēne [Gk. root *gen*, beget]. One of the theoretical particles of a chromosome that carries an hereditary character.

gen'era'tive [L. *generare*, beget]. Capable of reproduction, of procreation.

genet'ic [Gk. *genesis (-etic)*, generation]. Relating to heredity.

genet'ics [prec.]. The study of the laws and processes of heredity.

ge'notype [Gk. *genos*, birth + *typos*, an imprint]. The genetic constitution (combination of genes) of an organism.

ge'nus [L. birth, descent]. In the classification of animals or plants, the division next above the species; i.e., below the Family or the Tribe.

geriat'rics [Gk. *gerion*, an old man + *iatrikos*, medical care]. The branch of medicine concerned with matters pertaining to old age; *see* Ephebiatrics, Pediatrics.

glauco'ma [Gk. *glaukos*, bluish green]. Raised pressure within the eyeball due to an excess of fluid, the result in turn of blockage of the drainage system. It is a progressive disease leading to failure of vision.

gli'a. Neuroglia.

Gliss'on's capsule. The capsule of the liver.

glȳcogen'esis [Gk. *glykys*, sweet (sugar) + root *gen*, produce]. The formation of glucose from glycogen or of glycogen from glucose.

glȳcogenol'ysis [Gk. *glykys*, sweet (sugar) + *lysis*, dissolution]. The breakdown of glycogen to glucose.

glȳcol'ysis [prec.]. The breakdown of glucose to lactic acid or to carbon dioxide and water.

gly'coneogen'esis; glu'coneogen'esis [Gk. *glykys*, sweet (sugar) + *nēos*, new genesis, origin]. The formation of glucose from noncarbohydrate material, as from protein or fat.

gly'coprotein; glu'coprotein [Gk. *glykys*, sweet (sugar) + protein]. A conjugated protein containing a sugar group; it is present in mucin.

granula'tion(s) [L. *granulum*, diminutive of *granum*, a grain]. Masses of small grainlike bodies.

granulation tissue [prec.]. The vascular granular tissue that covers a healing open wound and becomes converted to scar tissue.

hap'loid [Gk. *haplous*, single]. Referring to the reduced number of chromosomes in the gametes; *see* Diploid.

heart block. Disease of the atrioventricular bundle that slows or blocks conduction of the impulse from the atria to the ventricles. In complete blockage the atria beat at the normal rate (70 per minute) but the ventricles beat at their own rate of about 40 per minute. The arterial pulse is, of course, at the ventricular rate.

he'matin [Gk. *haima (haimat-)*, blood]. The pigment (porphyin) of hemoglobin plus iron.

hemi- [Gk. half]. A prefix meaning half; *see* Semi-.

hemol′ysis [Gk. *haima,* blood + *lysis,* a setting free, dissolution]. The liberation of hemoglobin from the red cells.

Hen′le's loop. The U-shaped part of a renal tubule.

hep′ar [Gk. the liver]. The liver.

hepat′ic [Gk. *hēpar (hepat-),* the liver]. Relating to the liver.

het′ero- [Gk. *heteros,* other, different]. A prefix in words derived from the Greek, meaning different from, something else.

heterol′ogous [Gk. *heteros,* different, other + *logos,* relation]. Indicating a tissue or part derived from another species, or of a tissue or cells in a part not normal to them.

het′erotran′splant [Gk. *heteros,* different, other + transplant]. The grafting of a tissue or organ taken from an animal of one species to the body of an animal of another species. Except for certain tissues and under very special circumstances the operation is not permanently successful; i.e., the transplanted tissue dies.

hia′tus [L. an opening, fr. *hio (hiatus),* yawn]. A gap or opening, aperture, or fissure.

hiccup [imitative of the sound]. The spasmodic contraction of the diaphragm and the sound made thereby; should not be spelled or pronounced "hicough."

histol′ogy [Gk. *histos,* a web (tissue) + *logos,* treatise, discussion, word]. The microscopic study of tissues.

hol′ocrine [Gk. *holos,* all + *krino,* separate (secrete)]. Referring to a type of glandular secretion that consists of the cells of the gland itself.

ho′mo- [Gk. *homos,* same]. A prefix in words of Greek derivation meaning of the same kind or class, alike.

homoge′neous (j) [Gk. *homos,* same + *genos,* family, kind]. Having uniform structure and composition throughout.

homog′enous (j) [prec.]. Having the same consistency throughout and usually the same composition.

homol′ogous [foll.]. Referring to a homologue, having the characters of a homologue.

hom′ologue [Gk. *homos,* same + *logos,* relation, treatise, word]. Any organ or part of the body that resembles in structure or origin another organ or part elsewhere in the body; or an organ or part in one species that corresponds in some way with an organ or part in another species, such as the wing of a bird and the arm of a man.

ho′motransplanta′tion [Gk. *homos,* same + transplant]. The grafting of tissue or of an organ from one person to another, or from one animal to another of the same species.

hordeo′lum [fr. L. *hordeolus,* a sty]. A sty.

hōst [Gk. *hospes,* a host]. An organism that harbors and gives sustenance to another (usually pathogenic) organism.

hu′mor [L. *humor* (or *umor*), a fluid. (1) One of the body fluids, such as the aqueous humor of the eye which fills the space between the cornea and the lens. (2) A substance, such as a secretogogue (extractive) in food which is absorbed into the blood and stimulates a digestive secretion. (3) A substance liberated at nerve endings, e.g., acetylcholine, and acting locally. (4) One of the fluids of the body, e.g., blood, phlegm, black bile and yellow, upon which the ancient theories of disease were based (humoral doctrine).

hy′aloid [Gk. *hyalos,* glass + *eidos,* a resemblance]. Glasslike in appearance.

hy′drocēle [Gk. *hydor,* water + *kēlē,* swelling, tumor]. An abnormal collection of fluid in any saclike cavity in the body, especially in the tunica vaginalis of the testis.

hydrocephalus (hī-drō-sef'al-us) [Gk. *hydor*, water + *kephalē*, head]. Excessive amount of fluid in the ventricles of the brain *(internal hydrocephalus)*, or in the subarachnoid space *(external hydrocephalus)*.

hȳdrol'ysis [Gk. *hydor*, water + *lysis*, solution, dissolution]. The taking up of water by a compound that then splits into smaller molecules. It is brought about by certain enzymes and by the action of heat and strong chemicals—acids or alkalis.

hȳdrostat'ic pressure [Gk. *hydor*, water + *statos*, standing]. The pressure exerted by the weight of water or other liquid.

hy'per- [Gk. *hyper*, above, over]. A prefix indicating excess; above the normal.

hyperpla'sia [Gk. *hyper*, above + *plasis*, a molding]. Active multiplication of the cells of any tissue.

hyperpne'a [Gk. *hyper*, above + *pnoia*, the breath]. Exaggerated respirations, with an increase usually of the volume of air breathed per minute.

hyper'trophy [Gk. *hyper*, above + *trophe*, nourishment]. Increase in bulk of a tissue or organ caused by an increase in the individual cells.

hy'po- [Gk. *hypo*, under]. A prefix meaning under, beneath; less than normal.

incon'tinence of urine [fr. L. *in*, negative + *contineo*, hold together]. Involuntary passage or dribbling of urine.

inertia (in-ursh'ĕ-a) [L. *in*, negative + *iners* (fr. *in*, negative + *ars*, art), sluggishness, unskilled]. In physics, the "resistance" a body offers to a force tending to move it from a position of rest. *Inertia of the uterus*, sluggishness or absence of contractions of the uterus during labor.

in'guinal [L. *inguen (inguinis)*, the groin]. Relating to the groin.

inhibition [L. *hibeo (hibitus)*, keep back, fr. *habeo*, to have]. Depression or arrest of function of any organ, e.g., slowing or stoppage of the heart by stimulation of the vagus nerve, or the lessening of any process.

inos'culate [L. *in* + *osculum*, diminutive of *os*, mouth]. Anastomose.

insemination [L. *insemino*, sow or plant, fr. *semen (semin-)*, seed]. The deposition of semen in the vagina either during coitus or artificially.

in'sula [L. an island]. The small part of the cerebral cortex hidden in the Sylvian fissure. It is disclosed by raising the adjacent overlapping parts of the frontal and parietal lobes.

integ'ument [L. *integumentum*, a covering]. The skin.

in'ter- [L. between]. A prefix in words of Latin origin meaning between, within.

in'terocept'or [L. *inter*, within + *receptor*, a receiver]. A receptor in mucous membranes of the alimentary or respiratory tracts.

in'terofect'ive nervous system [L. *inter*, between + *facio*, do]. Professor Cannon's term for the autonomic nervous system.

interstitial (in'tur-stish'al) [L. *interstitium*, fr. *inter*, between + *sisto*, stand]. Relating to spaces between fibers, cells, etc., especially in the tissues generally, as *interstitial fluid*.

in'tra- [L. within]. A prefix in words of Latin derivation meaning within.

in'trader'mal [L. *intra*, within + Gk. *derma*, the skin]. Within the skin, into the skin, as pertaining to an injection.

in'tro- [L. into]. A prefix meaning into.

invag'ina'tion (j) [L. *in*, in + *vagina*, a sheath]. The pushing of one part of a hollow structure inwards towards its center; to ensheath.

inver'sion [L. *inverto (inversus)*, a turning about]. (1) A turning into a reversed position, as inversion of the uterus, in which the interior of the uterus is turned outward and the organ displaced downward. (2) A turning inward, as inversion of the foot. (3) The conversion of a disaccharide to a monosaccharide; e.g., of cane sugar to glucose and fructose.

i'soagglu'tinin [foll.]. An antibody present in the serum of a member of one blood group that agglutinates the red cells of the blood of another group; that is, causing agglutination of cells in blood of the same species.

i'soagglutin'ogen [Gk. *isos,* same, equal + L. *agglutino,* glue together]. A substance (antigen) associated with the erythrocytes that reacts with an agglutinin (antibody) in the serum of a member of the same species and causes clumping together of the cells; *see* blood groups (Ch. 7).

jaw jerk. Reflex contraction of the jaw muscles following a tap on the chin.

kar'yokine'sis (car'yo-) [Gk. *karyon,* a nut *(nucleus)* + *kinesis,* movement]. Mitosis.

kar'yoplasm (car'yo-) [Gk. *karyon,* a nut *(nucleus)* + *plasma,* a thing formed]. The nonchromatin substance of the cell nucleus.

ker'atin [Gk. *keras (kerat),* horn]. A protein in the outer layers of skin, and in horn, nails, etc.

kerati'tis [Gk. *keras (kerat),* horn, the cornea + *itis,* meaning inflammation]. Inflammation of the cornea of the eye.

kētogen'ic [*keto (ketone)* + root *gen,* produce]. Referring to certain foods, especially fats, which tend to cause the production of ketone bodies.

knee jerk. A quick extensor movement of the knee, a kick, caused by tapping the ligamentum patellae while the leg is hanging loosely in the flexed position. It is absent in certain nervous diseases and abnormally active in others.

Kup'ffer cells. Large star-shaped cells attached to the walls of the sinusoids of the liver. They belong to the reticulo-endothelial system and are phagocytic.

lacta'tion [L. *lacto (atus),* to suckle (fr. *lac,* milk)]. The secretion of milk.

lacu'na, -ae [L. diminutive of *lacus,* a hollow or a lake]. A hollow space or gap in any tissue or organ.

lamel'la, -ae [L. diminutive of *lamina,* a layer or plate]. A thin layer, plate, or stratum.

lat'eral [L. *latus,* side]. In a direction toward a side, away from the mid-line of the body.

lesion (le'zhŭn) [L. *laedo (laessus),* to injure]. Any injury or structural abnormality in a tissue, organ, or part due to disease; e.g., a tubercle of a lung in tuberculosis, or the pustule of the skin in smallpox.

leuce'mia; leuke'mia [Gk. *leukos,* white + *haima,* blood]. A disease of the blood in which the white cells are greatly increased in number, there being many abnormal and primitive forms in the circulation. The disease may be acute or chronic, and according to which type of cell predominates in the blood—lymphocyte, myelocyte or myeloblast, or monocyte—it is called *lymphatic, myelogenous,* or *monocytic* leukemia.

leucope'nia [*leuco (leucocyte,* fr. Gk. *leukos,* white + *kytos,* cell) + *penia,* poverty]. A pronounced reduction of leucocytes; scarcity of leucocytes.

lip'opro'tein [Gk. *lipos,* fat + *protein*]. A conjugated protein containing a lipid group in its molecule.

lob'ūle [L. *lobulus,* diminutive of *lobus*]. A small lobe, or a subdivision of a lobe.

lymphangi'tis [L. *lympha,* clear water + Gk. *angeion,* a vessel + *itis,* meaning inflammation]. Inflammation of lymph vessels.

ly'sin [Gk. *lysis,* disintegration, dissolution]. Any agent that destroys cells by breaking them up or dissolving them. One that destroys blood cells is a *hemolysin;* bacteria, a *bacteriolysin;* and cells in general, a *cytolysin.*

ly'sis [Gk. disintegration, dissolution]. Disintegration of any structure, red cells, bacteria, fibrin, etc. Also used as a suffix in words of Greek origin, meaning breakdown or disintegration; e.g., *cytolysis*.

macera'tion [L. *macero (atus)*, soften by soaking]. Softening or breaking up by soaking in water or other liquid.

mac'roscopic (k) [Gk. *macros*, large + *skopeo*, to view]. Capable of being seen by the naked eye.

mag'enstras'se [Ger. *magen*, stomach + *strasse*, road]. The part of the interior of the stomach extending along the lesser curvature from the cardia to the region of the pylorus that is first traversed by the food after it has entered the stomach.

maras'mus [Gk. *marasmos*, a withering]. A state characterized by dehydration, wasting, and weakness; seen especially in infants as a result of infection or faulty feeding.

me'deal. In a direction toward the mid-line of the body.

medul'la [fr. L. *medius*, middle]. Any very soft structure, or the interior of an organ; e.g., the adrenal medulla, as opposed to the outer part, or cortex; marrow, spinal cord, medulla oblongata.

Meibomian gland (mī-bo'me-an). One of the glands at the margin of an eyelid.

meiosis (mī-o'sis) [Gk. a lessening]. Reduction division.

Mende'lian laws. The laws of heredity discovered by Gregor Mendel, an Augustinian monk, of the 19th century, living in Brunn, Austria. Studying inheritance in pea plants, he found that characters were transmitted to the offspring as independent factors, or genes. When two varieties of plant, each pure for a different character (shortness and tallness) are crossed, their progeny (F_1 generation) will be all tall; but they received a gene for shortness from their short parent as well as a gene for tallness from the tall parent; the character tallness that appears is called *dominant,* the hidden character shortness is termed *recessive.* These hybrid individuals produce three types of gametes, 25 percent of which contain only genes for tallness (dominant), 50 percent genes for both tallness and shortness, and 25 percent genes for shortness (recessive) only. When these are interbred, the offspring (F_2 generation) will be 75 percent tall and 25 percent short; that is, only those that had not received a gene for tallness from either parent will be short.

menin'gocele [Gk. *meninx (meaning-)*, a membrane + *kēlē*, a swelling, tumor]. A protrusion of the meninges of the brain or spinal cord through a defect in the skull or vertebral column.

mer'ocrine [Gk. *meros*, a part + *krino*, to separate (secrete)]. A secretion, such as the gastric or pancreatic juice, which is merely a product of the gland cells, and not part of their substance; *see* Holocrine.

meta- [Gk. after, between, over, beyond]. A prefix meaning after, over, beyond; or indicating a transformation from something else that has gone before.

metamorph'osis [Gk. *meta*, prec. + *morphē*, form]. A change, usually radical, in form; transformation, as that of the tadpole into the frog.

metazoon, -a [Gk. *meta* + *zoon*, animal]. A member of any class of animal above the Protozoa; that is an animal composed of many cells.

minimal air. The air that remains in the lungs after their removal from the body, and that gives pulmonary tissue its buoyancy.

mōmen'tum [L. motion]. The quantity of motion, the product of mass and velocity; impetus, the tendency of a moving body to continue in its course.

mon'ocȳte [Gk. *monos*, single + *kytos*, a hollow (cell)]. A white blood cell with a single unlobed nucleus. It resembles a large lymphocyte, but its nucleus is more deeply indented, being kidney or horseshoe shaped. Monocytes constitute from 2 to 8 percent of the leucocytes. They are elements of the reticulo-endothelial system.

mononu'clear [Gk. *monos*, single + *nuclear* (nucleus)]. Referring to a cell with but one nucleus.

morbil'li [L. *morbillus*, diminutive of *morbus*, a disease]. Measles.

motor end plate. The structure on the muscle fiber in which the motor nerve terminates.

multicellular [L. *multi*, many]. Consisting of many cells.

my'eloblast [Gk. *myelos*, marrow + *blastos*, a germ]. A granulocyte in a very early stage of its development (in the bone marrow).

my'elocyte [Gk. *myelos*, marrow + *kytos*, hollow (cell)]. A granulocyte in a late stage of its development (in the bone marrow).

myogen'ic [Gk. *mys*, muscle + root *gen*, produce]. Originating in muscle or from muscle.

myoneur'al [Gk. *mys*, muscle + *neuron*, nerve]. Relating to both muscle and nerve. Myoneural *junction*, the connection between a motor nerve ending and the muscle fiber; it has the properties of a synapse.

navic'ular (k) [L. diminutive of *navis*, a boat]. Shaped like a boat; scaphoid.

ne'oplasm [Gk. *neos*, new + *plasma*, something formed]. A new growth, a tumor composed of masses of newly formed cells.

neuri'tis [Gk. *neuron*, a nerve + *itis*, meaning inflammation]. Inflammation of a nerve.

neurogen'ic [Gk. *neuron*, nerve + root *gen*, origin]. Of nervous origin.

neurohu'moral [Gk. *neuron*, nerve + *humor*, q.v.]. Relating to the theory that nervous effects are transmitted by chemical substances (humors) liberated at the nerve endings; e.g., acetylcholine.

no'tochord [Gk. *nōtos*, back + *chordē*, cord]. A flexible bar in the early embryo around which the vertebral column is developed.

nu'clease [*nucleus* + *ase*, meaning an enzyme]. An enzyme that splits nucleic acids.

nu'cleopro'tein. A conjugated protein containing nucleic acid. It is an essential constituent of chromatin.

nystag'mus [Gk. *nystagmos*, a nodding]. A rhythmical oscillation of the eyeballs occurring in certain disease, and normally after rapid rotation of the body. The movements are most commonly from side to side, but may be up and down or rotary.

ob- [L. against, toward]. A prefix in words of Latin origin, meaning against or toward.

odont'oid [Gk. *odous (odont-)*, a tooth + *eidos*, a resemblance]. Shaped like a tooth.

-oid [Gk. *eidos*, a resemblance]. A suffix in words of Greek derivation, meaning a likeness to, resembling.

oligu'ria [Gk. *oligos*, few, little + *ourēsis*, urination]. Scanty urine.

-oma. A suffix added to words of Greek derivation to indicate a swelling or tumor of any kind; e.g., carcinoma, sarcoma.

ontogen'esis; ontog'eny [Gk. *on*, being + *genesis*, origin]. The developmental history of an individual, as opposed to the history of a race; *see* Phylogeny.

ontol'ogy [Gk. *ōn (ontos)*, being + *logos*, discussion, treatise]. The study of the development of an individual; embryology.

onychia (o-nik'e-ah) [Gk. *onyx (onych-)*, nail]. Inflammation of the root of a finger- or toenail, with suppuration and usually shedding of the nail.

o'öcyte [Gk. *ōon*, an egg + *kytos*, a hollow (cell)]. The primitive ovum in the Graafian follicle.

op'sonins [Gk. *opson*, sauce]. Substances in blood that stimulate the leucocytes (neutrophils) to attack bacteria—fancifully speaking, they make the latter more appetizing.

oral [L. *os (oris)*, mouth]. Relating to the mouth.

order. A division in the classification of animals or plants between the Class or Subclass (above) and the Family (below).

organ'ic [Gk. *organikos*, relating to an organ]. (1) In chemistry, relating to compounds containing carbon. (2) Relating to a disease associated with a structural change in a tissue or organ, as opposed to functional. (3) Pertaining to animal or vegetable life, as opposed to the inorganic world.

or'ganism. Any living thing, animal or plant.

orthope'dic [Gk. *orthos*, straight, right, true + *pais (paid)*, a child]. Relating to the study and treatment of chronic diseases of bones and joints and the correction of deformities, not only of children.

orthostat'ic [Gk. *orthos*, straight, right, true + *statos*, standing]. Relating to the upright (standing) position.

os, ora [L. mouth]. A mouth.

os, ossa [L. bone]. A bone.

osteogen'esis [Gk. *osteon*, bone + *genesis*, production]. Bone formation.

ovariec'tomy [L. *ovarium*, ovary + Gk. *ektomē*, excision]. Excision of the ovaries; castration of the female.

ox'yphil [Gk. *oxys*, sharp, acid + *philos*, fond]. Acidophil, eosinophil.

oxytocin (oks-i-to'sin) [Gk. *oxys*, swift + *tokos*, childbirth]. A principle of the neural lobe (posterior lobe) of the pituitary that causes uterine contractions; pitocin.

palpa'tion [L. *palpatio*, fr. *palpo*, to touch]. Determining, usually with a finger or the fingers or palm of the hand by touching.

para- [Gk. alongside, near, beside]. A prefix meaning beside, on the side of, not quite normal.

para-aminobenzoic acid. A factor of the vitamin B complex essential for the growth of certain microorganisms. Some sulfonamides exert their antibacterial action by rendering this vitamin unavailable for the infecting bacteria.

paren'chyma [Gk. anything poured in beside]. The part of an organ or tissue composed of cells that perform the specific function of the organ or tissue, such as the contractile fibers of muscle or the secreting cells of a gland, as opposed to the nonspecific supporting tissue or stroma of connective tissue.

paren'teral [Gk. *para*, beside, contrary to + *enteron*, intestine]. Referring to a route of administering a drug or agent of any kind other than by the gastrointestinal tract; that is, subcutaneously, intravenously, etc.

path'ogen [Gk. *pathos*, suffering, disease + root *gen*, produce]. Any organism that causes disease; hence, *pathogenic.*

pectoril'oquy [L. *pectus (pector-)*, breast, chest + *loquor*, to speak]. In auscultation of the chest, the transmission of the sounds of the patient's voice to the examiner's ear.

ped'icle [L. a little foot, diminutive of *pes (ped)*]. A stalk.

pepsin'ogen [*pepsin* + Gk. root *gen*, produce]. The inactive enzyme secreted by the gastric glands and converted to active pepsin by acid.

per- [L. through]. A prefix denoting through, around; in chemistry, the highest compound in a series.

percussion [L. *percussio,* a beating]. A method of physical examination, especially of the chest, in which the nature of underlying structure is determined from the sound caused by tapping with an instrument or finger.

peri- [Gk. around, beyond, surrounding]. A prefix meaning around, surrounding, exceedingly.

pe′trous [Gk. *petra,* a rock]. Hard, like stone.

phe′notype [Gk. *phainō,* display + *typos,* model]. The appearance, structure, coloring, and other characteristics of an organism.

phlebi′tis [Gk. *phleps (phleb-),* a vein + *itis,* meaning inflammation]. Inflammation of a vein.

phlebot′omy [Gk. *phleps (phleb-),* a vein + *tomē,* a cutting]. Incision into a vein, as for withdrawing blood.

pho′bia [Gk. *phobos,* fear]. An unreasonable fear of some particular thing or condition; e.g., *claustrophobia,* a morbid fear of any closed space; *agoraphobia,* fear of open spaces. The term is also used to indicate hypersensitivity to some form of stimulation; e.g., *photophobia,* pain in the eyes and spasm of the lids to a light that normally would cause no discomfort.

phos′phagen [*phosphorus* (Gk. *phōs,* light + *phoros,* bearing) + root *gen*]. Creatine phosphate, phosphocreatine.

pho′tochem′ical [Gk. *phōs (phōt),* light + chemical]. Pertaining to a chemical reaction caused by light energy, as in the rods and cones of the retina.

pho′topho′bia [Gk. *phōs (phōt-)* + *phobia*]. Hypersensitivity of the eyes to light.

photop′ic [Gk. *phōs,* light + *ōps,* the eye]. Pertaining to vision in bright light, a function of the cones of the retina.

pho′tosyn′thesis [Gk. *phōs (phōt-)* + *synthesis*]. The formation of carbohydrate from carbon dioxide and water, and the liberation of oxygen by sunlight acting upon chlorophyll.

phren′ic [Gk. *phrēn,* diaphragm]. Relating to the diaphragm.

phreni′tis [Gk. *phrēn,* diaphragm, seat of the emotions (an ancient belief) + *itis,* meaning inflammation]. Delirium, inflammation of the brain.

phylogen′esis; phylog′eny [Gk. *phylē, phylon,* a tribe + *genesis,* origin]. The development (evolution) of a race of animals or plants; *see* Ontogenesis.

phy′lum [L. fr. Gk. *phylon,* a tribe, race]. In the classification of animals or plants, a large division below the Subkingdom and above the Subphylum or the Class.

pi′siform [L. *pisum,* pea + *forma,* form]. Resembling a pea in shape and size.

plank′ton [Gk. *planktos,* wandering]. Minute free-swimming or floating marine organisms, either of the animal or vegetable kingdom.

pleth′ora [Gk. *plethorē,* fullness]. A fullness, an excess, especially of blood; congestion.

pli′ca (-ae) circula′ris (-es) [fr. L. *plica,* a fold + *circularis,* in the form of a small circle]. One of the transversely circular folds of mucous membrane in the small intestine.

pol̄y-. A Greek prefix meaning many.

pol′ycythe′mia [Gk. *poly,* many + *kytos,* a hollow (cell) + *haima,* blood]. A blood condition marked by an abnormally large number of red cells.

polyneuri′tis [Gk. *poly,* many + *neuritis*]. A condition marked by inflammatory and degenerative changes in the peripheral nerves, a symptom of vitamin B deficiency (beriberi) or chronic alcoholism.

polyu′ria [Gk. *poly,* many, much + *ouron,* urine]. Excessive secretion of urine.

pro- [Gk. before]. A prefix denoting before, forward.

prolapse (prō-laps') [L. *prolapsus*, a falling]. The descent of an organ from its normal position; e.g., prolapse of the uterus.

proliferation [L. *proles*, offspring + *fero*, to bear]. Multiplication of the cells of any tissue, usually in the sense of excessive.

protozo'on, -a [Gk. *protos*, first + *zoon*, an animal]. An animal composed of a single cell; a unicellular animal.

pterygoid (ter'ĭ-goyd) [Gk. *pteryx (pteryg-)*, a wing + *eidos*, a resemblance]. Resembling a wing.

pto'sis [Gk. a falling]. A falling down, prolapse, of any structure, but especially drooping of one or both eyelids.

pulse pressure. The pressure in the arterial system in excess of the diastolic pressure. For example, if the diastolic pressure amounts to 80 mm of mercury and the systolic pressure to 120 mm, the pulse pressure will be 40 mm of mercury.

purpura (pur'pū-rah) [L. fr. Gk. *porphyra*, purple]. A hemorrhagic state in which spontaneous bleeding occurs into the subcutaneous tissues, deeper layers of the skin, into or from the surface of mucous membranes, or into joints and other structures. It is often due to a deficiency of platelets.

pўram'idal. Shaped like a pyramid.

pyr'iform [L. *pirium*, a pear + *forma*, form]. Pear shaped.

quadrigem'inal (j) [L. *quadri*, four + *geminus*, twin]. Referring to any structure having four similar parts, but especially to the four bodies on the dorsal aspect of the midbrain (quadrigeminal bodies, or colliculi).

quin'sy [ME. corruption of Med. L. *quinancia*, fr. Gk. *cyanche*, sore throat, dog-throttling dog collar (fr. *kynōn*, dog + *anchein*, to throttle)]. Inflammation of the tonsils, with suppuration (suppurative tonsillitis).

râle (rahl) [Fr. rattle]. A crackling, clicking, bubbling, rubbing, or whistling sound heard upon auscultating the chest in certain diseases of the lungs.

ra'mus, -i [L. a branch]. A branch, as of an artery or nerve; or a barlike part of a bone, such as the ramus of the mandible.

recessive [L. *recedo (recessus)*, draw back]. An hereditary character that is latent, or masked by another character called *dominant*.

regurgitation [L. *re*, back + *gurgito (atus)*, flood]. The movement of material in a direction the reverse of normal, as the passage of the stomach contents into the esophagus (usually without vomiting), of duodenal contents into the stomach, or of blood from the aorta during diastole into the left ventricle.

Reis'sner's membrane. The membrane of the internal ear that separates the scala vestibuli from the cochlear duct.

retention of urine. Inability to void urine either as a result of a mechanical obstruction of the urinary passage or nervous disease that abolishes the normal micturition reflex.

retic'ulo-endothe'lial sys'tem [L. *reticulum*, a network + *endothelial*, relating to the endothelial tissues]. A system of cells in, or associated with, various reticular and endothelial structures, and also present in the general connective tissues. They have diverse functions and there are several types of these cells; some of those in the connective tissues are wandering, others are fixed. Those in the reticulum of the spleen are very large and phagocytic *(macrophages)*, and those in the blood sinuses of the liver *(Kupffer cells)* as well as some in the general connective tissues convert hemoglobin into bile pigment. Others are found in the reticulum of the bone marrow. The monocytes of the blood and certain small cells in neuroglia *(microglia)* belong to this system.

retic'ulum [L. diminutive of *rete*, a net]. A fine network.

re'tro- [L. back, backwards]. A prefix meaning backwards, behind, posterior to.

rhe'obase [Gk. *rheos*, a stream (current) + *basis*, base]. The minimal strength of an electric current that, acting for an indefinite but fairly long time, causes excitation of a tissue, e.g., nerve or muscle.

rhom'boid [Gk. *rhombos* + *eidos*, a resemblance]. Resembling a rhombus, which is a figure (exclusive of the square) with four equal and parallel sides.

rhonchus (ron'kus) [L. fr. Gk. *rhenchus*, a snoring]. A rough, roaring, whistling, or snoring rale heard upon auscultation over the bronchi in certain abnormal states of the lungs.

sciatic foramen (sī-at'ĭk for-a'men) [corruption of Gk. *ischiadikos*, fr. *ischion*, the hip]. One of the two foramina, greater and lesser, formed by a ligament closing the gap of the corresponding sciatic notch of the os coxae.

sciat'ic notch [prec.]. One of the two notches, greater and lesser, of the os coxae. The greater sciatic notch is the large indentation on the posterior border of the ilium below the posterior inferior spine; the lesser sciatic notch is situated on the posterior border of the ischium just above the tuberosity. Both notches are converted into foramina in the living subject by ligaments.

sciatica (si-at'ika). Inflammation or pain in the sciatic nerve.

sclero'sis [Gk. *sklerosis*, hardness]. Induration, hardening of a structure, such as the walls of arteries (arteriosclerosis) due to the deposition of calcium salts, or of any tissue, such as nervous or hepatic, by the replacement of its parenchyma by fibrous tissue.

sco'topic [Gk. *skōtos*, darkness + *ōps*, the eye]. Pertaining to vision in dim light, a function of the rods of the retina.

se'bum [L. tallow]. The greasy secretion of the sebaceous glands.

semi- [L. *semis*, half]. Prefix meaning half, equivalent to Greek *hemi-*.

sig'moid [Gk. *sigma*, letter S + *eidos*, a resemblance]. S shaped, e.g., the *sigmoid colon* (iliac and pelvic colons), which together form an S-shaped curve.

spay'ing [Gk. *spadōn*, a eunuch]. Ovariectomy, castration of a female.

species (spe'shēz) [L. kind, form, appearance]. In the classification of animals and plants, the division next below the Genus; its members interbreed.

specific gravity (abbreviated sp. gr.). The weight of any given substance as compared with an equal weight of distilled water. Thus, water having a value of 1.000, the specific gravity of urine is 1.002-1.030 (depending upon the concentration); blood, 1.055-1.060; plasma, 1.022-1.26; and cerebrospinal fluid, 1.006-1.08.

sphyg'mogram [Gk. *sphygmos*, pulse + *gramma*, a record]. A pulse tracing.

sphyg'momanom'eter [Gk. *sphygmos*, pulse + *manos*, pressed (pressure) + *metron*, measure]. An instrument for measuring the blood pressure.

spi'na bif'ida [L. *spina*, a spine, thorn, the back + *bifida*, cleft into two parts]. A congenital anomaly in which the arches of the vertebrae of a portion of the spinal column are absent or defective, so that the spinal membranes, or even the cord itself, protrude, and come to lie just beneath the soft tissues of the back. It occurs most commonly in the lumbar region.

stel'late [L. *stella*, a star]. Star shaped.

steno'sis [Gk. *stenos*, narrow]. A narrowing, usually applied to an orifice or tube; e.g., aortic stenosis.

Stenson's duct. The duct of the parotid gland.

Stokes-Adams disease. Heart block, causing a slow pulse, with arteriosclerosis, the combination of the two conditions making for a low diastolic pressure and consequent interference with the blood supply to the brain. Attacks of syncope and convulsions result.

sto'ma, stomata [Gk. *stōma (-atis)*, a mouth]. Any mouthlike opening.

stomati'tis [Gk. *stōma (-atis)*, a mouth + *itis*, inflammation]. Inflammation of the mouth.

stro'ma, stromata [Gk. a bed, mattress]. The framework of any tissue or organ; it is usually composed of connective tissue.

sty; stye (stī) [fr. OE. *stigan*, to rise]. Inflammation of one of the small glands at the margin of an eyelid; hordeolum.

sub- [L. below]. A prefix indicating below, less than.

sul'cus (k), **sul'ci** (sī) [L. a furrow, a ditch]. A narrow, relatively deep depression in any structure, but especially in the cerebral cortex.

super-; supra- [L. above, beyond]. A prefix indicating above, beyond, greater than, on the upper side.

suppura'tion [L. *suppura (-atus)*, to form pus *(pur)*]. Pus formation.

sym'patholyt'ic [*sympatho* (fr. Gk. *syn*, with + *pathos*, feeling) + *lysis (lyt-)*, freeing from, dissolution]. Referring to the action of certain agents in temporarily paralyzing sympathetic nerve fibers.

sym'pathomimet'ic [*sympatho* (prec.) + Gk. *mimikos*, imitating]. Referring to any drug or other agent, e.g., adrenaline, that imitates the action of sympathetic nerve fibers.

syn-; sym- [Gk. together with]. A prefix meaning with, together, joined; equivalent to Latin *con-*.

synarthro'sis [Gk. *syn*, together + *arthrosis*, articulation]. An immovable junction between two bones without an intervening joint.

syncy'tium [Gk. *syn*, together, with + *kytos*, a hollow (cell)]. A mass of multinucleated protoplasm, such as the cardiac muscle, in which the cells are not distinct and separate units but are continuous with one another without an intervening cell membrane.

syndesmo'sis [Gk. *syndesmos*, ligament (fr. *syn*, together + *deō*, bind)]. A synarthrosis in which the opposed bones are held together by fibrous tissue, as at the lower ends of the tibia and fibula.

syndrome (sin'drōm or sin'drō-mē) [Gk. *syn*, together + *dromos*, a running]. A group of symptoms that together form the picture of a disease.

syn'thesis [Gk. *syn*, together + *thesis*, a putting, an arrangement]. A building up of smaller parts into a larger whole; the putting together of smaller chemical groups to form larger and more complex compounds.

ta'bes dorsa'lis [L. *tabes*, a wasting away + *dorsalis*, of the back]. A nervous disease affecting the ganglia of the posterior spinal nerve roots and posterior columns of the spinal cord. It is characterized by ataxia, loss of the knee jerks, severe shooting pains, and often atrophy of the optic nerve. It is usually the result of syphilis.

tach'ycar'dia (k) [Gk. *tachys*, rapid + *kardia*, heart]. Rapid action of the heart.

tach'yphylax'is (k) [Gk. *tachys*, rapid + *phylaxis*, protection]. Loss of or reduction in sensitivity to any agent; tolerance following repeated use.

tax'ia; tax'is [Gk. order, arrangement]. (1) A suffix in words of Greek origin. (2) Also used alone, meaning to correct a dislocation or to return a hernia by gentle pressure to its normal position. (3) The tendency for certain organisms to move toward or away from a particular thing or state, or to arrange themselves in a position relating to that particular thing or state; then usually used as in (1), i.e., *electrotaxis, chemotaxis, thermotaxis,* etc.

tel'erecept'or [Gk. *tēle,* distant + L. *receptor,* a receiver]. An end organ, such as the receptors of the retina or the olfactory organs, which perceives at a distance.

te'lophase [Gk. *telos,* end, fulfillment + *phasis,* appearance]. The final stage of mitosis.

ther'mola'bile [Gk. *thermē,* heat + L. *labilis,* perishable]. Susceptible to change or destruction by heat.

ther'mosta'ble; ther'mosta'bile [Gk. *thermē,* heat + L. *stabilis,* stable]. Not altered by moderate heat.

thrombo'sis [Gk. a curdling]. Clotting of blood within the vascular system.

throm'bus [Gk. *thrombos,* a clot, curd]. A clot within a blood vessel.

thymus [Gk. *thymos,* an excrescence, sweetbread]. A soft structure occupying the upper part of the mediastinum and lower extremity of the neck. It is relatively large in infants but shrinks in later childhood and is a mere vestige in adults. It consists of a reticulum, the spaces of which are packed with lymphocytes. Its outer part is called the cortex, its central part the medulla. Scattered throughout the latter are peculiar bodies, known as *Hassall's corpuscles* and composed of concentric layers of flat epithelial cells surrounding a large round granular cell. Though it has been suggested that the thymus is an endocrine organ, there is no definite evidence that it should be classed as such; its function is obscure.

ti'dal air. The air breathed during ordinary respiration; it amounts to about 500 cc in man.

tone [Gk. *tonos,* tone or a tone]. Continuous action as said of a nerve, such as the vagus, or the slight continuous contraction of healthy skeletal muscle.

trans- [L. across, through, beyond]. A prefix meaning across, through, beyond.

traum'a, traumata [Gk. a wound]. A wound or injury, usually one caused by violence or some mechanical agency.

tribe [L. *tribus*]. In the classification of animals and plants, a subdivision of the Family, frequently synonymous with Subfamily.

troch'lea (k) [L. a pulley]. A pulley.

troch'oid joint (k) [Gk. *trochos,* wheel + *eidos,* a resemblance]. A pivot joint, such as that between the odontoid process of the axis vertebra and the atlas.

tro'pism [Gk. *tropē,* a turning]. The tendency for certain organisms to turn toward something, as growing sprouts of plants turn toward the light, *phototropism,* and its roots into the ground, *geotropism.*

tu'bercle [fr. L. *tuberculum,* diminutive of *tuber,* a swelling]. (1) A small circumscribed elevation on a bone. (2) The lesion in tuberculosis.

tuberos'ity [L. *tuberositas,* an elevation, a swelling]. An elevation on a bone larger than a tubercle.

tympani'tēs [fr. Gk. *tympanon,* a drum]. Swelling of the abdomen due to gas in the intestine or, rarely, in the peritoneal cavity.

u'vea [L. *uvea,* a grape]. The middle coat of the eyeball, consisting of the choroid, ciliary muscle, and iris.

u'veal tract. Uvea.

va'gusstof'fe [Ger. *vagus,* substance]. The humor formed at the terminals of the vagus nerve; acetylcholine.

vallate [L. *vallo (ate),* surround with, fr. *vallum,* a rampart]. Referring to certain structures, e.g., papillae of the tongue, that are surrounded by a circular moatlike depression, bounded in turn by a slightly elevated rim.

vallec'ula (k) [L. diminutive of *vallis*, a valley]. The depression on either side of the tongue, or of the vermis of the cerebellum.

varicel'la (sel') [L. diminutive of *variola*]. Chickenpox.

var'icocēle [Gk. *varix (varic-)*, a dilated vein + *kēlē*, a swelling, tumor]. Dilatation of veins of the spermatic cord in the scrotum.

vario'la [L. diminutive of *varius*, spotted]. Smallpox.

văs [L. *vasa* (genitive plural, *vasorum*), a vessel, dish]. A vessel or tube; e.g., vas deferens.

va'sa vāsor'um [prec.]. The small blood vessels supplying the walls of the larger arteries.

vas'cular [L. *vasculum*, diminutive of *vas*, a vessel]. Referring to any tube or system of tubes containing fluid, but most commonly to the blood vessels or lymphatics.

va'somo'tor. Referring to changes in the calibers of the blood vessels.

vermic'ular (k) [L. *vermis*, a worm]. Wormlike.

vermiform [L. *vermis*, a worm + *forma*, form]. Wormlike; e.g. vermiform appendix.

ver'nix caseo'sa [L. *vernix*, varnish + *caseus*, cheese]. The fatty substance on the skin of the newborn.

vestib'ular membrane. Reissner's membrane.

vestib'ular organ. The utricle and saccule.

vi'ral. Relating to viruses.

vi'rus, viruses [L. poison]. One of a group of infecting agents of uncertain nature, but probably a large and complex nucleoprotein molecule near the border line between the living and the nonliving. Unlike bacteria, they can multiply only within cells. They are much smaller than bacteria, being able to pass through a filter with much finer pores than those required to hold back bacteria, hence the term *filtrable* viruses. Though viruses cannot be seen through an ordinary type of microscope, however powerful, the electron microscope reveals minute objects called *elementary bodies* that are probably the viruses themselves.

vis'cus (k), **vis'cera** (s) [L. an internal part]. Any internal organ, but especially of the thorax or abdomen.

Whar'ton's duct. The duct of the submaxillary gland.

whit'low [etymology dubious, perhaps corruption fr. OE. *quick (whick)* or *white* + *flaw*]. Inflammation of the soft tissue in the neighborhood of a nail; paronychia.

Wirsung's duct. The pancreatic duct.

wisdom tooth. One of the four molar teeth that erupt very late—from the eighteenth to the twenty-third year; it is the third molar on each side of the upper or the lower jaw.

zoology [Gk. *zōon*, an animal + *logos*, treatise, discussion]. The study of animals, their classification, structure, physiology, etc.

zy'mogen (j) [Gk. *zyme*, leaven *(enzyme)* + root *gen*, produce]. The substance from which an enzyme is formed; proenzyme.

Appendix
Weights and Measures

THE METRIC SYSTEM

Linear measures

The unit of the metric system is the meter, which is the one tenmillionth part of the meridian quadrant of the earth. In the nomenclature of the system, multiples of the meter are indicated by prefixes derived from the Greek, as follows:

Meter; decameter, 10 meters; hectometer, 100 meters; kilometer, 1000 meters.

Fractions of the meter are indicated by prefixes derived from the Latin, as follows:

Meter; decimeter, $\frac{1}{10}$ meter; centimeter, $\frac{1}{100}$ meter; millimeter, $\frac{1}{1000}$ meter.

In microscopy, the unit of measure is $\frac{1}{1000}$ of a millimeter, called the micron (symbol μ); $\frac{1}{1000}$ micron (or $\frac{1}{1,000,000}$ millimeter) called the millimicron (symbol $m\mu$), and $\frac{1}{10,000}$ micron, called the Angstrom unit (symbol Å, or abbr. Å.U.), are used as measures of the wavelengths of light.

Weights

The unit of weight is the gram, or gramme; abbreviation, usually g or gm. It is practically the weight of one cubic centimeter of distilled water at its maximum density (4° C). Multiples of this unit are designated by prefixes derived from the Greek numerals, as follows:

Gram; decagram, 10 grams; hectogram, 100 grams; kilogram (abbr. kilo), 1000 grams.

Fractions of the gram are designated by prefixes derived from the Latin numerals, as follows:

Gram; decigram, $\frac{1}{10}$ gram; centigram, $\frac{1}{100}$ gram; milligram, $\frac{1}{1000}$

701

gram; microgram, or gamma (symbol γ), $\frac{1}{1000}$ milligram (or $\frac{1}{1,000,000}$ gram).

Fluid measure; volume; capacity

The unit of volume is the cubic decimeter, called a liter; one liter of water weighs practically 1 kilogram. It is divided into the deciliter, $\frac{1}{10}$ liter (weight 100 grams); centiliter, $\frac{1}{100}$ liter (weight 10 grams); and milliliter (or cubic centimeter), $\frac{1}{1000}$ liter (weight 1 gram).

APOTHECARY AND AVOIRDUPOIS SYSTEMS

Weights

The apothecary system (or the metric) is used in the United States for measuring drugs and other medicinals. In Britain the avoirdupois system is used for the latter purpose, and, as in the United States, for measuring ordinary commodities.

Apothecaries' Weights (U. S.)

Pound		Ounces		Drachms		Scruples		Grains
1	=	12	=	96	=	288	=	5760
		1	=	8	=	24	=	480
				1	=	3	=	60
						1	=	20

Avoirdupois Weights

Pound		Ounces		Drachms		Grains
1	=	16	=	256	=	7000
		1	=	16	=	437.5
				1	=	27.34375

Fluid measures

United States

Gallon		Quarts		Pints		Fluid Ounces		Fluid Drachms		Minims
1	=	4	=	8	=	128	=	1024	=	61440
		1	=	2	=	32	=	256	=	15360
				1	=	16	=	128	=	7680
						1	=	8	=	480
								1	=	60

British (Imperial)

Gallon		Quarts		Pints		Fluid Ounces		Fluid Drachms		Minims
1	=	4	=	8	=	160	=	1280	=	76800
		1	=	2	=	40	=	320	=	19200
				1	=	20	=	160	=	9600
						1	=	8	=	480
								1	=	60

EQUIVALENTS

Linear measures

One kilometer = ⅝ mile, or 3281 feet; 8 kilometers = 5 miles; 1 meter = 39 inches; 1 centimeter = ⅖ inch; 1 millimeter = $\frac{1}{25}$ inch, or ½ line; 1 micron = $\frac{1}{25000}$ inch.

One mile = 1⅗ kilometers; 1 yard = 92 centimeters; 1 foot = 30.5 centimeters; 1 inch = 25 millimeters.

Weights

One kilogram = 2⅕ pounds, or 35⅕ ounces, avoirdupois; 1 gram = 15½ grains.

One pound avoirdupois = 453.6 grams; 1 ounce avoirdupois = 28.4 grams; 1 drachm = 3.89 grams; 1 grain = 0.065 gram.

To convert kilograms to pounds avoirdupois, multiply by 1000 and divide by 454; to convert pounds avoirdupois to kilograms, multiply by 454 and divide by 1000.

To convert grams to ounces avoirdupois, multiply by 20 and divide by 567; to convert ounces avoirdupois to grams, multiply by 567 and divide by 20.

Metric Equivalents of Apothecaries' Weights

Grains	Grams	Drachms	Grams
½	0.032395	1	3.88788
1	0.064798	4	15.55152
5	0.323990		
10	0.647980	Ounces	Grams
20	1.295960	1	31.10394
30	1.943940	4	124.41576

Metric Equivalents of Avoirdupois Weights

The equivalents for grams and fractions of a grain are the same as those of apothecaries' weights.

Drachms	Grams	Ounces	Grams
1	1.77182	1	28.34912
4	7.08728	8	226.79296
		16	453.58592

704 - Appendix

Equivalents of Metric in Apothecaries' or Avoirdupois Weights

Grams	Grains
0.1	1.54339
0.5	7.71699
1.0	15.43399
5.0	77.16995
10.0	154.33991

Kilograms	Ounces (Avoirdupois)	Kilograms	Pounds (Avoirdupois)
1	35.27	1	2.2048
5	176.37	5	11.0240
10	352.74	10	22.0480

Fluid measures

One liter = 1.76 imperial pints, or 2.1 U. S. pints; 1 cubic centimeter = 17 minims (British), or 16¼ minims (U. S.).

One imperial gallon = 4.55 liters; 1 U. S. gallon = 3.79 liters; 1 imperial pint = 568 cubic centimeters; 1 U. S. pint = 473 cubic centimeters; 1 fluid ounce (British) = 28.4 cubic centimeters; 1 fluid ounce (U. S.) = 29.5 cubic centimeters; 1 fluid drachm (British) = 3.5 cubic centimeters; 1 fluid drachm (U. S.) = 3.7 cubic centimeters; 1 minim = 0.065 cubic centimeter.

To convert liters to imperial gallons, multiply by 22 and divide by 100; to convert liters to U. S. gallons, multiply by 265 and divide by 1000 (by moving the decimal point three places to the left); to convert imperial gallons to liters, divide by 22 and multiply by 100; to convert U. S. gallons to liters, divide by 265 and multiply by 1000.

Metric Equivalents of U. S. Measures

Minims	Cubic Centimeters	Fluid Drachms	Cubic Centimeters	Fluid Ounces	Cubic Centimeters
1	0.061618	1	3.697086	1	29.576686
5	0.308091	5	18.485431	6	177.460116
10	0.616181			16 (pt.)	473.226976
15	0.924272				

Metric Equivalents of British (Imperial) Measures

Minims	Cubic Centimeters	Fluid Drachms	Cubic Centimeters	Fluid Ounces	Cubic Centimeters
1	0.059205	1	3.5523	1	28.4184
5	0.296025	5	17.7615	5	142.0920
10	0.592050			10	284.1840
15	0.888075			20 (pt.)	568.3680
20	1.184100				

Equivalents of Metric in U. S. Measures

Cubic Centimeters	Minims		Liter	Fluid ounces	Pints
0.1	1.62341		1	33.82108	2.11381
0.5	8.11706				
1.0	16.23412				
5.0	81.17061				
10.0	162.34122				

Equivalents of Metric in Imperial Measures

Cubic Centimeters	Minims		Liter	Fluid ounces	Pints
0.1	1.68911		1	35.19691	1.75984
0.5	8.44556				
1.0	16.89112				
5.0	84.45560				
10.0	168.91123				

MEASURES OF ENERGY

One kilogrammeter is the energy or force expended in raising a weight of 1 kilogram to a height of 1 meter. One foot-pound is the energy or force expended in raising a weight of 1 pound avoirdupois to a height of 1 foot.

One kilogrammeter = 7.24 foot-pounds.

One foot-pound = 0.1381 kilogrammeter.

SYMBOLS

℥	minim	>	greater than; whence, from which is derived	
℈	scruple			
ʒ	drachm	<	less than; from, derived from	
℥	ounce	∞	infinity	
O	pint	:	ratio; "is to"	
μ	micron	::	equality between ratios; "as"	
μμ	micromicron	*	birth	
℔	misce, mix	†	death	
+	plus; excess; acid reaction; positive	♀	female	
−	minus; deficiency; alkaline reaction; negative	♂	male	
±	plus or minus; either positive or negative; indefinite			

Comparative Temperature Scales

Centigrade.	Fahrenheit.
100	220
	210
90	200
	190
80	180
	170
70	160
	150
60	140
	130
50	120
40	110
	100
30	90
	80
20	70
	60
10	50
	40
0	30
	20
10	10
	0
20	10

The zero of the centigrade scale marks the temperature of melting ice (32° F); the zero of the Fahrenheit scale is an arbitrary point, that of the lowest temperature observed by the deviser of the scale during the winter of 1709, practically the temperature of a mixture of ice and salt; it corresponds to −17.77° C. The temperature of boiling water, at sea level, is marked 100° on the centigrade scale and 212° on the Fahrenheit scale. One degree F is therefore ⅝ degree C.

The following are rules for the conversion of the temperature of one scale into that of the other:

Above 0° C or 32° F

F to C: subtract 32, multiply by 5, divide by 9.
C to F: multiply by 9, divide by 5, add 32.

Between 0° and 32° F or −17.77° and 0° C

F to C: subtract from 32, multiply by 5, divide by 9.
C to F: multiply by 9, divide by 5, subtract from 32.

The Chemical Elements*

With their symbols, atomic numbers, and atomic weights
(Based on $C^{12} = 12$)

	Symbol	Atomic Number	Atomic Weight[a]		Symbol	Atomic Number	Atomic Weight
Actinium	Ac	89	[227]	Mercury	Hg	80	200.59
Aluminum	Al	13	26.9815	Molybdenum	Mo	42	95.94
Americium	Am	95	[243]	Neodymium	Nd	60	144.24
Antimony	Sb	51	121.75	Neon	Ne	10	20.183
Argon	Ar	18	39.948	Neptunium	Np	93	[237]
Arsenic	As	33	74.9216	Nickel	Ni	28	58.71
Astatine	At	85	[210]	Niobium	Nb	41	92.906
Barium	Ba	56	137.34	Nitrogen	N	7	14.0067
Berkelium	Bk	97	[249]	Nobelium	No	102	
Beryllium	Be	4	9.0122	Osmium	Os	76	190.2
Bismuth	Bi	83	208.980	Oxygen	O	8	15.9994[b]
Boron	B	5	10.811[b]	Palladium	Pd	46	106.4
Bromine	Br	35	79.909[c]	Phosphorus	P	15	30.9738
Cadmium	Cd	48	112.40	Platinum	Pt	78	195.09
Calcium	Ca	20	40.08	Plutonium	Pu	94	[242]
Californium	Cf	98	[251]	Polonium	Po	84	[210]
Carbon	C	6	12.01115[b]	Potassium	K	19	39.102
Cerium	Ce	58	140.12	Praseodymium	Pr	59	140.907
Cesium	Cs	55	132.905	Promethium	Pm	61	[147]
Chlorine	Cl	17	35.453[c]	Protactinium	Pa	91	[231]
Chromium	Cr	24	51.996[c]	Radium	Ra	88	[226]
Cobalt	Co	27	58.9332	Radon	Rn	86	[222]
Copper	Cu	29	63.54	Rhenium	Re	75	186.2
Curium	Cm	96	[247]	Rhodium	Rh	45	102.905
Dysprosium	Dy	66	162.50	Rubidium	Rb	37	85.47
Einsteinium	Es	99	[254]	Ruthenium	Ru	44	101.07
Erbium	Er	68	167.26	Samarium	Sm	62	150.35
Europium	Eu	63	151.96	Scandium	Sc	21	44.956
Fermium	Fm	100	[253]	Selenium	Se	34	78.96
Fluorine	F	9	18.9984	Silicon	Si	14	28.086[b]
Francium	Fr	87	[223]	Silver	Ag	47	107.870[c]
Gadolinium	Gd	64	157.25	Sodium	Na	11	22.9898
Gallium	Ga	31	69.72	Strontium	Sr	38	87.62
Germanium	Ge	32	72.59	Sulfur	S	16	32.064[b]
Gold	Au	79	196.967	Tantalum	Ta	73	180.948
Hafnium	Hf	72	178.49	Technetium	Tc	43	[99]
Helium	He	2	4.0026	Tellurium	Te	52	127.60
Holmium	Ho	67	164.930	Terbium	Tb	65	158.924
Hydrogen	H	1	1.00797[b]	Thallium	Tl	81	204.37
Indium	In	49	114.82	Thorium	Th	90	232.038
Iodine	I	53	126.9044	Thulium	Tm	69	168.934
Iridium	Ir	77	192.2	Tin	Sn	50	118.69
Iron	Fe	26	55.847[c]	Titanium	Ti	22	47.90
Krypton	Kr	36	83.80	Tungsten	W	74	183.85
Lanthanum	La	57	138.91	Uranium	U	92	238.03
Lead	Pb	82	207.19	Vanadium	V	23	50.942
Lithium	Li	3	6.939	Xenon	Xe	54	131.30
Lutetium	Lu	71	174.97	Ytterbium	Yb	70	173.04
Magnesium	Mg	12	24.312	Yttrium	Y	39	88.905
Manganese	Mn	25	54.9380	Zinc	Zn	30	65.37
Mendelevium	Md	101	[256]	Zirconium	Zr	40	91.22

[a] A value given in brackets denotes the mass number of the isotope of longest known half-life or the best-known isotope.

[b] The atomic weight varies because of natural variations in the isotopic composition of the element. The observed ranges are boron, ±0.003; carbon, ±0.00005; hydrogen, ±0.00001; oxygen, ±0.0001; silicon, ±0.001; sulfur, ±0.003.

[c] The atomic weight is believed to have an experimental uncertainty of the following magnitude: bromine, ±0.002; chlorine, ±0.001; chromium, ±0.001; iron, ±0.003; silver, ±0.003. For other elements the last digit given is believed to be reliable to ±0.5.

*Based on Table of Atomic Weights and printed by permission of the International Union of Pure and Applied Chemistry and the Butterworth Scientific Publications.

Classification of the Proteins

CLASS OF PROTEIN	CHARACTERISTICS	EXAMPLES
A. Simple proteins		
(1) *Albumins*	Soluble in water and coagulable by heat. Present in both animal and plant tissues	*Serum albumin, egg albumin, lactalbumin* and various vegetable albumins such as *leucosin* (in wheat, rye and barley), *legumelin* in lentils, soy-bean, beans and peas and *phaselin* in kidney bean
(2) *Globulins*	Soluble in dilute saline solutions; insoluble in water. Animal globulins are coagulated by heat. Vegetable globulins imperfectly or not coagulated by heat	*Serum globulin, fibrinogen* (and *fibrin*) *vitellin* of egg yolk and vegetable globulins such as *excelsin* (Brazil-nut), *edestin* (hemp), *phaseolin* (kidney bean), *legumin* (peas and lentils) and *tuberin* (potato). A number of other vegetable globulins have been isolated and named
(3) *Glutelins*	Found only in plants. Insoluble in water, saline or alcohol, but soluble in very dilute alkali	*Glutenin* of wheat, *oryzenin* of rice and *glutelin* of maize
(4) *Prolamines* or *Gliadins*	Found in cereals (except rice) soluble in 70-90 per cent alcohol. Insoluble in water. They contain a large proportion of proline and ammonia nitrogen	*Gliadin* of wheat, *hordein* of barley and *zein* of maize
(5) *Albuminoids* or *scleroproteins*	Especially resistant to the usual reagents. They enter into the construction of protective and connective tissues, e.g., skin, tendons, ligaments and bones	*Keratin* of hair, skin, bone, feathers, tortoise shell and egg-shell, *elastin*, *collagen*, *ossein* and *gelatin* of tendons, ligaments, bone, etc.
(6) *Histones*	Soluble in water and precipitated by ammonia solution and by alkaloids. They contain a large percentage of diamino acids (p. 625)	*Globin* of hemoglobin, *thymus histone; scombron* and *gadus histone* in spermatozoa of mackerel and cod-fish respectively
(7) *Protamines*	Found in combination with nucleic acid in heads of fish spermatozoa. Constructed predominantly of diamino acids	*Salmine* and *sturine* in spermatozoa of salmon and sturgeon respectively

B. *Conjugated proteins.* Proteins whose molecule is combined with another non-protein group

(1) *Nucleoproteins*	Nucleic acid in combination with a protein belonging usually to the class of histones or protamines. Found in cell nuclei	See ch. 48
(2) *Chromoproteins*	Protein in combination with a pigment (e. g., hematin) containing iron, copper or other metal	Hemoglobin, hemocyanin, etc.
(3) *Glycoproteins*	Proteins other than nucleoproteins in combination with a carbohydrate group	*Mucin* in salivary gastric and intestinal secretions; *ovomucoid* of egg white and *chondromucoid* of cartilage
(4) *Lipoproteins*	Proteins in combination with lipid	Present in plasma, milk, cell nuclei
(5) *Phosphoproteins*	Proteins other than nucleoproteins and lecithoproteins in combination with a phosphorus-containing group	*Caseinogen* (and casein), *vitellin* of egg-yolk

C. *Derivatives of proteins—derived proteins.* These are produced by the action of acids, alkalis or proteolytic enzymes upon certain of the proteins listed above

(a) *Primary derivatives* (1) *Proteans*	Insoluble products formed in the early stage of the action upon proteins of water, dilute acids and enzymes	

Classification of the Proteins (Cont.)

C. *Derivatives of proteins—derivated proteins.—Continued*

(2) *Metaproteins*	Formed in a later stage of the action of acid or alkali	*Acid* metaprotein, *alkali* metaprotein
(3) *Coagulated proteins*	Formed by the action of heat or of alcohol upon solutions of proteins	
(b) *Secondary derivatives*		
(1) *Proteoses*	Formed by the action of pepsin or trypsin upon proteins. They are soluble in water from which they are precipitated by saturation with ammonium sulphate. They are incoagulable by heat	*Albumose* from albumen, *globulose* from globulin, *caseose* from casein
(2) *Peptones*	These represent a further stage in action of proteolytic enzymes. They are soluble in water but are not precipitated from an aqueous solution by ammonium sulphate. They are not coagulated by heat	
(3) *Peptides, di-peptides, tripeptides and polypeptides*	Products formed in the final stages of proteolytic digestion	Glycyl-alanine, leucyl-glutamic acid, etc.

Amino Acids Present in Most Complete Proteins

I. ALIPHATIC AMINO-ACIDS

A. *Monoamino-monocarboxylic acids*

Glycine (or glycocoll) $C_2H_5NO_2$, or amino-acetic acid

$$CH_2—NH_2$$
$$|$$
$$COOH$$

Alanine $C_3H_7NO_2$ or α-amino-propionic acid

$$CH_3·CH—NH_2$$
$$|$$
$$COOH$$

Serine, $C_3H_7NO_3$, or α-amino-β-hydroxy propionic acid

$$CH_2·CH—NH_2$$
$$|\quad|$$
$$OH\ \ COOH$$

Threonine $C_4H_9NO_3$

$$CH_3CH·CH—NH_2$$
$$|\quad|$$
$$OH\ \ COOH$$

Valine $C_5H_{11}NO_2$

$$CH_3$$
$$\backslash$$
$$CH·CH—NH_2$$
$$/\qquad|$$
$$CH_3\qquad COOH$$

Norleucine $C_6H_{13}NO_2$

$$CH_3·CH_2·CH_2·CH_2·CH—NH_2$$
$$|$$
$$COOH$$

Leucine, $C_6H_{13}NO_2$,

$$CH_3$$
$$\backslash$$
$$CH·CH_2·CH—NH_2$$
$$/\qquad\qquad|$$
$$CH_3\qquad\qquad COOH$$

Isoleucine, $C_6H_{13}NO_2$,

$$CH_3$$
$$\backslash$$
$$CH·CH—NH_2$$
$$/\qquad|$$
$$CH_3·CH_2\qquad COOH$$

Sulphur-containing monoamino-monocarbox acids

Cystine, $C_6H_{12}N_2S_2O_4$,

$$CH_2—S—S—CH_2$$
$$|\qquad\qquad|$$
$$CH—NH_2\qquad CH—NH_2$$
$$|\qquad\qquad|$$
$$COOH\qquad\quad COOH$$

Amino Acids Present in Most Complete Proteins (Cont.)

Methionine, $C_5H_{11}SNO_2$,
thiol-*n*-butyric acid

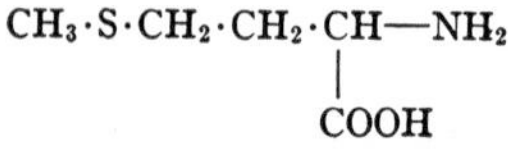

$$CH_3 \cdot S \cdot CH_2 \cdot CH_2 \cdot \underset{\underset{COOH}{|}}{CH} - NH_2$$

B. *Monoamino-dicarboxylic acids*

Aspartic acid, $C_4H_7NO_x$,

$$COOH \cdot CH_2 \cdot \underset{\underset{COOH}{|}}{CH} - NH_2$$

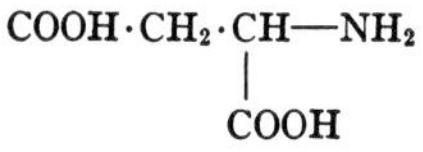

Glutamic acid, $C_5H_9NO_4$, or α-amino-glutaric acid

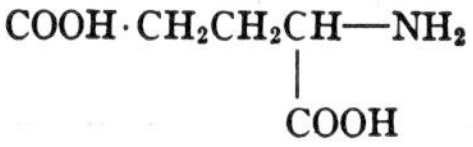

$$COOH \cdot CH_2CH_2 \underset{\underset{COOH}{|}}{CH} - NH_2$$

Hydroxyglutamic acid, $C_5H_9NO_5$,

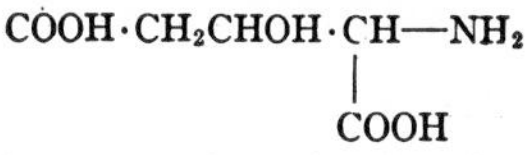

$$COOH \cdot CH_2CHOH \cdot \underset{\underset{COOH}{|}}{CH} - NH_2$$

C. *Diamino-monocarboxylic acids*

Arginine, $C_6H_{14}N_4O_2$,

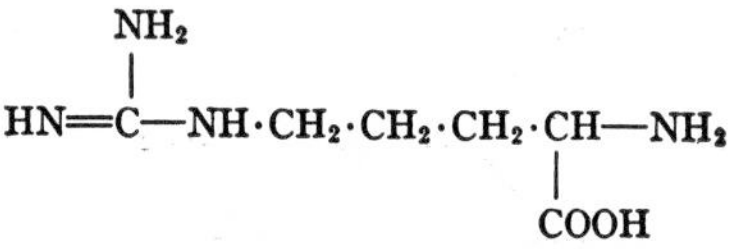

$$HN{=}\underset{}{C} - NH \cdot CH_2 \cdot CH_2 \cdot CH_2 \cdot \underset{\underset{COOH}{|}}{CH} - NH_2$$

Lysine, $C_6H_{14}N_2O_2$,

$$CH_2 \cdot CH_2 \cdot CH_2 \cdot CH_2 \cdot \underset{\underset{COOH}{|}}{CH} - NH_2$$

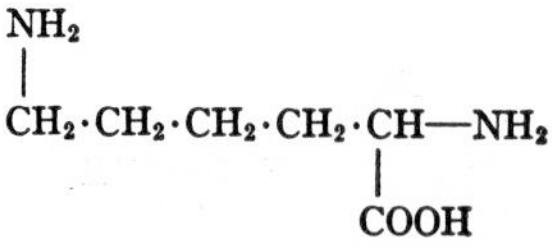

II. Aromatic Amino-Acids

Phenylalanine, $C_9H_{11}NO_2$,

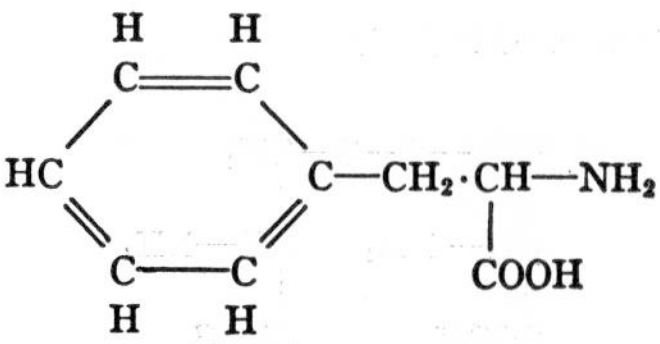

Tyrosine, $C_9H_{11}NO_3$,

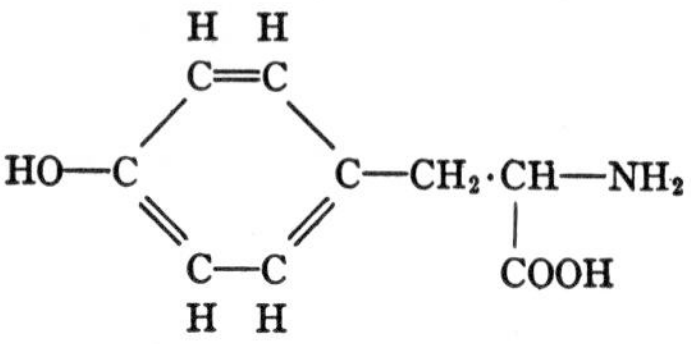

III. Heterocyclic Amino Acids

Tryptophane, $C_{11}H_{12}N_2O_2$,

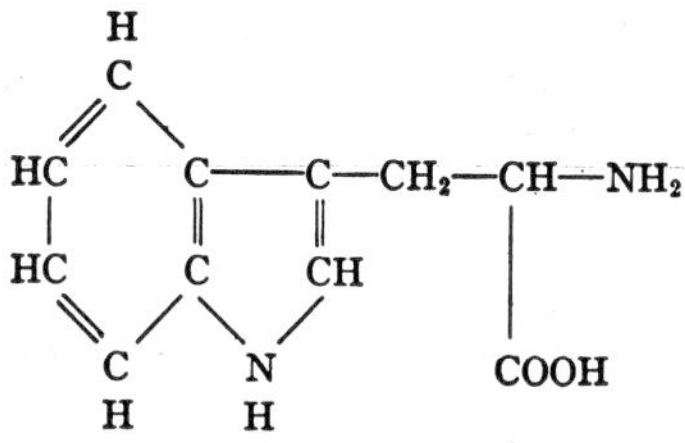

Indole nucleus

Histidine, $C_6H_9N_3O_2$,

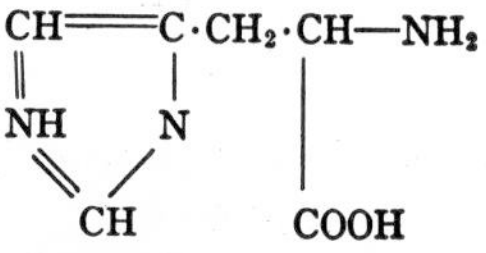

Imidazol ring

Proline, $C_5H_9NO_2$,

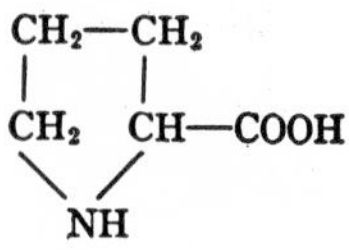

Pyrrole nucleus

Hydroxyproline (oxyproline), $C_5H_9NO_3$,

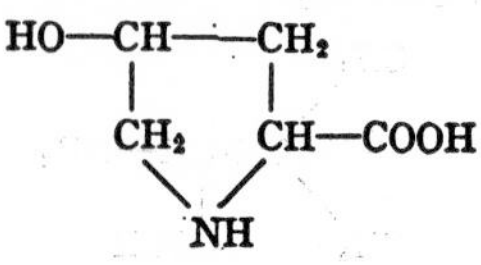

Ash Content of Edible Portions of Some Common Foods

(Modified from Lusk)

	IN 100 GRAMS FRESH SUBSTANCE						
	Iron	Calcium	Magnesium	Sodium	Potassium	Phosphorus	Chlorin
	mg.	mg.	mg.	mg.	mg.	mg.	mg.
Beefsteak, lean..	3.8	8	24	67	35	22	50
Liver (beef).....	8.0	11.0	....	....	....	....	....
Eggs............	3.0	67	9	15	14	16	100
Milk, whole.....	0.2	120	11	51	142	94	120
Cornmeal.......	1.1	....	....	....	....	....	....
Oatmeal........	3.7	93	127	81	380	380	35
Rice, polished...	0.7	8	27	21	68	89	50
Wheat flour.....	1.5	26	30	69	146	86	76
Wheat, entire grain........	5.2	44	170	106	515	469	88
Beans, lima, dried	7.2	71	187	245	1743	336	25
Beans, string, fresh..........	1.6	....	....	....	....	....	....
Cabbage........	0.9	49	14	20	243	27	13
Corn, sweet.....	0.8	....	....	....	....	....	....
Peas, dried......	5.6	100	145	118	880	397	40
Potatoes.......	1.2	11	22	19	440	61	30
Spinach.........	3.8	....	....	....	....	....	....
Turnips........	0.6	64	169	59	332	51	40
Apples.........	0.3	10	8	15	125	13	4
Raisins.........	3.6	57	9	141	830	126	70

Average Composition and Energy Values of Edible Portions of Some Common Foods

	PER CENT					ENERGY VALUE	
	Water	Protein N × 6.25	Fat	Carbo-hydrate	Ash	Per kg.	Per pound
	grams	grams	grams	grams	grams	calories	calories
Meat:							
Beef, round steak, medium fat..........	54.8	23.5	20.4	....	1.2	2,860	1,300
Mutton, leg roast.....................	50.9	25.0	22.6	....	1.2	3,125	1,420
Pork, ham, luncheon bacon, side....... {	49.2	22.5	21.0	....	5.8	2,870	1,305
	18.8	9.9	67.4	....	4.4	6,665	3,030
Chicken:							
Broilers................................	74.8	21.5	2.5	....	1.1	1,110	505
Fish, cod, whole.........................	82.6	16.5	0.4	....	1.2	715	325
Herring, whole.........................	72.5	19.5	7.1	....	1.5	1,455	660
Salmon, whole......................	64.6	22.0	12.8	....	1.4	2,090	950
Trout, brook, whole.............	77.8	19.2	2.1	....	1.2	980	445
Fats:							
Butter................................	11.0	1.0	85.0	....	3.0	7,930	3,605
Lard.................................	....	....	100.0	....	....	9,285	4,220
Suet.................................	13.7	4.7	81.8	....	0.3	7,790	3,540
Cheese:							
American, red.........................	28.6	29.6	38.3	....	3.5	4,765	2,165
Milk.................................	87.0	3.3	4.0	5.0	0.7	715	325
Eggs, hens', boiled.....................	73.2	13.2	12.0	....	0.8	1,685	765
Flour, white, wheat.....................	11.5	11.4	1.0	75.6	0.5	3,650	1,660
Bread, white...........................	35.6	9.3	1.2	52.7	1.2	2,650	1,205
Fruit:							
Apples................................	84.6	0.4	0.5	14.2	0.3	640	290
Banana...............................	75.3	1.3	0.6	22.0	0.8	1,010	460
Cherries..............................	80.9	1.0	0.8	16.7	0.6	805	365
Grape fruit...........................	93.6	0.6	0.1	5.7	....	267	120
Oranges..............................	86.9	0.8	0.2	11.6	0.5	528	240
Vegetables:							
Beans, dried..........................	12.6	22.5	1.8	59.6	3.5	3,530	1,605
Cabbage..............................	91.5	1.6	0.3	5.6	1.0	320	145
Lettuce...............................	94.7	1.2	0.3	2.9	0.9	206	90
Potatoes..............................	75.5	2.5	0.1	20.9	1.0	968	440
Sugar, granulated......................	....	....	....	100.0	....	4,090	1,860
Chocolate.............................	5.9	12.9	48.7	30.3	2.2	6,295	2,860
Cocoa, powder........................	4.6	21.6	28.9	37.7	7.2	5,105	2,320

Recommended Dietary Allowances*

(Food and Nutrition Board, National Research Council)

	CALORIES	PROTEIN GRAMS	CALCIUM GRAMS	IRON	VITAMIN A‡	THIAMIN (B₁)	RIBO-FLAVIN	NIACIN (NICO-TINIC ACID)	ASCOR-BIC ACID	VITAMIN D
				mg.	I.U.	mg.†	mg.	mg.	mg.†	I.U.
Man (70 Kg.)										
Sedentary..........	2500	—	—	—	—	1.5	2.2	15	—	—
Moderately active...	3000	70	0.8	12	5000	1.8	2.7	18	75	**
Very active........	4500	—	—	—	—	2.3	3.3	23	—	—
Woman (56 Kg.)										
Sedentary..........	2100	—	—	—	—	1.2	1.8	12	—	
Moderately active...	2500	60	0.8	12	5000	1.5	2.2	15	70	**
Very active........	3000	—	—	—	—	1.8	2.7	18	—	—
Pregnancy (latter										
half)............	2500	85	1.5	15	6000	1.8	2.5	18	100	400 to 800
Lactation..........	3000	100	2.0	15	8000	2.3	3.0	23	150	400 to 800
Children up to 12 years:										
Under 1 year§......	100/kg.	3 to 4/kg.	1.0	6	1500	0.4	0.6	4	30	400 to 800
1–3 years¶.........	1200	40	1.0	7	2000	0.6	0.9	6	35	**
4–6 years........	1600	50	1.0	8	2500	0.8	1.2	8	50	—
7–9 years..........	2000	60	1.0	10	3500	1.0	1.5	10	60	—
10–12 years........	2500	70	1.2	12	4500	1.2	1.8	12	75	—
Children over 12 years:										
Girls, 13–15 years...	2800	80	1.3	15	5000	1.4	2.0	14	80	**
16–20 years...	2400	75	1.0	15	5000	1.2	1.8	12	80	—
Boys, 13–15 years.....	3200	85	1.4	15	5000	1.6	2.4	16	90	**
16–20 years.....	3800	100	1.4	15	6000	2.0	3.0	20	100	—

* Tentative goal toward which to aim in planning practical dietaries; can be met by a good diet of natural food. Such a diet will also provide other minerals and vitamins, the requirements for which are less well known.

† 1 mg. thiamin equals 333 I.U.; 1 mg. ascorbic acid equals 20 I.U.

‡ Requirements may be less if provided as vitamin A; greater if provided chiefly as the pro-vitamin carotene.

§ Needs of infants increase from month to month. The amounts given are for approximately 6–8 months. The amounts of protein and calcium needed are less if derived from human milk.

¶ Allowances are based on needs for the middle year in each group (as 2, 5, 8, etc.) and for moderate activity.

** Vitamin D is undoubtedly necessary for older children and adults. When not available from sunshine, it should be provided probably up to the minimum amounts recommended for infants.

Further Recommendations, Adopted 1942:

The requirement for *iodine* is small; probably about 0.002 to 0.004 milligram a day for each kilogram of body-weight. This amounts to about 0.15 to 0.30 milligram daily for the adult. This need is easily met by the regular use of iodized salt; its use is especially important in adolescence and pregnancy.

The requirement for *copper* for adults is in the neighborhood of 1.0 to 2.0 milligrams a day. Infants and children require approximately 0.05 per kilogram of bodyweight. The requirement for copper is approximately one-tenth of that for iron.

The requirement of *vitamin K* is usually satisfied by any good diet. Special consideration needs to be given to newborn infants. Physicians commonly give vitamin K either to the mother before delivery or to the infant immediately after birth.

Standard Weight According to Height and Age

Men

Age	5 Ft.	5 Ft. 1 In.	5 Ft. 2 In.	5 Ft. 3 In.	5 Ft. 4 In.	5 Ft. 5 In.	5 Ft. 6 In.	5 Ft. 7 In.	5 Ft. 8 In.	5 Ft. 9 In.	5 Ft. 10 In.	5 Ft. 11 In.	6 Ft.	6 Ft. 1 In.	6 Ft. 2 In.	6 Ft. 3 In.	6 Ft. 4 In.	6 Ft. 5 In.
15	107	109	112	115	118	122	126	130	134	138	142	147	152	157	162	167	172	177
16	109	111	114	117	120	124	128	132	136	140	144	149	154	159	164	169	174	179
17	111	113	116	119	122	126	130	134	138	142	146	151	156	161	166	171	176	181
18	113	115	118	121	124	128	132	136	140	144	148	153	158	163	168	173	178	183
19	115	117	120	123	126	130	134	138	142	146	150	155	160	165	170	175	180	185
	5	1	2	3	4	5	6	7	8	9	10	11	6	1	2	3	4	5
20	117	119	122	125	128	132	136	140	144	148	152	156	161	166	171	176	181	186
21	118	120	123	126	130	134	138	141	145	149	153	157	162	167	172	177	182	187
22	119	121	124	127	131	135	139	142	146	150	154	158	163	168	173	178	183	188
23	120	122	125	128	132	136	140	143	147	151	155	159	164	169	175	180	185	190
24	121	123	126	129	133	137	141	144	148	152	156	160	165	171	177	182	187	192
	5	1	2	3	4	5	6	7	8	9	10	11	6	1	2	3	4	5
25	122	124	126	129	133	137	141	145	149	153	157	162	167	173	179	184	189	194
26	123	125	127	130	134	138	142	146	150	154	158	163	168	174	180	186	191	196
27	124	126	128	131	134	138	142	146	150	154	158	163	169	175	181	187	192	197
28	125	127	129	132	135	139	143	147	151	155	159	164	170	176	182	188	193	198
29	126	128	130	133	136	140	144	148	152	156	160	165	171	177	183	189	194	199
	5	1	2	3	4	5	6	7	8	9	10	11	6	1	2	3	4	5
30	126	128	130	133	136	140	144	148	152	156	161	166	172	178	184	190	196	201
31	127	129	131	134	137	141	145	149	153	157	162	167	173	179	185	191	197	202
32	127	129	131	134	137	141	145	149	154	158	163	168	174	180	186	192	198	203
33	127	129	131	134	137	141	145	149	154	159	164	169	175	181	187	193	199	204
34	128	130	132	135	138	142	146	150	155	160	165	170	176	182	188	194	200	206
	5	1	2	3	4	5	6	7	8	9	10	11	6	1	2	3	4	5
35	128	130	132	135	138	142	146	150	155	160	165	170	176	182	189	195	201	207
36	129	131	133	136	139	143	147	151	156	161	166	171	177	183	190	196	202	208
37	129	131	133	136	140	144	148	152	157	162	167	172	178	184	191	197	203	209
38	130	132	134	137	140	144	148	152	157	162	167	173	179	185	192	198	204	210
39	130	132	134	137	140	144	148	152	157	162	167	173	179	185	192	199	205	211
	5	1	2	3	4	5	6	7	8	9	10	11	6	1	2	3	4	5
40	131	133	135	138	141	145	149	153	158	163	168	174	180	186	193	200	206	212
41	131	133	135	138	141	145	149	153	158	163	168	174	180	186	193	200	207	213
42	132	134	136	139	142	146	150	154	159	164	169	175	181	187	194	201	208	214
43	132	134	136	139	142	146	150	154	159	164	169	175	181	187	194	201	208	214
44	133	135	137	140	143	147	151	155	160	165	170	176	182	188	195	202	209	215
	5	1	2	3	4	5	6	7	8	9	10	11	6	1	2	3	4	5
45	133	135	137	140	143	147	151	155	160	165	170	176	182	188	195	202	209	215
46	134	136	138	141	144	148	152	156	161	166	171	177	183	189	196	203	210	216
47	134	136	138	141	144	148	152	156	161	166	171	177	183	190	197	204	211	217
48	134	136	138	141	144	148	152	156	161	166	171	177	183	190	197	204	211	217
49	134	136	138	141	144	148	152	156	161	166	171	177	183	190	197	204	211	217
	5	1	2	3	4	5	6	7	8	9	10	11	6	1	2	3	4	5
50	134	136	138	141	144	148	152	156	161	166	171	177	183	190	197	204	211	217
51	135	137	139	142	145	149	153	157	162	167	172	178	184	191	198	205	212	218
52	135	137	139	142	145	149	153	157	162	167	172	178	184	191	198	205	212	218
53	135	137	139	142	145	149	153	157	162	167	172	178	184	191	198	205	212	218
54	135	137	139	142	145	149	153	158	163	168	173	178	184	191	198	205	212	219
55 & up	135	137	139	142	145	149	153	158	163	168	173	178	184	191	198	205	212	219

Standard Weight According to Height and Age

Women

Age	4 Ft. 8 In.	4 Ft. 9 In.	4 Ft. 10 In.	4 Ft. 11 In.	5 Ft.	5 Ft. 1 In.	5 Ft. 2 In.	5 Ft. 3 In.	5 Ft. 4 In.	5 Ft. 5 In.	5 Ft. 6 In.	5 Ft. 7 In.	5 Ft. 8 In.	5 Ft. 9 In.	5 Ft. 10 In.	5 Ft. 11 In.	6 Ft.
15	101	103	105	106	107	109	112	115	118	122	126	130	134	138	142	147	152
16	102	104	106	108	109	111	114	117	120	124	128	132	136	139	143	148	153
17	103	105	107	109	111	113	116	119	122	125	129	133	137	140	144	149	154
18	104	106	108	110	112	114	117	120	123	126	130	134	138	141	145	150	155
19	105	107	109	111	113	115	118	121	124	127	131	135	139	142	146	151	155
	8	9	10	11	5	1	2	3	4	5	6	7	8	9	10	11	6
20	106	108	110	112	114	116	119	122	125	128	132	136	140	143	147	151	156
21	107	109	111	113	115	117	120	123	126	129	133	137	141	144	148	152	156
22	107	109	111	113	115	117	120	123	126	129	133	137	141	145	149	153	157
23	108	110	112	114	116	118	121	124	127	130	134	138	142	146	150	153	157
24	109	111	113	115	117	119	121	124	127	130	134	138	142	146	150	154	158
	8	9	10	11	5	1	2	3	4	5	6	7	8	9	10	11	6
25	109	111	113	115	117	119	121	124	128	131	135	139	143	147	151	154	158
26	110	112	114	116	118	120	122	125	128	131	135	139	143	147	151	155	159
27	110	112	114	116	118	120	122	125	129	132	136	140	144	148	152	155	159
28	111	113	115	117	119	121	123	126	130	133	137	141	145	149	153	156	160
29	111	113	115	117	119	121	123	126	130	133	137	141	145	149	153	156	160
	8	9	10	11	5	1	2	3	4	5	6	7	8	9	10	11	6
30	112	114	116	118	120	122	124	127	131	134	138	142	146	150	154	157	161
31	113	115	117	119	121	123	125	128	132	135	139	143	147	151	154	157	161
32	113	115	117	119	121	123	125	128	132	136	140	144	148	152	155	158	162
33	114	116	118	120	122	124	126	129	133	137	141	145	149	153	156	159	162
34	115	117	119	121	123	125	127	130	134	138	142	146	150	154	157	160	163
	8	9	10	11	5	1	2	3	4	5	6	7	8	9	10	11	6
35	115	117	119	121	123	125	127	130	134	138	142	146	150	154	157	160	163
36	116	118	120	122	124	126	128	131	135	139	143	147	151	155	158	161	164
37	116	118	120	122	124	126	129	132	136	140	144	148	152	156	159	162	165
38	117	119	121	123	125	127	130	133	137	141	145	149	153	157	160	163	166
39	118	120	122	124	126	128	131	134	138	142	146	150	154	158	161	164	167
	8	9	10	11	5	1	2	3	4	5	6	7	8	9	10	11	6
40	119	121	123	125	127	129	132	135	138	142	146	150	154	158	161	164	167
41	120	122	124	126	128	130	133	136	139	143	147	151	155	159	162	165	168
42	120	122	124	126	128	130	133	136	139	143	147	151	155	159	162	166	169
43	121	123	125	127	129	131	134	137	140	144	148	152	156	160	163	167	170
44	122	124	126	128	130	132	135	138	141	145	149	153	157	161	164	168	171
	8	9	10	11	5	1	2	3	4	5	6	7	8	9	10	11	6
45	122	124	126	128	130	132	135	138	141	145	149	153	157	161	164	168	171
46	123	125	127	129	131	133	136	139	142	146	150	154	158	162	165	169	172
47	123	125	127	129	131	133	136	139	142	146	151	155	159	163	166	170	173
48	124	126	128	130	132	134	137	140	143	147	152	156	160	164	167	171	174
49	124	126	128	130	132	134	137	140	143	147	152	156	161	165	168	172	175
	8	9	10	11	5	1	2	3	4	5	6	7	8	9	10	11	6
50	125	127	129	131	133	135	138	141	144	148	152	156	161	165	169	173	176
51	125	127	129	131	133	135	138	141	144	148	152	157	162	166	170	174	177
52	125	127	129	131	133	135	138	141	144	148	152	157	162	166	170	174	177
53	125	127	129	131	133	135	138	141	144	148	152	157	162	166	170	174	177
54	125	127	129	131	133	135	138	141	144	148	153	158	163	167	171	174	177
55 & up	125	127	129	131	133	135	138	141	144	148	153	158	163	167	171	174	177

References

General anatomy

Cates, H. A., and Basmajian, J. V., *Primary Anatomy*. Williams & Wilkins, Baltimore.
Cunningham's Anatomy, Editor, Brash, J. C. Oxford University Press, New York.
Grant, J. C., *A Method of Anatomy*. Williams & Wilkins, Baltimore.
Grant, J. C., *An Atlas of Anatomy*. Williams & Wilkins, Baltimore.
Gray's Anatomy, Editors, Johnstone, T. B., and Whillis, J. Lea & Febiger, Philadelphia.

Bacteriology, viruses, and antibiotics

Hussar, A. E., and Holley, H. L., *Antibiotics and Antibiotic Therapy*. Macmillan, New York.
Park, W. H., and Williams, A. W., *Pathogenic Microorganisms*. Lea & Febiger, Philadelphia.
Rhodes, A. J., and van Rooyen, C. E., *Textbook of Virology*. Williams & Wilkins, Baltimore.
Wilson, C. L., and Loomis, W. E., *Botany*, 3d ed. Holt, Rinehart and Winston, New York.

Biochemistry

Harrow, B., *Textbook of Biochemistry*. Saunders, Philadelphia.
Hawk, P. B., Oser, B. L., and Summerson, W. H., *Practical Physiological Chemistry*. McGraw-Hill (Blakiston Division), New York.
Hoffman, W. S., *The Biochemistry of Clinical Medicine*. Year Book Publishers, Chicago.
Mitchell, P. H., *A Textbook of Biochemistry*. McGraw-Hill, New York.
West, E. S., and Todd, W. R., *Textbook of Biochemistry*. Macmillan, New York.

Biology and physical chemistry

Baitsell, G. A., *Human Biology*. McGraw-Hill, New York.

716

Clark, W. F., *Topics in Physical Chemistry*. Williams & Wilkins, Baltimore.

Strausbaugh, P. D., and Weimer, B. R., *General Biology*. Wiley, New York.

Blood and other body fluids

Drinker, C. K., and Joffey, J. M., *Lymphatics, Lymph, and Lymphoid Tissue*. Harvard University Press, Cambridge, Mass.

Gaunt, R., and Birnie, J. H., *Hormones and Body Water*. Charles C. Thomas, Springfield, Ill.

Leitner, S. J., Britton, C. J., and Neumark, E., *Bone Marrow Biopsy*. Grune & Stratton, New York.

Marriott, H. L., *Water and Salt Depletion*. Charles C. Thomas, Springfield, Ill.

Newburgh, L. H., *The Significance of the Body Fluids in Clinical Medicine*. Charles C. Thomas, Springfield, Ill.

Potter, E. L., *Rh, Its Relation to Congenital Hemolytic Disease*. Year Book Publishers, Chicago.

Quick, A. J., *The Physiology and Pathology of Hemostasis*. Lea & Febiger, Philadelphia.

Weisberg, H. F., *Water, Electrolyte, and Acid-Base Balance*. Williams & Wilkins, Baltimore.

Whitby, Sir Lionel E. H., and Britton, C. J. C., *Disorders of the Blood*. McGraw-Hill (Blakiston Division), New York.

Wiener, A. S., *Rh-Hr Blood Types*. Grune & Stratton, New York.

Circulation

Altschule, M. D., *Physiology in Diseases of the Heart and Lungs*. Harvard University Press, Cambridge, Mass.

Bell, E. T., Clawson, B. J., and Fahr, G. E., Editors, *Hypertension, a Symposium*. University of Minnesota Press, Minneapolis.

Gregg, D. E., *Coronary Circulation in Health and Disease*. Lea & Febiger, Philadelphia.

Hecht, Hans H., *Basic Principles of Clinical Electrocardiography*. Charles C. Thomas, Springfield, Ill.

Heymans, C., *Introduction to the Study of Blood Pressure and Heart Rate*. Charles C. Thomas, Springfield, Ill.

Krogh, A., *Anatomy and Physiology of the Capillaries*. Yale University Press, New Haven, Conn.

McMichael, J., *Visceral Circulation*. Little, Brown, Boston.

Moulton, F. R., Editor, *Blood, Heart and Circulation*. Science Press, Lancaster, Pa.

Schmidt, C. F., *The Cerebral Circulation in Health and Disease*. Charles C. Thomas, Springfield, Ill.

Wiggers, C. J., *Circulatory Dynamics*. Grune & Stratton, New York.
Youmans, W. B., *Hemodynamics in Failure of the Circulation*. Charles C. Thomas, Springfield, Ill.

Dictionaries

American Illustrated Dictionary, Dorland, W. A. N. Saunders, Philadelphia.
The Faber Medical Dictionary, Wakeley, Sir Cecil. Faber & Faber, London.
The Putnam Medical Dictionary, Taylor, N. B., and Taylor, A. E. Putnam, New York.
Stedman's Medical Dictionary, Editor, Taylor, N. B. Williams & Wilkins, Baltimore.

Digestion

Alvarez, W. C., *The Mechanics of the Gastrointestinal Tract*. Hoeber, New York.
Thomas, J. E., *The External Secretion of the Pancreas*. Charles C. Thomas, Springfield, Ill.
Youmans, W. B., *Nervous and Neurohumoral Regulation of Intestinal Motility*. Interscience Publishers, New York.

Embryology, genetics, and reproduction

Altenburg, Edgar, *Genetics*. Holt, Rinehart and Winston, New York.
Beck, A. C., *Obstetrical Practice*. Williams & Wilkins, Baltimore.
Corner, G. W., "The Nature of the Menstrual Cycle." *Medicine*, Vol. 12 (1933), p. 61.
Davenport, C. B., *How We Came by Our Bodies*. Holt, Rinehart and Winston, New York.
Davidson, J. N., *The Biochemistry of the Nucleic Acids*. Methuen, London.
Hamilton, W. J., Boyd, J. D., and Mossman, H. W., *Human Embryology*. Williams & Wilkins, Baltimore.
Hutchins, C. M., *Life's Key—DNA*. Coward-McCann, New York.
Reynolds, S. R. M., *Physiology of the Uterus*. Hoeber, New York.
Robson, J. M., *Recent Advances in Sex and Reproductive Physiology*. McGraw-Hill (Blakiston Division), New York.
Sutton, H. E. *Genes, Enzymes and Inherited Diseases*. Holt, Rinehart and Winston, New York.

Endocrinology

Albright F., and Reiffenstein, E. C., *The Parathyroid Glands and Metabolic Bone Disease*. Williams & Wilkins, Baltimore.

Cushing, H., *The Pituitary Body and Its Disorders.* Lippincott, Philadelphia.
Hartman, F. A., and Brownell, K. A., *The Adrenal Gland.* Lea & Febiger, Philadelphia.
Means, J. H., *The Thyroid Gland.* Lippincott, Philadelphia.
Pincus, P., and Thimman, K. V., Editors, *The Hormones.* Academic Press, New York.
Van Dyke, H. B., *The Physiology and Pharmacology of the Pituitary Body.* University of Chicago Press, Chicago.

History of medical sciences

Garrison, F. H., *History of Medicine.* Saunders, Philadelphia.
Marriott, H. J. L., *Medical Milestones.* Williams & Wilkins, Baltimore.

Histology

Bailey's Textbook of Histology, Smith, P. E., Editor. Williams & Wilkins, Baltimore.
Ham, A. W., *Histology.* Lippincott, Philadelphia.
Nonidez, J. F., and Windle, W. F., *Textbook of Histology.* McGraw-Hill, New York.
Sharpy-Schafer, Sir E., *Essentials of Histology,* Carleton, H. M., Editor. Longmans, Green, London.
Wilson, G. B., and Morrison, J. H., *Cytology.* Reinhold, New York.

Kidney

Bell, E. T., *Renal Diseases.* Lea & Febiger, Philadelphia.
Bradley, S. E., *The Pathologic Physiology of Uremia in Chronic Bright's Disease.* Charles C. Thomas, Springfield, Ill.
Fishberg, A. M., *Hypertension and Nephritis.* Lea & Febiger, Philadelphia.

Medicine

Boyd, W., *An Introduction to Medical Science.* Lea & Febiger, Philadelphia.
Harrison, T. R., Editor, *Principles of Internal Medicine.* McGraw-Hill (Blakiston Division), New York.

Metabolism and nutrition

Cruicshank, E. W. H., *Food and Nutrition.* Livingstone, Edinburgh.
Du Bois, E. F., *Basal Metabolism in Health and Disease.* Lea & Febiger, Philadelphia.

Du Bois, E. F., *Fever*. Charles C. Thomas, Springfield, Ill.

Evans, E. J., Editor, *The Biological Action of the Vitamins, a Symposium.* University of Chicago Press, Chicago.

Hutchison, R., Mottram, V. H., and Graham, G., *Food and the Principles of Dietetics*. Edward Arnold, London.

Jukes, T. H., *B-Vitamins for Blood Formation*. Charles C. Thomas, Springfield, Ill.

Lusk, G., *The Elements of the Science of Nutrition*. Saunders, Philadelphia.

Rosenberg, H. R., *The Chemistry and Physiology of the Vitamins*. Interscience Publishers, New York.

Sherman, H. C., *The Chemistry of Food and Nutrition*. Macmillan, New York.

Muscle

Schneider, E. C., and Karpovith, P., *The Physiology of Muscular Contraction*. Saunders, Philadelphia.

Nervous system

Adrian, E. D., *The Basis of Sensation*. Norton, New York.

Adrian, E. D., *The Mechanism of Nervous Action*. University of Pennsylvania Press, Philadelphia.

Adrian, E. D., *The Physical Background of Perception*. Oxford University Press, New York.

Barcroft, Sir Joseph, *The Brain and Its Environment*. Yale University Press, New Haven, Conn.

Brain, W. R., *Diseases of the Nervous System*. Oxford University Press, New York.

Brodal, A., *Neurological Anatomy in Relation to Clinical Medicine*. Oxford University Press, New York.

Cannon, W. B., and Rosenblueth, A., *Autonomic Neuro-Effector Systems*. Macmillan, New York.

Fulton, J. F., *Functional Localization in the Frontal Lobes and Cerebellum*. Oxford University Press, New York.

Fulton, J. F., *Physiology of the Nervous System*. Oxford University Press, New York.

Gantt, W. H., *Experimental Basis of Neurotic Behavior*. Hoeber, New York.

Hardy, J. D., Wolff, H. G., and Goodell, H., *Pain Sensations and Reactions*. Williams & Wilkins, Baltimore.

Kuntz, A., *The Anatomy of the Autonomic Nervous System*, Lea & Febiger, Philadelphia.

Mitchell, G. A. G., *Anatomy of the Autonomic Nervous System*. Livingstone, Edinburgh.

Pavlov, I., *Conditioned Reflexes*. Oxford University Press, New York.

Pavlov, I., *Lectures on Conditioned Reflexes*, International Publishers, New York.

Ranson, S. W., *Anatomy of the Nervous System*. Saunders, Philadelphia.

Sherrington, Sir Charles, *Integrative Action of the Nervous System*. Cambridge University Press, New York.

Strong, O. S., and Elwyn, A., *Human Neuroanatomy*. Williams & Wilkins, Baltimore.

Von Bonin, G., *Essay on the Cerebral Cortex*. Charles C. Thomas, Springfield, Ill.

Wolf, H. G., and Wolf, S., *Pain*. Charles C. Thomas, Springfield, Ill.

Physiology

Best, C. H., and Taylor, N. B., *The Physiological Basis of Medical Practice*. Williams & Wilkins, Baltimore.

Cannon, W. B., *The Wisdom of the Body*. Norton, New York.

Fulton, J. F., *Howell's Textbook of Physiology*. Saunders, Philadelphia.

Langley, L. L., *Cell Function*. Reinhold, New York.

Sodeman, W. A., *Pathologic Physiology*. Saunders, Philadelphia.

Starling, E. H. (revised by Lovatt Evans), *Principles of Human Physiology*. Lea & Febiger, Philadelphia.

Winton, F. R., and Bayliss, E. L., *Human Physiology*. McGraw-Hill (Blakiston Division), New York.

Wright, S., *Applied Physiology*. Oxford University Press, New York.

Respiration

Comroe, J. H., and Dripps, R. D., *The Physiological Basis of Oxygen Therapy*. Charles C. Thomas, Springfield, Ill.

Gray, J. S., *Pulmonary Ventilation and Its Physiological Regulation*. Charles C. Thomas, Springfield, Ill.

Haldane, J. S., and Priestley, J. G., *Respiration*. Oxford University Press, New York.

Purves-Stewart, J., and Worster-Drought, C., *The Diagnosis of Nervous Diseases*. Williams & Wilkins, Baltimore.

Sacklad, M., *Inhalation Therapy and Resuscitation*. Charles C. Thomas, Springfield, Ill.

Special senses

Camis, M., *The Physiology of the Vestibular Apparatus*. Oxford University Press, New York.

Davson, H., *The Physiology of the Eye*. McGraw-Hill (Blakiston Division), New York.

Duke-Elder, W. S., *Text Book of Ophthalmology*. Kimpton, London.

Granit, R., *Sensory Mechanisms of the Retina*. Oxford University Press, New York.

Moncrieff, R. W., *The Chemical Senses*. Wiley, New York.

Stephens, S. S., and Davis, H., *Hearing; Its Psychology and Physiology*. Wiley, New York.

Index

723